By Force of Arms

Volumes in The Journals of don Diego de Vargas

*The Text and Concordance of Correspondence of don Diego de Vargas
1675–1706*, The Vargas Project Microfiche Series, 1 (1988)

*Remote Beyond Compare: Letters of don Diego de Vargas to His
Family from New Spain and New Mexico, 1675–1706* (1989)

*Letters from the New World: Selected Correspondence of
don Diego de Vargas to His Family, 1675–1706*
(1992; Abridged edition of *Remote Beyond Compare*)

*The Text and Concordance of the Journals of don Diego de Vargas,
New Mexico, 1691–93*, The Vargas Project Microfiche Series, 2 (1992)

The Hopi Pueblo of Walpi, Ben Wittick, c. 1890
   Museum of New Mexico

By Force of Arms

The Journals of don Diego de Vargas,
New Mexico, 1691–93

John L. Kessell and
Rick Hendricks, EDITORS
The Journals of don Diego de Vargas

Meredith D. Dodge, Associate Editor
Larry D. Miller, Assistant Editor
Alison R. Freese, Research Assistant
Gerald J. Mandell, Research Consultant

A Volume in The Journals
of don Diego de Vargas

UNIVERSITY OF NEW MEXICO PRESS : *Albuquerque*

Library of Congress Cataloging-in-Publication Data

Vargas, Diego de, 1643–1704.
   [Selections. English. 1992]
   By force of arms : the journals of don Diego de Vargas, New
Mexico, 1691–93 / John L. Kessell and Rick Hendricks, editors ;
Meredith D. Dodge, associate editor . . . [et al.]. — 1st ed.
     p. cm. — (The Journals of don Diego de Vargas)
   Contains the journals, letters, and official papers of don Diego
de Vargas and related documents.
   "This is the second volume in the Vargas series"—CIP pref.
   Includes bibliographical references and index.
   ISBN 0-8263-1357-4
   1. New Mexico—History—To 1848—Sources. 2. Spaniards—New
Mexico—History—17th century—Sources. 3. Vargas, Diego de,
1643–1704. I. Kessell, John L. II. Hendricks, Rick, 1956– .
III. Dodge, Meredith D., 1950– . IV. Title. V. Series: Vargas,
Diego de, 1643–1704. Works. English. 1989.
F799.V281213 1992
978.9'02—dc20   92–4067
                                             CIP

The preparation of this volume was made possible in part by grants
from the Division of Research Programs of the National Endowment
for the Humanities and the National Historical Publications and
Records Commission.

Contents

Illustrations

Preface

Two centuries after its arrival in the New World, the banner of imperial Spain waved over a vast territorial expanse, from Valdivia to Cavite to El Paso. On the northern frontier of New Spain, presidial soldiers, settlers, and missionaries faced seemingly implacable indigenous foes and the threat of incursion by European rivals, Frenchmen and Englishmen. Only a decisive response could prevent the disintegration of the empire. Circumstances called for a latter-day conquistador, a new Cortés.

The ambitions of Diego de Vargas in the royal service coincided with this historical juncture. Following a long Vargas family tradition of military service, don Diego sought employ in the Indies. In the viceregal capital, Mexico City, he had recourse to powerful officials, particularly the Conde de Galve, through the kinship and clientele relationships that bound together the elite of Madrid. He advanced his career through diligent effort in fulfilling his duty, though his connections served him as well in his quest for preferment.

Although he made it abundantly clear he would accept almost any post worthy of a person of his illustrious lineage, don Diego welcomed the task of regaining New Mexico. Departing El Paso in August 1692, he intrepidly led his small band of Spaniards and Indian allies on the largely ceremonial reconquest of the kingdom and provinces of New Mexico. The responses to his feat were predictable rejoicing in Mexico City and puzzling quiescence by the Pueblo Indians.

The documents in this volume describe the preparations for Vargas's 1692 reconnaissance, the investigation into a legendary mercury mine in the Sierra Azul, and jurisdictional conflicts with the Franciscans, all within the context of the ebb and flow of bureaucracy. A wide variety of material is represented, including reports, testimony, letters patent, viceregal orders, and the deliberations of royal councils.

Most of what constitutes the actual daily campaign journal is a written record of what Vargas dictated to his scribe.

It is important to note that while the Pueblo presence is well documented, the Pueblos themselves are largely silent. Observations about Native American life are filtered through Spanish perceptions, and in this sense, an authentic Pueblo voice does not appear here. We have attempted to compensate for this in the annotation, based on modern sources, throughout this volume.

This is the second volume in the Vargas series. The first, *Remote Beyond Compare: Letters of don Diego de Vargas to His Family from New Spain and New Mexico, 1675–1706*, came as a surprise, welcome but wholly unanticipated. None of us knew when we began planning this multivolume documentary series that any personal correspondence of New Mexico's late-seventeenth-century governor and recolonizer had survived in Spain. Presented with several dozen Vargas letters, we judged the collection worthy of translation and publication, not only because such writings home from the Spanish Indies by a middle-ranking official are unusual, but also, and primarily, because they present a more complete picture of don Diego de Vargas, the central figure in the reconquest of New Mexico.

In contrast, the present volume and those to follow in the series redirect the emphasis from the man to the events of his time. They are the journals, the official government records of the Vargas years in New Mexico spanning his two terms as governor, 1691–97 and 1703–1704, and that of his interim successor and nemesis, don Pedro Rodríguez Cubero, 1697–1703. *By Force of Arms* covers the first period from 1690 to 1693, critical years for the reestablishment of the Spanish presence north of El Paso.

The introduction is not intended as a summary of the documents that make up the body of this work; rather it seeks to set the stage for Vargas's 1692 expedition and place events in New Mexico within the broader context of the Spanish empire. It focuses on those events, beginning with the 1680 Pueblo Revolt, that explain the situation of the colony in exile in El Paso and how it was viewed from both north and south of the ford on the Rio Grande.

The raw material of the *Journals*, with supporting documentation, is found in many locations. The work of copying and collecting has been made inestimably easier through the help of the directors and staffs of the State Records Center and Archives, Santa Fe, New Mexico; The Bancroft Library, University of California, Berkeley; The

Huntington Library, San Marino, California; The Newberry Library, Chicago, Illinois; Benson Latin American Collection, The University of Texas, Austin; Beinecke Rare Book and Manuscript Library, Yale University, New Haven, Connecticut; Library of Congress, Washington, D.C.; Archivo General de Indias, Seville, Spain; Archivo Histórico Nacional and Archivo Histórico de Protocolos, Madrid, Spain; and Archivo General de la Nación and Archivo General de Notarías, located in Mexico City.

In this volume, we have chosen in places, after much thought, to reorder the sequence of documents to reflect historical reality, as opposed to arbitrary archival organization. Doing so permits the unfolding of events in a straightforward, commonsense fashion.

Our philosophy of translation remains a faithful English rendering informed by historical sensibility. In light of this, textual errors, such as mistaken dates, have been preserved. The editorial procedure for this and succeeding volumes is based on the *Chicago Manual of Style* and is the same as that employed for *Remote Beyond Compare*. Should readers have need of fuller explication, they may consult that volume. All Spanish personal and place-names have been modernized; *Webster's New Geographical Dictionary* has served as the standard for the latter. The *Handbook of North American Indians* is the name authority for Native American names and places.

A special note on usage is pertinent here. As English has evolved, many words of Spanish origin have passed over into the language and become standard English usage. Hence, words that appear to be Spanish, such as alferez, malpais, llano, and Cadiz, occur throughout the text. These have been taken as they appear in *Webster's Third New International Dictionary of the English Language*.

Unlike the first volume, here the Spanish transcripts do not appear with the printed English text. Readers wishing to avail themselves of the Spanish text may obtain microfiche copies of the transcripts directly from the Vargas Project. The fiche include semipaleographic transcription of the complete Spanish text, an alphabetical key-word and text reference list, and a summary vocabulary and frequency list. By making the texts available in this way, we expect to reach scholars interested in linguistic studies of Early Modern Spanish, particularly as written on the far northern frontier of New Spain.

———

No scholarly work appears without the generosity and support of others, both intellectual and financial. The John Simon Guggenheim Memorial Foundation initially helped to establish the project by a fellowship to John L. Kessell in 1980. The National Historical Publications and Records Commission (NHPRC) and the National Endowment for the Humanities (NEH) have been instrumental in providing institutional support to the Project and its work in subsequent years. In addition, the NHPRC made available publication subventions for *Remote Beyond Compare* that permitted the University of New Mexico Press to keep the volume and its reprint very reasonably priced. The L.J. and Mary C. Skaggs Foundation supplied funding in 1989–90 that permitted a match of NEH monies. A timely grant from Tobías Durán, director of the university's Center for Regional Studies, and José A. Rivera, director of the Southwest Hispanic Research Institute, enabled the Project to complete preparation of the present volume. Joseph P. Sánchez, director, Spanish Colonial Research Center, the National Park Service, has provided the salary of a graduate student and collegiality as a neighbor. Beginning in 1988, the New Mexico State Legislature has given generously to the Project; for this assistance, we would particularly like to thank Sens. Michael Alarid and Tom Benavides.

While the present work encompasses among many others documents in J. Manuel Espinosa's *First Expedition of Vargas into New Mexico, 1692,* we hope we have presented the era in a fresh light through a new translation, broader documentary context, and a comprehensive scholarly apparatus. Because *By Force of Arms* is part of the multivolume *Journals of don Diego de Vargas,* the inclusion of Vargas's previously published campaign journal is justified in terms of continuity. The general unavailability of Espinosa's earlier work also argues for the appearance of this new edition. We remain indebted, however, to Espinosa's pioneering work on the Vargas period.

Over the past decade, we have been fortunate to collaborate with a number of outstanding individuals at the University of New Mexico. Special thanks are due Paul G. Risser, provost and vice-president for research; B. Hobson Wildenthal, dean of the College of Arts and Sciences; Ann W. Powell, director of Research Administration; Jonathan Porter, chair of the History Department; Robert Migneault, dean of Zimmerman Library; and Roger P. Thompson of Contract and Grants Accounting. Our colleagues in the Center for Southwest Research and in the Special Collections Department of Zimmerman Library at the University of New Mexico have lent unstinting aid since the Project began.

We would also like to acknowledge the contributions of Eleanor B. Adams, Martha L. Beebe, Myra Ellen Jenkins, J. William LaRue, William C. Martin, Gary A. Smith, Judy D. Woodward, and M. Jane Young.

As always, the staff of the University of New Mexico Press has been the very embodiment of cooperation. To Elizabeth C. Hadas, director; David V. Holtby, associate director and editor; and Emmy Ezzell, art and production manager, we extend our deep gratitude.

Individual contributors have also played an important role in the Project's continuing existence. Through La Compañía de Vargas, loyal supporters of the Project have time and again responded to our pleas for donations.

What errors may remain we claim as our own.

La Compañía de Vargas

Sargento mayor
Sam and Carrie Arnold
Marco Jesús González Peán
    del Valle y Rivera
Marvin D. and Stella Johnson
Federico Mora
Mr. and Mrs. James K. Walton

Capitán
Mr. and Mrs. Duncan E. Boeckman
Jack Burton
Tim Gallagher/Albuquerque Tribune
Manuel C. Kábana
Janet LeCompte
Joe and Katherine McClaugherty
Mountains and Plains Booksellers
Marc Simmons
Mark and B.J. Thompson

Capellán
Charles W. Polzer, S.J.

Teniente
Eleanor B. Adams
Nancy S. Arnon
Laughlin Barker
Richard K. Barlow
John O. Baxter
Carolyn R. Beske
William and Betsy Bayne
Paul and Marjorie Berman
Helen Greene Blumenschein
Nancy R. Briggs
William C. and Norma Briggs
Janey T. Brink
Hon. Tibo and Betty Jean Chavez
Norman Cleaveland
Saul and Anne-Lise Cohen
John B. Colligan
John P. Conron
Mr. and Mrs. Andrew P. Davis
The Gilberto Espinosa family
Mr. and Mrs. Jerald Friedman

Diana Hadley
G. Emlen Hall
Raymond and Lana Harrigan
Dr. and Mrs. Siegfried S. Hecker
Frank E. and Alice Carr
    Hendricks
Susan Cable Herter
Van Dorn Hooker
Frank Horan
Mrs. Jane H. Ivanovich
Myra Ellen Jenkins
Ken Johns Automotive Group
Marc and Marcia Johnson
Franklin Jones
Robert W. Kern
Jack and Patty Little
Mr. and Mrs. Harold L. Loyd
Tim and Becky MacCurdy
Raymona J. McAdams
Mr. and Mrs. Donald D. McBride
Zachary L. McCormick
Anne Doerfert McGoey
Mr. and Mrs. E.L. Mechem
Manuel J. Meléndez
Marshall R. Nason
Norman Neuerburg
John T. Nichols
Concha Ortiz y Pino de Kleven
George Clayton Pearl
Jennifer J. Pruett
Richard E. and Cecilia Ransom

Jeffrey Romero
Hon. Louis and Gail Saavedra
Jane C. Sanchez
Elynor R. Sass
Carl D. Sheppard
Wid and Katherine Slick
Mr. and Mrs. Robert J. Stamm
Joe and Diana Stein/La Galería
    de los Artesanos Books
R. Ted Steinbock
Patricia McEnearney Stelzner
Ernestino and Harriet Tafoya
Sallie Wagner
Robert and Dorothy Walker
Mr. and Mrs. Jim A. Watson
David J. Weber
Philip J. West
Victor Westphall
Elizabeth Wills
Spencer and Kathleen Wilson

Soldado

Charles B. and Joan Arnold
David V. Holtby
Dorothy D. Hughes
Ruleen Lazzell
Osvaldo Linares
Samuel P. Martin
Ray Martinez
Potter and Kelly, P.A.
Carroll L. and Brent Riley

Part 1

Uprisings against his royal superiority set bad examples for those barbarous nations who do not understand it, but must be made to see it. Thus, they must be made to understand by force of arms. Your excellency will see fit to leave the way this is done to such valiant captains as serve under your superior order.

——Dr. don Benito de Noboa Salgado, fiscal

Introduction

In 1692, when Gov. Diego de Vargas described his new post as "remote beyond compare,"[1] New Mexico was already nearly a century old. Vargas was its thirtieth governor. The colony, known in the documents as the kingdom and provinces of New Mexico, represented, from the vantage of the viceregal court in Mexico City, Spain's claim to the far north. Distant and ill-defined, except for its disputed southern boundary with New Biscay, New Mexico had evolved through two stages.

During the first and shorter—from its founding in 1598 to 1609—don Juan de Oñate governed as proprietor. A silver-mining magnate from Zacatecas, Oñate had negotiated a contract with the viceroy to pacify New Mexico, which he did. For him and his family, this was a business venture. Yet try as they might, the Oñates could discover no commodity or means to profit from their heavy investment. Finally, amid suggestions to abandon the colony, don Juan resigned.[2]

At times during New Mexico's second stage—from 1610 to 1680—Franciscan friars dictated the affairs of the colony. Their appeal to the Spanish crown had averted abandonment and resulted in a change of status from proprietary to government-subsidized royal colony. Although Spain was, to some degree, protecting its northern claim from English and French rivals, New Mexico existed for three generations, at a cost of nearly 2 million pesos, mainly as a Franciscan ministry to the Pueblo Indians.

The most sedentary native people on New Spain's northern frontier—and therefore the most exploitable from the European imperialist point of view—these town dwellers lived in notable contrast to the seminomadic peoples who shared their high, semiarid, basin-and-range landscape. When first contacted by members of Francisco Vázquez de Coronado's expedition in 1540, the Pueblos may have numbered sixty thousand or more. Their population declined stead-

3

New Spain
Map drawn by Jerry L. Livingston.

ily during the seventeenth century, the result of European diseases, famine, and warfare, until, by 1680, there were approximately seventeen thousand Pueblo Indians, counting the western Acomas, Zunis, and Hopis.[3]

Geographically, the Spaniards divided the wider world of the Pueblo Indians into seven or eight clusters, or provinces, based on the different languages they spoke. These Indians shared lifeways and values that were in many respects similar, though some sociocultural and linguistic traits gave individual Pueblo groups their distinctive identity. They lived in compact, multitiered stone and adobe communities, built around plazas representing the center of their universe. Sacred mountains in the four directions marked the outer boundaries of this world. The village and farmlands were considered the women's realm. Beyond lay the mountains, where men hunted and went on sacred pilgrimages. Each pueblo housed from several hundred to as many as two thousand people, who owed primary allegiance to their community, but carried on intricate reciprocal relationships of trade, ceremony, and intermarriage with others in the region. The Spaniards found them cultivating maize, beans, squash, cotton, and tobacco along the Rio Grande valley from the Piro-speaking pueblos in the area of present-day Socorro north as far as Taos, and from Pecos, east of Santa Fe, to the west past Acoma and the Zuni pueblos to the Hopi mesas of Arizona.

Without delay, the Spaniards had sought to impose their Christian sovereignty on the Pueblos. Oñate began by having Pueblo Indian governors in each community swear allegiance to the Spanish monarch. Franciscan friars moved in and induced the people to build adobe or stone and mud churches with their adjoining conventos. Through gifts, ritual, music, and coercion, stiffened by threat of corporal punishment, the missionaries sought to instill the Christian gospel.

The Pueblos already had their own rich and all-encompassing religious beliefs. They included an age-old curing and weather-control complex directed by medicine men or priests, who were entrusted with the well-being of the people, as well as the kachina religion, centered on fertility and the growth of crops. The broad outlines of the kachina cult had been introduced from the south several hundred years before the Spanish incursion, one of several successive waves of Mesoamerican influence.

The Pueblo world was not monolithic, and responses to Christianity varied greatly. For most Pueblos, the prospects offered by another religion were worthy of consideration, at least initially. Parallel rites such as head washing, or baptism, aspersal of holy water, singing, and the use of altars encouraged acceptance. As time wore on, however, Catholicism began to polarize the Indian community. Opinion ranged from those who embraced the new religion, often individuals who were not initiated into esoteric Pueblo rites, to those who rejected the friars' stringent regime and the suppression of indigenous religion; there were also those who incorporated some, but not all, elements of the Spanish faith. Still, before 1680, the Spaniards, a dominant but nervous minority, always managed to punish the murder of missionaries and other acts of Pueblo defiance.[4]

New Mexico's racially mixed Spanish population grew slowly from a few hundred during Oñate's proprietorship to almost three thousand by 1680. The royal governor, his appointees, the Franciscans, and members of some fifteen or twenty economically and socially prominent families formed the upper level of this frontier society. Most of the remaining colonists worked for them. Because New Mexico lay at the far reaches of the camino real and attracted few immigrants, its residents intermarried until almost everyone was related. Hispanic New Mexico became a colony of cousins. That, however, did not ensure harmony.

The community split over exploitation of the Pueblo Indians, the colony's primary natural resource. Missionaries and those colonists employed by them competed with other settlers, at times viciously, for Pueblo Indian labor, land, and loyalty. The Franciscans invoked the higher purpose of Christianizing the heathens, while other Spaniards, often with the governor's support, vowed that without more Pueblo Indian tribute, trade, or irrigable land, they could not hold and defend this land for the king of Spain.

While the division of legal jurisdiction between governors and friars was never clearly defined, especially with regard to the Pueblos, civil and religious power in the colony were remarkably concentrated. The royal governor and captain general exercised overall executive, legislative, judicial, and military authority. He appointed in each of six or eight districts a local official known as alcalde mayor and capitán a guerra who wielded similar delegated authority. Often the governor controlled the cabildo of Santa Fe, the pre-1680 colony's only chartered municipality. As the culturally Hispanic community grew, he named two lieutenant governors, one for the Río Abajo, the downriver jurisdiction below the prominent descent known as La Bajada, 30 kilometers south of Santa Fe, and another for the Río Arriba above.

In the king's name, the governor bestowed mercedes, or grants, of all kinds: of office, land, and Pueblo Indian tribute. This undivided patronage gave him dictatorial power. The several dozen encomenderos collected from all or a designated portion of the households in given pueblos the annual contribution owed to the Spanish crown. The Indians paid in kind: a piece of locally woven cloth, or manta, and a measure of maize from each head of household, or the equivalent. In return, the encomenderos swore to protect their tributaries, foster Christianity among them, and be ready with animals and weapons to answer the governor's call to defend the kingdom.

If civil authority in New Mexico was remarkable for its concentration in one man, religious authority was no less centralized. The Franciscan custos exercised quasi-episcopal powers as prelate over everyone in New Mexico, Indian and colonist alike. As a Franciscan, he was characterized by his asceticism and devotion, zealously seeking martyrdom in the service of God. About 1616, Franciscan authorities had elevated the New Mexican missionary field to the status of custody, a semiautonomous administrative unit meant in time to grow into a fully developed Franciscan province. New Mexico's Custody of the Conversion of St. Paul, however, because of Indian warfare, poverty, and lack of facilities for training novices, remained subordinate to the Province of the Holy Gospel in Mexico City during the entire Spanish colonial period.

Elected for a triennium by the governing body of the province, the father custos directed the friars' activities and represented them in their dealings with the governor and other authorities. He presided over the custody's convention, or chapter meeting, which he convoked as soon as practical after word of his election reached New Mexico. At all other times, a four-man council, the definitorio, advised him. Its members, called definitors, were elected at the convention.

Reassignment of missionaries regularly took place at the chapter meeting. The custos then forwarded to provincial headquarters in Mexico City a list of missionaries and their stations, upon which the number of royal stipends for the custody was based. The missionary in charge of a convento was entitled guardian. Often at a New Mexico mission, the father guardian was the only friar in residence. Because the custos frequently resided in the convento at Santo Domingo Pueblo, it became the colony's unofficial seat of ecclesiastical authority.

Additionally, as prelate, the Franciscan custos exercised the office of ecclesiastical judge ordinary, representing the distant bishop of Durango. This gave him jurisdiction in certain ecclesiastical cases brought for or against laymen in New Mexico, for instance, those relating to asylum in the churches of the colony.

For much of the century, the custos also wielded the formidable authority of the Holy Office of the Inquisition as its local agent. Too often, he used this power for economic gain and political ends. Although mission Indians were exempt from prosecution by the Inquisition, any colonist accused of bigamy, blasphemy, assent to false doctrine, seemingly Jewish practices, a pact with the devil, or the like, could become the object of a local investigation. Forwarded for examination to the tribunal of the Holy Office in Mexico City, such files of testimony in a few instances resulted in the issue of arrest warrants. When served on the accused in New Mexico, they resulted in seizure of property, confinement, a mortifying journey in chains to Mexico City, and trial before the Inquisition in the viceregal capital.

Because no bishop or other ranking churchman resided in the colony, its thirty or forty Franciscans enjoyed an effective spiritual monopoly. If the friars chose to withhold the sacraments of the church or report alleged crimes against the faith to the Inquisition, not even the governor had local recourse. Because appeal to Mexico City took months, governors and friars tended to confront one another in New Mexico. In this poor and remote colony, civil or ecclesiastical protocol seemed to matter as much as material advantage.

As a distant outpost in Spain's world economy, New Mexico figured mostly as an expense. The traditional view of the colony's economy in the seventeenth century is one of a geographically remote area dependent on the triennial mission supply caravans and local barter based on three sources: Indian trade and tribute, a large part of the former with Plains Indians and all of the latter from Pueblos; livestock, mostly sheep, raised on estancias, or ranches, especially in the Río Abajo; and subsistence farming, to which Spaniards added wheat and a variety of non-native fruits and vegetables. New Mexico's few exports included animal skins and hides, woven items of wool and cotton, salt, piñon nuts, criminals sentenced to work in mines or sweatshops to the south, and a good many non–Pueblo Indian slaves. [5]

A well-to-do citizen of New Mexico might have owned a few hundred head of cattle and sheep; a few dozen oxen, horses, and mules; several hundred varas of irrigated land; a few thousand acres of open range; a handful of Indian servants or slaves; the required metal farm implements, tools, and weapons; a sturdy wagon; and a number of prized household goods, imported at high cost, such as clothing, linen, dishes, and religious articles. Most furniture was locally made.

In reality, New Mexico's economy was somewhat more involved, inextricably linked as it was to the rest of the empire, including Peru and the Philippines. [6] From at least as early as the 1640s, only a decade after the silver bonanza at Parral in New Biscay, New Mexicans of means and government officials in the colony engaged in financial transactions with financiers and entrepreneurs in Parral. New Mexico's governors routinely arranged with agents there to process drafts from the viceroy in support of the colony and draw their salaries from the Treasury office in Durango or Zacatecas. These sums were then invested in merchandise and livestock and shipped to New Mexico.

A sophisticated system of credit, tied to some of the most prominent merchants in the viceregal capital, reached through Parral to Santa Fe. Pack trains and wagons owned by New Mexicans and freighters from New Biscay carried on fairly regular trade, with agricultural supplies, such as seed and breeding stock; manufactured goods; a few Black slaves; and venture capital moving north. The events of the 1690s would lead to the rapid reintegration of New Mexico into the imperial economy.

The composition of what could be called secular authority in late-seventeenth-century Pueblo Indian society was more complex than its Spanish counterpart. [7] Since perhaps as early as 1620, the Pueblos elected officials to fill administrative offices created by the Spaniards: pueblo governors, lieutenants, alguaciles, and priests' assistants, or fiscales. Often, these men who dealt regularly with the non-Pueblo world learned Spanish customs and the language. Some were related to Spaniards or were mixed-bloods themselves.

The Spaniards tried to transform these officials into dependent elites by bestowing on them the honorific "don" and granting them the outward signs of authority in the Spanish world, such as horses, European-style clothing, and canes. Yet despite such attentions, these officials tended to retain their primary allegiance to the na-

Two Pueblo Indians of San Ildefonso,
Edward S. Curtis, 1905
Museum of New Mexico

tive priests, becoming effective buffers between Spaniards and Indian religious leaders.

In addition, the Pueblos retained war priests and their captains. The war priest represented Sun Father and the captains the Twin War Gods. They were knowledgeable about and dedicated to indigenous ritual but also had proven themselves in war. They met and dealt with any form of danger from outside. Their followers seemed to be younger and in good physical condition—the mocetones described in the documents as Pueblo fighting men.

Religious authority among the Pueblos resided with the inside chief, or cacique, who was advised by a council composed of the leaders of sacred societies. Representing Earth Mother, he was to treat the people as a mother would her children. Responsible for the internal, spiritual life of the pueblo, he could not take an active part in violence. The war captains and the elected governor, along with their staffs, carried out the decisions of the inside chief and council.

In some respects, access to positions of authority among the Pueblos was more egalitarian than in Spanish society. Responsibility and influence were not as dependent on kinship and clientele relationships as among Spaniards. Maturity and living an exemplary life were keys to personal power, as was knowledge of life-giving myth, legend, and lore. Accumulation of personal wealth was not an acceptable end in itself; generosity and sharing of material goods were highly respected.

The Spaniards successfully played upon the religio-political factionalism that pervaded the Pueblos. The inherent divisions within Pueblo society, for example, alignments along moeity or clan lines, were exacerbated by the varying responses to the Spaniards, who were eager to exploit the resulting tensions. This explained in part the ease of Oñate's conquest and the continuing domination by relatively few Spaniards. Yet in the late 1660s and 1670s, a time of drought and food shortages, the Pueblos showed increasing signs of resentment. There had been sporadic outbreaks of resistance since Oñate's rule, but now, seemingly, more of the Pueblo people listened to leaders who urged drastic means to expel the Spaniards and cleanse the Pueblo homeland.

The all but inevitable Pueblo-Spanish War, fought between 1680 and 1696, occurred in three phases. In the first, the stunningly effective Pueblo Revolt of 1680, the Pueblo Indians rose suddenly in near unison, forcing the Spaniards to evacuate the colony and retreat downriver to the vicinity of El Paso. The much longer second phase, from 1681 to 1691, found the adversaries widely separated for the most part, each side beset by disunity and hardship. During the third and final phase, Spanish reconquest under Gov. Diego de Vargas, 1692–96, settlers and missionaries, relying on force of arms, Pueblo allies, and accommodation, reestablished themselves among the Pueblos. A momentous shared event, the Pueblo-Spanish War ensured the cultural diversity of New Mexico.[8]

Although experience had taught the Spanish citizens of New Mexico not to dismiss entirely rumors of revolt by Pueblo Indians, they could scarcely have imagined during the summer of 1680 the devastation about to envelop them.[9] Five years earlier, Gov. Juan Francisco de Treviño had arrested a number of Tewa ceremonialists for witchcraft and idolatry. Among those punished was a man from the Tewa-speaking pueblo of San Juan known only by his native name. In later documents, the Spaniards referred to him as Popé, master strategist of the 1680 revolt.[10]

The experience of Capt. Francisco de Anaya Almazán, a rugged, second-generation New Mexico rancher and soldier, was typical.[11] In the late summer of 1680, Anaya and a squad of eight armed men were guarding a horse herd in the Tewa district near the pueblo of Santa Clara. It was routine duty. Nothing suggested imminent danger. Then, at daybreak on a Saturday, shouting broke the calm. The usually peaceable Santa Claras, armed and roused for war, rushed the Spaniards with intent to kill. For an instant, the latter must have hesitated; had the Indians gone mad? Two of the guards, Felipe López and Marcos Ramos, died in the fighting, while Anaya and the others, driving the horses before them, made their escape toward Santa Fe.

That day, the feast of St. Lawrence, 10 August, similar and simultaneous violence erupted all over the northern Pueblo world. Actually, Gov. Antonio de Otermín had received messages from Taos, Galisteo, and Pecos that a general revolt was planned for 13 August. He promptly arrested two Tesuque messengers accused of carrying the word from pueblo to pueblo, and they corroborated the story. Otermín took quick action, sending warnings to his alcaldes mayores. Only gradually, however, as survivors made their way into Santa Fe, with stories of widely scattered death and destruction, did the governor grasp that the Indians had advanced the date. His messengers had not reached the outlying areas in time.

Mre. de campo Francisco Gómez Robledo, sent north to reconnoiter, returned on 12 August, confirming the worst. Already, rebellious Pueblos had killed scores of Spaniards, first the Franciscan missionary priests who lived with them in their pueblos, and then dozens of neighboring colonists, whole families.

Fearing that the northern Pueblos would soon unite in an effort to overrun Santa Fe itself, put its defenders to death, and desecrate the church, on 13 August, Governor Otermín sent urgent word to fray Francisco Gómez Cadena at the church and Franciscan convento east of the plaza. The friar was to consume the blessed sacrament; gather the holy images, vessels, and other items of divine worship; close up church and convento; and bring everything to the governor's more defensible residence on the north side of the plaza. There, several hundred desperate and incredulous Spaniards would make their stand.

Early on the morning of the fifteenth, Otermín spotted Tano and Pecos warriors approaching Las Milpas de San Miguel, south of the Santa Fe River. They looted the homes of Mexican Indians in that area and took up positions, waiting for Tewa, Taos, and Picuris reinforcements to join them in the battle against the Spaniards. Three days before, Otermín had sent a Tano named Juan with a message to the alcalde of Galisteo, but Juan had now returned as leader of the defiant warriors.

Entering the villa, Juan announced that he had come with two crosses. Otermín was to choose one or the other. The red cross meant that the Spaniards intended to fight; the white would signal the governor's willingness to withdraw. Declaring that the war was not of his choosing, Otermín refused both. Instead, he insisted that the rebels cease all hostilities, promising that he would pardon them for their treason and sacrilege.

Juan ignored the Spaniard and rode back to his followers, who sounded trumpets and rang the bells of the San Miguel chapel, shouting insults at the Spaniards. Then they destroyed the abandoned dwellings they had occupied and burned the chapel. Otermín decided to attack before the Tewas, Taos, and Picuris arrived. In the day-long battle that followed, the Indians suffered many casualties. Finally, their allies arrived and engaged the Spaniards in another part of the villa so the remaining Tano and Pecos warriors could escape.

With the Spaniards confined in the casas reales, the Pueblos diverted the ditch carrying water to the government complex. They sang victory songs, shouting that the God of the Spaniards, their father, was dead. Mary, their mother, and the saints, mere pieces of rotten wood, were all dead, but the Indians' god lived. During the week-long siege, Governor Otermín recorded the arrival of more and more refugees. For lack of water, cut off for two days and a night, the livestock in the casas reales began to die. Meeting with the most experienced colonists, the governor resolved that it would be better to die fighting than of hunger and thirst as prisoners trapped in the casas reales.

In furious combat on the morning of 20 August, armed and mounted Spaniards put their besiegers to flight. The three Franciscans present, along with civil and military leaders, signed an urgent petition to the governor to evacuate the capital. Hastily distributing clothing, provisions, and animals to the survivors, reportedly more than a thousand, Otermín on 21 August presided over the Spanish withdrawal from Santa Fe.

The Pueblos, content for the moment to let the refugees pass, kept close watch from the mesa tops. Proceeding along the Rio Grande southward, the Spaniards were repeatedly sickened by the sight of friends and relatives killed in the uprising. At Santo Domingo, five bodies lay grotesquely strewn behind the church, and inside, the corpses of three Franciscan missionaries further testified to the ferocity of this rebellion.

Five days after the escape from Santa Fe, just beyond the deserted pueblo of Sandia, a large body of Indians on horseback and on foot ventured down out of the hills to attack the refugees, shouting and firing harquebuses at them. Governor Otermín dispatched fifty armed men who drove them off. From a captured Indian, he learned that his lieutenant governor, don Alonso García, had already retreated south from the pueblo of Isleta with some fifteen hundred men, women, and children. Otermín wrote an angry letter summoning García. Those people had not been forced to fight as Otermín had; they had abandoned their base out of fear alone, not knowing whether their governor was dead or alive. The irate Otermín chose fray Francisco Farfán and four armed men for the dangerous business of delivering the letter.

As this small party pursued García, Otermín questioned the Indian prisoner, an eighty-year-old man from Alameda Pueblo, concerning reasons for the revolt. He stated that resentment toward the Spanish colonists and friars had been strong since the time the kingdom was discovered. The Spaniards took away the Indians' religious objects and forbade the ceremonies, dances, and ancient customs their elders taught them. He had heard Pueblos speak of this since he was of an age to understand. Other Indians spoke of mistreatment by Francisco Javier, Otermín's secretary of government and war, as well as Luis de Quintana and Diego López, who demanded Pueblo labor and burned kivas. Javier had carried out the sentences against the Pueblo leaders in 1675.

Farfán and the escort caught up with the others nine days later at the campsite known as Fray Cristóbal, where they delivered to Alonso García the first word that the governor and many families from the upriver district had survived. García and five or six men hastened north with Father Farfán to greet the governor. The rest of the people, who refused to go back, were, in an opinion attributed to Farfán, so grimly determined not to return to New Mexico that they would willingly die first.

García had scarcely embraced his governor before Otermín ordered him arrested. On review of the written proceedings explaining his subordinate's decision to vacate Isleta, however, the governor relented, acquitting García and releasing him. United finally on 14 September, all the survivors of the Pueblo massacre continued their march toward the mission of Nuestra Señora de Guadalupe at El Paso, where the Franciscan procurator general of New Mexico, fray Francisco de Ayeta, awaited them with meat, maize, and the loaded wagons of the triennial supply caravan.

When Governor Otermín at last took stock of the pathetic New Mexico colony in exile, which he did between 29 September and 2 October on the banks of the swollen river opposite La Salineta, some 16 kilometers northwest of El Paso and still within the jurisdiction of New Mexico, he understood the hopelessness of an immediate reconquest. Many refugees disobeyed him and continued on to El Paso and beyond. Furious, Otermín appealed to the governor and district officers of New Biscay to send the deserters back under threat of punishment. In all, 1,946 people of all ages and classes passed muster, of whom the governor deemed 155 capable of bearing arms.

Fray Francisco Farfán testified that some of the apostate Pueblo Indians, repentant of the atrocities they had committed, had summoned him to remain with them. He endorsed Father Ayeta's pledge to send friars and provisions whenever the authorities decided on a reentry; he, personally, stood ready to resume his ministry.

The colonists fortunate enough to have lived through attack, seige, and retreat had survived the Pueblo Revolt of 1680, the first phase of the Pueblo-Spanish War. In just over six weeks, the Pueblos had driven their former exploiters from New Mexico. For the first time, they had all but united, giving them numerical superiority of more than five to one in the war zone, perhaps fifteen thousand to fewer than three thousand. Moreover, they had taken the Hispanic community by surprise, a fact reflected in the number of casualties—some four hundred colonists killed, among them twenty-one Franciscan missionaries.

The Pueblos' resounding triumph of 1680 for a time obscured the tentative nature of their alliance. One Christian Tiwa Indian from Isleta, Alonso Shimitihua, turned back at La Salineta, intending to persuade his compatriots that they should atone for their grave sins and return to Christianity.[12] He took with him two Tiwas from Isleta, four Piros, and one Jemez. All declared the same purpose for their return, but the Piros disappeared when they reached their territory. The two others from Isleta told Shimitihua they wanted to travel ahead and announce the group in their pueblo, to which he agreed. After Shimitihua arrived, a captain from Alameda Pueblo rode up on horseback with a large retinue, a yellow standard at their head. He wore an alb and surplice with a scarlet band over it and a maniple for a crown. These Catholic vestments were thought to retain the power of the Christian God, and the Pueblos wore them as war trophies to bring whatever benefits they might, just as they venerated the scalps of brave enemies and adopted them into the tribe to bring rain and other blessings.

On the Indian captain's orders, Shimitihua and his companions were bound and escorted from Isleta, through Alameda and Sandia, finally reaching Santo Domingo. While they waited to be questioned by the mixed-blood Keres leader, Alonso Catití, Shimitihua's Tiwa companions revealed to him that they had returned not to beseech their brethren to surrender, but to seek their aid and with them return to El Paso and kill all the Spaniards. The brother of one of the Tiwas had remained with the Spaniards to rally the Mansos to the Pueblo cause, which the Tiwas and Piros also favored.

Betrayed, Shimitihua went to Catití's house, which was decorated with objects looted from churches; carpets and cushions furnished the rooms. A Navajo leader, wearing an alb and chasuble with an altar cloth tied around his head, was there to negotiate a peace with Catití. Next to him was a large chalice in which Catití offered the Navajo water, a traditional gesture of hospitality.

When questioned, Shimitihua responded that he wanted to open their eyes and convince them to repent and return to God. Catití scorned the idea and questioned Shimitihua's companions. Informed of their plan, Catití arranged for the prisoners to meet with Popé. When Popé heard Shimitihua's reason for returning, he reacted more violently than Catití, wounding the Tiwa with a knife and shouting that there was no God and that prayer would never bring mantas and other goods. Shimitihua was saved only because Catití restrained Popé.

Interrogating his Tiwa companions in front of Shimitihua and the Jemez the next day, Popé was pleased with their idea and joined in planning the assault on El Paso. The Tiwas and Piros who would accompany them south were to attack the ranchos of Juan Domínguez and Alonso García in the El Paso area, robbing and killing the inhabitants. The Mansos were to put the friars to death in their conventos. If the Sumas joined, they were to slay all the remaining Spaniards or steal their horses so they could never return to Pueblo territory. The two Tiwas departed for Isleta to complete preparations.

After seeing further acts of desecration at Taos and unwilling to witness any more of the idolatries he knew were being performed in the other pueblos, Shimitihua abandoned his mission and returned to El Paso, arriving there on 6 March 1681. The two Tiwas from Isleta, accompanied by a number of Tiwas and Piros, tried to put their plan into effect, but were intercepted by Faraón Apaches. Five Pueblos were killed, and the two Tiwas' confederates turned back.

Fearing Popé's wrath for this failure, Shimitihua's Isleta companions continued on to El Paso, where they arrived shortly after him. When he accused them of the conspiracy they had revealed to him, they responded that no such plans had been carried out. Instead, they claimed that when they had arrived in Isleta ahead of him, their relatives had warned them that if they showed any sympathy for Spaniards or their God, they would die. They had fabricated the conspiracy story to save their lives.

Popé's leadership, though short-lived, inspired an immediate return to indigenous religion. Shrines were reestablished in the pueblo plazas with offerings of maize meal and feathers. Once again, children learned the traditions of their ancestors. Kachina masks reappeared. Popé ordered everything Spanish destroyed. He prohibited the mention of Mary and Jesus and declared that all Pueblos were to drop their baptismal names. Men were to leave their Christian spouses and take others of their choice. They were to bathe in the rivers to cleanse themselves of holy water and the oils of baptism.

Unanimity, if it ever existed, was fleeting. There were serious differences about the future. Those Pueblos who had most openly rebelled would fight to the death to maintain their freedom. Others knew the Spaniards would inevitably return because they had been born in that land and had grown up with them. Discontent grew as the pace of Apache raids quickened, since the Spaniards no longer offered protection. Old animosities among the Pueblos were rekindled.

The second phase of the Pueblo-Spanish War, the agonizing period from 1681 to 1691, was for the residents of El Paso terribly discouraging. Every royal official in New Spain had heard the shocking news of the Pueblo Indians' revolt and the flight of New Mexico's royal governor. After that, it is not likely they heard much about the refugee colony.[13]

Life in the communities, strung out along the flood plains and the hills of the Rio Grande downriver from the ford that gave the district its name, was, by all contemporary accounts, wretched. Shortages of most everything, crowding and discord among neighbors, alleged profiteering by a greedy few, fears of attack by local Indians, drought and searing heat or flood, too little good farming or grazing land, and uncertainty about the future plagued the families who did not desert.

Gov. Antonio de Otermín, whose request to abandon his post for health reasons was repeatedly denied in Mexico City, decreed in vain that New Mexico survivors who had fled beyond the El Paso district should return. Late in 1681, he led an abortive reconquering expedition back up the Rio Grande. Inconclusive in a military sense, it proved that both Pueblos and Spaniards suffered from deep divisions within their ranks. Popé, the Spaniards learned, had tried to weld a Pueblo confederacy and rule almost in the manner of a Spanish governor. Resentful of his arrogance, other Pueblos deposed him in favor of Luis Tupatú, a less aggressive leader from Picuris Pueblo. For their part, the Spaniards, while ineffectually attempting reconquest, split into factions, each blaming the other for the expedition's failure.

Governor Otermín, who burned what he could of four deserted pueblos en route to Isleta, occupied the latter without a fight and dispatched part of his force under the command of Mre. de campo Juan Domínguez de Mendoza, the colony's most experienced mili-

ORACION
FVNEBRE,
QVE DIXO EL DOCTOR

D. YSIDRO SARIÑANA, Y CVENCA
Chantre de la Santa Iglefia Metropolitana de
Mexico, Cathedratico de Prima de Sagrada Efcritura en
la Real Vniverfidad, Calificador del Tribunal del Santo
Officio de la Inquificion, y Examinador Synodal del
Arçobifpado.

☞ *El dia* 20. *de Março de* 1681. ☜

Prefente el Ex.mo Señor Marquès de la Laguna,
Conde de Paredes, Virrey defta Nueva-Efpaña.

EN las Exequias de veinte y vn Religiofos de la Regular
Obfervancia del Seraphico P. S. Francifco, que murieron
à manos de los Indios Apoftatas de la Nueva-Mexico,
en diez de Agofto del Año de 1680.

Imprimela, y Dedicala à la Catholica, y Real
Mageftad de el Rey N. Señor

D. CARLOS SEGVNDO
(que Dios guarde.)

El R. P. Predicador Fr. FRANCISCO AYETA,
Cuftodio habitual de aquella Cuftodia, actual Vifitador
de ella, y Comiffario General del Santo Officio de la
Inquificion de la Nueva-Efpaña.

CON LICENCIA.

En Mexico, por la Viuda de Bernardo Calderon, año de 1581

Title page of the funeral sermon preached at the memorial service for
twenty-one Franciscan missionaries who died in the Pueblo Revolt of
1680, Mexico City, 20 March 1681

Henry E. Huntington Library and Art Gallery

tary veteran, to reconnoiter the pueblos farther upriver. Domínguez parleyed with Pueblo leaders at Cochiti and fearing a trap, withdrew in order. He met Otermín moving slowly northward, burning pueblos as he came. Reunited in council, the officers considered the fierceness of the winter and the poor condition of animals and men and resolved to turn back for El Paso. On their way south, they forced 385 Isleta Indians to join them and burned their pueblo.

The colony's two most prominent churchmen had accompanied the 1681 Otermín expedition, but fray Francisco de Ayeta and his secretary, fray Nicolás López, disagreed on the prospects of reconquest. Ayeta shared Otermín's pessimism. The Franciscans' chief supply officer, or procurator general, for the past six years, he had arranged in Mexico City and transported to New Mexico the relief caravans of 1677, 1680, and 1681. Shortly after Otermín's failed entrada, Ayeta was off again to negotiate for supplies to sustain the colony in exile. He had seen that the Pueblo Indians upriver despised Spaniards and Christianity and defended the governor's withdrawal of the expedition.

Father López, on the other hand, was deeply critical of Otermín. The governor should never have burned pueblos without first admonishing the Indians. López thought that most of the Pueblo Indians would welcome the Spaniards' return, if the governor's abusive secretary, the cruel and infamous Francisco Javier, were not among them. Fray Nicolás took the part of Juan Domínguez de Mendoza's faction, in control of the Santa Fe cabildo in exile. Mocking Otermín's threat of the death penalty for anyone who left El Paso without his permission, a cabildo delegation headed by the Taos sargento mayor, Fernando Durán y Chaves, set out for Mexico City in March 1682, carrying scathing charges against the governor.[14]

On 29 August 1683, don Domingo Jironza Petrís de Cruzate, a capable career officer from Aragon, replaced Otermín as governor at El Paso. Jironza struck a series of compromises. He had evidently brought with him and restored to their families the members of the cabildo delegation, who had been jailed in Mexico City. By supervising carefully his predecessor's residencia, he was able to send Otermín south with a clean record. In the interest of harmony, he chose not to proceed as instructed against Juan Domínguez de Mendoza. He then set about trying to consolidate and strengthen the El Paso settlements.

For three years, the presence of poverty-stricken New Mexico refugees, at first some two thousand of them and still more than half that number, had strained the meager resources of the El Paso district. Before that, on the south side of the river at the ford, the Franciscans had founded in the late 1650s the mission of Nuestra Señora de Guadalupe, where they congregated several hundred of the local Manso Indians. By 1668, when they dedicated a new church, the mission had a convento and two distant mission stations, or conversiones: one, San Francisco de los Sumas, 50 kilometers due south, near present-day Samalayuca, Chihuahua; and the other, La Soledad de los Janos, evidently at a distance of nearly 300 kilometers more west than south.

In the shadow of mission Nuestra Señora de Guadalupe, just below the ford where the camino real crossed the Rio Grande, a community of colonists had grown up. Whether they lived in New Mexico, whose Franciscan custody supplied the friars, or in New Biscay, whose governors claimed jurisdiction over the near side of the river, was debatable.[15]

After Governor Otermín had moved his New Mexico refugees across the river, he sought jurisdiction along the valley for at least 50 kilometers, as far downriver from El Paso as La Toma, near where don Juan de Oñate had first taken possession in 1598. At the far end, he established what he called the real of San Lorenzo de la Toma, which shared its patron saint's day with the anniversary of the Pueblo Revolt. Here, he and the cabildo of Santa Fe made their temporary headquarters, and here, in September 1681, he recruited the fifty-man presidio authorized in Mexico City. Other refugees, both colonists and Indians, sought to survive in mixed, makeshift settlements between San Lorenzo and El Paso.

Governor Jironza brought with him reconfirmation from the viceroy that El Paso and its district were to be considered part of New Mexico and held at all cost. Moreover, the governor's seat should be a villa, just as Santa Fe had been. If, however, reasoned Jironza, he were able to reoccupy Santa Fe, he could put the problems of sustaining the colony here behind him.

The testimony Otermín recorded of certain Pueblo Indians just before Jironza's arrival left the impression that some Pueblo factions would peacefully accept the Spaniards' return. In mid-November 1683, the new governor sent a small party under the leadership of Capt. Salvador Holguín up the valley to find out. Holguín got as far as Las Barrancas, somewhat south of present-day Albuquerque, where he fought a battle with Apaches and satisfied himself that the Pueblos did not want peace.[16]

In the spring of 1684, after a fruitless inspection of the terrain on both sides of the river, Jironza resolved to concentrate the dispirited population within 6 to 8 kilometers of the mission of Nuestra Señora de Guadalupe at El Paso, where he stationed the presidio. He had made his headquarters at El Paso as well, buying from the Mansos a site and several houses, and beginning construction of buildings to serve as the casas reales. When a widespread, Manso-led plot to massacre the Spanish refugees came to light, he postponed his resettlement plan for the moment.

Moving swiftly, Jironza had the eight alleged instigators arrested, interrogated, and tried. He noted especially in the testimony of the accused their awareness that the Pueblo Indians had not been punished. He sentenced all eight to be garroted that evening. Afterward, their bodies were to be displayed as a public lesson.

Alarmed, a gathering of colonists, accompanied by fray Francisco Farfán, at once appealed to the governor not to carry out the sentence for fear of massive Indian retaliation. They reminded Jironza that twenty-six of their armed men, who had left their families behind, were away on an expedition with Juan Domínguez de Mendoza and fray Nicolás López to the La Junta region and Texas. Jironza reconsidered. He stayed the sentence, but did not revoke it. As a result, most of the Christian Mansos fled northwest of El Paso to the rancheria of Captain Chiquito, leader of the unconverted Mansos.

Jironza then ordered the residents of El Paso communities, much against their will, to close ranks. At the closest site downriver, 2 or 3 kilometers from El Paso, he made them relocate the real of San Lorenzo. Then, moving southwest along the river, came the transplanted, mostly Indian communities: San Antonio de Senecú de los Piros, Corpus Christi de la Ysleta de los Tiguas, and Nuestra Señora de la Concepción de Socorro de los Piros, all three taking their names from abandoned, upriver New Mexico pueblos.

On 6 May 1684, the wide-ranging Sumas and Janos, neighbors of the Mansos to the south and west, rose in rebellion. They sacked and burned distant La Soledad, killing fray Manuel Beltrán and Antonio de Arvizu and his family. At Santa Gertrudis de los Sumas at Ojito, evidently a successor to San Francisco de los Sumas, the rebels murdered the Archuleta family but missed the missionary, who was away at the time. Fray Juan de Zavaleta and fray Antonio de Acevedo barely escaped to Parral from their remote stations in the La Junta area.

In response to an appeal from Capt. Francisco Ramírez de Salazar, alcalde mayor of Casas Grandes, 200 kilometers to the southwest, Jironza had sent his lieutenant governor, Mre. de campo Alonso García, with thirty men in April. In early June, they fought alongside troops from Sonora in a battle against a reported two thousand Mansos, Sumas, Janos, and others. García was wounded, and Afz. Juan de Lagos of the governor's household, along with nine of the Indian allies, died in combat.

The governor himself took the field in late July, with thirty-six soldiers and fray Antonio Guerra, in hope of convincing the rebel Mansos to return. Not far from Captain Chiquito's rancheria, some 80 kilometers northwest of El Paso, at the campsite called Doña Ana, they avoided a trap, engaged the Mansos, and put them to flight. This victory, coupled with the execution in El Paso of the accused Indian conspirators, whose number had increased to ten, resulted, according to Jironza, in new requests for peace.

In September 1684, when Ramírez and Capt. Juan Fernández de la Fuente appeared at El Paso in person to request aid, Jironza dispatched Capt. Roque Madrid with fifty soldiers and a force of allied Piros and Tiwas. Near Casas Grandes, they fought a fierce, day-long battle in which Madrid and eleven soldiers were wounded, along with four Indian allies. They claimed to have killed more than forty of the enemy, wounding many others. Everywhere, it seemed, the frontier was aflame.[17]

In utter desperation late that summer of 1684, the cabildo, in the name of all the suffering families of colonists, had petitioned Jironza to abandon El Paso and settle in the valley of San Martín or along the Río Sacramento in New Biscay. He refused, bound as he was by royal orders to hold El Paso, key to defense of the entire northern frontier. He provided for a census instead, which showed the surviving colonists gathered into three groups, each listed with an indication of their woefully inadequate stores of food, clothing, animals, and weapons. At El Paso, there were 53 households made up of 499 people; at San Lorenzo, 36 households and about 354 people; and at Ysleta, 21 households with 198 people, for a total non-Indian population of 1,051.[18]

The colonists' poverty continued unrelieved during the remainder of Jironza's term. The governor felt compelled in the spring of

1685 to defend himself in legal form against accusations by Alcalde mayor Ramírez de Salazar that Jironza had failed to provide sufficient aid to beleaguered Casas Grandes. In Mexico City, fray Nicolás López, who sought viceregal support for a missionary venture in the La Junta region and Texas, set about lobbying for the appointment of Juan Domínguez de Mendoza as governor to succeed Jironza.

The cabildo in El Paso, again in 1685 under the sway of the Domínguez faction, repudiated its earlier praise of Jironza and now damned his administration in a secret letter sent to the viceroy. With the unauthorized courier, Lázaro de Mizquía, rode Domínguez de Mendoza; his son, Baltasar; and his son-in-law, Diego Lucero de Godoy. The very day of their illegal departure for Mexico City, Governor Jironza opened the trial in absentia of Juan Domínguez de Mendoza. While selected witnesses in El Paso made him out a monster, and Domínguez himself presented in Mexico City a singularly impressive memorial of his long service, a most unlikely candidate had already won appointment as governor.

Inconspicuously, Pedro Reneros de Posada had passed muster before Governor Otermín on 12 September 1681, describing himself as a thirty-year-old bachelor, and eleven days later enlisted as a presidial soldier. Reneros, who must have gone on Otermín's bootless 1681 expedition, rose rapidly in rank to alferez and captain. Governor Jironza had sent him on a mission to Mexico City in 1684. Incredibly, on 19 September 1686, three weeks after Jironza had been in office for the normal three-year term, don Pedro reappeared in El Paso to assume the governorship.

Though he did not solve any of the problems of the New Mexico colony in exile, young Reneros governed vigorously, almost recklessly, as if assured of influence in high places. The most dramatic deed of his foreshortened two and a half years in office was a military reconnaissance in force north into Pueblo country, the first since Otermín's in 1681. Few details have survived. Apparently late in the summer of 1687, the Spanish column proceeded up the Rio Grande to the Jemez River, ascending the latter northwestward the short distance to the Keresan-speaking pueblo of Santa Ana.

Offered terms if they surrendered, the Indians refused, and the Spaniards attacked. The invaders must have overrun the pueblo, since Reneros reported burning it. Then, with four Pueblo leaders and ten other captives, they marched back to El Paso. He ordered the leaders executed. The other ten were found guilty of participating in the revolt of 1680, and Reneros dispatched them under guard to New Biscay, where they were sold as slaves for ten years and forbidden to return to New Mexico.[19]

In 1688 or early 1689, the governor had an encounter with a large gathering of Sumas who seemed inclined toward peace, though they evidently included those who had destroyed the mission station at Ojito five years earlier. Reneros relied on subterfuge. Summoning the Indians under a flag of truce, he attacked, killing many. Identifying nine as leaders, he had them shot and ordered forty more sold into slavery for ten years' labor in the mines, at the same time sending two little girls as gifts to the governor of New Biscay. Instead of praising him, his fellow frontier officers roundly criticized Reneros, asserting that such dishonorable behavior only served to incite the Indians further.[20]

Pedro Reneros de Posada's harsh administration ended much as it had begun, but with roles reversed. Domingo Jironza now replaced Reneros on 21 February 1689. Having cleared his accounts in Mexico City and received reappointment from Spain, Jironza was back for a second term, bringing needed horses, supplies, and weapons. He deflected from his predecessor's residencia to a separate lawsuit the soldiers' accusations that don Pedro had embezzled their pay. During subsequent litigation in Mexico City, when lawyers asked to review the residencia proceedings, it was discovered that the record had inexplicably vanished from the archives. Reneros lost and was ordered to pay.

Reestablished in his post, Governor Jironza led his own armed expedition upriver with 80 Spaniards and 120 Indian allies. Since 1680, year after year, New Mexicans in exile had commemorated vengefully the feast day of St. Lawrence, 10 August. Jironza chose that day in 1689 for their departure. Averaging more than 25 kilometers a day up the eroded and overgrown camino real, Jironza's force left the Rio Grande and rode along the valley of the Jemez River past the previously punished pueblo of Santa Ana as far as the neighboring, hilltop pueblo of Zia, where the Indians had fortified themselves and defiantly awaited the Spaniards. At dawn on the feast day of the beheading of St. John the Baptist, 29 August, the invaders attacked.

According to a laudatory certification the cabildo drew up a year later of Jironza's campaigns, the bloody battle raged all day, until eight o'clock that night, when the Spaniards proclaimed victory. Zia lay devastated and smoldering. The count of prisoners totaled seventy-odd. More than six hundred of the defenders had perished, many preferring death in the flames to surrender. Certain Apaches and other Indians, seemingly intimidated by word of the governor's triumph, came into the campsite at Fray Cristóbal in September to make peace with Jironza as the victorious Spaniards marched back toward El Paso.[21]

Five years later, one of the governor's nephews, Capt. Juan Mateo Manje, wrote another description of the sack of Zia in 1689. He added that fifty of Jironza's eighty Spanish soldiers had been wounded in the fighting. At least one seemed to have died on the way home. Manje also claimed that his uncle formed a pueblo with a missionary in the El Paso area for the Zia captives.[22] Local citizens requested that these captives be awarded to them to sell for ten years' servitude, which the viceroy in council approved on 18 January 1690. While extending thanks in the king's name, the viceroy also raised the annual salary of the El Paso presidial soldiers from 315 pesos to 450, which put them on a par with the soldiers of New Biscay. On 9 February 1690, the viceroy dispatched to Madrid news of the triumph at Zia, recommending that Governor Jironza be rewarded.[23]

Much later, in 1777 or 1778, fray Silvestre Vélez de Escalante, extracting documents in Santa Fe that are now missing, offered that at Zia, Jironza had ordered four allegedly notorious medicine men executed by firing squad in the plaza. The friar also related the story of another remarkable captive taken during the battle.

Spanish-speaking and literate, Bartolomé de Ojeda had fought with determination against the Spaniards. Twice wounded, once by musketshot and once by arrow, and fearing death, he repented and asked to confess to a Spanish priest. Afterward, Governor Jironza had the wounded Indian leader treated and carried along with the other prisoners. When he recovered in El Paso, Ojeda proved a rare source of information for Governor Jironza, who was already planning the reoccupation of New Mexico.

Especially encouraging was Ojeda's report of Pueblo Indian disunity. According to him, the Keresan-speaking peoples of Zia, Santa Ana, San Felipe, Cochiti, and Santo Domingo, along with the Jemez, Taos, and Pecos, were waging continuous warfare against the Tewa pueblos and Picuris. The Acomas had split, one faction still living atop their rocky eminence and the other at Laguna, where immigrants from Zia and Santa Ana had joined them. This Laguna aggregation warred against the other Acoma faction and Zia. Zunis and Hopis were also at war.

Bands of Apaches made peace with some pueblos and raided others whenever they could. The Utes had been hostile since 1680 to all the uprisen Pueblo Indians, punishing especially Taos, Picuris, the Tewa pueblos, and Jemez. The Tewas and Picuris in 1688 had relieved Luis Tupatú of command and reelected Popé, but they were the only ones who obeyed him. Bartolomé de Ojeda also related in detail how seven of the Franciscan missionaries had met their deaths in 1680.[24]

Jironza meant to avenge the dead friars and reconquer New Mexico on a second entrada, which he planned initially for May 1690. In March, however, hostilities flared again to the southwest, and the governor sent another relief detachment to Casas Grandes. The peace agreements he had made with the Mansos, Sumas, and others proved extremely unstable. Rumors of plotting abounded. Finally, having learned of a gathering of ten Indian groups bent on annihilating the El Paso settlements, Jironza took the field with seventy soldiers and a hundred Indian allies. Departing 28 October, they could not have gone far. On 1 November, they fell on a remnant of the gathering, killing some and taking the women and children captive. A few days later, at the Indians' request, Jironza again granted them peace.[25]

Although Governor Jironza may not have known it, his successor, Diego de Vargas, a man who would later criticize him for making peace too hastily, had already left Mexico City and was proceeding northward toward the frontier. As governor, Jironza might have expected to complete a full three-year term, as he had before. Moreover, on the strength of his dramatic victory at Zia, he expected reappointment so that he might carry through and restore the lost kingdom.

Late in 1643—a year that witnessed France's signal victory over Spanish forces near Rocroi; the birth in Normandy of explorer Robert Cavelier, sieur de La Salle; and, in New Mexico, the public execution of eight colonists accused of murdering the royal governor—Diego de Vargas was born in Madrid to an illustrious and indebted family of the middling nobility. His mother died when he was five. His father, a captain and knight in the Order of Santiago, departed soon after for the Indies to serve, remarry, and die in Guatemala. Diego; his older brother, Lorenzo; and their younger sister, Antonia, grew up secure amid a large extended family and the amenities of their class.

At age sixteen, don Diego became the sole male heir to the House of Vargas of Madrid when his brother died. Two years later, in 1662, he petitioned and received from the crown permission to act for himself in legal matters. He claimed to have attended classes at the University of Valladolid, but did not earn a degree. In 1664, when he was twenty, Vargas married Beatriz Pimentel de Prado, twenty-two. She and her prominent family were his neighbors in Torrelaguna, fewer than 50 kilometers north of Madrid, where the Vargases owned a great house and scattered properties. During the next six years, the couple had five children, all baptized in the parish church at Torrelaguna. Four survived infancy, two boys and two girls.

In 1666, Vargas learned that his father had died in Guatemala. Although he took formal possession of the family's properties in Madrid, Torrelaguna, and Granada, he evidently did not relish the responsibilities of a landed gentleman. By 1672, don Diego had resolved to go to the Indies, primarily to collect a share of his father's sizable Guatemala estate.

Leaving behind doña Beatriz and their four small children, Vargas, now twenty-eight years old, secured a one-time appointment as royal courier to the viceroy of New Spain. Witnesses testified before his departure that don Diego was his deceased father's only male heir, describing him as a young man of average stature, straight hair, and broad face. His most distinguishing feature, they noted, was a speech impediment; he lisped. Delayed for months in Cadiz, Diego de Vargas sailed at last aboard a packet boat in the spring of 1673.[26]

Amid the bustle of Mexico City, set on Lake Texcoco and rimmed by snow-clad volcanoes, Vargas found favor. The viceroy, the Marqués de Mancera, appointed him alcalde mayor of Teutila, a gold-mining district in the mountains of Oaxaca, a few days' ride from Guatemala. Here, he received the sad news from a brother-in-law that his wife, doña Beatriz, had died suddenly in Torrelaguna. By return mail, he provided for his young children, revealed the ruggedness of his first post in the Indies, and implied he would soon return to Madrid.

Nevertheless, five and a half years later, Vargas accepted promotion to a more prominent mining district. Tlalpujahua lay in the mountains 160 kilometers northwest of Mexico City. By this time, 1679, he was maintaining a residence in Mexico City and a woman

Diego de Vargas, the only known portrait,
Capilla de San Isidro, Madrid.
Estudio Portillo, Madrid.
Courtesy J. Manuel Espinosa

companion by whom, over the next several years, he had at least three natural children.

Vargas's career went well. On the strength of his energetic administration of the Tlalpujahua district, which saw crown receipts from local silver mines triple in five years, the viceroy, the Conde de Paredes, recommended Vargas for promotion. Although seeking a post in Guatemala or Peru, in mid-1688, he settled for the governorship of New Mexico, a colony in exile. Ten days after his agent at court in Madrid paid 2,500 pesos into the treasury of the Council of the Indies, the bureaucracy produced his royal title. Yet, more than two and a half years elapsed before Diego de Vargas assumed the governorship in El Paso.[27]

Whatever Vargas's abilities, he inhabited a world in which personal connections often counted more than accomplishments. He knew how to use family and elite networks in Madrid and Mexico City. It was no coincidence that his career flourished during the viceregal terms of don Tomás de la Cerda y Aragón, the Conde de Paredes, 1680–86; don Gaspar de la Cerda Sandoval Silva y Mendoza, the Conde de Galve, 1688–96; and don Francisco de la Cueva Enríquez, the Duque de Alburquerque, 1702–11, all of whom maintained homes and ties in Madrid. They and their families knew one other at court, and all were related by blood or marriage.[28]

Vargas's connections to these three powerful men owed much to the women in their lives. When don Tomás de la Cerda y Aragón, third Marqués de la Laguna, married doña Luisa Manrique de Lara y Gonzaga, eleventh Condesa de Paredes, in 1675, he added her illustrious title to his own.[29] In February 1684, while don Tomás was serving as viceroy in Mexico City, doña Juana de la Cerda y de Aragón, daughter of his brother, don Juan Francisco Tomás Lorenzo de la Cerda Enríquez de Ribera y Portocarrero, eighth Duque de Medinaceli, wed don Francisco de la Cueva Enríquez, tenth Duque de Alburquerque, viceroy of New Spain in the early eighteenth century.[30]

When Vargas's twenty-three-year-old elder daughter, Isabel María, married Ignacio López de Zárate, forty-one, in Madrid on 13 December 1688, don Diego, through no effort of his own, acquired further connections at court. Don Ignacio acted as legal adviser to the Council of War, the administrative body responsible for military matters throughout the empire. His elder brother, Juan Antonio, the first Marqués de Villanueva de la Sagra and knight in the Order of Santiago, served as its secretary. Boasting later, López de Zárate told his father-in-law that the whole court had attended the wedding.

The couple's marriage sponsors were the Duque and Duquesa de Fernandina, children of the Marqués de Villafranca.[31] In 1688, don Fadrique de Toledo y Osorio held the title as seventh Marqués de Villafranca and the Duque de Fernandina. Don Fadrique was also the father of doña Gelvira María de Toledo y Córdoba, the second wife of don Gaspar de Silva y Mendoza de la Cerda, eighth Conde de Galve.[32] Thus, through his daughter, don Diego enjoyed a quasi-familial relationship with the viceroy, the Conde de Galve, established at a most propitious moment in Vargas's career.

Understandably, don Diego sought to spin as broad a web of influence at court in Madrid as he could. From the beginning of their correspondence in 1690, he never scrupled to ask his son-in-law for favors. Moreover, he implored don Ignacio to act as a surrogate father to Isabel María's younger brother, Juan Manuel, nineteen, the family's sole surviving legitimate son and heir. Through him, too, Vargas enhanced his connections. Juan Manuel lived at the royal palace as a menino in the queen's household, then presided over by the former viceroy, the Conde de Paredes, and by the Duquesa de Alburquerque, Ana Rosalía Fernández.[33]

A close personal relationship also bound the Conde de Galve and the House of Alburquerque. In 1686, on the death of don Melchor de la Cueva y Enríquez, ninth Duque de Alburquerque, Galve had felt moved to wear a long mourning cloak, not because of family ties, but because it seemed appropriate.[34] Years later, after his long service in Mexico City and the voyage home, the moribund Conde de Galve was carried to the house of his dear friend, the tenth Duque de Alburquerque, in Puerto de Santa María, where he died.[35] Although Galve's death stripped Vargas of an influential patron, he continued to seek favor through the former viceroy's widow.[36]

Perhaps through her brother, a menino in the royal household where the Duquesa de Alburquerque occupied a place of great honor, Isabel María de Vargas seems to have become a friend of the women of the House of Alburquerque. She and don Ignacio, it would appear, named a daughter born in 1692 or 1693 for Ana Rosalía Fernández, ninth Duquesa de Alburquerque and mother of the tenth duque. Isabel María accompanied doña Ana Rosalía when she bade farewell to her son and daughter-in-law as they departed Madrid in 1702 for Mexico City. Doña Juana de la Cerda y de Aragón, the tenth duquesa and vicereine of New Spain, personally carried a letter from Isabel María to Vargas, who was then in Mexico City. After the Duque de Alburquerque acquitted him of the charges against him,

Carlos II and members of his court, 1684, detail from the painting "La Sagrada Forma" by Claudio Coello, 1685–90, El Escorial
From *El Escorial, 1563–1963* (1963)

don Diego urged his family to write the viceroy and thank him for his assistance. In Madrid, Isabel María and Ignacio called on the elder duquesa to express their gratitude. Finally, when Diego de Vargas died in New Mexico in 1704, the Duque de Alburquerque wrote a letter of condolence to the Santa Fe cabildo.[37]

The Conde de Galve, thirtieth viceroy of New Spain, assumed office in September 1688, although his public entrance into Mexico City was delayed until 4 December. Whether don Gaspar de la Cerda Sandoval and don Diego de Vargas Zapata, ten years younger, had actually known one other in Madrid, their families certainly did, and don Diego had an old friend in don Amadeo Isidro Zeyol, mayordomo of Galve's household.[38]

Galve's rule lasted seven years, during which he made lasting contributions to all aspects of life in the viceroyalty, religious, social, and military. In 1689, he instructed Dr. Juan de Aréchaga, senior judge of the audiencia, to supervise construction of a seminary for secular clergy, the Seminario Conciliar, which rose at a cost of 40,000 pesos on the east side of the cathedral facing the Calle del Reloj. Galve also encouraged the establishment of new parishes in Mexico City in 1689–90.

Taking a personal interest in the drainage system, or desagüe, designed to control the flooding of Mexico City, the viceroy enlisted the services of fray Juan Romero; Pedro de la Bastida, an audiencia judge; and engineer Jaime Franck. Between 1691 and 1693, with new infusions of funds and labor, they oversaw extensive cleaning and repair, bringing the desagüe into good working order for the first time in years. Another of Galve's projects, initiated but not completed during his administration, was a road connecting Guatemala and Yucatán.[39]

The Conde de Galve also witnessed New Spain's most serious internal crisis in the summer of 1692. Failure of the wheat crops in the Puebla region in 1691 had resulted in food shortages and high prices. Early in June 1692, widespread rioting broke out, particularly among the Indians and lower classes in Mexico City and Tlaxcala. A mob swept into the main plaza of the capital, setting fire to the cabildo building, the granary, a number of shops, and even the viceregal palace. Only through military mobilization of the city's elite were the disorders finally brought under control.[40]

Defense of his vast jurisdiction—stretching from Santo Domingo

in the east to the Philippines in the west—challenged the new viceroy of New Spain. Reports of European rivals, pirates, and rebellious Indians vied for his attention. Fortunately, for a period of five
months, the Conde de Galve benefited from the counsel and experience of the outgoing viceroy, the Conde de Monclova, who had
been posted to Peru.[41] Beginning in 1687, Monclova had put into
effect a series of measures designed to secure his far-flung jurisdiction. From mutinous Chamorros and English adventurers in Guam[42]
to La Salle's Frenchmen in Texas, the viceroy confronted numerous flash points, which, taken together, had ominous potential. His
swift responses apparently led Carlos II to name him to the Viceroyalty of Peru after only two years in New Spain.[43]

It is unclear why the king chose Galve as Monclova's replacement.
Neither is it known what had prepared him for the position. Yet, as
the two viceroys conferred through the winter of 1688 and early spring
1689, they doubtless fashioned strategies to deal with the multiple
threats. The plan that emerged contained much that Monclova had
begun, but must also have incorporated Galve's innovations.[44]

How they sought to defend New Spain and its dependencies Galve
revealed in confidential correspondence with his brother, the Marqués
del Cenete, the future Duque del Infantado.[45] Through his brother,
well placed at court, Galve was assured that his concerns reached
the king's ear. Not a comprehensive scheme, Galve's reaction to foreign interlopers and local insurgents included a wide range of defensive proposals, some of which were approved and implemented, while
others were ignored.[46]

One of the first alarms Galve heard on his arrival in Mexico City
was sounded by the governor of New León, who reported Frenchmen
in his jurisdiction—among them, Jean L'Archevêque and Jacques
Grollet, who had been with La Salle.[47] In 1689, Galve dispatched
Alonso de León on an expedition, suggested earlier by Monclova, to
find La Salle's French colony.[48] The following year, León ventured
into east Texas to found mission San Francisco de Tejas. The restive Tarahumaras in New Biscay, meanwhile, staged a major rebellion in 1690, which threatened the security of the entire northern
frontier. Galve's response was swift and effective.[49] That same year,
he sent two thousand soldiers to Santo Domingo to secure the northern part of the island against the French.[50]

Late in 1692, word reached the viceroy that Diego de Vargas had
reentered Santa Fe and reconquered New Mexico. All New Spain

celebrated the news, and Galve reported it in glowing terms to his brother and the king in Madrid.[51] In the spring of 1693, Andrés de Pez sailed across the Gulf of Mexico to a bay he named Santa María de Galve, and, in 1689, Spaniards erected the presidio of San Carlos de Panzacola nearby on the Florida gulf coast.[52]

Most of Galve's successes took place on land; his battles with English, French, and Dutch pirates preying on Spanish possessions in both oceans were less conclusive. Pirates interrupted the sailing of the Manila galleon from the Philippines, and their activity in Yucatán forced the viceroy to expend considerable resources on fortifications at Campeche, prey to the intrepid Lorencillo. Martín Rivas led a failed attempt to drive the English from the area in 1688–89. At Havana, the fortresses required constant vigilance, and the forces there dedicated much of their time to fitting out ships to hunt pirates. The Armada de Barlovento increased from seven to fourteen vessels and was then reduced to six during Galve's administration.[53] On balance, the defensive maneuvers of the Conde de Galve, including the reincorporation of New Mexico, more often than not produced the desired results.

Vargas must have looked forward with pleasure to Galve's coming. Although his record as alcalde mayor of Tlalpujahua had been commendable, by early 1687, during Monclova's brief tenure, Vargas found himself in Mexico City without a post. His 1688 appointment in Spain to the governorship of New Mexico stipulated a five-year term, the same 2,000-peso annual salary his predecessors received, and immediate action by the viceroy, even if a previous viceregal appointee's term had not ended. Galve, who assumed command from Monclova before Vargas's New Mexico appointment reached Mexico City, reappointed don Diego to Tlalpujahua early in 1689.

That convenient arrangement, however, went awry when a royal appointee to the same post appeared unexpectedly later that year. There was nothing Galve could do. Vargas had to relinquish Tlalpujahua again, which caused him severe financial hardship. As alcalde mayor and local administrator of the royal monopoly on mercury, an essential ingredient in the amalgamation of silver, he had advanced large quantities of mercury to miners on credit. Now, he had to appeal to them and their agents for early payment while Galve held the New Mexico appointment for him.

Early in 1690, the viceroy received news of Domingo Jironza's triumph at Zia and recommended the New Mexico governor to the king. It took months for the viceroy's report to reach Madrid and months for notice of any royal reward to Jironza, such as reappointment to the governorship of New Mexico, to arrive in Mexico City. Still, if he intended to fill the New Mexico post, don Diego had to get his affairs in order.

Fortunately, his longtime friend and principal creditor in Mexico City, financier don Luis Sáenz de Tagle, was one of the richest men in the capital. Buyer of unminted silver, outfitter of mine owners and administrators, and prominent member of the Consulado, or merchants' guild, Sáenz de Tagle had loaned Vargas large sums of money during his alcaldía mayor at Tlalpujahua. Don Luis and his nephew and son-in-law, don Francisco Díaz de Tagle, continued to do so while don Diego served in New Mexico. Don Francisco, an attorney, represented Vargas in Mexico City and arranged the provision and conveyance of supplies to the distant colony.[54]

On 25 September 1690, the Conde de Galve issued the dispatches ordering Vargas's accession to the governorship of New Mexico. As governor-designate, he received from the treasury office on 12 October two years' salary in advance, or 4,000 pesos, as well as an allowance of 800 pesos for moving and travel expenses. Assuring her that he was providing for her dowry, don Diego wrote a short letter to Isabel María in Madrid on 4 November, just before he set out for New Mexico. "Hence, I go," he told her, "not heeding a journey of five hundred leagues through the land of infidel, heathen, and barbarous Indians, one continually in a state of open warfare."[55]

As was his custom, Vargas kept separate his Old and New World lives. He mentioned to neither Isabel María nor don Ignacio in Spain the family he was leaving in Mexico City. By 1691, the eldest of his three natural children was about ten years old. He had given the boy the name Juan Manuel, the same as his legitimate son in Spain. The other two, Alonso and María Teresa, were about nine and five. Taking his leave of the children, who remained in the capital with their mother, forty-seven-year-old Diego de Vargas, accompanied by attendants and baggage, struck northwest from the valley of Mexico on the camino real, bound for the silver-rich city of Zacatecas and the high desert that lay beyond.

He was three months en route, "most nights," he related to his son-in-law, "sleeping with my boots on, horse saddled, and weapons at the ready."[56] Acceding formally to the governorship of New Mexico at El Paso on 22 February 1691, don Diego de Vargas evidently conducted don Domingo Jironza's residencia with gentlemanly dispatch, and the latter departed once again for Mexico City. Only then, beginning in mid-April, did Vargas report to Viceroy Galve the deplorable conditions of the place and turn his attention to coping with the morale, security, and supply of the New Mexico colony in exile.

Abbreviations

Type of Document

ADS	Autograph document signed
AL	Autograph letter
ALS	Autograph letter signed
C	Copy
DS	Document signed
L	Letter
LS	Letter signed

Works

CRG	J. Manuel Espinosa *Crusaders of the Río Grande*
HAHR	*Hispanic American Historical Review*
Handbook	Alfonso Ortiz, ed. *Southwest* vols. 9 and 10 of *The Handbook of North American Indians*
KCC	John L. Kessell *Kiva, Cross, and Crown*
NCE	*New Catholic Encyclopedia*
NMF	Fray Angélico Chavez *Origins of New Mexico Families*
NMFA	Fray Angélico Chávez "Origins of New Mexico Families, Addenda"
NMHR	*New Mexico Historical Review*
NMR	Fray Angélico Chávez *New Mexico Roots*
RAP	Michael P. Marshall and Henry J. Walt *Rio Abajo Prehistory*
RBC	John L. Kessell *Remote Beyond Compare*
RECOP	*Recopilación de leyes de los reinos de las Indias*

Archives

AASF	Archives of the Archdiocese of Santa Fe, Santa Fe, New Mexico
AGI	Archivo General de Indias, Seville, Spain
AGN	AGN Archivo General de la Nación, Mexico City, Mexico
AGNot.	Archivo General de Notarías del Distrito Federal, Mexico City, Mexico
AHN	Archivo Histórico de la Nación, Madrid, Spain
AHP	Archivo del Hidalgo del Parral (Chihuahua), Mexico
AHPM	Archivo Histórico de Protocolos, Madrid, Spain
BNM	Biblioteca Nacional de México, Mexico City, Mexico
BYU	Harold B. Lee Library, Brigham Young University, Provo, Utah
EBARN	Eleanor B. Adams, research notes
HL	The Henry E. Huntington Library, San Marino, California
LDS	Microfilm collection of the Church of Jesus Christ of Latter-day Saints, Salt Lake City, Utah
SANM I, II	Spanish Archives of New Mexico, New Mexico State Records Center and Archives, Santa Fe

Notes

1. Diego de Vargas to Ignacio López de Zárate, El Paso, 9 Apr. 1692, in John L. Kessell, Rick Hendricks, Meredith D. Dodge, Larry D. Miller, and Eleanor B. Adams, eds., *Remote Beyond Compare: Letters of don Diego de Vargas to His Family from New Spain and New Mexico, 1675–1706* (Albuquerque, 1989) (hereinafter RBC):167–68.

2. George P. Hammond and Agapito Rey, eds., *Don Juan de Oñate, Colonizer of New Mexico, 1595–1628* (Albuquerque, 1953), 1:6, 42–57; 2:1042–45.

3. Estimates of Pueblo population on contact in 1540 and at the time of the first permanent Spanish settlement in 1598 vary widely. Those presented here are conservative. A recent study postulates the total population of the Pueblo Southwest in 1500 as high as approximately 220,000, which includes 131,750 in the Rio Grande pueblos (excluding the Tompiro region), 66,967 people in the Western Pueblo region, and about 23,000 hunter-gatherers dispersed east and south of the Rio Grande pueblos. Unrecorded epidemics between 1540 and 1600

may have resulted in a dramatic population loss not corroborated by colonial documents. For the documented decline in one pueblo, see John L. Kessell, *Kiva, Cross, and Crown: The Pecos Indians and New Mexico, 1540–1840* (Washington, D.C., 1979) (hereinafter KCC): 489–92. Steadman Upham, "Population and Spanish Contact in the American Southwest" (Paper delivered at "Disease and Demographics: New World Peoples Before and After 1492," Smithsonian Institution, Washington, D.C., 2–3 Nov. 1989). Marc Simmons, "History of Pueblo-Spanish Relations to 1821," in *Southwest*, vol. 9 of *Handbook of North American Indians* (Washington, D.C., 1979):186. In the Vargas series, we are using Pueblos with uppercase P for the people and lowercase p for their communities, except when referring to a specific named pueblo, e.g., Pecos Pueblo.

4. Early efforts to understand the dynamics of Christian conversion and Pueblo reaction include Edward H. Spicer, "Spanish-Indian Acculturation in

the Southwest," *American Anthropologist* 56 (Aug. 1954):663–84, and Edward P. Dozier, "Rio Grande Pueblos," in *Perspectives in American Indian Culture Change* (Chicago, 1961):94–186. More recent discussions include David R. Wilcox, "Changing Perspectives on the Protohistoric Pueblos, AD 1450–1700," and Florence Hawley Ellis, "Comments on Four Papers Pertaining to the Protohistoric Southwest," in *The Protohistoric Period in the North American Southwest, AD 1450–1700* (Tempe, 1981):378–409, 410–33. A highly interpretive work is Ramón A. Gutiérrez, *When Jesus Came, the Corn Mothers Went Away: Marriage, Sexuality, and Power in New Mexico, 1500–1846* (Stanford, 1991).

5. For seventeenth-century New Mexico, the various studies by France V. Scholes, most of them published singly or serially in the *New Mexico Historical Review* (hereinafter NMHR), remain the most useful, among them "The Supply Service of the New Mexican Missions in the Seventeenth Century," 5 (Jan. 1930):93–115, (Apr. 1930): 186–210, (Oct. 1930):386–404; "Problems in the Early Ecclesiastical History of New Mexico," 7 (Jan. 1932):32–74; "Civil Government and Society in New Mexico in the Seventeenth Century," 10 (Apr. 1935):71–111; *Church and State in New Mexico, 1610–1650* (Albuquerque, 1937), also NMHR; and *Troublous Times in*

New Mexico, 1659–1670 (Albuquerque, 1942), also NMHR.

6. Felipe de la Cueva Montaño to Andrés Hurtado, Slave sale, Parral, 12 Nov. 1663, AHP, 1662B. Ana María Niño de Castro, Will for Bartolomé de Estrada Ramírez, Parral, 8 Dec. 1684, AHP, 1685B. Tomé Domínguez to Andrés Peláez, Bill of sale, Parral, 4 June 1641, AHP, 1641A. Juan Durán de Miranda to Domingo de la Puente, Power of attorney, Parral, 11 May 1671, AHP, 1671C. Juan Manso to Domingo de la Puente, Power of attorney, Parral, 13 Jan. 1662, AHP, 1662B.

7. This discussion is based on Rick Hendricks, "Observations of Pueblo-Spanish Relations in the Vargas Era" (Paper delivered at the New Mexico Historical Society Annual Conference, Socorro, New Mexico, 9 Oct. 1989). See also Alfonso Ortiz, *The Tewa World: Space, Time, Being, and Becoming in a Pueblo Society* (Chicago, 1969); Triloki Nath Pandey, "Images of Power in a Southwestern Pueblo," in *Anthropology of Power: Ethnographic Studies from Asia, Oceania, and the New World* (New York, 1977):195–215; and Edward P. Dozier, "Spanish-Catholic Influences on Rio Grande Pueblo Religion," *American Anthropologist* 60 (June 1958):441–48.

8. The concept of a continuous, three-act Pueblo-Spanish War, 1680 to 1696, is suggested by John L. Kessell, "Spaniards and Pueblos: From Crusading

Intolerance to Pragmatic Accommodation," in *Archaeological and Historical Perspectives on the Spanish Borderlands West*, vol. 1 of *Columbian Consequences* (Washington, D.C., 1989):127–38.

9. The seventeenth century witnessed several violent outbreaks of Indian resistance in New Mexico. Although the purpose of the conspiracies was to drive the Spaniards from the colony, Pueblo efforts were thwarted because of disunity and Indian informers who betrayed their compatriots to the Spaniards. In the mid-1640s, Gov. Fernando de Argüello Carvajal (1644–47) ordered twenty-nine Indians hanged at Jemez for plotting with Apaches to overthrow the Spaniards. A revolt of the Jemez, Keres, Southern Tiwas, and Apaches discovered in 1650 resulted in execution of nine‾ leaders and the enslavement of other participants for ten years. Piro rebels in the late 1660s met a similar fate, as did Esteban Clemente, a ladino Indian hanged immediately after disclosure of his plan for a general rebellion. KCC, 168, 225. Jane C. Sanchez, "Spanish-Indian Relations during the Otermín Administration, 1677–1683," NMHR 58 (Apr. 1983):133–51.

10. Moving from San Juan north to Taos, seemingly to take advantage of that pueblo's relative isolation and long tradition of resistance, Popé formed an alliance of Pueblo religious and war leaders that cut across linguistic bounds and all but united the Pueblo world. Charles Wilson Hackett, ed., and Charmion Clair Shelby, trans., *Revolt of the Pueblo Indians of New Mexico and Otermín's Attempted Reconquest, 1680–1682* (Albuquerque, 1942), 1:xix–xxviii. Alfonso Ortiz, "Popay's Leadership: A Pueblo Perspective," *El Palacio* 86 (Win. 1980–81):18–22. Joe S. Sando, "The Pueblo Revolt," in *Southwest*, vol. 9 of *Handbook of North American Indians* (Washington, D.C., 1979):194–97. A controversial interpretation that identifies an angry mulatto as mastermind of the 1680 uprising is Fray Angélico Chávez, "Pohé-yemo's Representative and the Pueblo Revolt of 1680," NMHR 42 (Apr. 1967):85–126. More recently, Stefanie Beninato, "Popé, Pose-yemu, and Naranjo: A New Look at Leadership in the Pueblo Revolt of 1680," NMHR 65 (Oct. 1990):417–35, has suggested that a thoroughly acculturated descendant of the mulatto might have served as a Pueblo war leader whose role in the revolt complemented Popé's.

11. The following description of events is based primarily on the introduction in volume one of Hackett and Shelby's *Revolt*. This standard, two-volume work presents translations of the contemporary documents.

12. The source for the Shimitihua account is Eleanor B. Adams's unpublished transcript of Silvestre Vélez de Escalante, Extracto de noticias, 1777–78,

BNM, 3:1 (19/397.1). Vélez de Escalante compiled the Extracto from documents, some now missing, in the governor's archive in Santa Fe. Eleanor B. Adams, "Fray Silvestre and the Obstinate Hopi," NMHR 38 (Apr. 1963):115–16. Sanchez, "Spanish-Indian Relations," 134–37, also relates the case of Shimitihua.

13. The most complete study of the New Mexico colony in exile is Vina Walz, "History of the El Paso Area, 1680–1692" (Ph.D. diss., Univ. of New Mexico, 1950). "Of the four governors who served in El Paso during this period," she writes in summary (pp. v–vi), "Otermín had the supplies and lacked the character; Jironza had character and wanted resources; Reneros had neither; Vargas had both."

14. This is not the conspicuous Río Abajo rancher of the same name. Fray Angélico Chávez, *Chávez: A Distinctive American Clan of New Mexico* (Santa Fe, 1989):35–37, and *The Origins of New Mexico Families in the Spanish Colonial Period in Two Parts: The Seventeenth (1598–1693), and the Eighteenth (1693–1821) Centuries* (1954; rpt., Santa Fe, 1975) (hereinafter NMF):21–22. Sanchez, "Spanish-Indian Relations," 133–51. Hackett and Shelby, *Revolt*, 2:32–375. Walz, "History of the El Paso Area," 51–103.

15. Anne E. Hughes, *The Beginnings of Spanish Settlement in the El Paso District* (Berkeley,

1935):295–391, carried the subject up to 1685 and was corrected in certain particulars by Walz, "History of the El Paso Area." For a general description of the Mansos, Sumas, Janos, and other neighboring hunting-and-gathering band people, see William B. Griffen, "Southern Periphery: East," in *Southwest*, vol. 10 of *Handbook of North American Indians* (Washington, D.C., 1983):329–42.

16. Certification by the cabildo, El Paso, 25 Nov. 1690, AGN, Civil 1743. NMF, 82. Sanchez, "Spanish-Indian Relations," 144–47.

17. Roque Madrid to Domingo Jironza, Casas Grandes, 3 Oct. 1684, and Muster, El Paso, 15 Nov. 1684, in Thomas H. Naylor and Charles W. Polzer, eds., *The Presidio and Militia on the Northern Frontier of New Spain* (Tucson, 1986), 1:506–27, 521 n37. Certification by the cabildo, 25 Nov. 1690. Walz, "History of the El Paso Area," 135–70.

18. Evidently, Jironza exhorted the alcaldes mayores of New Biscay and sent his lieutenant governor, Francisco Madrid, on a tour of the mines and settlements of that province to round up and return former New Mexicans. Madrid brought back thirty. Francisco R. Almada, *Diccionario de historia, geografía y biografía sonorenses* (Chihuahua, 1952):410–11. General muster, El Paso, 11–14 Sept. 1684, in Ernest J. Burrus, ed., "A Tragic Interlude in the Reconquest of New Mexico,"

Manuscripta 29 (Nov. 1985), 154–65.

19. Walz, "History of the El Paso Area," 187–244. Proceedings, El Paso, 12 Apr. 1685 and Muster, El Paso, 15 Nov. 1684, wherein Reneros appeared as Veneros de Posada, in Naylor and Polzer, *Presidio and Militia*, 1:514–47. Muster, San Lorenzo, 9–12 Sept. 1681, and List of soldiers, 23 Sept. 1681, in Hackett and Shelby, *Revolt*, 2:35–68, 134–42.

20. This Machiavellian victory over the Sumas has been somewhat confused. For one thing, a surviving document blamed it on Capt. Pedro Renedos, which led Guillermo Porras Muñoz, *La frontera con los Indios de Nueva Vizcaya en el siglo XVII* (Mexico City, 1980):89, 328, to make Renedos another man and describe two similar actions against the Sumas. Walz, "History of the El Paso Area," 227–28, correctly identified Renedos as Reneros, but also thought there were two battles. The second, she assumed incorrectly, took place after his term as governor of New Mexico, while Reneros was campaigning as a captain under the governor of New Biscay, which seems unlikely.

21. The similarity of certain particulars suggests that Jironza or members of the cabildo may have read the epic account of the Spaniards' victory at Acoma in 1599 in Gaspar Pérez de Villagrá's *Historia de la Nueva México* (Alcalá de Henares, 1610).

Certification by the cabildo, 25 Nov. 1690.

22. Five years after the fact, Jironza's nephew offered other variant details: the fighting lasted from dawn to ten o'clock at night; six hundred apostates were killed in battle, with many more, who refused to surrender, consumed in the flames; and the prisoners numbered ninety. Juan Mateo Manje, Diary of an expedition, 7–23 Feb. 1694, in Ernest J. Burrus, S.J. *Kino and Manje: Explorers of Sonora and Arizona, Their Vision and the Future* (St. Louis, 1971):286–87. Chávez, *Chávez*, 52.

23. Walz said the captives were indeed distributed among the soldiers, an act confirmed by the crown on 21 July 1691. Walz, "History of the El Paso Area," 250–51, 257. Treasury junta, Mexico City, 18 Jan. 1690, AGN, Civil 1743.

24. In his day, Vélez de Escalante could find no diary or other detailed account of the 1689 expedition in the Santa Fe archives. Vélez de Escalante, Extracto. Adams, "Fray Silvestre," 115–16.

25. Walz implied that Jironza marched to La Junta, some 300 kilometers down the Rio Grande. The dates of the expedition's departure and the battle, recorded by the cabildo, make that impossible. It is more likely the battle occurred on the way to La Junta. Certification by the cabildo, 25 Nov. 1690. Walz, "History of the El Paso Area," 259.

26. An extensive biographical sketch of don Diego is found in the introduction of RBC. Scholes, *Church and State*, 175–77.

27. Vargas's title as governor of New Mexico was dated in Madrid on 18 June 1688. RBC, 42–43.

28. Geographical proximity in Madrid likely played an important role in these families' personal relations. The family of the Conde de Galve, the House of Infantado, owned several properties in the parish of San Andrés, a short walk from the Vargas complex on the Calle del Almendro. Some ancillary Infantado buildings abutted the holdings of the Marqués de Villafranca, father of the Conde de Galve's second wife. The families worshiped at the church of San Andrés, adjoining the parish of San Pedro el Real, of which the Vargases were members. At some point, the family of the Conde de Paredes owned a house backing on the Vargas property. Only the Alburquerque residence in the Palacio de la Plazuela de la Encarnación was distant, just northeast of the Royal Palace. Francisco Fernández de Béthencourt, *Historia genealógica y heráldica de la monarquía española, Casa Real y grandes de España* (Madrid, 1920), 10:298. RBC, 111 n79. The Duquesa del Infantado, Censo, Madrid, 29 Nov. 1677, AHN, Clero, Libro 8258.

29. Diego Gutiérrez Coronel, *Historia genealógica de la Casa de Mendoza* (Cuenca, 1946):114.

30. Béthencourt, *Historia*,

10:298. Alberto García Carraffa and Arturo García Carraffa, *Diccionario heráldico y genealógico de apellidos españoles y americanos* (Madrid, 1955), 24:64–68.

31. RBC, 45, 275. Ignacio's use of the titles was confusing here, since at the time of the marriage, Fadrique held both titles.

32. Gutiérrez Coronel, *Historia genealógica*, 299, 406.

33. Letters of the Conde de Paredes, mayordomo of the queen's household, to the Duque del Infantado, 1689–90, AHN, Osuna, Cartas 115:4, 251:23. RBC, 47–49.

34. The Conde de Galve to the Marqués del Cenete, Madrid, 23 Oct. 1686, AHN, Osuna, Cartas.

35. Antonio Felipe de Mora, Certification of death, Puerto de Santa María, 12 Mar. 1697, AHPM, P. 12.118. RBC, 184.

36. Vargas also instructed his family to seek out the Condesa de Paredes as well as a trusted member of Galve's household, his secretary, Juan de Vargas Manuel de Lodeña. RBC, 193–94.

37. RBC, 144 n1, 224, 256, 310–11.

38. RBC, 152, 199.

39. José Ignacio Rubio Mañé, *El virreinato* (Mexico City, 1983), 3:192–94; 4:131–41, 198 n179, 306–308.

40. Carlos de Sigüenza y Góngora, *Alboroto y motín de México del 8 de junio de 1692: Relación de don Carlos de Sigüenza y Góngora en una carta dirigida al almirante don Andrés de*

Pez (Mexico City, 1932): 34–82.

41. Monclova did not take the first available ship to Peru; rather he remained in Mexico City until April 1689. Meanwhile, that ship, the almiranta of the Philippines fleet, stayed in the waters off New Spain to hunt pirates. The Conde de Galve to the Conde de Bornos, Mexico City, 28 June 1689, AHN, Osuna, Cartas. Antonio de Robles, *Diario de sucesos notables, 1665–1703* (Mexico City, 1946), 2:180.

42. The Spanish garrison on Guam was under siege by the local Chamorros when Monclova arrived in New Spain. Order was not restored until late in Galve's rule. Such notable English seamen as William Dampier also visited Guam during this period. The island, about two and a half months' sail from Acapulco, was an important stop for provisions on the long journey to the Philippines. Lucas Mateo de Urquiza, dispatched to the Pacific to assess conditions in the Ladrones Islands, Japan, and the Philippines, reported to Galve early in 1689. Lucas Mateo de Urquiza to the Conde de Galve, aboard the *San Cristóbal de Burgos*, 25 Jan. 1689, AHN, Osuna, Cartas. Charles Beardsley, *Guam Past and Present* (Tokyo, 1964):136–41. L.M. Cox, *The Island of Guam* (Washington, D.C., 1926):24–31.

43. Carlos II, Cedula, Aranjuez, 3 May 1688, cited in Juan

Bromley Seminario, "La ciudad de Lima durante el gobierno del Virrey Conde de la Monclova," *Revista Histórica* (Lima) 22 (1955–56):155–56.

44. In his seminal study of the viceroyalty of New Spain, José Ignacio Rubio Mañé dedicated two of four volumes to expansion and defense. In volume 2, pages 82–332 deal with the period under study; in volume 3, pages 1–246 are relevant. Rubio Mañé, *Virreinato*.

45. Cristina Arteaga y Falguera, *La Casa del Infantado: Cabeza de los Mendoza* (Madrid, 1944), 2:126–52. The Sección Osuna of the AHN contains many letters from the Conde de Galve to his brother and other influential people at the Spanish court.

46. Among the more interesting proposals not implemented, one called for a highly mobile, one-hundred-man cavalry detachment to respond to pirate activity on either coast of New Spain. Galve considered the plan militarily and economically sound. The Conde de Galve to the Marqués del Cenete, Mexico City, 14 July 1689, AHN, Osuna, Cartas.

47. An error has been perpetuated in the historiography of this episode. The Jesuit historian, Andrés Cavo (1739–1803), misreading Gabriel de Cárdenas y Cano's *Ensayo cronológico para la historia general de la Florida* (1723), attributed the report to the governor of New Mexico. This mistake was repeated by Rivera

Cambas, who used Cano as a source for much of his history. Manuel Rivera Cambas, *Los gobernantes de México* (Mexico City, 1872–73), 1:267. Gabriel de Cárdenas y Cano [Andrés González de Barcia Carballido y Zúñiga], *Ensayo cronológico para la historia de la Florida* (Madrid, 1723):288. The Conde de Galve to the Conde de Bornos, Mexico City, 28 June 1689, AHN, Osuna, Cartas. For a complete account of the Spaniards' response to the French presence in Texas, see Robert S. Weddle, *Wilderness Manhunt: The Spanish Search for La Salle* (Austin, 1973). See also the multidisciplinary study of Patricia K. Galloway, ed., *La Salle and his Legacy: Frenchmen and Indians in the Lower Mississippi Valley* (Jackson, Miss., 1982).

48. Weddle, *Wilderness Manhunt*, 175, 210, 260. Lillian Estelle Fisher, *Viceregal Administration in the Spanish-American Colonies* (Berkeley, 1926):267, 300.

49. Audiencia de México, Mexico City, 2 July 1690, AHN, Osuna. Tomás de Guadalajara, *Historia de la tercera rebelión Tarahumara* (Chihuahua, 1950).

50. Fisher, *Viceregal Administration*, 291.

51. The Conde de Galve to Carlos II, Mexico City, 8 Jan. 1693, AHN, Osuna, Cartas.

52. Fisher, *Viceregal Administration*, 272–73.

53. The Conde de Galve to Carlos II, Mexico City, 18 Dec. 1689, AHN, Osuna, Cartas. The Conde de Galve to the Marqués del Cenete, Mexico City, 13 Jan. 1693, AHN, Osuna, Cartas. The Conde de Galve to the Marqués del Cenete, Mexico City, 20 Feb. 1689, AHN, Osuna, Cartas. The Rivas journal and commentary on French activities follow in AHN, Osuna, Cartas. The Conde de Galve to the Conde de Bornos, Mexico City, 25 Mar. 1689, AHN, Osuna, Cartas. Fisher, *Viceregal Administration*, 263, 267, 295.

54. Because of his illustrious name and his contacts, Vargas was able to borrow heavily. He did not, however, possess great personal wealth, an assumption made by J. Manuel Espinosa in *Crusaders of the Río Grande: The Story of Don Diego de Vargas and the Reconquest and Refounding of New Mexico* (Chicago, 1942) (hereinafter CRG):32–33. RBC, 41–43, 117 n137, 182 n1, 200 n1.

55. RBC, 146–47. Disbursements, Mexico City, 1690, AGI, Contaduría 780.

56. RBC, 151–52.

Part 2

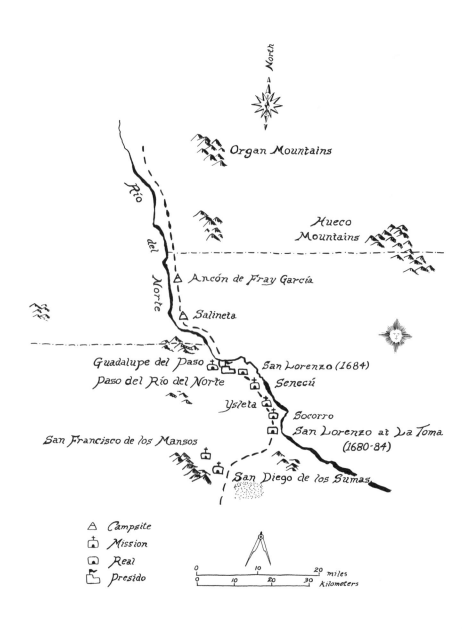

North

Organ Mountains

Hueco
Mountains

Río

del

Norte

△ Ancón de Fray García

△ Salineta

Guadalupe del Paso
Paso del Río del Norte

San Lorenzo (1684)
Senecú

Ysleta

Socorro
San Lorenzo at La Toma
(1680-84)

San Francisco de los Mansos

San Diego de los Sumas

△ Campsite
⌂ Mission
▢ Real
⌐ Presido

0   10   20   miles
0   10   20   30   Kilometers

The El Paso Settlements.
Map drawn by Jerry L. Livingston.

CONDITIONS AT EL PASO; PLAN FOR JOINT CAMPAIGN
ON THE SONORA FRONTIER; AND INCENTIVES TO
FORMER NEW MEXICANS SETTLED ELSEWHERE,
APRIL–DECEMBER 1691.*

Impatient to get on with the reconquest of New Mexico, don Diego de Vargas assesses the resources at his disposal in the El Paso district and requests aid from the viceroy. He proposes a reconnaissance to the villa of Santa Fe and objects when a plan by Capt. Juan Fernández de la Fuente of Janos presidio threatens to divert his energies into a combined campaign on the Sonora frontier. Fernández, don Diego points out, has no business corresponding directly with the viceroy and suggesting that thirty men from the poor presidio of El Paso take part. The governor of New Biscay, Fernández's proper superior, has ample manpower of his own. Moreover, it is Vargas's desire to rescue the apostate Indians of New Mexico from their slavery to the devil, which, he believes, should take precedence over fighting heathens.

The authorities in Mexico City disagree. A joint campaign should be waged first, against Apaches and allied tribes west of El Paso, then the matter of New Mexico considered, including return of its former citizens residing in New Biscay. Vargas, of course, obeys. Not only does he agree to outfit and send men, but also, as ranking officer, insists on commanding the western campaign in person.

Capt. don Juan Fernández de la Fuente

Proceedings of the joint entrada from the provinces of Sinaloa, Sonora, and El Paso
New Mexico

Diego de Vargas to the Conde de Galve, El Paso, 19 April 1691, LS.

Your excellency,

It is my duty to place myself humbly at your excellency's feet to demonstrate my fervent wish that your excellency may be in good health, as Our Lord saw fit to grant me on my journey and accession to the governorship on 22 February.[1] The soldiers of the company of this outpost passed muster before me. I found that they had 132 horses. Most of the men had neither leather jackets nor swords. The soldiers and citizens of this pueblo of El Paso and the inhabitants of the four pueblos and missions number scarcely one hundred. Together, the soldiers and the citizens have scarcely 200 horses and mules. Of these, according to my information, there are not 25 saddle and pack mules. The Christian Indians and the unconverted Indians (with whom there is a truce) in El Paso, the missions, and the four pueblos, do not number one thousand men and women.

Your excellency, the forces and settlements of this kingdom today have so few provisions that were I not to send to Parral for flour, even I would have to live on tortillas made from what little maize there is.[2] There are no cattle. As for sheep, there are some six hundred in the area, most of them belonging to the religious of the missions and custody.

The weapons Gen. don Domingo Jironza[3] gave me appear on my receipt. Of these, only six blunderbusses are serviceable, because the others must be assembled and made ready, attaching locks, stocks, bands, and screws, all of which may cause such senseless waste that it would have been better to buy good harquebuses with triggers, such as those used in the capital. The blunderbusses are heavy, like everything else, and the locks and bands are very flimsy. The only good thing about the barrels is that they are thick, but they are uncomfortably heavy for this kind of campaign since it is carried out on horseback. The soldier has to shield himself and does not perform the task as he may with a lighter weapon that neither exhausts nor encumbers him. Thus, it appears to me, sir, that should your excellency see fit, you could order forty or fifty harquebuses sent, such as those I refer to that are made in Mexico City. They should be kept here in the casas reales, charged to his majesty's account, and used to arm the settlers whenever a campaign is undertaken. The repaired and serviceable blunderbusses should also be held in reserve in the casas reales. The lieutenant general, whom the governor and captain general will appoint when he mounts a campaign, can arm the remaining settlers with them, since that is all they are good for and they are already in the casas reales.

There are also two bronze stone mortars, one larger than the other. Only the large piece has a breech, so I am sending the pattern of both so that one breech can be sent for the large piece and two for the small one. This small cannon cannot be used. It was filled with lead to within two fingers of a span because the priming hole exploded. A new hole was drilled in front of it, and the space behind filled in, thus reducing its power. The soldiers who went on campaign to Zia[4] told me they had tested it and were unable to achieve the effect they might have against adobe-wall fortifications if it could be operated without this defect. I am told that walls built in New Mexico are constructed of stone masonry and mortar. I deeply regret finding myself without an instrument of force to destroy the Indians' fortifications. In order to do damage to those within the walls, it would seem to me that some bombs or grenades would be very effective.

Your excellency, I am awaiting the religious who was with you and informed you that the rebel, apostate Indians of New Mexico wanted to make peace again, but could not, because the Spaniards were going to burn their pueblos and devastate them by fire and sword.[5] They caught them by surprise at daybreak and forced them to defend themselves. The Indians did not know, first, what kind of enemies they were, and, second, why the Spaniards would treacherously attack at such an hour if they wanted their friendship. As the religious told you, the truth of the matter is that the Indians had presented some letters or papers regarding their intentions. Your excellency favored me by making me a party to this information, ordering me to act in accordance with the Indians' wishes.

I hope the religious will come with the good weather. I also hope to gather together supplies, mules, and a few horses, even though I have to bring them from far away, financing them any way I can. I shall go on campaign, taking the religious in my company as an eyewitness, so that he may see that I fulfill my duty and protect the Indians while campaigning, entering into their pueblos without permitting a shot to be fired, even though they may force me to put myself on the defensive or the offensive and take up arms. I must make it known to the Indians that his majesty's will is that they should again be reduced to the brotherhood of our holy faith. Even if my life is at great risk, I must do this and see everything for myself. If I escape with my life, I shall report to your excellency as befits my zeal in the royal service, so that you may decide what is most appropriate.

Your excellency, I found neither surgeon nor armorer in Zacatecas, Sombrerete, or Parral, as was decided in Mexico City.[6] A citizen with the skill in this pueblo of El Paso says it is not in his interest to agree to do the work for a salary. In the interim, until an armorer may be sent to me from Mexico City, as your excellency has ordered, the man who is in this outpost will assemble the weapons. I shall respectfully send you a detailed account of what is being paid to him and his bill of sale for those guns, the cost of which your excellency will please order repaid to me through an agent. I shall do likewise for the expenses I may incur for the campaign. I shall send the total of what I take with me, according to what I have learned from my predecessor's experience. Thus, your excellency will please order everything according to your judgment, from which I expect the benefits of your greatness. May heaven grant you a long and happy life. From this pueblo of El Paso, 19 April 1691.

Most excellent sir, the least of your servants kisses your excellency's hand,

Don Diego de Vargas Zapata
Luján Ponce de León [rubrica]

Most excellent lord, the Conde de Galve

———

Cadena[7]

Mexico City, 26 May 1691
To the lord fiscal
[Galve's rubrica]

Benito de Noboa Salgado, Fiscal's reply, Mexico City, 2 June 1691, DS.

Your excellency,

His majesty's fiscal[8] has seen this letter from the governor of El Paso, don Diego de Vargas Zapata Luján Ponce de León. He states that for this government, on the occasions when its governors have requested weapons, they have all been sent those thought to be appropriate. For this reason, the fiscal was certain that this government would be well provisioned with weapons. Yet just recently, don Pedro Reneros,[9] having completed his term, led us to believe that many of them have been worn out, for which he would have us exonerate him.

The previous fiscal did not agree with that decision and pleaded before the Royal Tribunal of Accounts that Reneros be made to pay for their cost in full, as he has been informed. The tribunal will have proceeded in such a way that, should it please your excellency, you may order that weapons of the type this governor requests and that seem appropriate to you be bought in Mexico City and sent to him. The three breeches he requests for the stone mortars may be sent as well. As there is no armorer, one from the ranks should be sent so as not to increase the cost to the royal treasury. As always, your excellency will decide as you see fit, which will be, as always, for the best.
Mexico City, 2 June 1691.
Dr. don Benito de Noboa Salgado [rubrica]

The Conde de Galve, Decree, Mexico City, 4 June 1691, ADS.

Inform the royal tribunal of the cost of the weapons; issue a dispatch so that the factor, don Sebastián de Guzmán,[10] may commis-

sion the three breeches that are requested; and look for an armorer from the ranks for that province as the fiscal suggests.
[Galve's rubrica]

> *Tribunal of Accounts, Report, Mexico City,*
> *12 [June] 1691, DS.*

Most excellent sir,

This tribunal has reviewed the final accounting taken of don Pedro Reneros, former governor of New Mexico, about the weapons he alleges to have been worn out during his governorship. The results have been accepted for the reasons put forward by the governor and information presented. The following is provided for your excellency, so that you may know what was said to have been expended:

gunpowder count 44 quintals
50 firearms
150 carbines with flasks and
   priming flasks
6 blunderbusses
4 levers and crowbars
7 blunderbuss locks
9 pairs of shackles
some handcuffs
1 small artillery piece
1 bullet mold
12 cannonballs

4 quintals of bullets
a pair of tongs and a sack of
   bullets
4 lead base plates
3 hammers and 2 saws
13 chisels and 4 adzes
4 counter-plates with locks
8 padlocks with keys
4 benches with backs
3 large wooden tables
2 brushes

With regard to the aforementioned, your excellency might order an appraisal, because the tribunal has not been informed of the value. Your excellency will order as you see fit, which will be for the best. Mexico City, Tribunal of Accounts, 12 [June] 1691.
[3 rubricas]

———

Mexico City, 18 June 1691
Have this at hand when Vargas sends his report about the weapons his predecessor handed over to him.
[Galve's rubrica]

Diego de Vargas to the Conde de Galve, El Paso,
20 June 1691, LS.

Most excellent sir,

I have informed your excellency of my arrival at this plaza de armas
of El Paso and have reported the supplies of weapons and horses I
found and that this kingdom is without provisions. Because the season was so advanced, I had to direct attention and aid to the repair
of the acequias for the fields. I spent two months on these repairs,
and the main dam is still not to the point where it will control the
river and permit its current to be directed. Since the runoff is very
heavy during the springtime, because of the snows melting in the
ranges and mountains of New Mexico, it does great damage when
the current strays from its course and will not enter the acequias.
For this reason, it is necessary to build next year's dam in time, so
that it will channel some of the high water into the acequia, and if
there is no high water, the dam can hold it all. Because of these
repairs, the fields were planted late, with a modest amount of wheat
sown in May and maize during this month of June. This is because
of the fear that irrigation would be lacking at the height of the
growing season.

> Increase of soldiers of the presidio; he will make the entrada in October
> with the full company, leaving the citizens for defense

At present, your excellency, this kingdom suffers an unbelievable
dearth of provisions, and to this may be added the fact that there is
not a single head of cattle and the season is very dry. I have written
your excellency about the unavailability of provisions and the scarcity of horses. I am taking care that the horses be kept in the most
strategic outposts in order to have them at the ready to pursue the
enemy. I have taken every care to obtain some horses and mules to
hold in reserve, as well as some cattle. This is so that, once the growing season is over and I am assured that the Indians and the rest of
the community are harvesting their milpas, I can leave on campaign
around the middle of October, by whatever ways and means available to me, and reconnoiter as far as the villa of Santa Fe, as I have
already written to you.

Even though it is a very difficult time, because I am totally without the resources of provisions and horses, a question of greater con-

cern is that if I were to move my camp without the men having harvested their crops, it would render supply impossible.

This matter is worthy of concern, your excellency, as is the fact that this outpost is the farthest, surrounded on all sides by the enemy and lacking the resources of the kingdom of New Biscay,[11] which has so large a presidial force in its garrison. I have information that its captains from Janos and Conchos[12] have increased their forces in favor of the latter. With more consideration for this presidio, the same can be done for it, when for whatever crisis, its governor, soldiers, and citizens have no other recourse than to band together. Surely, your excellency, the captains of those presidios, joining hands, justified the need to increase their forces by asking how they could carry out their scouting missions and campaigns with fifty men, while having to leave twenty men as a garrison at the presidio. Of the thirty who would go, ten would be needed for escort and to guard the horses. With the twenty who remained, a capitán, cabo y caudillo would be hard pressed to take the positions by which the enemy could make their escape and still have men to destroy them in the heat of battle. The enemy is always camped on ridges, mesas, and canyons of very rugged mountains, as these are. It is even necessary to march all night in order to avoid being perceived by the enemy and, on occasion, into the morning because one cannot measure time by distance when it is over such difficult terrain. Even though the sallies those captains make are so brief and they have settlements of citizens, the additional forces have been given to them.

For reasons I judge obvious, most excellent sir, of even greater justification than what those governors proposed to your excellency would be for these men to be sent as reinforcements to this plaza de armas. With them, this governor[13] could set out from this outpost of El Paso for the interior, the kingdom of New Mexico, and the territory of the apostate Indians, a distance of 130 leagues to the villa of Santa Fe. The governor could ill afford to leave reinforcements. Even taking with him its company of fifty men, he would still be at great risk, since the enemy appear from all directions and might surround them, not only the common enemy, who have been forever and everywhere the Apache, but also those who are to be searched out and against whom the aim of his enterprise is directed—the rebels and apostates against our holy faith.

The governors who were my predecessors made entradas, taking some soldiers of this company and some citizens. I plan, your excellency, to undertake my campaign and entrada (in which I hope, by the grace of God, to succeed) to the kingdom of New Mexico and villa of Santa Fe at the time and season I have determined and with the supplies I may have at hand, taking only the full company of this plaza de armas for this purpose. In the midst of the harshest time of year, the enemy will be in their houses because of the cold. I shall seek them out to fight, not choosing the season when they might be scattered about in their milpas or hunting and fishing.

I want to jeopardize neither this outpost nor the lives of its citizens to protect myself and safeguard my life and those of the soldiers of this company. It will be left to the few citizens there, together with the Indians who remain, to guard the four pueblos of its jurisdiction and their churches, houses, and women. I offer this matter for your excellency's very just consideration, so that you may see that it must be attended to. If his majesty (may God keep him) seeks the reduction and restoration of the rebel and apostate nations who are our declared enemies in the kingdom of New Mexico, to this end and for this reason this presidio must be increased.

If it is to be the protection of a frontier in open warfare and the defense of all the other jurisdictions of Sonora,[14] Sinaloa, and the kingdom of New Biscay; and if those captains, united with one another and not having more than several similar enemy nations to destroy or reduce, increase their forces; with even more reason, your excellency, finding myself alone, surrounded and besieged by so many whom I must always face, I should be provided with this support. My duty is conquest and reduction, rather than chasing off and destroying a rancheria and a few bands of Indians who try to steal horses by the light of the moon.

What I am relating to your excellency is nothing more than a brief complaint about what burdens this plaza de armas that requires no justification or special privilege. It is apparent that the facts themselves baldly proclaim my interpretation. They define and clarify the information I may have failed to express. Thus, in all things I trust that I shall receive from your excellency's largess, should it be granted, not respite but strength by increasing the number of these soldiers who are needed so as not to waste time.

I am sending to your excellency with this letter those I received from the Jesuit fathers, Juan María de Salvatierra,[15] visitor of the missions of the provinces of Sonora and Sinaloa, and one from the father rector (whose name is Marcos de Loyola)[16] of the Chínapa mission,[17]

Juan María Salvatierra
   From Miguel Venegas, *Juan María de Salvatierra*,
   trsl. Marguerite Eyer Wilbur (1929)

in which he requested from me the assistance of Spanish-speaking Indians. Of record in that letter is the sending of the Indians, which I immediately requested, provisioning them with whatever they might have needed. Also, I am sending your excellency Capt. Juan Fernández de la Fuente's[18] letter, dated 16 April 1691 at Janos, and the reply I promptly made on 29 April. By these and other letters, your excellency will see how ready I am in everything concerning the royal service; their contents will demonstrate my hopes.

May your excellency enjoy every happiness, which, as your truly concerned servant, I wish. May God keep your most excellent person in your increasing greatness. Dated in this plaza de armas, 20 June 1691.

The least of your servants kisses your excellency's hand,

Don Diego de Vargas Zapata
Luján Ponce de León [rubrica]

To his excellency the viceroy, the Conde de Galve

———

New Mexico, 20 June 1691
Don Diego de Vargas Zapata y Luján
Received on 22 July

———

Mexico City, 23 July 1691
To the lord fiscal with the enclosed letters
[Galve's rubrica]

Marcos de Loyola to Diego de Vargas, Chínapa, 6 February 1691, ALS.

Dear sir,

For seven years in this province of Sonora we have been afflicted and tormented by the daily wars that the Jano, Jocome,[19] and Suma[20] nations wage against us, which we experience and suffer without remedy. We see ourselves obliged to try whatever means are available to bring peace and tranquility to this land and spread our holy faith, so that the king our lord may not lose ground that has cost and continues to cost him so dearly.

Janos, Jocomes, and Sumas

Thus, availing myself of your favor and protection, I ask and request in the name of all these missions that you appeal to the father minister of the pueblo of El Paso to allow one or two of the Manso Indians to be sent to me from that pueblo to see whether through them we can bring not only the Janos, but also the Jocomes and Sumas, who remain to be pacified, to peace as the other nations already are.

My superior, the father visitor of these missions, so informs you in his letter to you. Sir, after various encounters they had with the Spaniards while they were being pacified, I had some Manso Indians in my house, which was then in the district of Teuricachi.[21] During the time they were with me, I recognized that those Manso Indians had authority among the Janos and Jocomes, and especially Captain Chiquito,[22] whom I baptized and who stayed in my house many days. Because of my knowledge of the Mansos, the father visitor of these missions decided to see whether by means of these Indians we could achieve the peace and tranquility we hope for.

For this reason, I ask you that Captain Chiquito come, if he is alive and would want to. If he cannot, then the Indian named José, who was a catechist[23] in the church of El Paso, may come, and with him another Indian named Tomás, who is round-faced and good-natured. Since both speak Spanish, we may send them from here with messages of peace. Perhaps Our Lord may will or allow that in this way we may achieve the good we wish for.

I have no doubt that with your strong arm and great zeal for the honor of God and king, this land and all of us will achieve what I ask of you in humble submission in this letter. I shall see to it that the Indians who come are well paid and so forth. May God Our Lord keep you for me the long years I wish for you, in the good fortune you deserve and I wish for you. Chínapa, 6 February 1691.

Dear sir, the least of your chaplains and your devoted servant kisses your hand,

Marcos de Loyola [rubrica]

Juan María de Salvatierra to Diego de Vargas, Chínapa, 8 February 1691, ALS.

Dear sir,

I shall be happy if this letter finds your lordship in perfect health and with the fortuitous success at arms I so wish. With respect to the fulfillment of my duty, I am in the process of carrying out the visitation of these provinces of Sinaloa and Sonora.[24] I hope to seek all possible means to avoid hostilities with the many enemy nations who surround us. By the grace of God and the favor of the Queen of Victories, the Seris,[25] Cocomotaques,[26] Sobas,[27] and Pimas have already been pacified. I find myself face to face with the enemy Jocomes and Janos. With your good favor and love, I hope to have the best means for so desirable an end—some kind of peace or truce.

It has come to my attention that in the pueblos of El Paso there are some Christians of the Manso nation who are obedient to you. Some years ago, they were on the Sonoran frontier. They had frequent communication with Marcos de Loyola, the father rector, who wrote to you. I also enter my pleas to you, requesting that you deign to send one or two Mansos so that they may meet with the father rector.

You will please forgive me if I am mistaken about your given name and surname, because I am writing in haste and away from a settlement where I might learn the proper form. Although I know of your works by the general renown of your exploits and your good government, I hope you will excuse my ignorance and uncertainty about your name.

Without further ado, I am completely at your service. I pray to Our Lord and to the most holy Virgin that they may grant you every happiness. Chínapa, 8 February 1691.

The least of your subjects and your chaplain kisses your hands,

Juan María de Salvatierra [rubrica]

Lord Gov. Diego de Vargas

Diego de Vargas, Certification, El Paso,
22 March 1691, DS.

In the pueblo of El Paso, 20 March 1691, Juan de Valencia,[28] resident of the pueblo of Socorro and citizen of this jurisdiction, gave to me, don Diego de Vargas Zapata Luján Ponce de León, governor and captain general of this kingdom of New Mexico and its presidio for his majesty, a sealed packet that I opened, since it was addressed to me, the governor and captain general. I read the letter contained in this packet, as well as another from the father visitor, Juan María de Salvatierra, of the Company of Jesus. He states therein that he is making his way to the provinces of Sinaloa and Sonora. I find in these two letters that they propose to me the means to obviate the hostilities of so many enemy nations. They need to bring them together through pacification, which they base on the hope of having Indians who might understand, know, and speak their language and who are familiar with the mountain ranges of the three enemy nations of Jocomes, Janos, and Sumas. It is for this purpose that the father rector suggests to me in his letter the Indians who are present in El Paso. Having considered with care and regard the report in this letter and that of the father visitor, I ordered that the matter be attended to and that my officers and militia leaders should seek out the Indians mentioned in the letter. Of them, only the Indian he says he knows, who is named Tomás and has the features mentioned in his letter, is in this pueblo and presidio at present. I asked the Indian directly, because he speaks Spanish, and through the interpreter, whether he knows the father rector, Marcos de Loyola. He said that, yes, he knows him because he gave him food in his mission. He said that he was of the Manso nation. I ordered him to leave. Because the mission is 100 leagues from this presidio and in country threatened by enemies, for greater safety I appointed Juan, a Spanish-speaking Indian who has been governor of this pueblo, to accompany him. He is brave and fully trusted by the Christians and Spaniards to whom he has been a very good and faithful friend in whatever the governors, my predecessors, ordered him to do because they knew firsthand of his loyalty. I, the governor, wish for the good end sought by the pacification and bringing together of the rebellious nations who have risen in the provinces and missions of Sonora and Sinaloa, even though they are not in my jurisdiction. Considering what may redound to the service of both majesties, the following Indians are going: Juan, as their captain; Tomás; Francisco; Pedro de Santiago; Agustín; and Luis.

I gave a saddle mule for the journey to Captain Juan and provisions to him and the rest. I also gave them a horse to carry their provisions. So that it may be of record, I signed it in the presence of the secretary of government and war. These letters remain in this my court of justice so that it may be of record that today, 22 March 1691, these six Indians, having been provisioned as stated, are leaving on their journey.

Don Diego de Vargas
Zapata Luján [rubrica]

By order of the lord governor and captain general,
                              Don Pedro Ladrón de Guevara [rubrica][29]
Secretary of government and war

Juan Fernández de la Fuente to Diego de Vargas, Janos, 16 April 1691, LS.

Lord governor and captain general,

I received your letter, dated 22 March, with Juan, captain of the Mansos, and the other five who came with him. From it, I learned of the suggestion that the reverend father, Marcos de Loyola, made in his letter to you and the reverend father, fray Francisco de Vargas,[30] custos of that kingdom. I have seen what you and the reverend father custos provided with great zeal in the royal service to bring about the peace and tranquility of the rebel nations.

Do not let it be said that because the Indians did not come peace was not achieved. This will not be easy until the Janos and Jocomes, prime movers of the uprisings of all the nations who were pacified, are dealt with. It is common knowledge that they took the Christian Mansos from that pueblo and the heathens from up and down the river. They brought them, until I sent them off under the terms of the treaties granted in the province of Sonora, and they returned to that kingdom. The Christians have stayed there, even though, with the closeness of the Janos, they are constantly wavering. Because of the frequent rabble-rousing[31] among them by Captain Chiquito's heathens (and many others), we already see what they are about.

The Sumas of Ojito,[32] Guadalupe, and other pueblos also came with them until most of them perished in a rout we handed them three years ago come August. Nevertheless, there is no nation all along that river and its environs not acting cocky and taking up arms whenever it pleases, concerned only that no one pursue or punish it. In Candelaria,[33] they even murdered two young men, Jorge, and some other citizens. Since the camino real was closed, there was no one to open it until we went and punished them, as is common knowledge.

You will please forgive me, for they really require punishment and, believe me, it must not be light. Now we are seeing the Apaches enter that camp. They have come in two or three times, pretending to be peaceful, to sell their buckskin and later steal the horses. What this comes down to is that on these frontiers during this month alone the Apache leaders have made off with around a hundred animals, nearly fifty from two citizens of this presidio. Since I was away with all my men on the frontier of Sonora province, the enemy, who is from the Gila Mountains,[34] could not be pursued.

It seems to me that this summer, if it would please you, we shall give them a whipping. They have it coming, because they are the ones who harass both these frontiers and those. It is common knowledge that they are in league with the Janos, Jocomes, Pimas, Sobaipuris,[35] and Sumas, as shown by several statements that have been taken. It is now suspected that they took part in an ambush that occurred on 19 March in the pueblo of Bacoachito,[36] which is one of those the father, Marcos de Loyola, administers. They managed to kill sixteen people, carrying off eleven alive and burning Father Loyola's house and most of the pueblo. God willed that a few Indians who reached the church defended it.

That peace not be sought by the fathers, but that war be waged

In this light, having seen the robberies, deaths, and destruction these nations are committing, it does not seem right, either for us or the fathers, to seek peace with them.

Peace should not be sought by the fathers, and war should be waged on the enemy. We should wage war against them with fire and sword until they seek peace with us. Many times it has been granted to them, and they have broken it, and, sir, as the old saying goes: A hard war ensures a secure peace. When the war is not carried everywhere, they are victorious, because there are many of them and they are strongly united. We are spread thin and in disagreement. That is why they make war.

I cannot do everything. Let me assure you that in the five years since I arrived at this presidio, I have not even been in it. Instead, I have been out on the kingdom's many frontiers, on campaign for two years running. When one part is pacified, another bursts into flame.

So you will know whether the Apaches were in league, at the time the mares were carried off from this presidio, the soldiers who were chasing them found a cross, very well made, from a cane 6 spans long with a staff of justice as crosspiece. Above the arm, they put eleven lines that seem to me to stand for the eleven captives. Below they put sixteen lines on the cross for the dead Christians.

Having seen this, Captain Juan and the rest of the Mansos said that they felt it was not right to sue for peace, and for their part, they did not dare go alone. This was because they did not know the lay of the land or anything about it. They would only enter accompanied by some Spanish soldiers. This cannot be done now, because of the weakness of the horses, the harshness of the weather, and the hard work they have been doing. Seeing that the Indians were tired and that their animals arrived nearly dead at this presidio, I provisioned them so they could go with me to Father Horacio Polici's mission.[37] They told him this in my presence. The father, after examining the letter they gave him, wrote to Father Marcos de Loyola, sending your letter and the others they had brought with them. They are returning and will explain everything that happened.

If it would have brought about any useful end, I would have detained them. Some useful end might have been more easily achieved here than there, since every day they are within sight of that presidio. God grant that the horse herd recover and that the Indians do not make war as they do now.

Sir, we are all working toward the same end. As for me, I would like for his majesty's weapons to be used everywhere. The victories of the few are shared by the many. Whenever I can be of service to you, and nothing prevents me, I shall be at the ready for any- and everything that may further the royal service and please you.

May God keep you many years in the best posts you may obtain and we, your servants, wish for you. Janos, 16 April 1691.

Your foremost servant kisses your hand,

Juan Fernández de la Fuente [rubrica]

Lord governor and captain general, don Diego de Vargas Zapata y Luján

Diego de Vargas to Juan Fernández de la Fuente, El Paso, 29 April 1691, LS.

I received your letter while I was with Juan, the captain of the Mansos. I see that my wish to have the bearer place my response directly in the hands of Father Marcos de Loyola was not fulfilled. I sent it with the previous letter to him. I did this so that he might see the punctual demonstration of my regard for him in having sent the Indian and his companions and so that he might have the knowledge upon which the hope of reduction and pacification of the nations uprisen in the mountains is based. This is so that once and for all, one might carry out—based on this knowledge and revelation—the savage war and punishment that, as you state in your letter, their perversity merits.

With respect to what you state, do not think me a fool. Assuming that I do not give satisfaction in this matter, I reply that only you can judge. I am sorry that sending the Indian Juan and his companions, which Father Loyola prompted me to do, was a failure. I gave them exactly what they asked, in consideration of the royal service and zeal for both majesties. That effort went awry and was frustrated when the allied Janos, Jocomes, Pimas, and other nations invaded the village called Aguache,[38] belonging to Father Marcos de Loyola's mission, on 19 March.

In this regard, you tell me it has been recorded in the statements received that the Sumas, who are encamped by this river, were accomplices. I give you my word that at the slightest indication that may prove a conspiracy, they will find in me the punishment that fits such a crime, in addition to the many they have already committed. My predecessor granted them peace without thinking, in that they were the ones who, last year, were at La Junta de los Ríos[39] with the Janos, Conchos, and some rebellious Apaches, waiting for Gen. don Domingo Jironza to set out on the campaign he intended to undertake to the kingdom of New Mexico. Without the information from an Indian at the Socorro mission, they would have succeeded in laying waste to this pueblo of El Paso and the remaining missions, and this outpost would have been left totally defenseless. This information resulted in the general's going with all his men to the outpost of La Junta de los Ríos. Along the way, he had the good fortune to capture a scout, but such luck came to nothing, since he escaped from the man who was bringing him in. On the way to that outpost, they found the enemy lying in wait among the rocks, though most had fled because of the scout's escape. Having verified the crime against the Sumas, Gen. don Domingo granted them peace.

Later, I found the Sumas at peace in their heathen, free condition, encamped at Guadalupe mission, which they had destroyed and whose church they had burned. If the religious who was there had not fled, they would have killed him. The Suma nation lives on fish—for this reason they like to live at their camp by the river—and by stealing horses, without wanting to return to our holy faith, much less to be subjugated. They prefer their freedom instead, not planting crops to feed themselves. I find that what I am relating to you was covered up by General don Domingo, as was his having granted peace to the Apaches, which allowed them to reconnoiter the outposts where the horses and other animals were. In thanks for the peace, they carried off José de Padilla's[40] mares and mules and horses belonging to the custos, Father Guerra,[41] and other settlers.

Nothing you said to me in your letter was my responsibility, but that of General don Domingo, which is what I have been saying. You inform me that the Apaches who did the damage and stole the animals in the month of March are in the Gila Mountains. They have joined those enemy nations. That is why you propose that we strike out on campaign when the time is right, and I respond to you that, for my part, I shall leave whenever I have the opportunity.

Lack of horses and supplies and that he cannot help him or leave because of the distances

With respect to the lack of supplies and sufficient horses, I cannot tell you exactly when I shall be able to go. You should carry out the campaign with your men wherever you find the greatest assistance. Since I am surrounded by enemies, I find it necessary to attend to the most urgent defense. In addition, you are under your governor's orders and definitely cannot take it upon yourself to join me from such a distance. The Gila Mountains are more than 40 leagues from the New Mexico road, after which one must leave the road and head west for another 30 leagues, so that I am 70 leagues from there, and you would be 140. I would have been happy to see and serve you, as I shall, personally aiding you with my men on such occasions that you may have need of me. For now, I am closing the book on the Suma and Apache nations.

Only time will tell if fortune will help me with my men to under-take—as my sole responsibility—punishment of the enemy, thereby obtaining the revenge that is required. They will pay for what they have done, both here and there. I am confident you will be satis-fied, and you can be assured of my willingness, since the reasons I give you in this letter are so compelling.

May God keep you for many years. From this presidio of Nuestra Señora del Pilar y el Glorioso San José, 29 April 1691.

Your very affectionate servant kisses your hands,

Don Diego de Vargas Zapata Luján
Ponce de León [rubrica]

Lord capitán, cabo y caudillo, Juan Fernández de la Fuente

Benito de Noboa Salgado, Fiscal's reply, Mexico City, 28 July 1691, DS.

Most excellent sir,

His majesty's fiscal has seen this proposal don Diego de Vargas Zapata y Luján made to your excellency, the enclosed letters from the missionaries, and the one from Capt. Juan Fernández de la Fuente. In it he explains the shortage of provisions and the lack of horses in the El Paso area and the remedy he would apply, which, without doubt, will be consistent not only with his many responsi-bilities in aiding those citizens, but also with fulfillment of his majesty's service. He relates as well that in the other presidios, the number of soldiers has increased, which, with greater justification, should have taken place in that real, because of his intention to pacify all that district of New Mexico. On this point, the fiscal states that a combined force more effectively achieves notable successes than when war is waged on two fronts. Since they are required to provide mutual assistance, this kind of warfare might bring to an end the war with the Janos, Pimas, and other frontier tribes in the province of Sonora. Having successfully waged this battle, they can join in aiding the governor of El Paso so that he may bring to a close his own, which would be brought about by summoning all the former residents of New Mexico to resettle their properties,[42] safe in the knowledge that there will be soldiers in the villa of Santa Fe. The favors your excellency may see fit to grant this villa, as well as to whoever may care to settle there, will serve as an incentive. Thus, when everyone is united, there will be enough soldiers without it being necessary to increase costs with new recruitment, and events will be more certain. Your excellency will decide what you think most appropriate.

Mexico City, 28 July 1691

Dr. don Benito de Noboa Salgado [rubrica]

———

Mexico City, 30 July 1691

File with the completed proceedings concerning the combined forces of the provinces of Sinaloa and Sonora with those of El Paso and the proposal that Capt. Juan Fernández made about this matter in his letter of last 19 April. Bring to the junta a copy of this response to the governors of Parral, New Mexico, and Sinaloa, together with the correspondence concerning this same point. [Galve's rubrica]

Junta of the Treasury, Mexico City, 3 August 1691, DS.

In the Junta of the Treasury that his excellency the viceroy, the Conde de Galve, held on 3 August 1691, with Dr. don Juan de

Aréchaga[43] and Lic. don Francisco Fernández Marmolejo,[44] judges of this royal audiencia; don Andrés Pardo de Lago[45] and don Juan José de Veitia,[46] comptrollers of the Royal Tribunal of Accounts; the factor, don Sebastián de Guzmán, and don Antonio de Deza y Ulloa,[47] knight of the Order of Santiago, treasury officials of this court; don Fernando de Deza y Ulloa,[48] comptroller general of tributes and mercury, the letter from the governor and captain general of the provinces of New Mexico, dated 20 June of this year, was examined, together with the enclosures he sent; as well as the proceedings about the combining of forces from the provinces of Sinaloa, Sonora, and El Paso; and the proposal that Capt. Juan Fernández de la Fuente made in this regard. It was unanimously decided, having considered the information concerning the risk and threat at hand, that Capt. Juan Fernández de la Fuente should take all the proper steps set forth in the orders his excellency sent to the governors of New Biscay, New Mexico, and Sinaloa, so that they might carry out what is contained therein. It is presumed that they will have received the orders by now and will be executing them in accord with the dispatches and the junta's decision of 18 July of this year. Until now, there has been neither definite reason compelling the entrada the governor of New Mexico intends to make to the villa of Santa Fe nor cause for rebellion among the Indians of El Paso, where today they are at peace with its inhabitants. Compliance with what was ordered is also pending. It is reiterated so that it will be carried out and the governor of New Mexico will fulfill the orders dispatched because this is where the need is greatest and where they will help the most.

After achieving the ends to which the combining of all the forces referred to is directed (with the result of its progress, whatever else may happen, and time and weather permitting), it will be decided whether it is advantageous to carry out the entradas he intends to make to the villa of Santa Fe. Attention will be paid to the expenses the royal treasury may incur, because of the high costs already occasioned in the wars of the conspiracies in New Biscay and Sinaloa. The governor and captain general of New Mexico will doubtless keep this in mind for the future, as is to be expected from his zeal, which is proved by what he has done, and is in accord with his sense of duty and worth as a soldier. Knowing he is highly regarded, he will continue to foster the jurisdiction he defends, and the settlers and religious will be maintained in their pueblos by the means he has discussed and carried out with such punctual attention.

As for the future, if some aid is necessary, it will be granted him, inasmuch as it supports the maintenance of those outposts and their inhabitants. Because it is understood that the salaries and the number of soldiers have been increased in the presidios of New Biscay, he is to be informed that they are kept at the level of their original allotment in accord with his majesty's orders, without any increase. The only exception is the presidio of El Paso, which during his predecessor's term was modeled on the presidios of New Biscay, so the increase favored his presidio alone. Not only were the enlistments of the complement increased to the fifty they all now have, but also 450 pesos were paid to each soldier who had previously received less. Now they are all treated equally.

Dispatches are being sent so that the citizens of El Paso who had left for other places may be brought back or compelled to return from wherever they are, so that with the others, they may aid the governor in what he is doing in his majesty's service. This is also known from the orders he gave for sending the Indians to wherever they were requested. They so decided and signed with his excellency. Lords Aréchaga; Marmolejo; Pardo; Veitia; Guzmán; Deza; Deza [Galve's rubrica and two others]

The dispatches were made and delivered to the Secretariat of the Cámara.

Diego de Vargas to the Conde de Galve, El Paso, 14 August 1691, LS.

Most excellent sir,

Sir, the capitán, cabo y caudillo of Janos presidio, Juan Fernández de la Fuente, arrived at this plaza de armas of El Paso today with a letter from his governor and captain general of New Biscay, don Juan Isidro de Pardiñas,[49] dated 15 July of the present year. With that letter, he sends me your excellency's, dated in that court of Mexico City on 22 June of the present year. I have seen and read your excellency's letter with the respectful attention my duty demands. I have considered your proposal regarding the report that the capitán, cabo y caudillo, Juan Fernández de la Fuente, made to your excellency about the hostilities the various rebel Indian nations are committing in the area of Janos presidio in Sonora province and its frontiers. He suggests that in order to seek out the enemy, the forces of the presidios of Janos, Sinaloa, New Mexico, and El Paso should be combined. Your excellency gave this information to the governor of New Biscay so that he might make me a party to it as well, sending me your letter so that I might carry it out with dutiful attention.

Your excellency also advises me to leave the presidio and its environs with protection sufficient for its defense. This is the tenor of your excellency's order. Because of my humble sense of duty, I must report to your greatness that I, as the least of your servants who so reveres you, am unable to comply as promptly as you may wish. I say, most excellent sir, that this government is a constant—a frontier in open warfare and safeguard of the kingdom of New Biscay, Sonora, and Sinaloa—completely surrounded by numerous enemies. Though it will be up to your excellency to decide, there are many in that court who can so attest. This is my obligation and at my risk. It is of record, by virtue of the oath I am ordered to swear before your excellency by the royal title I have from his majesty, and you are to receive, that I shall have the fortress on guard and vigilant and defend it against the enemy. This is what his majesty orders me, because it seemed to him that the fortress had been constructed as he ordered in the year 1683, when don Domingo Jironza was governor. Pursuant to this, your excellency, I, having taken the oath, swore to carry out well and faithfully the responsibilities of governor and captain general: to maintain and preserve this presidio in safety and defense against the enemy, neither surrendering nor yielding, and obey all rights, royal laws, and ordinances.

This government is very much at my risk and my obligation, as is that in Parral and New Biscay to its governor. The difference is that Parral is prepared against its enemies, as its jurisdiction is so well supplied with presidios, haciendas, settlements, reales, and provisions, as well as seeds, cattle, horses, and mules. At this miserable, isolated spot, surrounded by enemies, the few citizens were so lacking in provisions, which are in short supply, that they have survived since they arrived on mesquite fruit, drinking atole made from it, and eating quelites. This is what they have lived on.

Sixty people without horses or weapons

For their protection, they have this presidio, which his majesty (may God keep him) assigned to them, based on truthful information provided by Gen. don Antonio de Otermín in the proceedings of the new entrada in the year 1681. He said that most of the citizens had abandoned that place and gone as fugitives to the jurisdictions of the kingdom of New Biscay and diverse parts of Sonora and Sinaloa. Even in Mexico City, there are people who obtained permission by cunning or favor and other fugitives. The fifty soldiers live here for the protection of the holy churches and families of the few citizens who have remained. There are scarcely sixty people, and of those, not even forty are fit to bear arms. They have neither horses nor weapons other than the matchlocks they may be issued from this royal armory for any call to arms.

The first time General don Domingo came, he established and built this presidio by order of the most excellent lord viceroy, the Conde de Paredes, Marqués de la Laguna.[50] It is some 8 leagues from this outpost of El Paso. Four or 5 leagues beyond the presidio was the real and villa of Spaniards given the name San Lorenzo, where his predecessor, Gen. don Antonio de Otermín, established his headquarters. He populated it with citizens who remained in this kingdom and many of those who had left as fugitives. The Indians living in this pueblo of El Paso, as well as others, were planning an act of treachery. The Mansos and Sumas gave some indication of this by striking their camps.

Recognizing the risk—and fearing they might conspire and arise all at once, burning the churches, and that other enemy nations could come and join them—it was decided to move the presidio to this pueblo of El Paso and transfer the Spaniards and citizens who were settled by his predecessor in the real and villa of San Lorenzo to a small settlement having few Indians. It was called then, as it is today, the real of San Lorenzo, not quite 2 leagues from this pueblo of El Paso. A few citizens remained in the next three pueblos, a little more than a league away, to raise some sheep and plant crops. They made their farms among the pueblos so that over a distance of 5 leagues they might lend a hand to one another, and the presidio might aid them in pursuing the enemy. Even though they are so arranged and only 5 leagues distant, they run the risk of their livestock crossing to the other side of the river where the Indians live.

The Apaches come when the moon is out and usually carry off some livestock. They also come during the planting season, when, as they know, the other Indians are guarding their milpas so the livestock neither eat nor damage the plants. I must form some squads and Indian troops, although few in number, to go out to different places. Some may alternate between different outposts in groups of fifty men. Your excellency, out of the soldiers and citizens, I shall scarcely be able to form a squad to be the main guard of the horses; the people necessary to guard this plaza de armas; and the people for the campaign, which is necessary to seek out and repulse the enemy's raids. When they are noticed, they can be followed, and the people of these pueblos can be armed and put on the defensive.

As I must repeat to your excellency, I do not have presidios where I can pluck handfuls of people to form a company. I shall be ever watchful and would gladly risk losing my life for my king and lord to fulfill my duty. I was given this presidio of soldiers without shelter or defense, as it is, having neither fortress, redoubt, nor small fort that was ordered built. For this reason, I was granted the title of governor, captain general, and castellan of the fortress of this kingdom of New Mexico. With the presidio, you order me to keep myself on the alert and defend it against the enemy, neither surrendering nor yielding. Thus, most excellent sir, you may consider this an explanation of my performance, but not of what may seem to be reasons for avoiding my duty. This is because his majesty (may God keep him) assigned the fifty soldiers to this presidio and outpost. Thus, the viceroy, the Conde de Paredes, and the council of ministers realized the greatest saving to the royal treasury. His excellency and his ministers saw from the report that it was only what was necessary and not in excess. They felt that with these soldiers the enemy could be resisted, if not destroyed. They could keep and protect whatever Indians there were. The number of Christian Indians increased because of my predecessor's entradas to the kingdom of New Mexico. Don Antonio de Otermín took 385 people from Isleta Pueblo, who were counted, as is recorded in his proceedings. Gen. don Pedro Reneros took those who were in Santa Ana Pueblo, and Gen. don Domingo Jironza, my immediate predecessor, those who were able to escape from Zia Pueblo.

Thus, most excellent sir, his majesty gave the presidios to the governor of New Biscay and assigned them where they are needed, should war break out among the Tarahumaras, who are already harassed by the Pima, Jocome, and Jano enemy, as well as the other Indian nations of Sonora. According to what Captain Fuente of the Janos presidio says, some Sumas, the Manso rancheria led by Captain Chiquito, and the Apaches from the extensive Gila mountain ranges will join them. More than the others, these last three nations have besieged and surrounded me. They are in close communication with the same group of Mansos who left when General don Domingo moved this presidio (from which I report to your excellency) to this outpost from where he founded it in 1683.

The very reverend father custos, fray Francisco de Vargas, worked for more than two years for the conversion of these Mansos, most of whom lived in this kingdom, until they were reduced to our holy faith. He founded their church, called San Francisco de los Mansos,[51] on the site they chose 8 or 9 leagues from El Paso. They received the water of holy baptism in April of the present year. The very reverend father was godfather of a captain I appointed governor of this rancheria. I acted as godfather[52] of another captain from another rancheria, so that they might remain happy and not become agitated. Since their rancherias are so remote, some Apaches from the mountains come and go in groups of two, four, or six. This communication, and that with the Sumas who are heathens, is so ready because they have rebelled and married Manso and Suma women, as have some Apaches. These are reasons, most excellent sir, for being suspicious of their loyalty, because they are only pretending. By not depriving them of contact with Apaches and Sumas, which are extensive nations where I am, we aim to keep the Mansos of the rancheria happy in our holy faith. It is our hope to see whether their example will be imitated by those who attack the area. It is only Captain Chiquito's rancheria, which is said to be in the Sierra Florida,[53] lying mainly in the provinces of Sonora. I do not intend to dwell on the details, but to go on with the report I should make to your excellency, as so great a prince representing his majesty (may God keep him), to whom those of the kingdom of New Biscay reported.

Trade would be very beneficial to both majesties, as would establishing Janos presidio to convoy silver and defend the farms and missions within its jurisdiction. This is the task Captain Fuente was ordered to carry out with some of the fifty men. Should the enemy be encountered there, he should go to the governor of New Biscay, since it is his responsibility to request aid of him as the one responsible for maintaining and preserving his kingdom, district, and jurisdiction. If it is in Sonora, its governor could give him five or six men. All Captain Fuente requests is thirty men to come to the aid of his jurisdiction, without wanting to weaken the others. Ordering six men with a strong leader from each company of the presidios was not to lose them, but to send them so that they might be under Captain Fuente's orders. This captain should not have presumed to make a report to your excellency. What he intended was to remove forces this kingdom does not have, which would leave it at great risk. The cost to his majesty has been great to preserve the souls of the Indians who are the care and responsibility of the apostolic missionary fathers and governors who were my predecessors. Removing the forces would place it in obvious danger because the enemy, seeing it unprotected, could fall upon this outpost again.

By the axioms and policies of good government, there is friendship and peace with the nations who live in and around the outpost. With regard to Mansos becoming Christians—an end that is hoped for—this hope is sustained; we trust in His Divine Majesty that the rest of their nation, which is in rebellion, may join them because they see them at home in the pueblo, and the apostates among them may ask for mercy and be absolved of their apostasy by the missionaries. In the same way, the other heathens may follow, asking for the water of baptism.

Note
Thirty men

Most excellent sir, in your wisdom you will see that these are urgent reasons for me to decide to remain and not leave this kingdom at risk. I am amazed that no one came the 70 leagues, from where the captain was, or the 140, from where his governor of New Biscay was, to give me reports and opinions about the combining of forces. That is, the governor of New Biscay could keep his forces in reserve, so that, as I have told you, his Captain Fuente could take the thirty men he requests. They should not presume to be worthy of judging and giving opinions, because they cannot know what may happen to each governor and whether there may be risk. One governor cannot comprehend what generally happens to all others. To try to do so is arrogant and vain, since the kingdoms are so different, each with its own customs and policy.

In responding to and satisfying your excellency's point that the Indians of New Mexico are not at war and thus the entrada could be postponed until another time, I find repugnant anything that may further such a proposition when the Christianity of the Indians is suffering every moment. I should be thanked and applauded for my zeal in seeing whether, by the hands of the apostolic missionary fathers,

I can snatch from the devil's clutches and reduce to our holy faith those I am able. This is so that they will cast off their apostasy and so that the freedom they enjoy in their thought will not take root in their hearts, for the devil has them in his grasp, possessing their souls as they die in apostasy so that they will be his slaves. Your excellency will see whether this matter is proof of my zeal, since I am undertaking this entrada at my own expense.

That he does not ask aid from the other presidios

I have neither requested an advance of funds from his majesty nor put his provinces and presidios at risk by asking them for men. I shall instead take only those from this company with me without disturbing and risking his majesty's frontiers and presidios by requesting men from them. If the Indians of New Mexico were only heathen enemies, as the Apaches and Sumas are, the entrada could be postponed. Citizens of the kingdom of New Biscay could then attend to the enemies of this kingdom of New Mexico without leaving their district and kingdom, except to go after prisoners from some rancheria, based on reliable information from scouts sent out to reconnoiter the countryside. The Indians of New Mexico, however, are rebels, not heathen but apostate. Three things are at risk if there is a delay in their reduction and conquest. First, if they die in apostasy as the devil's slaves, they are damned. Second, in their wickedness as apostates, they become evil and make their reduction impossible. Third, because they are so new to our holy faith, scarcely reduced, most are in danger of being lost. They may follow the evil sect their parents teach them and those who govern them order.

Your excellency can confirm this, as proof of my truthfulness, with the religious (of whom there are many elderly ones) in the convento of Nuestro Padre San Francisco in Mexico City. [54] You will understand the reasons for my response to your excellency's points.

Increase of men-at-arms and soldiers for the presidio

I would also have you know that after two couriers, I am still waiting for the response to my report to your excellency about the men-at-arms and the soldiers for this presidio. I have also expressed to your excellency the impossibility of provisions. The few fields were late and lightly planted, because of the time spent repairing and cleaning the acequias. I decided it was wise to stay in this kingdom's presidio and outpost during the summer, so that the citizens and Indians might plant, enjoy, and gather the seeds to assure their families' sustenance.

Had I gone on campaign, I would have done so without provisions. The horses were weak because it had not rained. I am hopeful that if it rains in September, they will fill out a little. With whatever horses I may have (it seems to me there will be more than one hundred, as well as fifty mules), I shall go on campaign with the supplies I have collected: biscuit made from one hundred fanegas of wheat flour; meat; sugar; chocolate; tobacco; paper; wine; cheese; wax; soap, so that the soldiers can wash their clothes; pinole; and maize flour. The last item will be given to the missionary fathers as a gift for their sustenance.

He will make an entrada around October

I have these supplies and have made preparations, should your excellency order me to undertake the entrada. I shall carry it out in the middle of October. Your excellency's order will find me prepared. I choose this season because I shall find the enemy, whom I am going to seek out to fight, gathered in their pueblos and houses because of the rigors of the cold and snows. In contrast, during the summer they are away from their pueblos. Most of them are scattered about: hunting, working their milpas, fishing, and in the mountains gathering the roots and fruits they eat. My plans in this government, where his majesty has installed me, are not only to see whether I can preserve it, but also to increase, as a result of the entradas to the kingdom of New Mexico, the number of Indians and restore some of them to obedience to both majesties.

It seems to me that it will be with the influence and support of his majesty, the king our lord (and your excellency, as the representative of his royal person), that I can entertain these thoughts and fulfill these passions. My wish will always be to be at your feet. I want you to know that I neither oppose nor am failing to comply with your order commanding me not to undertake this entrada to the kingdom of New Mexico, should your excellency repeat it to me in the second post, which I am awaiting.

As I have said in this letter, when the harvest is in I shall apply myself, this company's forces, and the supplies to make war on the

Apaches of the Gila Mountains. If the winter weather permits, I shall also carry out the task of making war in the Sierra Florida, where they say the rancheria of Captain Chiquito's Mansos is.

I offer your excellency in this letter the explanation of the points contained herein as the most proper representation to your most excellent person. I trust that, out of your understanding for the royal zeal, it will receive your attention as a matter redounding to the royal service. May Our Lord keep your most excellent person as shield and defense of all kingdoms of the realm. Dated in this plaza de armas of El Paso on 14 August 1691.

Most excellent sir, the least of your servants who venerates you kisses your feet,

Don Diego de Vargas Zapata Luján Ponce de León
[rubrica]

Most excellent lord viceroy, the Conde de Galve

———

El Paso
14 August 1691
Don Diego de Vargas Zapata y Luján
Received on 21 November

———

Mexico City, 22 November 1691

Put this letter with the one from the same governor of 4 October and those dated 14 August and 9 September that accompanied it, written to the governor of New Biscay and to the captain of the presidio of Janos, Juan Fernández de la Fuente, and the one I have from the governor of New Biscay of 26 October, together with the related proceedings on combining the forces of the three presidios of El Paso, Janos, and Sinaloa, and take them to the fiscal. [Galve's rubrica]

Diego de Vargas to Juan Isidro de Pardiñas, El Paso,
14 August 1691, LS.

Dear sir,

With yours of 15 July of the present year is included the letter
from the most excellent lord viceroy, the Conde de Galve, humbly
accompanied by my response to him given out of my reverent sense
of duty. I give his greatness the required explanation. Likewise, I
report on the clear and certain causes, motives, points, circumstances,
consequences, and opinions about the reasons I refer to for not being
able to give the aid of thirty men your lordship's captain, Juan de la
Fuente, of Janos presidio proposes and requests. He has informed
me that he finds himself overrun by the Pima, Janos, and Jocome
nations who have rebelled together with the Gila Mountain Apaches
and the Sumas, as well as Captain Chiquito's Manso rancheria in
the Sierra Florida. They rob, burn, and kill within the jurisdiction
of his frontier as in the pueblos of the kingdom of Sonora, which is
your responsibility and at your expense. Since you have so many
presidios well furnished with supplies, cattle, horses, and mules; haciendas; settlements of Spaniards and Indians securely at peace; and
reales, I am very much amazed that with your great understanding
you have not reproved the capitán y cabo, Juan Fernández de la
Fuente, for having made a report to his excellency, without first warning you of the state and condition of the enemies and the damages
they inflict and continually perpetrate in the jurisdictions of his presidio and those of Sonora. For a man of your good judgment and
experience, it would not be a burden to take six men from each of
your presidios and send them with a good cabo with whatever orders
seem appropriate, when all he wants is thirty to go on the offensive
against the enemy. Better yet, let him do what he knows how to do
where relief is needed and not make reports to his excellency.

There should be no combining of forces based on those from the
presidio of Sinaloa and from this presidio, which only has fifty soldiers for its minimal defense. I have divided them into three squadrons. One is for guarding the horses; another for the plaza de armas;
and another for patrolling the countryside and reconnoitering the
other bank of the river for enemy forays and camps, of the Apaches
or any others, who may come to steal the horses of the citizens and
Indians living in the pueblos of this district. Some of them, if they

did not have protection, could not safely leave their houses to care for their milpas.

I deeply regret that I cannot provide aid in this war, as I would, not excepting even myself, if I saw that Casas Grandes[55] and the Janos presidio were besieged and in danger. I would assist, I say, with everything, holding back nothing, paying no attention to this kingdom, which his majesty (may God keep him) has entrusted to me as my obligation and at my risk, as he has that one to you. You can see the difference. Your kingdom is fertile and better secured in every way by the presidios that fortify and guard it everywhere. For all this, you seem fearful and beg for men from a poor governor of a miserable, isolated spot whose protection and maintenance is his responsibility. He has neither more assistance nor more force than this company of fifty soldiers and fears seeing himself incessantly assailed by the Apache nations, surrounded by the Sumas and their allies. It is also to be feared that even those who are held to be friends may imitate the license, pillaging, and destruction of the others. With all I have to think about, being so hemmed in and close to these enemy nations, I neither ask you to give me men nor shall I petition his excellency. I leave it to his discretion and decision. As for mine, I do not inform his excellency just so that he will give me men for the enterprise at hand, because I do not ask for aid. As for me, I only want—once and for all—to put my life and that of these soldiers on the line.

I am awaiting the second courier, whom I sent to his excellency in June. If he gives me a different order, I shall abide by and fulfill it to the extent I am able. If his excellency, when informed, were to order me to carry it out, whatever risk or happenstance will be his excellency's responsibility. All testimony will be taken and the necessary protests lodged so that at all times his majesty may be given an accounting of everything that may result and that I have lived up to my well-known sense of duty. You know I am steadfast in serving you and returning your many favors. I am troubled that on the present occasion, I can neither give you this aid nor serve you as I would if I were able, going as your soldier with this company under your order.

My arguments counter those who are not dedicated to his majesty's service and would rather be grandees in Spain than take a pike and go out to serve him in areas where his greatness increases. In this way, I respond to all your arguments, except the one about the postponement of the entrada to New Mexico. I am making a distinction, relating the reasons to his excellency. As representative of his majesty's royal person, he will judge and weigh them, giving me the order or orders he decides upon, which I am humbly waiting to carry out.

May God keep you the many happy years I wish. El Paso, 14 August 1691.

Your most steadfast servant kisses your hand,

Don Diego de Vargas Zapata
Luján Ponce de León [rubrica]

Lord general, don Juan Isidro de Pardiñas

———

El Paso, 14 August 1691
Don Diego de Vargas
Written to don Juan Isidro de Pardiñas
Received 21 November

Diego de Vargas to Juan Fernández de la Fuente, n.p., 9 September 1691, LS.

Dear sir,[56]

His excellency (may God keep him) orders me to suspend the entrada at present to the kingdom of New Mexico and offer aid and protection where it is needed most. Thus, I advise you by this letter that on 10 October I shall have prepared my company and one hundred Indian warriors, who are among the best allies from these pueblos, and the supplies and munitions for my troops. With them, I shall personally serve his majesty wherever the need is greatest.

Notice to Fuente that he is coming for the union of arms with the aforementioned men

Please advise me where you want us to meet so that in every way his majesty's service may be fulfilled and his weapons well employed where the enemies' opposition and resistance is greatest. I think they are the Gila Mountain Apaches. Tell me where we can join forces, because I shall be ready to ride on 10 October. I shall count the days and the enemies destroyed on campaign. Time will tell us what we must do. You can always be sure that I hope you are in good health. May God keep you for many happy years. Dated today, 9 September 1691.

Your most affectionate and surest servant kisses your hand,

Don Diego de Vargas Zapata
Luján Ponce de León [rubrica]

Capt. Juan Fernández de la Fuente
New Mexico, 9 September 1691

———

Don Diego de Vargas Zapata y Luján
Received on 21 November
Written to Capt. Juan Fernández de la Fuente

*Diego de Vargas to the Conde de Galve, El Paso,
4 October 1691, LS.*

Most excellent sir,

Sir, in response to the recommendation I made to your excellency and sent on 20 June of this year, you send me your directive and order. The lords minister, in the general junta your excellency held with them, decided to give them to me. They appended to them the report Capt. Juan Fernández de la Fuente of Janos presidio made to your excellency on 19 April. On 14 August, he brought me a letter from your excellency in the packet from his governor and captain general of New Biscay, don Juan Isidro de Pardiñas. He also brought responses for your excellency and from his governor. It occurred to me to send copies of them to you with this courier so that, if you see fit, they may be examined by the Junta of War and Royal Treasury, where the very obtuse report was originally heard and is on file.

After your excellency has seen my response to the first order, which I repeat by this courier, and the one I gave to the governor, and after the lords minister have heard them, it could be that they may find that Captain Fuente's idea may be completely dismissed as merely seeking to avoid a loss of support for his governor and captain general of New Biscay. It is incumbent upon him, since the province of Sonora is his responsibility. He has such a large presidio of men-at-arms that Captain Fuente's aim comes down to asking for thirty men. As the governor is advised, he should reprimand his captain for making a report to your excellency and wasting the time that, of course, should have been applied wherever the enemy harasses, instead of getting involved in paperwork.

I must state in this letter the obstacles I encounter that must be added to my response in the copy with regard to your excellency's order, resolved on 3 August with a view to Juan Fernández de la Fuente's report on the combining of forces he proposes with this presidio of El Paso. The first observation of interest to your excellency, which must be taken into consideration, is that the Indians and nations who infest the provinces of Sonora are wandering rancherias. They also have scouts, who are undetected. They know, more or less, when the army is called to arms. It is very easy for them to take prisoners, watching for the return to this pueblo of El Paso of the men-at-arms who leave to pursue them.

It is certain, and very much without doubt, that they are to be feared. Their arrowheads provide their sustenance. In a day and a night, they walk 40 or 50 leagues without being noticed, since they travel through the mountains. Just when it seems that the enemy is going to be destroyed, on the contrary, they destroy these poor unfortunates.

The second observation is that the Indians who are at peace do not go beyond good intentions. They do not know how to fight in a different jurisdiction, and it can be said of them that they are as cowardly as a dog in a strange neighborhood. They go bad; by imitating the enemy's example, they would do the same in this land. They would like to remain sole owners of it.

They have better sites to fortify and defend themselves than any four nations Captain Fuente could imagine, without the men of all the presidios then being enough. He can join forces with the neighboring province of Sinaloa to hem in the enemies between them. He should ask his governor, if your excellency sees fit, to enlist for another year the thirty men he asks for from this presidio and not go around disrupting such important plans and decisions of men who so little value life and fulfill their duty, as I do.

To say to your excellency that I was ready to leave to reconnoiter the villa of Santa Fe is out of modesty in wanting to relate what was done and not what I promise. It is my intention, and that of my whole company, to triumph or perish until Santa Fe is restored. It would be necessary to conquer the first pueblo of Cochiti, San Juan, and Santo Domingo Paraguai.[57] Since the Indians would be fortified in the fortress and palace with earthworks they have thrown up, I would attempt to breech them by assault, without their killing my people. As I have no cannon with which to knock them down, I would take advantage of the night and stealth, leaning some poles with planks on top against the wall to make a cover so that, without being seen under it, a mine could be dug. Then I and my men would hurl ourselves through it, entering the fort sword in hand (or with lances for those who lack swords). In order to divert the enemy's attention, some of the men would make feints by leaning ladders against the wall as if assaulting it, firing at random, and using every trick to hide the mining operation from the enemy.

This could not be done any other way except tunneling, because of the thickness of the ramparts and the lack of cannon to knock them down, without the risk that my men might be killed. The tunnel would bisect the wall, as a transept would, going the distance necessary to come up within the plaza de armas. Having arrived by dead reckoning by this route and having covered the distance, I would tunnel and bore upward toward the sky, so as to break through and come out into the plaza de armas during the dawn watch with my men. From inside, the door would be broken down and opened. The men who had been readied and assigned could defend against the Indians' leaving until they were destroyed as wicked rebels who are not obedient to his majesty.[58] I am very troubled by the fact that I am ready and waiting for this campaign and undertaking, this year, once and for all, either to end my life or restore to his majesty his land and vassals, freeing them from the devil's slavery as apostates.

My wishes to serve his majesty may be frustrated by seemingly truthful reports that, well, I must say, I find spurious. It would be better if each governor defended his own territory and if Capt. Juan de la Fuente, being a subordinate and subject to his governor, did not attempt to lord it over me, making a report when it was legitimately his governor's place to do so. He also takes on the enemy nations of Sinaloa, when his majesty has already assigned a governor and presidio with men-at-arms for this. For the province of Sonora, the governor of New Biscay should have named a lieutenant general where he has his men and citizenry to guard his territory.[59]

> He would leave about 10 October from New Mexico, as he writes Fuente

If mine is calmed, it is not because I ask for aid, but because I maintain the vigilance of inspecting it and my men divided into three squadrons: one to guard the horses, one to keep watch over the territory the Apaches and other enemies enter, and another in this plaza de armas. I am assuming that your excellency will order me to go where aid is needed most, which is deemed to be the provinces of Sonora and Sinaloa. This is why I sent the letter I am sending with this one to your excellency to the capitán, cabo y caudillo, Juan Fernández de la Fuente. In it, I told him that I would leave this outpost and plaza de armas about 10 October, marching with my troops, taking provisions, horses, mules, and munitions, so that his majesty's weapons may be employed on the offensive and that he should advise me so we can join forces. He responds that it would be better for me to go with my troops to his presidio at Janos, whence we would go out together on campaign, which will best dictate its own course.

Most excellent sir, I recognize that the most important enemy infesting these provinces are the Apaches in the Gila Mountains. Even Juan Fernández de la Fuente (in his letter I sent to your excellency, which was discussed in the general junta held to decide upon the order your excellency gave me) realized that, first, it was necessary to destroy the Apaches of the Gila Mountains, the most powerful in bravery, skill, and number. If your response to his letter and to mine is completely in agreement with my opinion, it will still be to combine forces and carry out the invasion of the Gila Mountains. Given the number of men, they could be distributed in such a way as to carry out a slaughter of telling consequence, and the enemy might then leave the provinces of Sonora and Sinaloa calm for a time. The other enemies are but poorly established rancherias, or so I have been told.

I should like to be certain that your excellency recognizes my devoted vigilance in serving you in everything. I regret that I assured myself that your excellency would applaud my decision. I had hoped to subject the people of the villa of Santa Fe to his majesty's royal vassalage, given the means I had, without inconveniencing your excellency by asking you to remove forces from the presidios or give me anything in advance from the royal treasury. In 1681, a very considerable sum was spent,[60] and they did not advance beyond Cochiti and had to turn back.

I am here solely by my own will, driven by my Catholic zeal and as a vassal of his majesty (who is so revered) to undertake this enterprise, which is more necessary than any other. These enemies are of the greatest consequence, because Christianity suffers from them. They are the instrument and origin of all the other rebellions. Because they have not been punished, the others continue in their insolence. May the latter not be moved by having seen the former. They have not been discredited, and the required satisfaction has not been exacted.

Your excellency and the lords minister can rest assured that I wish this were word of having restored Santa Fe, rather than an expression of my feeling that a dubious report may have caused me to check my daring. Most excellent sir, if within sight of Parral the Indians, covered by presidios at a distance of 20 leagues, rob and kill, and if so many citizens and haciendas have not overcome these other Indians, and since Capt. Juan de la Fuente bases his recovery on the combining of forces of thirty men from this presidio, then his governor must have some other objective. After all, he allows him to report to your excellency on the small number of thirty men he asks for. It seems to me, most excellent sir, that the Tarahumaras[61] are about to come down from the mountains, and it is necessary to be on guard against this. The governor and Captain Fuente want to use this pretext to hold the presidial soldiers in reserve.

He leaves in person with the company and one hundred Indians with provisions and horses

I am leaving in person, most excellent sir, with my company and one hundred Indians to go on the offensive. I am of the opinion that this should always be done against the enemies in the Gila Mountains who are superior in everything, in force and the vastness of their territory. If contradicted, my opinion notwithstanding, I shall go to make war wherever it is decided. For my part, I shall take care to fulfill my duties in his majesty's service and take, as I repeat to your excellency, the previously mentioned quantities of provisions, men, weapons, and horses. In everything, I hope that the combining of forces will be achieved, and your excellency will recognize my blind obedience.

In obedience to orders

As always, I humbly obey and carry out your excellency's orders. May Our Lord keep your most excellent person in your increasing nobility for many happy years. Dated in this outpost of El Paso and its presidio on 4 October 1691.

Most excellent sir, the least of your humble
servants kisses your excellency's hand,

Don Diego de Vargas Zapata
Luján Ponce de León [rubrica]

Most excellent lord viceroy, the Conde de Galve

Juan Isidro de Pardiñas to the Conde de Galve, Parral, 26 October 1691, LS.

Most excellent sir,

Sir, I have received your excellency's first orders that the forces of the El Paso and Sinaloa presidios should be combined with those of Janos under the command of Capt. Juan Fernández de la Fuente to go on the offensive against the nations who harass those frontiers and Sonora province. Having sent them on to the governors of El Paso and Sinaloa, the latter informed me that in compliance with them, he would be in Sonora on the fifteenth of the present month with the forces under his command. The governor and captain general of New Mexico replied to me, placing obstacles in the way of their compliance and sending me the enclosed letter for your excellency. Now I have been notified in a postscript to the letter he wrote me that around the twentieth of this month, he would be at Janos presidio with Capt. Juan Fernández de la Fuente to begin the war as ordered by your excellency. Your opportune decision to repeat the orders, it seems to me, overcomes the obstacles first suggested. With regard to my own obedience, I sent Capt. Francisco Ramírez de Salazar[62] the order your excellency saw fit to issue about supervision of the forces and the ten presidial soldiers from here, so that, with the twenty from Sinaloa, the flying company your excellency has provided for Sinaloa will be formed.[63] Thus, your excellency is obeyed with regard to what you have seen fit to decide. May God keep the most excellent person of your excellency in the increasing nobility I wish and is so necessary. Parral, 26 October 1691.

Juan Isidro de Pardiñas Villar de Francos [rubrica]

Most excellent lord, the Conde de Galve

Parral, 26 October 1691
Received 21 November
Don Juan Isidro Pardiñas

Diego de Vargas to the Conde de Galve, El Paso, 4 October 1691, LS.

Most excellent sir,

Sir, I received your excellency's directives and orders of 3 August of the present year. I humbly and promptly sent the alcalde mayor of Casas Grandes two certifications from the person who came on behalf of his majesty's justices from the districts and jurisdictions where the citizens and other people belonging to this kingdom of New Mexico are, ordering them, by virtue of your excellency's order and directive contained therein, to return. Thus, in this way I sent him the second copy of the enclosed dispatch for the alcalde mayor, his lieutenant, and the remaining ministers of justice of the real of Santa Rosa Cosihuiriáchic.[64] Likewise, I sent to the governor of New Biscay the certification of your excellency's directive and the order for him that I received nominatim in the dispatches. I charge the justices to carry out promptly your excellency's order, advising me so that I can faithfully inform you so that you may know the result, as is my duty to your greatness.

I must warn your excellency of several objections and obstacles that will prevent the total fulfillment of your directives and orders with respect to where the citizens of this kingdom and others belonging to it are. The justices use the pretext of protecting these areas to impede your excellency's order, advising that these people live in mining camps and to comply would be detrimental to the royal treasury. They babble on with similar arguments to question, interpret, and criticize the orders of the most excellent lords viceroy, including your excellency. A governor of this kingdom only succeeds in alienating himself from the justices without achieving the desired end of bringing back the citizens to this outpost from where they have scattered.

Second, many are living under the protection of the royal standard, having enlisted in the presidial companies of Janos, Conchos, Cuencamé,[65] and Gallo.[66] They also work on cattle ranches and farms whose owners naturally take advantage of the privilege of royal laws and ordinances that speak in their favor, protesting damages, spoilage, losses, and the risks they face on their ranches from the enemy, even though they are peopled by their servants. I must inform your excellency of these excuses, because if the citizens and other people mentioned were in the reales, they would be protected by reason of the increase to the royal treasury. They are thus honored vagabonds, being neither mineowners nor fit to work in the mines, more like wasters and spongers off those who are in the presidios, given that your captains will have to defend them. They should be more aware that they should neither speak of nor discuss your excellency's directive and order with the soldiers and citizens who are from this outpost and legitimate natives of this kingdom. They will say that the order should not apply to well-established citizens who live in the presidios, haciendas, and ranchos of the jurisdictions that serve to grant a reprieve to and favor the areas the enemies harass. The citizens and people included will have to answer for these and many other stupidities, saying and alleging that they are settled in where they are and have established a way of life. They allege that his majesty gives them nothing here in this kingdom, so they cannot live in it since they have no way of acquiring what they need to sustain themselves. This is, or so they say, a barren land, because it does not have a rainy season to produce pastures for raising a few head of cattle, and crops are gathered only by conserving the few drops of water in the acequia from the Río del Norte.

These arguments, most excellent sir, are based on events that happened during my predecessors' time, as related to me as I passed through Parral, and in the short time I have resided in this government. With your great understanding, your excellency will see that for my part I have omitted nothing. The problem with the directives is that they do not come prepared for all these objections. It should be of record in them that all those to which I refer your excellency cannot be raised. These people should come and remain here, faithfully carrying out under pain of death his majesty's royal will, as expressed in your excellency's order and directive. Thus, the justices will carry it out, in the knowledge that these people are not going to be allowed to live in their jurisdictions. Each one in his own must carry out the order insofar as it concerns him with the threat of incurring penalties your excellency may reserve for him. I make all this known to you because in the junta the lords minister, who vote and advise your excellency, were not of the opinion that returning the people and soldiers of this presidio would be effective.

That fifty men be added to the presidio and the kingdom conquered

Your excellency can endeavor and order that they make entradas, reconnoiter, and patrol all over the land, with citizens and soldiers in sufficient number to go on campaign and still leave this country protected. What I consider most difficult will be to conquer the entire kingdom of New Mexico without his majesty giving me an additional fifty men for this presidio. Without taking one citizen from this kingdom and with only the one hundred men, I shall give you all the kingdom of New Mexico reduced by force of arms. By using my head, I shall do this well. I do not speak of peopling, but of conquering, because what is not very possible has no place in my sense of duty.

Your excellency will please advise me about all this, but not because I would stop, by virtue of your excellency's directives, seeking as many people as can be induced by all gentle means, by promising them land and that they may live wherever they choose. I shall try for all I am worth to defer them from campaigning. I shall take no one unless it is very much of his own free will and he offers to go. I shall pay his way, relieving him from guarding the horses. For my part, this is all I can do. I would have them recognize that if they come by virtue of this order, the reason is to carry out his majesty's royal will and for no other end.

I hope it will be duly fulfilled, and with equal humility, I place myself at your excellency's feet, hoping that Our Lord may keep your most excellent person many happy years. Dated in this plaza de armas of this presidio on 4 October 1691.

Most excellent sir, the least of your servants
humbly kisses your excellency's hands,

Don Diego de Vargas Zapata
Luján Ponce de León [rubrica]

Most excellent lord viceroy, the Conde de Galve

———

New Mexico, 4 October 1691
Don Diego de Vargas Zapata y Luján
Received on 21 November

Notice of the receipt of the directive on the return to El Paso and its district of all the citizens of New Mexico who are absent and scattered throughout the kingdom of New Biscay, the impossibility of executing this, and the difficulties that exist despite appearing reasonable to him. He reports on this point so that it will not be thought that he has more than enough forces for battles and entradas by simply having been sent what was reported.

———

Mexico City, 22 November 1691
To the lord fiscal with related proceedings that fifty men from the presidio be added and he will conquer the entire kingdom
[Galve's rubrica]

Benito de Noboa Salgado, Fiscal's reply, Mexico City, 26 November 1691, DS.

Most excellent sir,

His majesty's fiscal has reviewed this last letter, along with the earlier ones, from the governor of New Mexico, together with the other one from the governor of Parral of 26 October of this year. In it, it is of record that the governor of New Mexico has agreed to combine his forces with those of Capt. Juan Fernández de la Fuente, so that the reduction of those nations will be attained first, before going on to another enterprise. He will have already fulfilled this obligation, and the fiscal has no comment to make about it.[67] In the letter of 4 October, he relates to you the resistance he encounters in getting the settlers of New Mexico back to El Paso. They are already more or less used to their life and to the support they have from the captains, magistrates, and mine- and hacienda owners who aid them. Should your excellency decide, if you see fit, on an entrada to New Mexico, to overcome their feeling that the site of El Paso is very inhospitable and too poor to be settled, Santa Fe must be sufficiently populated and have everything needed, if it is to be permanent and produce good results. To achieve this, an edict should be issued and proclaimed that all Spanish men and women who left and return to New Mexico, as well as the other Spaniards who settle, whether as soldiers or citizens, will be considered hidalgos,[68] worthy of distributions of land and encomiendas, according to what each one deserves, should your excellency grant them this favor in his majesty's name. In contrast, if those who were citizens in New Mexico will not be led back to settle their land, they will be considered plebeians, unworthy of being able to aspire to positions of honor, military or civilian, and unworthy of the name Spaniard. With this, there will be no one so base that, like a brute, he values his creature comforts more than the honorable advancement of his lineage and family.

With regard to what the governor of El Paso proposes, that with one hundred soldiers—fifty he has and another fifty who will be added—he will conquer New Mexico, the fiscal states that there can be no secure conquest if there are no settlers who will support it later. This should not be done haphazardly, but very efficiently. For this reason, he has stated in his response on page four of these proceedings that once the uprising of the Janos has been put down, all the forces will go to the aid of the governor of El Paso for the battle for New Mexico. Anything more would be wasteful, to no advantage, and would give greater reason to the rebellious Indians for being more contumacious and wicked. In this way, the governor will consider the battle more certain and doubtless have many more men than what he proposes. Your excellency will provide in everything what is most advantageous to the royal service. Mexico City, 26 November 1691.

Dr. don Benito de Noboa Salgado [rubrica]

———

Mexico City, 26 November 1691
To the general junta [Galve's rubrica]

Junta of the Treasury, Mexico City, 4 December 1691, DS.

At the Junta of the Treasury held on 4 December 1691 by the most excellent lord viceroy of New Spain, the Conde de Galve, with the lords Dr. don Juan de Aréchaga, don Francisco Fernández Marmolejo, judges of this royal audiencia; don Mateo Fernández de Santa Cruz[69] and don Manuel Gerónimo de Tovar,[70] knight of the Order of Santiago, senior comptrollers of the Tribunal of Accounts; don Antonio de Deza y Ulloa, knight of the Order of Santiago, treasury official and comptroller; and don Fernando de Deza y Ulloa, comptroller general of tributes of New Spain: Having seen these letters from the governor of New Mexico, dated 9 September, 4 October, and 21 November regarding the matter of the entrada to the provinces the governor of New Mexico proposes and that he would conquer them by force of arms, it was decided that the governor, after finishing the battle for which the forces were combined, will propose on this point what occurs to him so that the decision that may be of service to his majesty may be made; that a dispatch may also be made so that the governor of Parral, having finished the battle, may assemble with the captains of the presidios in his charge and, interpreting the proposal the governor of New Mexico makes about the entrada, discuss and confer on what occurs to them and the differences in their opinions and his and of the governor of Par-

ral and transmit them to his excellency; that the dispatch be proclaimed wherever it seems appropriate to the governor of New Mexico,
so the notice reaches those people who may want to go settle those
provinces; and that they be given grants and distributions of land
and considered hidalgos and be given other honors according to what
each merits for himself and his family. Thus, they decided and signed
with his excellency. His excellency, Lords Aréchaga, Marmolejo,
Santa Cruz, Tovar, Deza, and Deza
[Galve's rubrica and one other]

All the dispatches of the junta have been made and delivered to the
office of his excellency's secretary.

Juan Isidro de Pardiñas to the Conde de Galve, Parral, 23 November 1691, LS.

Most excellent sir,

Lord don Diego de Vargas Zapata y Luján, governor and captain
general of New Mexico, has sent requisitions with an enclosure of
your excellency's directive so that all inhabitants and natives of New
Mexico should be ordered to leave and return there from the jurisdictions of this kingdom. After I made this public, the outcry and
demonstrations were so great that I find myself obliged to ask you on
their behalf for compassion. Ruined and miserable, they left that
province and have applied themselves on various frontiers of this kingdom, making their homes so as to maintain themselves. Many people have been moved to pity and supplied them with a great deal of
money. It will be difficult to pay their debts for years, and they have
only been given a few months. They also allege that they did not
receive pay from his majesty while in New Mexico. Many of them
left twenty, thirty, and even forty years ago. So it is that the outposts
of Casas Grandes and what they call Las Cruces[71] are garrisoned
with some of them. They have their dwellings there to the advantage and for the protection of these areas. They have meritoriously
served at their expense on all occasions Capt. Francisco Ramírez de
Salazar needed them. As volunteers, many of them took part in the
war with the Tarahumaras. Their misery is so well known that no
one can be ignorant of it. They make this plea with the abundant

tears that have obliged me to bring it to your excellency's attention in this letter, so that with your accustomed piety, it may be attended to, providing what may be most in the service of his majesty, whom I will obey, and that will always be for the best. May God keep the most excellent person of your excellency in the increasing nobility I wish and is so necessary. Parral, 23 November 1691.

Most excellent lord, the Conde de Galve,

Don Juan Isidro de Pardiñas
Villar de Francos [rubrica]

––––––––

Parral, 23 November 1691
Don Juan Isidro de Pardiñas
Received on 14 December
He presents objections to the order that the citizens of New Mexico who have left the country should be obliged to return.

––––––––

Mexico City, 14 December 1691
To the lord fiscal with the related material
[Galve's rubrica]

> *Benito de Noboa Salgado, Fiscal's reply, Mexico City, 15 December 1691, DS.*

Most excellent sir,

His majesty's fiscal has seen this letter from the governor of Parral and the report he makes about the difficulty of returning the citizens of New Mexico found in those districts. This was already reported by the governor of New Mexico on another occasion when the fiscal and your excellency responded. By dispatch on the fourth of the current month, with agreement of the general junta, it was ordered that a proclamation be published in the kingdom of Parral and other jurisdictions that seemed appropriate to the governor of New Mexico, so that all persons who may go to settle there as soldiers and citizens will be considered nobles, worthy of distributions of land and other grants. The governor of Parral will not yet have this dispatch. Now that there is an opportunity, it may be sent to them so that it can be proclaimed in his district and the other regions where it seems appropriate. The fiscal does not doubt that it will serve as an encouragement to the citizens and natives of New Mexico who may be there to return. Moreover, they are the first who should return. They will obtain greater benefits beyond recovering what they had—distributions of land, noble status, and reputation—than they are able to obtain now. In the interim, until the time comes for their return to New Mexico, they will be able to prepare themselves and make arrangements. Until then, they are not to leave. They will have time to get together the belongings they have where they are today, because making the proclamation now is not to say that they should go immediately, but to prepare them for when the time comes. Your excellency will decide what is most convenient. Mexico City, 15 December 1691.

Dr. don Benito de Noboa Salgado [rubrica]

Mexico City, 15 December 1691
As the fiscal proposes, the cited dispatch is inserted. [Galve's rubrica]
The dispatch is made and delivered in the office of your excellency's secretary.

---

*AGN, Historia 37:2. 46 folios, 90 written pages; and AGI, Guadalajara 139:4. First three folios are badly torn and lacunae have been supplied here from AGI, Guadalajara 139:4, fols. 1r–6v. Transcripts of various letters were published, some with omissions, in Otto Maas, *Misiones de Nuevo Méjico: Documentos del Archivo General de Indias (Sevilla) publicados por primera vez y anotados* (Madrid, 1929):122–33.

1. Vargas acceded to the governorship of New Mexico in El Paso on 22 February 1691. RBC, 151.

2. Maize, or Indian corn, became the principal foodstuff of Mexico, both of people and livestock, and spread from there to the rest of North and South America. Desired characteristics, such as drought resistance and size and type of kernel, were obtained

by selection. The variety that came to predominate in the Southwest was a flour-type maize that could be crushed and ground on a metate directly and did not require soaking in a lime solution to soften the hulls.

Vargas purchased and transported maize with him from north-central New Spain. In this passage, he is probably referring to white maize grown in the El Paso area. Wheat in New Spain was stricken by blight in the early 1690s, causing an increase in the demand for maize, higher prices, and a shortage in 1692. Enrique Florescano and Alejandra Moreno Toscano, *Bibliografía general del maíz en México* (Mexico City, 1987). Charles Gibson, *The Aztecs under Spanish Rule: A History of the Indians of the Valley of Mexico, 1519–1810* (Stanford, 1964):307, 308–23, 327, 554 n64. Antonio Manrique Chávez, *El maíz en el Perú* (Lima, 1987):34–47, 50–52.

3. Domingo Jironza Petrís de Cruzate y Góngora was born around 1650 in the Spanish province of Huesca. In Madrid in 1675, he executed the conveyance of a 3,000-peso credit to one Francisco Freire de Andrade, who from time to time had loaned him cash for various trips, illnesses, and other reasons. The conveyance of 3,000 pesos to Jironza two months earlier referred to him as licenciado, or licenciate, although when signing the second document he did not use the abbreviation Lic.

Jironza left Cadiz on 10 April 1680 aboard the warship *San José.* A captain commanding fifty soldiers, he had a dual appointment as inspector of the presidios of the Windward Islands and royal courier to the viceroy of New Spain, who had been instructed to give him a post as reward for Jironza's services.

Once in New Spain, Jironza received from the viceroy, don Payo de Rivera Enríquez, the only suitable available post, the alcaldía mayor of Mestitlán, near Mexico City. He served with distinction there until 1682.

Jironza twice served as governor of New Mexico, from 1683 to 1686 and again from 1689 to 1691. In 1684, he led an expedition against the Apaches. The following year, he was ordered to gather and return all the settlers who had fled New Mexico. Between 1686 and 1689, the inept administration of his successor, Pedro Reneros de Posada, apparently put the colony at great risk. One source indicates that had Jironza not been reinstated, New Mexico would have been lost.

Although Jironza's 1689 attempt to reconquer New Mexico was unsuccessful, he destroyed Zia Pueblo. During the battle, fifty of his eighty men were wounded, six hundred Indians killed, and seventy captives taken. Two years later, he began preparations for another expedition to New Mexico, but warfare with the Sumas in the south led to cancellation of the expedition. By 1691, Diego de Vargas had acceded to the governorship.

As a result of Jironza's services, described as receiving the applause of the kingdom, Carlos II granted Jironza membership in one of the military orders. He also instructed the viceroy, the Conde de Galve, to find a post other than the governorship of New Mexico for Jironza, if Vargas had already taken office. As a result, Jironza became in 1693 alcalde mayor of Sonora and captain of the flying company of Sonora, serving until 1698. In July of 1700, he was serving in San Juan Bautista. He was mentioned in Juan Fernández de la Fuente's journal as late as February 1701.

Jironza's steady advancement in his career may have been the result in part of family connections. Carlos de Sigüenza y Góngora, in a 1692 letter to Andrés de Pez, mentioned that Jironza was his uncle. He was, in all probability, married to the sister of Sigüenza's mother. He was also the uncle of Juan Mateo Manje. Francisco Eusebio Kino, *Kino's Historical Memoir of Pimería Alta* (Berkeley, 1948):192, 193 n29. Domingo Jironza Petrís de Cruzate, Report, San Juan Bautista, 15 July 1700, AHP 1700. Juan Fernández de la Fuente, Proceedings, Janos, 19 Feb. 1701, AHP 1701. Naylor and Polzer, *Presidio and Militia*, 1:512 n2, 574. Francisca María Osorio to Domingo Jironza, Conveyance, Madrid, 29 Aug. 1675, Archivo Histórico de Protocolos de Madrid, P. 11.319, and Jironza to Francisco Freire de Andrade, Conveyance, Madrid, 7 Nov. 1675, AHPM, P. 12.357. Juan Mateo Manje, Diary of an expedition, 7–23 Feb. 1694, in Ernest J. Burrus, *Kino and Manje, Explorers of Sonora and Arizona: Their Vision of the Future* (Rome and St. Louis, 1971):47 n4, 285–87, 278, 317, 321 n9, 353–56, 357–58, 469. Cabildo of Santa Fe, Certification of the Services of Domingo Jironza Petrís de Cruzate, El Paso, 25 Nov. 1690, AGN, Civil 1743. Carlos de Sigüenza y Góngora, *Alboroto y motín de México del 8 de junio de 1692: Relación de don Carlos de Sigüenza y Góngora en una carta dirigida al almirante don Andrés de Pez* (Mexico City, 1932):29.

4. The reference is to Jironza's 1689 attack on Zia.

5. The priest referred to is probably fray Francisco de Vargas and the battle, Jironza's attack on Zia in 1689.

6. Zacatecas was the principal Spanish settlement in New Galicia. A silver strike in 1548 attracted Spaniards in ever-increasing numbers to this isolated area, separated from other centers of Spanish habitation by desert and seminomadic Indians.

Zacatecas was the site of a Franciscan benefice, Nuestra Señora de los Zacatecos. The convento established there served as the center of the province of San Francisco de Zacatecas, which founded many missions to the north. In addition to the Franciscans, Dominicans ministered to Indian barrios, and the Augustinians had a convento with outlying doctrinal charges.

Although begun as an alcaldía, after 1580 Zacatecas was a corregimiento appointed directly from Spain. The discovery of the Veta Grande produced a bonanza that lasted from 1670 to 1690. From that time until the turn of the century, Zacatecas entered a period of decline, though the population continued to number in the tens of thousands.

Sombrerete lay 165 km northwest of Zacatecas, at 2,351 m in the Sierra de Sombrerete, a range of the Sierra de Zacatecas, in the kingdom of New Galicia. In 1570, the real of Sombrerete was granted the title of Villa de Llerena, after the mining center in the province of Badajoz, Spain. In 1646, rich silver ores were discovered in the area. An isolated pocket of Spanish settlement on the northern frontier, Sombrerete was frequently besieged by Zacateco-speaking Chichimecs.

The discovery of rich silver ore in the summer of 1631 led to the founding of San José del Parral in north-central New Biscay. Parral soon became the unofficial capital of the kingdom, and the governors, beginning with Gov. Luis Monsalve y Saavedra, usually chose to reside there instead of the official capital, Durango. After 1709, San Francisco de Cuéllar,

later renamed San Felipe el Real de Chihuahua, became the residence of the governors. San José del Parral was a benefice and site of a Franciscan hermitage. In the 1690s, discoveries of ores at Urique and Gaunaceví attracted miners and left Parral largely deserted. Peter Gerhard, *The North Frontier of New Spain* (Princeton, 1982):6–8, 43, 46–50, 130–32, 217–18. For an excellent discussion of the mining centers of the northern frontier of New Spain, see P.J. Bakewell, *Silver Mining and Society in Colonial Mexico: Zacatecas, 1546–1700* (Cambridge, 1971). See also Robert C. West, *The Mining Community in Northern New Spain: The Parral Mining District* (Berkeley, 1949) and Oakah L. Jones, *Nueva Vizcaya: Heartland of the Spanish Frontier* (Albuquerque, 1988).

7. Pedro Velázquez de la Cadena was the Conde de Galve's secretary. Velázquez de la Cadena was married to Elena Centeno. He died on 6 February 1697. Robles, *Diario*, 3:58, 73. The Conde de Galve, Mexico City, 22 Sept. 1692, AGN, Reales Cédulas, 24. Rubio Mañé, *Virreinato*, 4:132.

8. Dr. Benito de Noboa Salgado was named judge of the Audiencia of the Philippines in 1660, but declined the post. From 1662 to 1685, he was a judge of the Audiencia of Guatemala. In 1685–86, he was a criminal fiscal for the Audiencia of Mexico and from 1686 to 1692, a civil fiscal.

Noboa died on 1 November 1692. Robles, *Diario*, 2:275. Ernesto Schäfer, *El Consejo Real y Supremo de las Indias: Su historia, organización y labor administrativa hasta la terminación de la Casa de Austria: La labor del Consejo de Indias en la administración colonial* (Seville, 1947), 2:464, 466, 476, 521.

9. Pedro Reneros de Posada, born around 1651 in Ozeño in the mountains of Oviedo, was described in 1681 as of good physique with ruddy face and wavy, chestnut hair and beard. He succeeded Jironza as governor in 1686 under unexplained circumstances and held the post until 1689. Although extant records of Reneros's tenure are spotty, some proceedings survived. They deal with his prohibition on dueling, keeping cattle out of the fields, and his order for soldiers to refrain from selling their arms and horses.

He made an expedition to Santa Ana Pueblo in 1688 that very much resembled a slave raid and resulted in the destruction of the pueblo. He apparently attacked Zia Pueblo on that same expedition, but was forced to retreat, taking only human booty or sheep and horses, as Vélez de Escalante would have it.

Alleging in 1688 that Reneros had not paid them, presidial soldiers began a lengthy legal action that continued through the term of Gov. Domingo Jironza, Reneros's 1689 successor. This may actually have been a jurisdictional dispute between Reneros and Jironza. Fifty Soldiers of New Mexico vs. Pedro Reneros de Posada, El Paso and Mexico City, 20 Mar. 1689–16 Oct. 1690, AGN, Provincias Internas 35:5. Vélez de Escalante, Extracto. Jack D. Forbes, *Apache, Navaho, and Spaniard* (Norman, 1960):207–209. Hubert Howe Bancroft, *History of Arizona and New Mexico, 1530–1888* (1889; rpt., Albuquerque, 1962):194. Hackett and Shelby, *Revolt*, 2:32, 63, 134.

10. Sebastián de Guzmán y Córdoba, inspector, purveyor, and judge of the treasury, entered royal service in 1675. He arrived in New Spain in the flota of September 1675 with an appointment as comptroller of the Mexico City Treasury office. Shortly after, in 1677, he was described by the criminal judge and royal inspector, Juan Sáenz Moreno, as somewhat dim, but very zealous in the royal service. By 1690, he had completed one of several unpublished treatises, El régimen político de cajas reales, based on his experiences in the fiscal arm of government.

Before coming to New Spain, Guzmán had studied in Spain in the 1660s under the well-known Spanish mathematician, Francisco de Ruesta. Once in the New World, he followed his interests in hydrography and navigation, pursuits that eventually led to a close friendship with Carlos de Sigüenza y Góngora, the most prominent intellectual of his time in New Spain. Guzmán had access to at least four of Sigüenza's unpublished manuscripts, all of which were subsequently lost. For nine years, he personally retained the manuscript for Sigüenza's *Libra astronómica y filosófica* and was responsible for its publication in 1690. Guzmán died on 20 August 1697. Robles, *Diario*, 2:182, 183; 3:61. Carlos de Sigüenza y Góngora, *Libra astronómica y filosófica* (Mexico City, 1959):v, vii, 3, 13, 14, 15, 16, 17. Ismael Sánchez Bella, "El Tribunal de Cuentas de México, siglo xvii," in *Memoria del Cuarto Congreso Venezolano de Historia del 27 de octubre al 1° de noviembre de 1980* (Caracas, 1983), 3:120.

11. Initially a vast province, incorporating, from the midsixteenth century on, what later became New León, Coahuila, New Mexico, Sonora, and Sinaloa, New Biscay was a gobierno whose administrative head, the governor and captain general, was directly accountable to the viceroy in Mexico City for financial and military matters. The governor in turn supervised his subordinates, the justicias mayores, who handled administrative, judicial, treasury, and law-enforcement duties in all major Spanish settlements. Porras Muñoz, *Frontera*, 14–17, 40–44, 54. CRG, 5–6, 32 n24, 35–56, 118–19, 129. Gerhard, *North Frontier*, 164–67. See also Jones, *Nueva Vizcaya*.

12. Established in late 1685 approximately 68 km northeast of Parral, the presidio of Conchos was part of the renewed Spanish response to Indian activity sparked in part by the 1680 Pueblo uprising in New Mexico. From 1687 on, the presidial commander acted as the governor's deputy, or justicia mayor, of this frontier territory, which extended at times as far north as the Rio Grande and west to Tarahumara country.

The presidio of San Felipe y Santiago de Janos, established at Casas Grandes about 1685, was moved to Janos in the northwest corner of New Biscay around 1691. There, it defended the camino real, which passed through its jurisdiction to El Paso and into New Mexico. From 1684 to 1698, it also served as a staging area for campaigns against Indians raiding in New Biscay and Sonora. Juan Fernández de la Fuente served as captain at Janos and led campaigns against enemy Indians in the 1680s and 1690s. This presidio played a major role in military strategy designed to control the Janos, Sumas, and kindred tribes in the late seventeenth and early eighteenth centuries. Edward H. Spicer, *Cycles of Conquest: The Impact of Spain, Mexico, and the United States on the Indians of the Southwest, 1533–1960* (Tucson, 1962):98, 232–33, 236. Porras Muñoz, *Frontera*, 54, 179, 184–85, 241, 243, 244, 285, 291, 309, 328, 345. William B. Griffen, *Indian Assimilation in the Franciscan Area of Nueva Vizcaya* (Tucson, 1979):62, 90. Gerhard, *North Frontier*, 184–85, 230, 242.

Luis Navarro García, *Sonora y Sinaloa en el siglo xvii* (Seville, 1967):43–44, 277–80, 310, 311, 314–15, 316–17. Forbes, *Apache*, 206, 208, 226–27, 248, 278. Max L. Moorhead, *The Presidio: Bastion of the Spanish Borderlands* (Norman, 1975):21–23, 49–50, 64–65, 73, 79. Herbert Eugene Bolton, *Rim of Christendom: A Biography of Eusebio Francisco Kino, Pacific Coast Pioneer* (Tucson, 1984):245, 288, 290, 317–18, 382.

13. As a common mode of discourse, Vargas often refers to himself in the third person. Switching from first to third person as he does here often makes it difficult to follow the narrative. To make matters worse, Vargas, when writing in the third person, frequently substitutes "there" for "here" in relating his location.

14. Spanish exploration of Sonora began in the mid-1530s, but it was not until the early seventeenth century that permanent settlement took place. The Jesuits began their missionary work in the Cumuripa-Tecoripa area and by the 1640s, labored among the Pimas Bajos and southern Opata. Miners, eager to exploit Sonora's silver, followed.

Civilian control of the area was concurrent with the spread of Christianity. In 1641, Pedro de Perea, as justicia mayor y capitán a guerra, assumed jurisdiction of all the territory north of the Yaqui River, an area that came to be known as Sonora, or New Andalusia.

Sinaloa, bounded on the west by the Gulf of California, originally went north into what became in the seventeenth century the provinces of Ostimuri and Sonora. Its eastern boundary was New Biscay, while south lay Culiacán. Initially, the governor of New Biscay appointed its alcalde mayor, who, in the late sixteenth century, further acquired the title of teniente de gobernador and capitán general. At the time of the organization of Sonora in 1640, the viceroy designated the captain of the Sinaloa presidio as alcalde mayor, thus opening the way to jurisdictional disputes with the governor of New Biscay. Gerhard, *North Frontier*, 256, 272, 275, 279–84. Navarro García, *Sonora y Sinaloa*, 67–70.

15. Juan María de Salvatierra was born in Milan in 1648, son of a father of Spanish descent and an Italian mother, and entered the Society of Jesus in the province of Milan in 1668. After arriving in New Spain in 1675, he completed his studies in Mexico City. By 1680, he was active in Chínapa, founding two missions, and the area of the villa of Sinaloa. Professing in 1684, he continued his evangelizing and by 1690, had established two additional missions in the Chínapa area, one, San Francisco Javier de Serocahui, serving as a base for his explorations throughout the area. That same year, he was appointed visitor of the missions of Pimería Alta. Upon arriving at the Dolores

mission there in December 1690, he met Father Eusebio Francisco Kino, thus beginning a lifelong friendship and collaboration that included extensive exploration of Baja California. He returned reluctantly from the frontier in 1693 to become rector of the Jesuit colegio of Guadalajara and in 1696, went on to serve as rector and master of novices at Tepotzotlán. Throughout this period, he worked actively to raise support and money for the exploration and missionization of Baja California. In 1697, he won viceregal permission to undertake the enterprise of California, a task that occupied him almost without interruption until his death in 1717. Ernest J. Burrus, trans. and annot., *Juan María de Salvatierra: Selected Letters about Lower California* (Los Angeles, 1971):25–33, 41–52, 68. Bolton, *Rim*, 263–65. Francisco Javier Alegre, *Historia de la Provincia de la Compañía de Jesús de Nueva España* (Rome, 1960), 4:35–36, 97–99, 250 n16.

16. Marcos de Loyola was born in Toledo and came to New Spain in 1678. In 1693, Loyola began serving at Mátape, 120 km south of Arizpe, and was still there in 1701. CRG, 36–37. Gerhard, *North Frontier*, 280.

17. San José de Chínapa, a mission to the Opata, was one of three missions under the charge of fray Juan Suárez in the 1640s during a short-lived Franciscan penetration from New Mexico. It

was located northeast of Arizpe on the Sonora River. In the early 1650s, the Jesuits assumed control. In 1685, Chínapa served briefly as permanent mission, or cabecera, with Bacoachi as its charge, or visita. Francisco Javier de Mora supervised Arizpe and its two visitas, Bacoachi and Chínapa, for twenty-six years beginning in the late 1680s. Spicer, *Cycles*, 90, 97. Bolton, *Rim*, 593. Navarro García, *Sonora y Sinaloa*, 52, 268–74, 284–85, 313.

18. An indefatigable campaigner, Juan Fernández de la Fuente, born around 1650, served initially with the provincial militia from New Mexico at Casas Grandes from 1681 to 1684. In 1682, Fernández was described as captain and merchant resident in the real of Nacosari. During this time of unrest in New Biscay and Sonora, Fernández participated in repeated campaigns against the Janos, Sumas, and other Indians who had allied to attack the Spaniards in El Paso and in the northern settlements of New Biscay. After the jurisdictions of Casas Grandes and Janos were permanently divided in 1691, Fernández was referred to as general. He was thus an officer of equal military rank when he finally secured Vargas's temporary support in Sonora. At the time of his death in Mexico City on 2 December 1713, he was described as a bachelor who left no heirs. LDS, Asunción Sagrario, Mexico City, Deaths, 1693–1714, 35750. Navarro García, *Sonora y*

Sinaloa, 277, 285–86, 309–11, 314. Porras Muñoz, *Frontera*, 179, 182–85, 308–10, 324–45. Juan Fernández de la Fuente, Declaration, San Juan Bautista, 7 Nov. 1682, AHP 1682C. NMF, 30–31.

19. The Janos and Jocomes, small bands of wandering hunters and gatherers, lived in the extreme southwest corner of what is now New Mexico and in northern Chihuahua. Janos and Jocomes evidently spoke the same language, which may have been Athapaskan. After 1700, they appear to have merged. Occasionally, they warred against the Spaniards, but by 1706, had made peace. Thomas Hinton, "Southern Periphery: West," in *Handbook*, 10:324. Griffen, "Southern Periphery: East," in *Handbook*, 10:330. Jack D. Forbes, "Unknown Athapaskans: The Identification of the Jano, Jocome, Jumano, Manso, Suma and Other Indian Tribes of the Southwest," *Ethnohistory* 6 (Spr. 1959):97–144.

20. Nomadic hunter-gatherers, the Sumas lived in present-day northern Chihuahua, as far north as El Paso and as far south as La Junta de los Ríos. They apparently harassed the Franciscans at Teuricachi in the 1640s, though they later made peace with them, living at the mission at Casas Grandes. In 1684, however, they, along with the Conchos and others, revolted and sacked Casas Grandes, which led to harsh Spanish reprisals and the establishment of the presidio at Janos. Griffen, "Southern Periphery: East," in *Handbook*, 10:329. Spicer, *Cycles*, 321–23.

21. The mission of Nuestra Señora de Guadalupe de Teuricachi, established in 1645, was located approximately 50 km northwest of Arizpe. It was founded by fray Juan de San José to minister to the Opata. After the departure of the Franciscans, the Jesuits took over in 1653. With the addition of Cuchuta, the mission was then reestablished, with Cuquiárachi and Teras as visitas. In the 1680s, the Opata revolt, and subsequent attacks by Janos, Jocomes, Sumas, and Apaches, resulted in the posting of soldiers near the mission. Campaigns, including the joint 1691 Fernández de la Fuente-Vargas offensive, were mounted in the area around Teuricachi. Bolton, *Rim*, 247. Navarro García, *Sonora y Sinaloa*, 69–70, 252, 266, 277, 282, 309, 314, 319. Spicer, *Cycles*, 98, 232.

22. The Mansos were Apaches who lived in the El Paso region. The term Mansos, meaning tame, was first applied by Juan de Oñate in 1598. Beginning in the mid-1650s, some of these Indians were persuaded to live in missions, where they were catechized and taught the rudiments of European agriculture and livestock raising. The Mansos reportedly held sway over the Janos and Jocomes.

Captain Chiquito was the leader of the Mansos who, in 1667, left the area near El Paso to live apart from the Spaniards. Although they had not rebelled by 1682, they were responsible for raids and thefts of cattle and horses. The increased population of El Paso, the result of refugees fleeing New Mexico in 1680, and Piro and Tiwa conflict with local Indian residents, helped prevent a Manso uprising. Some of Chiquito's Mansos may have been involved in the Suma and Jano uprising at the mission of Nuestra Señora de la Soledad, near El Paso, in 1684. In July of the same year, Governor Jironza campaigned against the Mansos and burned Captain Chiquito's rancherias, though the Manso leader remained free and continued to harass the Spaniards. Forbes, *Apache*, 152–229. Griffen, "Southern Periphery: East," in *Handbook*, 10:339–40. Morris E. Opler, "The Apachean Culture Pattern and Its Origins," in *Handbook*, 10:388. CRG, 36 n37.

23. Translated here as catechist, the word temastián, meaning teacher, catechist, or preacher, derived from the Nahuatl temachtiani. The term was recorded by fray Alonso de Molina in his *Vocabulario en lengua castellana y mexicana y mexicana y castellana* (1555–57; rpt., Mexico City, 1977). Rémi Siméon, in his *Diccionario de la lengua nahuatl o mexicana, redactado según los documentos impresos y manuscritos más auténticos y precedido de una introducción* (Mexico City, 1981), says that the "ch" sound was

equivalent to the Portuguese "x," a palatal sibilant. The temastián was taught the necessary Spanish words and assisted the missionary with translation and instruction. Spicer, *Cycles*, 289–90.

24. After nearly ten years of missionary work in western New Biscay, Salvatierra was appointed visitor of the Jesuit missions in Sonora and Sinaloa in 1689. The beginning of his visitation coincided with a quickly suppressed revolt among the Pimas and Tarahumaras and ended in 1693. Miguel Venegas, *Juan María de Salvatierra of the Company of Jesus: Missionary in the Province of New Spain, and Apostolic Conqueror of the Californias*, ed. and trans. Marguerite Eyer Wilbur (Cleveland, 1929):121–37. Gerhard, *North Frontier*, 175. See also Bolton, *Rim*.

25. The Seris, nomadic gatherers thought to be related to Californian Indian groups, lived by the Gulf of California in the seventeenth and eighteenth centuries from near present-day Guaymas along a 300-km stretch to the north and ranged 100–150 km inland. Some Seris adjusted to the coming of the Spaniards by moving from the coast, raiding and stealing, taking advantage of a new resource in a harsh environment. Thomas Bowen, "Seri," in *Handbook*, 10:232–33. Hinton, "Southern Periphery: West," in *Handbook*, 10:324.

26. The Jesuit Adam Gilg,

missionary to the Seris, mentioned the "Cocomocaketz," probably the Cocomotaques (metathesis of t and k), as perpetrators of an attack on the Tepocas, a Seri band, whom he had persuaded to settle at San Eustaquio. Spicer, *Cycles*, 106.

27. The related Sobas and Upper Pimas were rancheria peoples who lived south of the Gila River in present-day Arizona and Sonora. Reduced to missions, employed as mine workers and on ranches, and struck by epidemics such as smallpox, their population declined steadily during the Spanish period. Bernard L. Fontana, "Pimas and Papagos: An Introduction," in *Handbook*, 10:125. Paul H. Ezell, "History of the Pima," in *Handbook*, 10:149, 150.

28. Capt. Juan de Valencia and his family fled Santa Fe in 1680. Their names appear on the El Paso muster roll of 1684. In 1692, Valencia, while deputy alcalde of Senecú, Ysleta, and Socorro del Sur, received Vargas's orders to assemble troops for his entry into New Mexico. In September of that year, Vargas stopped at Valencia's abandoned estancia near the present-day town of the same name. NMF, 109. J. Manuel Espinosa, *First Expedition of Vargas into New Mexico*, 1692 (Albuquerque, 1940):51, 67. See below, AGN, 37:6.

29. Pedro Ortiz Niño Ladrón de Guevara came to New Spain in 1682 and served as secretary of government and war to Gov.

Domingo Jironza. He married María Gómez Losada on 16 July 1684. He figured as a captain in a list of the fifty-man presidial company at El Paso signed by Governor Jironza on 18 April 1686. In 1692, he served as notary for the friars. His brother, Nicolás Ladrón de Guevara, accompanied Governor Vargas on the 1692 expedition. Fidelia Miller Puckett, "Ramón Ortiz: Priest and Patriot," NMHR 25 (Oct. 1950):267. Domingo Jironza, Muster, 18 Apr. 1686, El Paso, BYU, Spanish New Mexico Collection.

30. Fray Francisco de Vargas came to New Mexico from the Holy Gospel Province, into which he had been incorporated in 1665. In 1680, while assigned to the mission at El Paso, fray Francisco de Vargas was sent north with the relief party for the settlers fleeing the Pueblo Revolt. In February 1682 and January 1683, he was residing in El Paso. From August to November of 1683, he was at the mission of San Lorenzo. In 1685, Vargas was guardian at Guadalupe del Paso and three years later, was elected custos, a post he held from June 1688 to July 1691. From February to September 1693, he was president and guardian at El Paso. He served as vice-custos in El Paso and Santa Fe in 1694, then became custos again when he succeeded fray Salvador Rodríguez de San Antonio, holding that post from January 1695 to February 1697. Eleanor B. Adams and Fray

Angélico Chávez, eds. and trans.,
The Missions of New Mexico,
1776: A Description by Fray
Francisco Atanasio Domínguez,
with Other Contemporary
Documents (Albuquerque, 1975):49,
338. Bancroft, *Arizona and New*
Mexico, 192, 213, 220–21. Fray
Angélico Chávez, *Archives of the*
Archdiocese of Santa Fe, 1678–1900
(Washington D.C.):14, 16. J.
Manuel Espinosa, ed. and trans.,
The Pueblo Indian Revolt of 1696
and the Franciscan Missions of
New Mexico: Letters of the
Missionaries and Related Documents
(Norman, 1988):53–55, 57–58.
Libro de entradas y profesiones de
novicios de este convento del Padre
San Francisco de México,
1562–1680, The Bancroft Library,
Mexican Manuscripts 218.
Francisco Antonio de la Rosa
Figueroa, Becerro general
menológico y cronológico de todos
los religiosos que de las tres
parcialidades conviene, a saber
Padres de España, Hijos de
provincia y Criollos, ha habido en
esta Santa Provincia del Santo
Evangelio desde su fundación
hasta el presente año de 1764,
Newberry Library, Chicago, Ayer
Collection.

31. Here rendered as rabble-
rousing, the word tlatole is derived
from Nahuatl: tlatole, or speaker;
and tlatolli, or word, discourse,
exhortation, history, narration, or
message. Siméon, *Diccionario*,
677, 678. Molina, *Vocabulario*,
141.

32. Ojito may refer to Ojito de
Samalayuca, possibly the site of
the mission of Santa Gertrudis
near El Paso. Santa Gertrudis was
destroyed in 1684. Hughes,
Settlement, 368.

33. Candelaria was located
south of Samalayuca.

34. The name Gila usually
refers to the Gila River rising in
the mountains of southwestern
New Mexico. Here, the name is
used to designate the mountainous
area near the river, which includes
the Mogollon, Burro, Pinos Altos,
and Black ranges. Jerry L.
Williams and Paul E. McAllister,
eds., *New Mexico in Maps*
(Albuquerque, 1979):16. Opler,
"Apachean Culture," in *Handbook*,
10:388–89.

35. The Sobaipuris were Upper
Pimans, who spoke a Piman
language of the Uto-Aztecan
family. Before the arrival of the
Spaniards, they lived along the
upper San Pedro and Santa Cruz
rivers, just beyond the eastern
limits of the Sonora desert in what
is now southeastern Arizona.

First regular contact with the
Spaniards occurred in the 1680s,
when Father Kino and
accompanying Spaniards visited
the area. Over the next
seventy-odd years, the presence of
the missions attracted Apache
raids. The Sobaipuris allied with
the Spaniards, but were driven
west, where they joined the
Papagos of south-central Arizona
and eventually disappeared as a
separate entity. Ezell, "History of
the Pima," in *Handbook*, 10:149.

Fontana, "Pimas and Papagos," in *Handbook*, 10:125, 126, 131, 133; and "History of the Papago," in *Handbook*, 10:137. Spicer, *Cycles*, 119, 126–27.

36. San Miguel de Bacuachito, or Bácoachi, located about 55 km north and slightly east of Arizpe in Sonora, was at this time a visita of Chínapa. Paul M. Roca, *Paths of the Padres Through Sonora: An Illustrated History and Guide to Its Spanish Churches* (Tucson, 1967):150–51.

37. Born in 1654 in Naples, Horacio Polici entered the Jesuit order at the age of seventeen, professing his final vows on 2 February 1689. He arrived in Mexico City in February 1684. His first posting was to Los Santos Mártires del Japón under Father Antonio Leal in Sonora. In 1687, he was assigned to the mission of Bacerac, south of Bavispe in Opata country. He was named visitor for the missions of the area in 1696. During his lengthy tenure at Bacerac, he had a great deal of contact with Kino and dealt with Jironza and Fernández de la Fuente during their campaigns in the 1690s. He died in Bacerac in 1713. Bolton, *Rim*, 244, 332, 334–35, 339–42, 344–45, 357–58, 393, 532–33, 580, 593. Ernest J. Burrus, ed. and trans., *Kino Reports to Headquarters: Correspondence from New Spain with Rome* (Rome, 1954):100 n3, 117 n23. Naylor and Polzer, *Presidio and Militia*, 1:588. Francesco Maria Piccolo, *Informe*

del estado de la nueva cristiandad de California 1702 y otros documentos (Madrid, 1962):329 n3. Ernest J. Burrus, "Francesco Maria Piccolo (1654–1729), Pioneer of Lower California, in the Light of Roman Archives," *Hispanic American Historical Review* (hereinafter HAHR) 35 (Feb. 1955):65–67.

38. The settlement identified here as Aguache is likely Aguaje, near Teuricachi in Sonora, which was ministered to by the Jesuits. Alegre, *Historia*, 517–18. Gerhard, *North Frontier*, 283.

39. La Junta de los Ríos, present-day Presidio, Texas, at the confluence of the Río de los Conchos and the Rio Grande, is approximately 275 km southeast of El Paso. In the early seventeenth century, some missionary work was unsuccessfully attempted nearby. It was not until the early 1680s, however, that the Franciscans made a concerted effort to Christianize the area. During the Manso revolt of 1684 at El Paso, unrest spread to the Julimes living at La Junta de los Ríos. Christian Indians of the area helped the missionaries escape to Parral. By the end of Jironza's term in 1691, seven missions had been established in and around La Junta de los Ríos. Hughes, *Settlement*, 330–33, 357–58. Vito Alessio Robles, *Coahuila y Texas en la época colonial* (Mexico City, 1978):324.

40. José de Padilla Villaseñor, a native of Querétaro, born about 1647, came to New Mexico before

1668. He had served as an alcalde mayor for twelve years when he passed muster before Governor Otermín in El Paso in October 1681. Padilla participated in Otermín's attempted reconquest.

He made various trips to Mexico City. In 1683, he carried a petition on behalf of some of the settlers to the viceroy and the following year was dispatched from El Paso by the cabildo to report on conditions in New Mexico. Lorenzo Madrid and Sebastián González, members of the cabildo, brought suit against him for not reporting about this, whereupon Padilla sought asylum at the convento of Nuestra Señora de Guadalupe. At this time, he was described as former regidor de primer voto, alguacil mayor, and pendolero. In 1689, Padilla escorted some religious to Mexico City, where he also petitioned for payment of unpaid salaries.

Padilla was alcalde mayor and capitán a guerra of Senecú in 1692. According to a census in late December of that year, he and his wife, María López, had eight children: Felipe, nineteen; Juan Antonio, sixteen; Antonio, fourteen; Diego, twelve; José, nine; Cayetano, seven; Joaquín, three; and Luis, an infant. In addition, two orphans were living with the family: José, fourteen; and Juan de Dios, nine. Apparently, he remained in the El Paso area until his death sometime before August 1713. Fray Angélico Chávez, *New Mexico Roots Ltd.: A Demographic Perspective from genealogical,* *historical and geographic data found in the Diligencias Matrimoniales or Pre-Nuptial Investigation (1678–1869) of the Archives of the Archdiocese of Santa Fe; Multiple data extracted, and here edited in a uniform presentation by years and family surnames* (Santa Fe, 1982) (hereinafter NMR), 8:1439–40. NMF, 84. CRG, 51. Hackett and Shelby, *Revolt,* 1:cxxiii, clxxxvii; 2:132. Ralph Emerson Twitchell, comp. *The Spanish Archives of New Mexico: Compiled and Chronologically Arranged with Historical, Genealogical, Geographical, and Other Annotations, by Authority of the State of New Mexico* (Cedar Rapids, 1914), 2:74. Elizabeth Howard West, "The Right of Asylum in New Mexico in the Seventeenth and Eighteenth Centuries," NMHR 41 (Apr. 1966):121. J. Manuel Espinosa, trans., "Population of the El Paso District in 1692," *Mid-America* 23 (Jan. 1941):78–79.

41. Vargas was in error; fray Antonio Guerra was secretary, not custos, in April 1691. Fray Francisco de Vargas was custos at the time. While serving at El Paso in 1683, the Indians of the nearby mission of Socorro attempted to murder Guerra. He later accompanied Jironza on a mission to negotiate peace with the Mansos, at which time they tried to kill them. Later, during Vargas's administration, Guerra persuaded the Sumas to settle in the pueblo of San Diego de los Sumas, about

30 km south of El Paso. In 1701, he was elected custos. Chávez, *Archives*, 10, 14. Hughes, *Settlement*, 329, 349. Walz, "El Paso," 288. Forbes, *Apache*, 232.

42. Gov. Antonio de Otermín, who served from 1677 to 1683, and Gov. Domingo Jironza, who held the office twice, from 1683 to 1686 and from 1689 to 1691, used the term deserters to refer to those residents of El Paso who were absent without permission, a number of whom were living in New Biscay and Sonora. Otermín attempted to stop the flow of residents leaving El Paso by issuing an order on 5 April 1682 forbidding unauthorized departure on pain of death. Hughes, *Settlement*, 364–69. Walz, "El Paso," 84–85.

43. Juan de Aréchaga y Casas held a chair at the University of Salamanca before he came to New Spain. From 18 June 1671 to 13 November 1680, he held the post of criminal judge in the Audiencia of Mexico and from the latter date to 26 August 1694, that of judge. He served as the judge for the residencia of the Conde de Paredes, who was viceroy from 1680 to 1686. Aréchaga died 31 August 1694. Robles, *Diario*, 2:309–10. Hanke and Rodríguez, *Virreyes españoles*, 5:92 n6. Schäfer, *Consejo Real*, 2:457, 462.

44. Before coming to New Spain, Francisco Fernández de Marmolejo was a colegial, student or professor, at Salamanca. From 21 February 1673 to 23 July 1681,

he served as criminal fiscal of the Audiencia of Mexico. While holding this position, he received from the Council of the Indies the important commission to investigate the financial aspects of the viceregal administration of the Marqués de Mancera (1664–73) after his residencia. This resulted in nineteen charges, from which the former viceroy was completely absolved in 1681. On 23 July 1681, Fernández was promoted to judge of the audiencia, a post he filled until his death. In 1690, Fernández was also a member of his majesty's council and auditor general for war. He married Francisca de Sosa on 12 November 1676. Fernández died on 2 April 1693. Robles, *Diario*, 2:204, 286. Hanke and Rodríguez, *Virreyes españoles*, 5:10, 71, 88. Schäfer, *Consejo Real*, 2:458, 466.

45. Capt. Andrés Pardo de Lago, a native of Mexico City, was born in its cathedral parish on 13 February 1662. He inherited his position as comptroller in the Tribunal of Accounts of New Spain from his father, Capt. Gerónimo Pardo de Lago, who had originally purchased it for 13,000 pesos. He paid an additional 2,000 doblones in 1679, with the proviso that the office pass to his eldest son or to whoever might marry one of his daughters. On 13 January 1683, Andrés married in Pánuco María Magdalena de Medrano, a native of that city. They had at least one son, Gerónimo, born in Mexico City on 2 October 1692,

who entered the Order of Calatrava in 1718. Pardo de Lago died in Mexico City on 20 June 1700. Guillermo Lohmann Villena, *Los americanos en las órdenes nobiliarias, 1529–1900* (Madrid, 1947), 2:96. Sánchez Bella, "Tribunal de Cuentas," 3:82.

46. Juan José de Veitia Linaje was the son of a prominent peninsular official. His father, José de Veitia, after thirty-nine years of service in the Casa de Contratación and as the secretary for New Spain in the Council of the Indies, became secretary of the Despacho Universal in 1682, retiring because of poor health in 1685.

In the 1690s, Juan José, a member of the Order of Santiago, was comptroller of the Tribunal of Accounts in Mexico City. In a royal cedula of 29 June 1695, Carlos II chose him to be governor of Yucatán, a post he never filled. In 1697, he went to Puebla as superintendent and administrator of alcabalas and was appointed alcalde mayor in 1699. In 1702, he was still a member of the tribunal's mesa mayor, the body responsible for its day-to-day administration, and involved in the financial administration of the city. In the 1720s, he served as administrator and judge for the mercury monopoly. Mark A. Burkholder and D.S. Chandler, *Biographical Dictionary of Audiencia Ministers in the Americas, 1687–1821* (Westport, Conn., 1982):119. Sánchez Bella,

"Tribunal de Cuentas," 3:89. Juan José de Veita Linaje to Francisco de Oyanguren, Power of attorney, Mexico City, 1 June 1697, AGNot. 122. Schäfer, *Consejo Real*, 2:564. Rubio Mañé, *Virreinato*, 3:195 n165. Luis Navarro García, "El Real Tribunal de Cuentas de México a principios del siglo xviii," *Anuario de Estudios Americanos* 34 (1977):519. José Antonio Escudero, *Los secretarios de estado y del despacho, 1474–1724* (Madrid, 1976), 1:271–72; 3:661–62.

47. Antonio de Deza y Ulloa, knight of the Order of Santiago, the son of Fernando de Deza y Ulloa, was born in Huejotzingo and baptized on 29 August 1658. By 1680, he was serving as factor in the Mexico City Treasury office. During the tenure of the interim viceroy, Payo de Rivera Enríquez (1673–80), he also received an unspecified post in Saclatlán. In 1681, he became an infantry captain. Later, like his father, he was an alcalde mayor and administrative judge of royal tribute and mercury. He was a comptroller in Mexico City in 1691. On 22 July 1695, he was promised the post of governor of New Biscay, but did not fill this position until 1708–12. Schäfer, *Consejo Real*, 2:545. Lohmann Villena, *Americanos*, 1:132. Hanke and Rodríguez, *Virreyes españoles*, 5:88. Robles, *Diario*, 2:146.

48. Fernando de Deza y Ulloa was born in Peñaranda de Bracamonte (Salamanca) and

baptized on 13 January 1634. He went to New Spain as a page of the viceroy, the Duque de Alburquerque (1653–60). During the government of the Marqués de Mancera (1664–73), he received an interim appointment as treasurer of the Mexico City Treasury office and was assigned a salary of 2,876 pesos. When this came to light in the subsequent investigation of Mancera's handling of the viceroyalty's finances in 1676, the Council of the Indies ruled in 1681 that half the salary had to be repaid, since Deza was the interim, rather than the proprietary, holder. Deza was unable to make restitution himself, so it fell to Mancera to reimburse the treasury. Deza later became corregidor of Huejotzingo, and later of Zacatecas, and the administrative judge of róyal tribute and mercury. Lohmann Villena, *Americanos*, 1:133. Hanke and Rodríguez, *Virreyes españoles*, 5:77–78.

49. Juan Isidro de Pardiñas y Villar de Francos Camaño, knight of the Order of Santiago, a native of the city of Cadiz (Cadiz), was the son of Capt. Mauro de Pardiñas Villar de Francos y Camaño and Nicolasa María Fernández Franco. Pardiñas bought the office of governor of New Biscay for 35,000 pesos in 1684. While waiting for the incumbent governor, Gen. José Neira y Quiroga, to finish his term, Pardiñas served as alcalde mayor of Puebla. In 1687,

Pardiñas acceded to the governorship of New Biscay. Indian rebellion; disagreement with the viceroy, the Conde de Galve, over treatment of Indians; and lack of funds for defense plagued his term of office. On 28 October 1692, Pardiñas married Andrea Josefa Antonia Fernández de Córdoba Bocanegra de la Higuera Reynoso y Amarilla in Puebla.

On 23 June 1695, Pardiñas gave his wife power of attorney and power to make a will. Although he may have departed New Biscay in August 1695, by March of the following year he was again in Parral. Padriñas was buried in Puebla on 20 April 1707. LDS, Puebla, Sagrario Metropolitano, Deaths, 228701. Juan Isidro de Pardiñas to Juan Salaíces, Power of attorney, Parral, 7 Mar. 1696. Andrea Fernández de Córdoba to Baltazar de Castro, Power of attorney, Parral, 13 Aug. 1695, AHP, 1695. Juan Isidro de Pardiñas to Andrea Fernández de Córdoba, Power of attorney, Parral, 23 June 1695, AHP, 1695. Juan Isidro de Pardiñas to Andrea Fernández de Córdoba, Power to make a will, Parral, 23 June 1695, AHP, 1695. LDS, Parral, Marriages, 162555. Alonso de Herrera Barragán, Guarantee, Parral, 31 July 1693, AHP, 1693A. Forbes, *Apache*, 209–11, 215, 219, 223, 229, 233. Naylor and Polzer, *Presidio and Militia*, 1:574, 578.

50. Tomás Antonio de la Cerda y Aragón (1638–92), the Conde de Paredes de Nava, Marqués de la Laguna de Camero Viejo, served

two terms, from 1680 to 1686, as the twenty-eighth viceroy of New Spain. Jironza's establishment of a presidio near El Paso is discussed in Walz, "El Paso," 107–19. Rubio Mañé, *Virreinato*, 4:432. RBC, 39, 111 n79.

51. The mission of San Francisco de los Mansos was founded by fray Francisco de Vargas about 1690 and described as being approximately 25 km from the presidio of El Paso. Fray Joaquín de Hinojosa to fray Salvador de San Antonio, Senecú, 23 April 1693, AASF, Loose Documents, Mission, 1693.

52. Vargas routinely stood as godfather to children of Indian leaders, thus putting into place the compadrazgo, the special, reciprocal relation existing among parent, godparent, and godchild in Catholic, Spanish society. At the same time, he was performing a social function familiar to Indian peoples of New Mexico within their own cultural context. Rick Hendricks, "Levels of Discourse in Early Modern Spanish: The Papers of Diego de Vargas, 1643–1704," *North Dakota Quarterly* 58 (Fall 1990):124–39. Kessell, "Spaniards and Pueblos," 1:133. For a similar discussion of the compadrazgo in Latin America, see Paul Charney, "The Implications of Godparental Ties Between Indians and Spaniards in Colonial Lima," *The Americas* 47 (Jan. 1991):295–314.

53. The Sierra de Santa Rosa de la Florida, or the Florida Mountains, is located in present-day Luna County, New Mexico, just south of Deming.

54. The convento of San Francisco in Mexico City, or Convento Grande, was established in the 1520s. It served as the mother house of the Franciscan Order in New Spain and head-quarters of the Province of the Holy Gospel. In the late seventeenth century, the Convento Grande had two hundred cells and a refectory large enough to accommodate five hundred. Fray Fidel de Jesús Chauvet, *San Francisco de México* (Mexico City, 1985):41. See also Mario Ramón Campos Rebollo, *La casa de los Franciscanos en la ciudad de México: Reseña de los cambios que sufrió el Convento de San Francisco de los siglos xvi al xix* (Mexico City, 1986).

55. Casas Grandes was located in the fertile San Diego valley near the Casas Grandes river. When the Spaniards arrived in the sixteenth century, six to eight thousand people lived there and in adjoining valleys near the site of extensive pre-Columbian ruins. Most of the Spanish colonists arrived in the 1660s from New Mexico. By 1678, there was a Franciscan mission, San Antonio de Casas Grandes, of the province of San Francisco de Zacatecas.

In 1686, a fifty-man presidio was established with Juan Fernández de la Fuente named captain in mid-1687. With the founding of Janos presidio four years later, about 60 km upriver at Janos,

Casas Grandes was reduced to a forty-man post, headquarters for a flying company. Moorhead, *Presidio*, 21–22. Luis Navarro García, *Don José de Gálvez y la Comandancia General de las Provincias Internas del Norte de Nueva España* (Seville, 1964):27, 32–33. Gerhard, *North Frontier*, 231–32.

56. Of linguistic interest here are the differing forms of address Vargas uses with Fernández de la Fuente and Pardiñas. He addresses Fernández de la Fuente as vuestra merced, a polite, even courtly, form, but one lacking the connotation of nobility. With Pardiñas, Vargas chooses vuestra señoría, indicating that he considers him his social equal and of noble status. José Plá Cárceles, "La evolución del tratamiento 'vuestra-merced'," *Revista de Filología Española* 10 (July–Sept. 1923):245–80.

57. The document clearly reads Santo Domingo Paraguai, but this usage is not corroborated. Paraguai may refer to another pueblo, perhaps Pojoaque, one Spanish variant of which was Pajagüe. The confusion may be the result of either Vargas's or a copyist's error. John P. Harrington, "The Ethnogeography of the Tewa Indians," *Twenty-Ninth Annual Report of the Bureau of American Ethnology, 1907–1908* (Washington, D.C., 1916):334.

58. Vargas's description of his proposed attack against Santa Fe reflects his knowledge of seventeenth-century siege warfare. The use of a tunnel, or mine, to break through the enemy's defenses was standard siege strategy. Vargas could have learned about siege warfare from any of a number of sources. Aside from relatively contemporary writers, such as Juan Fernández de Espinosa and Diego de Prado, the classic military writers were available and widely read. José Almirante, *Bibliografía militar de España* (Madrid, 1876):286, 640, 778, 946–47. J.F.C. Fuller, *From the Defeat of the Spanish Armada, 1588 to the Battle of Waterloo, 1815*, vol. 2 of *A Military History of the Western World* (New York, 1955):129–30.

59. The governor of New Biscay appointed alcaldes mayores in important Spanish settlements in his jurisdiction, including Sonora and Sinaloa. If the posting included extensive military duties, the appointee might be called the teniente de capitán general. In 1690, the alcalde mayor of Sinaloa was Diego de Quirós. He served until 1693, when the new alcalde, Manuel de Agramont, arrived to succeed him. Lázaro Verdugo y Chávez held the post of alcalde mayor of Sonora from 1689 to 1690.

The province of Sinaloa was an area of conflicting jurisdiction beginning in the mid-1600s. It was never clearly established whether the right of appointment to the governments of Sinaloa and Sonora fell to the governor of New Biscay or the viceroy in Mexico

118   *By Force of Arms*

City. The problem of competing candidates, one sent from Parral and one from the capital, was finally resolved by the governor of New Biscay sending a list of three choices to the viceroy for final selection. Naylor and Polzer, *Presidio and Militia*, 1:575 n4. Navarro García, *Sonora y Sinaloa*, 291, 303–304. Gerhard, *North Frontier*, 166, 246, 272, 275.

60. To mount the 1681 entrada, the 150 citizens were to be provided 250 pesos' worth of supplies, while the 50 soldiers were to receive 350 pesos' worth. The minimum cost for the expedition would thus have been 55,000 pesos. Hackett and Shelby, *Revolt*, 2:10–12, 95–134.

61. The deep hostility of the Tarahumaras, who had initially welcomed contact with Jesuit missionaries earlier in the century, was provoked by the influx of Spaniards into the Cosihuiriáchic area following the discovery of silver. Although the 1660s and 1670s had been a fairly peaceful time between Spaniards and Tarahumaras, Spanish demands for labor, land, timber, and charcoal after 1683 put increasing pressure on the Indian community. The result, after four years of plotting, was the 1690 revolt, in which the Tarahumaras were joined by the Conchos, Sumas, Janos, Jovas, Julimes, Chinarras, Oclames, Tobosos, Chisos, and Apaches.

The uprising failed to drive the Spaniards from Tarahumara country, and in 1690, the Tarahumaras retreated to the mountains of the Sierra Madre Occidental. They remained a threat to New Biscay until 1697, when they revolted for the last time. Thomas E. Sheridan and Thomas H. Naylor, eds., *Rarámuri: A Tarahumara Colonial Chronicle, 1607–1791* (Flagstaff, 1979):8, 39–40, 44–45. Gerhard, *North Frontier*, 185–86. Porras Muñoz, *Frontera*, 203. Copies of letters concerning the Tarahumara revolt of 1690, Mexico City, 26 June 1690, AHN, Osuna.

62. Francisco Ramírez de Espinosa Salazar was born about 1628 in New Mexico. In 1663, he moved with his wife to El Paso and later to Casas Grandes where, in 1684, he became the second alcalde mayor, a post he held until his death. He led an attack in 1684 against the Sumas and Janos who had raided Janos presidio and were on their way to Casas Grandes. In 1692, the viceroy approved Ramírez's proposal for a flying company composed of fifty men. Ramírez, however, died that year in Zacatecas on his way home. Navarro García, *Sonora y Sinaloa*, 313. Naylor and Polzer, *Presidio and Militia*, 1:507, 521 n7, 528–33, 575 n6. The Conde de Galve, Decree, Mexico City, 8 July 1692, AHP, 1692A. NMF, 90.

63. The flying company, a highly mobile mounted force with fresh horses at hand and ready to respond in an emergency, permitted a reduced number of

men to protect a large area and avoided the expense of permanent presidios. The flying company patrolled most of the year, halting only when circumstances dictated or to winter over at a plaza de armas selected by the commander. Porras Muñoz, *Frontera*, 309–10. Roberto Mario Salmón, "Frontier Warfare in the Hispanic Southwest: Tarahumara Resistance, 1649–1780," *Mid-America* 58 (Oct. 1976):178 n9.

64. Santa Rosa Cosihuiriáchic, in New Biscay, about 95 km southwest of present-day Chihuahua, was the site of the discovery of rich silver ore in 1686. It soon became an administrative center of a district of the same name. It was a parish seat and the largest settlement of Spaniards in the area.

A number of former New Mexico residents lived in the area. In Papigóchic: Sgto. mayor Sebastián de Herrera, Pedro Varela de Losada, Nicolás Lucero [de Godoy], Sebastián de Herrera, Capt. Cristóbal Fontes, Francisco Fontes, Capt. Felipe de Arvizu, Nicolás Ruiz de Hinojos, and Juan Márquez. In Bachiniva: Capt. Esteban [López] de Gracia, Juan Esteban [López] de Gracia, Pedro de Fragua, and Luis de Ayala. In the area around San Juan de la Concepción, Las Cruces, and Valle de Torreón: Ignacio [López] de Gracia, Juan de Arzate, Diego Luján, Capt. Gonzalo de Paredes, Sgto. mayor Felipe Durán, Juan Mateo de Sandoval [y Manzanares],

Pablo de Ortega, Juan de Morales, Felipe García, Gregorio Cobos de la Parra, Felipe Baca, José [Durán] de Chaves, José Velásquez, Jacinto Madrid, Pedro [Durán] de Chaves, Bernabé Márquez, and two young men called Los Caravajal. In Sonora: Francisco Varela, Roque Varela, Juan Romero, Diego de Hinojos, José Gonzáles, Tomás Arvizu, Juan de Arvizu, Juan Ramos, Francisco Bernal, Cristóbal López, Cristóbal Nieto, Felipe de Arteaga, Francisco de Salazar, Cristóbal Varela, and José Varela. In the jurisdiction of Todos Santos [San Bartolomé]: Gen. Tomé Domínguez [de Mendoza], Juan Domínguez, Diego Domínguez, Francisco Domínguez, and Antonio Domínguez. List of former New Mexico residents who left with Antonio Otermín, Parral, 1684, AHP, 1684D. Gerhard, *North Frontier*, 190, 193.

65. In 1601, a real was settled at Cuencamé de Ciniceros, 150 km northeast of Durango in New Biscay. The indigenous people were Zacateco-speaking hunters and gatherers. By the early seventeenth century, there was an alcalde mayor and capitán a guerra for the mines at Cuencamé; it was also the seat of a jurisdiction of the same name.

A presidio, Nuestra Señora de la Concepción del Pasaje de Cuencamé, was established just north of Cuencamé in 1685. By 1687, the presidio had a garrison of fifty soldiers. The commander was also given the title of alcalde mayor and teniente de capitán general of the real of Cuencamé.

The Zacatecan Franciscan doctrina of Nuestra Señora de la Purísima Concepción de Cuencamé ministered to the Indian population, and the benefice of San Antonio Cuencamé served the Spaniards. Gerhard, *North Frontier*, 193–95.

66. The presidio of San Pedro del Gallo in the jurisdiction of Mapimí was also established in 1685 as part of the defensive cordon erected on the northern frontier to protect mining areas. Its foundation replaced presidios at Chametla and San Hipólito in western New Biscay. Luis de Quintana was named captain of the new presidio and its fifty-man contingent in 1687. Navarro García, *Gálvez*, 21, 32. Moorhead, *Presidio*, 121–22.

67. No journal of the expedition's military operations is known to have survived. See RBC, 155 n2.

68. In his original contract for the conquest of New Mexico, dated 21 September 1595, Juan de Oñate proposed that the settlers going on the entrada be recognized as hidalgos of noble lineage, enjoying the same honors and privileges as those of Castile. The precise wording of the provision was that of paragraph ninety-nine of the 1573 ordinances regulating new settlements in the Indies. Although the viceroy, Luis de

Velasco II, agreed to this, his successor, the Conde de Monterrey, over Oñate's strong objections, chose to modify the provision, stipulating that only those who persevered in the conquest for five years would be so honored. On 17 October 1601, a special junta advised the crown to incorporate this change, which Felipe III did in a cedula of 8 July 1602. The cedula was received and adopted by the viceroy and audiencia in Mexico City on 26 June 1604. Hammond and Rey, *Oñate*, 1:7, 10, 42–57; 2:743, 963, 974–75.

69. Mateo Fernández de Santa Cruz, the Marqués de Buena Vista, was born in Villada (Palencia) and baptized on 31 October 1651. He went to New Spain about 1680 with his uncle, fray Manuel de Santa Cruz, bishop of Puebla. He was a member of the Tribunal of Accounts's mesa mayor. By April 1702, he had died in Mexico City. Navarro García, "Real Tribunal de Cuentas," 519. Lohmann Villena, *Americanos*, 2:42.

70. Manuel [Francisco] Gerónimo de Tovar originally bought his supernumerary position on the Tribunal of Accounts in 1685 for 16,500 pesos. Although this post was suppressed in 1691, he had it reinstated. By 1702, he was, though blind, still serving on the tribunal. At this time, he was also in debt to the royal treasury for 68,000 pesos, the result of borrowing when he administered

the playing-card monopoly. A decision from the Council of the Indies in October 1702, aimed at reform of the tribunal, resulted in Tovar's retirement in 1703 at half-salary. Navarro García, "Real Tribunal de Cuentas," 519, 521.

71. The Las Cruces referred to here was located in the upper Santa María river valley in the jurisdiction of Cosihuiriáchic in New Biscay. The area suffered greatly as a result of the Tarahumara uprising in 1690–91. Gerhard, *North Frontier,* 185–87.

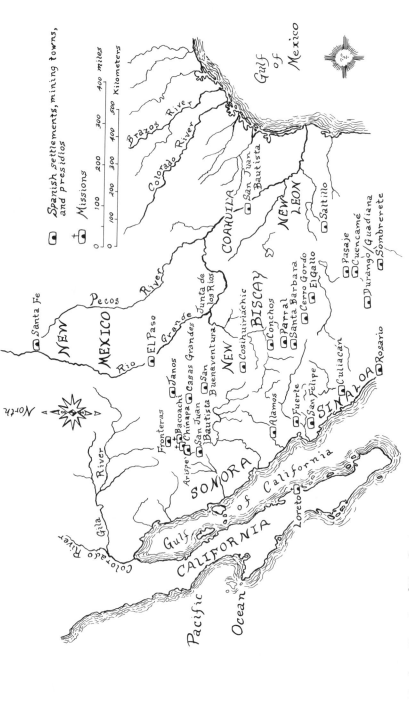

The Northern Frontier of New Spain.
Map drawn by Jerry L. Livingston.

TESTIMONY REGARDING AN ALLEGED MERCURY MINE
BEYOND ORAIBI; SETTLEMENT OF THREE HUNDRED
SUMA INDIANS; DISCOVERY OF SALINAS; PROPOSALS TO
RETURN FORMER NEW MEXICO CITIZENS SETTLED IN
NEW BISCAY; AND PLANS FOR AN ARMED ENTRADA INTO
NEW MEXICO, MAY 1691–MAY 1692.*

Even in his anger about being drawn into hostilities on the Sonora frontier, Governor Vargas hastens to comply with the viceroy's request for information about a rumored mercury mine beyond the pueblo of Oraibi in Hopi country. He takes testimony from three Franciscans and nine veteran residents. All have heard of the mine and know of the antiglare, cosmetic, and medicinal uses of a mercury-like substance in New Mexico. Boasting of his own considerable experience in mining, Vargas forwards the testimony to Mexico City.

As governor, don Diego does not scruple to compare his accomplishments, honor, and zeal to the alleged weaker performance of his predecessors. They could not control the Suma Indians; he has won them over and congregated some three hundred at a new mission 2 leagues downriver from Socorro del Sur. The governors who served before him could never find the so-called Apache salina in the rugged mountains east of El Paso; Vargas has discovered it and a dozen others. He wishes the sample he is sending to the viceroy were mercury instead of salt.

In Mexico City, the Conde de Galve routinely orders the fiscal to comment on Vargas's letters, and the file grows. Royal cedulas of 1683 and 1689 and the visionary scheme of Toribio de la Huerta to reconquer New Mexico are made part of the record. The viceroy orders two former governors living in Mexico City, Jironza and Otermín, to give their opinions about the mercury mine and reconquest. Otermín's response includes the suggestion for fifty or sixty well-armed soldiers and a hundred Indian allies to approach the Hopi pueblos without being seen and disarm the residents.

Galve, meeting with his junta, in August and December 1691 and May 1692 formulates policy and dispatches orders to Governor Vargas in the field. He decides that armed reconnaissance of New Mexico should come first and discovery of the mercury mine second. He approves don Diego's request for the aid of fifty additional paid soldiers to be detached from the presidios of New Biscay.

As for the return of former New Mexico residents now settled in New Biscay, the viceroy changes his mind. Instead of threats, they should be offered incentives: hidalgo status and land. Vargas disagrees. He thinks that, as loyal vassals of the crown, they should rally honorably to the royal standard whenever notified and condemns their excuses.

Year 2 1691
2nd

Acts and proceedings in fulfillment of the original letter of record therein from the most excellent viceroy, the lord Conde de Galve, that were recorded and are being sent to his greatness in his superior government in the city and court of Mexico in New Spain by the governor and captain general of New Mexico for his majesty and so forth.
[rubrica]

The Conde de Galve to Diego de Vargas, Order, Mexico City, 27 May 1691, DS.

From accounts of persons who have resided in those lands, I have it that in the rebellious region of New Mexico lies the province they call Moqui.[1] At a distance of 12 leagues from it toward the big river, there is a mountain range,[2] one of its most prominent, from which they extract metals or ore of cinnabar, which the Indians use to paint themselves. All sorts of people used it, especially Spanish women, to preserve their good complexions and so that smallpox scars on those who suffered from this ailment might not show. This metal is heavier than lead and so liquid and greasy that it soaks through the riding gear and saddle blankets of the packhorses on which it is carried. If rubbed, it leaves stains of royal purple and white and for this reason is commonly taken for mercury and very pure at that. There is a tradition that the mineral is very abundant. The range produces it as a pure liquid in some small lagoons and puddles, with the result that it can be tested and easily examined without much cost or risk.[3]

This information should not be neglected as it is so favorable to the common cause of the whole kingdom, the royal service, and the royal treasury. It occurs to me to inform you, so that, with the eldest and most respected people of my government, we may seek to examine the probability, advantages, disadvantages, difficulties, and expenses of going to that range. We may also examine its distance, cordillera, and routes, and then test the quality of the metals and find out if some citizens have extracted mercury from them for working local silver, as I understand they have. Maximum clarity in everything should be sought and advantage taken of Father José de Espínola[4] (if he is there), a criollo of the kingdom of Peru, who is said to have some knowledge of the matter.

Of all that may result and occur to you in this matter, and by means of the proceedings and acts that will be recorded, you will give me an account so that I, having seen it, may decide what is of most advantage to the royal service. May God keep you many years. Mexico City, 27 May 1691.

The Conde de Galve [rubrica]

Lord don Diego de Vargas Zapata y Luján

Diego de Vargas, Acts and proceedings, El Paso, 1–12 August 1691, DS.

Report of the date of the arrival of the courier dispatched by his excellency with this letter

In the pueblo of El Paso, kingdom of New Mexico, on 1 August 1691, the courier, don Diego Fernández de Aguilar, arrived with the dispatch from the postmaster[5] of the kingdom of New Spain. He was sent to return to this kingdom from the city and court of Mexico on 31 May, with the letter contained on these two sheets. It is from the most excellent lord, the Conde de Galve, dated in Mexico City on 27 May of the present year, and signed by his excellency. He is the representative of the king, our lord, and his viceroy, governor and captain general of all the kingdom of New Spain, and president of the royal audiencia of the city and court of Mexico. I, don Diego de Vargas Zapata Luján Ponce de León, his majesty's governor, captain general, and castellan of the fortress and presidio of this kingdom of New Mexico, have reviewed it.

Obedience

I receive and read it with proper respect and reverence and am ready with all diligence and efficiency to record the acts and carry out what the most excellent lord viceroy orders me. I desire that, at his direction and order, the effects may be achieved in the royal service and for the increase of the royal treasury, common good, and worth of the monarchy of this entire kingdom. I shall humbly and promptly go forth to properly carry out what the most excellent lord viceroy may order me.

So that the receipt of this letter and its fulfillment may be of record, I order it placed at the beginning of the acts and proceedings and that the persons should be examined and make their declarations according to the tenor and points his excellency refers to therein. So that it may be of record, I signed it on said day, month, and year ut supra.

Don Diego de Vargas Zapata Luján Ponce de León
[rubrica]

Act
Declaration of Father José de Espínola

In the pueblo and real of San Lorenzo, jurisdiction of this kingdom and provinces of New Mexico, on 3 August 1691, I, don Diego de Vargas Zapata Luján Ponce de León, his majesty's governor and captain general of this kingdom and its presidio in obedience to and fulfillment of the letter, placed at the beginning of these proceedings, from the most excellent viceroy, his majesty's representative for the entire kingdom of New Spain, dated 27 May of this year and signed by his excellency (may God keep him), departed from the plaza de armas and pueblo of El Paso, 2 leagues away, to the real of San Lorenzo, where I found Father preacher fray José de Espínola, who is ill in bed in its convento de San Lorenzo of our father St. Francis. I informed him of the letter from the most excellent lord viceroy, the Conde de Galve, and read it to him.

Having understood it, his reverence said that if the metal has the qualities expressed in his excellency's letter, there is no doubt that it must be very rich in mercury and, based on assays he has seen in the kingdom of Peru, it is what they call pepina.[6] If it is present, every effort should be made to extract the mercury, even though extracting all of it would be difficult because of the lack of tools for this operation. He says that the same report in this letter has been made to him by other persons to whom he has answered in the same way and said what is cited is true. Regarding that metal, he says that it is mercury. This is what he knows and declares. So that it may be of record, he signed it with me, the governor and captain general; Father preacher fray Miguel Muñiz[7] from this convento; and Afz. don Alfonso Rael de Aguilar,[8] a citizen in the pueblo of El Paso, present and as witnesses, to which I attest.

Fray José Espínola Almonacid [rubrica]

Fray Miguel Muñiz de Luna [rubrica]

Don Diego de Vargas
Zapata Luján Ponce de León [rubrica]

Alfonso Rael de Aguilar [rubrica]

The declaration continues

Furthermore, he added and said that for some eleven years, he, the declarant, has been living here as a resident in the pueblo of El

Paso in this kingdom of New Mexico, accompanied by Father preacher
fray Nicolás de Echevarría,[9] likewise a resident in that convento. The
latter related to him and recounted that he had lived in the provinces of Moqui and New Mexico for many years, having arrived at
an early age at those missions.

Father Echevarría told the declarant how, in the pueblo, while
he was guardian of Moqui, an Indian told him one day that he had
gone hunting over toward the mountain range referred to in his excellency's letter. He found a pool at the base of a rock and put his hands
into what appeared to him to be drinking water, and it slipped away.
The Indian saw that the water slipped away from him and that it was
as thick as atole. For this reason, Father Echevarría said it was mercury. So that it may be of record, I, the governor and captain general, sign it with the witnesses undersigned as before.

                                  Fray José Espínola Almonacid [rubrica]
                                   Fray Miguel Muñiz de Luna [rubrica]
Don Diego de Vargas
Zapata Luján Ponce de León [rubrica]
                                    Alfonso Rael de Aguilar [rubrica]

Declaration of the reverend father preacher and custos, fray Francisco
de Vargas

In the pueblo and plaza de armas of El Paso on 3 August 1691, it
seemed appropriate to me, the governor and captain general, to go
and receive the declaration from the reverend father preacher, fray
Francisco de Vargas, ecclesiastical judge and custos of these holy
missions of our father St. Francis of this kingdom of New Mexico,
in his cell in the convento of Nuestra Señora de Guadalupe del Paso.

I reminded his reverence of what we had spoken of in various con-
versations regarding the circumstances and things of the kingdom
because he had been there and also spoken with very old religious
who were present in this kingdom. To acquire the exact information
that his excellency (may God keep him), the most excellent viceroy,
the Conde de Galve, orders me by his letter of 27 May of this year,
which is at the beginning of these proceedings, I read it to the very
reverend father. Having heard it, he said that regarding the ore or
metal that his excellency mentions in his letter, he has seen it brought

from Zia Pueblo, where he was at the time it was burned and the rebellious, apostate enemy uprising was suppressed there.[10] The metal was as his excellency said in his letter, liquid and greasy, and when rubbed in the hands, a blue or purplish luster remained. The very reverend father asked the same Indians who went on that campaign whence they brought the ore. They answered him that they brought it from Zuni and Moqui.[11] He has heard some people say it contains mercury.

The very reverend father said that Father fray Nicolás de Echevarría had recently arrived at this convento of El Paso and is residing in it. He had served in the missions more than thirty years and was custos of the kingdom of New Mexico. He was a very old religious, more than seventy. One day, he was speaking with the father, the very reverend declarant, and another two or three religious who were, as well as can be remembered, Father preacher fray Juan Muñoz,[12] present guardian of the convento of Ysleta, and Father José de Espínola. Father Echevarría recounted that among the things to admire in the kingdom of New Mexico, there was one an Indian had told him about. This was when the religious was living in the land of the Picuris or Moqui—he does not remember which. The Indian said he had seen and found at the foot of a mountain range, trickling, what seemed to be water falling to the ground onto a rock that had a hollow, like a basin. When he tried to get some with his hand, it slipped away from him. Examining it, he said that it was as thick as atole. From this, Father Echevarría deduced that it could not be anything other than mercury. This is what he knows and has heard.

So that it may be of record, he signed it with me, the governor and captain general; the witnesses present were don Alfonso Rael de Aguilar and Capt. don Pedro Ladrón de Guevara.

Fray Francisco de Vargas [rubrica]
Alfonso Rael de Aguilar [rubrica]
Don Pedro Ladrón de Guevara [rubrica]

Don Diego de Vargas
Zapata Luján Ponce de León [rubrica]

Declaration of the father preacher and commissary, fray Juan Muñoz de Castro

In the pueblo of Ysleta on 4 August 1691, I, the governor and captain general, proceeded in fulfillment of what the most excellent lord viceroy orders me with attention to the preceding declaration of the very reverend father custos I received yesterday, 3 August of the present year, which records the information he heard about the mercury in conversation one day with Father preacher Nicolás de Echevarría, who was present for many years in the provinces and interior of this kingdom of New Mexico in its missions. The reverend father custos had this conversation with three religious, one of whom was Father fray José de Espínola, who was cited by the most excellent lord viceroy in the letter from his excellency, which is of record at the beginning of these proceedings, as is the fact that I gave it proper acknowledgment.

Having received the declaration of Father José de Espínola, recorded in these proceedings before that of the reverend father custos, who is cited together with Father Juan Muñoz de Castro, religious of our father St. Francis and commissary of the Holy Office, present guardian of the convento of Nuestro Padre San Antonio of Ysleta Pueblo, and having visited him in his cell there, I told his reverence, after kissing his hand, the reason for my visit.

I showed him the letter from the most excellent lord viceroy and read it to him. After he had heard it, I went on to receive his declaration according to the tenor of the information his excellency (may God keep him) requests. His excellency seeks to know whether it is true that there is a mountain range beyond the province of Moqui, in the uprisen kingdom of New Mexico, and whether cinnabar ore or metal occurs there, and if so, its requirements, circumstances, and whatever else seems appropriate. This is what the most excellent lord viceroy relates in his letter. His excellency has requested all the information he requires, and once the preacher and commissary, fray Juan Muñoz de Castro, guardian of this convento, learned of it, he stated the following.

One day in 1680, having recently come to this kingdom, he had a conversation about New Mexico in the convento of El Paso with Father preacher fray Nicolás de Echevarría, an elderly religious with much experience in and information about the kingdom. Among the things he reported was that, in the province of Moqui, there was a great quantity of mercury ore, so pure that it formed a pool or small lake in the hollow of a rock or cave. There was liquid, because the rocks were all metal, and it trickled drop by drop into the pool or small lake. This information was given to Father fray Nicolás de Echevarría. An Indian tried to get some of this liquid, which seemed to him to be water, but it went out of his hands, and he could not hold it because it seemed alive. The stones from which it trickled were extremely heavy, a reddish color, and so greasy that they stuck to one's hands and stained clothing and the saddlebags in which they were gathered.

The father related all this among other beneficial things the kingdom possessed; this particular one was communicated by an Indian. The father never saw it, nor was able to see it, but the many times he told about it, he always told it the same way. I know this and can declare it in good conscience.

So that it may be of record, he signed it with me, the governor and captain general. Present as witnesses were Afz. don Alfonso Rael de Aguilar and Afz. don Juan Severino Rodríguez de Suballe,[13] who also signed it. So that it may be of record, I so attest.

Fray Juan Muñoz de Castro [rubrica]

Juan Severino Rodríguez de Suballe [rubrica]

Alfonso Rael de Aguilar [rubrica]

Don Diego de Vargas
Zapata Luján Ponce de Leon [rubrica]

Declaration of Sgto. mayor Juan Lucero de Godoy

In the pueblo of El Paso on 8 August 1691, I, his majesty's governor and captain general of this kingdom of New Mexico, in fulfillment of and obedience to the letter of the most excellent lord viceroy, the Conde de Galve, of the kingdom of New Spain, dated 27 May of the present year, and so that the precise information the most excellent lord seeks may be sent him from people of the greatest confidence, fidelity, and intelligence who have seen the ore or metal of cinnabar, where it is brought from, and what its characteristics are, as his excellency's letter expresses, had appear before me the sargento mayor, Juan Lucero de Godoy,[14] citizen of the real and pueblo of San Lorenzo and native of the villa of Santa Fe, kingdom of New Mexico, sixty-six years old.

I read him the letter from the most excellent lord viceroy. Having heard it, he said all the circumstances the letter describes about the ore or metal specified in it are true, except the two about small lakes or puddles of mercury. Although they may exist, he cannot firmly declare that he has seen them or knows of them. He has no information about mercury having been extracted by any citizen or other person in that villa and kingdom of New Mexico to use in the processing of silver, of which he knows nothing.

Regarding the distance, direction, and cordillera, he made the following statement. He stated that the distance to the first pueblo, which is called San Bernardo de Aguatuvi,[15] is 100 leagues from the villa of Santa Fe. Counting from this pueblo of El Paso, it is about 200 leagues, as it seemed to him and everyone else. From the pueblo of San Bernardo to the last pueblo, San Miguel de Oraibi, is 7 leagues, and from Oraibi to the big river, as his excellency's letter says, would be 12 leagues. The mountain range is on this side of the river. The mine is in this range on a very prominent hill. The Indians from the province of Moqui said it took from morning to midday to climb it and until night the same day to come down loaded with ore. This was related to him by Antonio de Cisneros,[16] citizen and native of this kingdom, who is summoned so that he may declare it.

The declarant has commonly heard in the kingdom of New Mexico, as well as in Mexico City, that it was rich cinnabar, a metal rich in mercury. It was requested from his father for painting in that city where he had an uncle who practiced this art.[17]

The range where the hill is lies to the west. All that country from the time one leaves the pueblo of El Paso is dangerous, with enemies not only from the rebellious nations in the kingdom of New Mexico and its provinces, but also because it is surrounded by the very numerous Apache nations who are everywhere. To make the entrada to the province of Moqui and there discover and reconnoiter the hill where the metal is found, two hundred men-at-arms will be required with all the necessary outfitting for such a long journey and patrol. He thinks that, at the very minimum, going with some risk and a lot of work, one hundred and fifty men will be necessary, adding to either of the figures one hundred and fifty Indian warriors, recognizing that no more can be taken from these pueblos. He also knows that as many as two hundred Indians could be required and very necessary.

He stated that the cost for the moderate and very necessary number of one hundred and fifty men would be the following. He stated that the minimum needed would be fifteen mules and horses for each man. More than 8,000 pesos will be needed for food. To transport the supplies—because the land is harsh, very rocky, and barren and because of its vastness—many mules will be lost and more than 6,000 pesos needed for the round trip. This, which he declares on

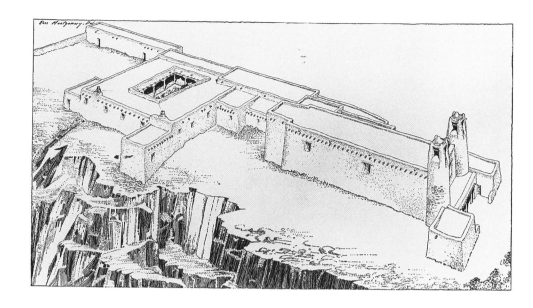

San Bernardo de Aguatuvi, conjectural restoration by Ross. G. Montgomery
From Montgomery, Watson Smith, and John O. Brew, *Franciscan
Awatovi* (1949)

the basis of these costs, is done with an eye to the greatest economy for the royal treasury. The 8,000 pesos are understood to be only for the supplies of the one hundred and fifty men, limiting the trip out, stay, and return to five months. This is what can be done and of no little importance when one is looking for some benefit to his majesty. To maintain the one hundred and fifty Indians with maize meal, pinole,[18] tobacco,[19] and animals, it is necessary to give them horses so that they can go without wearing them out. At two horses for each Indian, three hundred horses are needed. To carry their supplies of pinole, meal, and tobacco, they will need fifty pack mules. No remounts will be added for them, pursuant to the greatest savings for his majesty. As to sending the men-at-arms, his excellency will know best where they will be least needed by his majesty and also where he can give the order to recruit them for the journey.

The points in the letter have been fully responded to and declarations made. So that the report may be of record and set down thus, he signed it with me, the governor and captain general, with Capt. don Pedro Ladrón de Guevara and Afz. don Alfonso Rael de Aguilar as witnesses, citizens in this kingdom. They also signed it, to which I attest.

Juan Lucero de Godoy [rubrica]

Don Pedro Ladrón de Guevara [rubrica]

Alfonso Rael de Aguilar [rubrica]

Don Diego de Vargas
Zapata Luján Ponce de León [rubrica]

Statement of Antonio de Cisneros

In the pueblo of El Paso on 8 August 1691, I, the governor and captain general, refer to the declaration dated yesterday, 8 August 1691;[20] received; and made before me by the sargento mayor, Juan Lucero de Godoy, who, summoned in it, states that he knows the mine of the ore or cinnabar metal. It is beyond the last pueblo of Oraibi in the province of Moqui, kingdom of New Mexico. At a distance of 12 leagues, which is what his excellency, the most excellent lord viceroy of New Spain, says in his letter, is the big river, and on this side the mountain range. Antonio de Cisneros, citizen of the real and pueblo of San Lorenzo in this kingdom, told the declarant that in the range there was a very prominent hill where the mine is located. The Indians take from morning until midday to climb it and until night to return loaded with ore to the bottom.

To obtain the precise information the most excellent lord viceroy commanded of me, I had Antonio de Cisneros appear. Before me and the witnesses required by law, I read him the letter from the most excellent lord viceroy that is at the beginning of these proceedings. After he had heard and understood it, and after I had advised him by virtue of the declaration made by the sargento mayor, Juan Lucero de Godoy, he is summoned and advised in this regard that the most important thing is obedience to and fulfillment of his excellency's letter and he should declare and say all that he might know about the questions and points raised in the letter.

He made his declaration in the following manner. He stated that he is the Antonio de Cisneros who is cited by the sargento mayor, Juan Lucero de Godoy, whom he knows. It is true that his name is Antonio de Cisneros, and he is a native of New Mexico, born in the provinces of Zuni in the pueblo of that name. He came as a boy to live with his father downriver from the place called La Custodia, since it lies before the villa of Santa Fe. Afterward, he went with his father, whose name is Bartolomé de Cisneros.[21] The governor and captain general of the kingdom at that time—he does not remember exactly who, for he was very young—gave his father the grant of alcalde mayor for the provinces of Zuni and Moqui. When he was in the province of Zuni, he found out from the Indians that they were going to collect almagre.[22] Asking them where they collected it, they said they got it from a hill that is beyond the direct route to Moqui, taking half a day to climb it and half to come down. They said it was very large, and they had made a cave from which they extracted almagre. That was all they told him.

They used the ore to paint themselves red. It was also used by all sorts of women, Spanish as well as Indian, and he saw them anoint themselves with it. He saw the ore; it is heavy, liquid, and greasy, and when a woman would take it and rub it in her hand, her hand turned purple. He said that it seeped through the buckskin sacks the Indians brought it down in. They then took it to La Custodia. They sold it throughout New Mexico. He does not know whether they extracted mercury from the ore.

The mine seems to be toward the west, since from Oraibi, which is the last pueblo of the province of Moqui, the Indians pointed in that direction to show where they went to collect and bring this almagre.

He cannot really say how many leagues it is from El Paso to where the mine is in the province of Moqui. He knows it is a land full of both rebellious enemy Indians and Apaches. He does not know anything else.

So that it may be of record, a witness signed it for him at his request, because he did not know how. He stated that he was about twenty-eight years old. The following witnesses to these proceedings were present: Afz. don Alfonso Rael de Aguilar and Capt. don Pedro Ladrón de Guevara, who signed it with me, the governor and captain general. I so attest.

By request and as witness, Bartolomé Gómez Robledo[23] [rubrica]

Don Pedro Ladrón de Guevara [rubrica]

Alfonso Rael de Aguilar [rubrica]

Don Diego de Vargas
Zapata Luján Ponce de León [rubrica]

Statement of Sgto. mayor Bartolomé Gómez Robledo

In the pueblo of El Paso on 9 August 1691, I, the governor and captain general, in fulfillment of and obedience to the letter and so that his excellency, the most excellent lord viceroy of New Spain, may obtain in full the precise information he orders me therein to acquire, and so that it may be of record, had appear before me the sargento mayor, Bartolomé Gómez Robledo, of this pueblo of El Paso and kingdom of New Mexico. With him present and with the undersigned witnesses required by law, I read the letter from the most excellent lord viceroy, which is placed at the beginning of these proceedings.

Having heard it and familiarized himself with its points and questions, he stated that he has seen the almagre (for so it is called throughout New Mexico by both Spaniards and Indians) many times and held it in his hands. It is liquid, greasy, and extremely heavy and stains so that although one washes one's hands with hot water, the stains remain almost a month. They used it in snowy weather for eye strain, rubbing it on themselves.

In the time of Gen. don Luis de Guzmán,[24] the declarant's father, who was inspector of the provinces of Zuni and Moqui, brought back some small bags or sacks of ore. Although they were very small, each one weighed so much that it could scarcely be carried. The ore soaked through the packsaddle, sack, and blanket of the jack on which it was carried, which was also stained in such a manner that until the rains came, the stain would not go away.

He also declares that don Jacinto Muñoz de Moraza was living in the province of Sonora in the real of San Miguel. When the declarant was going to the province of Sonora on orders from the former governor and captain general of this kingdom, don Antonio de Otermín, don Jacinto Muñoz asked the declarant why they wanted more riches than they had from the mercury mine. It was almagre, and God had provided the mine with mercury of such purity that it could not be exhausted. The citizens of the kingdom of New Mexico did not have to look for silver mines, simply to work the metals they had. Although the mine belonged to his majesty, for the first year ~~the last year was for the discoverer~~ the discoverer benefited from it and was given grants of a robe of a military order and an income of 30,000 pesos a year. Once the year was over and the discoverer had profited, the mine passed to his majesty.[25] He also told him how he could extract the mercury from the metal. Because of what he told this declarant, he responds and states that it seems to him that it would be very easy, if one had the tools.

His cousin Bartolomé Romero[26] was killed in Taos by the Indians when they rebelled in the kingdom of New Mexico. He was an encomendero and had his encomienda in the last pueblo of the province of Moqui, which is called Oraibi, where he went every year to collect his encomienda. He told this declarant he had been at the hill where the mine was and seen and brought almagre from it. It is, in his opinion, 14 to 15 leagues from the pueblo of Oraibi. The Indians said it is a dry land and they carry drinking water to it in tecomates.[27] In his opinion, it is toward the western sea, and the mountain range or hill is very rich in almagre ore or metal. He stated that only the Indians had worked it, making a hole in the ground like a cave.

It was 100 leagues from the villa of Santa Fe. From the pueblo of El Paso, one can go without entering the villa by way of the pueblo of Acoma and the province of Zuni, which is, in his opinion, from 40 to 50 leagues from the villa of Santa Fe. The distances from this outpost of El Paso are: 50 leagues to Senecú, 30 to Acoma, 40 to Zuni, and as many again to Moqui. Traveling with a load, the trip takes five days. From Moqui to the mine, it is 15 leagues, as stated. In total, it is 175 leagues.

The way is passable, with some good and some bad water holes,

firewood, and pasture. From Senecú, one goes through piñon forests and rosemary thickets. He has traveled as far as the province of
Zuni and beyond to what they call El Cuartelejo.[28] The rest was told
him by his cousin, as has been said.

Since it is a land at war with the enemy and full of Apaches, it
seems to him that a hundred men-at-arms can make the entrada,
taking all that is necessary and spending eight months on the trip
out, stay, and return, to reconnoiter it well. It seems to him that
twelve animals for each soldier will suffice, four mules and eight
horses. Many supplies will be necessary. He stated it seems to him
that from six hundred to eight hundred Indians will be necessary
and also many supplies will be needed for the men-at-arms and soldiers. From all this, his excellency may determine as he sees fit.

He declared this and signed it with me, the governor and captain
general, with the attending witnesses. He stated that he was fifty-one
years old, and I signed it.

Bartolomé Gómez Robledo [rubrica]
Don Pedro Ladrón de Guevara [rubrica]
Alfonso Rael de Aguilar [rubrica]

Don Diego de Vargas
Zapata Luján Ponce de León [rubrica]

Declaration of Capt. Juan Luis Luján

On 9 August in this pueblo of El Paso, I, the governor and captain general, for the information his excellency orders me to obtain
by his letter, had Capt. Juan Luis Luján[29] appear before me. He is a
very old man and stated that he was eighty-six years old, a criollo of
the villa of Santa Fe. I read him the letter from the most excellent
lord viceroy, which is at the beginning of these proceedings.

He stated that he has seen the ore his excellency mentions. The
natives and citizens call it and consider it to be almagre. He has
held it in his hands various times, and it is very liquid and greasy;
rubbed between the hands, it leaves a purple stain. This declarant
went with his compadre, the maestre de campo, Francisco Gómez
Robledo,[30] who was going to the province as inspector. On his father's
orders, he brought a load in two cow hides, that is, two medium-
sized leather sacks. The ore or metal was so heavy and greasy that it
soaked through the packsaddle, straw pad, and saddle blanket and
even stained the animal. This declarant stated that he did not go to

see the mine. His compadre said that when he asked the natives of the province of Moqui for the ore, they refused, denying that they had it, which made him angry.

His compadre, the inspector, went to the mine, which he told him is on a wide llano; there is a round hill there. When it rains, everything becomes colored with reddish water for a distance of three harquebus shots around. From this, the inspector knew the mine to be very rich. Asked why, since he was in the company of the inspector, he did not go with him to see the mine, he stated that his compadre always traveled as inspector, but on this occasion he did not go with him.

He was asked to tell about everything his excellency, the most excellent lord viceroy, refers to and orders in his letter, that is, if he heard or has heard of seeing puddles or small lakes of mercury. He states that he does not know. The inspector only told him how far it was from Oraibi to the mine. He went, spent a day on the trip, and returned the next day. From this pueblo of El Paso, it seems to him that it is farther to the villa of Santa Fe than from the villa to the pueblo of Oraibi, in the province of Moqui. It is toward the west, which is the direction they indicate for the location of the mine from the pueblo of Oraibi.

It is a land at war. In some parts, they say there are Apaches, and in others there are Coninas.[31] To enter there, at least one hundred fully equipped men-at-arms will be necessary. Each soldier will need to take twelve horses and six mules, since it will be necessary for each to transport his suit of armor.[32] He states that because of the lack of peaceful Indians in that land, at least a hundred Indians will be necessary. He states that at least five months will be needed for the trip out, stay, and return. There are enough pastures, firewood, and water holes. In some areas they are scarce and far apart, and many supplies are necessary because they are spread out. The single most important and necessary consideration is to take supplies. He knows nothing more than what has been related.

He signed it with me, the governor and captain general, so that it may be of record, along with the undersigned witnesses. I so attest.

Juan Luis
Don Pedro Ladrón de Guevara [rubrica]
Alfonso Rael de Aguilar [rubrica]
Don Diego de Vargas
Zapata Luján Ponce de León [rubrica]

Declaration of Capt. José Téllez Girón

In this pueblo of El Paso on 9 August of this year, I, the governor and captain general, had Capt. José Téllez Girón[33] appear before me. He stated that he is about sixty years old and a native of the villa of Coyoacán, in the kingdom of New Spain. He has been living in this kingdom and provinces of New Mexico for forty-four years. He came to them, paid by the Royal Treasury of Zacatecas, with Gen. Hernando Ugarte y la Concha,[34] who came as governor and captain general when New Spain was governed by the bishop-governor.[35] I read him the letter from the most excellent lord viceroy of all this kingdom, the Conde de Galve, which is at the beginning of these proceedings.

Having heard the letter, he stated that it is true that, when Gen. Hernando Ugarte y la Concha governed the kingdom, he was one of the eight soldiers who remained in New Mexico serving in its palace. From information beyond what it says in the letter from the most excellent lord viceroy about the ore of almagre or cinnabar, the declarant knows that, as soon as it arrived with the military leaders who went to the provinces of Zuni and Moqui, the governor ordered it, and they brought him an animal with some very heavy sacks of ore or almagre. The declarant saw that the almagre had gone through the packsaddle and sacks to the animal; all were stained.

The Indians use two kinds of ore to paint themselves: one is yellow, and the other, from the province of Zuni, is greasy and red. He has heard from many people that the yellow becomes red and about the mine of almagre, or cinnabar, from the cabos y caudillos, now dead, who went to those areas, 12 leagues from the provinces of Moqui in the land of the Navajo Apaches.[36] That is where the ore is.

With regard to what has been said, he states that the sargento mayor, Juan Lucero de Godoy, should be called. He held that post and brought some of that metal to his father. He has nothing more to declare about this matter.

That area, according to indications, is to the west. From this pueblo to Moqui and to the last pueblo of Oraibi must be more than 200 leagues. Going directly would be even shorter. It is a hostile land belonging to the Apaches, with pasture, firewood and water, and many enemy peoples. Seventy well-armed soldiers and their horses will be needed for the entrada. This should be done with the understanding that the El Paso area will remain garrisoned and secure. Three or four hundred Indian allies and five to six long, hard months will be needed. No one knows what the future may bring. Regarding the supplies for the seventy men, more than 200 fanegas of biscuit will be required; the Indian people will need 150 of maize meal and pinole. In addition, 250 cattle, 15 arrobas of chocolate and the same of sugar, and 400 hands of tobacco must be supplied.

He has nothing more to say. He signs it with me, the governor, and attending witnesses, so that it may be of record, as I attest.

José Téllez Girón [rubrica]
Don Pedro Ladrón de Guevara [rubrica]
Alfonso Rael de Aguilar [rubrica]

Don Diego de Vargas
Zapata Luján Ponce de León [rubrica]

Declaration of Capt. don Fernando Durán y Chaves

In the pueblo of El Paso, on 9 August 1691, I, the governor and captain general, in fulfillment of and obedience to the letter of the most excellent lord viceroy of record in these proceedings, had Capt. don Fernando Durán y Chaves[37] appear before me. He is a citizen of this pueblo, a criollo of New Mexico, and forty-five years old. In the presence of my attending witnesses, I read him his excellency's letter.

He stated that it is true that there is such an ore. He has seen it and brought it back from Moqui. It is public knowledge, and all the citizens and natives of New Mexico know that there is such ore or metal. He does not know where the mine is. Those who do know are the Moquinos and natives of the pueblo of Oraibi in the province of Moqui. It is very heavy, so much so that a person can scarcely lift a tercio. One can only lift a very small amount. He stated that he learned about it from Antonio Montoya,[38] who told him that when his brother-in-law brought a load, Montoya could not lift a tercio when unloading it.

He also says that he knows the ore or almagre has mercury in it, because this declarant's grandmother told him that a religious of that custody named fray Gerónimo de Pedraza,[39] who knew a lot about medicine and was a great doctor, mixed it with an unguent that required mercury. The declarant's grandmother asked the religious why he was putting in that ore or almagre, and he answered that it was because it contained very fine mercury. The declarant stated that it was so liquid and greasy that, when rubbed on the hand, it looked as if it were smeared with lard.[40]

He stated that he was a good friend of Father fray Nicolás de Echevarría, who was guardian among the Picuris of the kingdom of New Mexico.[41] One day, in this pueblo of El Paso, he was told how once, when the father was in his guardianship, an Indian he knew went hunting with another, whom the Apaches killed. He escaped and since he was very tired, lay down to sleep where the night had overtaken him in a mountain range before Picuris Pueblo toward the east. He got thirsty and noticed that water was falling drop-by-drop from one rock on to another with a hole in it, like the hub of a cart wheel. He put his hand into the hole and saw that it was not water, because it was very heavy.

He came and told all that to the father, who sent with the Indian an acquaintance of his named Juan de Herrera,[42] now dead, who lived in the cañada 8 leagues before the guardianship. In fact, it was Juan de Herrera with that Indian who took him to see the mercury. The Indian recognized it when Juan de Herrera poured it out of a little tube to show it to him. He said it was what he saw at the rock in the range. For that reason, the father decided to go see it. His prelate assigned him to another mission as guardian, which he lamented, then saying that he was sent elsewhere by his prelate so suddenly that it must not have been God's will for him to find it.

From the villa where this happened to the father to Picuris, it must be about 12 leagues. He states that the father told him that the Indian said it is a day's travel from Picuris. From this, he infers that it must be another 10 or 12 leagues to the mountainous country. It is true that women and Indians use almagre to paint themselves red. It is 100 leagues from the villa of Santa Fe to the province of Moqui, where he has been twice. This is what he knows and has declared.

Asked how many men-at-arms and soldiers it would be necessary to take to reconnoiter the provinces of Moqui, as his excellency, the most excellent lord viceroy, says in his letter, and Picuris Pueblo, he stated that it seems to him that from 100 to 150 men and twelve to fifteen animals each will be needed, of which at least twelve should be horses and two mules. It seems to him that for the trip out, stay to reconnoiter everything, and return to this pueblo of El Paso, about six months will be needed. It is a hostile land full of enemies, Apaches as well as rebellious, apostate Indians, enemies of the kingdom and provinces of New Mexico. It will be necessary to provision the 300 Indian warriors and the 150 men-at-arms who are going. Each person, soldier and Indian, will require four fanegas of provisions. This is assuming that there will be an opportunity in one of the pueblos of the province of Moqui to obtain some provisions, meat and maize. For the trip out, stay, and return, they will need to take at the very least 300 cattle, chocolate, sugar, soap for washing clothes, and tobacco for the Indians and soldiers, likewise for the men-at-arms. This will be as his excellency sees fit.

So that it may be of record, he signed it with me, the governor and captain general, and my attending witnesses. I so attest.

Don Fernando de Chaves [rubrica]
Don Pedro Ladrón de Guevara [rubrica]
Alfonso Rael de Aguilar [rubrica]

Don Diego de Vargas
Zapata Luján Ponce de León [rubrica]

Declaration of Capt. Roque Madrid

In the pueblo of El Paso on 11 August 1691, I, the governor and captain general, in fulfillment of and obedience to the letter referred to and placed in these proceedings from the most excellent lord viceroy of all this kingdom of New Spain, had the maestre de campo, Roque Madrid,[43] appear before me. He is currently capitán, cabo y caudillo of the company of this presidio, a person who has traveled through various parts of this kingdom of New Mexico. In my presence and that of my attending witnesses, I read him the letter from the most excellent lord viceroy. He heard it and the points by which his excellency seeks to learn the truth about the metal or cinnabar ore.

He stated that he has seen the metals or ore called almagre in New Mexico; it is heavy and has all the characteristics his excellency states in his letter. From what he was told by the Spaniards and natives of the pueblo of Oraibi, the last in the province of Moqui, there is a big river 12 to 14 leagues from the pueblo of Oraibi. On the other side, the river beats against a large rock. Above the rock is the vein containing the ore or metal. He brought some from the pueblo of Oraibi on a pack animal. It seeped through the bag, or buckskin sack, placed inside the cow hide he was carrying it in and almost through the animal's packsaddle. He neither knows about pools or puddles that produce this ore, nor has he seen them. In the villa of Santa Fe, they used it for one thing and another.

The distance from El Paso to the pueblo of Isleta is 80 leagues, and from Isleta to Moqui and the pueblo of Oraibi would be 90 to

100 leagues. Although there are pasture and firewood, there are, in his opinion, only two shallow water holes, and at times there is no water at all, and he has made the trip.

This is a land of enemy Apaches. It seems to him that at least 150 or 200 soldiers will be needed and at least 100 Indian warriors. Four or five months will be necessary for the task to be carried out well. Each soldier will require at least twelve good horses and four mules. These men should go well armed with all their weapons; the horses bearing their armor; the soldiers with their leather jackets, leather or iron morions (whichever they have), harquebuses, lances, swords, and shields.[44] Each Indian should be given at least one horse.

He also stated that each man will need a sack of biscuit each month made from 2 fanegas of flour. If there is not enough wheat to make the biscuit, 1/2 fanega of maize meal and another 1/2 of pinole, as well as a fanega of wheat, which will make a half-sack of biscuit, can be given as ration each month. This is the minimum a soldier should have to eat each month. In addition, with one head of cattle a soldier will have enough meat to eat for two months. He will also need all the rest—chocolate, sugar, tobacco, and some wine from Castile to heal wounds—and whatever else his excellency may also be pleased to give, such as soap, for washing the soldiers' clothes. All he has stated is what he declares and knows. Also, 2 fanegas of maize for each of the hundred Indians will be needed, for they are hearty eaters, and some tobacco.

So that everything in his declaration may be of record, he signed it with me, the governor and captain general, and my attending witnesses. He stated that he is forty-six years old. I so attest.

Roque Madrid [rubrica]

Don Pedro Ladrón de Guevara [rubrica]

Alfonso Rael de Aguilar [rubrica]

Don Diego de Vargas
Zapata Luján Ponce de León [rubrica]

Declaration of Capt. Juan de Dios Lucero de Godoy

In the pueblo of El Paso on the same day, month, and year, I, the governor and captain general, in fulfillment of and obedience to the letter from his excellency and, if possible, to obtain clearer information, as the most excellent lord viceroy orders me, had Capt. Juan de Dios Lucero de Godoy[45] appear before me. He is a citizen and native of the kingdom of New Mexico and at present lives in this pueblo of El Paso serving his majesty as soldier and leader of one of the squads of this presidio and plaza de armas. In the presence of my attending witnesses, I read him the letter the most excellent lord viceroy sent me, which is placed at the beginning of these proceedings.

After he heard it, he stated that he has been in the pueblo of Oraibi, which is the most distant of them all, in the province of Moqui. He was there for six months. While there, he got a small bag of ore. He had collected it in the pueblo from the Indians. He does not know what the Moquinos of the province call it, but in New Mexico and the villa of Santa Fe, they called the ore or metal almagre. It is very heavy, liquid, and greasy, as his excellency says. When smeared on the hand, it turns bright purple, as if smeared with lard. This is how it is done. It is true that it seeps through the packsaddles and blankets of the pack animals. What happened to this declarant was that the bag he was bringing was wrapped up in a bundle of sixty mantas from the region, and it soaked through all of them.

He heard his uncles, Francisco Gómez Robledo and Bartolomé Romero, say that this ore or metal is in an area one day's travel from the pueblo of Oraibi. His uncles had not heard anything else from the Indians of the Moquino pueblos. He also heard them say that it was only one day's travel and that a river ran below the hill containing the almagre toward where the sun sets. The Indians also told him that two days' travel from that place was another very big river. Because it was so large and the Moquino Indians do not know how to swim, they did not cross it. From this pueblo of El Paso, one can make the trip directly, if desired. It is some 80 leagues, and from Isleta, about another 80, but these are very long leagues, to the pueblo of Oraibi.

It is a hostile, enemy land, inhabited by Apaches. If one enters the heart of their land by way of the province they call Navajo, there are, besides these enemies, the apostate, uprisen enemies of the kingdom and provinces of New Mexico. The land has pasture, firewood, and water, although some days' journeys are necessarily longer to reach the water holes. On the way, there is a stretch of rocky malpais that bruises and peels the horses' hooves. As a result of the difficulty of the terrain and because of the enemies, at least a hundred mounted soldiers will be needed. Each one should take twelve horses and four mules. The trip out, stay, and return will require at least four months.

Each soldier will need a sack of biscuit monthly, made from 2 fanegas of flour, and a two-year-old calf for jerky. With a large cow, he would have enough meat for two months. In addition, each month he should have his hand of tobacco, paper, chocolate, and whatever his excellency may wish to give. Two hundred Indian warriors will need to go. Each Indian should be given a good horse. Every month, each Indian will need a fanega of maize, pinole, and tobacco. He declares this and gives his age as thirty-six.

So that it may be of record, he signs it with me, the governor and captain general, and my attending witnesses. I so attest.

Juan de Dios Lucero de Godoy [rubrica]
Don Pedro Ladrón de Guevara [rubrica]
Alfonso Rael de Aguilar [rubrica]

Don Diego de Vargas
Zapata Luján Ponce de León [rubrica]

Declaration of Capt. Antonio Jorge

In the pueblo of El Paso on 12 August 1691, I, the governor and captain general, in fulfillment of and obedience to his excellency's letter, which is of record at the beginning of these proceedings, had Capt. Antonio Jorge[46] appear before me. He stated that he was a criollo, a native of the estancia of El Alamo, 5 leagues from the villa of Santa Fe, in the province and kingdom of New Mexico. He stated that he is thirty-nine years old. I read him the letter referred to from the most excellent lord viceroy.

After he heard it, he stated in the presence of my attending witnesses that he has been in the provinces of Zuni and Moqui, where he lived in the last pueblo, Oraibi, and in Halona in the province of Zuni, with his father, Capt. Antonio Jorge. His father was alcalde mayor three times in those provinces for former governors and captains general of the province of New Mexico. They were don Fernando de Villanueva, don Juan de Miranda, and don Juan de Medrano.[47] This declarant was the lieutenant of the alcalde mayor, his father, in the provinces of Zuni and Moqui.

He stated that it is true, according to the Indians, that walking six days from the pueblo of Oraibi, there is a hill where there is an opening like a mine. They extract the ore they call almagre from it. The ore is very heavy, in his opinion, as heavy as lead. After the Indians smear their faces with it, they look shiny, as though they have smeared themselves with tallow and stained themselves purple. This declarant tried it by taking a small amount in his hand, which was left stained with a purple color, as if smeared with oil. It soaks through the sacks and packsaddles of the pack animals. They traded the almagre ore, taking it down for barter to the pueblos of Taos, Pecos, and the rest of the custody. He neither heard of pools or puddles of mercury nor did he ask about them.

He stated that the mountain is beyond the pueblo of Oraibi. There is a big river to the west they call the Coninas; he recognizes it since it is the direct route to the Conina nation, whence the river takes its name.

It was a new mission where Father fray José de Espeleta,[48] former custos of those missions of New Mexico, was beginning to make conversions. He lived before and after in those provinces, particularly at this outpost. The distance from El Paso to Isleta is 80 leagues. From Isleta to the pueblo of Oraibi, the last of the provinces of Zuni and Moqui, it is, in his opinion, 100 leagues, and from the pueblo of Oraibi to the river and rancheria of the Coninas, 14. The land along the way has pasture, firewood, water holes, and a level road. There are five pueblos in the province. The first is called Awatovi; the second, Walpi; the third, Mishongnovi; the fourth, Shongopavi; and the fifth, Oraibi. They have many people. It seems to him there must have been more than three thousand warriors at that time, and today there must be even more, unless there has been some plague among them, because it has been eleven years since the uprising of Indians against the kingdom of New Mexico.

This land is surrounded by Apaches. If one leaves this outpost, there are Apaches of the Organ Mountains and of the Gila Mountains, which are extensive, beginning at Acoma mesa about 50 leagues from the villa of Santa Fe and extending to the Florida Mountains and toward the province of Sonora. Apaches live in various parts of them. He reckons that 150 men-at-arms—soldiers—will be needed. In his opinion, the trip, leaving El Paso at the beginning of August, will require twelve horses and four mules. Moving at the company's pace, it seems to him, as an experienced traveler on the road to the pueblo of Oraibi, that four months' time is needed to get to Coninas, reconnoiter the mine, and return to El Paso.

Also, it seems to him that with a load of biscuits (made of 4 fanegas of flour and 1/2 fanega of pinole) and two head of cattle, a soldier will have enough food for the trip. It is also necessary to take a hundred Indian warriors with three horses each to carry their loads. Each will need 3 fanegas of flour and pinole as well as some tobacco.

So that his declaration may be of record, he signed it with me, the governor and captain general, with my attending witnesses. I so attest.

Antonio Jorge [rubrica]

Don Pedro Ladrón de Guevara [rubrica]

Alfonso Rael de Aguilar [rubrica]

Don Diego de Vargas
Zapata Luján Ponce de Leon [rubrica]

Diego de Vargas to the Conde de Galve, El Paso, 26 August 1691, LS.

Most excellent sir,

Sir, with humble attention to my duty, I put into execution your excellency's letter dated 27 May of the present year. I have received the declarations of both the religious and the best-informed citizens. There seemed to me to be a sufficient number for a full investigation: three religious and nine of the most experienced people currently living in these pueblos. Since the uprising in the year 1680, the people who had experience in this kingdom immediately left this land, living spread throughout the jurisdictions of New Biscay, Sonora, Sinaloa, San Buenaventura,[49] Casas Grandes, and the presidio of Janos. I recognize, most excellent sir, that in seeking the greatest economy for the royal treasury, because the provinces of Zuni and Moqui are the most distant of the kingdom of New Mexico, precisely these must be sought if it is desired that they should be reduced and the apostate Indians give their obedience.

Reduction and proof of the mines

At the same time, one can obtain the principal end and extract along the way the proof, which your excellency still doubts, of the report made to your greatness about the mine of metal or cinnabar ore being 12 leagues away. It is very true that there is ore in great abundance, so much so that the natives of those pueblos marketed it

and other natives brokered it. Spaniards who went there also transported it for profit. There was little use of it among the Indians of
the area, although it was among the goods they bartered. They also
kept what they needed to use when there was snow. When they
went out on campaign, they smeared themselves with the ore to
protect their vision. Women also used it on their faces and for
smallpox scars.

According to what they say, it is heavy, liquid, and greasy and
leaves a purple luster when rubbed on the hands. It has the sheen of
mercury in its greasiness. Thus, in his declaration, Father Espínola,
a criollo from Peru, states that if the qualities are as related to your
excellency, it is not only mercury, but pepena metal,[50] the very rich
Peruvian kind or better, thus returning, most excellent lord, the greatest saving to the royal treasury. Two things may be obtained. The
first is reduction of the apostate and rebellious peoples in those
provinces. The second is to determine the truth and find out whether
there is a mine and if so, send your excellency one or two loads
of the metal so that it may be assayed by both physical and chem-
ical analyses.

Flasks to be sent in 3/4-vara boxes

In order to ascertain its purity and so as not to lose it because of
the wetness of the mercury, which soaks through the bags, packsaddles, and blankets, it should be bottled in some large, doubled-walled,
square tin flasks,[51] made in Mexico City. The boxes in which they
would fit should be made there as well. As heavy as they say the ore
is, it will suffice that the boxes be made 3/4 of a vara long and 1/3
wide. In this manner, the pure metal, which is mercury, can be
transported without waste, because, as is understood, it soaks through
the buckskin sacks and hides. Besides, on such a long trip, of about
600 leagues from this province and the mine to the court in Mexico
City, one can see that by transporting it in buckskin bags, the purest
part would be lost. As a result, the ore would lose its value by losing
its mercury content on the trip, but the effort that might have been
made to analyze it completely would not be.

The undertaking could be financed by using the profit it produces,
and the balance could go to the royal treasury. It would be good
fortune to obtain a proven source of mercury in this kingdom,[52] so
that there would always be reserves of mercury needed in mining

districts and the nearby reales of Los Frailes, Parral, Guadiana, and Rosario, as well as the others of Guadalajara and Zacatecas. [53] It would be fortunate if most of these reales could be given mercury with the greatest largess for refining ores and to have mercury in these reales and those of Sonora, Santa Rosa de Cosihuiriáchic, and elsewhere. They will save the silver they now lose by smelting, since the ore is so finely crushed and the metal so dispersed that only mercury can incorporate the salt and magistral added to it. [54] The crushed ore is processed with them until it renders the silver it contains, of whatever purity. Then the amalgam is washed, and the mercury is removed and recovered.

Increase of the fifty-man company

I have considerable experience in mining, and it is true that I shall be happy, most excellent sir, if we have the good fortune to find the mine. To this end, should your excellency see fit, you may examine the declarations. Seeking only to accomplish this in the shortest time, I shall personally take the risk of going with the men your excellency may choose to add to the fifty-man company.

No more than a hundred Indians can go

I advise your excellency that no more than a hundred Indians can go. I shall make the trip with them and the soldiers your excellency may indicate for this company. Your excellency should believe that I shall take whatever actions appropriate to discover the mine: inquiring of the Indians regarding it, taking them along, and treating them well. Doing everything possible, I shall take great pride in serving his majesty.

At this time, your excellency is the instrument and guide who motivates it. Your excellency will be uniquely responsible for informing this whole New World of this benefit, this hidden treasure, should God be pleased to grant me such good fortune. The processing of ores would bring great increases to the royal fifth. [55] Although the ores may be rich in silver that must be processed with mercury, they are neither discovered nor worked for lack of it. Even with silver that can be smelted, they leave veins containing even more silver that must be processed with mercury. If they are worked, it is only to discard this ore to reach what can be smelted lying in the lode visible between veins that sometimes surround the lodes and consist of silver that must be processed with mercury.

The last witness holds steadfastly that there is a mine. He also states in his declaration that eleven years ago, there were more than three thousand Indian warriors, and Apaches on both sides of the river surround them in those provinces. First, we shall seek to reduce the apostates as gently as possible, and if some rebel, they will be consumed once and for all. Those who obey will be safer. Afterward, we shall seek to treat them kindly. We shall cross the river and nation of the heathen Coninas and seek through an interpreter to assure them they need not be disturbed because no harm will come to them. I shall have reconnoitered whatever mountain ranges or hills we encounter.

If we discover the mine, I shall see where the lode goes. We shall prospect for it everywhere, reconnoitering its whereabouts and the direct route. We shall see whether it is a solid hill big enough to be permanent, whether the terrain is broken, and whether it is on the slope of the range. I shall become thoroughly familiar with that place and what is found and make a report to your excellency, placing before it the investigation of the route and the log of the journey, all signed by two witnesses and my secretary of government and war. In my unworthiness, it seems to me this is all I can report to inform your excellency. Yielding in everything to your excellency, may my sense of duty ensure the results (which may serve Our Lord). I leave the disposition of the appropriate means to the judgment and wisdom of your greatness. I shall deliver them immediately, not reserving even a crust of biscuit for my mess. I shall take the provisions necessary not only for my household and me, but also those required by the religious, the chaplains who will go with the soldiers and the apostolic missionaries for the reduction of the Indians.

Nota bene; means applied to provision men and chaplains

The authority of your support gives credence to and assures his majesty's intent with the pardon he offers them to return to the yoke of our holy faith, as is his wish. For this, he is sending me to punish those who oppressed them, freeing them from their slavery. Your excellency will decide about all this and send me as your least servant, who will be flattered to serve you in every way and please his majesty, the king, our lord, for whom I do what looks not only to the expansion of the royal crown, but also to the increase of the royal treasury.

May God keep your excellency's most excellent person many very happy years, as I wish. Done in this plaza de armas of El Paso on 26 August 1691.

Most excellent sir, your least and humblest servant kisses your excellency's hand,

Don Diego de Vargas
Zapata Luján Ponce de León [rubrica]

Most excellent lord viceroy, the Conde de Galve

These acts and proceedings are on ordinary paper because the stamped variety is not available here. So that it may be of record, I, the governor and captain general, signed it. I am sending them to the most excellent lord viceroy of this kingdom of all New Spain. In the presidio and plaza de armas of El Paso, 4 October 1691.

Diego de Vargas to the Conde de Galve, El Paso,
4 October 1691, LS.

Most excellent sir,

Sir, now that these proceedings have been closed, as well as the letter of transmittal to your excellency, I have received information from a certain Diego de Hinojos,[56] who tells me that he knows the mine and has been to it. He gives a very favorable account. The ore is so damp that to extract it they first squeeze it to expel the water. They do this to transport it better, because it is very heavy, and so that it will not soak through the blankets and packsaddles. Diego de Hinojos is a criollo of this kingdom and enlisted as a soldier in the presidio of Janos. I have written his captain and shall pay the 300 pesos owed him for next year. That will be when he sends me this soldier, after the campaign is over. Thus, I shall have him enlisted and ready in this presidio, so that, should your excellency give the order, it may be executed immediately.

I repeat to your excellency that I shall take the risk, in spite of the consequences, of reconnoitering the mine and staying the worry of the rumors and fabrications, which is all they are. Don Fernando de Chaves, one of the principal citizens of this kingdom, told me that his grandfather had told him that in New Mexico, when digging a grave for a burial, a body was found. Many grains of mercury were on the body, so much so that they decided to see who had been buried. They found out it was a prominent woman of the villa. They wondered, from the great amount of ore she had smeared on herself, whether the mercury or grease of the ore had soaked through because her skeleton was saturated.

For the army to cross the river, I shall have many rafts built, and we shall cross although it may be high. According to Diego de Hinojos, the mine is on the other side, about 15 leagues away. He advised me by way of a soldier from this presidio. May God keep your excellency many happy years, as I wish. Done at this plaza de armas of El Paso, 4 October 1691.

Most excellent sir, the humblest and least of your servants kisses your excellency's hand,

Don Diego de Vargas
Zapata Luján Ponce de León [rubrica]

Most excellent lord viceroy, the Conde de Galve

The Conde de Galve, Order, Mexico City,
22 November 1691, ADS.

Mexico City, 22 November 1691

I am aware of the gravity of this matter and the results of the proceedings, carried out by virtue of my order of last 27 May, and what accords with what was proposed to his majesty in this matter by Capt. don Toribio de la Huerta[57] and ordered by his royal cedula of 13 September 1689 regarding its support. I expect him soon in these kingdoms, although he has not yet arrived, and the reason for his delay is unknown. Because this may be detrimental to the royal service and the common good of these kingdoms and the rest of his majesty's dominions, the lord fiscal should review these proceedings, the royal cedula, and the copy of don Toribio de la Huerta's report that accompanies it so that after reviewing it he may propose and request what is most appropriate. [Galve's rubrica]

Benito de Noboa Salgado, Fiscal's reply, Mexico City, 24 November 1691, DS.

Most excellent lord,

I have seen all the proceedings consisting of your excellency's letter and the information the governor of El Paso, don Diego de Vargas Zapata Luján, gathered by virtue of it. The contents, don Toribio de la Huerta's report, and the royal cedula issued about the Sierra Azul and a mercury mine 100 leagues from New Mexico should be read carefully. There are very old accounts that the Sierra Azul has a great quantity of gold, and it is conjectured that the Cerro de Tierra Colorada is mercury, because Indian and Spanish women paint their faces with the ore, tinting them purple. It has the same effect on the sacks and packsaddles used to transport it. The ore is also heavy and greasy. Although from very early times they have brought many bags of it to New Mexico—as so many are greedy for its advantages—no one has tested it to prove that it is mercury. As a result, it all comes down to assumptions, which is no reason to spend the amounts from the royal treasury the witnesses propose. The amounts will always more than double. It will be very expensive to determine the truth. If it were true, to resettle the mine would double the expense.

For one action to produce two favorable results, either of which would be a success, the fiscal has already reported many times how important it is to again subject New Mexico, thus preserving the former dominion and removing the example the rest of the nations have for carrying out insurrections at every turn. Once the Spaniards resettle the villa of Santa Fe, they will find the reconnoitering of the Sierra Azul and the Cerro Colorado easier, since they are 100 leagues away from the villa and very close to the provinces of Zuni and Moqui where there were Spanish alcaldes mayores.

The witnesses state that some 100 (others say 200) soldiers will be needed, some Indians, and their expenses. The fiscal will consider appropriate whatever your excellency may see fit to apply to the reduction and settlement of New Mexico and the villa of Santa Fe. From there, what those hills may hide can be revealed, given that don Diego de Vargas, son of one of the principal families of Madrid, whose sense of duty encourages him in the royal service, is governor in El Paso. With 150 men-at-arms, he should proclaim that all the families of New Mexico should return to their homeland. He should also pardon the Indians and rigorously oblige the Spaniards not to demand personal services from them; rather they should leave them in reasonable and Christian freedom, without punishing them with death for the past uprising. Thus, their reduction and friendship would be inevitable. They will help us as they used to in the wars against other barbarians.

Although the royal cedula grants this commission to don Toribio de la Huerta, a very good and honorable man, your excellency knows well that even though he may greatly desire to act in the royal service, the undertaking is large, and he cannot have the means for its execution. With the financial assistance he will ask for at each step, it would be the same as if his majesty were to do it on his own account. Because the area is so vast, no sort of reduction could be achieved. If such a battle is to be won, it will be only because of your excellency's strength, skill, and industry. The longer the delay, the greater the loss. Don Toribio is in Spain and too far away to carry out this matter. It is unreasonable to expect any one person to finance something so expensive, to which is added the uncertainty of his advanced age. Your excellency will provide whatever you see fit. Mexico City, 24 November 1691.

Dr. don Benito de Noboa Salgado [rubrica]

The Conde de Galve, Decree, Mexico City,
28 November 1691, ADS.

Mexico City, 28 November 1691

Have the former New Mexico governors, don Antonio de Otermín and don Domingo Jironza, who are present in this city, report in sufficient detail about this material and the points that my letter of last 27 May contains so that the best judgment can be made. Place a copy of his majesty's royal cedula of 4 September 1683 about this kingdom with the proceedings, and once done, bring it. [Galve's rubrica]

Carlos II, Cedula, Madrid, 4 September 1683, C.

The King

To the Conde de Paredes, Marqués de la Laguna, my kinsman; of my council, chamber, and Junta of War of the Indies; my viceroy, and governor and captain general of the provinces of New Spain; president of my royal audiencia in Mexico City; or the person or persons who may be in charge of its government.

In the letter of 22 December of last year, 1682, you report that you have given me an account of the miserable state of the provinces of New Mexico, as the result of the uprising of the Indian warriors, in confederation with many of the converts. On our behalf, you undertook the first and second military entradas to ascertain whether by this means some of what was lost could be recovered. You provided the necessary amounts and ordered the establishment of a presidio with fifty soldiers at the ford they call El Paso. You considered them indispensable to protect and defend the convento of religious of St. Francis there and the three missions of Suma Indians, the only ones that had remained in that custody, the Nueva Conversión de Nuestro Padre San Francisco de los Mansos. To be safe, the Spaniards retreated and gathered there. They, the Indians who left the first time, and those they brought from Isleta the last time numbered more than 1,300. Since there was no presidio to hold those who had left on the first and second retreats, the fear was that, because of their inconstancy, the Indians would rejoin the apostates, drawn by homeland, kinship, and liberty. Because the religious who are the missionaries there and the Spaniards lack this protection and defense, they would abandon the site. They would thus leave the new conversion of the Suma and Manso nations exposed to loss, which would also endanger the other new conversions at Casas Grandes and all those that follow each other down one side of the province of Sonora. This would leave the whole border of Parral exposed. They feared and expected very grave damages and hostilities there, with obvious risk to those who had remained. Were this ford to be lost, all hope of restoring the province would vanish. It would be necessary to abandon the new conversions and many in the province of Sonora, in addition to bringing the enemy's hostility nearer to all the kingdom of New Biscay.

The cedula dispatched on 25 June 1680[58] was very influential and persuasive in the maintenance of the presidio and the expenses incurred. In it, you were ordered, as is of record, since there was progress in the conversions in the provinces and the ministers of the doctrine were complying with their obligation, to apply all possible means for their aid and defense in the manner you might think most appropriate to obtain the reduction of the Indians to our holy faith and preservation of what has been and will be discovered. In light of these considerations, you had ordered, with agreement of the general junta, that the presidio should be maintained there. In the interim, with the more detailed report contained in the proceedings you sent, I ordered you to determine whether it was necessary to maintain and proceed with the recovery of those provinces and the province of New Mexico. You were not to have paid for this, so as not to increase the expense to my royal treasury, without a direct order from me.

The contents of your letter have been considered in my Royal Council of the Indies, along with the results of the proceedings you attach, especially those of the general junta held in Mexico City on 28 July 1682. I have at hand the cited cedula of 25 June 1680, what my fiscal requested with regard to it, and his opinion. In view of all this, I have decided to approve, as I do by this cedula, the formation of the presidio with the fifty soldiers you refer to in the place they call the Río del Norte. It is my will that it should be preserved and maintained in the form you have arranged and was decided in the general junta referred to. In this way, not only will the missions and conversions made up to now, those that will be made, and the Spaniards and Indians gathered together be safeguarded, but also the security of the provinces of New Mexico and the mines of Parral, which is so important for their preservation and increase.

Nota bene

Regarding the recovery of what has been lost in those provinces, I charge and order you that, with all possible diligence expected from your zeal and attention to my royal service, you should seek to make the provision that seems most appropriate to you to accomplish the restoration with the greatest economy possible to my royal treasury. You will immediately give the orders for each item necessary as a result of receiving this dispatch. So that I may know what may be done in fulfillment of it and this cedula, my accountants on my Royal Council of the Indies and my treasury officials in Mexico City will record it. Done in Madrid on 4 September 1683.

I, the King

By order of the king our lord
Don Francisco de Salazar[59]
Signed with four rubricas of the royal council

Obedience

In Mexico City, on 1 March 1684, the most excellent lord, the Conde de Paredes, Marqués de la Laguna, my lord viceroy and governor and captain general of this New Spain: Having received this royal cedula from his majesty, I obeyed it and ordered that it be kept, fulfilled, and carried out with the proper respect, in accord with what it provides.

The Conde de Paredes, Marqués de la Laguna
As ordered by his excellency.
Francisco Rico de Arce

———

This agrees with the copy of the cited royal cedula filed with the original proceedings done in this superior government by the cabildo and regimiento of the villa of Santa Fe and don Diego de Vargas Zapata, to which I refer. So that it may be of record, I so certify in Mexico City on 28 November 1691 and make my sign in testimony of the truth. [rubrica]

Cristóbal del Castillo y Tejeda[60]
Royal scribe [rubrica]

———

Toribio de la Huerta to Carlos II, Petition, n.p.,
[1688], C.

My lord,

Capt. don Toribio de la Huerta, a gentleman privileged by the sovereign lords of Castile, your majesty's predecessors, one of the first conquistadores of the kingdom of New Mexico and the provinces of Sinaloa and Sonora, and discoverer of the kingdom of Gran Quivira,[61] which has four kings and an emperor, where Christianity has been destroyed: He says that he has served your majesty for more than forty years in the kingdoms and provinces referred to, in which time more than thirty settlements and reales have been established, and many churches and conventos built, in all of which the petitioner has participated as one of the principal conquistadores. In addition, he has discovered a place more than 200 leagues long, composed entirely of silver ore, from which great quantities are extracted at present. They call this the Sierra Azul. If the site were settled and defended as it merits, it would yield an endless supply.

Likewise, he has discovered another mine containing mercury, from which this whole kingdom, the kingdom of New Spain, and the rest of the provinces and kingdoms already discovered could be supplied. This would be of great utility to the royal treasury, because of the increased expenses that your majesty incurs in transporting this commodity to that kingdom. This mine is between Zuni and Moqui. At present it is beyond the jurisdiction of the royal crown, because the kingdom of New Mexico rose up eight years ago.

This misfortune came about as the result of the limited knowledge that some governors had of the nature of the inhabitants. They burdened them with too many tributes and new taxes without paying attention to the fact that in that province there were neither minerals nor trade goods other than clothing and handwork. This motive obliged them to rise up, to the grave detriment of God Our Lord and your majesty. On that occasion, twenty-two religious and more than eight hundred Spaniards died, and more than sixty churches and conventos were destroyed.[62] The most regrettable matter was their having reverted to being idolaters. The petitioner, recognizing the grave damage that can follow if this province is not subjected to the royal crown, has come to bring this information to your majesty's attention. Various Indian nations are beginning to enter there and little by little taking control of whatever they can, strengthening themselves. If no remedy is sought, the former provinces will end up being lost.

Nothing moves him to this but the cause of God, the service of your majesty, the common good of your vassals, and his love of those lands, since he spent so much time conquering them. For this reason, he offers to subject those rebels to the royal crown at his own expense, if your majesty grants him as a reward for his many services the area from La Toma on the Río del Norte to Taos with the title of marqués with jurisdiction.[63] For the duration of the war, he should be given the military and political government of Sinaloa and Sonora, and in the event of his death, his sons, don Pelayo and don Sebastián de la Huerta, can succeed him.

It is very necessary to secure the area, provide appropriate refuges, and give aid. Should your majesty make him this grant, and give him the convicts, wagons, arms, and munitions as is customary, then he will immediately go to begin the conquest. For it, he will take 1,000 horses, 500 foot soldiers, 2,000 head of cattle, and 6,000 sheep and goats. Thus, he may settle those lands, taking also his children and family. With this, the reputation he has there because of his deeds of forty years, and their awareness of his experience and knowledge of the land, he hopes to accomplish this new service for your majesty.

My lord, regarding what he requests of your majesty, since the region is tyrannized by the enemy and beyond the royal jurisdiction, it seems to the petitioner that if you make this grant to him, the royal patrimony will not be defrauded; rather benefit will result. More than 300,000 pesos will have been wasted without any improvement in the situation. By carrying out what he proposes, he can restore what was lost. There can be great profit to the royal treasury in the future and the assurance that the enemy will not make intrusions there. Moreover, if there is a mercury mine there, it could be a great advantage, because of the scarcity of this commodity in that kingdom and provinces. The petitioner will bring the mine into production, should your majesty see fit to give him the contract[64] for it, in accord with the one for Huancavelica in the kingdom of Peru, and the right to appoint four treasury officials to begin collection of the royal fifths and the rest of the taxes belonging to your majesty.

Until now, the governors of those provinces have only worked for their own self-interest, without regard for the preservation of your majesty's vassals or the royal patrimony. This was the case when don Bartolomé de Estrada[65] and don José de Quiroga[66] were governors. Since these provinces are more than 300 leagues from Parral, where they lived, they sent don Francisco Cuervo y Valdés[67] to travel through them, having delegated all their powers to him. He ruined the entire real of San Juan,[68] took the lives of more than twenty caciques, and caused the rest to revolt by imposing various taxes on them and taking a great part of their wealth.

All this resulted in the ruin and loss of Sonora. On that occasion, he defrauded your majesty of more than 200,000 pesos. Because the administration of seven mines was in the petitioner's care, it seemed to him very much in your majesty's service to give an account of these excesses to the Audiencia of Guadalajara so that a remedy might be provided. After this was done, he was appointed judge for the investigation. He arrested don Francisco, who asked the petitioner to post bail for him, as in fact he did. He put up the amount of 200,000 pesos, risking his estate, so that the defrauded funds might be restored to your majesty. More than 12,000 pesos have been spent on these proceedings, because of the great distance of more than 600 leagues from Sonora to Guadalajara. Besides these expenses, they wasted what was sent to don Francisco Cuervo and he himself more than 40,000 pesos, all out of hatred, at which the petitioner sought to prevent the royal treasury from being defrauded.

Don Francisco Cuervo fled from the Guadalajara jail before measures could be taken, having been assisted by the guarantors, who posted bail of more than 3 million. When the royal audiencia recognized the truth of the petitioner's accusation, it ordered his estate returned, freeing him from the bond he had posted. Having seen that no decision was made regarding the fraud don Francisco had perpetrated, the petitioner appealed to your majesty's Royal Council of the Indies, where the suit is at present. From this, it will be seen that everything he has said is true as are the rest of the documents he has presented at the office of the secretary of the president of the Royal Council, and others he will present when your majesty so orders to justify this petition. He requests that your majesty make him the grant he asks for in remuneration of his services and because he wishes to continue them. This will be in accord with your majesty's justness and Christian zeal.

Since the fleet is about to sail, may your majesty please see fit to order that the grant be dispatched in time to go with it.

———

This is a copy of the petition that remains at the office of the secretariat of the Council and Cámara of the Indies that handles matters pertaining to the provinces of New Spain, which is in my charge. It was sent from here to the lord Conde de Galve, viceroy of that kingdom, with a dispatch dated today from his majesty, Madrid, 13 September 1689.

Don Antonio Ortiz de Otalora [rubrica]
Copy
Corrected

Carlos II, Cedula, Madrid, 13 September 1689, C.

The King

To the Conde de Galve; kinsman; gentleman of my bedchamber; my viceroy and governor and captain general of the provinces of New Spain; president of my royal audiencia in Mexico City; or the person or persons who may be in charge of its government.[69]

Don Toribio de la Huerta's petition has been considered in my Junta of War for the Indies with the report on this matter by don Lope de Sierra Osorio[70] of the Council of the Indies, the rest of the papers on the matter, and what my fiscal requested and advised me. I have resolved to order and command you (as you will see by the dispatch dated today, which don Toribio will present to you) to listen carefully to his proposals expressed herein. Once this is done, you should take the appropriate measures you think necessary to verify and learn what can be granted to him from all that. For his part, if he provides the means and avails himself of the help of his friends and relatives to accomplish what he promises, you will give him the title of marqués. I shall give don Toribio de la Huerta grants and honors corresponding to the fruit of the services he may perform and whatever else corresponds to his merits and the services I expect from his zeal. I shall take care to liberally reward his descendants and those who aid him personally and with their wealth in the attainment of the cause, which is in God's service and pleasing to me.

It occurs to me to advise and order you, as I do, not to neglect this matter; rather you should attend to it with all the care and zeal that is expected from your Christianity and sense of duty. So that you might better inform yourself of all that is related and offered by don

Toribio de la Huerta, I am sending you with this dispatch a copy of the report he put in my royal hands, which was signed by my secretary below. When you see it, you will make a special investigation into its content, as I order you. You will seek out zealous, prudent people from among the best informed in that kingdom and those places and provinces to instruct you and make you competent to decide what should be done and whether don Toribio de la Huerta, his sons, relatives, and friends have the means and abilities for an undertaking of such consequence. When this individual arrives, if you find that the aim can be advanced, you will honor, favor, encourage, and assure him that I shall award him grants of the greatest honor and esteem, earned by the service he and his associates may perform.

For this enterprise, you will see that he posts bonds satisfactory to the treasury officials for whatever goods and other things they may provide him. As soon as you know the fruit and effect of his promise, you will give the appropriate orders so that the governor and my royal justices of New Biscay may encourage him and prudently give the aid and assistance necessary, attending to the state and relief of my royal treasury. In this way, it is possible that very great service to me will be brought about, as well as an imponderable good for the provinces adjoining New Mexico, and principally the goal of restoring the souls of those miserable Indians to the profession of our holy Catholic faith, from which they have parted, and attracting many others to the same knowledge.

You will give me a clear, organized, and detailed account on the first occasion that presents itself of the receipt of this dispatch and the report that goes with it, which don Toribio de la Huerta carries and will present to you, and what you decide and do about this. You will send the originals or faithful copies to the Junta of War of the Council of the Indies in confirmation of what don Toribio says he will do to accomplish what he has proposed and the bond he may post to assure it is done. It has been brought to my royal attention that if the reduction of New Mexico does not proceed, to discuss the advantages that could follow from working the mercury mine this individual says he discovered and examined between Zuni and Moqui would be in vain. Once brought into production, it could be the greatest treasure of those provinces and the greatest increase to my royal treasury, but its existence cannot be verified, since it lies deep within the lands of the rebel, enemy Indians.

Please be informed that since don Toribio de la Huerta is at present short on funds, I have ordered him to be given 200 pesos, silver escudos, as assistance, drawn on my treasurer of my Council of the Indies, to aid him. By the dispatch of this date, 400 silver pesos of 8 reals, which in Spain are escudos of 10 reals, are ordered drafted on and paid at my Royal Treasury office of Veracruz, so that he can pay his passage and return to that kingdom. You are thus advised so that you will have this information. Done in Madrid on 13 September 1689.

I, the King [rubrica]

By order of the king our lord
Don Antonio Ortiz de Otalora[71] [rubrica]
[5 rubricas]
Copy
   To the viceroy of New Spain, with a copy of the report that don Toribio de la Huerta has presented about the proposals he makes to undertake the conquest of the provinces of Zuni and Moqui in New Mexico, so that he will carry out what is ordered and give an account of what will be decided and done.
Officially issued.[72] Corrected. [rubrica]

Domingo Jironza Petrís de Cruzate, Opinion, Mexico City, 1 December 1691, DS.

Most excellent sir,

   I hereby comply with your excellency's order in your decree of 28 November of this year in which you see fit to order me to report in sufficient detail to promote a full understanding of the matter and points contained in your letter of 27 May, written to the current governor of El Paso. After review and examination of the measures taken in its fulfillment and the depositions of the witnesses, I recognize that in a practical sense this matter is impossible to carry out. If the cause is not removed, then the desired effect cannot be achieved, as the lord fiscal says in his reply, which is in these proceedings, and as experience has taught me on entradas I made on various occasions when I held the post of governor and captain general. In the provinces of New Mexico, there is a long-standing tradition about the existence of a Sierra Azul and gold deposits. None of our men, however, has managed to examine it in person, since it is so far from El Paso. Although it is true that the ore, or cinnabar, exists, it is impossible to report the specific details required, much less with the certainty needed.

Regretting the loss of such extensive provinces, my zeal for the greatest service to his majesty compelled me to inquire at length and in written reports about those losses. I carried this out with people who were knowledgeable about the land and sent the information to the most excellent lord viceroy, the Conde de Paredes, Marqués de la Laguna, in my report of 12 May 1686,[73] which will be in the offices of the secretary of your excellency's superior government.

He saw it and ordered it brought for a test, which was made; no mercury was found

In it, the distances from one place to another, the terrain, climate, and water holes are described clearly and distinctly, especially those of Zuni and Moqui, with maps. Just last year, when I made an entrada on 7 August 1689, I had information about the cinnabar ore—one of the points in your excellency's letter—and had some brought to me. After I saw it, I arranged to test its mineral content by assay. I made vessels for this purpose. An assayer very knowledgeable about such matters carried out the assay. He found nothing that might indicate the presence of mercury, although it may have been that some necessary ingredient for the essential extraction was lacking and not available there. It might have been possible to attain this end had there been a substantial supply of this ore to test carefully to see whether it had mercury. I am convinced that the long-time residents of that kingdom, if they knew of it, would not have assayed it, because it is so far away and in enemy territory, where one could not enter without being well-armed and provisioned. This is what I am able to report, in obedience to your excellency's orders. Mexico City, 1 December 1691.

Don Domingo Jironza
Petrís de Cruzate [rubrica]

Antonio de Otermín, Opinion, Mexico City,
11 December 1691, DS.

Most excellent lord,

This is in fulfillment of what your excellency orders me by decree of 28 November. I have seen what your excellency wrote to don Diego de Vargas, governor of New Mexico, what you ordered him, and what he answered; the declarations of those he examined to this end; the opinion of the lord fiscal by your excellency's decree of the twenty-second of last month; and the two cedulas from his majesty. I now turn to the execution of my report, limiting myself solely to the points in your excellency's letter, which seems to be your intention, although it seems inexcusable to me not to touch on the point of the reduction of the apostates, which one supposes is an essential point in the decision about discovering whether there is mercury.

From my limited talent for understanding New Mexico and its disposition, it seems that today the essential and even principal reason for bringing about the reduction has become the undertaking of the journey to Moqui to discover the mercury, rather than dealing with the reduction of the apostates. As the experience of all the conquistadores, beginning with Cortés, shows us, all their conquests and reductions were as by accident or as if subsidiary, since the lure of gold and silver was foremost. New Mexico lacks these, leaving aside rumors about its great wealth, and also everything necessary for the families who would have to settle there. There are not even houses to live in. Because of this, one can understand that the ones who left, defeated by the insurrection, have a great loathing for that region. For this reason, and fearing they might be forced to return, they left for distant jurisdictions, so that of the places they left, only the one on the Río del Norte remains. As a result, one can understand the difficulty of dealing with the reduction and settlement of the apostates.

Although one might want to do this first, as we all want, it would always be necessary to make an entrada to investigate their current situation first. This is because, aside from their obstinate loathing of the holy faith, we know they have returned to their enmities, as to their former ways, warring against each other. We know neither their present circumstances nor whether there are fewer now than when we left them. Spaniards cannot maintain themselves without Indians.

Therefore, since we must make the entrada to reconnoiter, for which expenses will be incurred, I think it better to enter the province of Moqui first because of the mercury. Should it require processing, then reduction of the Indians will be very easy, since this will require settlement in the same part of the mountain range where the mines are and reduction not only of the apostate Indians of Moqui, but also obedience and subjugation of the Cruzados,[74] Coninas, Apaches, and other Indian nations that may be around the mines to work them. Later it will be necessary to reduce the pueblo of Zuni and the mesa of Acoma for free passage on the trip by the people, wagons, and pack animals for transport, as well as the rest of the custody. In this case, as I say, little will need to be done to reduce them.

I see, sir, the conflicting opinions of the witnesses in don Diego de Vargas's proceedings, especially regarding the number of soldiers necessary for the journey to Moqui. Some say that two hundred are required and others seventy. I am not unaware, sir, that there are enemy Apaches on the road that goes to Zuni and from there to Moqui, but I also know they were there before the revolt. Ten or twelve men, and sometimes fewer, used to go between the custody and the province of Moqui as escort of the religious and the person going to inspect the province; the trip never required more.

Sixty soldiers and a hundred Indians

The province of Moqui, which comprises five pueblos from what I remember, may have as many as five hundred Indians able to take up arms. We also know they have had setbacks, so that today there must be fewer of them, so they may cause less concern. One of the declarants exaggerates the risk, which I consider none at all for fifty or sixty well-armed soldiers and a hundred Indian allies, even in that part of the range where the mines are. That is where the Cruzados and the Coninas are, and they are neither numerous nor very warlike. Assuming that they are at peace with the Moquinos and learn of the Spaniards' departure before they arrive at Moqui, the Indians may band together to offer some resistance, which I consider impossible. It would be advantageous to take care to arrive at Moqui without being noticed and strike the first two pueblos at dawn. Having disarmed them, the Spaniards could then go on to the other pueblos and do the same thing. They could then go in complete safety to the mountain range to finish unhurriedly what they set out to do.

For this reason, in my previous report, I told your excellency that if it were possible to go by Zuni without being seen, it would be better. In this way, they could not warn the Moquinos that the Spaniards were going there—not so much for the risk to the Spaniards, as for their carrying off supplies and the little livestock they may have, risking a lack of supplies for the Spaniards' return trip. If they could not get by without being seen by the pueblo, or because they lack provisions or water in that territory, they could make a dawn attack. The Indians could all be secured and their weapons taken from them. Without doing this, no one would dare to go on to Moqui or return to the custody.

Provision that the El Paso presidio not be left without men

It seemed appropriate to me to give these warnings to ensure the greatest safety, but not from fear of risk. Numerous times I have seen 40 men with 300 Indians go in and out to punish the Apaches in the heart of their lands without any significant misfortune. That being the case, once they noticed the soldiers, they would warn each other with smoke signals, and the surrounding rancherias would gather quickly. Even so, I am certain, sir, that 50 or 60 well-armed and -mounted soldiers can enter with 100 or 150 Indian allies to undertake the action without risk. Supposing that the presidial soldiers enter to undertake this action, they should be equipped with everything necessary: weapons, horses, mules, and supplies. Regarding this, I suggested in my previous report that this journey would not be very expensive. I also suggested what the expense would be for the Indians and some extra volunteers. It seemed to me then, as it does now, that they should go as well. I also remember proposing to your excellency that, because of the threat to El Paso in the absence of the presidio, Capts. Juan de Retana[75] and Juan de la Fuente should order some soldiers from their presidios to go there until the return of the El Paso presidial soldiers.

All the declarants in don Diego's proceedings seem to agree that there is a cinnabar mine, where it is, and its quality, although they do not know whether it contains mercury. Gov. don Domingo Jironza seems to indicate that he tested it and did not find any sign that the cinnabar contained mercury. He does not say who the assayer was, so that based on his reputation or qualifications one could evaluate his assay and the cinnabar, which is what is being sought. It is just a matter of finding out what I can already assure your excellency with complete certainty. As I have told you before, the sargento mayor, Diego del Castillo,[76] was in the province of Moqui for five years in the post of alcalde mayor. From him we learned about the cinnabar, that it contained mercury, and about the Sierra Azul. As someone interested in mining, he extracted the ore that was necessary from the mine for assay. This same man brought a blue stone veined with gold from the Sierra Azul as a sample. He gave it to his brother-in-law, the maestre de campo, Francisco Javier,[77] so that its proceeds might be brought from Parral for the most holy Virgin.

Even though this is not pertinent to the matter at hand, I wanted to mention it here so that you might know that someone has been to the Sierra Azul. He was the only Spaniard who went. We and everyone else found out about it from him and that he extracted mercury from the cinnabar. He was also the one in the story about the Indian who drank hard water from the pool, which ran right through him. As I have told your excellency, I met the Indian and have spoken to him many times. He always confirmed what he had said the first time.

The reckoning of the distance from the villa of Santa Fe to the province of Moqui varied, as it did in the declarations don Diego de Vargas took. Some thought it was 100 leagues from the villa, and others, from Isleta. It is 30 leagues from the villa to Isleta. What they do agree on is that from Isleta to Oraibi, the farthest pueblo of Moqui, is 89 leagues. Going on in this manner, from Isleta Pueblo to that of Acoma, it is 18; from Acoma to Zuni, 24; and from there to Oraibi, 47. With the 12 from this pueblo to the mountain range where the mine is, that makes 101 leagues in all. Today, though, to go from El Paso to the province of Moqui, it is not necessary to go up as far as Isleta. One can leave from the former pueblo of Senecú, 30 leagues this side of Isleta Pueblo, and take the direct route to the pueblo of Zuni, or one can pass to one side and from there to Moqui. I find little difference in going from Senecú or Isleta to Zuni because of how much worse the road gets toward the west from Isleta by way of Acoma and from Zuni to Moqui. From Senecú to get to the route, one travels to the northwest, so that, as I say, there is little difference, unless it is finding water holes along the way. Since the road from Senecú to Zuni is little used, a judgment cannot be made and an exact location of water holes cannot be given. There are, however, many Indians in El Paso from Senecú and the pueblo of Socorro, 12 leagues above Senecú, who have knowledge of the land from when they used to campaign there with the Spaniards. They will know the water holes.

Should the decision be made, the most propitious time to leave on that journey would be as soon as the snows have melted, around April, which is when the water holes are full and everywhere. They would be able to take advantage of the summer for the trip out and back.

This is what I have to say, fulfilling what your excellency commands me. Mexico City, 11 December 1691.

Don Antonio de Otermín [rubrica]

Mexico City, 28 December 1691
To the lord fiscal
[Galve's rubrica]

Benito de Noboa Salgado, Fiscal's reply, Mexico City, 4 January 1692, DS.

Most excellent sir,

His majesty's fiscal has seen these two reports from the former governors of New Mexico. Referring completely to everything in the reply of 24 November 1691, he says that with regard to don Antonio de Otermín's report, because he was governor when New Mexico was lost and this unfortunate situation continued when he returned to restore the province, it is not surprising that he speaks with so many misgivings and precautions about the difficulty of reduction. This should be done only upon your excellency's effective decision, for his majesty desires it, according to the royal cedula placed in these proceedings and issued to the most excellent lord, the Conde de Paredes. Uprisings against his royal superiority set bad examples for those barbarous nations who do not understand it, but must be made to see it. Thus, they must be made to understand by force of arms. Your excellency will see fit to leave the way this is done to such valiant captains as serve under your superior order. They will obey it with devoted affection. When your excellency is no longer viceroy, your generous spirit will continue to inspire such an important undertaking, securing the lost dominions and preserving those at peace for his majesty. Thus, your excellency should seek, first and before anything else, to resettle New Mexico. For, if it is said that with 50 men and some Indian allies, it is possible to go where the mercury is, then with 150 men there will be enough people to defend the settlement and reduction of New Mexico, together with its settlers, and send some of them on to the discovery, so that they may deliver to this city twelve loads of ore, half blue and half red, so that the assay can be made in the appropriate manner. Your excellency will provide in everything what you judge most advantageous to the royal service, and, as always, the best. Mexico City, 4 January 1692.

Dr. don Benito de Noboa Salgado [rubrica]

———

Mexico City, 5 January 1692
To the junta
[Galve's rubrica]

Diego de Vargas to the Conde de Galve, El Paso, 30 March 1692, LS.

New reduction of Indians of 30 March

Most excellent sir,

Sir, at the time I entered and took possession of this government, I found living in the pueblo of Socorro (5 leagues from this presidio and pueblo of El Paso) the nations who are natives of the kingdom of New Mexico and some Christian Sumas. From the time of their second uprising and general conspiracy, when don Pedro Reneros de Posada was governor, and during it, they were living in the pueblo of Guadalupe. There, with increased expense and care, the former father custos, fray Nicolás López[78] (who died in the convento of El Paso), took great pains to carry out perfectly the work on its church and convento, as I say.

This very reverend religious, and his predecessors who were in that prelacy, believed in the Indians' truthfulness. Because the outpost was flourishing with an increased number of cattle, they allowed the Indians to enjoy their freedom and generously gave them cattle. Nevertheless, they rebelled and burned the holy church and convento. Its father guardian and minister, who assisted them in order to free them from savagery, had the good fortune of being away. There is no doubt the Indians would have taken his life. I was told they tore to pieces everything the religious had in his cell.

The uprising caused the governor to seek appropriate punishment for such an outrage. He had the skill and cunning to bring the Indians together, where he surrounded them with the men-at-arms of this presidio, though they were disbanded. He ordered the soldiers to kill some of them. By chance, one of the religious who live in this holy custody arrived at the time of this skirmish and managed to help some escape and save them from perishing. Even though barbarians, they understood that he had sheltered them from danger. I also saw this very thing when I arrived on my entrada.

Likewise, in the two Piro pueblos that are called Ysleta and Senecú,[79] some twenty heathen Sumas and a very few Christians live. They used to be at Ysleta and Socorro, where they elected a governor and alcaldes from their own nation, so that they might be more secure, living with some government. Those who had risen up, their allies, and relatives were found encamped and living in this place, which is as good as lost, at risk because of their treachery and infidelity. They were absolute lords of this place. It is 14 leagues from this outpost of El Paso, and from there, they went wherever they wanted, because they were free to, and communicated with the people camped at those pueblos. They came and went, although as secretly as they could, in order to communicate with them. They dissimulated about the hope of their reduction, always responding with opposition and equivocal words every time it was proposed by those who lived in the pueblo of Socorro that they should return to the pueblo, to have their church and lands to plant. Because they were so free, they responded in such a way that they were left alone. It was thought there was no hope for them because of their evil nature, their well-known treachery, and the repeated attempts at their reduction. Our Lord was pleased to dispose circumstances in such a manner that they might move me, with the obligations of my position, to make them understand by demonstration how knowledgeable I was about them.

The first method I employed was to treat kindly and with much affection the ones who live in those pueblos, having them tell the others how much I wanted them to be at peace. For this, it would be good for them to come and settle, because I had letters from the captain of the presidio of Janos complaining about them. He advised me that it was the Sumas of Guadalupe and Ojito who were entering in the company of the Janos and Chinarras[80] to raid the pueblo of Casas Grandes and the provinces of Sonora. If they did not come in to settle, for that reason he would have to destroy them there, if he could. They lived there, sustaining themselves on fish and grain that the place provided them. It also had a great abundance of mescals and tunas in season. They stole two horses belonging to the Keres nation at Socorro,[81] which made things worse for me. Its governor considered the matter in writing, warning me that the Sumas were evil and their rancherias rising in rebellion as quickly as they could and leaving the pueblo. This forced me to leave the rancheria of the Mansos where I had received the document, taking with me twenty soldiers, the captain, and the alferez of this presidio, to go out and verify its contents. Finding the Sumas in the pueblo, even though they were frightened, I tried to dissuade them from their intentions to assure they would not leave. They supposed, since they are such suspicious people, that the occasion of my sudden trip and arrival there was because I had information that the Chinarras and Conchos[82] had made a strike against the wagons leaving the salina. When I was alone with the governor who wrote the document, I told him to advise me what they might do and try to collect payment for their horses, using me as a threat. He did so later, and they were paid in buckskins.

In the month of July, I had occasion to sound a call to arms, in response to another document I received with information that Apaches had carried off the horses from the pueblos of Socorro and Ysleta. I was obliged at midnight, for that was when I received word, to get up and send for enough horses for mounts for two squads and give orders to send the allied Indian warriors ahead to follow the enemy's tracks from those pueblos. After the horses arrived, I mounted up at dawn with the squads and the captain of the presidio. I went to the pueblo of Senecú, where the scouts informed me about the enemy's route and of their tracks apparently leading toward the Hueco Mountains. Then I ordered the captain to cross the river with his soldiers and follow the enemy's route and tracks. When they found them, they should advise me so that I could provide according to the number of tracks made out and the direction of their route.

After I had issued the order and was about to go straight to where it was thought the enemy was going, the governor of Socorro arrived at the pueblo of Senecú, where I was. He told me he was coming to give me word that the Indians who carried off the horses were not Apaches but Sumas, and were from Guadalupe. For this reason, it was necessary for me to send the captain a new order so that he might approach through the wooded area along the river, lying in ambush with his men. I would return to mount up another two squads so that they might go to Guadalupe, and as soon as the enemy noticed them, kill as many as they could. He should destroy and kill those who might flee to the other bank of the river, lying in wait until the battle might break out on this bank. He would be able to tell by the shots and the noise.

I left for the pueblo of Socorro with the squads, going as far as the place they call Presidio Viejo[83] on the following day, where the father chaplain came with the squad leader. I gave the latter the order that, if there were no tracks, he should go to Guadalupe, and if the Indians did not flee and were peaceful, he should do them no harm. It happened that, when the soldiers arrived, the Indians approached them, laying down their weapons. When the captain of the presidio noticed them, he crossed the river with the men in his charge to that place. The Indians greeted them with fish they caught in the river and told them among other things that they were happy the soldiers had come and seen that they were not stealing horses. They were told on behalf of our men that they could now see the trouble we had gone to and that, if they did not live right, they would be punished and thrown out of that place. The arrival of the soldiers left them confused, since they had not committed such a crime on that occasion. In the interim, I ordered the horses rounded up in the pueblos. They were in the bosque, and it could not be determined whether this was the result of a stampede. This is likelier than that they were taken by Indians. The people who went on that mission realized they could scarcely make out three or four trails and that even these could not be said with certainty to be Apache or Suma. Thus, everyone lived in fear, especially the Indians.

With respect to my first skirmish with the Apaches, they were friendly with some rancherias from among the Indians I took for the battle. This was a troop of Indians who lived in the pueblo of Socorro with their governor. They were in the skirmish and much disliked. Then I realized that this could be the basis, as was said, for the beginning of their affection for the father, who favored them in their difficulty. His name is Father fray Antonio Guerra, and he was guardian at the convento of El Paso and secretary of the very reverend father custos. I conferred with the father about whether it would be wise for him to go with an escort of some soldiers to see the captain of the nation and rancheria of Guadalupe. He was a Christian who had rebelled at that time. The father should tell him he could also assure him of a pardon from me or the punishment I could give him and the rest of his rancheria for having committed such a great crime. They should come to see me, because the father would have assured them I would do them no harm. Regarding the question of whether the father has, in his opinion, the confidence, or is motivated by his fervor and apostolic state, he responded that he appreciated the escort, but said he did not need it. He would go alone with the governor and some Spanish-speaking Indians of the pueblo of Socorro, so that with them, he could reassure them of my good will and my wish for them to return and be reduced to our holy faith and give obedience to his majesty, in whose royal name I would pardon them.

They should choose a place

Thus, he immediately set out on his trip, and, going to Guadalupe, saw that the captain they call don Felipe had gone to the interior to live. The father went there and found him after walking a great distance. He asked him why he lived so far away. He responded that the Suma Indians of Guadalupe had done something, and he did not want to live there with them, being made to pay for them. He lived quietly and wished only good for the Spaniards. He said other things that enabled the father to move him to be reduced so effectively that the father told me how tenderly the Indian responded to him and the tenderness with which he listened to him. This had the effect of his coming with him, accompanied by those who were of his nation. Its governor, with some who were newly arrived, came to this outpost into my presence and that of the father. I spoke to, embraced, and treated that Indian and the rest kindly. I told them what I desired: their return to our holy faith. I would pardon them in his majesty's name, and they should tell the rest of their rancheria, relatives, and friends that they should select the best place next to the pueblo of Socorro, so they might be safe from the Apaches, as were the rest. They would have their pueblo and church and open their acequia, thereby assuring the fields they had planted. They would have everything they needed, as they saw the other Indians had.

I told them this, because I pitied them and wished them well, and that they should come. If my intention had been to destroy and kill them for their great crime, I would have already done it, as I had with the Apaches, which the governor and the others had seen. They responded through the father that they would come after harvesting their grain and go to collect their people and tell them they could come safely. They did so, after having fought with a rancheria of Apaches where they killed four and captured a few, though it cost them two of their own. When they arrived, those who were in the pueblo of Socorro pointed out the site. After having seen it, they thought it was good. They saw the intake for water from the river and the path of the acequia.

So that this would be fully carried out, the current very reverend father custos, fray Diego de Mendoza[84] (during whose tenure what is related occurred), ordered Father fray Antonio Guerra to go assist with the intake and the acequia, so that the Indians might attend to the work on it. With great zeal, the father has served God Our Lord and his majesty by his punctual assistance. He carried out his prelate's order with great kindness, and his assistance has shone with pains-taking care. As of the date of this letter, the Indians have finished the intake and the acequia in that place, which is 7 leagues from here and 2 from the pueblo of Socorro, so that they are within sight of each other.

Three hundred Indians reduced

They number some three hundred Christians and heathens, who, it is hoped, will become Christians too. One lives in the hope that they will be steadfast by having labored joyously at that task, without asking for anything, building their houses and beginning to build their church.

This is to inform your excellency of this new mission and pueblo reduced to our holy faith and that this is their only land and that it is next to Estero Largo. Should the Divine Majesty permit the con-quest of New Mexico, and his majesty order the natives of the rest of the pueblos to move, then those of the Suma nation, who are natives of this land, will always remain, with their present pueblo and newly founded outpost, if God sees fit. Your excellency should also be informed that since it is a new church, it should be aided with the usual contribution his majesty has ordered for the bell, vestments, missal, and the rest.

For this reason, I have given your excellency such a detailed report, and I shall be pleased in every way if my wish is appropriate. From what has been written, your excellency will see that the foregoing is both cause and effect of what follows. You should also know that the very reverend father custos and the other fathers of this holy custody humbly wish for the increase of our holy faith and, with the vigilance of their apostolic zeal, eagerly wish for its spread. As loyal vassals, they fully obey what his majesty orders them, always stopping short of saying what they might about their activities and their duty.

May God keep the most excellent person of your excellency in your ever-increasing nobility the many happy years I wish. El Paso, 30 March 1692.

Most excellent lord, your humble and dutiful servant kisses your excellency's hands,

    Don Diego de Vargas Zapata
    Luján Ponce de León [rubrica]

Most excellent lord viceroy, the Conde de Galve

———

El Paso, 30 March 1692, don Diego de Vargas Zapata y Luján
Received 20 May

He advises about the new reduction, pacification, and congregation of as many as three hundred Suma Indians at a distance of 7 leagues from El Paso and asks for a bell and sacred vestments for the church they are building.

———

Mexico City, 21 May 1692
To the lord fiscal
[Galve's rubrica]

Benito de Noboa Salgado, Fiscal's reply, Mexico City, 21 May 1692, DS.

Most excellent sir,

His majesty's fiscal has seen this letter from the governor of El Paso in which he gives an account of the reduction of three hundred Suma Indians of those who had rebelled. Today they reside in the place described, 7 leagues from El Paso and 2 from the pueblo of Socorro, at the insistence of the governor and of Father fray Antonio Guerra. Thus, your excellency will be pleased to order that thanks should be given to both for this battle and reduction, and also that sacred vestments should be sent immediately, as well as a chalice, paten, and bell, in conformity with Law 7, Title 2, Book 1 of the *Novísima Recopilación de Indias.* Your excellency will order what is best. Mexico City, 21 May 1692.

Dr. don Benito de Noboa Salgado [rubrica]

Diego de Vargas to the Conde de Galve, El Paso, 7 April 1692, LS.

Salinas
Most excellent sir,

Sir, because the Apaches' raids are continuous and repeated on moonlit nights, I determined that the only thing needed in this area was the direct route to their salina and the Sierra Negra.[85] The salina is necessary to this settlement because of the lack of this ingredient. The small salina they had on the other bank of the Río del Norte in past years was submerged by the flooding and swelling of the river, so that they lost that source, leaving them totally without a place where they could supply themselves. They have got by, relying on the extraction of some coarse salt from the small salina on the road to Casas Grandes. It is used in Parral for the processing of ore with mercury. In the time of my predecessors, don Pedro Reneros de Posada and don Domingo Jironza, they sent troops of soldiers and some citizens at various times to find the Apaches' salina. They returned so as not to perish on the way, because there is no water.

Route to Apache salina has no water

Those who went told me that, having traveled two hard days and a night, they returned. They did not continue the search for lack of water and because they knew neither the distance nor the direction where they would find the salina. They traveled to within sight of the mountain range they knew of, the landmark of the salina. They did not find it, and so as not to get lost, they returned, and because of the risk that their animals might tire, took the shortest route to the river to provide relief for themselves and their horses.

He took twenty-two people and sixty Indian allies
From Saturday

Despite what has been said, I wanted to try my luck, relying on the Apache Indian who has been my prisoner since my first skirmish with his nation last September. I left, taking with me no more than twenty-odd people, soldiers, officers of this company, and two citizens who also wanted to go, in addition to sixty allied Indian warriors. I spent the night, Saturday, 8 March, in the pueblo of Socorro, next to the Río del Norte, about 5 leagues from this outpost.

I left on Sunday, the ninth of the month, between eight and nine in the morning with the men-at-arms and the Apache Indian as guide. He took me toward the Hueco Mountains through sand dunes and lands with many boxwood bushes.[86] We reconnoitered as we traveled. As the sun was setting behind the Hueco Mountains, I advanced with a few men on fast horses to see whether there were any Apaches, because this was their land and where they hunt. The rest of the camp arrived after vespers. The march must have been about 12 leagues.

On the following day, Monday, at ten, I left the mountains. The scout went, taking the route to a shallow water hole called El Alamo. Since there was no water for the horses and at vespers it was still a long way, I ordered a halt on the savanna along the route, and the men-at-arms and I slept there. Since there was no water for the horses, I sent a troop of twenty Indians ahead so they might reconnoiter the mountain range and El Alamo water hole—in case the enemy was camped there—since they had never set foot there. When the morning star appeared, we rode to the water hole, arriving at ten o'clock.

I reckoned the distance to be about 18 leagues, with some stretches of malpais and land all covered with boxwood bushes.

I found the scouts at El Alamo water hole, and they told me the water hole scarcely had enough water for the people. We drank our chocolate there, because we could not build a fire the night before lest we be discovered by the enemy thought to frequent that water hole.

I greeted the Apache scout warmly and asked him through an interpreter where there was water for the horses. He pointed to some mountains that could be made out from the rise and hill at the water hole El Alamo, taking a route due east. Apparently, they are between 9 and 10 leagues away. Having arrived at the mountains, I crossed the cañada that divides them. On the right side of the mountains was some green underbrush where there seemed to be water, and so there was. We found a pool of rainwater, where some of the horses drank, and my vanguard and I continued on.

After finding the tracks of three Apaches, I ordered the captain and the sergeant with some Indians to enter through the cañada in the mountain range on the left. While they kept watch and reconnoitered, I skirted its washes and ravines with another few Indians and three soldiers, not waiting for the rest of the men and thereby losing the advantage our luck might offer us. After having gone more than 4 leagues, we came upon a pool of rainwater in the wash of a ravine, which made us very happy. We halted, awaiting our company, and saw some deer. The captain and the sergeant arrived, coming out of another ravine in the range. They said they had neither found Indians nor seen tracks. They found water and many deer there and said it was full of tunas and mescals. The Apache scout said that during the rainy season there are tunas, and Apaches live there. Since the men-at-arms were all together, I ordered them to halt there, and we spent the night at that place.

On the following day, Wednesday the twelfth, after warmly greeting the Apache scout, I asked him where the salina was that the Apaches took salt from, which he had promised to tell me. He pointed to the path next to a very high mountain range that could be made out and above it, a mountain with a pointed crest. It appears to be split in half and in the direction of the rising sun; that is where the salina is. By traveling hard, we could be there that day by sunset. As a result of the Apache's declaration, I ordered the captain and ten soldiers to come with me on their fastest horses and that each should lead another by the bridle. I also ordered the twenty fastest Indians to come and the rest of the camp to follow my tracks with their horses. I was going on ahead with the men, taking the scout along on one of my horses, so that we could arrive earlier to see whether the enemy was there, look for water and pasture for the horses, and reconnoiter the salina. The captain and the men-at-arms mounted up and carried out my order.

We left about seven in the morning. Traveling at a good pace, I ordered at midday that the mounts should be changed rapidly and drank some chocolate with the men-at-arms. Going at a harder pace, at a gallop I came to where I could see the salina from a little hill and high rise at around three in the afternoon. From there, we saw the salina. Happy and content, we thanked God for our success in having discovered this place.

What the salina is like

After a little more than a league, we arrived at the salina, which is like a laguna. At its widest, it seems to be between 40 and 50 varas and as long as a musket shot.[87] Its banks are exposed and dry for 5 to 6 varas, and all the rest of the laguna proper has water that comes up to the calf in places and in others to the knee.

The sediment of the salina is so thick and hard that we chopped it up with a mason's pick and a carpenter's hatchet. We took some pieces, thicker than a span and as wide as we wanted and could get out. The hardness of the sediment is determined by the thickness and density of the crust, which is very white and salty, like the sample I am sending in the little bag. How I wish, most excellent lord, it were from the mine of cinnabar ore, that is, mercury, reported to be in the province of Zuni on the hill near the river where the Coninas Apaches live.

I saw and reconnoitered the salina and surrounding area, and there seemed to be others. Later, the Apache took me on toward a vega, where he thought the enemy might be and there might be fresh water for the men. Having gone more than a league and a half, we found that the springs he talked about were dry. We only found one with a little water; only one horse drank, and the water was all gone. We had to return to the tulare and the area that drops down to the salina.

Having returned, we found it to be a ciénaga and discovered that the water, although hard and brackish, could be drunk out of necessity, as we did. So that the horses might not get bogged down in the ciénaga, as happened with the first horses, which fought to get to the water because of their thirst, I ordered the men to perform a task. With the hoes[88] I brought along as a precaution, they were to make some furrows, drainage ways so the water could get out to firmer ground and pools or puddles so the horses could drink from them without risk. The undertaking was achieved, and they drank very happily.

That night, I brought the Apache scout to my tent. I asked him various questions: whether, in the mountains that flanked us and extended so far, another salina could be hidden in the distance where the enemy might be or where there might be water. He answered me that he thought most of the Apaches would be gone from the mountain ranges. They would have gone to the Río Salado, which would be as far again as I had already gone. The mountain range ahead was the Sierra Negra, where the high peak was, and in front of it water would be found, and there could possibly be a rancheria there.

Nota bene

The following day, Thursday, it was necessary to stay where we were so the horses could recover because they were exhausted from the excessive cold and the long days' journeys to the water holes found by means of divine providence and even chance. Therefore, it occurred to me that we should not leave without searching and reconnoitering the Sierra Negra, locating the water hole to see whether the enemy was there. Thus, that night I ordered the captain to guard the camp and horses and the Indians to do the same and extract their salt and have some ready and collected for everyone. Of the soldiers there were, I chose nine with their squad leader to mount their best horses and lead one by the bridle. Likewise, he was to summon the Indian war captains for me. I ordered that only twenty Indians should come with me. I chose them and ordered him to have them ready that night, so that at daybreak, we might leave and still have time to return, since we had a lot of ground to cover.

Other salinas, and in all, thirteen

So, on the following day, Thursday,[89] I left on horseback at daybreak with ten soldiers and twenty Indian warriors. Heading straight toward the salina we had discovered, we went by it and headed in the direction of the mountains and high peak. Having gone through a vega with many boxwoods for some 3 leagues, I reconnoitered and carefully investigated salinas that followed one after another into the distance, some larger and some smaller. I saw and counted thirteen. In some along the route of our march, I found salt that was very fine and white, which they call flor de sal.[90] Having gone that distance from the vega, I skirted the Sierra Negra, because there was a trail I discovered with the experienced men. I split off from this Apache trail, having the adjutant take the hillside and the rise of the mountains on the right-hand side. Using the trail as guide, I followed it in with six men, going up and down many hills of malpais and mountains into a funnel-shaped canyon where we found ourselves unable to get out, because the heights of the range reached to the sky. We saw the high peak rising like a wall.

We waited there for the adjutant and his compañeros, who came two hours later. They said they had discovered on the top of the hill in the direction they had taken a sabino and, at its foot, a spring of flowing fresh water and another, further along. He would take me and show me that water hole. The two water holes would be sufficient for the horses when it was necessary to make the expedition and campaign to the Río Salado and reconnoiter that terrain. Realizing I could do no more, and since it was already late and I had to go 7 or 8 leagues more to where I had changed horses, we changed horses again and returned. On leaving the funnel-shaped canyon, the adjutant showed me that one could make out on the high rise what seemed from below to be someone scouting our camp at a canter.

Friday

On the following day, Friday, at one in the afternoon, I ordered the horses brought up and departed with the men, who took all the salt they could carry. We traveled very contentedly for having discovered it and reconnoitered the enemy's land, their water holes, hiding places, hunting grounds, and pasturage.

Then, the scout told me he would take me a new, shorter way to get to the river, even though we would pass through a stretch of mountainous country and a funnel-shaped canyon with very rough going, sleeping without water for two nights, and traveling altogether three and a half days.

Until Monday

This was how long it took to travel the new route and way, entering the pueblo of Socorro, Monday, 17 March, and El Paso, Tuesday, the eighteenth, to celebrate the feast day of the patriarch St. Joseph,[91] patron of this presidio.

Until Tuesday
Eleven days

This was the successful conclusion of this expedition and the previous campaign to the Florida Mountains in pursuit of the enemy Sumas, in which they were killed and imprisoned. This new discovery was requested by my previously mentioned predecessors at the urging of the father custos, fray Nicolás López, who died in this holy custody.

In everything, I shall wish for success in properly serving your excellency, and so that you may be informed, I shall maintain this kingdom as carefully as I can, which is my duty. May God keep your most excellent person in your ever-increasing nobility many happy years, with a long succession of so royal a lineage, as your humble servant wishes. El Paso, 7 April 1692.

Most excellent sir, your least worthy and most indebted servant humbly kisses your excellency's hands,

Don Diego de Vargas Zapata
Luján Ponce de León [rubrica]

Most excellent lord viceroy, the Conde de Galve

———

Mexico City, 21 May 1692
To the lord fiscal
[Galve's rubrica]

Benito de Noboa Salgado, Fiscal's reply, Mexico City, *21 May 1692, DS.*

Most excellent sir,

This letter is devoted to relating to your excellency that the governor of El Paso has made a trip to discover the salinas from which the Apaches supplied themselves, as in fact he did, along with other water holes and various places, of which your excellency may consider yourself notified for whatever importance this may have in the future. Mexico City, 21 May 1692.

Dr. don Benito de Noboa Salgado [rubrica]

Diego de Vargas to Juan Isidro de Pardiñas, El Paso, *9 April 1692, LS.*

Dear sir,

Notwithstanding the two directives issued by his excellency, the most excellent lord viceroy of this kingdom and that of New Spain, with agreement of the general junta—the first on 4 August of last year, 1691, and the second, whose contents I am sending you on this date by the same courier, who is Capt. José de Padilla—the citizens who withdrew from this kingdom to different areas and settlements of New Biscay did not show the care, obedience, and humility they should in fulfilling these directives. Instead, they are rebels who neither do their duty nor recognize the benignity that the greatness of his excellency's royal lineage freely bestows upon them in this second directive. Many of the citizens and other people respond with equivocal and imaginary arguments, saying that for the entrada to the kingdom under control of the uprisen, apostate Indians, they will gladly take part promptly, if advised in time, because they most eagerly desire it. They will live in that kingdom if it is reconquered. So that the citizens and other people who are in your kingdom and government of New Biscay may understand and be notified of my decision, it has occurred to me to notify you in great detail what I have decided, which is to depart this presidio with its company in early July.

I shall begin by ferrying the provisions and military supplies for war from this pueblo and ford of the Río del Norte, first sending the horses and mules ahead. The people referred to who agree to make the entrada need to know how long it will take and that they must equip themselves with horses and weapons. I shall give them munitions and, from the day they enter this plaza de armas, order their meals provided, and that they have their chocolate to drink, morning and afternoon. I shall do this during the period of their stay, service on campaign, and return (should God see fit to grant us life), and also for the time they may be resting in this pueblo of El Paso, and not hinder their return to their homes. I shall provide weapons to those who are without lances or escopetas.[92] I shall relieve them during their service on campaign from being assigned by the militia leaders to any quarter watches[93] or being selected for squads that may be necessary to reconnoiter the enemy.

Regarding everything mentioned, my decision, and the preparations I have made, my intention is to assist these people by feeding them, giving them ammunition, and providing them weapons. Moreover, if the war, which must be carried out justly against the rebels,[94] should produce captives, I shall favor these people in their distribution. This is all I can do in the royal service.

So that they may learn of it, I ask you to order this letter made public on a feast day at the time when most of the citizens and other people are gathered, so that it may come to their attention. Be good enough to see that your secretary of government and war certifies it and that it is witnessed by the public or royal notary who may be in that real. May God keep you for the many years I wish. El Paso, 9 April 1692.

Your most affectionate and surest servant kisses your hands,

Don Diego de Vargas Zapata
Luján Ponce de León [rubrica]

Lord governor and captain general, Juan Isidro de Pardiñas

Diego de Vargas to the Conde de Galve, El Paso,
17 April 1692, LS.

Conquest
Most excellent sir,

Sir, I am sending this courier, as is my humble duty. In your excellency's order of last 4 December, passed with the agreement of the Junta of the Royal Treasury, your greatness orders me, after I have returned from the expedition to and campaign in the province of Sonora, to inform you about the conquest of New Mexico, whose nations have been in rebellion since their uprising in 1680. In 1681, Gen. don Antonio de Otermín made an entrada with a substantial number of soldiers; a large stock of provisions, horses, and mules; many suits of armor; and thirty-two wagons, which were all that this holy custody had at that time. The men-at-arms were veterans of this kingdom and still had passionate feelings about the loss of their kin, property, and homes. All these circumstances must have provoked them to seek satisfaction by punishing the enemy. In addition, royal providence, through the person of the most excellent lord, the Conde de Paredes, then viceroy, provided the amounts of record in the royal account books.

Most excellent sir, although my adverse fortune has ridden roughshod over me and finds me in this region, I wish to dedicate myself in service and loyalty to my king, to see the extent of his dominion, and try if I can—without causing concern, much less difficulty, to your excellency and the lords of that royal junta—to restore that kingdom with the pride of my well-known sense of duty and lineage. I am making preparations to go there. I have only a few horses guarded in the summer pastures with the mules, and I shall have those only if the enemy Indians do not force me to take part of the herd to follow and destroy them. I am also supplied with provisions: cattle, rations of biscuits, pinole, flour, chocolate, sugar, wine, panocha, cheese, wax, medicines, soap, tobacco, paper, and besides this, the accouterments for the religious who will go with me. In this way, God willing, I shall, without the slightest doubt, begin to ferry the supplies and other military equipment, munitions, and tools, with a crate of harquebuses I find satisfactory to replace the men-at-arms' worn-out weapons.

Then, on 12 July, I shall first have the squad that guards the horses leave from this pueblo of El Paso. Once it has crossed to the other side of the river, it will receive the horses, along with the provisions. Afterward, I shall cross with the people of this company, a hundred Indian allies, the muleteers with their trains, and cattle on the hoof with their escort, all equipped with horses and mules, also at my expense.

It is my responsibility to conclude the entrada to the pueblo of Cochiti[95] and on to the villa of Santa Fe, even if all the power of the world opposes it. I shall overcome or reduce them, first making them recognize that the intent and desire of the king our lord is that they give obedience to God and king. If they do not avail themselves of my suggestion by means of the three or four apostolic fathers of this holy custody (who will be chosen by the very reverend father custos and whose care will be my responsibility and who will eat with me as brothers), I shall repeat it to these nations through the interpreters. If they still do not avail themselves of it, I shall destroy them by force of arms, saving only the little boys and girls.

This, most excellent sir, is my firm resolve. I repeat that fifty soldiers would be necessary for this presidio, and with them, I would conquer all the kingdom of New Mexico. The Indians would then see that they are vassals and would worship in our holy faith. I repeat that I shall make an entrada with the soldiers into those nations of the interior. Wherever camp is made, the place will be held securely and the royal standard raised in front. Likewise, if the enemy Apaches who infest the whole region should dare take a few horses or mules or attack the camp, it will have the necessary protection.

After the kingdom has been conquered, if his majesty intends for it to be resettled, the soldiers of the garrison and others will serve as a reserve in order to escort the supplies, the soldiers' families, settlers, and religious who go there. It is necessary to thoroughly patrol where the enemy may come and go to commit robberies. This is common among Apaches from different rancherias, such as the Faraones of the Llanos, Siete Ríos, Salineros, the ones from Chilmos, those of the Río Salado, and many others.[96] They were all at war, committed many robberies, and caused deaths when New Mexico was under their control. They had frontier pueblos with cuarteles and towers with stone mortars, and in some, they tell me, they also had an artillery piece. Your excellency will see that, with no remedy at present, the increased number of citizens and their ranchos, haciendas, and pueblos would be at risk, such would be the enemy's boldness. Because of that, as I have said, fifty additional soldiers will be necessary for this presidio for the conquest, and if the region is to be settled, for the escort of the families and to protect them for three or four years from the Indians, as much from those newly conquered as for safety from the Apache nations. When that period, or whatever one his majesty thinks appropriate, has passed, you can decrease the number of soldiers as you see fit, leaving those necessary.

I have nothing more to report to your excellency and the lords of the Junta of the Royal Treasury. About all this, your excellency will command me as your greatness sees fit. I repeat and affirm in this letter that with fifty soldiers added to this presidio, I shall conquer the kingdom of New Mexico, where the rebels have risen against our holy faith and the royal crown. He who will put this to the test with the fifty men and his person where the greatest opposition is, in Cochiti and the villa of Santa Fe, is the one who has this presidio at present. He will hurl himself with the additional fifty men into battle against the rest.

May God keep the most excellent person of your excellency the many happy years in your ever-increasing nobility, as I wish and is so necessary. El Paso, 17 April 1692.

Most excellent sir, your most dutiful and least worthy servant humbly kisses your hands,

Don Diego de Vargas Zapata
Luján Ponce de León [rubrica]

Most excellent lord viceroy, the Conde de Galve

———

El Paso, 17 April 1692
Don Diego de Vargas Zapata y Luján
Received on 20 May

He says he is leaving around July by way of the cordillera of Santa Fe, New Mexico, to fight the Indians and their intervening settlements as far as the capital and custody. He gives a reason for the preparations he has made for this operation. With the additional fifty salaried soldiers, he will conquer New Mexico, restoring it to its former state.

———

Mexico City, 21 May 1692
To the lord fiscal
[Galve's rubrica]

> *Benito de Noboa Salgado, Fiscal's reply, Mexico
> City, 22 May 1692, DS.*

Most excellent sir,

The governor of El Paso offers to reduce to its former state all the kingdom of New Mexico, which is in rebellion. For this he may be given fifty paid soldiers above and beyond the ones the presidio has, facilitating, as much as he is able, the reduction of that kingdom. In the fiscal's opinion, the governor will need to take one hundred effective soldiers with him. In addition, thirty will remain in the presidio of El Paso with a good leader satisfactory to the governor for reserve, defense, and security of the presidio and its inhabitants. The hundred men with the Indian allies are needed for the expedition to the villa of Santa Fe, to settle and maintain it while your excellency decides what needs to be done. The fiscal does not doubt that, decisively entering that villa and peaceably informing the pueblos, they will be reduced without force of arms. An uprising is never so deep-rooted that there are not many people, though in the minority, of a contrary opinion. Thus, for success, the fiscal thinks it appropriate that at least those hundred men should go to do battle, leaving, as was said, thirty in the presidio.

Your excellency, with your great providence and understanding, will do what you judge most appropriate, for our good name requires the restoration of New Mexico. Mexico City, 22 May 1692.

Dr. don Benito de Noboa Salgado [rubrica]

> *Diego de Vargas to the Conde de Galve, El Paso,
> 17 April 1692, LS.*

Conquest

Most excellent sir,

Sir, I received your excellency's order passed on last 4 December, with agreement of the Junta of the Royal Treasury and its lords minister. In it, your excellency orders me to send it to the jurisdictions where the citizens and natives of this kingdom are found, so they may be informed about the privilege your excellency in the name of his majesty grants to those who return to this kingdom and provinces of New Mexico. I carried it out in this way, ordering it made public. It is true, most excellent sir, that my short discourse aroused opposition and made the order difficult to carry out. They offered arguments against the measures necessary for the fulfillment of the order, much to my sorrow. In the face of this resistance, I struggled because of my great lack of knowledge. I was saying, How is it that the love of a vassal for his majesty becomes opposition? I was saying that only out of the goodness of your excellency's heart and royal lineage could you make such a concession to those vassals who had abandoned their legitimate homeland. If you consider that one reaps what one sows, I would have expected your excellency, by means of the preceding order agreed upon in the same acuerdo of last 4 August, to order me not only to have the magistrates compel those citizens to come, but also to advise you of those who did not comply with it properly.

It occurred to me to tell your excellency my opinion in my letter of 4 October about the difficulties that present themselves to me to advise you, for the consideration of your excellency's nobility, that just and proper execution was lacking, since you repeat those provisions in your present directive of 4 December. When I was confident they would go, you ordered me to go in person to wherever the citizens were living in freedom, camped out on small hills, in cañadas, and on savannas, and demolish their dwellings and bring them to this kingdom. They deserved this because of their rebelliousness, in addition to having their leaders and instigators punished, separating the rebellious from those who willingly followed the directive. I see that your excellency bestows the privilege of hidalgo status and other grants upon those who may come. They have found, as I repeat, the antidote for the venom of their guilt in your excellency's greatness, for you not only absolve, but also reward them. I fully recognize, most excellent sir, that those who attended the junta, which your excellency has frequently attended and presided over as their prince on his royal throne, would propose to you such absolution. It would seem to them the easiest way, but not the harsh one these people deserve.

Nevertheless, I cannot avoid responding to your excellency, explaining about my opposition to the execution of your order. I carried it out to the letter, as you ordered me, with one exception and comparison *interminis*, deriving from it the proof and consequences of my blind ignorance and difficulty in opposing fulfillment of your order, which was determined, premeditated, examined, and reviewed in such a serious, grave tribunal as a junta of the royal treasury. The lords of the junta decide, having at hand his majesty's laws and cedulas, so they can give the correct summary of your excellency's provision. The one exception is, sir, that if all the delinquents do not take advantage of sanctuary in sacred places,[97] we should identify and except those who should be reprimanded and excluded from the prerogative because they should assist them. These citizens of New Mexico claim, regarding its reduction, that: laws of reales apply to those who live in them; laborers' ordinances apply to those on farms; and whatever laws apply to those in presidios, either as enlisted men or others living there covered by the laws, ordinances, and privileges. His majesty concedes this to people who are at liberty, free and without obligation, and distinguishes them from people like those of New Mexico, for the force of being compelled and the rigor of the law coincide.

They should not be looked upon as free, because they are under the obligation of being original settlers, and children and grandchildren of such. The cost to his majesty at the time this kingdom was conquered is of record. He assisted them again, when, in 1680, Gen. don Antonio de Otermín was governor and sought to restore it to the royal crown from the uprisen enemy nations, in rebellion since that time and to this day. At that time, he brought suit against some of these citizens for disobedience and rebellion against his majesty's order by refusing his directive. These suits can be found in the government office where they were sent.

From this, most excellent sir, in addition to proving my difficulty, I reach this conclusion based on my exception regarding the difficulty and opposition to obeying your directive. If the delinquent citizens should be distinguished and defined as such, then the laws and royal ordinances do not apply. Should the royal justices wish to interpret, they may be favored when they should be excluded, considering that they are original citizens at the royal crown's expense. As such, they are of a different nature than those covered and protected by such laws and royal ordinances. On the contrary, they bear the blot and stain of having failed law and king, denying their homeland by fleeing it. Some were eyewitnesses to and others heard evidence of the crime of lese majesty in the uprising against the royal crown. The Indians rose against his law, killing the religious and priests and profaning the churches and divine images of God Our Lord, His most holy Mother, and the saints. They committed every atrocity, sacrilege, and iniquity possible, and some that cannot be imagined, as though forsaken by God and possessed by the devil.

Most excellent sir, if this did not move the citizens, How could honor and the natural love for their relatives and descendants who perished at the hands of the enemy? They abandon the kingdom and leave, living with this outrage, without taking into consideration this cause—so much a part of their reputation—abandoning their law, their king, and their country. I am not going to try to persuade them with love, because I can scarcely trust them for any undertaking requiring people who have remained loyal and have concern and zeal for their reputation. These are the ones I love and esteem; they are the ones who in the crucible of their labors, hunger, and nakedness have borne up well. Cheerful and loyal to their king, these, most excellent sir, are the ones worthy of such privileges, to be preferred to all others who may participate in the division of lands and other grants so much in your excellency's royal and magnanimous breast.

I beg you to receive from my loyal heart in the service of his majesty and your excellency these poorly drawn sketches. Without flattery, but out of my strong, sure desire, I shall always live humbly at your feet. May God keep the most excellent person of your excellency in your ever-increasing nobility. From this plaza de armas of El Paso, 17 April 1692.

Most excellent sir, your least worthy but most dutiful servant humbly kisses your excellency's hands,

Don Diego de Vargas
Zapata Luján Ponce de León [rubrica]

Most excellent lord viceroy, the Conde de Galve

———

Mexico City, 21 May 1692
To the lord fiscal
[Galve's rubrica]

*Benito de Noboa Salgado, Fiscal's reply, Mexico
City, 22 May 1692, DS.*

Most excellent sir,

His majesty's fiscal has seen this letter from the governor of El
Paso, the one attached dated 9 April, and the copy of the one he
wrote to the governor of Parral so that his planned expedition to New
Mexico in the coming month of July may be made public. This was
to conform with your excellency's orders to settle New Mexico. He
reports at length on the little effect that numerous dispatches have
had, since none of the refugees, citizens, and settlers who left New
Mexico have wanted to return, excusing themselves with various pre-
texts. Your excellency will see fit to order new dispatches issued,
declaring in them that those citizens who will not return will be considered unfit for and unworthy of royal service and offices of the republic, which will be recognized once the expedition is under way. Your
excellency will order in everything what is for the best. Mexico City,
22 May 1692.

Dr. don Benito Noboa de Salgado [rubrica]

*Diego de Vargas to the Conde de Galve, El Paso,
9 April 1692, LS.*

Conquest

Most excellent sir,

Sir, the time has passed during which the refugee and native citizens of this kingdom could have obeyed the two directives provided
by your excellency with the agreement of the Junta of the Royal Treasury on 4 August 1691. For my part, I have humbly carried them
out to the letter, sending the certifications of the directives to the
governor and captain general of New Biscay, his lieutenants general, alcaldes mayores, and other magistrates, as well as to his lieutenant and alcalde mayor of the province of Sonora. I also sent my
lieutenant governor and captain general to the pueblo of Casas Grandes and its jurisdiction of the outpost of San Buenaventura where
more than twenty-five or thirty of the original, legitimate citizens of

this kingdom are settled. They all departed, as did the rest of the fugitives, leaving this kingdom unprotected, and against all that was provided, ordered, and arranged by the most excellent lords viceroy, your excellency's predecessors.

Your greatness may be certain that neither the privilege, nor honor, or your excellency's promise to those who come that they would be considered hidalgos and participate in the distribution of lands and other grants that in your magnanimity you may see fit to give, has been the means to achieve its reduction. Instead, they fail to recognize their obligation, for which their only excuse is their inability, because they say they are responding and confront the people I have sent who have carried the certifications of your excellency's directives. As far as coming to live here, they decline and absolutely refuse. As for the entrada to the kingdom of New Mexico against the rebellious, apostate Indians, they will come when called.

To see whether their words are pretense, because mine are constant, I have decided they should know my intention and the means— the how and the when. I am sending the original of the copy of that letter to the governor and captain general of the kingdom of New Biscay, his lieutenants, and alcaldes mayores. After having seen and examined it, I ask that they make it public and that my wish and what I am prepared to do be made known to those concerned.

I would like to have everything for your excellency, without pointing out or proposing anything, not even the opinion you ordered me to give, except to give an account of my humble desire to restore that kingdom of New Mexico. I have nothing more to add but that I have responded, demonstrated, and reported to your excellency all that occurs to me. It only remains for me to address the question of the means for my entrada, whose results may be as I hope, trusting in divine mercy.

May your excellency's greatness prosper and your most excellent person for countless ages, as I need. El Paso, 9 April 1692.

Most excellent sir, your least worthy and humblest servant kisses your excellency's hands,

Don Diego de Vargas
Zapata Luján Ponce de León [rubrica]

Most excellent sir, the Conde de Galve

———

Mexico City, 21 May 1692
To the lord fiscal [Galve's rubrica]

> ### *Benito de Noboa Salgado, Fiscal's reply, Mexico City, 22 May 1692, DS.*

Most excellent sir,

His majesty's fiscal refers to the reply, dated today, to the other letter from this governor on the same point about which he speaks here. Mexico City, 22 May 1692.

Dr. don Benito de Noboa Salgado [rubrica]

———

Mexico City, 23 May 1692

Take to the junta all these letters from the governor of El Paso with the replies the lord fiscal has given to them. [Galve's rubrica]

> ### *Junta of the Treasury, Mexico City, 28 May 1692, DS.*

In the Junta of the Treasury held on 28 May 1692 by the most excellent lord Conde de Galve, viceroy of this New Spain, with the lords Dr. don Juan de Aréchaga and Lic. don Francisco Fernández Marmolejo, judges of this royal audiencia; don Andrés Pardo de Lago and don Mateo Fernández de Santa Cruz, comptrollers of the Royal Tribunal of Accounts; don Sebastián de Guzmán, don Antonio de Deza y Ulloa, don José de Urrutia,[98] treasury officials of this court: Five letters written to his excellency by don Diego de Vargas Zapata Luján, governor and captain general of the provinces of New Mexico, dated 30 March and 7, 9, and 17 April of this year, were examined in this junta. In the first, he gives an account of his decision about the entrada he has considered for the conquest he intends of the rebellious nations of those provinces. He has planned it in such a way that he will be ready to carry it out on 12 July of this year. No other help with the expenses will be necessary for this purpose than the fifty soldiers he has requested. With this assistance, he will assure the performance and execution of what he promises. He explains in this letter and the previous ones about this subject, the mode and circumstances he brought to your excellency's attention because they were noteworthy and very weighty matters. He goes on to say that a proposition of such consequence needs closer inspection and greater means to obtain so effective an end, and that he has made such a decision.

This intent is supported by the proceedings undertaken by virtue of the letter-order placed at the beginning about the reconnoitering and exploration of the Sierra Azul where there is said to be mercury. Two royal cedulas, dated 4 September 1683 and 13 September 1689, followed, because they were necessary for the matter at hand. At the same time, a report about their contents was made, and they were carried out to the letter. Their tenor and that of the proceedings informed one precisely how to proceed in the resolution of this enterprise. Having executed it in this way and after having discussed it, everyone was of the opinion and agreed that the means proposed by the governor of New Mexico for the reduction and conquest of the rebels, as well as the very words of those two royal orders, coming so close together and for the same end, seemed to be not by chance, but by special divine providence.

The first royal cedula ordered the recovery of those provinces with all diligence so that their restoration may be obtained with the greatest economy to the royal treasury, approving everything else spent on this matter for the preservation of what had remained. The second concluded that, unless the reduction of New Mexico comes first, it is useless to discuss the advantages that might follow from developing the mercury mine, since it is in enemy territory.

Also advanced for your excellency's consideration and wisdom is that the individual who had promised the entrada and reconnaissance of the mine had not come to this kingdom and his delay was detrimental not only to the royal treasury, but also to the common good. At the same time, and with a similar decision (as is of record in his letters), there is a man with the sense of duty and lineage of don Diego de Vargas. By all that was related, it had come to be perfectly understood that the entrada for the conquest and restoration of the provinces of New Mexico should be carried out in the form the governor and captain general had proposed. There was no doubt that these two royal cedulas favored and supported this decision because it conformed to the royal will, which explains the form it takes. The royal will was for them to be restored with royal Catholic zeal so that the apostate rebels might be returned to our holy faith, which is more clearly stated in the second cedula. In it, he orders that the reduction was to be carried out first, instead of pursuing the advantage of development of the mines and savings to the royal treasury.

For now, the governor asks for no other means than the support of fifty men-at-arms, who are indispensable, because he demonstrates the lack of citizens in that place he can avail himself of. As will be arranged, they must be presidial soldiers from Parral, whom his majesty pays.

It is also the case that the governor is a person of such outstanding qualities, lineage, and sense of duty that he far outdistances the other candidate, don Toribio de la Huerta, who, according to available information, could not dutifully carry out the task completely. For the stated reasons, this can be expected from the governor's zeal, because only with his valor and great nobility could such a proposal have promise.

So that your excellency and all the lords of this junta may give him many thanks and so that he may promptly know that, in appreciation for the way he has proceeded, he will be assisted with the aid he requests, the governor and captain general of Parral should be ordered that, as soon as he receives don Diego de Vargas's letter requesting him to send the fifty soldiers, he should do so. He should take them from the four newly established and the old presidios of that kingdom, removing some of the fifty men from each presidio in such a way that their absence will not be greatly felt, as it will not be if done under this arrangement. They should be sent with their weapons and horses wherever don Diego de Vargas directs them, so that they will be at his disposal and under his orders, until they have another order from his excellency. The governor and captain general of New Biscay is to carry this out promptly and in such a manner, neither delaying sending nor detaining them under any pretext, motive, or argument, with the warning that if he does not do so, a most serious charge will be made against him at his residencia. Sending the soldiers wherever don Diego de Vargas requests them will result in the least delay in this particular for what can be produced and expected to be of usefulness in the greatest service to his majesty. These are the means chosen in this junta as most advantageous, because he does not imply that they are necessary for the entrada.

By sending them to him wherever he asks for them, he can avail himself of and use them as he sees fit. In this manner, the plan is better assured.

It is also declared in this junta that the time has not arrived for the reconnaissance of and prospecting for the cinnabar mine in the Sierra Azul, because further investigations and details are necessary. The governor, don Diego de Vargas, making the mentioned entrada to the villa of Santa Fe, will be able to request and make further inquiries, availing himself of whatever means seem most advisable. He will send the information to his excellency, whenever there is occasion, also informing him of the results his entrada may be producing when he sends to Parral for the soldiers or whenever he has an opportunity. His discretion will devise means for everything, and he will continue to show the same concern, as much for his person as for any event caused by war. If there are any objections, they may be dealt with over time, notwithstanding the confidence his good character assures, for which his majesty (may God keep him) will honor him, upon notice of his labor and desires in the royal service, responding through his excellency with the rewards that will be his.

Regarding the citizens who have withdrawn from those provinces of New Mexico, so that they may return to them, let the dispatches the fiscal requests be carried out subject to their penalties. As for the information about the discovery of the salinas, the governor should be thanked and his excellency advised about what may be of importance in the future. Also, thanks should be given to the father custos and to fray Antonio Guerra for the reduction of the three hundred Suma Indians. For this, send vestments, a chalice with paten, and a bell as the fiscal asks. Carry this out through an agent as soon as possible.

So that all the points included in this decision may be understood, issue the dispatches and in the one about the entrada, insert an exact copy for Gov. don Diego de Vargas, so that he may understand the contents. Thus, they resolved and signed with his excellency. His excellency; Lords Aréchaga, Marmolejo, Pardo, Santa Cruz, Guzmán, Deza, and Urrutia [4 rubricas]

---

*AGN, Historia 37:3. 77 folios, 157 written pages. Also in AGI, Guadalajara 139:4, fols. 61r–175v. A translation of the Conde de Galve's 27 May 1691 letter to Vargas and some of the Sierra Azul testimony are in Maas, *Misiones*,

139–49, with omissions. A translation of the Galve letter is in J. Manuel Espinosa, "The Legend of the Sierra Azul with Special Emphasis upon the Part it Played in the Reconquest of New Mexico," NMHR 9 (Apr. 1934):130–31. Fragments of letters from Vargas to Galve are in the same article, 140–43. J. Manuel Espinosa has published a translation of the junta document of 28 May 1692, "Report of the Finance Committee of the Government of New Spain, March 28, 1692, Officially Authorizing Governor Vargas to Reconquer New Mexico," NMHR 14 (Jan. 1939):76–81 and in *First Expedition*, 43–47.

1. The term Moqui (Móokwi) is the tribal name for a people and area now designated Hopi. In Vargas's day the Spanish pronunciation would have been Moqüi (Mókwi). Because early Spanish was usually written without diacritics, later observers assumed Moqui (Móki) to be the proper pronunciation. When anthropologist Jesse Walter Fewkes discovered in the 1890s that Moqui closely resembled the Hopi word móki, meaning dead, which was offensive to the Hopis, he pushed to change the accepted form to Hopi. In Third Mesa dialect, hópi means "good in every respect," while in Mishongnovi, on Second Mesa, hópi is "wise, knowing." John C. Connelly, "Hopi Social Organization," in *Handbook*, 9:551. John P. Harrington, "Notes on the Names Moqui and Hopi," *American Anthropologist* 47 (Jan.–Mar. 1945):177–78.

2. The river referred to here is the Little Colorado and the prominent mountain range, the San Francisco Peaks.

3. The Spanish phrase los metales o tierra de bermellón is translated as metals or ore of cinnabar. Bermellón and cinabrio were synonyms in this period for a heavy, red ore that contained mercury.

The ore identified here as cinnabar, however, is either hematite, an iron oxide, or red ocher, a mixture of hematite and clay. Europeans reportedly mixed red ocher with wax and applied it to the skin to fill in hollows and scars. The Pueblo Indians continue to use both hematite and red ocher today as red pigments for ceremonial purposes and pottery decoration. Hopi red ocher sources in the past included the San Francisco Peaks area; Red Butte, south of the Grand Canyon; and Cataract Canyon, a tributary of the Grand Canyon, on the Havasupai reservation about 175 km west of Hopi. The variety of sources may account for variations in distance, travel time, and direction in testimony New Mexicans gave.

Havasupai red ocher is the source Hopis prefer today. They either trade the Havasupais for this ocher, which is considered special throughout the Pueblo world, or collect it themselves, after four days of purification, in a location described as being high up in a canyon wall. The properties of red ocher samples obtained in 1990 at Hopi and originating from the Havasupai area correspond closely to the description in the document. Even in powder form, the ocher is heavy, and when rubbed on the skin, a purplish, metallic sheen appears. This sheen indicates the presence of hematite, however, not mercury, as the Spaniards assumed. A cinnabar crystal ground for purposes of comparison did not produce a similar effect, although mercury content was high.

This confusion between ore containing hematite (iron oxide) and cinnabar was not uncommon. Biringuccio wrote in 1540 that native mercury was often found in a dark red stone almost like cinnabar and that ore containing mercury was sought amidst an earthy red mineral he referred to as the substance of Saturn (lead). To complicate the matter further, cinnabar deposits occur in several locations in southern Arizona, often in association with hematite, clays, and schists. The closest sources to Hopi country are in the Mazatzal Mountains to the southwest and in Copper Basin, 16 km southwest of Prescott. Native mercury is found on the surface in both these formations, although geological reports do not mention pools of the substance. An earthy variety of cinnabar in these areas contains iron oxides and clay as impurities, producing a brownish-red powder when crushed, the same color as Hopi red ocher.

Spaniards in sixteenth-century Peru similarly confused hematite (or red ocher) and cinnabar in their initial search for mercury sources. They found natives of the area using a red pigment, called llimpi, to paint themselves for war and festivities. The Spaniards believed it to be cinnabar. When the Spaniards asked the Indians to lead them to the source of their llimpi, they found it contained too little mercury to mine profitably. They later discovered the rich mercury ore and native mercury deposits near Huancavelica. As in Arizona, hematite is associated with veins of cinnabar ore in that area of Peru. The Inca Garcilaso de la Vega wrote that the Incas knew of native mercury, but prohibited it because they recognized its harmful effects on those who gathered it. Nevertheless, a crimson-colored pigment called ichma, derived from ore associated with native mercury—most likely cinnabar— was used by young women of royal blood during certain festivals. Llimpi, Garcilaso claimed, was of a less delicate, purplish color obtained from another mineral, most probably hematite or red ocher. El Inca Garcilaso de la Vega, *Comentarios reales de los incas* (1609; rpt., Buenos Aires, 1943):213–14. Modesto Bargalló, *La minería y la metalurgia en la América española durante la época colonial* (Mexico City, 1955):78–79. José de Acosta, *Historia natural y moral de las Indias* (Mexico City, 1979):161. Carl Lausen and E.D. Gardner, *Quicksilver (Mercury) Resources of Arizona* (Tucson, 1927):11. John W. Anthony, Sidney A. Williams, and Richard A. Bideaux, *Mineralogy of Arizona* (Tucson, 1977):137. Vannoccio Biringuccio, *The Pirotechnia of Vannoccio Biringuccio* (1540; rpt., New York, 1942):82. Walter Hough, "A Collection of Hopi Ceremonial Pigments," *Annual Report of the Smithsonian Institution, 1900* (Washington, D.C., 1902):469. John C. McGregor, "Burial of an Early American Magician," *Proceedings of the American Philosophical Society* 86 (Feb. 1943):290. Georg Agricola, *De Natura Fossilium (Textbook of Mineralogy)* (1546; rpt., New York, 1955):35. Personal communication with Dr. Gary A. Smith, Senior Research Associate, Dept. of Geology, University of New Mexico, July 1990.

4. In 1694, fray José de Espínola (or Spínola) Almonacid was incorporated into the Holy Gospel Province in Mexico from the province in Charcas (Bolivia). From 1682 to 1696, Espínola was in the El Paso area. Rosa Figueroa, Becerro. Chávez, *Archives*, 10, 15, 17.

5. Regular outgoing mail from New Mexico was usually sent with the supply caravans that went there every three years. Important mail was carried by a mounted courier. By the late 1680s, it had been determined that expenses would be paid by the postmaster in Mexico City for one courier for each round trip. The average day's travel was from 60 to 75 km. The average time for the trip from Santa Fe to Mexico City was about two months. A special courier Governor Vargas sent from Santa Fe in 1693 covered the distance of about 2,500 km in thirty-six days. Lansing B. Bloom, "The Vargas Encomienda," NMHR 14 (Oct. 1939):376 and "New Mexico under Mexican Administration, 1821–1846," *Old Santa Fe* 1 (July 1913):14–16. Walz, "El Paso," 229–30. *Recopilación de leyes de los reynos de las Indias* (hereinafter *Recop.*), Lib. 5, tít. 15, ley 10 and Lib. 9, tít. 7, leyes 1–28.

6. Pepina refers to ore found in the center of a lode. For a description of the mercury mines at Huancavelica, see Bargalló, *Minería*, 254–55, and Guillermo Lohmann Villena, *Las minas de Huancavelica en los siglos xvi y xvii* (Seville, 1949).

7. Fray Miguel Muñiz de Luna professed in Puebla on 17 February 1684. By 1691, he was ministering in the El Paso area and accompanied Governor Vargas on the 1692 expedition. He remained in the El Paso district through 1696, serving as president, notary, and missionary. From 1697 to about 1718, he was in New Mexico, where he served in a variety of posts. He was custos in 1708 and, toward the end of his career, returned to the El Paso area. Chávez, *Archives*, 12, 252. EBARN.

8. Alfonso Rael de Aguilar, a native of Lorca in the Spanish province of Murcia, was married to Josefa García de Noriega in El Paso in 1683. They had six children: Alonso, Eusebio, Juan, Antonia, Francisca, and Feliciana. Rael served as Vargas's secretary of government and war and lieutenant general during the 1692 reconquest and 1693 recolonizing expedition. During a long civil and military career, Rael served as alcalde of Santa Fe, protector of Indians, mayordomo of the Confraternity of Our Lady of the Rosary, sargento mayor, and captain. In 1709, Rael was unofficially acting as scribe in Santa Eulalia de Chihuahua (present-day Aquiles Serdán), site of a major silver strike. Pedro de Arizaga, Obligation, Santa Eulalia de Chihuahua, 24 Nov. 1709, AHP, 1709. CRG, 247. Naylor and Polzer, *Presidio and Militia*, 1:521. NMF, 263.

9. Fray Nicolás de Echevarría (or Echavarría) was born about 1616 in Sierra de Pinos, Zacatecas, the son of Juan de Echevarría and María Ramírez. At the Convento Grande on 2 May 1637, twenty-one-year-old Echevarría professed in the Franciscan Order. Although he was in New Mexico by 1644, he did not appear on the 1659 roster. In 1663, he served at Picuris and was definitor of the custody. By March 1666, he was named guardian at Pecos and served at Sandia in 1668. KCC, 210, 497, 532 n54.

10. This is a reference to Governor Jironza's sack of Zia in August 1689 and would indicate that Father Vargas was chaplain of the expedition.

11. The red ocher from Zuni and Moqui may have traveled along the major trade route that linked the Zuni-Cíbola area with the Tiguex province of the middle Rio Grande, branching then north, south, and east toward the remaining Pueblo settlements and extending onto the Plains. Other routes radiated out from Zuni, leading northwest to Hopi; west to the Havasupai, the Pacific Ocean, and the Gulf of California; and south to the Mesoamerican area. Ernest Beaglehole, *Notes on Hopi Economic Life* (New Haven, 1937):84–85. T.J. Ferguson and E. Richard Hart, *A Zuni Atlas* (Norman, 1985):48–49. Carroll L. Riley and Joni L. Manson, "The Cíbola-Tiguex Route: Continuity and Change in the Southwest," NMHR 58 (Oct. 1983):347–67.

12. Born in New Spain in 1638, fray Juan Muñoz de Castro, a Discalced of the Province of St. James, arrived at El Paso with fray Francisco de Ayeta in 1680. He served as commissary of the Holy Office and vice-custos. To collect alms, he went several times on preaching missions to the mines of Cosihuiriáchic. He left for New Mexico with Governor Vargas. Having completed twelve years of service in New Mexico, Muñoz was incorporated into the Holy Gospel Province on 22 April 1694.

During the absence of fray Francisco de Vargas in 1698, Muñoz served as custos. EBARN. Fray Juan Muñoz de Castro, Petition regarding service in New Mexico, 25 June 1692, BNM 4:3 (22/456.1).

13. Juan Severino Rodríguez de Suballe was born about 1655 in Seville. The son of Capt. Clemente Rodríguez, Juan Severino was included on 27 February 1677 in a list of convicts bound to serve as soldiers to relieve the provinces of New Mexico. He was enlisted indefinitely at regular pay. Deputy alcalde of the Sandia district in 1680, he retreated to Socorro with his grandfather-in-law, Alonso García, and on 26 August 1680 witnessed a document regarding the deaths of friars and settlers from Taos to Santo Domingo. His wife was Ana María Varela. NMF, 95. Twitchell, *Spanish Archives*, 2:29. Hackett, *Historical Documents*, 3:319.

14. Juan Lucero de Godoy was born in New Mexico about 1624 to Pedro Lucero de Godoy and Petronila de Zamora. In 1663, he served as secretary of government and war to Gov. Diego de Peñalosa. He was a sargento mayor and alcalde ordinario of Santa Fe in 1680 and escaped the revolt with his wife, four sons, and four daughters. Lucero de Godoy was appointed interpreter for the Tewa language on several occasions in the 1680s when Spaniards ventured north into Pueblo country. He and his third wife,

Isabel de Salazar, returned with Vargas. He claimed in 1693 to have been in the royal service for fifty-two years, having resided in Santa Fe for forty. Hackett and Shelby, *Revolt*, 1:137; 2:107, 232, 250. NMF, 60.

15. San Bernardo de Aguatuvi was founded in 1629, under the patronage of St. Bernard of Clairvaux. It stood about 17 km southeast of First Mesa on Antelope Mesa. Awatovi was destroyed by Hopis in late 1700 or early 1701. Rick Hendricks, "Forgotten Lessons and Missing Links: Bandelier as a Pioneering Scientific Historian" (Paper delivered at the Bandelier Sesquicentennial Conference, Albuquerque, New Mexico, 7 Aug. 1990), 3. John P. Wilson, "Awatovi—More Light on a Legend," *Plateau* 44 (Win. 1972):125–30. Ross Gordon Montgomery, Watson Smith, and John Otis Brew, *Franciscan Awatovi: The Excavation and Conjectural Reconstruction of a 17th-Century Spanish Mission Establishment at a Hopi Indian Town in Northeastern Arizona* (Cambridge, Mass., 1949):121–25.

16. Antonio de Cisneros, mixed-blood son of Capt. Bartolomé de Cisneros and Ana Gutiérrez, was born about 1653, possibly in the jurisdiction of Zuni and Moqui, since it is known that his father was living there in 1662. Antonio passed muster before Governor Otermín at San Lorenzo de la Toma on 12 September

1681. The December 1692 census of the El Paso area lists him as a bachelor, living in San Lorenzo with his widowed mother and five siblings. Cisneros married Josefa Luján, also of mixed blood and Santa Fe native, on 1 January 1695. Her parents, both deceased, were Miguel Luján and Elena Ruiz. In 1698, he was alcalde mayor of Galisteo. By 1706, Cisneros was serving in the same post at Zuni. In August of that year, he died as a result of wounds inflicted by Apaches. AASF, Diligencias matrimoniales, 1698:14. Espinosa, "El Paso District in 1692," 78–79. NMF, 289. NMR, 10:1843.

17. Antonio Palomino, a contemporary of Vargas, described various red pigments in paints. Mineral vermilion was made from cinnabar from the mines. The process of preparing vermilion was to grind it well with white wine and then make small tablets of the paste. Before use, the tablets were tempered with linseed oil on the palette. Artificial vermilion was made from sulfur and mercury, calcined together, and gave the most beautiful red (encarnado). Red ocher was also used as a red pigment. Antonio Palomino de Castro y Velasco, *El museo pictórico y escala óptica* (1715; rpt., Madrid, 1947):488–90, 1144–45.

18. Pinole (Nahuatl pinolli from pinol-atl) is a meal or flour made from parched maize or other grains and used, when beaten into cold or hot water, as a drink.

Sometimes honey, sugar, chocolate, cinnamon, vanilla, or other ingredients are added. The term also refers to the drink itself.

19. Nine varieties of the some seventy-odd tobaccos were cultivated in the New World as a ceremonial adjunct, medicine, and drug. The favored variety, *Nicotiana tabacum*, was native to Mexico, Central America, and the Caribbean. Others, such as *N. rustica* (known as punche in New Mexico), *N. attenuata*, and *N. trigonophylla*, were cultivated or gathered by Indians.

Tobacco was widely grown in New Mexico among both Spaniards and Pueblo Indians before the establishment of the tobacco monopoly in 1765, not only for local consumption, but also for trade with those Indians who did not grow it. Hands of tobacco, small bundles of five or more leaves, were carried for smoking. The leaf was shredded or powdered and wrapped in the inner leaves of maize husks to form cigaritos. Men also smoked pipes. E. Boyd, "The Use of Tobacco in Spanish New Mexico," *El Palacio* 65 (June 1958):103–106. Lawrence Kinnaird, "The Spanish Tobacco Monopoly in New Mexico, 1766–67," NMHR 21 (Oct. 1946):328, 330. George A. West, *Tobacco, Pipes and Smoking Customs of the American Indians* (1934; rpt., Westport, Conn., 1970):30, 33, 48, 59, 60–61, 65.

20. Either Governor Vargas misstated the date or the scribe incorrectly wrote 8 August for 9 August when Antonio de Cisneros actually testified.

21. In 1662, Bartolomé de Cisneros lived with his brother, Vicente, in the Zuni-Moqui jurisdiction. On 7 October 1670, Cisneros was absent from Hawikuh when fray Pedro de Avila y Ayala was attacked and killed. Cisneros and his wife, Ana Gutiérrez, had at least three children: two sons, Alonso and Antonio, and a daughter, Catalina. Bartolomé was dead by 1694, but his wife was still alive and residing in El Paso. NMR, 10:1843. NMF, 104. Fray Agustín de Vetancurt, *Teatro mexicano: Descripción breve de los sucesos exemplares de la Nueva-España en el nuevo mundo occidental de las Indias* (Madrid, 1961), 4:287.

22. In the viceroy's letter at the beginning of this testimony, mercury-bearing ore is referred to as bermellón, while all the native New Mexicans call the ore almagre. In Vargas's report to the viceroy at the end of the testimony, he uses bermellón or almagre to clarify that both terms are being used to indicate the same ore. While almagre is associated today with red ocher, the New Mexican witnesses considered almagre to bear mercury, which red ocher does not. In late-sixteenth-century mining terminology, almagre and bermellón were used interchangeably to mean mercury-bearing ore, or cinnabar. In Peruvian Spanish-Quechua dictionaries of the time, bermellón and almagre were both translated as puca alpa, literally red earth, or puca llimpi, the red pigment Indians used for face painting, thought to be cinnabar.

Capt. Juan Mateo Manje, accompanying Father Kino on an expedition north through southern Arizona in 1697, also used the terms bermellón or almagre finísimo to describe a red pigment he saw a young man wearing as face paint in Pima country, near present-day Sacaton in Pinal County. Because it was heavy, liquid, and oily, and seeped through the buckskin bag the youth carried it in, Manje assumed the ore contained mercury. The young man told Manje the pigment could be found five days' journey to the northwest and toward the Colorado River, the same general area the New Mexicans describe in this document, in Havasupai country west of Hopi. Juan Mateo Manje, *Luz de tierra incógnita en la América septentrional y diario de las exploraciones en Sonora* (Mexico City, 1929):254. Domingo de Santo Tomás, *Lexicón, o vocabulario de la lengua general del Perú* (1560; rpt., Lima, 1951):35, 58. Diego González Holguín, *Vocabulario de la lengua general de todo el Perú llamada lengua qquichua o del inca* (1608; rpt., Lima, 1952):401, 431.

23. Bartolomé Gómez Robledo, born around 1640, was the son of long-time New Mexico residents

Francisco Gómez Robledo and Ana Vicente. He and his brothers, Francisco and Andrés, were principal figures in the colony before 1680. He was Bartolomé Romero's cousin. In 1663, he was single and holding the position of alferez. That year, he fled New Mexico with the tribute from Acoma and the horses belonging to his brother who was on trial in Mexico City. He was still single in 1681 when he was a sargento mayor in El Paso. At that time, he had a natural son, Bartolomé, with him. They did not join the recolonizing expedition of 1693. NMF, 36–37. Scholes, *Troublous Times*, 214.

24. Luis de Guzmán y Figueroa was governor of New Mexico from 1647 until 1649.

25. What is being described here in imperfect fashion is the asiento, or contract, system in force for mercury mining. Based largely on the Spanish experience with the mines in Huancavelica, Peru, the system provided for the orderly and profitable exploitation of mercury deposits. Although all mines belonged to the crown, gold and silver mining operated largely within the context of a free market. Mercury, however, was much more strictly regulated. Beginning with the premise that mercury mines belonged to the crown in perpetuity, the crown exerted a monopoly over the production and distribution of mercury. Although the discoverer of a mercury mine in theory had usufruct for thirty years, after which the mine would revert to the crown, in practice the crown asserted its ownership from the beginning, entering into contracts with those wishing to undertake exploitation. *Recop.*, Lib. 8, tít. 23, leyes 1–12. Lohmann Villena, *Huancavelica*, 59–89. Gaspar de Escalona Agüero, *Gazofilacio real del Perú: Tratado financiero del coloniaje* (1647; rpt., La Paz, 1941):132–45.

26. Bartolomé Romero was a cousin of Bartolomé Gómez Robledo and the uncle of Juan de Dios Lucero de Godoy. In 1662, he became embroiled in a conflict with Gov. Diego de Peñalosa. Scholes, *Troublous Times*, 198–99, 214, 231.

27. A tecomate (Nahuatl tecomatl, clay vessel or bowl) is a common clay vessel in the shape of a gourd.

28. The term cuartelejo seems to be have been applied to distant, inhabited areas. Here it is not to be confused with the area in present-day western Kansas where Apaches lived in the 1690s. Marc Simmons, "History of Pueblo-Spanish Relations," in *Handbook*, 9:187.

29. Juan Luis the Elder passed muster in 1680. He had a wife, one grown son, and three small children. In 1689, he was living among the refugees at El Paso and was a captain. Later, he appeared as Luis Luján and Ruiz Luján. Apparently this Luis family belonged to the Ruiz Cáceres Luján line. NMF, 62.

30. Francisco Gómez Robledo was the scion of one of New Mexico's oldest families. He was born around 1630 in Santa Fe to Francisco Gómez, a native of Portugal, and Ana Robledo. His father had joined Alonso de Oñate's household and accompanied him from Spain. In 1660, Francisco the Younger served as alcalde ordinario of Santa Fe. Over a three-year period, 1661–64, Gómez Robledo was the subject of Inquisitorial investigation to examine his unfavorable attitude toward New Mexico's clergy and ascertain whether he might be a crypto-Jew. The question of Gómez's alleged Jewishness was primarily based upon his suspect Portuguese ancestry and the fact that his father, accused of being a Jew, never denied it. Francisco defended himself before the Holy Office in Mexico City, was acquitted, and returned to New Mexico. In 1680, he passed muster as maestre de campo and Governor Otermín's lieutenant in the Río Arriba district. Gómez Robledo was married, had one grown son, two small ones, five daughters, an unmarried sister, a sister-in-law with seven children, and twenty other people in his household. By the 1660s, he had become mayordomo of the Confraternity of Our Lady of the Rosary, a post he was again occupying in 1684. In 1685, he was alcalde ordinario and acting as juez receptor, the magistrate commissioned to take testimony, in El Paso. By 1693,

Gómez Robledo was dead. Naylor and Polzer, *Presidio and Militia,* 1:539–40. NMF, 35–36. Maureen Flynn, *Sacred Charity: Confraternities and Social Welfare in Spain,* 1400–1700 (Ithaca, 1989):33. AGN, Inquisición 583:3. Scholes, *Troublous Times,* 190–94.

31. Informants in the El Paso area did not always clearly distinguish between Apaches and Coninas. Vargas made the mistake of initially considering them a single group. Later, he referred to them as two different groups. When he went to Walpi in 1692, he saw many warriors who were obviously not Hopis. He was informed that they were Utes, Apaches, and Coninas. The Indians referred to as Coninas are Havasupais, a Yuman-speaking group of northwestern Arizona. The origin of the word Coninas is uncertain, though a number of variants appear in Indian languages of the Southwest. The Havasupais are direct descendants of the prehistoric Cohonina, a culture that appeared in the plateau region south of the Grand Canyon around A.D. 600. Douglas W. Schwartz, "Havasupai," in *Handbook,* 10:13–24. Forbes, *Apache,* 241–42.

32. Terno, or terno de armas, is generally translated as suit of armor. Although armor was becoming less and less useful in Europe by the beginning of the seventeenth century with the increasing use of firearms, it was still functional in the New World

for defense against stone-tipped arrows, lances, and war clubs.

Muster rolls of soldiers, such as the one in El Paso, 15–16 September 1681, indicate that various individuals had suits of armor; others had only cuirasses, consisting typically of breastplate and backplate. Some had cueras, multilayer leather jackets, and the poorest had no armor at all. Marc Simmons and Frank Turley, *Southwestern Colonial Ironwork: The Spanish Blacksmithing Tradition from Texas to California* (Santa Fe, 1980):26. Muster roll, El Paso, 15–16 Sept. 1681, in Hackett and Shelby, *Revolt*, 2:74–86.

33. José Téllez Girón was born in Los Altos de San Jacinto in Coyoacán around 1631. In New Mexico, he held encomiendas at San Felipe and Cochiti in 1661. In 1667, he was living in Senecú. He married Catalina Romero in 1680 with whom he had three sons and four daughters. From 1684, he was living in Ysleta del Sur. He took part in a junta of war in Santa Fe in December 1693. He died, as did so many others, in 1695 as the result of epidemic or battle. CRG, 155, 239. NMF, 106.

34. In 1650, Gen. Hernando Ugarte y la Concha, governor of New Mexico from 1649 to 1653, discovered a plot by Tiwas, Keres, Jemez, and Apaches to drive the Spaniards from the province. Tiwas of Alameda and Sandia were found to have handed over horses from Spanish herds to the Apaches. Nine leaders from Isleta, Alameda, San Felipe, Cochiti, and Jemez were hanged after an investigation. Many inhabitants of the conspiring pueblos were sold into slavery for a period of ten years. Apache captives were also sold into slavery during Ugarte's term. Francisco de Lima to Bartolomé Hernández, Transfer of slaves, Parral, 11 July 1654, AHP, 1654B. Hackett and Shelby, *Revolt*, 2:245, 246, 299.

35. Marcos de Torres y Rueda (1588–1649), acting as viceroy of New Spain in 1648–49, was born in Almazán (Soria). He was canon of Burgos (Burgos) and was later promoted to the bishopric of Yucatán, a position he filled from 1646 to 1649. He concurrently held the post of interim viceroy of New Spain from 1648 until his death on 22 April 1649, though his actual title was governor of the viceroyalty. Rubio Mañé, *Virreinato*, 1:149. Schäfer, *Consejo Real*, 2:605. Hanke and Rodríguez, *Virreyes españoles*, 4:109–12.

36. From the arrival of the Spaniards in the late sixteenth century until about 1850, Athapaskan peoples of northwest New Mexico and northeast Arizona, that is, east of the Hopis, north of Zuni and the Western Keresans, and west of the northern Pueblos, were usually referred to as Navajo Apaches. David M. Brugge, "Navajo Prehistory and History to 1850," in *Handbook*, 10:489–90. Forbes, *Apache*, xiii, 11.

37. Born in New Mexico about 1650, Fernando Durán y Chaves II was a descendant of the Chaveses who arrived in 1600 with the second consignment of settlers. In 1670, he was serving as an alferez and soon after married Lucía Hurtado de Salas. They had four children by 1680 and were living in the ancestral estancia of El Tunque, somewhere in the vicinity of present-day Ranchos de Santa Ana. A captain at the time of the Pueblo Revolt, he fled south with his family. Durán y Chaves participated in the 1692 expedition as alferez real and returned with his wife and numerous children to settle in 1693, the only Chaveses to do so. By 1696, he was alcalde mayor of Bernalillo. When Vargas fell ill in 1704 during a campaign against Apaches in the area, he was carried to Fernando's house, where he died. By 1707, Durán y Chaves had moved south to Atrisco, in the Albuquerque area, where many of his children were living. He died there sometime between 1712 and 1716. NMF, 20–21, 160–61. Chávez, *Chávez*, 3, 41–72.

38. Antonio Montoya was born around 1647, the son of Diego de Montoya and doña María de Vera. In 1680, he left New Mexico, fleeing from the Pueblo Indians. He and his wife, María Hurtado, brought a number of children when they returned with Vargas in 1693. In that same year, he was described as a leading citizen of New Mexico.

CRG, 155. NMF, 78, 235. NMFA, 63:373.

39. Fray Gerónimo de Pedraza, a native of Mexico City, professed there as a lay brother on 2 December 1608. By 1618, he was a missionary in New Mexico, having accompanied Gov. Juan de Eulate. Over the years, he gained a reputation as a healer, as in the 1620s when he cured the Apache chief Quinía of an infected arrow wound by applying a copper medal with the images of the Virgin Mary and St. Francis. Pedraza died at San Felipe Pueblo on 5 May 1664. KCC, 109, 139. Frederick Webb Hodge, George P. Hammond, and Agapito Rey, *Fray Alonso de Benavides' Revised Memorial of 1634* (Albuquerque, 1945):89, 259–60, 311. Vetancurt, *Teatro mexicano*, 3:270, 4:118.

40. This testimony indicates that doctors may have considered the metallic, greasy properties of crushed hematite, or red ocher, evidence of fine mercury. Hematite, red lead, and Armenian bole (a red clay) were common ingredients in unguents and other medicinal preparations of that time. Hematite, or red ocher containing hematite, was used in powder form mixed with water as an astringent to heal wounds, stop bleeding, and treat ulcers. Preparations containing mercury and cinnabar were rare. Fray Agustín Farfán's *Tractado breve de medicina* calls for both azogue muerto, or extinguished mercury, and cinnabar in an unguent as a

treatment of last resort for syphilitic patients. Farfán was aware of the dangers of mercury poisoning and warned his readers that careless or unnecessary use could lead to death. If used properly, however, Farfán claimed that mercury had the ability to draw out the humors from deep within the body by anointing a patient's joints. At this time, mercury treatment was the only therapy successful in alleviating some of the suffering from syphilis, though the side effects were often as harmful as the disease. Stanislav Andreski, *Syphilis, Puritanism and Witch Hunts* (London, 1989):7, 75. Fray Agustín Farfán, *Tractado breve de medicina* (1592; rpt., Madrid, 1944):94–98. Agricola, *De Natura Fossilium*, 88.

41. Durán y Chaves's declaration is thoroughly confused. He refers to Picuris as the pueblo in the province of Moqui that is elsewhere identified as Oraibi. He places the alleged mercury mine to the east of Picuris, while the other declarants stated that it was west of Oraibi.

42. In early seventeenth-century New Mexico, there were a number of individuals named Juan de Herrera. NMF, 45.

43. Born in New Mexico about 1644 to Francisco Madrid and Sebastiana Ruiz Cáceres, Roque Madrid was the younger brother of Lorenzo and like him, a survivor of the 1680 Pueblo Revolt. He escaped with his wife, Juana de Arvid López, and children. In 1685, he was named head of the El Paso presidio and a sargento mayor and captain. He served Vargas on dozens of military campaigns and eventually settled at Santa Cruz. From 1699 to 1707, he was alcalde mayor. He rose to the rank of maestre de campo before his death sometime between 1716 and 1723. Barnaby Thomas, *After Coronado: Spanish Exploration Northeast of New Mexico, 1696–1727* (Norman, 1935):87. NMF, 66, 216. NMFA, 63:318. Naylor and Polzer, *Presidio and Militia*, 1:509.

44. The term chimal (Nahuatl chimalli), translated here as shield, refers to a small round shield or target. Siméon, *Diccionario*, 103.

45. Juan de Dios Lucero de Godoy was born in 1656 and in 1681 married María Varela. In 1693, he was serving as a sargento mayor in New Mexico and considered a leading citizen of the colony. Deputy alcalde in El Paso in 1705, he was still there in 1718. CRG, 155. NMF, 61.

46. Born in New Mexico about 1654, Antonio Jorge II was the son of Capt. Antonio Jorge de la Vera I and Gertrudis Baca. His grandfather, Manuel Jorge, was a Portuguese merchant in Parral, a native of Tangier, in North Africa. Antonio II fled south in 1680 with his mother and two sisters. During the 1692 Vargas entrada, Jorge served as a captain. The following year, he was a sargento mayor and leading figure in the colony. In 1694, he married Catalina de

Espínola in Santa Fe. While alcalde mayor and capitán a guerra of Santa Cruz, he died in 1695. CRG, 57, 155, 203, 226, 238. NMF, 51. Manuel Jorge, Will, Parral, 7 June 1655, AHP, 1654B. Hackett and Shelby, *Revolt*, 2:83, 102.

47. Little is known about midseventeenth-century New Mexico governors. Fernando de Villanueva served from 1665 to 1668. He was followed by Capt. Juan Rodríguez de Medrano y Mesía, who acceded to office in November 1668, remaining until 1671. Gen. Juan [Durán de] Miranda was governor of New Mexico from 1664 to 1665 and again from 1671 to 1675. Juan Miranda to Gerónimo de Vega y Salazar, Power of attorney, Parral, 26 Jan. 1664, AHP, 1663A. Juan Miranda to Domingo de la Puente, Power of attorney, Parral, 12 May 1671, AHP, 1671C. KCC, 219.

48. Fray José de Espeleta began his ministry around 1650 at Zuni. Later he served at various Hopi pueblos and learned to speak the language. From 1663 to 1669, he was at Awatovi and from 1669 to 1672, at Oraibi. He was killed at Oraibi, along with fray Agustín de Santa María, in 1680. The Indian Francisco, who gave Vargas information about the Sierra Azul, claimed to have murdered Espeleta. Hodge, Hammond, and Rey, *Revised Memorial*, 298. CRG, 102, 345.

49. San Buenaventura, New Biscay, was located in the fertile Santa María river valley. It experienced two influxes of settlers from New Mexico, one in the 1660s and one in the 1680s. Gerhard, *North Frontier*, 232.

50. The term pepena refers to a bagful of high-quality ore that mine workers, mostly Indians, were allowed to collect after fulfilling their daily quota. Although mineowners lost some high-grade ore as a result of this practice, it served as an incentive for the workers to continue exploring for better ore. Pepena was sold to small smelting operations and the mineowners, or processed to spend or sell. Bakewell, *Silver Mining*, 125.

51. Tinplate flasks for mercury were custom-made for the transportation of mercury ore. Although metallic tin was mined in Mexico to some extent even before the arrival of the Spaniards, by 1618 it was more cheaply obtained from Spain and Peru. It is not known whether tinplate was produced in New Spain. Vargas's request for metal flasks may have derived from the manner individual miners used in transporting small amounts of mercury. Regulated as early as 1679, transportation of mercury was to be effected in badanas, or sheepskin containers, like wineskins, packed in stout crates. The containers consisted of two or three skin bags, each made of three layers. A skin held from 1/2 to 1 quintal of mercury. Sometimes casks were substituted for crates. West, *Parral*, 34. Bargalló,

Minería, 577, 578. Bakewell, *Silver Mining*, 171. Manuel Carrera Stampa, "The Evolution of Weights and Measures in New Spain," HAHR 29 (Feb. 1949), 10, 14. Elinore M. Barrett, *The Mexican Colonial Copper Industry* (Albuquerque, 1987):91–101.

52. Silver mining in New Spain relied heavily on mercury. In the patio process, one of the amalgamation methods of refining silver or gold, mercury was mixed with a slurry of crushed ore, stirred by workers or by driving animals through it, until, after several weeks or months, the mercury was thought to have combined with all the precious metal in the ore. The slurry was then washed, and the dross carried off by water. The heavier amalgam went to the bottom of the vats, from where it was collected. Free mercury was extracted by compressing the amalgam in sturdy canvas bags; the resulting silver product was referred to as piña. Finally, the piña was heated in furnaces that drove the mercury off as vapor, which was collected and condensed for reuse. Bargalló, *Minería*, 127–29.

53. There were numerous silver mines in the districts of Los Frailes, Parral, Guadiana, Rosario, and the regions of Guadalajara and Zacatecas. The real of Los Alamos was developed as a result of the discovery of silver at Los Frailes, Sinaloa (present-day Alamos, Sonora), in 1683. In 1631, a rich silver strike was made at San José del Parral; subsequent strikes at

Guadamecí and Urique depopulated Parral in the early 1690s and 1700s. Guadiana (present-day Durango) was important because it had a royal treasury office through which all silver produced locally had to pass to be taxed. Rosario is in southern present-day Sinaloa. Salt extracted nearby from the tidal flats along the Río Chametla (or Baluarte) was used in amalgamation. In addition, the discovery of gold and silver in 1655 gave rise to the mining center of Nuestra Señora del Rosario. Guadalajara also played an important role in the mining industry. First, as the seat of a royal audiencia, it exercised important political and administrative control and, like Guadiana and Zacatecas, had an office of the royal treasury. For a discussion of Zacatecas as a mining center, see Bakewell, *Silver Mining*, 140–44, 180–86. Bargalló, *Minería*, 127–29. C.H. Haring, *The Spanish Empire in America* (1947; rpt., New York, 1963):74. Gerhard, *North Frontier*, 217, 277.

54. The term magistral refers to copper sulfate, $CuSO_4$; the salt is sodium chloride, $NaCl$. Bargalló, *Minería*, 194.

55. As early as the late fourteenth century, the Spanish crown had established the principle of royal ownership of all mines and ores and its concomitant right to tax production. By the seventeenth century, for silver, this generally meant a tax of 20 percent, the quinto, or fifth. The fifth could be

reduced to as low as 5 or 10 percent to encourage production in newly discovered mines or for areas where production had fallen off severely or costs were very high. Bargalló, *Minería*, 81–82. Juan de Solórzano Pereira, *Política indiana*, Lib. 6, cap. 1, art. 21. Escalona Agüero, *Gazofilacio*, 132–33.

56. Diego de Hinojos passed muster in 1681. He was twenty-three, a bachelor, and a native of New Mexico. NMF, 49.

57. Toribio de la Huerta, born in Asturias about 1630, had lived in New Mexico, where he was a citizen, beginning in 1653. Testimony of Capt. Toribio de la Huerta against Diego de Peñalosa Briceño y Verdugo, Mexico City, 5 July 1663, AGN, Inquisición 507:1. RBC, 172 n3.

58. In the first cedula mentioned, dated 25 June 1680, the crown generally charged the Conde de Paredes with supplying aid to New Mexico to further the cause of recolonization and evangelization. By the later one of 4 September 1683, the crown approved Paredes's earlier establishment of a fifty-man presidio at El Paso and ordered him to continue with plans for the restoration of New Mexico. Hackett, *Historical Documents*, 3:307–308, 349–50.

59. Francisco de Salazar was the secretary of the Council of the Indies. He had previously occupied the post of secretary of Negociación del Norte from 7 July

1683 to 21 September 1684. Carlos I (1519–56) had divided his single secretariat of state in two: North, to deal with northern European matters; and Italy, to handle Mediterranean affairs. After 1586, secretariats proliferated, with secretaries of war, state, the royal household, treasury, and so forth established. In the seventeenth century, the multiplying secretariats were placed under the Secretario del Despacho Universal. Salazar also served as secretary for New Spain and Peru. Schäfer, *Consejo Real*, 1:371. Juan Beneyto Pérez, *Historia de la administración española e hispanoamericana* (Madrid, 1958):350.

60. Cristóbal de Castillo y Tejeda must have functioned only in the capacity of royal scribe at the viceregal court in Mexico City. Neither his name nor his records appear among the public scribes whose books are preserved today in the Archivo General de Notarías in Mexico City.

61. The kingdom of Quivira lay to the east of New Mexico on the plains of present-day Kansas. Francisco Vázquez de Coronado explored it in 1541; Juan de Oñate traveled there in 1601. Neither found the wealth they sought. As late as 1689, Toribio de la Huerta alleged that he was a discoverer of Quivira, a claim previously advanced by Diego de Peñalosa. While governor of New Mexico (1661–64), Peñalosa had arrested Huerta, a favored servant of his predecessor. Huerta avenged

himself in 1663 in Mexico City, testifying against Peñalosa before the Inquisition. Later, as part of a scheme to interest the French court in an invasion of New Spain, the expatriate Peñalosa fabricated a *Relación del descubrimiento del país y ciudad de Quivira*, based on a fictitious expedition of discovery in 1662. Here, Huerta takes a similarly contrived page from his former enemy. See Scholes, *Troublous Times*, 40, 229–30, 242–43.

62. Twenty-one Franciscans perished in the 1680 uprising: in San Diego de Tesuque, Rev. fray Juan Bautista Pío, a native of Vitoria in the province of Alava; in Santa Cruz de Galisteo, the custos, fray Juan Bernal, and fray Domingo de Vera, natives of Mexico City; in San Bartolomé de Shongopavi, the first guardian and prelate of the convento de San Cosme, fray José de Trujillo, a native of Cadiz; in the convento of Porciúncula in the pueblo of Pecos, fray Fernando de Velasco, a native of Cadiz; in San Francisco de Nambé, fray Tomás Tórrez, native of Tepozotlán; in San Ildefonso, fray Luis de Morales, native of Ubeda or Baeza in the province of Jaén, and fray Antonio Sánchez de Pro, former resident of the Discalced convento in Mexico City, a native of Mexico City; in San Lorenzo de los Picurís, fray Matías Rendón, a native of Puebla; in San Gerónimo de los Taos, fray Antonio de Mora, a native of Puebla, and fray Juan de la Pedrosa, a native of Mexico

City; in San Marcos, fray Manuel Tinoco, a native of the province of San Miguel in Estremadura; in Santo Domingo, fray Francisco Antonio Lorenzana, a native of Galicia, and the perpetual custos, fray Juan de Talabán, a native of Seville with twenty years' experience as a missionary, and fray José de Montesdoca, a native of Querétaro; in San Diego de los Jémez, fray Juan de Jesús, a native of Granada; in San Esteban de Acoma, the definitor, fray Lucas Maldonado, a native of Tribujena; in La Purísima Concepción de Alona, fray Juan del Val, a native of Castile; in San Bernardo de Aguatuvi, fray José de Figueroa, a native of Mexico City; in San Francisco de Oraibi, the perpetual custos, fray José de Espeleta, a native of Estela in Navarre, with thirty years' experience as a missionary, and fray Agustín de Santa María, a native of Pátzcuaro. The king, following Huerta, seems to have included another, as yet unidentified, individual to arrive at twenty-two martyrs. All other sources give the number of dead as twenty-one friars and about three hundred and eighty colonists. Isidro Sariñana y Cuenca, *Oración funebre* (Mexico City, 1681), HL, Rare Book 106425. Vetancurt, *Teatro mexicano*, 3:269–79.

63. Huerta wanted jurisdiction, that is, to govern, make laws, and administer justice, rather than a purely honorific title. Joaquín Escriche, *Diccionario razonado de*

legislación y jurisprudencia (Bogotá, 1977), 3:558.

64. The mercury mines at Huancavelica were a royal monopoly. Exploitation was leased to the mining guild through asiento, or contract, whereby miners pledged to produce a given amount of mercury during a specified time, in return for the crown's provision of Indian labor, cash advances, and the promise to buy the mercury at a predetermined price. Arthur Preston Whitaker, *The Huancavelica Mercury Mine: A Contribution to the History of the Bourbon Renaissance in the Spanish Empire* (Cambridge, Mass., 1941):9–12. See also Lohmann Villena, *Huancavelica*.

65. Bartolomé de Estrada y Ramírez, a native of Oviedo (Oviedo), served as comptroller general of accounts for New Spain. He was a member of the Order of Santiago and married to Ana María Niño de Castro y Córdoba, a native of Puebla. Together they had six children: Micaela, Gregoria, Felipe, José, Manuel, and Bartolomé Miguel. Estrada also had two natural sons, José and Miguel Antonio. In 1670 and 1671, Estrada acted as interim governor of New Biscay. On 31 December 1677, he secured the future of the title of governor and captain general of New Biscay. He served a full term in that office from 1679 to 1684, when he died in Parral. Bartolomé de Estrada, Will, Parral, 21 Aug. 1684, AHP,

1685B. Naylor and Polzer, *Presidio and Militia*, 1:491. Schäfer, *Consejo Real*, 2:545. García Carraffa, *Diccionario heráldico*, 30:205.

66. José de Neira y Quiroga, knight of the Order of Santiago, secured the future for the title of governor of New Biscay on 19 June 1680. He served in that office from 1684 to 1688. Neira was a native of the villa of Villabad in Galicia, the son of Gómez de Riomol y Quiroga and Catalina Santiso y Neira. Neira resided in Parral and married María de Apresa e Ibarra. They had three sons: Diego Francisco, Manuel Ignacio, and Isidro José. After his term of office, Neira pursued diverse business interests in Parral. He was buried on 7 July 1705. LDS, Parral, Burials, 162563. José de Neira y Quiroga, Will, Parral, 2 July 1705. Schäfer, *Consejo Real*, 2:545.

67. Francisco Cuervo y Valdés, son of Alonso Cuervo and Ana Suárez, was baptized on 16 June 1651 at the family seat of Llamero in the municipality of Grado (Asturias). By 1678, he was serving in Sonora at San Juan Bautista as an infantry captain; he also had an interest in two local stores. In the following years, he served as inspector general in Sonora and in 1681, alcalde mayor and capitán a guerra and lieutenant governor of Sonora. In 1681, he was accused of abandoning his post by the alcalde mayor of Ostimuri and jailed, though he was later acquitted.

Cuervo served as an infantry captain in New Biscay (1684); interim governor in New León (1687); and treasurer and agent of the royal treasury in Guadalajara. From 1690 to 1695, he was imprisoned in Madrid for charges leveled against him for his role as a treasury official. On leaving prision, he married Margarita de Alderete in 1695. Her dowry included a robe in the Order of Santiago.

Back in the Indies by June 1696, Cuervo had secured the future for the governorship of Coahuila and served in that post from 28 May 1698 to 28 May 1703. Cuervo acceded as provisional governor of New Mexico on 10 March 1705 and remained in office until 1 August 1707. By 1711, Cuervo had received the corregimiento of Zacatecas for five years, with the right for his son, Francisco Cuervo y Torres, to succeed him.

At the time of his death, on 23 April 1714 in Mexico City, Cuervo was described as the widower of Margarita de Alderete and residing on the Calle del Colegio. He was buried at the convento of San Agustín. LDS, Mexico City, Sagrario, Burials, 0035750. Francisco Cuervo de Valdés, Inspection, San Ildefonso de Ostimuri-Parral, 24 July 1681–17 July 1682, AHP, 1682A. NMF, 183. Luis de Morales, Proceedings, San Juan Bautista, 15 Oct. 1682, AHP, 1682C. Francisco Cuervo de Valdés to Francisco Antonio de Mendibil, Power of attorney,

Mexico City, 6 June 1696, AGNot. 692. Ovidio Casado Fuente, *Don Francisco Cuerbo y Valdés, Gobernador de Nuevo México, fundador de la ciudad de Alburquerque* (Oviedo, 1983):17, 19, 20, 24, 34, 99, 115. Eloy Benito Ruano, "Nuevos datos biográficos sobre don Francisco Cuervo y Valdés, fundador de Alburquerque (Nuevo México)," in *Boletín del Instituto de Estudios Asturianos*, Separata, no. 3 (Oviedo, 1984):332–40. Marc Simmons, "Governor Cuervo and the Beginnings of Albuquerque: Another Look," NMHR 55 (July 1980):194–96, 203–204.

68. First settled in the 1640s, the real of San Juan Bautista was about 40 km southeast of Arizpe in Sonora. Beginning in the 1650s, it flourished as a mining center and became the provincial capital in 1658. Because of its exposed location and the flooding of its mines, it was abandoned in the mideighteenth century. Gerhard, *North Frontier*, 282–85. Naylor and Polzer, *Presidio and Militia*, 1:585 n3.

69. Here much of the text of Huerta's petition is repeated.

70. Bachiller Lope de Sierra Osorio was a judge of the Audiencia of Mexico from 19 June 1670 to 5 November 1677, when he was named interim president of the Audiencia of Guatemala. He served in that post until 1680, when he was named judge of the Chancillery of Granada. At some point he might have completed his

licentiate, because he is referred to by that title while serving in Guatemala. From 12 May 1684 to 27 April 1702, he was president of the Audiencia of Guatemala. He was also an interim member of the Cámara of the Council of the Indies from 7 February 1696 to 4 March 1697, when he became a full member. While on the council, he was a member of the Junta of War. Schäfer, *Consejo Real*, 1:364; 2:457, 538.

71. Antonio Ortiz de Otalora served as secretary of the Junta de Descargos of the Council of the Indies from 3 November 1684 to 26 March 1691. He also served as secretary for New Spain and later for Peru. In June 1695, he was named secretary of the Council of Italy for Milan. Schäfer, *Consejo Real*, 1:371.

72. The legal term oficio, translated here as officially issued, identifies a document or letter in which a public official gives an order or provides advice in some matter dealing with his post or replies to an order or advice given him. Formally naming it an oficio distinguishes it from other types of documents, such as petitions, acts, powers of attorney, and so forth. Escriche, *Diccionario razonado*, 4:195.

73. Walz, writing in 1950, stated that she was unable to locate this document; it has not yet come to light. "El Paso," 292–93.

74. The Indians referred to by the Spaniards as Cruzados are the Yavapais of northwestern Arizona.

They speak a dialect of Upland Yuman and are closely related to the Havasupais and Walapais. The first recorded mention of the Cruzados was made during the Oñate expedition in 1598. The name comes from the Indians' practice of wearing a cross made of two pieces of cane in their hair. From 1686, the Yavapais were also referred to as Apaches. Yavapai did not come into use until 1774, when it was employed by fray Francisco Garcés. Sigrid Khera and Patricia S. Mariella, "Yavapai," in *Handbook*, 10:38–45. Hammond and Rey, *Oñate*, 2:1015. Douglas W. Schwartz, "Havasupai," in *Handbook*, 10:13–24.

75. Gen. Juan Fernández de Retana was a Basque, born in Nanclares de Gamboa (Alava) around 1652. By 1678, he had arrived in Parral and was involved in freighting. Referring to himself in 1684 as a citizen and merchant of the city, Fernández de Retana was by May of that year its justicia mayor, as well as the lieutenant governor of New Biscay.

In the mid-1680s, he won appointment as the first captain of the newly established presidio of San Francisco de los Conchos. Responding to French expansion into Texas, he led an expedition there in 1688. Throughout his tenure, he dealt with extensive Tarahumara raids and uprisings occurring in his jurisdiction. His harsh reprisals against them caused him to be ordered exiled from New

Biscay, although he remained during the legal proceedings and was eventually exonerated. Sometime before 1694, he acquired extensive agricultural properties in and around Conchos, about 60 km north of Parral. At his death in 1708, Fernández de Retana was buried in Parral on 25 February. LDS, Parral, Burials, 162563. Juan González de Retana and Juan Bautista de Ibabe, Inventory of the estate of Juan de Retana, Parral, 24 Oct. 1708, AHP, 1708. Naylor and Polzer, *Presidio and Militia*, 1:549, 553 n8. Juan Bautista de Ibabe and Juan González de Retana, Will for Juan de Retana, Parral, 3 Nov. 1708, AHP, 1708. Juan de Retana, Proceedings, Parral, 30 Mar. 1684, AHP, 1684A.

76. Diego López del Castillo, born around 1600 in Seville, came to New Mexico about 1634. He was married twice: to María Barragán and to María Griego (also known as María de la Cruz Alemán). In 1664, he was residing in Santa Fe. By 1680, he was sargento mayor and alcalde mayor of Moqui. Mustered before Governor Otermín at La Salineta in September of the same year, he stated that he was more than eighty years old. In San Lorenzo the following year, again before Otermín, López del Castillo gave his age as ninety-six. He was still active in 1682. Hackett and Shelby, *Revolt*, 1:143; 2:34, 106, 367. NMF, 55.

77. Francisco Javier Casero (or Casado) was the brother-in-law of Diego López del Castillo. Javier was born in 1630 in Seville and came to Santa Fe with the escort of the wagon train led by Gov. Bernardo López de Mendizábal. In 1660, Javier was the captain in charge of a trade caravan to Parral. By 1663, he had married Graciana Griego, daughter of Juan Griego. In the ensuing years, Javier also served as secretary of government and war, alcalde ordinario, and maestre de campo. He fled the Pueblo Revolt with four daughters and two sons and declared himself to be a widower the following year. Javier left Guadalupe del Paso for New Spain in 1682 because of ill health. Mre. de campo Juan Domínguez de Mendoza complained to Governor Otermín about Javier's cruelty to the Indians. Javier, as collector of encomienda tribute; Luis de Quintana; and Diego López denounced Indians for witchcraft so they could confiscate their livestock. Otermín had promised the Indians he would not allow Javier and his comrades to return to New Mexico. His son, Francisco Javier II, acted as secretary of government and war in the mid-1680s, serving Gov. Jironza. Fernando Ocaranza, *Establecimientos franciscanos en el reino misterioso de la Nueva Mexico* (Mexico City, 1934):95, 96. NMF, 113. Hackett and Shelby, *Revolt*, 2:366. Naylor and Polzer, *Presidio and Militia*, 1:514, 539–40.

78. Fray Nicolás López Jardón, native of New Spain, professed on 1 November 1654. He preached at the Capilla de San Cosme of the Province of the Holy Gospel in Mexico City on 13 January 1675. As fray Francisco de Ayeta's secretary, López arrived in El Paso with the supply caravan in the summer of 1680. Ayeta chose him to carry the first news of the Pueblo Revolt to Mexico City. Having returned to El Paso, López accompanied Ayeta on the 1681–82 Otermín expedition.

In 1683, López went with Mre. de campo Juan Domínguez de Mendoza on an expedition to Texas. López helped fray Antonio de Acevedo and fray Juan de Zabaleta in the establishment of missions at La Junta de los Ríos and among the Jumano Indians. López found the Indians of Texas favorably disposed to receiving missionaries and set himself to the task of providing them.

In October 1683, López was procurator and vice-custos. Having been selected by the religious to seek assistance in Mexico City for the expansion of the missions into Texas, he spent much of 1685–86 with Domínguez de Mendoza in that effort. In 1687, López was custos and by 1692, was dead. EBARN. Chávez, *Archives*, 11. Elizabeth A.H. John, *Storms Brewed in Other Men's Worlds: The Confrontation of Indians, Spanish, and French in the Southwest, 1540–1795* (College Station, Tex., 1975):176–77, 179.

Hackett and Shelby, *Revolt*, 1:93. Vetancurt, *Teatro mexicano*, 3:220. Rosa Figueroa, Becerro.

79. Here Vargas incorrectly identifies the Southern Tiwa pueblo of Ysleta as Piro.

80. The Chinarras ranged south of Casas Grandes on the upper San Miguel and Santa María rivers in present-day Sonora. They were nomadic hunters and extended their hunts into the high valleys located east of the principal ranges of the Sierra Madre. According to one scholar, the Chinarras were desert-dwelling relatives of the Conchos who lived in the area of the Florido, Concho, San Pedro, and Chuvíscar river systems. Griffen, "Southern Periphery: East," in *Handbook*, 10:331. Naylor and Polzer, *Presidio and Militia*, 1:528.

81. Evidently, this is a reference to Keres Indians associated with Bartolomé de Ojeda, who is likely the unnamed, but literate, Indian governor mentioned here by Vargas.

82. The Conchos were probably speakers of a Uto-Aztecan language. They were semisedentary agriculturalists living in the Conchos river valley and along the Rio Grande. Their territory lay north of the desert area of the Bolsón de Mapimí, some 225 km northeast of Durango. Forbes, *Apache*, 39. Naylor and Polzer, *Presidio and Militia*, 1:304–305. Griffen, "Southern Periphery: East," in *Handbook*, 10:330.

83. Presidio Viejo was probably the site of the presidio first established for the El Paso district sometime in the spring or summer of 1682. It was located halfway between El Paso and San Lorenzo. By the spring of 1684, it had already been moved permanently to El Paso. Walz, "El Paso," 73, 118, 133 n60.

84. Fray Diego de Mendoza was one of the survivors of the Pueblo Revolt. At the time, he was guardian of the convento of Nuestra Señora del Socorro. Hackett and Shelby, *Revolt*, 1:30–31, 57.

85. The Sierra Negra is in the Guadalupe Peak range, midway between El Paso and the Pecos River. The range rises in southern Chaves County, New Mexico, then passes through the corner of Otero County and extends along the western boundary of Eddy County.

86. This terrain was covered with what the Spaniards termed bojedal (boj, boxwood; bojedal, stand of boxwood). Since the boxwood, a woody shrub or small tree of the family Buxaceae, is native to neither Texas nor New Mexico, the Spaniards were obviously applying a name they knew to a plant new to them. The bush referred to may have been from the genus *Bumelia*, tough, spiny trees or shrubs, sometimes referred to as ironwood. These may be found around salt marshes or in the gravelly hills associated with them. Personal communication with William C. Martin, curator of the Herbarium of the Department of Biology, University of New Mexico, 15 Aug. 1988.

87. A seventeenth-century smoothbore musket had a range of approximately 90 m. Personal communication with J. William LaRue, colonial-firearms expert, 12 Aug. 1988.

88. Translated here as hoe, the word coa (Nahuatl cuahuitl, or digging stick) means "a broad, flat metal blade resembling a one-sided spade, with a socket in which a long wooden handle was fitted in the same axis as the blade." Simmons and Turley, *Ironwork*, 84–85.

89. The second successive day labeled Thursday, this was apparently Friday the fourteenth and the next day, Saturday the fifteenth.

90. The phrase sal de flor, or flor de sal, refers to salt formed by the evaporation of rainwater on desert playas. "Light rains provided the best condition for the rapid crystallization of salts from capillary waters, resulting in an abundant deposition of fairly pure salt, called *sal de flor*." West, *Parral*, 37, 38.

91. The feast of St. Joseph is 19 March.

92. Here Vargas uses escopeta in the general sense of firearm, rather than his usual word, harquebus. The terms were synonymous, as was fusil, and by this time, referred to a flintlock firearm, in contrast to the

mosquete, which was a matchlock. Fray Francisco de Ayeta, commenting on the request of the Santa Fe cabildo for supplies for the refugees from the Pueblo Revolt, specified that they needed flintlock harquebuses with six thousand additional flints (1 January 1681). In the early sixteenth century, the term harquebus referred to the firearm supplied with a matchlock, but by the turn of the century had begun to be applied to the one with a wheellock. During the early eighteenth century in New Spain, the harquebus could be fitted with a flintlock. Harold L. Peterson, *Arms and Armor in Colonial America*, 1526–1783 (New York, 1956):12–13. Hackett and Shelby, *Revolt*, 1:238.

93. Sentinels divided the night into three watches, or cuartos. The first was the cuarto de la prima, or first watch; the second, the cuarto de la modorra, time of the deepest sleep, before sunrise; and the third watch, the cuarto del alba, or dawn watch. Vargas Machuca, in a discussion of the manner in which a military encampment should be set up, advised that two guards should be on duty on each watch, circling the camp on horseback. Bernardo de Vargas Machuca, *Milicia y descripción de las Indias* (1599; rpt., Madrid, 1892), 1:213.

94. The tradition of just war can be traced to Augustine, Aquinas, Francisco de Vitoria (c1486–1546), and Francisco

Suárez (1548–1617). Vitoria declared "the only just cause to declare a war is having received some injury." Spanish law delineated situations in which war could be made against Indians subject to the crown: when Indians initiated hostilities or became apostates and rebelled against local authorities. RECOP, Lib. 3, tít. 4, ley 9. Ramón Menéndez Pidal, *El P. Las Casas y Vitoria con otras temas de los siglos xvi y xvii* (Madrid, 1966):9–48. Francisco de Vitoria, *Relecciones sobre los indios y el derecho de guerra* (San José, Costa Rica, 1988):138.

95. Vargas alludes specifically to Cochiti here evidently because at that pueblo, in 1681, the advanced detachment of Otermín's unsuccessful reconquering expedition had sensed a trap and turned back. Hackett and Shelby, *Revolt*, 1:cl–clxvii.

96. All of these designations for different Apache groups are now obsolete. The Apaches of the Llanos were probably not an entity; rather the name was applied to several groups who gathered on the Plains to hunt bison. The Faraones were first mentioned in 1675. The name is derived from the Spanish Faraón, or Pharaoh. The Faraones have not been identified with any modern Apache group, although they may have merged with the Mescaleros. The Apaches de Siete Ríos are so called because they occupied the area between the Guadalupe Mountains and the Pecos River called Los Siete Ríos.

The name first appeared in 1659. These same Indians were often called Faraones. The term Salineros was used to describe several different Apache groups widely separated geographically. All were in some way associated with salinas. Gila Apaches living south of the Zuni salt lakes, others near the Manzano Salines in present-day Torrance County, and a group living on the Río Salado (Pecos River) were all referred to as Salineros at one time or another. The Apaches de Chilmo, or Chilmos, lived west of the Rio Grande, north of the Mansos (on an El Paso-Tucson axis), and south of Acoma. They were considered separate from the Gila Apaches. The term appeared first in 1667 and seems to come from the name of a chief, El Chilmo. Opler, "Apachean Culture," in *Handbook*, 10:389–92.

97. Although both secular and ecclesiastical authorities recognized the right of asylum, its development was marked by jurisdictional conflict. Felipe II (1527–98) abolished this right in all his possessions in 1570, but Pope Sixtus V (1520–90) issued a bull in 1573 prohibiting civil authorities from apprehending criminals who had taken refuge in places of asylum. The Royal Council, as was its prerogative, declined to make this bull public. More than a century later, the *Recopilación* stated that the church had to conform to secular law on matters of asylum, thus underscoring the lack of accord surrounding this issue. Barred from asylum were: highwaymen guilty of murder or robbery; those who burned or otherwise destroyed vineyards, croplands, and forests; those who killed or wounded someone in a church or cemetery while seeking asylum; and church arsonists.

A cleric was bound to give asylum to anyone else seeking sanctuary and provide them food and protection. He was to prevent forced removal of his charge. If, however, removal could be negotiated, the cleric had the responsibility to act as an intermediary to ensure the prisoner would be neither harmed nor killed, asking first that the authorities pardon him before leaving the church. Alfonso X, El Sabio, *Primera Partida según el manuscrito Add. 20.787 del British Museum* (Valladolid, 1975), Par. 1, tít 11, leyes 3, 5–6. Jaime Uyá, ed., *Fuero juzgo o libro de los jueces* (1815; rpt., Barcelona, 1968), Lib. 6, tít. 5, ley 16; Lib. 9, tít. 2, ley 1. Antonio Domínguez Ortiz, "Regalismo y relaciones iglesia-estado en el siglo xvii," in *Historia de la iglesia en España* (Madrid, 1979), 4:95–96. RECOP, Lib. 1, tít. 5, ley 2. *Enciclopedia de la cultura española* (Madrid, 1963), 1:515. Pedro Benito Golmayo, *Instituciones del derecho canónico* (Madrid, 1896), 2:92–93.

98. José de Urrutia, a native of Rentería (Guipúzcoa), came to Mexico City in 1676, where he lived on the Calle del Parque. He

served as a senior comptroller in the royal treasury. On 6 April 1684, he married Margarita de Arana y del Castillo, a native of Puebla who had been living in Mexico City for four years; the marriage produced several children. Urrutia died on 27 January 1709, after having made his will before Nicolás del Castillo, a royal notary, on 19 February 1708. J. Ignacio Rubio Mañé, "Gente de España en la ciudad de México: Año de 1689," Sobretiro del *Boletín del Archivo General de la Nación,* 2d ser., 7 (Mexico City, 1966):331.

ENLISTMENT OF MISSIONARIES FOR THE CONVERSION OF THE APACHES, AUGUST 1691.*

Father Francisco de Vargas, apparently chaplain on Gov. Domingo Jironza's devastating foray against the Pueblo Indians fortified at Zia Pueblo in 1689, evidently witnessed the peace entered into by Apaches in September of that year as the victorious Spaniards marched back toward El Paso. Here, almost two years later, he appeals to the missionary zeal of his Franciscan brethren, some of them newly arrived, to go out and work among these former enemies. He writes this letter the day after testifying before Governor Vargas about the rumored mercury mine. Two of the friars who vow in response to enter the Apache field, fray Cristóbal Alonso Barroso and fray Francisco Corvera, will accompany Vargas on his armed reconnaissance of New Mexico a year later.

> *Fray Francisco de Vargas, Letter patent, El Paso, 4 August 1691, LS.*

Summons to the infidel Apaches
Reverend father preachers and apostolic missionaries of this our holy custody
Brother missionaries
Jesus, Mary, and Joseph
Read in the convento of El Paso. Read in the real of San Lorenzo. Read in San Antonio de Senecú. Seen in Corpus Christi de la Ysleta. Read in La Purísima Concepción del Socorro. Read in Nuestro Padre San Francisco de los Mansos.
In attendance.

A Franciscan missionary, after Diego
Valadés, *Rhetórica Christiana* (1579)
  From John L. Kessell, *Kiva, Cross, and
  Crown* (1979)

Inasmuch as we are obliged by our duty to repeatedly suggest to your reverences that the commands of our reverend father superiors should be observed, kept, and carried out, as should what I have ordered by my letters patent (the first of which I made known after having received the office of custos of this Holy Custody of the Conversion of St. Paul of New Mexico),[1] I order that they be read again in each convento so that ignorance of them cannot be alleged at any time, unless the letters patent[2] have already been presented again. There is not the least need to come together at this convento of El Paso, as the letter patent says, and so forth.

God Our Lord in His majesty saw fit that in the year 1689 in the month of September, the barbarous Indians of the Apache nation made peace with the Spaniards of this kingdom, something many apostolic ministers who had lived in this holy custody had wished for with fervor and spirit. Even with the information about this nation and its vastness, many father preachers from other holy provinces had so wished. It was the most rebellious nation and did serious damage to the Spaniards and other people of this kingdom, by carrying off horses and other livestock and through hostility, infesting the countryside and killing many Christians of this kingdom. Today we see that this nation is tame, coming in peace into most of the pueblos of this kingdom. Because we, the religious of this our holy custody, as apostolic missionaries, should not lose this opportunity, we suggest to your reverences and ask that each one of you put all your painstaking effort and care into trying to reduce the souls of the Apache nation to the brotherhood of our holy Catholic faith. I have no doubt that with your reverences' spirit and fervor, you will achieve this end. As we know, the meekness of our Order has achieved more than the clash and force of arms. Our reverend fathers superior suggest this to us, making it known to us by the letter patent given to the father preacher, fray Antonio de Acevedo,[3] in his commission to bring religious from our holy mother province.

I remind your reverences of the spirit and yearning for martyrdom of our father, St. Francis, with which he infused his first sons, who showed acceptance, love, and gentle treatment for the most barbarous nations; and of my well-known experience of having been summoned by the Apaches to the sierra they call the Organ Mountains,[4] 30 leagues beyond El Paso, where I was for two days. I found myself among a very large number of Indians, having neither reinforcement of Spanish soldiers nor defense to resist such a profusion of barbarians should they have tried to kill me. Yet, I saw they were docile. Beyond this, we have other experiences with the nations around the jurisdiction of the real of Parral. We know that, after having captured some religious from our holy Order, they set them free, without harming them whatsoever, having fed them from their own food.

Thus, any omission and lack of spirit in the sons of the holy family of our father, St. Francis, will be very blameworthy, whether from fear of martyrdom, which contradicts the apostolic spirit and their vows, or for personal safety and comfort. We who live in such safety and with such outstanding examples are those with least right to fear. In any event, all will achieve the happiest merits and rewards through their apostolic rule.

If I have previously omitted this suggestion and exhortation, which is so full of grace, it was in consideration of the lack of ministers in this holy custody. Today, though, we have the necessary number here; with a minister in each of the six missions, there are enough for the administration of the holy sacraments. Thus, to the reverend father preacher apostolic missionaries who are not engaged in this activity, but who have a zeal for souls and have fervent spirits, I give them—beginning now—my blessing and permission in the name of our father, St. Francis, to go out apostolically to reduce the barbarous nations of these areas and in particular, the Apaches. Because of their rebelliousness, this is what has been wished for. It is thought that if our end is achieved through valor and effort, they will steadfastly embrace the holy faith.

I do not excuse myself from being the first because of my responsibility as custos, so that we shall not fail in this holy effort. Therefore, I order this letter patent to be made known. So that this information may reach all your reverences, it will be read in every convento. So that we may see which religious dedicate themselves to such a holy and exalted ministry, at the foot of this letter patent, each one should sign, that is, those who wish to go out voluntarily on such an exalted undertaking. They will leave from this convento of El Paso on the date cited, 15 August of this year, day of the Glorious Mystery of the Assumption of Our Lady, the Virgin Mary, who will serve as our guide and true pole star. May God Our Lord inspire your reverences most appropriately for His holy service and keep your reverences for me for many happy years in His holy grace. Convento of Our Lady of Guadalupe of El Paso, 4 August 1691.

Your reverences' friend and brother in the Lord who loves you and kisses your hands,

Fray Francisco de Vargas

Custos [rubrica]

———

Fray Cristóbal Alonso Barroso.[5] With the blessing of God and your reverence,[6] I shall go to those conversions of that nation or another or wherever God inspires me. In obedience to the present letter patent, I signed it with my name on 5 August 1691.

Fray Cristóbal Alonso Barroso [rubrica]

———

In accord with what was ordered and arranged in the letter patent contained above, I, fray Agustín de Colina,[7] missionary preacher of this holy custody of New Mexico, say that immediately when my will was disposed by holy obedience—to which it submits in every-thing through the vocation the Lord saw fit to give me—I have answered the call to this ministry twice already.

Notwithstanding that my imperfections do not merit such an exalted happiness, I shall gladly and humbly go. The Lord who governs my superiors' hearts will direct and govern all our actions. So that it may be of record, I signed in the same way as the father preacher, fray Cristóbal Alonso Barroso. If by chance my intent is not achieved among the nearest nations, because they are without fixed settlements, I shall go until I encounter others, those the Lord may see fit, if it is His divine pleasure. Today, 5 August 1691.

Fray Agustín de Colina [rubrica]

———

In conformity with and in the same way as the above fathers, I say that I shall go. I signed it as the truth. Today, 6 August 1691.

Fray Francisco Corvera[8] [rubrica]

———

Letter patent from fray Francisco de Vargas, given in the year 1691
The year 1691
So that the religious who wish to go to the conversion of the Apaches
may be enlisted

*AASF, 1691:5. 2 folios, 3 written pages.

1. The Custody of the Conversion of St. Paul—so named in commemoration of the assistance of St. Paul on the feast day of his conversion, 25 January, at the battle of Acoma in 1599—was a semiautonomous administrative body within the Franciscan Holy Gospel Province in New Spain. As a result of church-state jurisdictional conflicts from 1612 to 1616, the New Mexico mission field was raised to the status of a custody. Previously, its superior had been a commissary, but with the new status as custody, New Mexico gained a father custos, its own chapter, and definitors. RBC, 179 n2. KCC, 96, 103.

2. A patente, or letter patent, was a copy of a letter from major Franciscan superiors, often sent when the religious were being informed, consulted, or moved from one convento to another. Chávez, *Archives*, 5.

3. Fray Antonio de Acevedo, who professed in Puebla on 29 June 1674, was a native of Veracruz. He was serving as secretary at the mission of Ysleta del Sur in 1682. In 1683–84, Acevedo accompanied fray Nicolás López and Capt. Juan Domínguez de Mendoza to La Junta de los Ríos, after a delegation of Indians from there requested missionaries for their Jumano communities and for the central Texas tribes. Fray Antonio and fray Juan de Zabaleta remained in La Junta when the expedition turned east toward Texas. After only a few months, however, the pair apparently had to flee for their lives. They went to Parral, where Custos fray Salvador de San Antonio found them in 1685, and returned to El Paso with him. Fray Antonio subsequently worked in the missions of Corpus Christi de Ysleta and the real of San Lorenzo. In 1695, he was at Nambe Pueblo and a definitor of the custody. He served as guardian in Santa Fe from early 1695 to late 1696 and was still in the New Mexico mission field in 1702. Espinosa, *Pueblo Indian Revolt of 1696*, 156–57, 165, 204, 208, 253. Chávez, *Archives*, 8, 18. J. Charles Kelley, "The Historic Indian Pueblos of La Junta de los Ríos," NMHR 27 (Oct. 1952):266–70. Adams and Chávez, *Missions*, 261 n34, 329.

4. The Organ Mountains are at the south end of the Rocky

Mountain range in central New Mexico, about 16 km east of Las Cruces.

5. Fray Cristóbal Alonso Barroso, born in Lisbon, professed as a Franciscan at the Convento Grande in Mexico City on 5 March 1685. Barroso arrived at El Paso in 1691 and accompanied fray Francisco Corvera and fray Miguel Muñiz de Luna as chaplains on Vargas's first expedition to New Mexico the following year. In 1694, Barroso sailed with the flota for Spain to report to his superiors and press Vargas's request for more priests. From February 1698 to November 1699, he was in Santa Fe and in 1700, at Pecos. He died after 1703. Adams and Chávez, *Missions*, 330. Espinosa, *Pueblo Indian Revolt of 1696*, 63, 67, 82, 83. KCC, 497, 535 n18.

6. Reverence, an honorary title equivalent to provincial father, or father of the Order, was, with other titles, privileges, and exemptions, abolished—with some limitations—by Pope Urban VIII's (1623–44) 1639 brief. The reforms, however, did not persist, and the titles reappeared. Lázaro Iriarte de Aspurz, *Franciscan History: The Three Orders of St. Francis of Assisi* (Chicago, 1979):255–56.

7. Fray Agustín de Colina, who had earlier been custos of the custody in the province of Zacatecas, served in various capacities in the mission field of El Paso between 1689 and 1692. He then spent several years as a missionary to the Jumanos, submitting a report in 1693 concerning the state of the missions at La Junta de los Ríos. Between 1703 and 1707, fray Agustín labored at Zia, Santa Ana, Bernalillo, Jemez, San Ildefonso, and Tesuque. In 1707, he was custos of the New Mexico missions. Chávez, *Archives*, 9, 22, 245. Adams and Chávez, *Missions*, 259, 329.

8. Born in Manila, fray Francisco Corvera professed at the Convento Grande in Mexico City on 8 February 1684. He was apostolic notary in El Paso in 1691. In 1692 and 1693, Corvera participated in Vargas's two expeditions and served as assistant at Santa Fe in 1694. Assigned to San Ildefonso and Jacona in October 1694, he ministered there until June 1696, when he died inside the church at San Ildefonso, which was set on fire by Pueblo Indians. KCC, 252, 275, 287–88, 535 n18. Adams and Chávez, *Missions*, 331.

From the tone of this letter, it is obvious that former Gov. Pedro Reneros de Posada considers himself Diego de Vargas's friend, but also his social equal. Although he writes mainly to clear up rumors about the marital status of the Black drummer and herald, Sebastián Rodríguez, he takes the opportunity to congratulate don Diego and inform him of the deaths in Mexico City of several prominent people.

*Pedro Reneros de Posada to Diego de Vargas,
Mexico City, 4 April 1692, LS.*

I received your letter and am pleased you are in good health. I congratulate you on your victories in the wars in Sonora and the Organ Mountains, where you demonstrated your great valor. It is obvious that your deeds correspond to the great sense of duty with which you were born.

All your friends, as well as the viceroy, have been very pleased with your successes because there is no certain information from Spain, although there are rumors in which one should not take great stock. This land is in serious decline because of the great scarcity of everything.

God has taken lord don Fernando Valenzuela,[1] the Marqués de Guardiola,[2] don Juan de Urquiola,[3] don Fernando de Haro Monterroso,[4] and the wife of don Jacinto de Vargas.[5] I was very ill, but at present am in good health, which is what matters. As for the rest, God will dispose as He sees fit. As I say, my health is good as are the horses I ride, and everything else is all right, for which I thank God. Order me as you wish. You can count on me, with the zeal of a good friend, come what may, here or anywhere.

Moving on to respond to what you propose to me about the Black, Sebastián,[6] I made the effort and looked for the individuals from whom I had heard rumors about his being married. I asked them what they knew about the matter and whether Sebastián Rodríguez had married in Veracruz. They replied to me that they knew no such thing, I had misheard them, and such a conversation must have been about another Black, not Sebastián Rodríguez. I say I heard wrong and thought they were talking about him in that conversation.

So I say it is time he got married. Having satisfied myself that they were talking about another and not him, I can raise no objection. The reason for having raised any at all was the rumors I had heard from another. Because my memory is failing, I thought they were talking about him. I also thought you would agree with me because you like him so much.

May God Our Lord keep you many years. Mexico City, 4 April 1691.

Your friend and sure servant kisses your hands,

Pedro Reneros Posada [rubrica]

I am writing to Capt. Diego Arias[7] and Tomás de la Carrera.[8]

Lord governor and captain general, don Diego de Vargas Zapata Luján Ponce de León, my friend and lord

---

*AASF, 1691:1. 2 folios, 3 written pages. This document is misdated; by internal evidence, it had to have been written in April 1692, not 1691.

1. Fernando Valenzuela y Enciso was an unlettered, ambitious man who rose to great influence as a valido, or favorite, during the regency of Mariana de Austria (1634–96) and the reign of Carlos II (1661–1700).

In January 1677, however, Valenzuela was dismissed and subsequently exiled to the Philippines for a period of ten years. He languished in exile, having left his wife in New Spain. Later, while waiting in Mexico City for permission to return to Spain, he died in January 1692 after being kicked by a horse. John Lynch, *Spain Under the Habsburgs* (New York, 1984), 2:262–67. Robles, *Diario*, 2:236–37.

2. Dr. Juan de Padilla Guardiola y Guzmán, first Marqués de Santa Fe de Guardiola, was born in Seville, where he was baptized in the parish church of San Vicente on 29 August 1643. On 4 May 1670 in Madrid, in the parish church of San Ginés, he married Gerónima de Arratia y Cisneros, a native of the city, baptized in the parish church of San Andrés on 1 October 1636.

He received appointment as judge of the Audiencia of Santo Domingo on 18 July 1669. After completing his term on 23 May 1678, he returned to Spain for three years. A promotion to judge of the Audiencia of Guadalajara came on 8 April 1680.

Padilla was appointed judge of the Audiencia of Mexico on 10 April 1683. During his service in this capacity until his death, sometime before April 1692, he was nominated to serve on the Chancellery of Granada.

With the judicial career came other honors. He was recognized as royal councillor and, on 6 July 1682, inducted into the Order of Calatrava. His marquisate was issued on 6 March 1691. Both his sons, Juan Ildefonso de Padilla Gómez de Arratia, baptized in Santo Domingo on 19 February 1673, and Gaspar Raimundo de

Padilla y Guardiola, baptized in Santo Domingo on 9 February 1676, followed him into the Order of Calatrava in 1690. Lohmann Villena, *Americanos*, 2:93, 95. García Carraffa, *Diccionario heráldico*, 65:92. Schäfer, *Consejo Real*, 2:448, 458, 496. Ampelio Alonso-Cadenas López, Julio de Atienza et al., *Elenco de grandezas y títulos nobiliarios, 1981* (Madrid, 1981):550.

3. Juan Bautista de Urquiola y Elorriaga began his judicial career as a fiscal for the Audiencia of Guatemala on 10 April 1669. On 23 June 1671, he was elevated to judge of the audiencia until his promotion on 12 April 1680 to criminal judge of the Audiencia of Mexico. He served until 19 December 1686, when he became judge. He died in Mexico City on 16 February 1692. His funeral two days later in the church of San Pedro y San Pablo was attended by the viceroy, the audiencia, and the cabildo. Schäfer, *Consejo Real*, 2:458, 462, 477, 479. Robles, *Diario*, 2:240, 241.

4. In 1669, Lic. Fernando de Haro Monterroso was serving as solicitador fiscal of the Council of the Indies in Spain. As a subordinate of the Spanish ambassador to the Vatican, he was responsible for preparing business matters of the council and seeing to their dispatch with the ambassador's help. On 10 July of that year, he received his first American appointment as fiscal of the Audiencia of Guadalajara.

Haro became a judge on 19 November 1672. From there, he was promoted to criminal judge for the Audiencia of Mexico on 13 November 1680, filling this position for six years and becoming a civil judge on 23 December 1686.

In Mexico City, Haro lived on the Calle del Reloj with his wife, María de Vivanco. He died on 12 March 1692 and was buried the following day in the parish church of Santo Domingo. The Conde de Galve, the audiencia, and members of both the ecclesiastical and civil cabildos attended the funeral. Robles, *Diario*, 2:242. Rubio Mañé, "Gente de España," 187–88. Schäfer, *Consejo Real*, 2:206 n57, 458, 462, 496, 497.

5. Lic. Jacinto de Vargas Campuzano had been serving as a judge on the Audiencia of Mexico since 5 June 1685. His long career in the Indies began with his 24 December 1658 appointment as fiscal of the Audiencia of Santo Domingo, a position from which he was promoted to judge on 27 May 1661. On 2 October 1664, he was transferred to the Audiencia of Panama and from there to Santa Fe de Bogotá on 23 January 1666. He became criminal judge with the Mexican audiencia on 23 May 1674, serving until his last promotion to civil judge.

Vargas Campuzano was born in Toledo where he was baptized on 6 April 1628. He was the son of Juan de Vargas, a native of Dosbarrios in Toledo, and Lucía de Puelles.

While living in Madrid, he married Juana de Deza y Ulloa on 8 September 1658. She was from Peñaranda de Bracamonte (Santander), the daughter of Juan de Deza y Ulloa, a native of Toro, and Antonia de Vallejo, from Fuentidueña (Segovia).

In February 1692, doña Juana died in Mexico City. Her husband survived until 19 April 1697. They left one child, Juan José de Vargas, who, with Fernando de Deza y Ulloa, served as executors for Vargas Campuzano's estate. He had lived on the Calle de los Donceles and was buried in the Convento de Santa Teresa. Schäfer, *Consejo Real*, 2:447, 450, 458, 462, 470, 502. Rubio Mañé, "Gente de España," 154. Robles, *Diario*, 2:239.

6. Sebastián Rodríguez Brito, the son of Manuel Rodríguez and María Fernández, was most likely born in the 1650s in or near Luanda, Angola. How or when he came to the New World as a slave is unknown. By July 1687, however, he was in the domestic service of Governor Reneros de Posada. By May 1689, Rodríguez was free and living in El Paso. He was attempting to secure permission to marry Antonia Naranjo, the mulatta daughter of Pascual Naranjo and María Romero, citizens of New Mexico then resident in El Paso. The marriage bid was apparently unsuccessful because of unsubstantiated rumors that he already had a wife in Veracruz.

In 1691, still single, Rodríguez again sought permission to wed. He arranged a marriage contract with Isabel Holguín, a citizen of New Mexico. This only resulted in a brief union, for by 1696, Rodríguez was a widower living in Santa Fe and again seeking a wife. At this time, he was employed as the drummer of the presidio's company. He eventually married Juana de la Cruz, a native of Las Salinas, but of unknown descent, on 12 May 1697.

Rodríguez continued to live and work as the company's drummer in Santa Fe. By 1706, he was married yet again, this time to Juana de Arzate y Apodaca, the mestiza daughter of Caterina López de Yracia, a single woman, and an unknown Spaniard. Arzate had at one time been an Indian captive. She had at least two children with Rodríguez, Melchor and Margarita, and a daughter named María Rosa de Apodaca from an earlier liaison with a man known only as Domingo who was living with them. Rodríguez was dead by 1717. AASF, Diligencias matrimoniales, 1689:1, 1690:5, 1691:3, 1694:32, 1696:26, 1697:7, 1698:6, 1717:15. Juana de Arzate y Apodaca, Declaration, Santa Fe, 11 March 1706, AGN, Inquisición 735.

7. Diego Arias de Quirós was a native of Asturias and the son of Juan de Quirós Prieto and Inés Arias. He married María Ana Montoya, widow of Nicolás Márquez, on 20 July 1694. At that time, he was serving as royal alferez of Santa Fe. He received a grant of land just east of the Governor's Palace in Santa Fe and was a member of the Confraternity of Our Lady of the Conquest. Arias de Quirós's wife died in 1712, and he married María Gómez Robledo two years later at San Ildefonso. He served as alcalde mayor and alcalde ordinario in Santa Fe into the late 1720s. NMF, 134. NMR, 1:118.

8. Tomás Gutiérrez Carrera was born around 1665 in the pueblo of Cianca y Parbayón, municipio of Piélagos, located in a mountain valley in the Spanish province of Santander. Once two towns, Cianca and Parbayón were united as a result of declining population caused by an epidemic in the 1640s. Tomás was the son of Juan Gutiérrez Carrera and Catalina del Cotero. He was at Zacatecas in 1689 when he came to El Paso as an aide to Governor Reneros de Posada. In 1692, at age twenty-seven he married María Baca, age fifteen, either the daughter or the niece of Sgto. mayor Ignacio Baca, deceased, and Juana Anaya Almazán. He participated in Vargas's entrada later that year, but in 1695, was still living in El Paso. AASF, Diligencias matrimoniales, 1692:2, 1695:1. Pascual Madoz, *Diccionario geográfico-estadístico-histórico de España y sus posesiones de ultramar* (Madrid, 1845–50), 6:382–83; 13:25. Espinosa, "Population," 61–84.

PROCEEDINGS IN THE JURISDICTIONAL DISPUTE BETWEEN THE FATHER PRESIDENT, FRAY JOAQUIN DE HINOJOSA AND GOV. DIEGO DE VARGAS, EL PASO, JUNE 1692.*

As the years wore on, the unusual circumstances of Spanish refugee families living interspersed among Indians in the mission pueblos of the El Paso district caused friction between Franciscan missionaries and civil authorities. The friars continued to exercise a spiritual monopoly in the exiled colony, administering the sacraments to both Indians and Spaniards. Because they considered New Mexico an active missionary field, this was, to their way of thinking, as it should be. When fray Joaquín de Hinojosa, the interim superior in 1692, sought to define and control Indian lands—citing the ideal of separating Indians and Spaniards—he tested not only the expedient status quo, but also the authority and mettle of Gov. Diego de Vargas.

The documents that follow reveal one aspect of the dispute. Father Hinojosa wants an official copy of the proceedings of an earlier confrontation explained in the next section below. Governor Vargas denies the Franciscan's request. Let the viceroy decide who is correct, he admonishes. Indignant, friar and governor accuse each other of violating the spirit of the patronato real, the Spanish crown's patronage of the church in the Indies. Several local citizens, summoned by the friars, find themselves caught up in the controversy.

Fray Joaquín de Hinojosa, Petition for a copy of proceedings, El Paso, 2 June 1692, DS.

Fray Joaquín de Hinojosa,[1] son of the Holy Gospel Province of the Order of Our Seraphic Father St. Francis, preacher, missionary, president in capite,[2] and interim ecclesiastical judge of this Holy Custody of the Conversion of St. Paul of New Mexico for the Apostolic Holy See, and so forth: Today, Monday, 2 June of this year 1692, when I was in this convento of Nuestra Señora de Guadalupe del Paso, don Diego de Vargas Zapata Luján Ponce de León, the lord governor and captain general, castellan of the fortress of this presidio of El Paso, sent to me by his secretary of government the proceedings he was to and did make known to me before four witnesses: Sgto. mayor Francisco de Anaya Almazán,[3] alcalde de primer voto; Capt. Juan García de Noriega,[4] alguacil mayor; Capt. don Fernando de Chaves; and Sgto. mayor Juan Lucero de Godoy. Before them, he made known to me the proceedings in which, responding to a petition I had presented before the lord governor, I asked him to see fit to give me a copy of the proceedings he saw fit to provide in response to the presentations I have made. Contained in them is not only that I do not deny royal authority and usurp that of the patronato real,[5] but also that I am supported by it, royal cedulas, and the orders of the Royal Audiencia of Mexico. For proof of this, I refer to the presentations mentioned. So that it might and may be of record in any court that it is untrue that I deny or usurp royal jurisdiction, I asked the lord governor for a copy of what had been provided and presented that might serve as an instrument of his allegation, since according to law, an authorized copy should not be denied the party requesting it. Although at the end of the proceedings made known to me, he promises this copy, at the beginning, he refuses it. I summoned as witnesses of the notification made to me those people referred to above, before whom the proceedings were made known to me and that he did not even give me time to reply.

For this reason, I recognize that if the lord governor says that the reverend fathers, my predecessors, have not raised this point, it will have been because I have raised it, since I am being denied the justice of a copy and of being heard. It is being falsely imputed to me that I deny the patronato real, when it is of record from my presentations that I rely on it for the use of my jurisdiction and success of the missionary endeavor in these lands, for which I have presented a

cedula from the king our lord (may God keep him) and cited the ordinances of the Royal Audiencia of Mexico. So that for all time and before any competent judge it may be of record, I protest the implication that I do not accept the patronato real and, what is more, deny the slander of my denying it. I ask once, twice, and a third time for a legal, faithful, and authorized copy from the secretary of government and war, inserting in it as well the last proceedings made known to me today. I neither wish, intend, nor presume to prefer the Indians or that the citizens and other people of this kingdom not be attended to with total love. I say they are aided with every loving kindness, and in proof of these truths, I refer to what has been presented. So that this my notification may have the proper form, I order our secretary and apostolic notary to make it known to the lord governor before the same witnesses who served for the notification from him, putting at the end of these proceedings what he may see fit to reply before those witnesses, made legal with their signatures, to which our secretary and apostolic notary will attest. Done in this above-mentioned convento on the day, month, and year ut supra.
Fray Joaquín de Hinojosa [rubrica]
Interim ecclesiastical judge

Before me,
Fray Agustín de Colina [rubrica]
Secretary and apostolic notary

———

I, fray Agustín de Colina, missionary president of this convento of Nuestra Señora de Guadalupe del Paso, secretary of this Holy Custody of the Conversion of St. Paul of New Mexico, and apostolic notary, state that I went to comply with the order from the reverend father, fray Joaquín de Hinojosa, preacher, missionary, president in capite, and interim ecclesiastical judge of this kingdom of New Mexico, in which he ordered me to make known the above proceedings to the governor, captain general, and castellan of the fortress of this presidio of El Paso for his majesty. Brought into the lord governor's presence and after he gave me a seat with his customary politeness, I greeted him and asked him to listen to the proceedings referred to. He denied me the presence of the witnesses cited in it and refused in every way to allow me to read it. I stated that the three Divine Persons—Father, Son, and Holy Spirit—would be my witnesses. Having denied the copy, he did not want to hear the request of appeal and protest that his reverence in no way denied the patronato real. When the lord governor heard my words, which implored the highest and holiest tribunal of the Most Holy Trinity, he ordered the four witnesses called to make it known to them how he was ready to give the copy, but that it would be stamped and sealed with the letter of transmittal to the most excellent lord viceroy. Before these witnesses, I, as apostolic notary, made the proper protest, as was my responsibility, summoning them as witnesses, that the reverend father president did not deny the patronato real, but supported it for the better success of his office. I summoned them as witnesses that the lord governor did not listen to the above proceedings. So that it may be of record, the witnesses, Sgto. mayor Francisco de Anaya Almazán, alcalde de primer voto of the cabildo; Capt. Juan García de Noriega, alguacil mayor; Sgto. mayor Juan Lucero de Godoy; and Capt. don Fernando de Chaves, signed it with me on 2 June 1692.

I, Juan Lucero, state that what I sign is what the lord governor promised: to give the copy.
Juan Lucero de Godoy [rubrica]
Stamped and sealed

I, fray Agustín de Colina, missionary president of this convento of Nuestra Señora de Guadalupe del Paso, secretary of this Holy Custody of the Conversion of St. Paul of New Mexico, state that I called to this convento of El Paso don Fernando de Chaves as a witness summoned in the presence of the lord governor so that he might sign my protest that the lord governor promised to give a stamped and sealed copy with the letter of transmittal to the most excellent lord viceroy of New Spain. He stated that it was true and that he did not dare sign, because he had seen eight men in the province of New Mexico beheaded over a signature.[6] When I told him to sign his statement, he refused completely. So that it may be of record, I attest to it as apostolic notary.

Before me,
Fray Agustín de Colina [rubrica]
Secretary and apostolic notary

I, fray Agustín de Colina, missionary president of this convento of Nuestra Señora de Guadalupe del Paso, secretary of this holy custody, and apostolic notary, state that I called Capt. Juan García de Noriega,[7] alguacil mayor of the cabildo, for the summons in the above proceedings in which I called him in the presence of the governor and captain general of this kingdom. I attest and give truthful testimony that after reading it to him, he stated that it was so, but he would not sign it until such time as the governor and captain general gave the copy he promised in the form and manner stated above. He qualified this by stating they had not advised him from the time he was called until today when I sent him the document as apostolic notary. So that it may be of record, I attest to it and sign as notary on 5 June of this year 1692.

Before me,
Fray Agustín de Colina [rubrica]
Secretary and apostolic notary

I, fray Agustín de Colina, missionary president of this convento of Nuestra Señora de Guadalupe del Paso, secretary, and apostolic notary, state that Sgto. mayor Francisco de Anaya Almazán,[8] alcalde of the cabildo, having come when he was called for the summons, and being asked to state whether it was so as he heard it in the above proceedings, he stated it was true. When asked to sign, since he was summoned as a witness, he replied that he could not, because he could not be a witness either for the lord governor in his last proceedings or for the reverend father president and ecclesiastical judge, notwithstanding that, before the governor, no one gave any reason to be excused from the summons. So that it may be of record, I attest to it as apostolic notary on 6 June 1692.

Before me,
Fray Agustín de Colina [rubrica]
Secretary and apostolic notary

Fray Agustín de Colina, Letter of transmittal, El Paso, 6 June 1692, LS.

Letter of transmittal

In this convento of Nuestra Señora de Guadalupe del Paso on 6 June 1692, having completed the actions that were my responsibility as notary in compliance with what the reverend father, fray Joaquín de Hinojosa, preacher, missionary, president in capite, and ecclesiastical judge ordinary of this kingdom, ordered, I, fray Agustín de Colina, missionary president of this convento of El Paso, secretary of this holy custody, definitor, and apostolic notary, summoned and called the witnesses referred to so that they might sign what was contained in the summons. One signed and wrote two lines in his own hand, as contained herein, and the document has a blank two fingers wide where the other three witnesses will sign. As they were called under bond and did not agree, using the authority of the office of apostolic notary, I wrote two of them a document signed in my name with the title of my notarial office, so they would not excuse themselves. When Capt. don Fernando de Chaves came, he responded with what is contained in his statement, to which I attest, and what followed, as the document contains in its entirety. I am writing a letter of transmittal to his reverence, so that he may provide what is most appropriate. I attest to everything stated in these proceedings and swear *in verbo sacerdotis* that I have faithfully and legally fulfilled the office of notary, without adding or removing anything from what they replied. So that it may be of record, I signed it with my name on the day, month, and year ut supra.

Fray Agustín de Colina [rubrica]
Secretary and apostolic notary

Fray Joaquín de Hinojosa, Order to covene the definitorio, El Paso, 17 June 1692, DS.

Fray Joaquín de Hinojosa of the Regular Observance,[9] son of the Holy Gospel Province, preacher, missionary, president in capite, and ecclesiastical judge ordinary of these provinces and kingdom of New Mexico: Having seen the above letter of transmittal from our secretary, definitor, and apostolic notary, and what he did as notary, the following seemed appropriate to me. The lord governor and captain general of this kingdom notified me that he was dispatching the courier to Mexico City to the most excellent lord viceroy, sending the proceedings and what was done about what was asked of him, stamped and sealed before witnesses. He was offering to send for me anything I might have for his excellency or our prelates. I replied before the same witnesses, who are the lords of the illustrious cabildo of this kingdom, and summoned them. Before his secretary of government and war, I responded *in voce* that I valued the lord governor's attention and that he might send his courier as he saw fit.

Nevertheless, I insisted and asked him for a faithful and legal copy of everything that had been done, according to law. Because he neither gave nor had given this copy, I summoned the same witnesses of this, my repeated request. Since today, Tuesday, 17 June 1692, having given ample time, I have not been considered worthy of this copy for my argument and presentation, I ordered our secretary and apostolic notary that, by the twenty-second of this month, he should summon to and convoke at this our convento of El Paso the very reverend and venerable definitorio of the Order. This is so that together, I can inform them and ask them to come as the definitorio with all attention to ask and request the lord governor and captain general of this kingdom, don Diego de Vargas Zapata Luján Ponce de León, to see fit to provide the copy I have requested of him. Since I have not been considered worthy of it, perhaps the authority of such a reverend definitorio of the Order will.

Once the reverend definitorio has asked for the copy and the lord governor has provided it, our worthy apostolic notary will present it to us to do with whatever may be appropriate within our rights. Should he not provide it—which I find hard to believe—this reverend definitorio of the Order will see fit to attest in writing as witnesses of what may result from its request. This will be done in the customary way, signed by all its fathers, countersigned and authorized by the junior definitor as secretary of the definitorio.

At the conclusion of all this, we may do as the law stipulates and present it before the most excellent lord viceroy of New Spain in his royal acuerdo by means of our very reverend fathers prelate, observing the order in this holy custody in a letter patent from our very reverend father commissary general, fray Fernando de la Rúa.[10] Thus, his reverence provided, ordered, and signed

on 22 June 1692, before me, the undersigned apostolic notary
and secretary.
Fray Joaquín de Hinojosa [rubrica]
President in capite

Before me,
Fray Agustín de Colina [rubrica]
Secretary and apostolic notary

Meeting of the definitorio, El Paso, 22 June 1692, DS.

In this convento of Nuestra Señora de Guadalupe del Paso on 22
June 1692, all the reverend fathers definitor of this Holy Custody of
the Conversion of St. Paul of New Mexico appeared, convoked by
the father, fray Agustín de Colina, missionary, secretary, and apostolic notary, by order of the reverend father, fray Joaquín de Hinojosa,
missionary, president in capite, and ecclesiastical judge ordinary of
this kingdom and provinces. This was so that, together, the reverend fathers definitor might go to the house or palace of the governor
and captain general of this kingdom, don Diego de Vargas Zapata
Luján Ponce de León, to request and ask him to see fit to provide a
copy of what was requested, asked, and presented by the reverend
father president.

In fulfillment of this order, we immediately went to make this request
with all propriety and respect. In reply to the request, the governor
and captain general stated that he had already issued the dispatch and
sent the authorized copy to the most excellent lord viceroy of New
Spain and that the judgment was already signed in the superior tribunal, for which reason he neither had provided nor would provide
the copy requested. The lord governor alleged by the words he spoke
that they attempted to impede or had impeded his exercise of the
patronato real, to which they said to him that it was not so. Instead,
they implored him to grant it in favor of the Indians for which he
had been given a cedula from his majesty (may God keep him). They
had also made some allegations, always under royal protection.

The members of the cabildo and regimiento of this kingdom were
present for all this as were most of the citizens. Perhaps they were
present because of an edict from the lord governor, convoking them
to form a general muster. The reverend father, fray Juan Muñoz de

Castro, senior definitor and commissary of the Holy Office, stated and asked all those present whether perhaps his reverence or any of the other ministers and religious who today are in this holy custody had thrown the Indians out of the pueblos and whether his reverence had not been a father to all in their need. To this, no one replied anything to the contrary.

With this, the reverend definitorio took its leave. So that what was done may be of record for your reverence, we certify that everything referred to was this way, faithfully and legally, as it happened before all who were summoned above. The reverend definitorio signed it before my secretary of the definitorio on this day, month, and year in the above convento ut supra.

Fray Juan Muñoz de Castro [rubrica]
Definitor
Fray Antonio de Acevedo [rubrica]
Definitor
Fray José Espínola Almonacid [rubrica]
Definitor

> By order of the reverend definitorio
> Fray Agustín de Colina [rubrica]
> Definitor and secretary

Fray Joaquín de Hinojosa, Letter of transmittal, El Paso, 22 June 1692, LS.

Letter of transmittal

Fray Joaquín de Hinojosa, preacher, missionary, and president in capite of this Custody of the Conversion of St. Paul of New Mexico and ecclesiastical judge ordinary of this kingdom: I have seen and understood the proceedings and certification of the venerable and reverend definitorio of this custody and what is contained therein. I am preparing this letter of transmittal to our very reverend father, fray Juan Capistrano,[11] retired lector, father of the Holy Province of Los Angeles, and commissary general of all those of New Spain, and also a faithful copy, legally made, to send to our reverend father, fray Diego Trujillo,[12] retired lector, chair of the theology of Duns Scotus, and provincial minister of the Holy Gospel Province, so that their reverences may decide what is most appropriate and, if necessary, present it to the most excellent lord viceroy of New Spain, inasmuch as I cannot appear in this without the blessing and permission of my superiors. So that we may observe in everything what is ordered by the cited letter patent from our very reverend father, fray Fernando de la Rúa, the reverend definitorio signed it with me. Stamped with the seal of our office and countersigned by our secretary, it was sent to these our superiors. Thus, his reverence provided and ordered it on 22 June of this year, 1692, before me, the undersigned secretary and apostolic notary.

Fray Joaquín de Hinojosa [rubrica]
President in capite
Fray José Espínola Almonacid [rubrica]
Definitor

Fray Juan Muñoz
de Castro [rubrica]
Definitor
Fray Antonio de Acevedo [rubrica]
Definitor
Fray Agustín de Colina [rubrica]
Definitor and secretary

Notification and protest about the untrue slander with transmittal of the proceedings
1692

*AASF, 1692:5. 4 folios, 7 written pages with superscription.

1. Fray Joaquín de Hinojosa, born around 1661, professed in Puebla on 5 May 1677. In early 1687, he was at La Junta de los Ríos, accompanied by fray Agustín de Colina and another Franciscan, where he remained for a year and eight months. He was at El Paso in March 1689 and in 1690, at Socorro. On the death of Custos fray Diego de Mendoza, Hinojosa became the president in capite of the custody. Adams and Chávez, *Missions*, 260, 264, 334.

2. The early Franciscans of New Spain gave the titles president, caudillo, or commissary to friars with delegated authority who led groups of their brethren into unorganized areas. In New Mexico, after the founding of the Custody of the Conversion of St. Paul about 1616, the term commissary continued in use in the above sense. The title president

in capite, literally president-in-chief, for the superior of the custody, regularly the custos, and president for the superior of a convento, instead of guardian, is exceptional. It resulted here from the death in office of Custos Diego de Mendoza and the election in chapter of Father Hinojosa as interim head of the custody, approved by the superiors in Mexico City on 30 June 1692. Fray Joaquín de Hinojosa, Letter patent, El Paso, 25 Aug. 1692, AASF, Loose Documents, Mission, 1680–1850, 1692:6. Scholes, "Early Ecclesiastical History," 39, 45–47.

3. Francisco de Anaya Almazán II, son of Francisco de Anaya Almazán and Juana López, was born in New Mexico about 1633. He and his first wife, Gerónima Pérez de Bustillo, had two children, a daughter born in 1654 and a son in 1658. Upon Gerónima's death, he married Francisca Domínguez, daughter of Capt. Tomé Domínguez and Elena Ramírez de Mendoza. Anaya served as alcalde mayor of the Tanos pueblos. During the Revolt, in which his wife and children were killed, he participated in the defense of Santa Fe. He later joined Otermín's attempted reconquest in 1681. In 1682, Anaya married again, this time to Felipa Cedillo Rico de Rojas. The couple returned to Santa Fe with Vargas in 1693, where their family grew to include two sons and a daughter. He died

sometime between 1713 and 1716. NMF, 3–5, 125. Personal communication with Myra Ellen Jenkins, 31 Jan. 1989.

4. Born about 1658 in New Mexico, Juan García de Noriega was the son of Alonso García and Teresa Varela. Alonso, a native of Zacatecas, owned the estancia of San Antonio, about 85 km south of Santa Fe. Juan married Francisca Sánchez de Iñigo on 4 May 1681 and took part in the Otermín expedition that same year. He also participated in Vargas's first expedition in 1692, but remained afterward with his family in the El Paso area. The 1692 census of the the El Paso area listed Juan as the alguacil mayor of the cabildo, living there with his wife and four children: Juan Antonio, eleven; Francisco, seven; José, five; and María, two. NMF, 33–34. NMFA, 63:171. AASF, Diligencias matrimoniales, 1681:7. Espinosa, "Population of El Paso," 61–84.

5. By papal delegation in the early sixteenth century, the crown exercised the right of universal patronage in the Indies. The monarchy enjoyed the privilege of nomination for positions in the secular clergy, and while the papacy retained the right of rejection, it rarely failed to approve a candidate. For its part, the crown pledged to protect and support the ecclesiastical establishment in the Indies. To aid in the financial burden this imposed, the crown received the proceeds of the

ecclesiastical diezmo, or tithe.
RECOP, Lib. 1, tít 6, leyes 1–51.
Solórzano Pereira, *Política
indiana*, Lib. 4, caps. 1–4. John
Frederick Schwaller, *The Church
and Clergy in Sixteenth-Century
Mexico* (Albuquerque, 1987):4.

6. Fernando Durán y Chaves
was alluding to the public
execution, attended by his father,
Pedro Durán y Chaves II, in Santa
Fe on 21 July 1643 of eight
colonists implicated in the defiance
and murder of Gov. Luis de Rosas
(1637–41). NMF, 20. Scholes,
Church and State, 175–77.

7. See fray Agustín de Colina
to Juan García de Noriega,
Summons, El Paso, 5 June 1692,
below, page 291.

8. See fray Agustín de Colina
to Francisco de Anaya Almazán,
Summons, El Paso, 6 June 1692,
below, page 291–92.

9. The Observant movement
grew out of a conflict within the
Franciscan Order over the Rule.
The struggle began in the early
fourteenth century and led to
schism in 1517. The Observants
pursued the right to strict
observance of the Rule,
emphasizing poverty, simplicity,
and individual worship. They were
opposed by the Conventuals, who
preferred communal living. Over
time, regular observance came to
mean uniformity, especially in
dress and tonsure. The Holy
Gospel Province was an Observant
province. For a complete
discussion, see Iriarte de Aspurz,
Franciscan History.

10. Fray Fernando de la Rúa, a
retired lector from the Province of
La Concepción, came from Spain
to Mexico City in 1666. As
commissary general, he was
responsible for new construction
and repairs at the conventos and
administrative reforms regarding
the collection and use of income of
female religious. Confirmed as
commissary general in 1670, he
was apparently removed the
following year as a result of
disagreements with Archbishop
fray Payo de Rivera Enríquez.
Among the long list of complaints
about De la Rúa was that he wanted
to take the franchise for the wagons
to supply New Mexico away from
the holder, because the latter would
not give him the money the king
provided. He was replaced and
ordered to go as vice-commissary
general to Nicaragua while his
residencia was pending. He went
to Spain instead, where the case
was resolved in his favor. He
remained there and was designated
a revisor of the constitution in the
General Congregation at Madrid.
Fray Isidro Félix de Espinosa,
*Crónica de los Colegios de
Propaganda Fide de la Nueva
España* (1746–47; rpt., Washington,
D.C., 1964):257, 259–60. Robles,
Diario, 1:98–100. Vetancurt,
Teatro mexicano, 3:218; 4:387.

11. In 1689, fray Juan de
Capistrano was sent from Spain to
Mexico City, where he served six
years as commissary general of
New Spain. During his term, he
was responsible for founding a

hospice and new seminary in Guatemala City in 1692. Fray Fidel de Jesús Chauvet, *Franciscanos memorables en México: Ensayo histórico, 1523–1982* (Mexico City, 1983):163. Vetancurt, *Teatro mexicano*, 4:388.

12. Fray Diego Trujillo occupied the Scotus chair at the university in Mexico City from 1678 until 1686. John Duns Scotus (1266?–1308), the Subtle Doctor, was an extremely influential Franciscan scholastic figure, usually seen as the intellectual adversary of St. Thomas Aquinas. Although a difficult and complex thinker, Scotus had more followers than St. Thomas or St. Bonaventure well into the seventeenth century and continued to be studied in the undergraduate arts course of the university at Mexico City. Paul Edwards, ed., *The Encyclopedia of Philosophy* (New York, 1967), 2:436. NCE, 4:1102–1106; 12:1226–28. John Tate Lanning, *Academic Culture in the Spanish Colonies* (London, 1940):43. Vetancurt, *Teatro mexicano*, 3:127.

The Franciscan Convento Grande, Mexico City, 1695, from a painting
by Diego Correa
   From Fidel de Jesús Chauvet, *San Francisco de México* (1985)

POSSESSION OF CHURCHES IN THE EL PASO DISTRICT;
DISPUTE BETWEEN THE FRANCISCANS AND THE GOVERNOR
OVER JURISDICTION; AND PROVISION OF FIFTY SOLDIERS FROM
NEW BISCAY TO AID IN THE RECONQUEST OF NEW MEXICO,
AUGUST 1691–NOVEMBER 1692.*

Diego de Vargas, his hopes set on the reconquest of New Mexico, resents having to do battle with the Franciscan father president, fray Joaquín de Hinojosa. He expresses his frustration, but refuses to be intimidated. In mid-June 1692, he orders that a copy for the viceroy be made of all the proceedings to date in the jurisdictional conflict with the friars.

It had begun amicably enough, the previous August, when the custos, fray Francisco de Vargas, requested that the governor grant to the Franciscans, in the king's name, formal possession of the churches, conventos, and enough land to maintain the missionaries in each of the El Paso settlements. Don Diego agreed. Then, fray Francisco's successor died suddenly, and the friars elected Hinojosa as interim superior.

In his petition of 16 May 1692, Father Hinojosa enlarges on the earlier request. He wants Indian lands set apart and pueblo boundaries marked. This, he insists, will permit the friars to better protect Indian interests and, at the same time, minister to non-Indians. In the churches and conventos of El Paso, Ysleta, Socorro, Senecú, and San Lorenzo, Governor Vargas goes through the ritual act of granting possession. As for anything further, he denies the father president's request.

For the viceroy, Governor Vargas explains the dire consequences that will result if the Franciscan has his way. He describes incidents of church-state discord reminiscent of New Mexico earlier in the seventeenth century. He implores the Conde de Galve to consider the record and decide the matter. Deliberations in Mexico City follow.

Somewhere en route, the southbound courier passes his northbound counterpart. The latter carries viceregal authorization for the fifty additional soldiers. Eagerly, don Diego resumes planning the entrada upriver. Even in that context, however, he chooses not to hide his displeasure with the Franciscans. He does not know if the Apaches will aid the apostate Pueblo Indians. Still, he assures Galve, they are dangerous enemies.

1692
Proceedings regarding the possession of the churches and conventos in the pueblo of El Paso, as well as in the rest of its district, requested by the very reverend father, fray Francisco de Vargas, who was custos of this kingdom in August 1691, followed by the petitions and proceedings provided for them by the reverend father, fray Joaquín de Hinojosa, president of this holy custody and interim ecclesiastical judge in capite,[1] who took possession of them in May 1692. Also included are the proceedings of the appeal, which was denied him, and the copy for his prelates dated 31 May 1692. They sent it to him for his information, and it was also conveyed to the most excellent lord, the Conde de Galve, viceroy, governor and captain general, and president of the Royal Audiencia of Mexico, so that his excellency, when he has seen the proceedings and letter of transmittal, may decide and order what he sees fit.
Gratis[2]
Judge
Don Diego de Vargas Zapata Luján Ponce de León, governor and captain general of the kingdom and provinces of New Mexico, castellan of its fortress and presidio for his majesty, and so forth.
Secretary

The alferez of the presidio, Juan Páez Hurtado,[3] secretary of government and war
Gratis

Proceedings, El Paso, 21–30 August 1691, C.

21 August 1691

Lord governor and captain general,

Fray Francisco de Vargas, minister, custos, and ecclesiastical judge ordinary of this Holy Custody of the Conversion of St. Paul and the provinces of New Mexico by apostolic authority, and so forth: I state that I have examined the archive where this holy custody's records are kept to see whether there were or had been acts of possession of the conventos standing today, which are Nuestra Señora de Guadalupe del Paso, that of the real of San Lorenzo, San Antonio de Senecú, Corpus Christi de la Ysleta de Tiguas, Nuestra Señora de la Limpia Concepción de los Piros del Socorro, and the new conversion of Nuestro Padre San Francisco de los Mansos, and have found no documents for any of them relating to possession. What is essential is for his majesty (may God keep him) to give possession to us as our royal patron and universal lord of these kingdoms and provinces, which are under his monarchy. Because in this province you are in his stead as governor and captain general of this kingdom and provinces of New Mexico, and I, as head and unworthy prelate of this holy custody, ask and request in the name of my sacred Order, that you see fit to grant possession of the conventos. For their maintenance, their lands should be measured and boundaries marked.

Please order that all the necessary instruments be provided so that the possession will always be of record. You will please see fit to grant it with your authority and privileges as governor and captain general. In this, my sacred Order will receive a singular favor. I and all the religious of this holy custody, your chaplains, shall receive this honor like the many others that with Catholic zeal you, as our singular benefactor, see fit to bestow upon us as the children of our seraphic father St. Francis.

Lord governor and captain general, I ask and beseech you to provide as I have requested in the name of my holy Order to enjoy the possession with more justice. By right and triumph of so many years, it is owed to the current and past missionary fathers of this holy custody. Despite their solicitude and the change in the stipend his majesty (may God keep him) sees fit to provide every three years,[4] the churches and things related to divine worship are in a disgusting state, as is manifest. Thus, I ask for justice. So that my request may be of record, I signed, and so forth.

Francisco de Vargas
Custos

Presentation

In this plaza de armas of the pueblo of El Paso in the kingdom of New Mexico on 21 August 1691, before me, don Diego de Vargas Zapata Luján Ponce de León, governor and captain general of this kingdom and castellan of its fortress for his majesty: The very reverend father, fray Francisco de Vargas, ecclesiastical judge and current custos of this holy custody of our father, St. Francis, now founded on the pueblos mentioned in his request, presented on this date.

Proceedings

Having seen how justified his report was, I am ready to give him possession of the conventos and churches in the pueblos of this district of El Paso, together with the convento and church called Nuestra Señora de Guadalupe in this pueblo. With respect to assigning land and marking boundaries so that with every care he should be given possession, I am ready to give it to him in this pueblo of El Paso, as well as in the five established at present and referred to in his request. I shall give and award him possession of the lands, according to the distribution of inhabitants of this pueblo of El Paso and real of San Lorenzo, both Spaniards and Indians, in these two pueblos as well as in the rest.

So that I might fulfill my wish to provide with justice for the very reverend father in the name of his holy Order, his reverence should designate the area that appears most fertile to him, in this pueblo and in the others of the holy custody, distinguishing one parcel of land from another as he sees fit. This is so that he can better guard against the uncertainties of the weather in the harvest of his plantings. He should state how much wheat, maize, and other seed should be sown in all the pueblos, according to the amount of each crop determined for each pueblo. Providence may provide a time for all things and in the greatest measure to the very reverend father.

Having done what was necessary, justly and in the presence of people I, the governor and captain general, shall name, I shall give possession entirely to his reverence. The proceedings that I, the governor and captain general, in the presence of my secretary of government and war, shall provide him will serve as title and privilege. So that it will be forever of record, I, in his majesty's name, shall determine, mark boundaries for, and set landmarks with the people I have mentioned and shall name. My secretary of government and war will notify and give the very reverend father a copy of these proceedings, so that in a period of exactly nine days, beginning with the day of his notification, the father may consult with whomever he chooses and gather information from the missionary fathers who are very worthily placed in charge of the conventos. With the definite notice of the selection of the lands, I, the governor and captain general, shall show favor and order that any and all citizens and Indians, whatever their station, should be favored. Once the land has been chosen, the very reverend father custos will give me a listing of what he chooses and designate it in the missions of this holy custody. So that the proceedings may be of record, I provided and signed this in the presence of my secretary of government and war on the aforesaid day ut supra.

Don Diego de Vargas Zapata Luján Ponce de León
Before me,
Juan Páez Hurtado
Secretary of government and war

Notification of the above proceedings

On the said day, month, and year, I, Juan Páez Hurtado, secretary of government and war, read and made known the above proceedings to our very reverend father custos, fray Francisco de Vargas, in his presence, to which I attest. Having heard and understood, his reverence stated that he would gather information from the fathers minister about the lands they might need to maintain and support themselves and the conventos in their charge. With the information from each one of the fathers, he will go to you so that you may provide what is most appropriate. So that his notification may be of record, he signed it with me, the secretary

of government and war, and the witnesses who were present on the said day ut supra.
Fray Francisco de Vargas
Custos
Roque Madrid
Tomás Gutiérrez Carrera
Before me, which I attest,
Juan Páez Hurtado
Secretary of government and war

Petition

On 30 August 1691

Lord governor and captain general,

Fray Francisco de Vargas, minister, custos, and ecclesiastical judge ordinary of this Holy Custody of the Conversion of St. Paul and provinces of New Mexico by apostolic authority, and so forth: With respect to the petition I have had placed before you, asking you to grant me possession of the conventos in this holy custody and the land for their support, I would have you know that it was because I did not find proof of possession in the archive of this holy custody. You had decreed and so ordered in the proceedings made known to me on 21 August of the present year 1691. In these proceedings, I note the promptness, care, and painstaking attention with which you seek the well-being of this custody, what would serve it best, and the support of its ministers. Although you suggested that the land necessary for this end in each convento should be examined, I have already complied with an investigation and been informed by the missionary fathers now at the conventos who have the necessary knowledge about what can be sown in each one for its subsistence and for those present in the conventos, in the following way: at the convento of Nuestra Señora de Guadalupe del Paso, 4 fanegas for wheat and 1 for maize; in the real of San Lorenzo, 2 for wheat and 1/2 for maize; in San Antonio de Senecú, 4 for wheat and 1 for maize; in Corpus Christi de los Tiguas, 3 for wheat and 1 for maize; in Nuestra Señora de la Concepción del Socorro, 2 1/2 for wheat and 1 for maize; and in the new mission of Nuestro Padre de San Francisco de los Mansos, 2 for wheat and 1 for maize.

Even though at three of these conventos they have not planted this year because of a lack of water, they could in the future. For this reason, and so that there will be successful harvests, I ask that you see fit to grant us in his majesty's name the land that would be used for the previously mentioned planting of wheat, maize, and vegetables. You could graciously do this wherever the father minister of each convento wills and is able to sow land under irrigation. Because the acequias provide so little and the river's course changes, which we experience each year, one cannot choose a permanent place. Beyond this difficulty, there is another no less troublesome. Having continued to plant the same land for two years, by the third year it is invaded by sandbur and moss. This permits the gathering of only a third of what could be harvested from newly worked land.

Lord governor, I ask and request that you order that I be given what I have referred to in my statement. I hope to receive justice and great favor from you, which I shall esteem, and it will be received by my holy Order. May you provide as I have requested, doing so for God Our Lord, acting with your Catholic zeal and justice, and so forth.

Fray Francisco de Vargas
Custos

Presentation

On 30 August 1691, the very reverend father, fray Francisco de Vargas, ecclesiastical judge in capite, appeared before me, don Diego de Vargas Zapata Luján Ponce de León, governor and captain general of this kingdom and provinces of New Mexico and castellan of its fortress and presidio for his majesty. His reverence, as custos, head, and prelate in this holy custody, in its name and that of his holy Order, requests that I give him possession of the land he designated in this pueblo of El Paso and the other pueblo missions of its district that are at present established and inhabited. In the request, he states that he cannot designate the exact site of the land so that I, the governor and captain general, could give him possession of it nominatim. He says this, stating that because the river changes course, he should be given fanegas of land under irrigation that can be planted in wheat, maize, vegetables, and seeds. Because he is fully justified in everything, with this I concede and grant to him, in the name of his majesty the king, whatever parcels he thinks safest and most fertile, so that the fanegas of wheat, maize, and other seeds and vegeta-

bles he mentions in his request can be planted. He can do this in the pueblo of El Paso, as well as in the others. He will be given possession, as he has asked, of the conventos, holy churches, and everything else. So that these proceedings may be of record, I provided, signed, and ordered with my secretary of government and war on the said day, month, and year ut supra.
Don Diego de Vargas Zapata Luján Ponce de León
Before me,
Juan Páez Hurtado
Secretary of government and war

Proceedings, El Paso, 16 May–2 June 1692, C.

Petition on 16 May 1692

Lord governor and captain general,

Fray Joaquín de Hinojosa, of the Regular Observance of our father, St. Francis, missionary father, president in capite of this Holy Custody of the Conversion of St. Paul of New Mexico, apostolic commissary, and delegate of his holiness in this kingdom and environs by apostolic authority: I state, sir, with respect to the reverend father, Francisco de Vargas, who was minister and custos of this holy custody, that he has presented a petition to you in which he requested and asked that he be given possession of the churches and conventos the reverend fathers, missionaries of this holy custody, have built over the past twelve years, such as Nuestra Señora de Guadalupe del Paso, where he was before, as well as the newly begun mission and conversion of the Indians of the Suma nation, which is called San Diego. Attention should be paid to the favorable concession and privilege from the holiness of our very holy father, Leo X,[5] of happy memory, so that the religious missionaries who serve in lands of the infidel and the newly converted might raise and construct churches and dwellings in which the true God and His holiest name will be praised. In them, the infidel can thus be educated more suitably, and with all reverence may be administered the holy sacraments. Also, conventos and living quarters should be built for the religious in which to better observe the regular cloistered and monastic rule, thus permitting greater fulfillment of their holy Rule. In addition, the ministers can make do with some assistance for their support, which is very worthy of consideration and just common sense. For this, some land is necessary on which they can cultivate grain to support themselves and provide for the missions they will newly establish. It will also provide for the necessities of the poor and the Indians when they need it, even though they pay the missionaries with grain for administration of the holy sacraments, because by all ecclesiastical right they are obligated to do so. Because it is incumbent upon me to make this request and leave the matter in the best condition the scarcity of these places allows, I ask and request with all humility that, by the time of the next inspection by your office in this kingdom, you see fit that I, or whoever may be the reverend father missionary president, may have the possession of churches, conventos, and land. This is so that from his majesty (may God keep him), the missions may have the authority and right of being in accord with his royal will, which is that his ministers possess them. With his sponsorship and through the patronato real his majesty enjoys in this region, the religious of this holy custody will have the security necessary for themselves and for the Indians who reside in the pueblos where today there are lands, water holes, pastures, and related property that his majesty (may God keep him), by so prudent a decision, sees fit to grant them by his royal cedulas, as contained therein. It is up to me, as their father, to request for them the comfort, not only spiritual, which is so beneficial, but also temporal, which is so necessary because it is the missionary fathers' duty. This was decided by the Holy Council of Lima (in the third session, chapter 3, page 148), so that the Indians would not be harmed in their pueblos and could live peacefully with moral customs.[6] I ask again, with all humility, that you see fit to provide everything referred to and requested by the reverend father, providing with justice what has been requested. Save error, and so forth, I swear *in verbo sacerdotis* that this petition is not malicious but in accord with my right. I hope to receive every favor in whatever may be approved and so forth.

Fray Joaquín de Hinojosa

Presentation

In the pueblo of El Paso on 16 May 1692, the very reverend father minister, fray Joaquín de Hinojosa, president and ecclesiastical judge of this holy custody and kingdom, presented to me, don Diego de

Vargas Zapata Luján Ponce de León, governor and captain general of this kingdom of New Mexico for his majesty and castellan of its fortress and presidio, the petition on the back of this page. Having seen it, I, the governor and captain general, order it added to the petition and proceedings I provided. The very reverend father president repeatedly cites the contents so that everyone may be in agreement. The very reverend father should be given a copy of the proceedings, so that if he has anything to question or add to what is decided in them, I shall await and listen to the satisfaction of full compliance with justice and what is most favorable to God, all of which I must keep in mind. So that the very reverend father may understand everything, at the same time I order my secretary of government and war to make known to him the proceedings I provide. I signed together with my secretary, who will record whatever the very reverend father may tell him. Done ut supra.

Don Diego de Vargas Zapata Luján Ponce de León
Before me,
Juan Páez Hurtado
Secretary of government and war

Notification of the above proceedings

On this day, 16 May 1692, in compliance with and obedience to the above proceedings, I came to this convento of Nuestra Señora de Guadalupe del Paso. After I read them to the very reverend father president, he stated, "Having read and understood the proceedings that you send me, I would say that they appear to be completely in agreement with what was requested and suggested by the reverend father, fray Francisco de Vargas. Given that you will so providently see fit to grant in the name of his majesty (may God keep him) what was requested in the petition, you should be given many thanks for being ready and disposed to immediately give possession of the churches, conventos, dwellings, and necessary land. With respect to the tranquility, peace, and calm of the Indians of the pueblos of these missions, which I cite again in my petition, may you see fit to provide that the land they are to sow be indicated to the Indians, ordering and informing them that they are not granted the land to alienate it; rather that, in his majesty's name, they are granted it for their support. Also, you should indicate the limits of each pueblo with some crosses or other signs, which would mark them. Then I can put in order for the reverend fathers what belongs to each of their jurisdictions, for better administration of the holy sacraments to the faithful. This is all that is asked for now with a newly emended request, always leaving the door open for whatever might occur in the future, hoping for favor and justice in everything and achieving grace from you for the best and according to law." So that it may be of record, the very reverend father president signed it with me, the secretary of government and war, on said day ut supra.

Fray Joaquín de Hinojosa
Before me,
Juan Páez Hurtado
Secretary of government and war

Proceedings

Immediately after, I, the governor and captain general, saw the above answer given by the very reverend father president, ecclesiastical judge in capite of this holy custody and kingdom of New Mexico, to the notification of the proceedings provided at his request, I ordered the execution of the proceedings I provided on 30 August 1691 in response to the petition made by the very reverend father custos, who at that time was fray Francisco de Vargas, according to what is contained therein. I ordered that acts of possession for the holy churches and conventos standing and established in the pueblos of the kingdom of New Mexico be kept, carried out, and fulfilled. The same should be done for sufficient land to plant the crops required for subsistence, which the very reverend father, fray Francisco de Vargas, expressed and designated. This is what is of record in the proceedings; everything should be granted to him as he has asked.

With regard to what has been reported, the current petitioner, the very reverend father, fray Joaquín de Hinojosa, president and ecclesiastical judge in capite of this holy custody and of this kingdom, should be given the possession he cites again in his request and would receive in the name of this holy custody as its head and in favor of his holy Order. With respect to what relates to the rest of the Indians, it is denied, and there is no reason for such a position. If there were, the reverend fathers would have presented it through their procurator general so that he might apply to me, upon whom the responsibility of their support is exclusively incumbent. Given the tranquility the Indians enjoy, and since the Spaniards act harmoniously toward them, one could neither support nor maintain itself, or even live in this kingdom, without the other. It would do serious harm to introduce mistrust between them. Thus, I again order my secretary of government and war to inform the very reverend father to refrain from getting involved in more than what concerns him and is his responsibility. I shall listen to him and deal justly with what he may ask of me. I shall administer justice with care and reverent attention, as is my duty, failing in nothing in the service and according to the royal will of his majesty (may God keep him). So that these proceedings, and that they have been provided, may be of record, I signed in this pueblo of El Paso, together with my secretary of government and war, on 17 May 1692.

Don Diego de Vargas Zapata Luján Ponce de León
Before me,
Juan Páez Hurtado
Secretary of government and war

Notification of the above proceedings

On this day, month, and year, I, the secretary of government and war, read the above proceedings to the very reverend father president. Having heard and understood, he stated, "With respect to the special possession he grants of what was requested by the father, fray Francisco de Vargas, I shall accept it, but with respect to the Indians, it is very much the responsibility of the missionary fathers. They have experienced what has already been suggested to you in the response to your proceedings. The very reverend missionary fathers have very sufficient basis to protect the Indians. His majesty was so much in agreement that he saw fit to give them the cedula I present, in which he makes the Indians the first who are deserving of our teaching. The terms explain very well his intention, which does not mean that the missionaries are fervent in spiritual matters and faint-hearted in the necessary methods conducive to firmly establish Christianity among the Indians. One grows with the help of the other. If the Indians say nothing, it is because of their extreme lack of spirit. Were it not for this knowledge, the reverend missionary fathers would not intercede in their favor. Those who can defend the Indians and do not, sin mortally. Therefore, because the missionaries have set this precedent, it continues to be very much their duty. This is a course of action that, had the protectors seen to their clear duty,[7] the lords governor might have put into practice the orders expedited by the Royal Audiencia in Mexico City during the loss of this kingdom. In them, you will see (if by chance they are in the archive) how his majesty's plan for support of the Indians, which is so necessary, is explained, even though support of the poor citizens may be in need of remedy. This will have been understood, without dwelling on the damages the Indians incurred (not just the temporal ones of record for you in some reports), among them, those relating to their land. Seeing that this mistrust was not the principal responsibility of those whom we may watch over forced me to subrogate what was beneficial and necessary for their good. Even though for the moment my request does not have support, it is not because I deny that the ministers are their most immediate protectors. To argue the contrary is to directly oppose what was expressed by the Holy Council of Lima, which I cited to you. Upon reflection, well advised and clearly seen, who could not have granted what was requested in such express terms, thereby impeding what is so much our responsibility? My intention is nothing more than that you gather and sign material about past abuses, and as his majesty's loyal vassal carry out his orders. The protectors, and I cannot imagine where they got that title, cannot have done their duty to avoid confusion." So that it may be of record, the very reverend father president signed it with me, the secretary of government and war, on the said day.

Fray Joaquín de Hinojosa
Before me,
Juan Páez Hurtado
Secretary of government and war

Possession of the convento of El Paso

In the pueblo of El Paso on 17 May 1692, in compliance with the foregoing proceedings, which I provided, and my secretary of government and war made known today by my order, I, the governor and captain general, came to this convento of our father, St. Francis, with my secretary of government and war, the two squads from the plaza de armas who guard this presidio, and the captain of its company, Mre. de campo Roque Madrid. I asked for the father president, fray Joaquín de Hinojosa, and his reverence immediately came out, accompanied by his secretary and guardian of the convento, fray Agustín de Colina. While we were outside the convento in the patio of his holy church, called Nuestra Señora de Guadalupe del Paso, he asked me to give him possession of the holy church and the rest.

I, the governor and captain general, in accord with the proceedings I provided on 30 August 1691 and those dated today, entered the holy church, leading the very reverend father president by the hand, and gave him possession in the name of his majesty.[8] His reverence took it de facto and de jure, walking around the church. Making the sign of the cross, he lifted and replaced on its high altar the holy cross, the altar cloths, and everything else the church had. In like manner, I led him by the hand into the baptistery, opening and closing the door and examining the font. The sacristy was entered as well, closing and opening its door and examining the vestments and other furnishings pertaining to the use of the holy church.

He came out to the patio with me, the governor and captain general, and I again took him by the hand. Making witnesses of those present, with the attendance of my secretary of government and war, I stated in a loud and clear voice how in his majesty's name I also gave him possession of the convento. I led him by the hand through the door, and he took possession de facto and de jure. We walked through the cloister and entered hand in hand into his cell and into the others, opening and closing their doors. I gave him the two documents of possession in his majesty's name, which he took quietly and peacefully, gainsaying nothing. Having come outside again, in the presence of the witnesses and with the attendance of my secretary of government and war, I repeated in a loud and clear voice the proceedings I provided on 30 August of last year, 1691, and 10 and 17 May of the present year, 1692.

Possession of land

In compliance with them, I stated that I was likewise giving him the documents of possession and indicated the amount of 4 fanegas of wheat for seed planting; 1 for maize; and other land to sow beans, squash, and other vegetables, and for a garden. Since this was by declaration, I indicated the lands I gave him possession of in his majesty's name, so that he could receive them for himself, as he received and accepted them, de facto and de jure. As head of this custody and in the name of his holy Order, he received it and would make use of it. With respect to the tenor of the proceedings I provided on 30 August of last year, 1691, the acequia, as is of record in the foregoing proceedings, does not have a fixed location, since the course of the river moves. The land is such that it cannot be sown continually, because by the third year, it is infested with sandburs and other briers. As a result, I did not give him possession in the land he indicated. I instead specified the lands I was indicating and giving him possession of in his majesty's name, with the distinction and stipulation I give and indicate that it is by declaration that the citizens and Indians must be given preference, both in terms of the quality and richness of the lands and the water of their acequia and irrigated land. I declare that I am indicating and giving possession in his majesty's name and that the reverend father president received it, accepting for himself and as head of this holy custody in the name of his holy Order. So that this may be of record, I signed it with my secretary of government and war, all the aforementioned people being present on the said day ut supra.

Don Diego de Vargas Zapata Luján Ponce de León
Before me,
Juan Páez Hurtado
Secretary of government and war

Possession of the church and convento of the pueblo of Ysleta

In the pueblo of Ysleta of this district of El Paso in the kingdom of New Mexico on 19 May 1692, I, the governor and captain general, have come to carry out the general inspection, which is my responsibility, and as his majesty, the king our lord, so orders me. The very reverend father, fray Joaquín de Hinojosa, president of this holy custody, in compliance with the proceedings I provided on 16 and 17 May of the present year, asked me to give him the possession contained herein and reviewed by me, the governor and captain general.

In the presence of the captain of this company, some soldiers, and other people who are citizens of this pueblo, and with the attendance of my secretary of government and war, on the patio before the door of the pueblo's church, called Corpus Christi de los Tiguas, I, the governor and captain general, led the very reverend father, fray Joaquín de Hinojosa, president of this holy custody and ecclesiastical judge in capite, by the hand through the door of the church and gave him possession of it. He took it de facto and de jure for himself, as head of this holy custody and in the name of his holy Order. Walking through the church, he saw on its high altar the depictions of images and saints, the cloths, and the cross, moving them in sign of possession. In like manner, I led him by the hand through the door of its sacristy, where he examined some vestments and other furnishings of the church's use. He went out into the church again and examined the baptismal font and removed and then replaced the lid as a sign of possession. He received possession quietly and peacefully, gainsaying nothing.

At the door of its convento, he asked me for possession, and in the presence of the customary witnesses and my secretary of government and war, I led the reverend father president by the hand and, in his majesty's name, gave him possession of it both de facto and de jure, which he took for himself, as head of this holy custody, and in the name of his holy Order quietly and peacefully, gainsaying nothing. He walked through the cloister, entering and leaving the cells of the convento and its workrooms, opening and closing the doors as a sign of possession, which I gave in his majesty's name, as is stated, to the reverend father.

Possession of land

Having come out to the patio of the convento and church again, I stated in a loud and clear voice that I also gave and indicated to the reverend father president in his majesty's name, the possession of 4 fanegas of land for wheat and 1 for maize, as well as the land required for a garden and planting the other foodstuffs, beans and squash, as they see fit. It is by declaration that I gave him possession and indicated the land in his majesty's name, with the stipulation that the citizens and Indians must be given preference, both in terms of the richness and quality of irrigated land, with the water from the acequia for irrigation to ensure the harvest, as specified in the preceding possession I order kept, complied with, and carried out, according to the proceedings expressed in it. So that the possessions in this pueblo of Ysleta of the church, convento, land, and everything else contained in these proceedings of possession that took place in the presence of the witnesses and persons contained herein may be of record, I signed it on the said day, month, and year with my secretary of government and war.

Don Diego de Vargas Zapata Luján Ponce de León
Before me,
Juan Páez Hurtado
Secretary of government and war

Possession of the church and convento of the pueblo of Socorro

In the pueblo of Socorro on 20 May 1692, in pursuance of the general inspection, while I, the governor and captain general, was on the patio at the door of the church with the captain, some soldiers, and some other people, with the attendance of my secretary of government and war, the very reverend father president, fray Joaquín de Hinojosa, asked me to give him the possession of this holy church and convento.

In compliance with the proceedings I provided, I led him through the door of the holy church, whose name is Nuestra Señora de la Concepción de Socorro, and having taken him in by the hand, I gave him possession, de facto and de jure, in his majesty's name. As a sign of it, he walked up the steps of the high altar and moved the ramilletero[9] and cloths. As a sign of possession, he moved and returned the furnishings to their places. Likewise, I led him by the hand into the sacristy, where he unfolded, looked at, and straightened up some furnishings and vestments. He came out with me, the governor and captain general, through the church and saw and examined the baptismal font.

When he was on the patio, he asked me to give him possession of the convento. Taking him by the hand, in the presence of the witnesses and with the attendance of my secretary of government and war, I gave him possession, de facto and de jure, in his majesty's name, which he took as head of this holy custody, for himself and in the name of his holy Order. He walked through the convento, entering and leaving the cells, examining the workrooms, and opening and closing the doors as a sign of possession.

Possession of land

Having come outside to the patio of the convento, in the presence of the witnesses and with the attendance of the secretary of government and war, I told them in a loud and clear voice that in his majesty's name, I also gave to the very reverend father president possession of the land he might need and indicated 2 1/2 fanegas for planting wheat, 1 for maize, and what might be needed for a garden, together with other grains and vegetables, as specified as to preference in the proceedings I provided and according to their clauses and the foregoing possessions. So that the possession and what was reported, as has been stated, may be of record with the attendance of the witnesses, other people, and my secretary of government and war, I signed it with him in this pueblo on the said day, month, and year.

Don Diego de Vargas Zapata Luján Ponce de León

Before me,

Juan Páez Hurtado

Secretary of government and war

Possession of the convento and church of the pueblo of Senecú

In the pueblo of Senecú, in pursuance of the general inspection, I, the governor and captain general, arrived today, 21 May 1692, in the company of the very reverend father president, fray Joaquín de Hinojosa, as well as the captain, soldiers, and other people who have followed me and been present on this general inspection, with the attendance of my secretary of government and war. I carried out the inspection of this pueblo, and the president asked me to give him possession of its church, convento, and the land indicated, according to the proceedings I provided on 30 August of last year, 1691, and on 16 and 17 May of the present year, 1692.

In compliance therewith, at the door of the church, I, the governor and captain general, with those in attendance took the reverend father, fray Joaquín de Hinojosa, by the hand and led him into the church, stating that in his majesty's name, I was giving his reverence possession of the church, the name of which is San Antonio de Senecú. He walked through the church and examined its high altar, moving from one side to the other the furnishings adorning it. He likewise entered the sacristy and there examined the vestments, opening and closing the boxes. Having come out into the church, he examined the baptismal font. In his majesty's name, I gave him possession, de facto and de jure, which he took for himself, as head of this holy custody and in the name of his holy Order.

Possession of land

Outside on the patio of the church, in the presence of the aforesaid people, with the attendance of my secretary of government and
war, I indicated to him 4 fanegas of land for wheat, 1 for maize, and
what is necessary for a garden and planting other grains and vegetables. Everything that has been related I stated in a loud and clear
voice, saying that in his majesty's name I was giving the father president possession, de facto and de jure, with the stipulation of preferring, in the land I indicated and gave to him in his majesty's name,
any persons and the water from their acequia, as expressed in the
proceedings and other foregoing possessions. So that it may be of
record that possession took place as has been stated in the presence
of witnesses and with the attendance of my secretary of government and
war, I signed it together with him on the said day, month, and year.
Don Diego de Vargas Zapata Luján Ponce de León
Before me,
Juan Páez Hurtado
Secretary of government and war

Possession of the church and convento of the real of San Lorenzo,
a Spanish settlement

On 21 May 1692, in pursuance of the general inspection, I, the
governor and captain general, arrived at about five o'clock in the
afternoon at the real of San Lorenzo, a pueblo of Spaniards, in this
district of El Paso of this kingdom of New Mexico, accompanied by
the reverend father president, fray Joaquín de Hinojosa, the other
people named in the foregoing proceedings regarding possession, and
my secretary of government and war. I carried out the inspection of
the real and the Mexican natives gathered together there. On the
patio at the church door, the very reverend father, fray Joaquín de
Hinojosa, president of this holy custody and interim ecclesiastical
judge in capite, asked me for the possession of the church and convento.

In the presence of the people who have followed me, the governor and captain general, and assisted in the general inspection, as
well as members of this cabildo and other citizens of this real, in the
presence of all, I led the reverend father president by the hand through
the door of the church, stating that, in his majesty's name, as they
were all witnesses, I was giving possession of the church to the rever-

end father president. He accepted it de facto and de jure in the royal name, for himself, as head of this holy custody and in the name of his holy Order. As a sign, he walked through the church, looked at the high altar and the others, on which he moved their images from one side to the other, and then returned them. He entered its sacristy and looked at and examined the furnishings and clothing used in the church and while in the church also examined its baptismal font.

When he came outside, I, the governor and captain general, led him by the hand through the door of the convento, in the presence of the people in attendance and my secretary of government and war. He walked through, entering and closing the doors of its cells and other workrooms. In his majesty's name, I gave him possession, de facto and de jure, which he accepted for himself, as head of this holy custody in the name of his holy Order, gainsaying nothing.

Possession of lands

Having come outside to the patio, I, the governor and captain general, stated in a loud and clear voice to the people in attendance and in the presence of my secretary of government and war that in his majesty's name I was likewise giving possession to the father president of 2 fanegas of land for wheat, 1 for maize, as well as the land required for a garden and planting other grains and vegetables, favoring any- and everyone with lands under irrigation and with the necessary water. I repeated to those in attendance the proceedings I provided and in compliance with them, indicated and gave him possession in his majesty's name, which the reverend father president accepted. So that the possession and what was reported in it, which took place in the presence of those named in these proceedings of possession, may be of record, I signed it with my secretary of government and war. I, the governor and captain general, don Diego de Vargas Zapata Luján Ponce de León, in this real on this day, month, and year.
Don Diego de Vargas Zapata Luján Ponce de León
Before me,
Juan Páez Hurtado
Secretary of government and war

Petition

On 31 May 1692

Lord governor and captain general,

Fray Joaquín de Hinojosa, minister, president in capite, and interim ecclesiastical judge of this kingdom of New Mexico by apostolic authority, and so forth: I appear before you in the manner most in accord with the law. I state that I asked you to substitute my petition for the one the reverend father, fray Francisco de Vargas, former minister and custos of this holy custody, had made to you, so that you would see fit in all wisdom to give me possession in the name of his majesty (may God keep him) of these churches and conventos. I accepted and received them in the name of my holy Order. I give repeated thanks for the prompt fulfillment of what was requested. In my petition, I noted two very necessary and useful points that looked not only to the good of the Indians, but also to the defense of my right and compliance with what our reverend fathers superior ordered. They have so ordered in this holy custody, and it is a point for which I can be held accountable if I do not fully comply with their proper orders, of which there was no approval. This was a decision I asked for and requested from them in the most appropriate manner, with honest intentions and lofty goals. I ask you to see fit to order that I be given a copy of my petition; what you provided in the proceedings of notification; and my response, in the form, manner, and style in which these proceedings have been carried out up to now. For the satisfaction of my right, I ask for justice and in all things await your favor. Salvo, and so forth.

Fray Joaquín de Hinojosa

~~Proceedings~~ Presentation

In the pueblo of El Paso on 31 May 1692, before me, don Diego de Vargas Zapata Luján Ponce de León, governor and captain general of this kingdom of New Mexico and castellan of its fortress and presidio for his majesty, the very reverend father minister, fray Joaquín de Hinojosa, president in capite and ecclesiastical judge of these holy missions and custody of this kingdom of New Mexico, presented to me, by his secretary's hand, the petition on the verso of this sheet.

Proceedings

I, the governor and captain general, having seen the petition and its contents, of course refuse him the copy of the proceedings and other matters expressed in them. The very reverend father president ecclesiastical judge of this holy custody and kingdom wishes to appeal the proceedings I provided in answer to his petition, presented on 16 May of the present year. He may do so by placing the appeal before the king, our lord, in his Supreme and Royal Council of the Indies as the source of royal jurisdiction, which I defend, and before the judge legislator to determine whether the royal cedula issued in the Supreme Council of the Indies has the character of renouncing the patronato real that it so clearly charges the governors and royal justices to defend and support.

The royal cedula was obtained by the apostolic missionaries of the provinces of Sonora, representing the vexations suffered by the Indians who live there under their administration by being compelled by the officials to go to work in the mines and the province's silver-refining haciendas.[10] Its content is different from the request and causes for wanting to adjudicate for themselves the lands they enjoy, which are currently being worked by Indians and Spaniards who inhabit the pueblos and missions of this district of El Paso in the kingdom of New Mexico. They mutually enjoy the lands in peace and friendship. They live on those they have without lawsuits or dissension, which would arise were I, the governor and captain general, without careful consideration to give the possession to the very reverend father. This he insisted upon in his request, again citing in it that of his predecessor, the very reverend fray Francisco de Vargas. Of record in the possession are the proceedings of distribution, which he requested and indicated in each of the pueblos of the missions inhabited today. This being the case, he would like to avail himself of the royal cedula and the session of the Lima Council he cites, which apply to recently converted Indians.

For security from the enemy, the present inhabitants are in pueblos and missions established within a district of not quite 5 leagues. The Indians live in three pueblos, and among them, some Spaniards. Each pueblo is divided, which was not done by my predecessors, from the time the Indians of New Mexico rebelled. The few here are from nations loyal to God and king. They left, as did those my predecessors had removed. As I repeat, the missionary fathers have their parishes divided according to their will. None of my predecessors interposed themselves, nor shall I, the governor and captain general, intervene.

In the present year, the Indians of Socorro will seek to have those of Ysleta ordered not to intrude on their lands. Desiring the fair administration of justice, I asked the reverend father president, as well as the father missionary, fray Antonio Guerra, the former guardian of the pueblo of Socorro who built its church and convento, that they both tell me, as prelates and former ministers to these Indians, how far the inhabited land extended at the time of the flight from New Mexico. They answered that it extended to Juan de Valencia's rancho,[11] and they administered and recognized it as a parish and its citizens as parishioners. Having visually judged the distance, I saw it to be a very legitimate and justified distance. I ordered them to use the acequia that crosses it in a straight line in the direction of the rancho as a sign that no one should pass from one bank to the other. I offer this as proof that the very reverend fathers custos, the predecessors of the aforesaid president, have neither promoted nor aspired to such adjudication under secular right, which would be to usurp everything from his majesty, the king our lord (may God keep him), not only his patronato real but also his royal jurisdiction and exclusive dominion.

I could not have made a grant of lands that had been taken from and adjudicated to be the possession of the missions. His predecessor legitimately and justifiably requested what pertained to him, and I, the governor and captain general, have provided it.

Today the very reverend father bases himself on laws of which I am unaware, in so polished, subtle, and elegant a style and depth of sententious eloquence that I naturally yield to him on this point. My inadequacy, however, does not admit the subtle implication of the petition presented. In it, he did not request the copy he should have to have recourse to the most excellent lord viceroy as representative of his majesty's person. After having seen the proceedings, the viceroy may justly decide either to reprimand me for my ignorance and lack of intelligence made evident to him in them or give me restrictively the order and the tenor of its provision.

This is what should be done without the very reverend father avoiding this knowledge, which I recognize as my superior to direct and inform me. He should not resort to subterfuges to show he was not subjected to a residencia of his time in office for failure to inform his superiors, the reverend fathers prelate. If the reverend father ingenuously appeals my proceedings and the royal jurisdiction of the patronato real to the most excellent lord viceroy, of course I am ready to send the copy to the most excellent lord viceroy as soon as it is safe for a courier. I shall inform the reverend father president through my secretary of government and war with the knowledge and assurance that I send the proceedings and information that I have done so to his prelates. If they go before your excellency requesting the copy or copies of whatever occurs to them, I, for my part, would not grant them such recognition. By this means, they want to claim jurisdiction in the patronato real.

The only thing that remains for the greatness of your excellency's justified consideration is changing the system and custom that has existed since the time the land was won. In particular is the observance of the good relations since 1680 (the year of the uprising of the Indians of New Mexico), in which the citizens and Indians who left have lived and are living, as I report, without the slightest controversy. Instead, the poor Spaniards are the ones who live at the mercy of the Indians, behaving as his majesty's vassals in obedience to royal justice, sacrificing their comforts. They confine themselves to whatever land is left for them. If they request the land, the governor will point it out, favoring the very reverend fathers in every way. Thus, the lands indicated, as well as water from the acequia, are subject to their will, and likewise the Indians.

The citizens are last in everything and have no privileges, which in justice they should have. They are the ones who aid and defend against enemy invasions during the absence on campaign of the forces of this presidio, taking their place, standing guard at the missions, and making raids against the enemy. His majesty could bring in citizens, and the missionary fathers could better instruct the Indians in our holy faith if they did not fear that they would be without aid.

In the pueblos where there are ministers, they treat the Indians with gentleness and with rigor, whipping them so that they learn and do not shirk instruction and divine offices. With wariness and ritual, they seek by plea and request to administer those Indians who are only there part of the time. They know that they would risk their lives were they to mete out such punishment to them, for these Indians would go to the mountains, and their conversion would be lost.

As a loyal vassal of his majesty, I inform your excellency by these proceedings that what is reported therein is what you have seen and reviewed, which pertains to you in your office. I order my secretary of government and war to notify the reverend father in the presence of four witnesses: Sgto. mayor Francisco de Anaya Almazán, alcalde ordinario de primer voto; the alguacil mayor, Juan García de Noriega; Sgto. mayor Juan Lucero de Godoy; and Capt. don Fernando Durán y Chaves. So that his reverence may understand the tenor of the proceedings, and should he ask for a copy of all the aforesaid in the form expressed in the proceedings, I shall order it given to him in response to the petition he may present for this, unless he requests in it more than he has requested and may occur to him to request before the most excellent lord viceroy as his majesty's representative. I also order my secretary to respond to him without recording anything that his reverence may say to him. So that the proceedings may be of record, I provided, ordered, and signed them with my secretary of government and war, together with the four witnesses I called and ordered to be present at the reading of these proceedings, which I signed ut supra.

Don Diego de Vargas Zapata Luján Ponce de León

Francisco de Anaya Almazán

Juan García de Noriega

Juan Lucero de Godoy

Don Fernando Durán y Chaves

By order of the lord governor and captain general

Juan Páez Hurtado

Secretary of government and war

Reading of the previous proceedings

On 2 June 1692, I, Juan Páez Hurtado, alferez of the company of the presidio of El Paso and secretary of government and war for lord don Diego de Vargas Zapata Luján Ponce de León, governor and captain general of this kingdom of New Mexico and castellan of its fortress and presidio for his majesty, certify, as required by law and according to my office, that in compliance with the previous proceedings of the lord governor and captain general and with the witnesses named therein, ordered and signed, I notified the reverend father, fray Joaquín de Hinojosa, interim president of this holy custody and missions of our father, St. Francis, and ecclesiastical judge in capite of this kingdom. I informed him personally of these proceedings, to which I attest, in the presence of the four witnesses in his cell in this convento of El Paso, reading to the reverend father the proceedings the lord governor and captain general provided on 31 May of the present year. I read them to his reverence *verbo ad verbum* with every care. So that the reading of the proceedings, according to what is contained in them, may be of record, I certify it and signed on the said day, month, and year, to which I attest.

In testimony of the truth, I signed it.

Juan Páez Hurtado

Secretary of government and war

———

This agrees with the original proceedings of the legal action that remain in the archive and court of law that are the responsibility of lord don Diego de Vargas Zapata Luján Ponce de León, governor and captain general of this kingdom and provinces of New Mexico and castellan of its fortress and presidio for his majesty, from which I, the alferez of the presidio and secretary of government and war, by his order had copied, to which I attest. Present as witnesses to see it corrected and emended were those called who signed and were named in the proceedings of 31 May. So that it may be of record, they signed it with me, the secretary of government and war. The copy and attested copy of the proceedings, in whole and in part, are on thirty-one sheets signed with my customary signature. This copy is made in this pueblo of El Paso on 16 June of the present year 1692 on ordinary blank paper, because stamped paper is not available in this area.

Francisco de Anaya Almazán [rubrica]

Juan Lucero de Godoy [rubrica]

Juan García de Noriega [rubrica]

Don Fernando Chaves [rubrica]

With testimony of the truth, I sign and make my customary rubrica,

Juan Páez Hurtado

Secretary of government and war [rubrica]

Diego de Vargas to the Conde de Galve, El Paso,
17 June 1692, LS.

Most excellent sir,

Sir, I am sending the proceedings originated and continued
before me by the very reverend fathers. One was custos last year,
1691, and the other, who has brought up the matter again, is at
present interim president because of the death that same year of the
reverend father, fray Diego de Mendoza, who succeeded the custos
from the year before. The current president could have followed
everything contained in the requests I cite, brought up, and asked
for in the possession sought by the reverend father, fray Francisco
de Vargas.

If the latter, with such mature judgement and experience, having
been in this area for twelve years, considered it his duty to ask for
possession of the land, pastures, waters, and water holes of all the
Indians settled in this pueblo of El Paso and those of its district, he
would have done so as well. The current president, by his argument,
tried to extend the claim. He asked not just for possession, bringing
up for this purpose the requests and proceedings from 30 August 1691
of the reverend father, fray Francisco de Vargas, of record in the
proceedings I provided. I ordered that he be given, for the holy
churches, conventos, and land, the possession he requested in his
petition. He should be given those that are indicated in this pueblo
and the rest of the district, which he cites in his request.

The reverend father president took the proceedings for the request
he presented on 16 May of the present year 1692, which consist of
the proceedings in which he brings up his claim. At the same time,
he asks that he be given possession of the land, pastures, water, and
water holes for the Indians by proceedings I provided for this on 17
May. In the proceedings, the granting of possession he requests of
the holy churches and conventos of this pueblo and those of its district is of record.

With respect to the land pointed out to them, the proceedings I
provided on 30 August 1691 should be fully kept, complied with,
and carried out. With respect to the possession he requested for the
Indians, there is no reason for such an action, which is denied, or
anything else that is of record in the proceedings, to which I refer
and about which my secretary of government and war notified him

at my order. He responded, as is of record in the notification of the proceedings. In it, one can see the father's boldness in suggesting that I, a loyal vassal of his majesty, did not follow orders. He told me I should have complied, which I let pass.

With all courtesy and care, on 16 May in this pueblo of El Paso, I gave him possession of its holy church, called Nuestra Señora de Guadalupe, and its convento. Having come out, in the presence of a group of several people from the two squads that had accompanied me, I told them the tenor of the proceedings: possession of 4 fanegas of land for wheat; 1 for maize; and the rest for other grains, beans, vegetables, and gardens, giving preference in the richness of irrigable land and water from the acequia. It was announced that I was giving him possession in his majesty's name. I continued this in the other pueblos according to the proceedings I provided, to which I refer. Having done so, I carried out what I was supposed to do as provided for in the proceedings issued on 30 August 1691. I order here that it be kept and complied with.

The reverend father president presented me with a petition his secretary hand delivered in which he thanks me for the possessions I have given him. He asks me to give him an authorized copy of all the proceedings to send to his prelates so that this may be of record for them and he will not be charged with not having given an account at the time of the residencia of his term in office. It is of record that I denied his request for a copy in the proceedings I provided on 31 May. If he would like to place the appeal before the king, our lord, in his Supreme and Royal Council of the Indies, he may do so. I shall give the copy to the person whose exclusive responsibility it is, as the source of royal jurisdiction I defend, who is legislative judge to determine whether the royal cedula issued in the Supreme Council of the Indies has the character of renouncing the patronato real, which the king entrusts to his governors and his royal officials to defend.

I state that I shall also give your excellency, as his majesty's representative, a copy of the rest of what is of record in the proceedings and whatever else occurs to me, not failing to recognize this knowledge as my superior, which can order and accuse me.

The remaining cases and explanations that are of record in the proceedings were made known at my order by my secretary of government and war with the attendance of the four witnesses who signed and are named and ordered. Nevertheless, the reverend father president, after the reading of the proceedings on that day, sent another petition with the secretary. I responded to him that I would neither accept nor admit it because it was denied, and I did not yet know what he had sent to your excellency. When he sends the proceedings to his prelate, and likewise expresses whatever he has to allege and say, your excellency will hear him and order. Replying, I said, "Look, my father, your reverence is denied." He protested, saying that even a post would listen to him, and no judge would refuse to listen. I responded, "My father, his excellency, the most excellent lord viceroy, will listen to what the very reverend prelate or prelates may express and allege and to what your reverence and the very reverend father president may advise and report." In this way, I advised the very reverend father in my proceedings. In his majesty's name I provide and so order.

Then the father secretary became angry and got up from the chair, shouting loudly, chastising me, saying that he took as his witness the holiest Trinity: God the Father, God the Son, and God the Holy Spirit. I told him in very polite and humble words that he should calm down, restrain himself, and see that such extremes were uncalled for. Because he persisted with a new outburst, I said, "Calm yourself, your reverence. Do not make such a commotion." I called the witnesses, and in their presence, he repeated that I had to give him the copy of the proceedings for his prelate. I replied that I did not have to give it to him, because he had no jurisdiction and was not my superior with respect to the post I exercised for his majesty, that of governor and captain general of this kingdom. I should instead give the copy to the most excellent lord viceroy, the Conde de Galve, who could command me, and whom I would humbly serve and obey. I would order a copy made and sent to his excellency. I would call the reverend father president, so that in his presence it might be examined and he might assure himself that the copy was legal and not doubt that I was carrying out my duties. In front of his reverence, I would enclose the letter of transmittal with the proceedings, sealing and addressing them to the most excellent lord, don Gaspar de Sandoval Cerda Silva y Mendoza, Conde de Galve, viceroy, governor and captain general of all New Spain and this kingdom, and so forth.

The father recognized my integrity and that the severity of his outburst, which I want to emphasize, did not cause me to lose my respect for him or respond rashly. He came to his senses and stated before the witnesses that he recognized me as governor and captain general, calling me by my first and last name, and listing offices I have held in which his majesty placed me. He stated that he and the father president were very obedient vassals of his majesty and they would obey me and comply with everything I might order, regardless of my post, since they respected me for being don Diego de Vargas and therefore worthy of esteem. He also stated that legal disputes do not lead to either good will, courtesy, or consideration.

I responded that even my posts could not take away who I am, which is enhanced by the honor he was showing me. As a lowly ant, I was at his feet, those of the very reverend father, and other fathers. My care and goodwill were steadfast in the sincerity and simplicity of a mutual, good friendship, which suffered the misfortune of question and dispute. I attribute this to my great ignorance. I wanted to serve his majesty effectively. With knowledge of the proceedings, your excellency will order me as you see fit, and I shall not exceed your orders.

All this took place, as I say, in the presence of the witnesses and soldiers who were in the guard and other people who came together when they heard our voices. At midday, the very reverend president sent me a plate of refreshments, and I answered him that I greatly esteemed the gift and the warmth with which he sent it to me. Because it happened to be the novena to Our Lady of the Conquest in this holy church, I went to the rosary in the afternoon.[12] The father secretary, who is guardian, did me the favor of coming out to greet me. I kissed his hand and his holy habit respectfully.

In the afternoon, he went in search of the same people, asking them to come to his cell so they could sign, as I had not wanted to give them the copy. They made one of them sign, and he left me his signature as I gave it to your excellency. They forced him, threatening him with censure. He came to advise me of what had happened to him and that in the same way they called everyone. The others excused themselves, saying that they did not have to sign; that I did not deny the copy to them, but to his superior; and that they could not be excommunicated without cause.

The day of the celebration of Corpus, they denied me the peace,[13] which they had given me since I arrived, as they had given it to my predecessors. I did not try to reach an understanding with the father, because the cabildo, as well as the others, were at the solemn ceremony, and they objected enough to all these points to provoke a bronze statue, as your excellency must see. An inquiry was begun to see whether in my absence they could excommunicate me (I cannot be convinced of such a thing). I have made up my mind and resigned myself to His Divine Majesty in all things and do not give cause for them to deprive me of such a benefit by separating me from the church. Your excellency may provide whatever you decide in your justified care, ordering me to do as you see fit.

Even if they continue to deny me the peace, I shall not ask for satisfaction so that such a change may be made. If they have an order from a competent judge, they should show it to me so that I may recognize whether it was or is their responsibility. If it is gratuitous, I do not wish to give myself more than the prelate may give me. For this favor, I would esteem him; it is the privilege and honor of the post I occupy. As such, denying it is not subject to the fathers' will. Administration and giving of the peace to all the governors and captains general who have been my predecessors has been instead a necessary and proper duty, practice, and observance since the land and this kingdom were won. Thus, there is no reason to remain silent without seeking your excellency's decision, for if I have this prerogative and privilege by virtue of my office, I should not be deprived of it. Even in the alcaldías mayores of this kingdom, on first-class feast days,[14] the priests give the peace to the alcaldes mayores. Your excellency will see how much greater right the person has who occupies the post of governor and captain general of the kingdom and provinces of New Mexico or any other, whatever it may be.

With respect to the contents of the proceedings, the reverend father, fray Joaquín de Hinojosa (whom the reverend missionary fathers of the custody named president and interim ecclesiastical judge in capite of this holy custody according to their statutes), wants to interpose adjudication of the land, water, pastures, and watering holes. It occurs to me to warn and demonstrate to your excellency the reasons and difficulties that seem to me—given my limited understanding—most compelling, from among the many reasons to deny the fathers such a wish.

In the adjudication, they are less impartial judges and more owners of the Indians' land. As his majesty's vassals, we must recognize laws based on singular reports from people with qualifications and approval, which is what the cedulas his majesty (may God keep him) promulgates are. Nevertheless, I would not consider it a disservice to his sublime majesty to suspend carrying out a cedula if by its fulfillment damage and risk to his royal crown would follow. Future contingencies cannot be prepared for. Therefore judges should carry out the required fulfillment of laws that do not allow for taking circumstances into consideration. Yet, in those laws where a risk may be seen in a future contingency, an accounting should be given to his majesty in his Royal and Supreme Council of the Indies, so that, as legislative judge, he may provide according to the future contingency and either amend or repeal the cedula. Or he may order, the future notwithstanding, that it be kept, complied with, and carried out.

I say this regarding the royal cedula to which the father president, fray Joaquín de Hinojosa, refers. It is not what he wishes. He wants to gloss and interpret it enough to corroborate his claim and wants it reissued. I have carefully repeated in the proceedings that it is different from the mandate and royal will. When it was promulgated, the future contingencies had not occurred, and I do not concede that the royal cedula speaks to and directs what he would have his wish extend to. There will be other cedulas, many later ones his majesty (may God keep him) may provide.

The new cedulas, and not the old, should always be obeyed, and they are. I do not remember, according to what I have seen and read, that his majesty, the king our lord, Carlos II (may God keep him), ordered in his new compilation of laws that the governors and corregidors were to inform themselves and restore all the pueblos of their districts and jurisdiction and that the citizens were to have knowledge of the royal cedula. One sees that superior judges, who are the most excellent lord viceroys and presidents, are exempt from it. This law has greater force, because his majesty has all-embracing dominion and enjoys, by papal authority, the patronato real and the right to give to the fathers. What pertains to them is jurisdiction in ecclesiastical matters, beyond conversion and reduction. This is so that they do not impinge on secular rights: the preservation, protection, and defense of the Indians; and jurisdiction in their civil and criminal proceedings.

For whatever future contingency, I explain to your excellency that in this land Indians and citizens live together uneasily in the pueblos, within a distance of 5 leagues. From the time of the uprising and loss of New Mexico, they have lived as guests and eat from the four pueblos' little irrigated land, which they plant and maintain.

Thus, if this cedula were put into effect and such a provision unthinkingly made, we would end up losing this kingdom for the following reasons. First, there are citizens and Indians here today who left the kingdom. It would introduce dissent and disturbance were everyone together as a group to follow the fathers' faction, because for the Indians to escape their savagery, they must satisfy the priests. As a barbarous people, these Indians and those who fled into the woods, deserts, and mountains would rise up and use treachery among all, with no possible remedy. By stealing horses that belong to this presidio and some citizens within 8 or 9 leagues, or at the least 4 to 6, they would make themselves lords of the land, killing all the soldiers and citizens. Without them, the Apaches and other enemy nations will also enter to rob, kill, and burn, and the kingdom and these provinces would be lost once and for all.

If they do not rise up, it is because they find themselves lords of the land, because the citizens have neither irrigated land to sow nor the assurance of water or security in their outpost. Also, because of the enemies referred to, it would be necessary for them to go and seek out a safe place and land to dry-farm in order to support themselves and their families. Without the citizens, his majesty's presidio, because it is in the interior, would be in the unfortunate circumstance of having its soldiers also in need, with no access to fields and having to go elsewhere. They could not support themselves on their salaries.

It would be difficult for the men of the presidio permanently to have to buy all their supplies from the Indians, who are lazy and for the most part idlers and shirkers. Some scarcely plant enough to sustain themselves, while others harvest more than those and squander it on themselves. They trade the goods they customarily use among themselves. When the citizens arrive at their houses wanting to buy goods, they either refuse or sell to them at an excessive price.

Thus, the people of this outpost would always be totally hungry and unhappy from the misery of having to go out to seek relief. Should they persevere, living with such difficulty, they could not resist the Apaches and other enemies, who would join together and have the audacity to destroy and ruin them completely. All would be lost.

In the twelve years since the uprising and loss of this kingdom and don Antonio de Otermín's departure from it, the presidio was placed at the outpost of Guadalupe[15] to give it that additional distance, about 14 leagues. His successor, don Domingo Jironza, moved the presidio don Antonio had established and founded during his tenure (by order of the most excellent lord, the Conde de Paredes), closer, placing it at the midpoint of the 14 leagues, better to favor the villa settled in the outpost of Guadalupe, and called it the real of San Lorenzo.

In that time, he had to deal with the Mansos, who were leaving and moving their rancherias, and was suspicious that they wanted to provoke the other nations to rebel. This reason obliged him to restrict the settlement and reduce it to the five pueblos within not quite 5 leagues.

Since that time, we have seen and experienced among the Indians their evil intention, attempted and carried out through the Mansos' departure, which is what I am saying. If they did not carry it out because they were detected, they did rebel, moving their rancherias until they themselves returned within sight of this district. The very reverend father, fray Francisco de Vargas, who was custos, went out and reduced them, persuading them to return. He assured them of the pardon of the lord governor and captain general, my predecessor don Domingo, so that they would be calm. Some of them stayed to live as they live today in this pueblo, and the others, with some heathens and their captains, settled in this outpost, which was indicated to them and where they are today.

Later in the time of General don Domingo, another rancheria of Captain Barbón of the Suma nation (which was the one I told your excellency at the end of February of the present year that I had captured and destroyed) from the Sierra Florida rose up in the outpost called Ojito, burning the holy church of Santa Gertrudis and killing a Spanish settler named Archuleta, together with his wife and children, who were camped in the district. A week later, they burned another mission called Soledad and killed Father fray Manuel Beltrán,[16] lay religious, as well as a settler named Antonio de Arvizu,[17] his wife, and children.

Later, during the time of Gen. don Pedro Reneros de Posada, who succeeded don Domingo, the Sumas who were camped in the outpost of Guadalupe rose up and burned its holy church and convento, though it was not God's will to permit them to kill its father minister guardian. The father, one of our father, St. Francis's, is fray Diego de Chavarría,[18] who is in the Convento Grande in that court. He will tell what happened and how they destroyed everything he had in his cell. In addition, one can find Gen. don Pedro Reneros, who was succeeded by Gen. don Domingo Jironza, in that court.

At the end of the year 1690, another junta of many nations was discovered. It was found out by an Indian of the Piro nation, who said that those nations were about to fall upon all these pueblos at the same time and burn their churches. General don Domingo went to the area the Indian pointed out where the allies were, close to Guadalupe, where they were encamped in a large cañada of more than 3 leagues. The allies fled, because an Indian scout who had been captured along the way escaped from our men. Since he was one of the enemy, he was able by means of his flight and escape to give notice of our many men who were coming to destroy them. Thus, the rancheria fled without waiting for the general's troops, who arrived in time to find the last of the allies, who were caught and killed. General don Domingo, at that court, will be better able to report on this.

It seemed to me most essential that these uprisings should be brought and placed before the greatness of your excellency for your consideration, and that in so short a time we have experienced such repeated events and occurrences. For these barbarous people, loyalty lasts as long as it suits them. As I repeat, if a Spanish citizen could live in front of every Indian's house, his majesty would be assured of their steadfastness and that they were purely Christians, as they are not today by entreaty and request. Thus, I repeat that wherever there might be settlements such as this, the father minister missionary will halfheartedly reprimand the Indians and order a few whipped, because he recognizes that his life is secure in such a settlement. In the pueblos where there are no settlements of Spaniards, he will not have the resolve even to reprimand them, much less whip them. What he will do is make the empty threat of telling them that he will report them to the governor and captain general.

I give so prolix an explanation to show that the policy and royal ordinances by which the Indians of the kingdom of New Spain are governed are not appropriate for these Indians. I am not unaware that based on the number of Indians, the designation of principal town is given to the pueblo. It consists of as many Indians as citizens. It must have, as it does, a governor the Indians choose, and the other minor officials in all the other pueblos. The land is given to them by measure if it is where his majesty can give or sell it to the people as he sees fit. In other places and pueblos, it remains vacant royal property, and the Indians use it together with their own, the 500 varas[19] measured from the door of the church in the four directions.

It is ordered that they should not allow citizens of just any character to live among them in their pueblos. Because with those who have different natures and customs, we see that many have caused various disturbances, breaking royal law and losing respect for his majesty. A short time ago, well, it was in 1690, there was an uprising in Celaya and Querétaro. Were it not for the protection of so large a population of Spanish citizens, people of a different character, and haciendas, the valleys and richest haciendas might have been cause for great concern. Nevertheless, there was an uprising against the citizens, and there were deaths and other damages.

Your excellency should understand that this land is spread out and inhabited not by trustworthy people, but by barbarous Indians. Every step of the way, there are Apaches, who are the far-ranging enemy, and many other nations. As I have written in the opinion your excellency (in accord with the Royal Junta of the Treasury and its lords minister) ordered me to give for the conquest of this kingdom, and have repeated, since it was won, there has been no distribution of land among the Indians. The Spaniards who founded their haciendas and ranchos were given grants of land in amounts based on character, merit, and duty. The governor and captain general had the authority to give them in his majesty's name. The title had the force of a grant by virtue of the directive and royal dispatch from the most excellent lord viceroy, who provided it as if it had come from the Supreme and Royal Council of the Indies, since it did not need to be confirmed. Thus, one must attend to his majesty's royal service by maintaining and preserving this kingdom. Altering the form that the civil government of the Spanish citizens and the Indians of reduced nations, as well as those who may be newly reduced, would be to risk not only the increase of what there is, but also its loss once and for all, making restoration impossible.

Thus, I have given your excellency my opinion, even though the fathers may try to censure me for it. In my humility and dutiful zeal, there is no one I would prefer to my king and natural lord (may God keep him). What I have done in his royal service on five campaigns and other raids is public knowledge. All these have been financed by my honor and out of my pocket, as will be the expected cost of the entrada I am about to make to the kingdom of New Mexico and the villa of Santa Fe.

I have given an account of this to your excellency with the letter in which I summon for the entrada the citizens from the kingdom of New Mexico who are in New Biscay. I promise them that from the day they arrive until they return to their homes, I shall set them an open table and provide chocolate in the morning and evening. I shall provide lances I have paid for completely, as well as the necessary firearms and bullets. Though wanting to carry it out so much, had I not promised your excellency the entrada, I might have postponed it, because of the uneasiness I have suffered in my spirit about this circumstance. It is not good for one who should have a calm spirit and be prepared (if God sees fit) to lose his life in such an enterprise to have such anxiety, the more so when he is taking with him the cause of it, which could be his relief in that critical moment.

Thus, I conclude by saying to your excellency that it would be better for the reverend father president and his secretary and guardian to occupy themselves with teaching our holy faith to the Indians. All the very reverend missionary fathers should tell, counsel, and order them to obey the Spaniards, who will love them very much, and to live in a civil and upright way, instructed in the practices of our holy faith. Because of the Spaniards, they will be kept safe from their enemies. They will not be killed, but defended, and not only them, but also their women and children.

It would not have much effect were I to tell them if the fathers do not, because as their servants, [20] cantors, and other workers, they civilize them. They learn to speak Spanish and persuade and influence the others about what they see as the fathers' will. What I have regretted most is their limited understanding. They can be moved to disobedience by example, such as the novelty of the priests' denying me the comfort and grace of the honor of the peace on so festive a day as Corpus Christi, when on weekdays since I came, they have punctually administered it to me. This is the reason I have been distressed, not because I am vain, which I do not feel except for what is lasting, my sense of duty, well-known character, and lineage, for which I do. In keeping with these, I have made this long report to your excellency and in it expressed my opinions, so that your greatness and the lords, having seen it, will order (if you see fit for the royal junta to do so) that I be corrected if need be, for in all things I am always at your feet.

Likewise, I humbly ask your excellency to decide and order once and for all with respect to the fathers, so that for as long as his majesty and your excellency see fit and would keep me, we shall all comply with those orders, as befits our station and office. I am only defending the royal jurisdiction and patronato real without interfering to usurp ecclesiastical jurisdiction, because even though ignorant, I know very well what is incumbent upon me. This is the reason for not allowing writings that might take my jurisdiction from me through absurd proposals, interpreting and glossing his majesty's laws and royal cedulas.

I also humbly make the request of your excellency with respect to their corrupt use of spiritual censures. They want the citizens to come to their cells and, by means of verbosity and Latin texts, want to persuade them to sign whatever they place before them for their consideration. As proof of this truth, I am sending your excellency the two papers the father secretary guardian of this convento of El Paso wrote and signed in which he calls the alguacil mayor of the cabildo of this kingdom, Juan García de Noriega. It is signed by the father secretary, fray Agustín de Colina, apostolic notary, and dated El Paso, 5 June 1692. In the father secretary's second paper, in his hand and signed by him, dated El Paso, 6 June 1692, he calls the lord alcalde, Francisco de Anaya, and tells him to come for the tranquility, better government, and peace of the citizens and the Indians, under threat of whatever penalty your excellency may determine. The fathers persuade, terrorize, and move them. Since they have an interest in this business and case, they want them to sign against their own case, and it is illegal to be a witness for both sides in the same case. By intervening, they infringe upon the jurisdiction of royal justice and the patronato real, as in this type of competing jurisdictions, and even more so when the judgment originates in the greatness of your excellency. Because this is well known, the religious will know what they can and must do. I only assure your excellency that in my case, I am not asking anything of anyone that I would not know how to reciprocate.

May God keep your excellency's most excellent person many very happy years in your increasing greatness. Done in this pueblo of El Paso, 17 June 1692.

Most excellent sir, your humble servant who venerates you kisses your excellency's hand,

Don Diego de Vargas
Zapata Luján Ponce de León [rubrica]

Most excellent lord viceroy, the Conde de Galve

———

El Paso, 17 June 1692, Don Diego de Vargas Zapata Luján
Received on 24 July

Fray Agustín de Colina to Juan García de Noriega, Summons, El Paso, 5 June 1692, ADS.

The lord alguacil mayor, Juan García de Noriega,

Twice I have sent you the message that you should come to this convento, and now, to be even more in accord with justice, I do it for a third, as I am apostolic notary of the ecclesiastical judge of this kingdom. Having summoned you in the presence of the lord governor and captain general of this kingdom, you should see fit to come here. You should take note that, in accord with the legality of the office I hold, I must swear and attest to the reasons why those who have been summoned excuse themselves or do not appear when they are called. I say this hoping that you will see fit not to make matters worse. From the convento of El Paso on 5 June 1692.

I kiss your hand,

> Fray Agustín de Colina [rubrica]
> Apostolic notary

To the captain, Juan García de Noriega (may God keep him many years), alguacil mayor of the cabildo of this kingdom, and so forth
Hand delivered

Fray Agustín de Colina to Francisco de Anaya Almazán, Summons, El Paso, 6 June 1692, ADS.

Jesus, Mary, and Joseph

The lord alcalde, Francisco de Anaya,

Before the father guardian of this convento, you agreed the other day to come sign (with the other companions I summoned as witnesses in the presence of the lord governor), the proceedings that, as apostolic notary, I wrote to attest, as is my duty and charge. The term of two days has passed without your having appeared, so now, under my signature and with the title of apostolic notary I hold, I call you to this convento of El Paso. Since your just reasons did not come in writing, you should take note, for I am the apostolic notary of the ecclesiastical judge of this kingdom. Let this be a warning so that I may proceed in a more justified manner in the cares of my office. El Paso, 6 June 1692.

I kiss your hand,

> Fray Agustín de Colina [rubrica]
> Apostolic notary

To the sargento mayor, Francisco de Anaya Almazán (may God keep him many years), alcalde of the cabildo of this kingdom, and so forth Real

Diego de Vargas to the Conde de Galve, El Paso, 19 June 1692, LS.

Most excellent sir,

Sir, after I had informed your excellency, the old citizens told me that lawsuits over conflicting jurisdiction were continual in the kingdom of New Mexico. The motive and means for them was the collection of royal tribute that his majesty transferred to the forty worthiest citizens, with the obligation of maintaining the kingdom, in peace and war, by having arms and horses at the ready. During the time of Gov. don Pedro de Peralta[21] or his successor, when the most excellent lord viceroy, the Conde de Monterrey,[22] was governing New Spain, the competition and cases over jurisdiction were such that they occasioned a report to be made to his excellency, as was done. To remedy the situation, a royal provision was decided upon. After review by the lords minister and with their agreement, the most excellent lord viceroy prepared his ordinances for the governance of the missions, respectfully ordering and directing the fathers prelate custos, whoever they might be, and the other ministers.[23] It was also pointed out to them in one of the chapter meetings that they were to have nine servants, in addition to the bell ringer, all of whom it was declared should be relieved from paying tribute. In another chapter meeting, which I also cite as proof to deny possession, the Indians of each guardianship were to give the father minister doctrinero 12 to 15 fanegas of maize each year and 33 to 35 of wheat for his subsistence. They were to take care to sow in such a way that they could securely provide and give that amount to the father.

Thus, one concludes that the fathers still neither had, nor were given, the right to have lands designated for their sustenance, which was the Indians' responsibility. Therefore, they can expect even less action on, adjudication about, and legalization of their possession of the Indians' land, when they themselves refuse to recognize that they are given and indicated land that was rightfully theirs, so that they might sow the grains, seeds, and other foodstuffs for their sustenance as they wish. Should your excellency see fit to do so, it would be very advantageous to have this royal provision searched for in the office of government and war, where the archive of dispatches and royal cedulas pertaining to this kingdom is found. I am passing over in silence the rest of the information the citizens have given me. May God keep your most excellent person in your increasing greatness many happy years. El Paso, 19 June 1692.

Most excellent lord, the least and humblest of your servants kisses your excellency's hands,

Don Diego de Vargas Zapata
Luján Ponce de León [rubrica]

Most excellent lord viceroy, the Conde de Galve

———

El Paso, 19 June 1692, don Diego de Vargas Zapata Luján
Received on 24 July

———

Mexico City, 24 July 1692
To the lord fiscal with the copy of the proceedings that accompanies the letter of 19 June from the informant. Before anything else, have

those in charge of the Government section make an authorized copy of the dispatch from the time of the lord Conde de Monterrey, cited in the letter, or indicate that it does not appear in the books of Government in this case. [Galve's rubrica]

————

In compliance with what your excellency ordered, we have searched in this office and examined all the books of general materials and the registries of dispatches during the time when the most excellent lord viceroy, the Conde de Monterrey, governed, which was from the year 1595 until 1603. Likewise, we have examined the books where some old royal cedulas from the year 1606 to 1627 are registered. For now, the royal decree the governor of New Mexico refers to does not appear. Thus, I certify it in Mexico City on 1 August 1692. Don Diego José de Bustos [rubrica]

————

I swear and attest that I have searched in this office of government and war, of which Capt. don José de la Cerda Morán was in charge, for the royal decree cited in this letter in the year referred to in the above certification. For now, there is no record in the books of its having been sent by this superior government. So that it may be of record, I provide the present document in Mexico City on 1 August 1692.
Juan de Aguirre Vidaurreta[24] [rubrica]
Royal notary and senior official of government

Benito de Noboa Salgado, Fiscal's reply, Mexico City, 7 August 1692, DS.

Most excellent sir,

His majesty's fiscal has seen this letter from the governor of New Mexico, together with another from him of 19 June of this year and the copy of the attached proceedings that record the request the father custos made last year for possession of the churches, conventos, and land for planting. It was ordered granted to him, as in fact was done in the time of the current custos or president, without indicating any land in particular, except what might seem to him most appropriate for planting the wheat and maize all those conventos or missions needed. At the time the father custos or current president expedited the assignment of land for the Indians, it appears that the governor did not agree for the reason, which can be inferred despite its absence, that the Spanish citizens and Indians are united, the land is common to everyone, and he did not wish to cause novelties and disturbances with the assignment.

It appears that the father custos resented this, asking him for a copy of the proceedings for his prelate, as he would have it understood, and stated that he had to care for the well-being and defense of the Indians. Because he was denied the copy, he refused the governor the peace, as was customarily given to governors. Other matters are of record in the two enclosed papers, from which the governor concludes that there are competing jurisdictions. In his second letter, he asks for jurisdiction, which had been recognized at an earlier time by reason of the tributes his majesty transferred to forty of the worthiest citizens on condition of maintaining that kingdom in peace and war. The most excellent lord, the Conde de Monterrey, designated this, issuing a royal provision with ordinances for its governance, allotting to the missionaries nine servants and a bell ringer, excusing them from tribute. The Indians of each guardianship were to give to the minister 12 to 15 fanegas of maize and 33 to 35 of wheat, without land being indicated for the fathers, as is of record at greater length in the letters and proceedings referred to. Even though your excellency ordered this royal provision searched for in the offices, certification has been provided that it did not appear.

The fiscal states that in the matter of looking out for the Indians, the missionary fathers are not their sole protectors; rather any Spaniard can ask for what would benefit them, and the governor should execute it as principal protector, looking in the first place to their comfort and then that of the Spaniards and other inhabitants. Even though land is distributed to the pueblos in accordance with the ordinances, aside from this, it so happens that the Spaniards are as guests until, with your excellency's favor, New Mexico is pacified. There Indians and Spaniards may go to make their homes, planting where it appears best to them. Because once the land where they plant becomes sterile, it is necessary to move to another site.

In this way, they have always managed in El Paso in all peace and quiet until today. The missionary fathers, in accordance with the sacred statute of the Rule of their Order, cannot own land. According to custom, they choose the land most appropriate for the necessary planting of maize and wheat for the sustenance of their custody and other missions. The citizens should show themselves to be prepared, so that they have extra and the fathers do not lack the necessary sustenance.

With this satisfactory plan and in friendship they have lived until now. Your excellency could, should you see fit, provide that it continue (since the governor has arranged it) until sometime in the future when a new arrangement is required. Because very slight dissensions at the beginning usually disturb the admirable zeal with which new conversions are entered upon, your excellency will please see fit to order a dispatch of entreaty and request to the religious and of advice to the governor, so that they will treat each other with all harmony and politeness, honoring each other, and that the religious give peace to the governor, as has been the custom. Among barbarous nations, much attention is paid to the authority and respect in which governors are held, and very favorable results are achieved. In this matter, your excellency, to whom the religious will have recourse if they have anything to offer, will provide in everything what is best.
Mexico City, 7 August 1692
Dr. don Benito de Noboa Salgado [rubrica]

Mexico City, 8 August 1692
To the junta [Galve's rubrica]

Junta of the Treasury, Mexico City, 16 August 1692, DS.

In the Junta of the Treasury that was held on 16 August 1692 by the most excellent lord, the Conde de Galve, viceroy of this kingdom, with the lords Dr. Juan de Aréchaga, senior judge of this royal audiencia; don Andrés Pardo de Lago and don Mateo Fernández de Santa Cruz, comptrollers of the Royal Tribunal of Accounts; don Antonio de Deza y Ulloa and don José de Urrutia, treasury officials of the royal treasury of this court; don Fernando de Deza y Ulloa, comptroller general of tributes and mercury of this New Spain: Having seen in this junta the letters from the governor and captain general of the provinces of New Mexico, don Diego de Vargas Zapata Luján, dated 17 and 19 June of this year; the copy of the proceedings wherein the governor appears to explain that there are competing jurisdictions with the father custodians and missionaries of the Order of our father, St. Francis, of those provinces and about the father custos having last year asked for the possession of its churches, conventos, and land for planting, and the rest that is of record at length; and what his majesty's fiscal requested about this particular, it was unanimously decided that his response should be followed and complied with on all points of its contents and that the necessary dispatches be issued. Thus, they decided and signed it with his excellency.

[Galve's rubrica]

His excellency. Lords Aréchaga, Pardo, Santa Cruz, Deza, Urrutia, Deza

Carlos II, Cedula, Madrid, 21 July 1691, C.

The King

To the Conde de Galve, kinsman; gentleman of my bedchamber; viceroy; governor and captain general of the provinces of New Spain; and president of my Royal Audiencia of Mexico; or the person or persons who might be discharging his duties: With the letter of 9 February of last year, 1690, you send the copy of the letters don Domingo Jironza Petrís de Cruzate, governor of the provinces of New Mexico, wrote you with regard to the entrada he had carried out against the uprisen and apostate Indians who have rebelled in that kingdom, and how he won, by fire and sword, the pueblo of Zia, where the rebels were fortified. In one of his letters, that of 27 October 1689, he says that in the presidio of El Paso, the citizens cannot be provided for. This is why during the government of the Conde de Paredes the governor had informed him that the most acceptable plan was to return them to the villa of Santa Fe in New Mexico and other closer places, wherever it might be most advantageous. He made the same report to you, so that you might arrange what should be carried out and how, regarding the points you express in your cited letter and the documents you send in it.

You will understand my decision from the other dispatches you will receive with this letter. With respect to what is included in the report that governor made to you, having seen it in my council, it occurred to me to order you that nothing new need be done regarding what relates to the presidio of El Paso; rather it should remain where it is today. In the rest that is suggested, it has been considered important that the new settlement of Spaniards should be in Zia Pueblo, rather than in another pueblo or in the villa of Santa Fe as is proposed by the governor, since it is so distant and remote with respect to where the previously mentioned presidio is.

Nevertheless, whatever might be best and most advantageous is left up to you, hearing and conferring on this point in the general junta and carrying out what might be decided in it, taking into consideration the state the conquests of don Domingo Jironza may be in at the time this matter is provided for. Considering the state of things as they may be, it is very natural that another adjustment and decision may be required. I hope that upon reflection on everything, you will apply your great zeal to what you judge most appropriate for the end that will result from that deliberation. Give me an accounting of what you decide and determine. Done in Madrid, 21 July 1691.

I, the King

By order of my lord the king

Don Juan de Larrea[25]

Signed with four rubricas of the lords of the council

Mexico City, 22 September 1692

The most excellent lord, the Conde de Galve, my lord viceroy, governor and captain general of this New Spain, having seen and obeyed this royal cedula ordered that it should be recorded in the books of Government, a copy placed with the proceedings from New Mexico about its reduction and entradas, and the lord fiscal should take it.

The Conde de Galve

By order of the conde, my lord

Don Juan Francisco de Vargas Manuel de Lodeña[26]

––––––

This is in accord with the original royal cedula in the office of the secretary of his excellency's Cámara. So that this copy could be made, I was shown it by virtue of his excellency's order.

Mexico City, 5 October 1692
Carlos de Sigüenza [rubrica]
His majesty's notary[27]

———

Mexico City, 22 October 1692
Put it with the proceedings on the matter.
[Galve's rubrica]

Juan de Escalante y Mendoza, Fiscal's reply, Mexico City, 31 October 1692, DS.

Most excellent sir,

His majesty's fiscal[28] for criminal matters of this royal audiencia has seen the copy of the royal cedula that appears to recommend the most appropriate places for the foundation of the villa of New Mexico, which is Zia, and not Santa Fe, where it previously was. This is according to what the fiscal has understood about this point, which is an assumption based on what don Domingo Jironza wrote when he was governor of those provinces. At present, there are different orders being expedited for the entrada that, according to the information your excellency has, don Diego de Vargas is carrying out to reconnoiter all of the uprisen places, of which we await the record of the completed actions and effects that may result. Compliance with the royal cedula cannot be considered until receipt of the reports on reconnoitering the area that will be the most appropriate. With respect to moving the presidio of El Paso, it is appropriate where it is today, as has been stated in various junta decisions. No more appropriate place is to be found for the defense and security of the missions and Spanish citizens who withdrew to it after the general uprising. Thus, on this last point, what his majesty orders, which is keeping the presidio where it is, is done on the basis of well-founded knowledge. Above all, your excellency will provide what you decide to be most advantageous, which will be, as always, the best. Mexico City, 31 October 1692.
Dr. don Juan de Escalante y Mendoza [rubrica]

Mexico City, 4 November 1692
As the fiscal proposes in all things [Galve's rubrica]

In the documents about the Vargas entrada

———

Mexico City, 22 October 1692
Put this with the related proceedings.
[Galve's rubrica]

*AGN, Historia 37:5. 73 folios, 138 written pages. Transcripts of various documents regarding possession of churches and the jurisdictional dispute were published in Maas, *Misiones*, 156–87, with omissions.

1. The civil authorities did not always render Father Hinojosa's title accurately. It should be president in capite and interim ecclesiastical judge ordinary.

2. The term gratis indicates that the scribe did not charge for these pages. Ordinarily, there was a set rate for each page, composed of a certain number of lines and words per line. Vicenta Cortés Alonso, *La escritura y lo escrito: Paleografía y diplomática de España y América en los siglos xvi y xvii* (Madrid, 1986):23.

3. Juan Páez Hurtado was born in Villafranca y los Palacios (Seville) on 2 February 1663 to Domingo [Páez] Hurtado and Ana Josefa Rubio (or Rubia). He first appeared in El Paso as an alferez in August 1692. Páez served as justicia mayor in El Paso during Vargas's colonizing expedition in 1693. His first wife, Pascuala López Vera, died in 1693, leaving him with one daughter, Ana. On 20 June 1704, Páez married Teodora García de la Riva. They had three children: Antonia, Gertrudis, and Juan Domingo. He served as acting governor from the time of Vargas's death in 1704 until 2 March 1705. From that time through the administrations of the Marqués de la Peñuela (1707–12), Flores Mogollón (1712–15), and Félix Martínez (1715–17), Páez served in various posts. In 1717 and again in 1724, he was acting governor. From 1731 to 1736, during the administration of Gov. Gervasio Cruzat y Góngora, Páez continued to served as lieutenant governor. By 1739, the versatile veteran had become alcalde mayor of Santa Fe. Páez died in Santa Fe on 5 May 1742 and was buried under the main altar of La Conquistadora. He had been an active mayordomo of the Confraternity of La Conquistadora and member of the Confraternity of San Miguel. Madoz, *Diccionario geográfico*, 16:142. CRG, 51, 52, 71, 72, 73,

Possession of churches 301

108, 131, 187, 204, 212, 220, 221, 282, 285, 290. West, "Right of Asylum," 123, 124, 126. Ted J. Warner, "Don Félix Martínez and the Santa Fe Presidio, 1693–1730," NMHR 45 (Oct. 1970):270, 271, 279, 282, 328, 361. NMF, 254. Parroquia de Santa María la Blanca, Villas de los Palacios y Villafranca (Seville), Bautismos, 1663, Lib. 5 (1664–67). Casamientos, Lib. 5 (1651–52). Bloom, "Vargas Encomienda," 398, 403, 410–11. Myra Ellen Jenkins, "Taos Pueblo and its Neighbors, 1540–1847," NMHR 41 (Apr. 1966):91.

4. As a result of the Pueblo Revolt, fray Francisco de Ayeta proposed to the viceroy on 3 January 1681 that for new reduction and conquest, only a third of the funds usually assigned should be given to the religious as stipend. The following month, the viceroy, in his report to the king, indicated that although one-half of the previously allocated assistance was owed the remaining priests, Ayeta had agreed it could be reduced by two-thirds, until it was again necessary to increase the number of priests in New Mexico. Hackett and Shelby, *Revolt*, 1:239; 2:11.

5. Giovanni de Medici was born into one of the most powerful families in medieval Italy in 1475. He became Pope Leo X in 1513 and served until his death in 1521. Eric John, ed., *The Popes: A Concise Biographical History* (New York, 1964):329–30. For an extensive, if biased, biography of Leo X, see William Roscoe, *The Life and Pontificate of Leo the Tenth* (London, 1846).

6. The Third Council of Lima was convened by Archbishop Toribio de Mogrovejo and met during 1582 and 1583. The council emphasized religious instruction and determined that Indians should be catechized in their native languages. In addition, the bishops reaffirmed their roles as protectors of the Indians. The reference here is to Actio III, cap. III, *De protectione et cura indorum*. Enrique Dussel, *A History of the Church in Latin America: Colonialism and Liberation, 1492–1979* (Grand Rapids, Mich., 1981):55–57, 268–69.

7. The protector de indios was to act as mediator between the Spanish legal system and the Indians, legally considered minors who would eventually be incorporated into society as adults. By 1589, the office was definitively established by royal cedula. Regulations regarding the office appear in the RECOP, Lib. 6, tít. 6, leyes 1–14. Charles R. Cutter, *The Protector de Indios in Colonial New Mexico, 1659–1821* (Albuquerque, 1986):5–7, 19, 31–34.

8. In contrast to the churches north of the El Paso area, the structures mentioned here had not been profaned in 1680. At the time possession was granted to President Hinojosa, the churches had been blessed and were being used for the

administration of the sacraments. Therefore, despite some similarities with the ritual concerning the blessing or consecration of a church, as contained in the Roman Ritual and Roman Pontifical, the ceremony performed by fray Joaquín was not, strictly speaking, a sacred rite of the Catholic church.

As the highest ecclesiastical authority on the scene at the time, President Hinojosa was sanctioned by canon law to take possession of ecclesiastical goods as the rightful property of the Universal Church or the Apostolic See and sacred goods as those things dedicated by blessing or consecration to divine worship. The churches were in use, and therefore in effective possession of the Franciscans, but the transfer from secular authority to ecclesiastical did not have the force of law derived from recording the transaction in the local church archive. Governor Vargas, as the representative of the king, and therefore the highest secular authority in New Mexico, was required by the laws of Castile and the Indies to grant possession of land for the erection of churches to the Franciscans. Seen in this light, the right of possession as recorded is the embodiment of the patronato real. Vargas, serving in lieu of the king, exercised his royal prerogative and fulfilled his responsibility to Hinojosa, the representative of the church.

The ceremony itself is an ecclesiastical variant of the act of possession of real property practiced in Spain since time immemorial. The toma de posesión, or act of possession, involved walking around the property, picking up dirt or stones and tossing them, pulling up grass, and proclaiming possession in a loud and clear voice. This physical act of possession is a symbolic representation of possession as derived from Roman law, where possession was related to use of real property. In English Common Law, the livery of seisin, which was a ceremony that involved the transfer of a twig, piece of grass, or a key, is of like origin. Seisin belonged to someone who used the land, the person who plowed it. President Hinojosa ritually reestablished the possession that was already established in fact by using the sundry church furnishings.

The rites for the dedication of a church are among the oldest in the Catholic church. Those contained in the Roman Pontifical remained largely unchanged from 1644 until 1961, when the rites were simplified and reformed. Laws pertaining to temporal goods of the church are contained in canons 1491–97. Stanislaus Woywod, *A Practical Commentary on the Code of Canon Law* (New York, 1957):189–202. *Pontificale Romanum: Ritus Solemnis pro Dedicatione Ecclesiae et Consecratione sive unius sive plurium altarium tam fixorum quam portatilium* (Cincinnati, 1890).

Rituale Romanum (Madrid, 1776). Rick Hendricks, "Franciscan Ritual in Seventeenth-Century New Mexico: Possession of Churches" (Paper delivered at the World History Association, Rocky Mountain Regional Conference on Religion in World History, Snowbird, Utah, 8 June 1990):20–23.

9. A ramilletero is a vase of artificial flowers, made of silk or metal, that sits on the altar. The use of flowers was traditional, but their placement on the altar varied from region to region. The NCE states that they were acceptable on the altar only in the sixteenth century, although our text indicates their use in the late seventeenth century. NCE, 1:350. J.G. Davies, ed., *A New Dictionary of Liturgy and Worship* (London, 1986):2.

10. On 16 December 1686, Father Eusebio Francisco Kino made a petition to the Audiencia of Guadalajara, complaining that Indians of New Biscay were impressed into service at the mines, which was preventing their effective conversion to Christianity. He recommended that they be exempt from this practice until five years after their conversion and compensated fairly for work they voluntarily carried out. A royal cedula from Carlos II dated 14 May 1686, which dealt with this matter, arrived before Kino's request. The cedula recognized the abuse and danger to newly converted Christians and provided that Indians throughout the New World should not be impressed into service until twenty years after their conversion. Bolton, *Rim*, 234–35. Bolton, *Kino's Historical Memoir*, 108–109. Antonio Muro Orejón, *Cédulas de Carlos II, 1679–1700*, vol. 1 of *Cedulario americano del siglo xviii: Colección de 248 disposiciones legales indianas desde 1680 a 1800, contenidas en los cedularios del Archivo de Indias* (Seville, 1956):248.

11. This rancho is not to be confused with Valencia's estancia upriver. A native of New Mexico, Juan de Valencia was the son of Francisco de Valencia and María López Millán. The family had an estancia in 1680 on the site of present-day Valencia. Juan; his wife, Juana Martín; their six children; and his mother escaped the revolt. Widowed of Juana Martín about 1688 in Ysleta, on 28 June 1689, Juan married Juana Madrid, the daughter of Juan de Madrid, living in El Paso, and Ana Holguín, deceased. The 1692 census of the El Paso district indicated Juan was living in Socorro with his wife, five children of his first marriage, one of his second, and thirty-two servants. He agreed to resettle in New Mexico with his large household if he received assistance, for he claimed to be too poor to do so without it. NMF, 109. NMR, 11:2027. Espinosa, "Population of El Paso," 61–84.

12. The novena of Our Lady of

the Conquest, also known as Our Lady of the Rosary or Our Lady of Remedies, is a nine-day devotion that begins on the first Sunday after Corpus Christi. Adams and Chávez, *Missions*, 8 n7, 358.

13. Dar la paz, or give the peace, as it is used here refers to the traditional embrace and kiss on the cheek in sign of friendship, rather than a part of the Mass. Corpus Christi, the Feast of the Holy Eucharist, is celebrated on the Thursday following Trinity Sunday, the first Sunday after Pentecost. Adams and Chávez, *Missions*, 354.

14. The term first-class days refers to the most important feast days of the Catholic church. Before the Code of Rubrics (1960), feasts were classified as double feasts of the first class, double feasts of the second class, major, or greater and minor doubles, or doubles, simple feasts, and commemorations. The term double is used to indicate *duplex officium*, the ceremony that the celebrant of the Mass performs: at the beginning of the Psalms, the entire antiphon is repeated, rather than just the beginning of the antiphon as in the semidouble feasts. It can also refer to the recitation of two sets of matins on the greater feasts. The number of all the feasts included fixed and movable feasts and octave days and at the time of Pope Urban VIII (1623–44), totaled 176. NCE, 8:917; 10:543.

15. This Guadalupe, below San Lorenzo, is not to be confused with Guadalupe del Paso. Walz, "El Paso," 227.

16. Fray Manuel Beltrán, a native of New Spain, professed in 1675. He was killed on 6 May 1684. Forbes, *Apaches*, 201. Naylor and Polzer, *Presidio and Militia*, 1:542.

17. Capt. Antonio de Arvizu was killed in the 6 May 1684 Jano and Suma revolt at the Soledad mission. He is variously referred to as Alviso (AGN 37:5; Forbes, *Apaches*, 201), Arbizu (EUI; Espinosa, *Pueblo Indian Revolt of 1696*), and Arvizu (*Diccionario Porrúa*). His brother, Capt. Felipe de Arvizu, was living in Papigóchic, New Biscay, by 1684. List of former New Mexicans, AHP, 1684D.

18. Fray Diego de Chavarría was born in 1661 in Tacuba, Mexico, and professed on 6 March 1679. He was in the El Paso area in the late 1680s and knew the Suma language. By the mid-1690s, he was serving upriver in New Mexico and was a chaplain on the August 1696 expedition to Acoma. In 1698, he became vice-custos and in 1699, was at Pecos. EBARN. CRG, 230, 275, 345.

19. On 13 July 1573, Felipe II provided ordinances for the establishment of towns, based on Greek and Roman concepts of city planning. Ordinances 111–37 describe the method of laying out a town, which included such matters as its location in a ventilated, healthy site; the size and

arrangement of streets and plaza; and their relationship to public buildings and the church. Indian pueblos were separate from Spanish towns and were delineated by a measurement that came to be known as the fundo legal. A 1567 ordinance declared that there must be 500 varas separating Spanish and Indian houses. Another, of 1687, added 100 varas to the distance measured in the cardinal directions. This arrangement could be abused by simply building a shack in one of the agricultural fields surrounding the pueblo. As a result, a 1695 cedula declared that the measurements should be made in those directions from the church. Dora P. Crouch, Daniel J. Garr, and Axel I. Mundigo, *Spanish City Planning in North America* (Cambridge, Mass., 1982):11, 13–18. Guillermo F. Margadant S., "Mexican Colonial Land Law," in *Spanish and Mexican Land Grants and the Law* (Manhattan, Kan., 1989):90, 92, 97. Mariano Galván Rivera, *Ordenanzas de tierras y aguas, o sea formulario geométrico judicial* (Mexico City, 1851):135, 156–57.

20. The term pilguanejo, translated here as servant, derives from the Nahuatl pilhuan, meaning sons or children. It is the plural form of pilli and with the Spanish depreciative suffix -ejo, means one in the service of the religious or a child raised at a convento.

21. Gov. Pedro de Peralta arrived in New Mexico early in 1610, during the second term of Viceroy Luis de Velasco II (1607–11), not that of the Conde de Monterrey. KCC, 93–99.

22. Gaspar de Zúñiga y Acevedo, the Conde de Monterrey, was the ninth viceroy of New Spain. He served from 5 November 1595 until 27 October 1603. Rubio Mañé, *Virreinato*, 1:292.

23. In 1648, Governor Guzmán y Figueroa issued an order exempting from tribute Indians needed for routine mission administration: an interpreter, a sacristan, a cantor mayor, a bell ringer, an organist, a herdsman, a cook, a porter, and a horsekeeper. In addition to these required servants, the friars employed others to cultivate fields and care for livestock. His action was based on a cedula issued on 30 January 1635 in Madrid. Scholes, *Troublous Times*, 25, 27, 109. Hodge, Hammond, and Rey, *Revised Memorial*, 187–89.

24. According to the register in AGNot., Juan Aguirre Vidaurreta worked as a royal scribe from 1680 to 1711.

25. Juan de Larrea, knight of the Order of Santiago, was a senior official in the Secretaría de la Negociación del Norte, Secretario de la Nueva España, beginning 26 March 1691. On 18 April 1694, he became a secretary of the Council of the Indies and on 18 April 1697, a councillor. He served in the latter post until his death on 21 June 1706. Schäfer,

Consejo Real, 1:365, 371. Robles, *Diario*, 2:275.

26. Juan Francisco Vargas Manuel de Lodeña served as the Conde de Galve's secretary when he was viceroy of New Spain. RBC, 193, 194 n1.

27. Carlos de Sigüenza y Góngora (1645–1700) was one of the leading intellectual lights of seventeenth-century Mexico. He served intermittently as a royal scribe from 1667 to 1678. Sigüenza's erudition encompassed history, mathematics, ethnography, linguistics, and cartography. He moved in elevated circles, serving as an informal advisor to several viceroys of New Spain; he was particularly close to the Conde de Galve. He died in Mexico City on 22 August 1700. Robles, *Diario*, 3:106–108. See Irving A. Leonard, *Don Carlos de Sigüenza y Góngora: A Mexican Savant of the Seventeenth Century* (Berkeley, 1929).

28. Juan de Escalante Colombres y Mendoza, a native of Santa Fe de Bogotá, was baptized there on 23 November 1655. He was the son of Dr. Manuel de Escalante y Mendoza, a Limeño and knight in the Order of Santiago (1655) who served as an audiencia judge in Mexico City in the 1650s, and Ana María de Laínez Clerque from Madrid; he was educated at the University of Salamanca where, after ten years, he graduated as a doctor of law.

Escalante's first position was as judge on the Audiencia of Santa Fe de Bogotá in 1681, but he traded appointments with Simón Ibáñez Lezcano that year to serve in the same capacity at Guadalajara. He was promoted to criminal fiscal of Mexico on 25 December 1686, then to civil fiscal (20 April 1693), and finally to judge on 17 May 1694. His last post was the presidency of the Audiencia of Guadalajara. He died in Mexico City on 3 September 1706 while serving his term.

Although Escalante was unmarried, he had family in the capital. One brother, Capt. Pedro de Escalante y Mendoza, held the title of the Conde de Loja. His wife was Josefa Gertrudis Saravia de Rueda. Another brother, Dr. Manuel de Escalante y Mendoza, was in the 1690s treasurer of the Mexico City cathedral. Like his father, Escalante was inducted into the Order of Santiago in 1696. Rubio Mañé, *Virreyes*, 4:40 n73. Schäfer, *Consejo Real*, 2:458, 464, 466, 496, 503. Robles, *Diario*, 3:24.

Seemingly to strengthen the Franciscans' hand, the father president, fray Joaquín de Hinojosa, begins an investigation of mission administration, summoning Spanish citizens to testify to the good conduct of the ministers. Governor Vargas protests. He orders the investigation stopped on the grounds that it may be violating his majesty's jurisdiction. Citing the friars' hasty and unwarranted resort to excommunication and their lack of respect for the royal governor, Vargas vents his frustration.

Diego de Vargas, Proceedings, El Paso area, 23-28 June 1692, C.

Don Diego de Vargas, governor
Concerning the jurisdictional dispute with the religious

Proceedings

On 23 June 1692, the sargento mayor, Francisco de Anaya Almazán, alcalde ordinario de primer voto of this cabildo, came before me, don Diego de Vargas Zapata Luján Ponce de León, governor and captain general of this kingdom and provinces of New Mexico for his majesty and castellan of its fortress and presidio, and gave me the following information. It was just past midday when he was in his house in the real of San Lorenzo and was called to the convento of our father, St. Francis, by the father missionary, fray Francisco Corvera, religious of this Order, who showed him the letter patent from the apostolic notary issued by the reverend father, fray Joaquín de Hinojosa, interim president of this holy custody. After having praised him for the offices he has held, he told him that he could neither refuse nor fail to answer the questions of the interrogatory, which he had to answer by virtue of it, this letter patent, and his superior's order. [1]

The alcalde ordinario signed the three questions of the interrogatory he was asked. One was whether the father guardian[2] of this convento lived well, properly kept the furnishings needed for worship and had added to them, and whether he has placed the Host in the ciborium, which he had not done before, so that he is prepared to administer the sacraments. There were other questions, and reference will be made to them. The alcalde signed these three questions. So that it may be of record, he tells me and discreetly reports this investigation, so that those people Father fray Francisco Corvera may call will not excuse themselves from giving statements when he introduces the three questions referred to above and interferes, usurping his majesty's royal jurisdiction.

I, the governor and captain general, as the king's legitimate representative, should conduct this investigation, if it is important to his right and the proof appropriate. This is the same as when the procurator general asks me to certify the number of religious to collect the contribution for those who serve in the missions of this holy custody, and whether I can attest to the continual burning of the lamp in the sagrario[3] of the main chapel of this holy church of El Paso, to ask for the alms of wine and oil[4] his majesty, the king, our lord, gives to them as the universal patron of these holy churches and all those in the entire kingdom of New Spain.

In the same manner he could ask me, if his excellency so ordered, and not introduce this investigation without cause. This clearly indicates the malicious intent to prejudice the jurisdiction of the patronato real. Because I take this act to be harmful to it, I suspend any further statements, because without knowing, people go obediently, having been called by an apostolic notary, and because of the fear that motivates them, not realizing that he is not their legitimate judge in this royal jurisdiction.

So that these proceedings and the investigation referred to may be of record, I order my secretary of government and war to notify the apostolic notary to desist from carrying out the prelate's order, because this pertains to the secular right of the royal jurisdiction of the patronato real, as I presented it, and as legitimately belongs to it. If he brings an order from his excellency the viceroy, the king's representative in all this kingdom of New Spain, once it is shown, he will make the investigations his excellency may see fit to command. He is the one I have informed and to whom I have transferred cognizance in the proceedings with the reverend father president. Thus, there is no need to confuse what is of record with new arguments. His excellency will provide as he may see fit regarding legality and reality.

These proceedings will be made known to the father apostolic notary, fray Francisco Corvera, with the secretary and witnesses I order to go: the alcalde, Sgto. mayor Francisco de Anaya Almazán; Sgto. mayor Lorenzo Madrid;[5] Afz. Francisco Lucero de Godoy;[6] and Capt. Sebastián González,[7] all of whom are citizens of the real of San Lorenzo. The secretary is ordered to do no more than attest to the notification and reply to the father that his prelate, the interim father president, will present these new proceedings and whatever else he may have to allege to the most excellent lord viceroy. I shall send him the copy, making it from this, the original, in the presence of the four witnesses cited in it who were present to see it corrected, copied, and countersigned by my secretary of government and war. I shall send his excellency the viceroy the copy. So that these proceedings and what is provided herein may be of record, I signed it with the alcalde ordinario and my secretary of government and war on this day, month, and year ut supra.

Don Diego de Vargas Zapata Luján Ponce de León
Francisco de Anaya Almazán
Before me, Juan Páez Hurtado, secretary of government and war

Record of the action taken

In the pueblo of the real of San Lorenzo on this day, 23 June 1692: I, the alferez, Juan Páez Hurtado, secretary of government and war of the governor and captain general of this kingdom and provinces of New Mexico, came to the real in fulfillment of the above proceedings. By the sargento mayor and alcalde ordinario, Francisco de Anaya Almazán, I first advised the witnesses the governor and captain general ordered and named in these proceedings, so that with their attendance and in their presence, I, the secretary of government and war, might notify the father preacher and apostolic notary, fray Francisco Corvera, of these proceedings. When the witnesses were all together, I entered the convento of our father, St. Francis.

The governor and captain general was visiting in his cell the father preacher, fray Antonio de Acevedo, guardian and minister of this convento and pueblo of the real of San Lorenzo. Mre. de campo Luis Granillo,[8] lieutenant of the governor and captain general, entered the cell while the witnesses who had been called and named remained outside. The governor ordered them to enter the cell with me, the secretary of government and war. He said to the father guardian that he had been informed that Father fray Francisco Corvera had been conducting investigations as apostolic notary, newly appointed by the reverend father interim president of this holy custody, interfering in the royal jurisdiction of the patronato real. If his reverence needed certification of his timely presence and fervent zeal in worship; the addition of having placed and situated the ciborium for the administration of the beatific Eucharist; and his virtue, learning, and other merits, it was unnecessary to use these means. He was worthy not only of the high offices attained by the reverend fathers superior of Mexico City, his prelates in the Convento Grande, but also the miters of this kingdom of New Spain and even, in his estimation, the papal throne.

The reverend father, with the modesty of his virtue, thanked him and asked whether Father fray Francisco Corvera were in one of the cells. He replied that not long ago, he had gone to the pueblos of Senecú and Ysleta and he did not know definitely in which of these he could be found.[9] In view of this, the governor and captain general ordered me to go with the witnesses and carry out the notification of these proceedings. So that what is contained in this record of the action taken, which happened as described, may be of record, I, the secretary of government and war, certify and sign it with the witnesses referred to herein, called and named in these proceedings. Done in this real and pueblo of San Lorenzo on this day, month, and year ut supra.

Luis Granillo
Francisco de Anaya Almazán
Lorenzo de Madrid
Sebastián González
Before me, Juan Páez Hurtado, secretary of government and war

Notification

In the pueblo of Senecú, on this day, 23 June 1692: I, the secretary of government and war, in fulfillment of the order and proceedings provided today, the day of this date, by the governor and captain general of this kingdom and provinces of New Mexico, came to and arrived at this pueblo of Senecú with the witnesses mentioned above, brought together and named in these proceedings. Having arrived at the residence of the father guardian of this pueblo, I found that he was in the company of the father preacher, fray Francisco Corvera, appointed apostolic notary by the reverend father interim president. In the presence of the witnesses, I, the secretary of government and war, greeted the father guardian, fray José de Espínola Almonacid, religious of our father, St. Francis, and minister of this pueblo. I said to the reverend father that, with his reverence's permission, I would inform Father fray Francisco Corvera of the proceedings I brought, which had been provided and ordered by the governor and captain general. The father said yes, I might go ahead and notify him.

Pursuant to this and with this permission, I the alferez, Juan Páez Hurtado, secretary of government and war, notified him of these proceedings according to what is contained there, reading them *verbo ad verbum* to the father apostolic notary, fray Francisco Corvera. I notified him in person, to which I attest, with the proper attention and in the presence of the witnesses. The father apostolic notary replied that, as his majesty's loyal subject, he would obey him and his excellency, who represented the royal person, but as a religious, he had to obey his prelate. So that this notification and the reply, which happened as described herein, may be of record, I, the secretary of government and war, certify and sign it with the witnesses named above in these proceedings in this pueblo of Senecú on this day, month, and year ut supra.

Luis Granillo
Francisco Anaya Almazán
Lorenzo de Madrid
Sebastián González
Before me, Juan Páez Hurtado, secretary of government and war

Certification

Further, I, the secretary of government and war, certify that the father apostolic notary, fray Francisco Corvera, on leaving the pueblo of Senecú, said to the alcalde ordinario, Francisco de Anaya Almazán, in the presence of the witnesses that he was excommunicated and should go be absolved. So that it may be of record, he signed it with me, the secretary of government and war, on this day, 23 June.

Francisco de Anaya

Before me, Juan Páez Hurtado, secretary of government and war

Presentation

On 24 June 1692, the sargento mayor, Francisco de Anaya Almazán, alcalde ordinario de primer voto of the illustrious cabildo of this kingdom, came before me, don Diego de Vargas Zapata Luján Ponce de León, governor and captain general of this kingdom and province of New Mexico and castellan of its fortress and presidio for his majesty. He reported to me that today, when he was at the real and pueblo of San Lorenzo, between nine and ten in the morning, he received a message from the reverend father interim president of this holy custody, fray Joaquín de Hinojosa.

By this message, he ordered him to come see him at the convento. The alcalde ordinario went and entered the cell of the father preacher, fray Antonio de Acevedo, guardian of this convento. His reverence was in the company of the father guardian and Father fray Francisco Corvera, appointed apostolic notary, who had yesterday summoned the alcalde ordinario. The reverend father asked him if he did not know he was excommunicated. He replied that if the law excommunicated him, he would obey the order, touching it to his forehead as a Catholic Christian. If he had erred in any way, he asked for mercy. He asked the father president why he had been excommunicated. His reverence replied that he had been excommunicated because he had revealed an excommunication made in the secrecy of the confessional and reported to the governor.

What he had said is of record in the proceedings that I, the governor and captain general, provided yesterday. Because he replied to the father that he was going to appear before and report to me, the father replied that he should go. The father did this, giving an order to the reverend father guardian to make the excommunication public, but postponing this action until the father came to report to me, the governor and captain general.

Later, changing the way he had spoken to him, the reverend father told him that he had spoken as a friend, and he might speak to the governor, telling him this might be postponed: "As an alcalde and a citizen, you can intervene." He replied to him, "We shall see. I shall go kiss the hand of the lord governor and communicate this to him." What he has stated is what he reports to me, the governor and captain general.

I am regretful and grieved that I caused him such vexation without reason and would like to ask what may be convenient for him. So that this information may be of record, I noted it as a completed action. Present were Mre. de campo Luis Granillo, my lieutenant governor and captain general, and Sgto. mayor Lorenzo Madrid. They signed it with the sargento mayor and alcalde ordinario, together with me, the governor and captain general, and my secretary of government and war on this day, month, and year ut supra.

Don Diego de Vargas Zapata Luján Ponce de León
Luis Granillo
Francisco de Anaya Almazán
Lorenzo de Madrid
Before me, Juan Páez Hurtado, secretary of government and war

Proceedings

Immediately after, on this day, month, and year, I, the governor and captain general of this kingdom of New Mexico, having seen the above information from the sargento mayor, Francisco de Anaya Almazán, alcalde ordinario, told him that he should advise me if the guardian of this convento went ahead to make his excommunication public, so that with this information I might provide the appropriate solution. So that it may be of record from these proceedings that he was present at their provision and knew of them, he signed with me and the above witnesses, with my secretary of government and war.

Don Diego de Vargas Zapata Luján Ponce de León
Luis Granillo
Francisco de Anaya Almazán
Lorenzo de Madrid
Before me, Juan Páez Hurtado, secretary of government and war

Report of the father guardian, fray Agustín de Colina, who came to the casas reales

In the pueblo of El Paso on 28 June 1692, at about seven or eight o'clock at night, the father minister of this convento of El Paso, fray

Agustín de Colina, came to visit me. [10] He brought several books, one large and one small. I did not stop to find out who the author was. He told me that by these books, I might see that I had incurred one of the censures of *In cena Domini*[11] because the proceedings I provided interfered with ecclesiastical jurisdiction. I replied that I was not interfering with ecclesiastical jurisdiction and referred to my proceedings. My obligation was to carry out my duty and not to know the summae of the confessors. [12] In the first place, if his reverence considered that I had incurred censure, he should absolve me because I was unaware of it. [13] I did not want disputes on this point and was leaving it up to him.

He told me that today he was about to order the alcalde ordinario, Francisco de Anaya Almazán, to leave the church. Did I not see that he had been called to the sacristy and told he had been absolved? He said, "Yes, the father president had done it." I replied to him that on St. John's Day, [14] he had told me nothing and said he knew nothing. Kneeling, I said to him, "My father, I do not wish to speak without your reverence absolving me first." He insisted that I examine the points he had marked in those books. Given the attention he owed me, he had not called me to the sacristy. To this I replied, "Your reverence, absolve me if you think I have incurred censure, because I am unaware of it. As a Catholic obedient to the holy mother church, I ask you to absolve me if you find I may have incurred censure. I am unaware of it." He absolved me *sub condicione si forte incurristi*. [15]

I summoned my secretary of government and war and asked that he be absolved in case he had incurred censure, and he absolved him. He said to me he knew nothing, and it had not been decided until the father president told him yesterday. He lectured me, insisting to my secretary that he did not need to satisfy me because I was satisfied by my proceedings and intention. For my part, as a Catholic I had asked him for and received absolution. If his reverence thought I had incurred censure, then it was so. I thanked him anyway, saying that Our Lord could take me now. He could go with this burden and he left. So that it may be of record in these proceedings for his excellency, the most excellent lord viceroy, the Conde de Galve, I signed it with my secretary of government and war on this day, month, and year ut supra.

Don Diego de Vargas Zapata Luján Ponce de León

Before me, Juan Páez Hurtado, secretary of government and war

---

This agrees with the original proceedings that remain in the archive and tribunal of the governor and captain general of this kingdom and provinces of New Mexico. By his order, I, the secretary of government and war, copied it, the witnesses to seeing this copy was correct and in agreement being Mre. de campo Luis Granillo, the lieutenant governor and captain general; Sgto. mayor Francisco de Anaya Almazán, alcalde ordinario de primer voto of this illustrious cabildo; and Capt. Sebastián González, citizens of this kingdom. So that it may be of record from this copy, they signed it with me, the secretary of government and war, to which I attest on this day, month, and year ut supra.

Luis Granillo
Francisco de Anaya Almazán
Sebastián González
Before me, Juan Páez Hurtado, secretary of government and war

*Diego de Vargas to the Conde de Galve, El Paso,
28 June 1692, C.*

Letter

Most excellent sir,

It is not well, sir, to go on without first putting myself at your excellency's feet, informing you through these proceedings about what has occurred since I dispatched the courier to your excellency with the proceedings of the jurisdictional dispute.

The reverend father interim president held to his intention of continuing his investigation. With the proceedings and letter of transmittal, I am sending your excellency the papers of his apostolic notary as proof of my truthfulness. This is my obligation and accords with my sense of duty, as I have said to your excellency, my prince and lord, who represents his majesty the king, our lord. It appears from the notification and record of the action taken that my secretary of government and war made that day that, not having obtained what he sought, it occurred to the reverend father to avail himself of introducing it with the information the alcalde ordinario gave me. I refer to this in the proceedings of 23 June that I am sending at present to your excellency. From among the newly named witnesses the apostolic notary called for the investigation; he imposed censure on the alcalde ordinario, but not on the alferez, Francisco Lucero de Godoy.

He knows (from the timing, what came before he sought out the witnesses through his insistence, and the documents to which I refer) that it is not legitimate for him to say that I interfere in his right and ecclesiastical jurisdiction, justifying himself and his decision by saying the alcalde ordinario and I incurred censure. It is true that I am confused because the father wishes with these books to make points and cases apply, though the present ones are different. Thank God I was born and raised in your excellency's native land.[16] I trod the halls of the University of Valladolid,[17] where I studied my first years. Though ignorant, I am not so much so that the father president, the guardian, and the rest of his followers can convince and persuade me to accept the points they mention as my fault. They take their investigation to be legitimate, and it should be free of the burden of the circumstances I note in this letter.

I humbly request, your excellency, that these proceedings be reviewed, because it is not well for me to pass over my point in silence. These difficulties should be recognized. They are a source of disquiet to those citizens and the one who is at each step at risk from the enemy and those who may cause him disrespect. It is not well that, although the father president's predecessors have governed with calm, this one tries to introduce letters patent of the most reverend father, fray Fernando de la Rúa. He was commissary general of the Order of our father, St. Francis, for all New Spain when the lawsuits occurred in the kingdom of New Mexico. The fathers should continue to use the most recent ones. After the loss of this kingdom, they were sent by the reverend father, fray Juan de Luzurriaga,[18] who was also commissary general of the Order. They only concern and pertain to this district. By means of the reform the most reverend father is making, he wants to conceal them because they are in accord with reports by men with good intentions who experienced the loss of this kingdom of New Mexico and are God-fearing and fervent in devotion to his majesty. This is not well because this kingdom enjoys such great tranquility, having passed through its troubles. The citizens are filled with hope of obtaining the relief of regaining their land. His majesty the king, our lord, will look to them as his humble vassals with their love and loyalty for him, worthy of any remuneration and assistance.

The reverend fathers may have been moved for these reasons to revive their intention of returning to their predecessors' time, that of the most excellent lords viceroy who were your excellency's, and mine, Gen. don Domingo Jironza. I responded to them by the proceedings that they should have recourse to your excellency. Nevertheless, they presented me with another petition, asking me for other documents. I replied to them that I would show them the papers from the archives, that they might copy what they wished, and might have recourse to your excellency by means of the copy.

I repeat to your excellency that for my part, I am careful not to give cause for such novelties. The fathers could have avoided such an attempt. The only one in which his majesty will consider himself served is if they conduct themselves in such a fashion that they take into consideration the respect owed to their governor and captain general and that the Indians see this. In this way, by their example, the Indians and citizens may have respect and go about unafraid of being run over roughshod by their excommunications. This is the terror that moves them whenever they think of it.

I trust your excellency will provide the means so that the results his majesty the king, our lord (may God keep him), seeks will be attained, the reduction and calm of these his vassals. Once they are, both Indians and citizens will be urged on and encouraged in the royal service, and if not, their spirits will be much vexed.

Had the entrada to New Mexico and the conquest of the villa of Santa Fe and the pueblos of its district not been promised and contracted for, I would abandon it, and the courier of this letter would go on the swiftest of horses. If the fathers have found a governor they can walk all over and insult, thanks be to God, I am accustomed to tolerating vulgarities with suspicions and fabrications, like the present one. The father passes judgment on the investigation through his notary, when he could do it himself on a visitation.[19] It would not appear suspicious and malicious like the present one. His decision came before the investigation he sought through the witnesses, which I refer to in the letter of transmittal of those proceedings. At the time of his *litis*, which is assumed to be for a preliminary trial alleging some calumny by the citizens and resulting from the charge in the proceedings, the investigation invalidates the allegation.

Thus, I state and realize with the knowledge that the investigation was improperly carried out for the father president. According to the investigation he had previously sought at the time of the *litis*, it must be seen as certain that I could not have incurred this excommunication. By my proceedings, what I ordered was that the apostolic notary cease and desist from the investigation in case he might be usurping his majesty's jurisdiction and that of his patronato real.

Nevertheless, I say in the proceedings that, once an order from your excellency is shown to me, he will have and receive whatever investigation your greatness may order. It is easy to see in the proceedings how pure and simple my intention is from the points to which I refer, so that the quality of the care I had for the father guardian of the real can be seen in the record of the action taken that my secretary certifies. What was said by the alcalde ordinario and his information served as the basis for my judgment as well as providing these proceedings and records of actions taken that I send to your excellency so that you may order me as you see fit.

For my part, I am humbly at your feet. May God keep your excellency in your increasing nobility the many happy years I wish. El Paso, 28 June 1692.

Most excellent sir, your humble and obliged servant kisses your excellency's hand,

Don Diego de Vargas Zapata Luján Ponce de León

Most excellent lord viceroy, the Conde de Galve

Decree

Mexico City, 22 October 1692
To the lord fiscal, don Juan de Escalante, because of the illness of lord don Benito de Noboa, with the proceedings about the matter and the copy that accompanies them

*BNM, 4:4 (22/453.1). 11 folios, 21 written pages.

1.   On 23 June, Father Corvera summoned Lt. gov. Luis Granillo, who refused to testify; Anaya Almazán; former alcalde ordinario, Capt. Sebastián González Bas; Afz. Francisco Lucero de Godoy;

and Sgto. mayor Cristóbal de Tapia. Each was instructed to reveal nothing of the investigation on pain of excommunication. Proceedings, El Paso, 20–29 June, 1692, AASF, Loose Documents, Mission, 1692:4.

2. The guardian at San Lorenzo was Antonio de Acevedo. Walz incorrectly concluded that Hinojosa was soliciting testimony about his own conduct rather than Acevedo's. Walz, "El Paso," 312–19. See discussion in text below. Chávez, *Archives*, 17.

3. The term sagrario here refers to the tabernacle, the niche, or construction used to house the pyx, or ciborium, containing the consecrated host. The use of a continuous light in front of a tabernacle containing the reserved sacrament dates from about 1250 and symbolizes the presence of Christ. After the Council of Trent (1545–63), the tabernacle was fixed on an altar, not necessarily the main altar. NCE, 8:753. Davies, *Dictionary*, 137–38.

4. As of 1631, the alms of wine and oil the king furnished annually to each priest included about 45 l of sacramental wine, 10 kg of prepared candle wax, and 30 l of oil for illuminating the Holy Sacrament. The total allowance for wine, tapers, and oil had been reduced from 400 to 300 pesos. Each priest's initial allotment of supplies furnished the necessary vestments and missals for worship, as well as food, clothing, utensils, tools, and other necessities of daily life in the mission. Scholes, "Supply Service," 100–10.

5. Lorenzo de Madrid, a New Mexico native born about 1634, was the son of Francisco de Madrid II, who was married to a daughter of Juan Ruiz Cáceres, and was the brother of Roque Madrid. In 1677, Lorenzo was a member of the cabildo of Santa Fe. In 1680, he was a sargento mayor, living in El Paso with his wife Ana Ortiz [Baca] and one son. In 1693–94, having returned to New Mexico with his second wife and their six adopted children, Madrid was an encomendero of Pecos. At Santa Cruz in 1696, he served as alcalde. The following year, charges were leveled against him that he was living in concubinage with Juana Domínguez, which both parties denied; they were married in 1707. Madrid was an alcalde in Santa Fe in 1703. He prepared his will in 1715. Hackett and Shelby, *Revolt*, 1:29, 35, 40; 2:66, 129. NMR, 6:1040. NMF, 66, 216. Twitchell, *Spanish Archives*, 1:4, 5, 97, 145.

6. Francisco Lucero de Godoy was born in New Mexico about 1645. He owned property near Santa Fe on the road to La Ciénega. He fled the Pueblo Revolt in 1680 and passed muster with twenty-two family members at La Salineta. Lucero de Godoy accompanied Vargas as a captain of artillery and armorer on the first expedition and the colonizing expedition and served as an interpreter for the Pecos as late as

1694. When his first wife, Josefa López de Grijalva, died in 1695, Lucero married Catalina de Espínola. NMF, 60–61. KCC, 257, 260. Hackett and Shelby, *Revolt*, 1:148; 2:19, 135, 197.

7. Sebastián González Bas [Vaz], who returned with Vargas, was married to Lucía Ortiz. He served in 1693 as an officer of the Confraternity of Our Lady of the Conquest. He died in Santa Fe on 11 June 1726, his wife on 3 March 1738. Although he had no children, he named as his heirs in Santa Fe Sebastiana González and Salvador González, orphans he had raised. NMF, 189.

8. Luis Granillo was born about 1641. He was described in 1680 as being sargento mayor, alcalde mayor, and capitán a guerra of the jurisdiction of Jemez and the Keres nations, procurador general of New Mexico, and regidor of the villa of Santa Fe. He was in Jemez when he was warned by an Indian ally about the revolt and was able to flee south. Granillo was listed as lieutenant governor, while living in San Lorenzo in 1692, a post he also held the following year during the recolonization expedition. In 1698, his title was maestre de campo, captain, and justicia mayor of El Paso. Granillo was married to Magdalena Varela de Losada. War proceedings, El Paso, 3 Apr. 1699, AHP, 1699. Naylor and Polzer, *Presidio and Militia*, 1:543 n14. Hackett and Shelby, *Revolt*, 1:xlvi–xlix, 80.

9. Corvera had moved the same day to the Piro pueblo of Senecú, where he heard the testimony of the native governor, Lucas Bachalo, as translated by Juan Esteban. At six in the afternoon, Páez Hurtado and the others arrived. Proceedings, 20–29 June 1692, AASF 1692:4.

10. By order of Hinojosa, the friars had met at Ysleta on 27 June to consider the crisis. The consensus was to give Anaya Almazán a second chance before posting his excommunication. At eight that night, Anaya came to Ysleta, pled ignorance, retracted everything, and was absolved by Hinojosa. Proceedings, 20–29 June 1692, AASF 1692:4.

11. Martin V, whose pontificate lasted from 1417 to 1431, was responsible for the bull *In cena Domini* (1420), although his successors made additions to it. This bull comprehensively treats matters of clerical jurisdiction and pertains to all Christendom. It was read publicly every year in Rome on Maundy Thursday, as well as in Spain and in the principal churches of the Indies. Antonio Joaquín de Ribadeneira y Barrientos, *Manual compendio de el regio patronato indiano, para su más fácil uso en las materias conducentes a la práctica: Dedicado al rey nuestro señor d. Fernando VI, El Amado* (Madrid, 1755):131.

12. A summa refers to a highly organized theological treatise, such as the Summa Theologica of St. Thomas Aquinas.

13. According to canon law, its strictures and those of civil law must not be confused. Although a person may commit an infraction against canon law, censure does not apply if that person is unaware of the law, because the person is not rebelling against church authority. In addition, civil laws are established to prevent and punish crimes, while canon laws provide for punishment that benefits the person who commits the infraction and suppose rebellion against ecclesiastical authority. Vargas claimed ignorance of any canon law he had contravened, yet asked for absolution of any possible infraction of which he was unaware. Golmayo, *Derecho canónico*, 2:405.

14. St. John's Day is 24 June.

15. "with the stipulation that you incurred it without knowing"

16. Vargas was alluding to the fact that Corvera was a native of Manila, not a peninsular Spaniard.

17. On several occasions, Vargas stated that he attended the University of Valladolid. Nevertheless, a review of the university's books of incorporation and matriculation for the 1660s turned up no mention of Diego de Vargas. RBC, 19, 107 n39.

18. Fray Juan Luzurriaga, born in Cantabria province in northern Spain, served as an apostolic preacher there and later, as a priest in Valencia province. He was named commissary general of New Spain on 16 May 1682 at the general chapter meeting of the Franciscan Order in Toledo. This was confirmed by the minister general, Father Marino Sormano, in Madrid on 26 June 1682. Luzurriaga left for the Indies on 4 March 1683. During his tenure, he wrote *Paraninfo celeste: Historia de la mística zarza, milagrosa imagen y prodigioso santuario de Aránzazu*, which was published in 1686. The Virgin of Aránzazu had long been celebrated in Mexico. A chapel to honor her at the convento of San Francisco de México was begun in 1682 and inaugurated in 1688. In the same year, Luzurriaga was succeeded by fray Juan de Capistrano. Espinosa and Canedo, *Propaganda Fide*, 165, 168. Vetancurt, *Teatro mexicano*, 4:164, 388. Robles, *Diario*, 2:28.

19. Vargas treats the more informal ecclesiastical visitation as though it were a civil one. Ordinarily, the religious visitor's presence was temporary and did not have as its purpose the administration of justice through legal formulae; rather it sought to correct and reform manifest abuses. The visitor did not impose penalties, strictly speaking, but corrections. He used his authority, rather than his judicial power, to govern. Golmayo, *Derecho canónico*, 1:172.

*When the viceroy, in consultation with the Junta of the Trea-
sury, reached decisions that required implementation, orders were
dispatched, often the same day and in the same words, to the
appropriate officials. In response to such an order, dated 4 December 1691, Gov. Juan Isidro de Pardiñas and seven of his captains offer their opinions about Diego de Vargas's proposed
entrada into New Mexico. None doubts that Vargas can enter
New Mexico; all doubt that he can hold it without great expense
to the treasury.*

*The two veteran captains who have campaigned with don
Diego and know him personally, Juan Fernández de la Fuente
and Francisco Ramírez de Salazar, are the most critical of his
plan. They have not changed their minds. They insist that all
available resources should be employed first against Apaches and
other more immediate enemies. Their responses reach Mexico
City too late. The viceroy has already dispatched to Governor
Pardiñas an order to provide Vargas with an additional fifty
soldiers from the presidios of New Biscay. The reconquest of New
Mexico is about to begin.*

1692
Opinions of the captains of New Biscay given by order of the most
excellent lord, the Conde de Galve, viceroy of New Spain, about

the entrada for the restoration the governor and captain general of El Paso and the province of New Mexico intends to make, which the governor and captain general of New Biscay sends to his excellency.

Juan Fernández de Retana to Juan Isidro de Pardiñas, [Parral], 15 March 1692, LS.

Lord governor and captain general,

The captain, Juan Fernández de Retana, currently serving his majesty in the presidio of San Francisco de Conchos, has seen the dispatch from the most excellent lord viceroy that you made known to him, so that he might give his opinion about the proposal the governor of New Mexico made to his excellency to restore that province, adding fifty soldiers to those he has. In fulfillment of his duty, Capt. Juan de Retana states that this proposal seems to him of no little advantage to the royal treasury, if by it and with this number of soldiers that province might be resettled with Spaniards as it was—all of which he doubts.

He is, however, certain that the governor will be able to enter the province and overcome the difficulties that present themselves. Because those areas are at hand and his responsibility, he will have sounded it out. If he does achieve this, it will of course be necessary to attend to its preservation by settling Spanish families where they lived before. They will have to be aided as well, so they can return and support themselves. Because of the great distances, they must be protected by presidios. The apostate rebels have maintained themselves so many years in their license and apostasy that they will easily repeat their rebellions for little reason, if the necessary inconvenience of taking precautions is not provided for in time.

Although the proposal itself for the retaking of New Mexico is tenuous, its preservation will cost the royal treasury great sums. According to experiences in those areas, it is understood that his majesty incurred expenses for more than ninety years in its preservation, even without war. The goal of his majesty's royal zeal is nothing more than reducing those apostates to the brotherhood of our holy Catholic faith, which is why he maintains so many ministers. It seems to him that at the sight of weapons, they will seek reduction to the faith through the preaching of the Holy Gospel alone. If not, it will be

necessary to pay for many years, because it is not a matter of pacification, but of preserving so remote a region. This is his opinion,
and his excellency will decide what is best about everything. [Parral],
15 March 1692.
Juan de Retana [rubrica]

Juan Bautista Escorza to Juan Isidro de Pardiñas, Parral, 15 March 1692, LS.

Lord governor and captain general,

The sargento mayor, Juan Bautista Escorza,[1] captain of the presidio of Pasaje in this kingdom of New Biscay, has seen the dispatch
that the most excellent lord, the Conde de Galve, viceroy of New
Spain, sent to you, so that he could give his opinion about the proposal to reduce the provinces of New Mexico and about what don
Diego de Vargas Zapata, governor and captain general, has proposed
about it. He states that with regard to his having been in the environs of that province when he was a captain of the militias in the
province of Sonora, he was at various times within the borders of
New Mexico. In 1680, when it was lost and the Spaniards deserted
it, he was about to go to its aid when word arrived about its complete
abandonment, which is why he did not go. He has reason to know
in detail what is of record and what is necessary for the preservation
of that province.
What he can state is that he has no doubt that don Diego de Vargas
will enter it in the way he proposes to his excellency, because of his
wish to employ himself in the royal service. Nevertheless, the sargento
mayor doubts that with just the fifty soldiers the governor proposes,
in addition to the fifty he currently has in his presidio, he can maintain provinces so vast, with unknown boundaries, presently surrounded
by innumerable enemy Indians. He would need much aid from the
royal treasury for the necessary settlements, more united and numerous than before, to avoid another misfortune such as the one that
occurred and contain the Indians, because their inconstancy should
be feared even when they are reduced. This is his opinion. With his
great zeal, his excellency will order about this what is most suitable
for the royal service. Parral, 15 March 1692.
Juan Bautista Escorza [rubrica]

Martín de Hualde to Juan Isidro de Pardiñas,
Parral, 16 March 1692, LS.

Lord governor and captain general,

I[2] have seen the dispatch from the most excellent lord viceroy of New Spain about what the governor and captain general has proposed to justify his conquest and that with fifty soldiers who will be added to those he has, he will achieve it. In accordance with his excellency's dispatch, you order me to state what I feel about this matter. In compliance, with respect to the fact that I have not been in that area and have no knowledge of those rebels and apostates, it only occurs to me to say that the governor and captain general making the proposal will have thought about it beforehand, with the prudence required by what he proposes to his superiors. If the cost is only that of the fifty men he requests, it could not be of less expense and more relief to the royal treasury.

It seems to me, however, that it is also my duty to advise that once the entrada to these provinces is achieved, it will be necessary to settle them with Spaniards, if it is to be successfully maintained. Although the Indians may be reduced through punishment at that time, it will be necessary to keep them subjected. Since there are numerous pueblos separated by such long distances in those provinces, the Indians must be constantly feared, even more so because the long time they have remained in their rebellion has induced arrogance in them. They are accustomed to their free way of living without religion. It would not be so necessary to take precautions if they were immediately subjected by arms.

Given the estimated small cost the governor and captain general proposes, I do not see any obstacle other than the large expenditures that will increase in the preservation and settlement of these provinces and the transportation of the citizens to them. This is what I can say about this matter, whose remedy his excellency's judgment will see to, with his great zeal for the greatest service to his majesty, providing the best for it, as is his excellency's custom. Parral, 16 March 1692.

Lord governor and captain general, your servant kisses your lordship's hand,

Martín de Hualde [rubrica]

Juan Fernández de la Fuente to Juan Isidro de Pardiñas, Janos, 29 April 1692, LS.

The captain, Juan Fernández de la Fuente, captain and protector for his majesty of the royal presidio of San Felipe and Santiago de Janos: I have just received an order from the most excellent lord viceroy, governor and captain general of this kingdom of New Spain, and president of the Audiencia of Mexico, the Conde de Galve, sent to my governor and captain general for his majesty of this kingdom of New Biscay, don Juan Isidro de Pardiñas Villar de Francos, who orders me to give my opinion about, and what pertains to, the points proposed by the governor and captain general of New Mexico, don Diego de Vargas Zapata y Luján. That order was dated Mexico City, 4 December of the past year 1691.

Opinion

Replying to the first point the governor makes, that by having left to make war against the Indians of Parral, one should consider his distress at not having carried through the entrada he had decided upon for the conquest of the villa of Santa Fe and the pueblos he mentions, first, I state that the entrada we made together with the governor and captain general of New Mexico, who directed the military forces, was not made against the Indians who infest the environs of Parral, but against the Apaches who made war in the kingdom of New Mexico when the Spaniards inhabited it. After it was abandoned, they have continued to wage a very harsh war by fire and sword on the frontiers of El Paso, those of this presidio, and the province of Sonora.

As has been seen and experienced, after the withdrawal of the forces from their lands and after all the camp had arrived at this presidio around the end of last October, the Apaches formed a mighty junta of all the people of their nation and those of the Janos, Jocomes, and Sumas. They followed us along the same track we traveled with the camp. Within sight of this presidio, they positioned themselves to cut off the camino real, which goes to the province of Sonora. We fought them this past 25 February when they sued for and accepted peace. Having a second time affirmed and recorded it, as his majesty commands, I left them very satisfied with some gifts of clothing and supplies I made to the captains and the rest of the leaders. I took my leave of them, and they agreed to come and go in this presidio.

Seeing that more than twenty days had passed and not one of them had come, I suspected they were planning some treachery. Such a junta could not maintain itself without inflicting serious damage, avenging the deaths and captures that occurred during the entrada made with that governor.

Before I discovered the junta, he wrote me a letter, dated 27 December. In it he states that he had an Indian of the Jumano nation, who was a captive of those Apaches. He had fled because they had killed all their captives from other nations. They were forming a junta of many peoples to destroy El Paso and all its pueblos and come do the same to this presidio and its frontiers, as is of record in the letter I have. Seeing what had happened to me both times I was with them and that they had not come to this presidio as they had agreed, I readied fifty well-armed soldiers and citizens with a few Indian allies from the Concho nation.

Although I was about to leave on 24 March, going personally for the third time to learn their plans, I could not. Because I had an ailment and was unable to sit my saddle, I ordered my alferez, Juan de Cantos del Castillo,[3] to go to that rancheria. Keeping the peace, he should ask them why they had not come to this presidio, as they had agreed with me. I ordered him to treat them with great kindness and listen to their reply.

Having done this, he was with them all day, the twenty-seventh. That night they took leave of one another very satisfied. On 28 March, the rest would come with the alferez to this presidio. That morning, he had all the men mount up. While they were loading the last of the supplies, the Apaches came down from the sierra in two flanks. They grabbed a citizen who was drinking from the water hole about an harquebus shot from the camp and wounded him once with a lance and four times with arrows. They raised the war cry, at which the soldiers appeared, killing and wounding many of the Indians who had gravely wounded the citizen, who died within six hours. One soldier from this presidio also died from other wounds. The alferez and others were wounded, the field remained ours, and the Indians were put to flight into the most rugged part of the mountains. They have withdrawn to their lands, which does not support the idea of easily conquering that kingdom with the use of only the fifty soldiers he requests beyond those of the complement of that presidio.

The entrada may be successful if these frontiers and those are secured, after having first conquered or reduced to peace all the rancherias, uprisen and at war, on both sides of the camino real[4] from the pueblo of El Paso to the villa of Santa Fe, for 100 leagues, with the risk of the Spaniards being noticed all along the way. Both the countryside and settlements are at very great risk. A deadly defeat could occur in either place, with nothing useful or advantageous for the two majesties following upon this conquest. In this regard, I know that even were he to go on campaign with the one hundred soldiers and win a pueblo or the villa of Santa Fe, it may not be possible to strengthen or preserve the countryside, because what happened on the entradas Gens. don Pedro Reneros de Posada and don Domingo Jironza made will happen again. Even though they succeeded in making a dawn raid on a pueblo without being noticed, they were unable to persevere or remain, because on learning this the remaining pueblos joined together. This forced them to withdraw in great haste the same day, in spite of the fact that they sometimes followed them. It was the same with the entrada Gen. don Antonio de Otermín made, just after the kingdom had been lost, with more than one hundred harquebusiers at the expense of the royal treasury and the trifling result following upon it.

Because of all this, it seems to me that the stratagems of war and conquest the governor proposes to carry out with the hundred men, conquering and reducing that kingdom by force of arms, are very arduous and difficult matters to undertake without first attaining peace and reducing the nations mentioned above. Even with everything, it seems that after the one hundred soldiers have settled in and fortified that kingdom, it will not be easy to come and go, searching out what is needed, without risk. I am of the opinion that, in order to achieve that conquest, settle the kingdom, come and go freely, and colonize it, much time, many people, the necessary provisions, and expense to the royal treasury are required. It is common knowledge that after they dispossessed the Spaniards of that kingdom, they fortified themselves in their pueblos and attracted as allies many nations who, during the time the Spaniards had settled, were enemies of both the Spaniards and the Indians of that kingdom.

I have reported what I think about the proposals made by the governor and captain general of New Mexico to the most excellent lord viceroy. In good conscience, with God as my witness, and based on my experience, I know these proposals are ineffective. So that it may be of record, I signed it at this royal presidio of San Felipe and Santiago de Janos on 29 April 1692.

Juan Fernández de la Fuente [rubrica]

Francisco Ramírez de Salazar, Parral, 19 May 1692, DS.

In the real of Parral, 19 May 1692, the lord sargento mayor, don Juan Isidro de Pardiñas Villar de Francos, knight of the Order of Santiago, governor and captain general of this kingdom of New Biscay for his majesty, stated that with respect to the fact that Capt. Francisco Ramírez de Salazar is at present in this real and is a person who has served his majesty in the province of New Mexico and has experience in and knowledge of it, he should state his opinion, as his excellency orders. He ordered him to appear and made known the dispatch for him to give his opinion about the proposal the governor and captain general of the province of New Mexico makes for the entrada to the villa of Santa Fe. Capt. Francisco Ramírez, being present and informed of the content of the dispatch, spoke in the following manner.

The joining of forces the governor and captain general of New Mexico refers to was directed against the enemies close to New Mexico and not against those of New Biscay or Parral, as he states, because it is many leagues from one place to the other. New Mexico is surrounded by the Apache nation and other rebel nations who are always at war. Unless settlements are made, the difficulty of being unable to preserve what may be conquered will always remain. Even if they enter, occupy, and restore the pueblos the governor and captain general refers to, it seems to Capt. Francisco Ramírez that they will be unable to maintain them without very great expense to the royal treasury. Even if the pueblos are won, the rebel enemies will return to others, and in this way, it will be a never-ending action. The Spaniards will scarcely be able to support themselves without the Indians. It will not be easy for them to sow for their sustenance, because there is no doubt they will be invaded regularly.

It also seems to him that, when the governor and captain general enters the villa of Santa Fe, the rebels will be able to seize the 100 leagues from El Paso to that villa, leaving the Spaniards unable to support themselves. With further assistance, they could take control of the areas that border this kingdom. In addition to the Indians of New Mexico being many, the nations here, such as the Apaches and others, are so great and numerous that they will extend themselves and begin to destroy both areas. They may do what they have never done before, extending themselves from the Río del Norte to this area. The major difficulty for the citizens in New Mexico is their ability to support themselves without having the roads clear and safe.

He notes that, although the expense the governor and captain general currently proposes is not very great considering the result, other, greater ones must follow. They will continue over time since it will take two or three years for the reconquest, in the event it is achieved. It is his opinion that they should first try to propose peace to those rebels, and if some pueblos agree to it, they should be accorded good treatment. It may be that the rest will be reduced by this example. If not, they should try to put them in need, laying waste to their fields at harvesttime, because by force of arms, he will encounter the obstacles he refers to. Above all, they should rid the countryside of enemies and reduce those on this side of the Río del Norte, since after the Jocomes, Janos, Sumas, and Apaches are brought into obedience, it will be possible to use all the arms in this conquest. He stated that this is his opinion and signed it with the lord governor and captain general.

Don Juan Isidro de Pardiñas
Villar de Francos [rubrica]

Francisco Ramírez
de Salazar [rubrica]

Before me,
Don Luis de Valdés [rubrica]
Secretary of government and war

Antonio de Medina, Parral, 20 May 1692, DS.

In the real of Parral, 20 May 1692, the lord governor and captain general, in compliance with the dispatch from the most excellent lord viceroy of New Spain, requested that Antonio de Medina,[5] currently captain of the campaign company of thirty soldiers of this kingdom, give his opinion and view about what his excellency orders with regard to the proposal made by the governor and captain general of New Mexico for the conquest or restoration of that province. After having seen the dispatch, he stated that with regard to the matters of the province of New Mexico, he has neither experience nor knowledge of its peoples. He has, however, heard of it from various men who have served there.

Of course, what can be discussed about the proposal of the governor and captain general of New Mexico is that he will have looked at it carefully in order to propose it to his excellency. He has no doubt that, because of his zeal and courage, he will enter, as others have, but he does doubt whether it will be possible for him to keep what he may restore. From the information he has about the Indians of that province, they are obdurate and under the press of arms will withdraw. For the Spaniards to settle, much aid in the form of continued great expense to the royal treasury is necessary. If the Indians are not reduced, the same difficulty remains. Regarding the entrada of the governor, he has no doubt, as others have done it, but he has his doubts about its preservation, about which his excellency will provide what he sees fit. This is what he can state, what he thinks, and his opinion. He signed it with the lord governor and captain general.

Don Juan Isidro de Pardiñas
Villar de Francos [rubrica]

Antonio de Medina [rubrica]

Before me,
Don Luis de Valdés [rubrica]
Secretary of government and war

Juan de Salaíces to Juan Isidro de Pardiñas, n.p., [May 1692], LS.

Lord governor and captain general,

I[6] have seen the most excellent lord viceroy's dispatch and have become aware from it of the proposal of the governor and captain general of New Mexico. In compliance with the command, I state, sir, that although I am without the experience of having been in that kingdom, from having listened for more than twenty years to various people who have been in and left that kingdom and also some of its pueblos, and especially since 1680, when that province was lost, I have no doubt that, with the fifty extra soldiers the governor requests, he can accomplish the conquest, as he proposes to his excellency. I have no doubt he will have examined it with the prudence and deliberation the question requires.

With reference to the new expense to the royal treasury, I know it to be the least that the governor and captain general can have proposed for the greatest achievement and success of this conquest. It seems to me, sir, that if the families do not enter to settle in the villa of Santa Fe or wherever the governor thinks most suitable when the forces enter making war, the expenses his majesty incurs for the preservation of the Indians who may be reduced will be many and much increased, because of the vastness of that kingdom and the distance from El Paso to the villa of Santa Fe. It is no fewer than 100 leagues, and within these limits and over this distance these Indians have acquired the custom of living freely for twelve years. Without being subjugated, they may undertake a new uprising. In the future, greater difficulties and increased expenditures to his majesty for their reduction may arise.

Likewise, I think the conquest more certain and of greater foundation, as I have said, if the families who would be settling enter with the soldiers. This would make it easier for the continuation and force of the war, both offensive and defensive. Dawn raids on the enemy can be repeated with fewer difficulties with the Spanish population in the center of that kingdom, which to my mind is the greatest difficulty of the matter for the preservation of the Indians reduced to royal obedience. For this, it will be necessary to transport new families in sufficient number for the secure and greater foundation and preservation of the conquest, attending to the greater service of God Our Lord, his majesty's Catholic zeal, and the good of those wretched Indians' souls. This is what, in accord with my experience, occurs to me, and his excellency will decide as he sees fit.

Your greatest servant,

Juan de Salaíces [rubrica]

Juan Isidro de Pardiñas to the Conde de Galve, Parral, 24 May 1692, LS.

Most excellent sir,

In compliance with your excellency's order, the captains of this kingdom have given their opinions, which accompany this letter, about what don Diego de Vargas, governor and captain general of New Mexico, proposed to your excellency. To give mine, as your excellency commands me, I do not have the essential information about what that region, so remote and distant from this one, requires. What I have tried to obtain is extremely varied. At present, communication with those rebel and apostate pueblos is cut off. There is no doubt that it would be advantageous to reduce them gently or by arms, to keep them in obedience.

It is neither easy to understand what this would cost nor whether war will be provoked, either by their obstinacy, or in its absence, with the Spaniards' entry. This would be more practicable, if the enemies in the immediate vicinity and confines of this kingdom and that of New Mexico were defeated and the entrada made more secure by not leaving such declared enemies at our backs. The joining together of forces of that presidio with those of this kingdom was against the Apaches, who are of that jurisdiction and not of this one, whence ordinarily they have left to invade and stir up trouble by their example, having expelled the Spaniards more than ten years ago. This causes more arrogance in these enemies.

As the one who has the matter at hand, the governor will have considered, according to the information he will have had, how he should express to your excellency the most appropriate action. Those who have lived in that kingdom and are now in that court can do this for your excellency as well. Capt. Francisco Ramírez de Salazar, although he has given his opinion in writing, can repeat it verbally more personally to your excellency, since he has been in New Mexico for so many years, having served his majesty both here and there. Your excellency will order what is most fitting and appropriate in everything. May Our Lord watch over your excellency for many years, as He may and I wish. Parral, 24 May 1692.

Don Juan Isidro de Pardiñas
Villar de Francos [rubrica]
Most excellent lord, the Conde de Galve

———

Received on 10 August

He sends his opinion and report about the entrada of the governor of El Paso to restore New Mexico with those of the captains of his government that accompany it, by his excellency's order.

———

Mexico City, 11 August 1692
To the lord fiscal, with the enclosed papers
[Galve's rubrica]

Benito de Noboa Salgado, Fiscal's reply, Mexico City, 14 August 1692, DS.

Most excellent sir,

His majesty's fiscal has seen this letter from the governor of Parral, along with the opinions, which, at your excellency's order, the captains of that kingdom have given about the entrada by the governor of El Paso for the restoration of the villa of Santa Fe in New Mexico. The fiscal states that your excellency, in response to the governor of El Paso's proposal, already allowed him to undertake this entrada, ordering him to be aided with fifty men chosen from the presidios of Parral. According to the information he has, it seems the governor of El Paso will have already left on the entrada during this month of August; hence, these reports have arrived late. The advantage of this entrada is deduced from all of them, but also the difficulty of maintaining the reduction without increased cost to the royal treasury, because of the need to establish presidios to secure the rear against the multitude of nations and the freedom to come and go and because of the need to introduce families.

Only Juan Fernández de la Fuente thinks this entrada absolutely inefficacious, bringing forth examples of others who have tried it. Instead, the governor of El Paso will have already begun it, as is his wish. It does not seem to the fiscal that he would rush to propose it without having first thought about and discussed it with the citizens of El Paso and others, according to what he will have recognized during the time that has passed of his governorship. What your excellency will be able to order for now is that these proceedings should be placed with the others in which the governor made the proposal and in which your excellency agreed to this entrada. Until the results that may come of it are known, and from which will be selected and discussed what your excellency may do, you will order in everything what is for the best. Mexico City, 14 August 1692.

Dr. don Benito de Noboa Salgado [rubrica]

Mexico City, 21 August 1692
Place with the proceedings on the matter.
[Galve's rubrica]

*AGN, Historia 37:4. 10 folios, 20 written pages. Also in AGI, Guadalajara 139:4.

1. In 1681, Juan Bautista Escorza was commissioned to pursue and punish Indians from more than thirteen nations who were conspiring against the Spaniards in the Bacadéguachi district in Sonora. Named captain of the new presidio of San Antonio de Cuencamé in 1685, Escorza became capitán vitalicio (for life or until removed at the king's pleasure) two years later. The following year, he served at the presidio of El Pasaje and guarded the borders of the Parras and Saltillo regions. By 1691, Escorza was a sargento mayor in New Biscay and protector of the Indians of Coahuila. Escorza was still campaigning in 1693. Porras Muñoz, *Frontera*, 180, 242, 245, 320–22. Naylor and Polzer, *Presidio and Militia*, 1:550 n3, 577 n13.

2. Martín de Hualde served as captain of the presidio of Santa Catalina de Tepehuanes from 1684 to May 1687 when he was named capitán vitalicio of the presidio of

Cerro Gordo (at this time, he is identified as Martín de Ugalde Anarivar). In 1691, he accompanied other captains from New Biscay in the recruiting of soldiers to retaliate against the Indians. Hualde remained in the Conchos region of New Biscay and served during the Tarahumara uprising. Although there is some confusion regarding his name in the documents, he signed Hualde. He was married to María de Lisalde. By 1708, Hualde was dead. Inventory of the estate of Juan Fernández de Retana, LDS, Parral, Burials, 162562. Juan Fernández de Retana and Martín de Hualde, Opinion, Papigóchic, 21 May 1701, AHP, 1701. Porras Muñoz, *Frontera*, 242, 274, 284, 323. Gerhard, *North Frontier*, 187–89.

3. Juan de Cantos del Castillo was serving as lieutenant governor and alcalde mayor of Casas Grandes in 1695. Naylor and Polzer, *Presidio and Militia*, 1:655 n95.

4. The camino real was the

2,560-km route that connected Mexico City with Santa Fe, by way of Querétaro, Zacatecas, Sombrerete, Nombre de Dios, Durango, and the Valle de San Bartolomé. Max L. Moorhead, *New Mexico's Royal Road: Trade and Travel on the Chihuahua Trail* (Norman, 1958):1–2. Rick Hendricks, "Road to Rebellion, Road to Reconquest: The Camino Real and the Pueblo-Spanish War, 1680–1696," in *Essays on the History of the Camino Real de Tierra Adentro* (Santa Fe, 1989): 39–48.

5. Capt. Antonio de Medina, in command of a company of Spanish soldiers and Indian allies, was at the presidio of San Miguel de Cerro Gordo in February 1687, where he met other military leaders to request additional men and mules for the Indian campaigns from the governor of New Biscay, José de Neira y Quiroga. Juan Bautista Escorza, Antonio de Medina, Domingo de Arzavalo, and Luis de Quintana to José Neira y Quiroga, Cerro Gordo, 12 Feb. 1687, AHP, 1687A.

6. Capt. Juan de Salaíces, a native of New Biscay, was described as a foundling raised in the home of Lic. Antonio de Salaíces, a secular priest living in Parral. Antonio and his brother, Sgto. mayor Juan, were natives of Budia, northeast of Madrid. Captain Salaíces was alcalde mayor of the real of San Diego by January of 1690. Juan de Salaíces, Pedro del Poso, Pedro de Quiroga et al., Opinion, 2 Jan. 1690, San Diego de las Minas Nuevas, AHP, 1690. Juan de Salaíces, Will, Parral, 28 Dec. 1675, AHP, 1676C. Antonio de Salaíces, Will, Parral, 6 Apr. 1696, AHP, 1696. Tomás de Guadalajara, Codicil to the will of Antonio de Salaíces, Parral, 19 May 1696, AHP, 1696.

Part 3

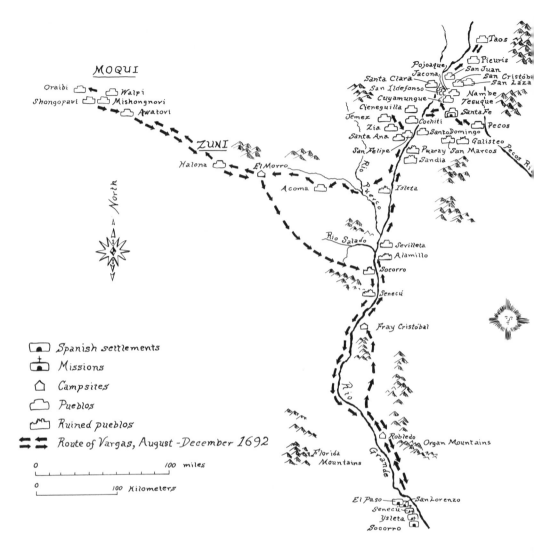

New Mexico. Map drawn by Jerry L. Livingston.

Aware of the tension between the governors in Parral and El Paso, the viceroy emphasizes that Governor Pardiñas will aid Governor Vargas promptly or face serious charges. A joint campaign on New Biscay's Sonora frontier has been attempted. Discovery of the rumored mercury mine can wait. Although Vargas's entrada is anticipated in this order, the courier bearing it is en route for a month and a half.

The Conde de Galve to Diego de Vargas,
Directive, Mexico City, 28 May 1692, DS.

Don Gaspar de Sandoval Cerda Silva y Mendoza, the Conde de Galve; gentleman of his majesty's bedchamber; comendador of Zalamea and Ceclavín in the Order and Knighthood of Alcántara; viceroy and governor and captain general of this New Spain; and president of its royal audiencia: In the Junta of the Royal Treasury I held today, five letters that don Diego de Vargas Luján y Zapata, governor and captain general of the provinces of New Mexico, wrote me, dated 30 March and 7, 9, and 17 April of this year, were seen. In the first, I was given a report about his decision to carry out the entrada he has considered for the conquest of the uprisen nations of those provinces, how he has prepared, and the way in which he is ready to leave to carry it out on 12 July of this year, without requiring any other financial assistance other than the fifty soldiers he has requested. He assures me that with this aid, the fulfillment and carrying out of what he pledges remain his responsibility.

In this letter and the previous ones about this matter, he explains the method and circumstances he took into consideration because they are of note and concern such a serious matter. He goes on to state that a proposal of such consequence required more careful inspection and means to achieve so important a result as any similar decision might. The proceedings, made by virtue of the letter-order at the beginning of them about the reconnoitering and prospecting of the Sierra Azul, where there is said to be mercury, supported this intent.

The two royal cedulas of 4 September 1683 and 13 September 1689 were placed after the record of these completed actions as necessary to them. At the same time, it is as though a report had been made from their contents, following them word for word. Their tenor and that of the proceedings would have formally included what should be followed in the decision about the enterprise. Because he carried it out in this way, all the lords minister in attendance, after having conferred in the junta, were in agreement that the means the governor of New Mexico proposed for the reduction and conquest of what was uprisen, as is literally expressed in the two royal orders, were so much as one, with the same result that this did not appear to be by chance, but by special divine providence.

The first royal cedula orders that every effort be made in the recovery of the provinces, so that the restoration might be achieved with the greatest savings to the royal treasury, approving everything expended for the preservation of what remained. In the second, it is concluded that, if the reduction of New Mexico does not come first, it would be vain to discuss the advantages that might follow from working the mercury mine since it is in enemy land. It was also advanced in the proceedings that the person who had promised to make the entrada and reconnoiter the mine[1] had not come to this kingdom from those of Spain and his delay was prejudicial not only to the royal treasury, but also to the public good. At the same time and with a decision similar to the one expressed in the former's letters, a man with the sense of duty and lineage of don Diego de Vargas Zapata offered himself.

Because of all that was related, the junta was in perfect agreement that the entrada for the conquest and restoration of the provinces of New Mexico should be carried out in the form the governor and captain general, don Diego de Vargas, arranged and prepared. Without the slightest doubt, the two royal cedulas favored and assisted this decision, since it is in accord with the royal will. This explains their form, giving it with the royal Catholic zeal for the restoration, from which will result the restitution of the uprisen apostates to our holy faith. It is ordered even more clearly in the second cedula that the reduction must be made first instead of pursuing the advantage of working the mines, likewise resulting in a savings to the royal treasury. For now, the governor requests no means other than the aid of the fifty soldiers. As he explains, they are indispensable, given the lack of settlers there of whom he can avail himself. They must be presidial soldiers from Parral whom his majesty has paid, as will be provided.

In addition, Gov. don Diego de Vargas is a person of such eminent talents, lineage, and sense of duty, with many advantages over the candidate don Toribio de la Huerta, who, according to the information available, would not fulfill his duty as precisely. Fulfillment can be expected from the governor's zeal for these reasons. He could only commit himself to such a proposal out of his valor and great nobility. This is why I, with all the lords minister of the junta, repeat to him many thanks, so that he may know punctually and in appreciation of his conduct that he will be assisted with the aid he requests. By dispatch of the same date as this one, the governor and captain general of Parral is ordered that as soon as he receives a letter from don Diego de Vargas asking for the fifty soldiers to be sent, he should do so, taking them from the four newly erected presidios and from the old ones of the kingdom. The fifty men will be taken proportionately from all the presidios so that their absence will not be greatly felt (as cannot be done with the aforesaid arrangement), sending them with their weapons and horses wherever don Diego de Vargas may designate, so that they may be at his disposal and under his orders until they have another order from me.

The governor and captain general of Parral is to promptly carry it out in this way. He is neither to postpone nor forbear sending the soldiers for any pretext, reason, or objection, with the understanding that acting to the contrary will result in a very serious charge during his residencia, as would the slightest delay in this matter for the good it can produce and is hoped for in the greatest service to his majesty. This method of sending the soldiers to the place Gov. don Diego de Vargas might request has been chosen in the junta as being the most appropriate, because don Diego de Vargas does not indicate they are necessary for the entrada. By sending them where he might request them, he may avail himself of them, using them as he sees fit, and in this way more fully assure this provision.

It was also declared in this junta that the time for the reconnoitering and prospecting of the cinnabar mine in the Sierra Azul has not arrived, because more effort and information are necessary. In carrying out the entrada to the villa of Santa Fe, Gov. don Diego de Vargas will be able to seek and inquire about other information. Once advised, he can avail himself of the means that may occur to him. He can send the information to me when there is an opportunity, communicating to me the results of his entrada when he sends for the soldiers at Parral or whenever he has the opportunity.

His discretion will find means for everything and advance his concern, both for himself and for other circumstances the war occasions. If difficulties arise, they may nevertheless be prevented in time by the confidence that assures his good character. To this belong the rewards his majesty (may God keep him) honors him with, with word of his hopes and employ in his royal service, and for my part, for his great dedication. This is the decision about everything referred to, and I agree on all its points. At present, I again thank Gov. don Diego de Vargas and order him to understand what this dispatch encompasses and concerns for its observance and fulfillment. Mexico City, 28 May 1692.

The Conde de Galve [rubrica]

By his excellency's order,
Don Pedro Velázquez de la Cadena [rubrica]

[rubrica]

So that the governor and captain general of New Mexico, don Diego de Vargas, may understand the decision of the junta that this dispatch includes, with a review of the one he has taken for the entrada to the villa of Santa Fe and so that he may carry it out, thanking him and notifying him that he is to be given the fifty men he requests

Signed [rubrica]

———

In those about Vargas's entrada

Diego de Vargas to the Conde de Galve, El Paso,
13 July 1692, LS.

Most excellent sir,

Sir, today, 13 of the current month, I received your excellency's
directive with the decision of the Junta of the Royal Treasury and its
lords minister, dated 28 May of the present year. I am ready to go
tomorrow to aid the crossing of the soldiers and victuals on rafts at
the ford of the Río del Norte, since it is very high, and later I shall
cross to enter the villa on the specified day.

So as not to fail to recognize my proper humility and the order
your excellency decided upon with the agreement of the lords minister, with proper submission and careful attention to my duties, I
humbly thank your excellency and the lords for providing the fifty
soldiers who, for the moment, are the responsibility of the governor
and captain general of the kingdom of New Biscay. Through your
excellency's order, he advises me by this post that when he hears
from me, he will immediately order them to go anywhere I say. With
regard to prompt execution, it has occurred to me to send a courier
to the governor, so that as soon as my letter arrives, he may order
the fifty soldiers to the plaza de armas of this pueblo of El Paso.

Here, from the day of their arrival until the day of their return to
their presidio, during their participation on the campaign, I shall
sustain and supply them with ammunition. If they lack weapons
or lances, I shall provide them and aid them with complete regard,
only after advising the governor and captain general to send me
soldiers and not citizens and that they should come well supplied
with animals. With the great burden of victuals, other army stores,
and ammunition to be carried, I shall do no small thing by supplying them with mules to carry the load, muleteers, and guards for
the cattle on the hoof I am taking to provision the men. I shall also
supply the two small carts or gun carriages and the large bronze
stone mortar, which I am taking to protect the camp in the plaza de
armas I shall choose. I am going to set it up in the midst of a great
many enemies.

I do not know whether the Apaches will also help the apostates. It is necessary to know the opinion both of the lord fiscal and of the other lords who may follow. The Apaches, even though they destroy each other, and kill, rob, and enslave one another, are all allies against the Spaniard. Thus, this argument would have been well founded, had the Apaches held to it. These Indians are different, since they are our barbarous enemy, even though the fathers will have exaggerated and informed your excellency that they are as sheep and little lambs. I would like to have the fathers at my side one day, so that I might lead them by the sleeve, and they might see how meek the Indians are. It is not good that they should try by interpretation to undermine decisions they should respect. I can only assure your excellency that it may be that Captain Ramírez will have been informed by the governor of New Biscay and his captains regarding this point. I repeat to your excellency that the reports will reinforce my decision. I shall endeavor, Our Lord giving me life, to perform according to the judgment by which you ennoble and favor me, which is the attribute of a prince and lord honoring his servants.

I conclude by saying to your excellency that I shall leave from this outpost, if God sees fit, with its presidial company and the fifty men from New Biscay. From the kingdom of New Mexico, I shall take two surgeons, a gunsmith, a miner, and two military leaders, as well as one hundred Indian allies. I shall leave the citizenry and other Indians with the necessary protection, having divided their five pueblos with their captains and lists of the citizens who should be under their command, as well as the Indian people of each one. I shall give orders to my lieutenant general, who is in charge of everything, and each and every individual, about the duties of his position. They must make raids to the other side of the river because of enemy forays, so that, having seen fresh tracks of the horses and allies on foot, the enemy will think that they cannot carry out their ambushes without first being noticed. Then, the captains should lend each other a hand, and my lieutenant general may execute my orders. After they have passed muster and I have examined their weapons and usable firearms, I shall leave them a supply of ammunition.

It appears to me that with this rule and form of governance, this government will be secured and defended in case the enemy cannot be pursued. In this way, they will maintain themselves. I shall seek to act quickly, most excellent sir, and even though the operation and undertaking is lengthy, nevertheless, I shall do my part to work day and night to save time and return to this area as soon as possible, if the Divine Majesty so permits it.

I shall then send your excellency the proceedings of the campaign, which make up its journal, reporting the daily events, marches, assaults, and invasions carried out against the rebel pueblos. I shall punctually give your excellency legal compliance in all things, as is my custom. Your excellency, having informed his majesty of such gloomy opinions, may decide to determine for yourself to remove doubts and opinions that have silently kept at bay the will to make a decision about the means for the battle in which I shall have success, should Our Lord God grant it to me. Thus, for the means I have applied, I shall consider them well spent in the service of his majesty. I only wish that on this occasion my fortune were not so lost to me, that I could place it, were I prosperous, at your feet. Please accept my zeal and will as the least of your loyal vassals who venerates and humbly wishes to serve your excellency, wishing that Our Lord keep your most excellent person many happy years. El Paso, 13 July 1692.

Most excellent sir, your least and very submissive servant humbly kisses your hands,

Don Diego de Vargas
Zapata Luján Ponce de León [rubrica]

Most excellent lord viceroy, the Conde de Galve

———

El Paso, 13 July 1692
Don Diego de Vargas
Received on 21 October

Diego de Vargas to Juan Isidro de Pardiñas, El Paso,
13 July 1692, C.

Sir,

You compliment me greatly by the honors you are pleased to do me in your letter, for which I return my best wishes and offer to serve you however I may. In view of the directive and order I received from his excellency, in which I am assigned fifty soldiers under the command of your government, you may choose from which presidios to send them to me. It is true that I was already prepared to leave on the undertaking tomorrow, 14 of the present month. Because of this order, I postponed it only for the time it would take for the sargento of this presidio to arrive with this letter to you. This is so that by virtue of his excellency's order, which you have, you may immediately decide to carry it out by ordering the men to depart.

I ask this of you: that they pass muster before you and you specify the weapons, horses, and mules with which each soldier comes, so that with the copy of it you will send me, I may reexamine the muster in this plaza de armas to record it in the proceedings of this campaign to be sent to the most excellent lord viceroy. The men should come well provisioned with weapons, horses, and mules. The responsibility of feeding them will be mine, from the day they arrive in this plaza de armas, for the duration of the march while on campaign, and the return. Likewise, I shall provide them with ammunition, and I hope you will favor me by sending completely satisfactory men. It would not be good for the captains to hold back those who could bring about the completion and triumph of this enterprise. If they are any less, it will not achieve this end.

I did not hold anything back from you on the Sonora frontiers; rather I happily brought even more than I was ordered to. Your captain at the presidio of Janos knows this. In a gentleman of your qualities, I have no doubt that this care will have been taken by my lords, the captains of the soldiers you are to send me. I beg you, for whatever it is worth, to send them to me, for I shall carry out the enterprise with great pleasure. May God keep you many years. El Paso, 13 July 1692.

Your most affectionate and surest servant kisses your hand,

Don Diego de Vargas Zapata Luján Ponce de León

Lord Gen. don Juan Isidro de Pardiñas

Juan Isidro de Pardiñas, Musters,
25 July–14 August 1692, C.

Parral, 25 July 1692: Put this letter at the head of the proceedings for sending the fifty soldiers the most excellent lord viceroy ordered dispatched to the governor and captain general of El Paso in New Mexico. Send the orders, so that from the three presidios of Pasaje, Gallo, and San Francisco de Conchos, they might come well armed and prepared for that end. Likewise, the captain of the presidio of Cerro Gordo[2] should dispatch five men for the complement of the fifty. This adjustment is made in view of the fact that the presidio of Janos has fifteen fewer men than those his excellency ordered to go to Sonora. I, the lord sargento mayor, don Juan Isidro de Pardiñas Villar de Francos, knight of the Order of Santiago, governor and captain general of this kingdom of New Biscay for his majesty, decree, order, and sign.
Don Juan Isidro de Pardiñas Villar de Francos
Before me,
Don Luis de Valdés,
Secretary of government and war
On the said day, the orders contained herein were sent.

———

In the real of Parral on 13 August 1692, the lord sargento mayor, don Juan Isidro de Pardiñas Villar de Francos, knight of the Order of Santiago, governor and captain general of this kingdom and provinces of New Biscay for his majesty, stated that since the soldiers from the presidios of Pasaje, San Francisco de Conchos, San Pedro del Gallo, and Cerro Gordo had just arrived so that fifty of them might go to El Paso in New Mexico for the recovery of that province in accordance with the order and dispatch of the most excellent lord viceroy of New Spain, I ordered that the soldiers pass muster, and that the supply of provisions they will carry be examined. For this, the lord factor and accountant of the royal treasury office of this kingdom, don José de Urzúa,[3] was present, and he examined them, as is customary. Because of the urgency of the case and to avoid further delays, the muster was passed today. Thus, I provide, order, and sign.

Don Juan Isidro de Pardiñas Villar de Francos
Before me,
Don Luis de Valdés,
Secretary of government and war

———

In the real of Parral on 13 August 1692, the lord sargento mayor, don Juan Isidro de Pardiñas Villar de Francos, knight of the Order of Santiago, governor and captain general of this kingdom and provinces of New Biscay for his majesty, complies with the foregoing proceedings. In the presence of lord don José de Urzúa, factor and comptroller of the royal treasury office of this kingdom, after a company of various squads arrived in accordance with the order he gave to the captains of the presidios to send them for which they turned in lists to him, he orders them to pass muster. He also orders the examination of the supply of provisions, weapons, ammunition, and horses with which they go to carry out what his excellency orders, to aid and assist the governor of El Paso of New Mexico on the entrada for the recovery of the province. They passed muster in the following form and manner.

Soldiers from the presidio of Cerro Gordo

José de Acosta,[4] fully armed, with munitions, six horses, and one mule
Francisco de Acosta, with five horses, an harquebus, shield, gunpowder and bullets, without leather jacket or coat of mail
Bernardo Delgado, fully armed, with eight horses, and munitions
Francisco López, six horses, harquebus, shield, gunpowder and bullets, without leather jacket
Juan de Mendoza, five horses, harquebus, shield, gunpowder and bullets, without leather jacket

Soldiers from San Pedro del Gallo

Tomás de la Mora,[5] fully armed, ten horses, one mule, gunpowder and bullets
Cristóbal de Mendoza, with his weapons, seven horses, gunpowder and bullets

Antonio Núñez,[6] fully armed, with eight horses, gunpowder and bullets

Bernardo de Gavidia, fully armed, with eight horses, gunpowder and bullets

José Muñoz, fully armed, eight horses, gunpowder and bullets

Juan Luján, fully armed, eight horses, gunpowder and bullets

Pedro Juárez Ochoa, fully armed, eight horses, gunpowder and bullets

Isidro de Santiago, fully armed, six horses, gunpowder and bullets

Juan de Vargas, fully armed, seven horses, gunpowder and bullets

Gerónimo de Gres, fully armed, six horses, gunpowder and bullets

José de Soto,[7] fully armed, eight horses, gunpowder and bullets

Pascual de Uribe, fully armed, eight horses, gunpowder and bullets

Cristóbal Pérez, fully armed, six horses, gunpowder and bullets

José Ochoa, fully armed, twelve horses, gunpowder and bullets

Lorenzo Quejada, fully armed, six horses, gunpowder and bullets

Soldiers from the presidio of Pasaje

Francisco de Almazán, leader of the fifteen soldiers from the presidio of Pasaje, passed muster fully armed, with thirteen horses, one mule, gunpowder and bullets

Juan García, fully armed, nine horses, one mule, gunpowder and bullets

Antonio Pérez, fully armed, eight horses, one mule, gunpowder and bullets

Nicolás de Zamudio, fully armed, nine horses, one pack and saddle mule, gunpowder and bullets

Bernardo de Sepúlveda, fully armed, eight horses, one mule, gunpowder and bullets

Gregorio Rodríguez, fully armed, eight horses, one mule, gunpowder and bullets

Gabriel de Alarcón, fully armed, eight horses, one mule, gunpowder and bullets

Juan de la Cruz, fully armed, nine horses, one mule, gunpowder and bullets

Lucas de Alarcón, fully armed, eight horses, one mule, gunpowder and bullets

José de Molina, fully armed, nine horses, one mule, gunpowder and bullets

Lucas de Cárdenas, fully armed, nine horses, one mule, gunpowder and bullets

Antonio de Contreras,[8] fully armed, eight horses, one mule, gun-
   powder and bullets
Ignacio González, fully armed, nine horses, one mule, gunpowder
   and bullets
Manuel Fernández, fully armed, twelve horses, gunpowder and bullets
Tomás de Mesta,[9] fully armed, fifteen horses, gunpowder and bullets
   The thirty-five soldiers who together make up three squads passed
muster as contained herein. What was recorded was examined. In
view of the fact that they have to go by way of the presidio of San
Francisco de Conchos, whence their captain has sent the list and
muster to him, he ordered and orders that it be placed in these pro-
ceedings and that the captain should return it after muster is passed
in due form at the time of the soldiers' departure. Accordingly, the
lord factor and accountant signed it with him.
Don Juan Isidro de Pardiñas Villar de Francos
Don José de Urzúa
Before me,
Don Luis de Valdés
Secretary of government and war

———

   In the presidio of San Francisco de Conchos on 10 August 1692,
Gen. Juan Fernández de Retana, captain of the presidio for his majesty, in fulfillment of the order from the lord governor and captain
general of this kingdom that fifteen soldiers be prepared for the New
Mexico expedition by virtue of the order from the most excellent
lord viceroy of New Spain, ordered the fifteen men to pass muster
in the following way:

From the presidio of Conchos

Lt. Martín de Alday,[10] fully armed, twelve horses, and three mules
José Navarro,[11] fully armed, nine horses, and one mule
José Antonio Carrasco, fully armed, eleven horses, and two mules
Tomás de Soto, fully armed, eight horses, and two mules
Antonio de Soto,[12] fully armed, eight horses, and two mules
Matías Cebreros, fully armed, nine horses, and one mule
José Santiago, fully armed, eight horses, and one mule
Simón de Aguirre, fully armed, nine horses, and one mule

Antonio Ruano, fully armed, eight horses, and one mule
Antonio de Morales,[13] fully armed, eight horses, and two mules
Francisco Perea, fully armed, eight horses, and one mule
Agustín del Río, fully armed, eight horses, and one mule
Juan de Chavarría,[14] fully armed, eight horses, and one mule
Andrés González, fully armed, eight horses, and one mule
Francisco de Herrera, fully armed, eight horses, and two mules

Accordingly, the fifteen soldiers of my company fully armed with harquebuses; leather jackets; swords; and one hundred fifty-two horses, mules, and other animals; well supplied with gunpowder, bullets, and victuals passed muster before me, the captain. So that it may be of record, I signed it.
Juan de Retana
Before me,
Fernando de Hinojos
Military scribe

———

In Parral on 13 August 1692, the lord sargento mayor, don Juan Isidro de Pardiñas Villar de Francos, knight of the Order of Santiago and governor and captain general of this kingdom of New Biscay: Having seen this list that Capt. Juan de Retana, currently of the presidio of Conchos, sent because the soldiers are in that outpost, which is along the way the others are taking to El Paso in New Mexico, he ordered and orders that they join forces in that presidio to make the trip. In accordance with the order from his excellency, the most excellent lord viceroy, he appointed and appoints as leader of the fifty soldiers, the alferez, Martín de Alday, current lieutenant of the presidio of San Francisco de Conchos, and directs that an order to this end be sent to him and that he take command of the thirty-five soldiers who have passed muster and the fifteen contained in the preceding list. He should immediately leave with the fifty soldiers under his command and go to aid the governor and captain general of New Mexico. The soldiers, contained herein, should follow the leader's orders. Thus, he ordered it recorded as proceedings and signed it.
Don Juan Isidro de Pardiñas Villar de Francos
Before me,
Don Luis de Valdés
Secretary of government and war

The order contained herein was sent, and the previously mentioned soldiers departed on this day.

————

This is in accord with the original list in the military proceedings recorded for this reason. By order of the lord governor and captain general, I copied it to inform the most excellent lord viceroy of New Spain that his order was fulfilled. Parral, 14 August 1692.
It is on six sheets and goes with this letter.
Don Luis de Valdés [rubrica]
Military scribe
Officially issued [Valdés's rubrica]

> *Juan Isidro de Pardiñas to the Conde de Galve,*
> *Parral, 6 October 1692, ALS.*

Most excellent sir,

Sir, in fulfillment of your excellency's order, I sent the fifty soldiers from the presidios of this government to the governor and captain general of New Mexico with a completely satisfactory leader for what your excellency orders. Their musters are in the enclosed copy I thought to place in your excellency's hands so that the promptness of my obedience, which I shall always exercise as is my duty, will be of record for you. May God keep your excellency's most excellent person in the greatnesses that are necessary to me. Parral, 6 October 1692.

Don Juan Isidro de Pardiñas
Villar de Francos [rubrica]

Most excellent lord, the Conde de Galve

————

Parral, 6 October 1692
Received on 21 October
Don Juan Isidro de Pardiñas

*AGN, Historia 38:1. 3 folios, 6 written pages.

1. This is a reference to Toribio de la Huerta's proposal for the reconquest of New Mexico.

2. AGN, Historia 37:5 (cont.). The presidio of Cerro Gordo was located about 65 km southeast of Parral in the present-day municipio of Hidalgo in north-central Durango. The 1631 silver strike at Parral had brought cattle ranchers into the region and a trade route passing through Cerro Gordo. Founded in 1646 at the behest of Luis de Valdés, governor of New Biscay, Cerro Gordo was initially considered part of the alcaldía mayor of the mines of Indé. The commanding officer at its founding was Gen. Juan de Barraza, cavalry captain, whose annual salary was 1,000 pesos; serving as alferez was his son, Carlos de Barraza. With a complement of thirty presidial soldiers, the presidio was at the time the largest on the north frontier. Gerhard, *North Frontier*, 179–81. Naylor and Polzer, *Presidio and Militia*, 1:379. List of soldiers at the presidio of Cerro Gordo, August 1646, AHP, 1646A.

3. Capt. José de Urzúa, born about 1649, was a native of Ascona (Navarre), the son of Tristán de Urzúa and Francisca Díaz de Ascona. Urzúa had at least two relatives living in Mexico City: Sgto. mayor Martín de Urzúa and Francisco de Urzúa, a cousin. By 27 February 1691, José was factor and accountant at the royal treasury in Durango. In 1691, he married María Teresa González Ramírez. During the mid-1690s, Urzúa remained factor and accountant of the royal treasury and was also the administrator of mercury in Parral. He was buried in the city of Durango on 1 April 1707. LDS, Durango, Burials, 654847. José de Urzúa to María Teresa González Ramírez, Power to make a will, Parral, 28 Jan. 1706, AHP, 1706. LDS, Durango, Marriages, 654837. José de Urzúa to Martín de Urzúa, Power of attorney, Parral, 25 Apr. 1691, 1691A. José de Urzúa to Francisco de Urzúa, Power of attorney, Parral, 27 Feb. 1691, 1691A.

4. A cabo, José de Acosta passed muster with all his weapons as a part of Gen. don Domingo Terán de los Río's company for the campaign against the Pimas on 17 July 1695 at Cocóspera. Another José de Acosta passed muster in the company of Gen. Domingo Agramonte y Arce from the presidio of Sinaloa for the same campaign. Naylor and Polzer, *Presidio and Militia*, 1:601, 604.

5. During the 1695 muster for the campaign against the Pimas, Tomás de la Mora was ill and remained in Janos. Naylor and Polzer, *Presidio and Militia*, 1:601.

6. Antonio Núñez was also a member of the company commanded by Terán de los Ríos in the 1695 campaign against the

Pimas. Naylor and Polzer, *Presidio and Militia*, 1:602.

7. José de Soto passed muster under command of Terán de los Ríos in the 1695 campaign against the Pimas. Naylor and Polzer, *Presidio and Militia*, 1:601.

8. Antonio de Contreras served under Terán de los Ríos in the 1695 Pima campaign. Naylor and Polzer, *Presidio and Militia*, 1:601.

9. Tomás de Mesta was described in 1681 as a New Mexico native, in his early twenties, and a widower. He and his brother Juan escaped the 1680 revolt. NMF, 73. Hackett and Shelby, *Revolt*, 1:148; 2:50, 105.

10. Martín de Alday was born in Escoriaza (Guipúzcoa) around 1657 to Martín de Alday y Aguiriano and Catalina de Lamariano y Arroaga. He was ranking officer of the fifty-man column from New Biscay and later held the post of governor of that province from 1720 to 1723. For the final two years of his life, he was on active duty as captain for life of the presidio of Pasaje. Alday was married to María Isabel Maldonado y Zapata. By 18 August 1724, he was dead. Juan de Veitia, Settlement of debt, Parral,

19 Jan. 1724, AHP 1724C. Martín de Alday to María Isabel Maldonado and Juan Blanco, Power to make a will, Parral, 9 Sept. 1722, AHP, 1722B. Thomas H. Naylor and Charles W. Polzer, *Pedro de Rivera and the Military Regulations for Northern New Spain, 1724–1729: A Documentary History of His Frontier Inspection and the Reglamento de 1729* (Tucson, 1988):77 n38.

11. An individual named José Navarro and his wife, Antonia Archuleta, had a daughter, Rosa, who married Cristóbal Durán at Socorro del Sur in 1719. At that time, he gave his residence as Ranchos del Paso in the jurisdiction of Socorro. NMR, 3:446. NMF, 242.

12. Antonio de Soto passed muster 17 July 1695 at Cocóspera. Naylor and Polzer, *Presidio and Militia*, 1:602.

13. Antonio de Morales was a lieutenant at San Juan Bautista in 1698. Bolton, *Rim*, 382. Gerhard, *North Frontier*, 282.

14. Juan de Chavarría appears to have been a prerevolt colonist of New Mexico who did not return to settle. Hackett and Shelby, *Revolt*, 2:156, 210, 362.

Armed Reconnaissance and Ritual Repossession by Diego de Vargas of Santa Fe and Twelve Pueblos of the Tewa, Tano, and Taos Indians, 9 August–16 October 1692.[*]

As field commander, chief of staff, and civil executive, Gov. Diego de Vargas exercises total control over the only official account of the reconquest—his sworn campaign journal—from which he emerges the hero. Throughout, Vargas demonstrates bravery, strength of character, and diplomatic skill. The results he achieves are phenomenal. Despite the vast numerical superiority of the Pueblo Indians and the bad weather, don Diego reports to the Conde de Galve that he has restored to the Spanish crown Santa Fe and twelve other pueblos.

Obviously, the Pueblo Indians are disunited, and Vargas courts them as allies. Some see advantages. Once they join him, he promises that he will make peace with their enemies or annihilate them once and for all. Many remember the brutal destruction of Santa Ana and Zia by Vargas's predecessors. They are moved by his boldness before Santa Fe and his restraint at Pecos. For now at least, all the resplendent Spanish governor demands is passive participation in ceremonial acts. Then, he and his column move on.

Wisely, Vargas dispatches the first half of his campaign journal from Santa Fe in mid-October. Its arrival by fast courier in Mexico City causes a sensation. In a year of natural calamity, famine, and riots, here is good news—a Spanish victory. Over-

Nuestra Señora de los Remedios
From Aline C. Ussel, *Esculturas de la Virgen María en Nueva España* (1975)

night, don Diego de Vargas becomes the talk of the court, the new Cortés. The Conde de Galve, who had begun to despair on 5 November, can scarcely do enough for don Diego on 24 November. The mood of the court prevails. The reconquest of New Mexico is accepted as a fait accompli.

Diego de Vargas, Campaign journal, New Mexico, 9 August–15 October 1692, C.

1692
Military proceedings of the campaign and conquest of the kingdom of New Mexico that, through divine favor, don Diego de Vargas Zapata Luján Ponce de León, governor and captain general of the land and provinces of this kingdom and castellan of its fortress and presidio for his majesty, has achieved at his expense. [rubrica]

Edict

Don Diego de Vargas Zapata Luján Ponce de León, governor and captain general of this kingdom and provinces of New Mexico, castellan of its fortress and presidio for his majesty: The most excellent lord viceroy of this kingdom and all New Spain, the Conde de Galve, after seeing my advisory letter, with the agreement of the Junta of the Royal Treasury and its lords minister, saw fit, as so great a prince, to issue to me his order and directive of 28 May, dated in Mexico City this present year, sending me the assistance of fifty soldiers from the presidios of Parral.

He is to leave on Saturday, 16 August, because the fifty soldiers from Parral have not arrived

I postponed the entrada, although I was ready to leave for the conquest of the villa of Santa Fe, principal city of this kingdom of New Mexico, and the pueblos of its district, because I received this notice and receipt of the directive on 13 July of the present year, in which the governor and captain general of the kingdom of New Biscay wrote me that as soon as I advised him, he would send me the fifty soldiers. I sent the sergeant of this presidio's company, so that the governor might send me the soldiers immediately. The sergeant returned with a verbal response that the governor was not answering my letter then, but would do so with the leader who would bring those men. The sergeant was to return to give me this explanation, and the men would come as soon as possible.

Until 16 August, he waited for the men from Parral
Three squads from the presidio's company, one hundred Indians

Because so much time has passed, to make it up, it has occurred to me to indicate by this edict when it would be best, as well as the last possible day, for the men-at-arms in my charge to depart from this outpost of El Paso. This is so that I, the governor and captain general, may leave rapidly to join the camp if the men from Parral do not arrive soon. Thus, I choose Saturday, the sixteenth of this month of August, for the departure of the three squads of this presidio's company; the captain and maestre de campo, Roque Madrid; the pack animals, wagons, livestock; and the hundred Indian allies indicated.

I am indicating to them that day, Saturday, for the departure from this plaza de armas of the pueblo of El Paso as far as the outpost they call Robledo,[1] 29 leagues away. I am designating it as a plaza de armas where the captain will halt. As soon as the men-at-arms from Parral come, I, the governor and captain general, shall leave with them and the squad that will remain on guard, the military leaders and officials, alferez, and sergeant, to join them at the plaza de armas and outpost of Robledo. So that they may be informed, I ordered it made public, preceded by the sounding of drum and bugle,[2] with the leaders, military officials, and my secretary of government in attendance. I order him to certify that it was made public. So that this edict and order may be of record, I provided, signed, and ordered it in this plaza de armas of the pueblo of El Paso, on 9 August 1692. I also ordered my secretary of government and war to sign it.

Don Diego de Vargas Zapata Luján Ponce de León
By order of the lord governor and captain general,
Juan Páez Hurtado, secretary of government and war

Attestation of the publication

In the pueblo of El Paso, on 10 August 1692,[3] I, Juan Páez Hurtado, alferez and secretary of government and war of this kingdom, fulfilled what I am ordered by the preceding edict made public with the sounding of drum and bugle with customary solemnity in the most public places in the loud and clear voice of Sebastián Rodríguez. A great crowd was present for its publication, including the captain, officials, and soldiers of this company. So that its publication may be of record, I so certify and attest. Present for all that was referred to were the alferez, don Alfonso Rael de Aguilar, and Tomás Gutiérrez Carrera, who signed it with me, the secretary of government and war.

Alfonso Rael de Aguilar

Tomás Gutiérrez Carrera

Juan Páez Hurtado, secretary of government and war

> Directive for the alcalde mayor of the Piros to notify those named in the edict not to fail to be present on the day indicated

Don Diego de Vargas Zapata Luján Ponce de León, governor and captain general of this kingdom and provinces of New Mexico and castellan of its fortress and presidio for his majesty: In this pueblo of El Paso, I have published this edict, citing in it the date of departure for the conquest of the provinces of New Mexico from the apostate, uprisen Indians, traitors to his majesty. On Saturday, the soldiers of this presidio will go, as well as the allied Indian warriors, muleteers, and escorts I have named and indicated for the convoy of provisions, other army stores, and cattle I take to supply this army. By the present edict, I order the alcalde mayor and war captain, José de Padilla, of the pueblos of Senecú, Ysleta, and Socorro; the teniente of the alcalde mayor, Juan de Valencia; and the captain, Diego de Luna,[4] all three in their districts and the pueblos where they live, to order on that day, Saturday, 16 August, that all the people included in this edict and command should be present in this plaza de armas of this pueblo of El Paso at eight o'clock in the morning. So that it may be understood by the governors of the pueblos, they will be ordered by the edict, as will the rest of the other people in the same manner. So that these and the others keep, fulfill, and carry it out, I, the governor and captain general, provide it. I signed it with my secretary of government and war in this pueblo of El Paso on 14 August 1692.

Don Diego de Vargas Zapata Luján Ponce de León

By order of the lord governor and captain general,

Juan Páez Hurtado, secretary of government and war

Carrying out of the above directive

In the plaza de armas of this presidio in the pueblo of El Paso on 16 August 1692, before me, don Diego de Vargas Zapata Luján Ponce de León, governor and captain general of this kingdom of New Mexico: Having ordered and prepared for the men-at-arms to be present by the directive contained above and the rest that is of record, I indicate that all were there at about ten o'clock in the morning, as were the horses, mules, and other livestock to supply the men-at-arms. I ordered them to take their provisions and army stores to the river crossing. I also ordered them to take the horses, mules, and livestock, separating those of the squad designated to leave as my personal guard. This was done by about two o'clock this afternoon.

Departure of the three military squads and the Indian allies

I, the governor and captain general, went accompanied by the capitán, cabo y caudillo, Roque Madrid; the officials of the company; its soldiers; my lieutenant governor and captain general, the maestre de campo, Luis Granillo; the sargento mayor and alcalde ordinario, Francisco de Anaya Almazán; and many settlers from this pueblo. I was there to watch many people crossing the river with provisions and livestock. It took until vespers for everything to get safely to the other side of the river. The men-at-arms made camp in the cañada, since it was late. So that the departure may be of record, I ordered it to be recorded as a completed action, which I signed with the aforesaid, together with my secretary of government and war.
Don Diego de Vargas Zapata Luján Ponce de León
Luis Granillo
Francisco de Anaya Almazán
Lorenzo Madrid
Roque Madrid
Diego Arias[5]
Juan López Holguín[6]
Before me, Juan Páez Hurtado, secretary of government and war

Departure of the wagons, the cannon, and a large, bronze stone mortar

On 17 August 1692, I, the governor and captain general, ordered the sergeant of this company and presidio, Juan Ruiz de Cáceres,[7] to convoy the two small wagons with some provisions, the cannon, and large, bronze stone mortar,[8] and deliver them to the outpost of Salineta,[9] where today the capitán y cabo, Roque Madrid, has orders from me to stop for the night with that camp. He will return to this plaza de armas to give me word of the delivery, as well as the report about that camp. If something is lacking, he will advise me. So that it may be of record, I ordered that it be recorded as a completed action. I signed, together with my secretary of government and war.

Don Diego de Vargas Zapata Luján Ponce de León

Before me, Juan Páez Hurtado, secretary of government and war

Order sent to the captain of the presidio for him to go to the outpost of Robledo where he should halt with that camp

By the nineteenth, no information had arrived about the soldiers from Parral

In the pueblo of El Paso on 17 August 1692, the captain of this company returned from delivering the two wagons, the cannon, and the large, bronze stone mortar to the capitán, cabo y caudillo, whom he found already quartered at the outpost of Salineta with the men-at-arms of the camp, in accord with the order contained above. Because it was after vespers, and I had no word that the fifty soldiers from New Biscay had come and did not know whether they had left, I sent a letter to Capt. Roque Madrid telling him to wait for me at the outpost of Robledo where I, the governor and captain general, shall go to join the camp. It is five days' journey from Salineta, where he is now. Thus, he will wait until I arrive. So that everything may be of record, I signed it with my secretary of government and war.

Don Diego de Vargas Zapata Luján Ponce de León

Before me, Juan Páez Hurtado, secretary of government and war

Don Diego de Vargas Zapata Luján Ponce de León, governor and captain general of this kingdom and provinces of New Mexico and castellan of its fortress and presidio for his majesty, and so forth: I received an order from the most excellent lord, the Conde de Galve, viceroy, and governor and captain general of this kingdom and all New Spain, with agreement of the general Junta of the Royal Treasury, dated last 28 May of this present year. His greatness agreed with what was decided at that royal junta and sent an order to the governor and captain general of Parral, so that once he had seen it, with no excuse or pretext, even for legitimate reason, he should order immediately readied and prepared fifty soldiers from the four presidios, apportioning them in such a way that their absence would not be so greatly felt.

The governor and captain general writes me in this regard and about receipt of the directive. I order the original letter placed with the military proceedings of the campaign of the entrada that I, the governor and captain general, have proposed to his excellency and decided to make and carry out myself, at my expense, without asking his majesty to repay me for whatever expenses I may incur. I only admit my humble and fervent zeal for his royal and sovereign person, whom I greatly venerate. The fifty men are those who, with great prudence and fervent initiative, the most excellent lord viceroy, with agreement of the lords minister of the Royal Junta of the Treasury, decided to order the governor of Parral to send me for this purpose. They will be under my command, carrying out the operations entrusted to me.

Despite the fact that I was ready to leave on 14 July with the camp and men-at-arms, provisions, and other army stores, as is public knowledge in all this republic and among the citizens of this pueblo of El Paso and its district, on the thirteenth, I received the dispatch contained and cited herein. Having read and understood it, I obeyed with the proper respect, as is my reverent duty, postponing the march. I immediately went on to thank the most excellent lord viceroy in writing, dispatching a courier, as in fact I did, to the real of Parral, sending with that packet a letter for the governor and captain general with the sergeant of this presidio's company, Juan Ruiz de Cáceres, who punctually and assiduously arrived there with that dispatch.

He delivered it by hand to the governor and captain general, don Juan Isidro de Pardiñas. He read my letter in which I told him about the fulfillment of the order and directive from the most excellent lord viceroy and his own letter in which he stated he would carry it out properly and promptly, telling me in it that as soon as I sent for the fifty solders of those presidios, he would give the order for them to leave immediately, without delay. He told the sergeant to return and tell me that he was not replying to me, because it would be done by the leader who would bring the men-at-arms. He had ordered and dispatched him to the captains of the presidios so that they would send the men.

When the sergeant arrived with the reply, I calculated the length of time the governor had the order; the time it had taken the same courier to come to me, the governor and captain general of this kingdom; the time taken by the trip there and back by the sergeant with my letter; and, not knowing at the time of this report where the men were, decided to leave on this enterprise. This is so as not to waste time and to avoid the rigorous winter expected in this kingdom which could make travel impossible and keep me from the battle I have so longed for.

> Order left for the lieutenant governor and captain general and the appointment of the captain of the men-at-arms from Parral and of the secretary of government and war; record that they waited for those men until today, 21 August, in the afternoon
> Likewise, until 21 August, without the soldiers from Parral having come, he decided to leave on Thursday, the twenty-first, with the company and three squads

Because of this, I decided to leave on the conquest today, Thursday, 21 August, taking the men of this company. I had sent ahead its capitán, cabo y caudillo to the outpost of Robledo with the provisions, the three squads, and the rest, as is of record in these war proceedings, as is their departure and crossing of the Río del Norte on the sixteenth of this present month.

> Order left for the quartering of the fifty soldiers from Parral

So that the fifty men-at-arms should not fail to carry out a superior mandate and order from the most excellent lord viceroy, I provide and leave as capitán, cabo y caudillo of the fifty men-at-arms the alferez of this company, Juan Páez Hurtado, secretary of government. Aided by my lieutenant governor and captain general, he should have them immediately cross to the other side of the river on the day of their arrival to find quarters where it would be best for the horses. Mre. de campo Luis Granillo, my lieutenant governor and captain general, will accompany him as far as the outpost they call Estero Largo.[10] From there, he will return to this outpost, leaving the alferez I indicate and select as captain of the company in his charge and under his command. I order him to divide up each day's journey, so that he will arrive in Santo Domingo Pueblo in twelve days. If he sees it is necessary to delay two or three days to rest the horses, he will do so.

When he arrives at the pueblo of Santo Domingo, he will immediately send me word, so that I may give him the order I find most appropriate. He will send the report with the four swiftest soldiers most familiar with the road, since the tracks from my camp will take them to where I am, should God see fit. I leave this order and directive entrusted to these men, so that it may be carried out properly. Each one, faithful to his duty in what he is responsible for, will carry out, keep, and give it the proper fulfillment.

So that the lieutenant governor and captain general, with the assistance of the appointed captain, may supply the soldiers, I leave him the key to a chest, full of chocolate and sugar, which I opened for him in the presence of witnesses. I also left bread, pinole, ten hands of tobacco, soap, and two fat beefs I have, so that they can take some jerky. I would like to have definite information about their departure so as to leave them the largest provision of meat, which is all they might need and the lack of which they will blame on their leader. He has not had the good judgment to make the arrangements he should have for the departure and campsite where he was. On that day I, the governor and captain general, could have decided to make the entrada with the company, had I known. I do not object to my increased expenses, but only express the feeling of failure of all to depart in a group for the best success in the operations against the apostate, uprisen enemy who is going to be reduced or conquered by force of arms.

So that the measures I have taken, the arrangements, motives, means, and everything else—such as the reason for my departure on the conquest—may be of record, I ordered the alferez, Alfonso Rael de Aguilar, to record it in the military proceedings of this campaign. I have designated and selected as captain and leader, Afz. Juan Páez Hurtado, who held the office of secretary of government and war, which I transfer to Alfonso Rael de Aguilar, whom I select, appoint, and designate, so that he may use and exercise it in accord with the title I shall give him, written and signed by me. I grant him the authority the law requires, so that he may use that office on the campaign and as long as I wish. So that everything may be of record, I, the governor and captain general, signed it with my lieutenant governor and captain general and the capitán, cabo y caudillo of the reinforcements. The witnesses to everything were the captains, José Téllez Girón and Lázaro de Mizquía,[11] and the sargento mayor, Juan Lucero de Godoy. They signed it with the newly appointed

secretary of government and war in this pueblo of El Paso on
21 August 1692.
Don Diego de Vargas Zapata Luján Ponce de León
Luis Granillo
Juan Páez Hurtado
Lázaro de Mizquía
Juan Lucero de Godoy
José Téllez Girón
By order of the lord governor and captain general,
Alfonso Rael de Aguilar, secretary of government and war

> Letter, the original of which the governor and captain general left for
> the alcalde mayor of Senecú to send to his excellency with the cou-
> rier to Parral

Most excellent sir,
   Sir, I am waiting for the fifty soldiers from Parral to finally come.
Their governor wrote me by the courier who brought your excellency's order that as soon as he had my letter, he would order them to
go. I then sent for them with all possible haste, dispatching to the
governor a courier who arrived on 21 July at the real of Parral. Having seen my letter, he ordered the courier to return, bringing me the
verbal reply he had given him, and that he would give a written reply
to the leader in whose charge the men-at-arms would come.

> Nota bene

   I calculated that fifty days had passed, during which not only might
the men have arrived at this outpost, but also I could have completed with them a good part of the march, which will necessarily be
a slow one because of the camp's pace. Seeing that it was necessary,
and delay inexcusable, I decided on the sixteenth to send ahead the
provisions, army stores, livestock on the hoof, and two wagons drawn
by oxen. As a result of the additional men ordered to come, I needed
to add to the provisions. I also sent the cannon and large, bronze
stone mortar in two small carts drawn by mules. The one hundred
Indian allies and three squads with the captain took horses, mules,
pack animals, and the order that they should stop at the place called
Robledo, where they would be well quartered, about 29 leagues
from El Paso.

Since today is 21 August and I have had no report about their coming, which the leader of those men might have sent me, I did not want to risk the enterprise and proposed conquest of the villa of Santa Fe, the pueblo of Cochiti, and the others of their district as I confirm and repeat in this letter. So that this may be recognized, I am departing today, Thursday, at four o'clock in the afternoon, from this pueblo of El Paso with the rest of the company. I am leaving an order for my lieutenant governor and captain general, having named as capitán, cabo y caudillo of the company of reinforcements my alferez and secretary of government and war. He has been with me and served his majesty since I came with the army. Over a period of two weeks, he will take them under his command to a pueblo called Santo Domingo, 10 leagues before, and on the road to, the villa and advise me of his arrival. I leave bread, pinole, sugar, chocolate, meat, tobacco, and soap for my lieutenant to supply the men-at-arms.

This was my final decision, so that my honor may be of record for all time for your excellency and the world and so that my wishes and ardor as a vassal of his majesty and a servant of your excellency not come to naught. To delay would be to make the enterprise impossible, and everyone will think that I ruefully await assistance. This aid—if it ever arrives—will bear witness to my accomplishments, which I hope Our Lord will grant me, equal in every way to casting aside my wishes and exalting once and for all His holy faith. Thus, I trust in His infinite mercy that your excellency will prosper and He will keep your most excellent person many happy years in your greater nobility. El Paso, 21 August 1692.

Most excellent sir, your least worthy and most indebted servant humbly kisses your excellency's hand,

Don Diego de Vargas Zapata Luján Ponce de León

Most excellent lord, the Conde de Galve

Departure

In the pueblo of El Paso on 21 August 1692, I, the governor and captain general, delivered the preceding letter into the hands of Capt. José de Padilla, so that he might send it to the real of Parral.

Journal

At about four o'clock in the afternoon, with the squad that had remained as a guard assembled, mounted, and ready to go with me, following the royal standard, I ordered the newly appointed alferez, Juan de Dios Lucero de Godoy, to raise it. Also present in this plaza de armas were the military leaders and some people who will be on the muster, who were in march formation. With the solemnity of the military instruments I ordered played, I mounted my horse. I left, as has been stated and in this manner, accompanied by my secretary of government and war and the reverend apostolic missionary fathers who come as chaplains of the army and to reduce the uprisen, apostate Indians of the kingdom of New Mexico.

Arrival at Ancón de Fray García

Having successfully crossed the Río del Norte, I arrived at Ancón de Fray García,[12] 5 leagues from El Paso, where I called a halt with the men for the night. So that the departure and march may be of record, I signed it with the military leaders, alferez, and my secretary of government and war in this outpost of Ancón de Fray García, on the bank of the Río del Norte on the day, month, and year ut supra.
Don Diego de Vargas Zapata Luján Ponce de León
Cristóbal de Tapia[13]
Juan de Dios Lucero de Godoy
Before me, Alfonso Rael de Aguilar, secretary of government and war

Arrival at Robledo

In the outpost of Robledo on 24 August 1692, I, the governor and captain general, arrived at this place at about six o'clock in the evening and found the capitán, cabo y caudillo, Roque Madrid, the men-at-arms of record in these proceedings as having departed, the provisions, and the rest, with nothing worthy of note having occurred to record. The march was 24 leagues. I designate this place as the plaza de armas to arrange the departure. So that the arrival may be of record, I signed it with the capitán, cabo y caudillo; the alferez; the artillery captain, Francisco Lucero de Godoy; and my secretary of government and war.

Don Diego de Vargas Zapata Luján Ponce de León
Roque Madrid
Francisco Lucero de Godoy
Juan de Dios Lucero de Godoy
Before me, Alfonso Rael de Aguilar, secretary of government and war

Arrival at San Diego

Today, Tuesday, 26 August 1692, having left the outpost of Robledo with the camp, I, the governor, arrived at this place called San Diego,[14] 4 leagues away. At about noon, the four soldiers I had sent to see whether El Perrillo[15] water hole had enough water arrived here. They said there was only enough for the pack mules, oxen, and other livestock. So that it may be of record, I signed it with the captain, the alferez of this company, and my secretary of government and war. Done ut supra.
Don Diego de Vargas Zapata Luján Ponce de León
Roque Madrid
Juan de Dios Lucero de Godoy
Before me, Alfonso Rael de Aguilar, secretary of government and war

Arrival and order to the captain, who is preceding us with the provisions, to go to El Perrillo and Las Peñuelas because of the shallow water holes

Today, Wednesday, 27 August 1692, as a result of the above information about the shallow water holes, at about three o'clock in the morning, I sent the captain of this company ahead with a squad of soldiers to go as escort and convoy of the pack animals, wagons, carts carrying provisions, and other army stores, so that they would be at El Perrillo. Because the water hole was shallow, they were to leave at four o'clock in the afternoon for the place that is called Las Peñuelas.[16] If they find water, they should call a halt until I, the governor and captain general, join them with the camp, whose departure was delayed until sunset, since the water was so distant. So that it may be of record, I signed it with the captain, the alferez, and my secretary of government and war.
Don Diego de Vargas Zapata Luján Ponce de León
Roque Madrid
Juan de Dios Lucero de Godoy
Before me, Alfonso Rael de Aguilar, secretary of government and war

Departure with the whole camp for Las Peñuelas

On this day, at about four o'clock in the afternoon, considering the shallow water holes and doubting there could be, for the camp I have with me, enough water at Las Peñuelas, the outpost indicated in the order above; and that the 32 leagues between San Diego and Fray Cristóbal and the Rio Grande are without water, except for what has been discovered, I can only be partially assured that all the oxen, the livestock to supply the camp, and the pack mules carrying provisions will not be lost. Also, regarding the risk and doubting that the water hole at Las Peñuelas can supply the whole camp, I, the governor and captain general, ordered them to go ahead for the two days' journey of record in the above order of this date to Capt. Roque Madrid.

I left this outpost before sunset with the whole camp. I arrived with it at eight o'clock at night at the place they call El Perrillo, Our Lord having seen fit in His divine providence to give us rain showers that began at vespers and continued until about midnight. Although all the men of the camp were exhausted from being wet, we were assured of having water and that there would be some at the outpost of Las Peñuelas. At dawn, I ordered the men-at-arms from the camp to ride there. So that it may be of record, I signed it at the outpost of El Perrillo at nine o'clock at night on 27 August with my secretary of government and war, the alferez, and the captain of the horse guard.
Don Diego de Vargas Zapata Luján Ponce de León
Juan de Dios Lucero de Godoy
Diego Arias de Quirós
Before me, Alfonso Rael de Aguilar, secretary of government and war

Arrival at Las Peñuelas

Today, Thursday, the twenty-eighth of the present month, after having attended mass, I, the governor and captain general, left, having sent the allied Indian warriors from this place of El Perrillo to that of Las Peñuelas. About a league before arriving, I met Capt. Roque Madrid on the road with the convoy of wagons and pack mules. He informed me that there was sufficient water, because they had had abundant showers the night I arrived at the outpost of Las Peñuelas. In the ciénaga in the cañada, I found a water hole sufficient for the whole camp. I called a halt there for the night until the following day. I immediately sent six soldiers to reconnoiter the water hole of El Muerto, [17] 6 leagues away. So that it may be of record, I signed it with the captain, the alferez of the company, and my secretary of government and war.

Don Diego de Vargas Zapata Luján Ponce de León
Roque Madrid
Juan de Dios Lucero de Godoy
Before me, Alfonso Rael de Aguilar, secretary of government and war

> Information from a soldier following the above order who went to reconnoiter the water hole of El Muerto

On that day, before vespers, one of the soldiers from among those of the above order arrived, having returned from the place called Paraje del Muerto. He reconnoitered it and saw the water hole, which barely had enough for the pack animals, livestock, and oxen. For this reason, I, the governor and captain general, gave an order to Capt. Roque Madrid at two o'clock on Friday morning, 29 August, that the wagons, pack animals, and livestock should be prepared and that he go with a squad of soldiers as its escort and convoy to that outpost and water hole of El Muerto, where he should stay until after midday. He should leave then, proceeding to the place called Fray Cristóbal[18] on the Río del Norte. He should stop for the night on the road without water, if they do not find any in the low ground or pans there may be because of the rain. I, the governor and captain general, shall leave, with the camp that follows me, to overtake him over that distance. I can join them about halfway, because the enemy Apaches frequent the mountain ranges and lands where we are traveling. So that the order may be of record, I signed it with the captain, the alferez of the company, and my secretary of government and war.

Don Diego de Vargas Zapata Luján Ponce de León
Roque Madrid
Juan de Dios Lucero de Godoy
Before me, Alfonso Rael de Aguilar, secretary of government and war

> Departure for the outpost of Fray Cristóbal and the Río del Norte

Today, Friday, 29 August, since the captain has carried out the above order, seeing that the trip to Fray Cristóbal and the Río del Norte is a long one and the day favorable—cloudy with a north wind—I, the governor and captain general, am leaving this outpost of Las Peñuelas at about eleven o'clock in the morning. I arrived with the camp at El Muerto when the captain was about to leave and stayed there until about five o'clock in the afternoon. When we all were together, we left, halting on a llano where we found a dry ciénaga, called La Cruz de Anaya.[19] That night, I ordered the captain to ride ahead early enough tomorrow, Saturday, to reach the river and outpost of Fray Cristóbal, so as not to risk exhausting the cattle and pack animals. So that the order and arrival at this outpost may be of record, I signed it with the captain, the alferez, and my secretary of government and war.

Don Diego de Vargas Zapata Luján Ponce de León
Roque Madrid
Juan de Dios Lucero de Godoy
Before me, Alfonso Rael de Aguilar, secretary of government and war

Arrival at Fray Cristóbal and the Río del Norte

Today, Saturday, 30 August, God Our Lord saw fit that I, the governor and captain general, and the camp should arrive at this outpost of Fray Cristóbal and the Río del Norte, without encountering any difficulties despite the length of the march. So that it may be of record, I signed it with the captain, the alferez, and my secretary of government and war.

Don Diego de Vargas Zapata Luján Ponce de León
Roque Madrid
Juan de Dios Lucero de Godoy
Before me, Alfonso Rael de Aguilar, secretary of government and war

Arrival at Senecú, whose pueblo is abandoned

Today, Sunday, 31 August, I, the governor and captain general, left Fray Cristóbal and arrived with the camp in front of the pueblo of Senecú,[20] which is 5 leagues away from the river on this side of the Río del Norte. So that it may be of record, I signed it with the captain, the alferez, and my secretary of government and war.

Don Diego de Vargas Zapata Luján Ponce de León
Roque Madrid
Juan de Dios Lucero de Godoy
Before me, Alfonso Rael de Aguilar, secretary of government and war

Arrival at the abandoned outpost of Juan García

Today, Monday, 1 September 1692, I, the governor and captain general, arrived with the camp at this outpost called Juan García.[21] The march was about 5 leagues. So that it may be of record, I signed it with the captain, the alferez, and my secretary of government and war.

Don Diego de Vargas Zapata Luján Ponce de León

Roque Madrid

Juan de Dios Lucero de Godoy

Before me, Alfonso Rael de Aguilar, secretary of government and war

Arrival within sight of the abandoned pueblo of Socorro

Today, Tuesday, the second of the present month, I, the governor and captain general, arrived with the camp at the abandoned and destroyed pueblo of Socorro,[22] a march of 7 leagues over a bad road. For the small wagons to pass, it was necessary to send the pack animals to carry their load, so that they could arrive at this place empty. So that it may be of record, I signed it with the captain, the alferez, and my secretary of government and war.

Don Diego de Vargas Zapata Luján Ponce de León

Roque Madrid

Juan de Dios Lucero de Godoy

Before me, Alfonso Rael de Aguilar, secretary of government and war

Arrival at the abandoned pueblo of Alamillo

Today, Wednesday, 3 September, I, the governor and captain general, arrived at this pueblo of Alamillo[23] with the camp. Halfway up the road, it was necessary to send the pack animals on because of the bad stretches so that the empty small wagons could get here. It was a march of 5 leagues. So that it may be of record, I signed it with the captain of the presidio, the alferez, and my secretary of government and war.

Don Diego de Vargas Zapata Luján Ponce de León

Roque Madrid

Juan de Dios Lucero de Godoy

Before me, Alfonso Rael de Aguilar, secretary of government and war

Arrival at the abandoned estancia that belonged to Felipe Romero

Today, Thursday, the fourth of the present month, I, the governor and captain general, arrived with the camp at this abandoned pueblo of Sevilleta.[24] To provide for the horses and mules, I went on ahead to the estancia they say belonged to Felipe Romero.[25] I called a halt there since the site had abundant pasture. Because the road was long and rough, it was necessary to send the pack animals on, so that empty, the small wagons, could make it here. The march was 6 or 7 leagues. So that it may be of record, I signed it with the captain of the presidio, the alferez, and the secretary of government and war.
Don Diego de Vargas Zapata Luján Ponce de León
Roque Madrid
Juan de Dios Lucero de Godoy
Before me, Alfonso Rael de Aguilar, secretary of government and war

Arrival at the hacienda of Francisco Gómez in the outpost of Las Barrancas

Today, Friday, 5 September, I, the governor and captain general, arrived at this outpost of Las Barrancas,[26] stopping with the camp next to the abandoned hacienda they say belonged to Francisco Gómez. The march was slightly more than 3 leagues. So that it may be of record, I signed it with the captain, the alferez, and my secretary of government and war.
Don Diego de Vargas Zapata Luján Ponce de León
Roque Madrid
Juan de Dios Lucero de Godoy
Before me, Alfonso Rael de Aguilar, secretary of government and war

Arrival within sight of the hacienda of Tomé Domínguez

Today, Saturday, 6 of the present month, I, the governor and captain general, arrived with the camp within sight of the hacienda they say belonged to Tomé Domínguez.[27] The march was 5 leagues. Because the road was very sandy, it was necessary to send the pack animals to bring the loads from the wagons so they could arrive there. So that it may be of record, I signed it with the captain, the alferez, and my secretary of government and war.

Don Diego de Vargas Zapata Luján Ponce de León
Roque Madrid
Juan de Dios Lucero de Godoy
Before me, Alfonso Rael de Aguilar, secretary of government and war

Arrival at the outpost and ruined estancia of Juan de Valencia

Today, Sunday, the seventh of the present month, after the very reverend apostolic missionary fathers celebrate mass, they can administer the holy sacrament of penance to the men of this camp who follow me tomorrow morning, the Day of Our Lady. [28] I stayed in this outpost called Valencia, having gone about 2 leagues. So that it may be of record, I signed it with the captain of the presidio, the alferez, and my secretary of government and war.
Don Diego de Vargas Zapata Luján Ponce de León
Roque Madrid
Juan de Dios Lucero de Godoy
Before me, Alfonso Rael de Aguilar, secretary of government and war

Arrival on the other side of the river opposite the hacienda of Juan Domínguez de Mendoza

Today, Monday, 8 September, after the very reverend apostolic missionary fathers had celebrated mass and administered the holy sacrament of penance to most of this army, I, the governor and captain general, left with two squads, the military leaders and officials, and the six citizens from El Paso. We were already well within the kingdom of New Mexico to reconnoiter whether there were any uprisen, rebel, apostate enemies in the pueblo of Isleta and the haciendas from there to the one belonging to Mre. de campo Juan Domínguez de Mendoza. [29]
I went ahead with these men. At my order, some soldiers scouted that land and went as far as the pueblo of Isleta, which is on the other side of the river and in sight of the camino real. No one was found, but they made out some tracks that were a few days old and headed in this direction. At the hacienda, which has some fruit trees in its garden, they found the same tracks. From this, it can be deduced that some of the uprisen Indians had come through to raid and, on the way, stopped to pick fruit from the trees. The march to where I called a halt and quartered the men was 8 or 9 leagues. So that it

may be of record, I signed it with those who went to reconnoiter the pueblo and hacienda, the sargento mayor, Alonso García;[30] the captain and squad leader, Juan Holguín; the alferez; and my secretary of government and war.
Don Diego de Vargas Zapata Luján Ponce de León
Alonso García
Juan López Holguín
Juan de Dios Lucero de Godoy
Before me, Alfonso Rael de Aguilar, secretary of government and war

Arrival at this hacienda they say belonged to Mejía

Today, Tuesday, the ninth of the present month, I, the governor and captain general, arrived with the men-at-arms at this hacienda of Mejía,[31] which borders on the road and is destroyed and abandoned, as are the rest. Seeing that this place was advantageous, level, and clear of bosque with water and some pastures, it occurred to me to leave the unnecessary oxen, wagons, cattle, and provisions here with some pack animals, together with the wagoners and a leader I leave with three soldiers. Thus, I am selecting this campsite to serve as a reserve for the provisions, so that the livestock and the horses, which are thin and tired, may recover so as not to risk losing them. To this end, I ordered a soldier to overtake the captain of the presidio, who had left with two squads for the convoy and escort of the camp, so he could come here. He arrived with everything at about eleven o'clock in the morning. So that it may be of record, I signed it with the captain, the alferez, and my secretary of government and war.
Don Diego de Vargas Zapata Luján Ponce de León
Roque Madrid
Juan de Dios Lucero de Godoy
Before me, Alfonso Rael de Aguilar, secretary of government and war

Appointment and order left for the leader staying at this outpost to guard the provisions, oxen, livestock, and horses

On 9 September, I, the governor and captain general, arrived at the outpost of Mejía, some 28 to 30 leagues from the villa of Santa Fe in the kingdom of New Mexico. The transportation of the provisions, small wagons, and livestock may hinder me in the entrada, conquest, and reduction of the uprisen, traitorous, treacherous, and apostate Indians who are in control of this kingdom. To make this entrada without any hindrance that might disturb my carrying out, arranging, and deciding upon the entradas to the villa and the pueblos of the apostates, I leave Rafael Téllez Girón appointed campaign captain and leader of those men in this outpost and hacienda of Mejía, so that he may be in charge of the guard and defense of the provisions I am leaving stored in this hacienda and also of the livestock, oxen, and horses.

> Reserve for the provisions and horses in the hacienda of Mejía with fourteen men and ten expected from Parral

For this, I am leaving him at present fourteen men with their weapons, horses, and munitions to maintain the necessary watch and guard over everything and patrol the countryside.

Since I am awaiting the fifty-man company from Parral, I leave an order for the captain for him to leave ten men from it who have the most fatigued animals, as well as their tiredest horses, so that guarding them as a unit may be in the charge of Rafael Téllez Girón. The ten men with the fourteen I am leaving are also to be under his command. They are to keep, fulfill, and carry out the orders he will give them as their captain and leader and should obey him completely without failing in the punctual attendance to everything, standing their watches and taking the necessary precautions.

So that the provisions, livestock, horses, and oxen may have greater security and defense, I am leaving it to him to corral the livestock and horses. I order him to round them up at about eight or nine o'clock at night and guard them. They are to sleep corralled until the third watch, when he and the men he thinks he needs will let them out. He is also to reconnoiter the countryside. Assuming that the men-at-arms from Parral arrive, if he thinks he needs to find a better campsite because of the pastures, he can go on to the hacienda and outpost I took a look at with him today, the one called Doña Luisa's,[32] where he can go with his men for its sheltered and fertile pastures.

In case the men from Parral do not come, he is to remain at this campsite until I, the governor and captain general, decide, order, and direct something else. So that what was referred to may be of record, I signed it with the captain of the presidio, the alferez, the newly appointed captain, and my secretary of government and war.

Don Diego de Vargas Zapata Luján Ponce de León
Roque Madrid
Juan de Dios Lucero de Godoy
Rafael Téllez Girón
Before me, Alfonso Rael de Aguilar, secretary of government and war

> Letter and order to the captain of the reinforcements whom the governor and captain general leaves as leader and campaign captain for the reserve of the provisions and guard of the livestock and horses

Once I had arrived at the abandoned outpost and hacienda of Mejía, I recognized the difficulty of transporting the provisions, livestock, oxen, and tired horses. Since I was ready to decide about the entrada to the pueblos of the traitorous, apostate rebels and the villa of Santa Fe of this kingdom of New Mexico, it seemed to me advantageous to rid myself of this burden to succeed in the operations and decisions with the boldness my zeal demands. Disregarding the small number of men for such an undertaking, I am leaving in this outpost the horses, mules, oxen, and provisions as a reserve.

I have appointed Afz. Rafael Téllez Girón as leader of its guard with the title of campaign captain. I leave only fourteen men, because I have so few with me, so that he will have some protection and be able to resist the enemy, whether Pueblos or Apaches. Thus, despite this small number, I leave him those men. I command and order that from those who are being brought, ten soldiers be left at his order and remain as reinforcements under the orders of Rafael Téllez Girón. They should be the ones with the tiredest animals. Likewise, the rest of the animals the soldiers bring can recover, leaving them all together. I also leave at present the supplies of meat and biscuit they will need and the order that he should assist them in everything they ask. By this letter, I also order and command him to go with the forty men of their company to the villa of Santa Fe by way of Santo Domingo without delay.

> The governor continues the trip with forty soldiers and ten citizens from El Paso to Cochiti to make a dawn raid with the missionaries and fifty Indians

I am leaving this afternoon, St. Nicholas's Day,[33] by the grace of God Our Lord, trusting in His divine mercy, with forty soldiers, leaving six with the provisions and horses I bring. Ten citizens are also in the convoy. They followed me from El Paso so that they could accompany the provisions and horses with the Indians when they overtook me. As I repeat, I am leaving this afternoon with the forty soldiers and two reverend missionary fathers, fray Miguel Muñiz and fray Francisco Corvera. The reverend missionary father, fray Cristóbal Alonso Barroso, will remain with the camp. Only fifty Indians will be able to follow me, because I shall be going so fast that I shall leave this outpost with only two horses per man, in addition to the one that is saddled, to make a dawn raid and lay siege to the pueblo of Cochiti, since it is the most populous and strongest. From there, if God sees fit, I shall go on to San Felipe and Santo Domingo to leave them in such a state that the gentlemen soldiers may pass unimpeded. I am sorry the most excellent lord viceroy gave them such an order. Until I see them in the villa of Santa Fe, should God see fit to give me success, I shall not be persuaded of their arrival. I hope they will be safe and sound in your company. May God keep you many years. From this outpost and abandoned hacienda of Mejía, 10 September 1692.

Don Diego de Vargas Zapata Luján Ponce de León
Lord Capt. Juan Páez Hurtado

> Departure with the forty soldiers and fifty Indians I take for the dawn raid and siege to reduce or conquer Cochiti

At this outpost and abandoned hacienda of Mejía on the tenth of the present month of the current year, having already ordered that the tired horses, mules, oxen, provisions, and men to guard and escort them be handed over to the campaign captain named in these proceedings, I, the governor and captain general, realized at about noon that I was in a place from which to make a dawn raid at one of the pueblos on the road and main route to the villa of Santa Fe, principal city of this kingdom of New Mexico.

I remained waiting for the reinforcement of the fifty soldiers the most excellent lord viceroy, the Conde de Galve, ordered to come from the presidios of Parral. Their arrival at El Paso and departure are doubtful, and I do not know of them. For these reasons, I had to leave on 21 August of the present year. Because of the possibility of being noticed by Indian hunters from the uprisen, apostate rebels of this kingdom, and in order neither to lose nor miss the opportunity to reduce or conquer them by force of arms, I am ordering Mre. de campo Roque Madrid, alferez and sergeant of the presidio of El Paso under my command, to immediately prepare forty soldiers. They should each take two extra horses as remounts, not counting the ones they are riding. They should be ready at two o'clock in the afternoon at the gate of this hacienda and guard post with fifty swift Indian allies.

Order to make the dawn raid at Cochiti and how it will be done

They and the two very reverend apostolic missionary fathers, fray Miguel Muñiz and fray Francisco Corvera, should go with me to make a dawn raid against the pueblo of Cochiti. Having arrived there, we will lay siege, surrounding it so as to better assure that no one can leave. The order I give them all is that they praise the blessed sacrament and the name of His Most Holy Mother five times. Neither the soldiers nor Indians, who will be given the order by interpreters, are to fire or begin the fight without my order, on pain of death. Although the rebels may answer me stubbornly and rebelliously in their apostasy and not accept the goal I wish for them, to give the proper humble obedience to the two majesties, the two very reverend fathers will persuade and exhort them through interpreters, in accord with their fervent spirit. If this is not obtained, I shall give the order through the general adjutant, Diego Varela.[34]

Order left for the sargento mayor so that he may go with the men who remain as escort of the convoy of provisions, pack animals, horses, mules, and Indians of the camp

For the convoy and escort of the provisions I bring and guard of horses, mules, pack animals, and Indian allies, I ordered Sgto. mayor Cristóbal Tapia to follow me with the men, horses, mules, six soldiers, and ten citizens with the artillery captain to the pueblo of Cochiti. They should conceal themselves and avoid the Indians from Santo Domingo and San Felipe in such a way that, considering the few men I have, he may arrive to assist me. He is aware of the fortifications and population at the pueblo of Cochiti. Since this is so, the pueblos of Santo Domingo and San Felipe are to be left until after Cochiti's surrender, Our Lord seeing fit. The sargento mayor will order the men in his charge and the pack animals to be ready by two o'clock in the afternoon.

Three missionary fathers

So that the departure may be of record, as well as the order for the entrada, siege, and the manner of its reduction; and the order for the sargento mayor, accompanied by the reverend missionary father, fray Cristóbal Alonso Barroso (for the three apostolic fathers come both to further the goal of His will and administer the holy sacraments to the army), I signed it with the military leaders named and my secretary of government and war on the day, month, and year ut supra.

Don Diego de Vargas Zapata Luján Ponce de León
Roque Madrid
Cristóbal Tapia
Francisco Lucero de Godoy
Juan de Dios Lucero de Godoy
Before me, Alfonso Rael de Aguilar, secretary of government and war

Entrada to the pueblo of Cochiti

Today, Thursday, eleventh of the present month, having traveled since yesterday afternoon, Wednesday, when I left the outpost of Mejía with the men whose departure is of record to make a dawn raid at this pueblo of Cochiti, I, the governor and captain general, have not stopped since that time until entering this pueblo of Cochiti.

Entrada to Cochiti at daybreak on 11 September

At daybreak, I arrived, surrounded it, and entered its plaza, where its cuarteles and dwellings are. They are in poor condition because they are abandoned, as is the pueblo. Riding with the soldiers to lay siege, I saw at the entrance as I passed, a very large milpa of maize, melons, and squash. I had decided with everyone's agreement to pursue the opportunity and enterprise of seeking the surrender of the people presumed to inhabit the pueblo. All the citizens of El Paso and those who came with me held this opinion. The Indians who guided me assured me of it as well. Even in the pueblo of El Paso, it was presumed to be so. It was an established opinion that the surrender of the pueblo would be a victory of greater consequence and triumph than even that of the villa. It is said that the Indians who inhabited the pueblo, however, have abandoned it for their safety and because of their fear of the Spaniards, selecting a place more to their liking.

He found it abandoned

So that the vigilance and resolve with which I left the outpost of Mejía, not stopping the march, whose apparent distance, from the time it took, was 16 to 18 leagues, and so that the entrada and discovery that the pueblo was abandoned and ruined, as were Puaray[35] and Sandia, which I passed, may be of record, I signed it today, on this date, with the captain of the presidio, the alferez, and my secretary of government and war.

Don Diego de Vargas Zapata Luján Ponce de León
Roque Madrid
Juan de Dios Lucero de Godoy
Before me, Alfonso Rael de Aguilar, secretary of government and war

Entrada to the pueblo of Santo Domingo

Immediately after, on the morning of 11 September in the plaza of the abandoned pueblo of Cochiti, because I was some distance from the pueblo called Santo Domingo, and the opinion held in the pueblo of El Paso was that it was inhabited by many Indians and nearby on the camino real that goes to the villa of Santa Fe, I, the governor and captain general, ordered the men-at-arms of my company to remount. They had just made a foray and entrada, and so that they could make another to the pueblo of Santo Domingo before it grew later in the day, I commanded and gave the order to the captain and leader of the presidio for him to cross with a squad to the other side of the river. This is so that if the Indians thought to be in the pueblo see the dust from the horses, discover me, and flee from the pueblo, they can be turned back and surrounded by the men I have with me.

Order about the pueblo of Santo Domingo and arrival there, finding it abandoned

I left there, arrived at, and surrounded the next pueblo. Entering its plaza, I examined the pueblo and found it very strong with high walls and abandoned dwellings and cuarteles. It is about 3 leagues away, rather more than less. So that the entrada and discovery of the abandoned pueblo may be of record, I signed it with the captain of the presidio, the alferez, and my secretary of government and war.
Don Diego de Vargas Zapata Luján Ponce de León
Roque Madrid
Juan de Dios Lucero de Godoy
Before me, Alfonso Rael de Aguilar, secretary of government and war

Arrival of the sargento mayor and artillery captain with the provisions and horses

Immediately after, on the same day, month, and year, at about ten in the morning, the sargento mayor and artillery captain arrived at this pueblo of Santo Domingo. I had sent two soldiers to him to give him the information that I was at this pueblo, so that he might not go on to Cochiti. In compliance, they arrived with the provisions, horses, and men under his command.

Information they give about the Indians of San Felipe

He gave me the information that, as they were going along the road, they found the Indians from the pueblo of San Felipe who formerly lived down by the riverbank living on the mesas. As soon as they descried the Spaniards from the mesas, they all left their houses.

Information about having seen Indians of the pueblo of San Felipe, who fled as soon as they saw our men

Sgto. mayor don Fernando de Chaves and Capt. Antonio Jorge were in the escort and had advanced ahead of it on point. They stated that they saw an Indian in the distance and called him, signaling him to come to them. They stated that the Indian came on horseback. They told him that he and all the people of his pueblo should come down, that we were coming neither to make war on them nor to harm them. The Indian answered them in Castilian that they did not want war but peace with the Spaniards. Because the Tewas and Tanos, who all speak the same language, were making war against them and causing much damage, they celebrated the coming of the Spaniards and would help them and go kill the Tewas. The Indians told them they should wait in the pueblo and they would go call the people who were fleeing. The Spaniards replied that he had come down at just the right moment. In fulfillment of my order, these declarants carried out the one I had given the sargento mayor, and under it followed the march. They do not know if he returned or not. They saw that the Indians were taking their sheep, goats, and other animals that were in the cañada when they left, fleeing their pueblo. When they spoke with the Indian, they also saw a little corral with sheep and goats. The escort neither harmed the Indians nor entered the pueblo to sack it, which might frighten them. Instead, they did not follow them, though they could have easily run roughshod over them, plundering, and taking the livestock. They harmed neither their persons, property, nor milpas. So that it may be of record that they persevered and persisted in their flight and that their proposition about peace between us is fraudulent, I signed it with the sargento mayor and Capt. Antonio Jorge, with the witnesses of these proceedings, the captain of the presidio, the alferez, and my secretary of government and war.

Don Diego de Vargas Zapata Luján Ponce de León
Roque Madrid
Cristóbal de Tapia
Don Fernando de Chaves
Antonio Jorge
Juan de Dios Lucero de Godoy
Before me, Alfonso Rael de Aguilar, secretary of government and war

Departure from the pueblo of Santo Domingo for the dawn raid at the villa of Santa Fe

On that day, 11 September, the Indian Esteban came. In accord with the information above, I had sent him to the lomas and mesas of the pueblo of San Felipe. The Indian saw that there was no one in either place. So as not to delay myself with a matter that can be attended to on the return trip, if God Our Lord sees fit, I, the governor and captain general, ordered all the men to prepare to leave to march to the villa of Santa Fe. When we were all together at about five o'clock in the afternoon, I left the pueblo with the camp.

To the villa of Santa Fe

Less than a league away, we found the road and a cuesta composed of malpais, so eroded by continuous rain and the passage of time that it could not be crossed. It was necessary to clear the way by hand and move the two small wagons, gun carriages with the bronze cannon, and large stone mortar by brute strength. This forced a halt at a place called Las Bocas,[36] with the camp arriving after vespers. Because the road was so difficult and filled with gullies, we had to spend the night at a campsite on the plain surrounded by mountains. The distance of that march was 3 leagues. So that it may be of record, I signed it with the captain of the presidio, the alferez, and my secretary of government and war.
Don Diego de Vargas Zapata Luján Ponce de León
Roque Madrid
Juan de Dios Lucero de Godoy
Before me, Alfonso Rael de Aguilar, secretary of government and war

The march continues to the pueblo of Cieneguilla

Today, Friday, 12 September of the current year, I, the governor and captain general, arrived at this pueblo called Cieneguilla,[37] which I reconnoitered and found abandoned. Since the road seemed to have moved, because it was bad for 3 leagues, eroded and filled with gullies by the continuous rains, I halted with the camp, waiting for sunset. At that time, I advised and ordered the men-at-arms to be prepared for the entrada. Once they were ready, I left with the camp.

Words the governor and captain general speaks to the men-at-arms of the camp

On a plain, before vespers, I told them all that, as loyal vassals of his majesty, they should carry out their duties and attend to the fast-approaching enterprise and battle at hand, which were such important obligations. As Catholics, it was our responsibility to defend our holy faith and, as vassals of his majesty, the reputation of his arms. Among other things, I told them that although we had so few men for the enterprise, I was confident of their sense of duty. Because of the respect they owed me, I trusted they would carry it out for me and I would achieve the triumph I wished for the honor and service of both majesties.

Traveling until about eleven o'clock at night, I called a halt at the end of the treeless plain on the bank of an arroyo called Arroyo Seco, although at the time there was water in it. I stopped with the camp to await the appropriate hour, which I told the captain of the presidio, other leaders, and war officials, would be three o'clock in the morning, based on their knowledge of the position of the stars. So that it may be of record, I signed it with the captain of the presidio, the alferez, and my secretary of government and war.
Don Diego de Vargas Zapata Luján Ponce de León
Roque Madrid
Juan de Dios Lucero de Godoy
Before me, Alfonso Rael de Aguilar, secretary of government and war

Entrada to the villa of Santa Fe

Today, Saturday, 13 September of the current year, 1692, at about two in the morning, the captain of the presidio, in compliance with my order, ordered the men-at-arms to mount up with their weapons. He reported to me, the governor and captain general, that they had mounted their horses a little after three when the whole camp was ready to follow me. As a result, I mounted up, and having gone along the camino real, came upon a tumbledown hacienda, which the captain of the presidio said was his. I halted there to pass the time while the camp gathered, since it was spread out and the bosque thick.

Once we were all together, I continued the march. On a llano, I stopped again so that the men might gather, because it was a dark night. While there, I asked one of the reverend apostolic missionary fathers to grant absolution to me, as well as the men of the camp who requested it. Once it was given and received, we again marched toward the bajada from the vega and open country where they said the villa would be, a quarter-league away. At that place, I again halted to collect the men-at-arms.

Order the governor and captain general gives his camp within sight of the villa of Santa Fe

Once they were all together, I told them that my order was that, after entering the plaza of the villa[38] in sight of and near the fortress of the apostate, rebel, treacherous traitors, and their pueblo, the whole camp was to say five times, "Praise be the blessed sacrament of the altar." No one was to begin the battle, neither the men-at-arms nor the Indian allies, who are to be told this by the interpreters, although most of them and their captains speak and understand our language. The signal I would give to all to begin the battle and start the war with all force and courage was for me to unsheathe the sword I carried.

Having given the order, I continued the march, going in close formation. After a short distance, I found myself in the villa's milpas, which surround its plaza, and we gave praise to the Lord. Having done so, the people of the villa immediately came out onto the ramparts of the fortress, occupying them from end to end with all sorts of people, men, women, boys and girls, and children. As dawn was breaking, their forms could be distinguished, and "Praise be the holy sacrament" was repeated to them. The interpreters, Sgt. Juan Ruiz de Cáceres, Pedro Hidalgo,[39] Sebastián de Monroy Mondragón,[40] and Pedro de Tapia, spoke to them in their languages, Tewa and Tano, which are one and the same.

They replied that they believed we were not Spaniards, but Pecos and Apache liars. I, the governor and captain general, repeated the alabado to them, ordering the interpreters to say it. Having said it to them, they replied that if we were Spaniards, why were we not shooting? and that I should shoot an harquebus into the air. I replied to this that I was a Catholic and they should calm themselves. As the sun came up, it would grow lighter, and they would see the image of the Blessed Virgin carried on the standard.

To the Blessed Virgin

They replied, doubting this, saying that the bugle should be sounded to see with certainty that we were Spaniards. At this, I then ordered not only that the bugle be sounded, but also the war drum, ordering the squadron to pass the word that no one should get excited or begin the war. I also ordered each squad and the captain of the presidio to take the corners and positions of the fortress, seeing whether there were more gates than the one I, the governor and captain general, was laying siege to. They did so, and I remained with a squad made up of the leaders, the six citizens who had followed me, and the interpreters.

They are in a fighting mood and reply that they have to kill all the Spaniards

Having sounded the instruments of war, they replied that they were ready to fight for five days, they had to kill us all, we must not flee as we had the first time, and they had to take everyone's life. At the same time, they began a furious shouting that must have lasted more than an hour.

Shouting for one hour

With the interpreters and the men-at-arms, I saw at the same time the growing number of people hurriedly going about filling in the gaps in the ramparts, newly fortifying them with many round stones, large stones from the metates, and objects to take the offensive against our men and kill them as they advanced, if they could not breach the walls because of their height. This was done with considerable risk and danger to our lives, because of the massive, connected nature of the walls. The Indians were safe from anyone killing them. In the interim, while they were shouting and screaming, some of their leaders stood up, shouting many shameful things in their language, which the interpreters, including the sergeant of the company and the others, told me. I ordered him to tell them to calm themselves and be assured that I was not coming to do them any harm whatsoever. To this, they replied that we should not let the horses eat from the milpas. I said to them that the milpas were safe and would not be damaged. I had so ordered and had men and soldiers guarding them.

After sunrise, I approached about twenty paces closer with the interpreter, my secretary of government and war, and the captain of the presidio, telling them that I had come, sent from Spain by his majesty, the king, our lord, to pardon them and so that they might again be Christians, as they had been, and the devil would not lead them astray. This was so they might be assured of my truthfulness, given that they knew the Virgin, our Lady, whose image was on the standard, as witness to the truth I was telling them so that they might believe and be assured of my good intentions. I ordered the royal alferez to show them the image of the Virgin, as I myself took it in my hand, showing it and saying to them that they had but to look at her and recognize her to be our Lady the Queen and the Blessed Virgin and that on the other side of the royal standard were the arms of the king, our lord, so that they might know he sent me. The soldiers had come under my command by his order, and I was his governor and captain general, as I was theirs. They should not doubt what I was telling them, but see I was telling them the truth. I pitied them because they believed in the devil, who deceived them, and not in God Our Lord, and they should see that they were Christians like us.

They replied to this that if it was true I was the new governor, I should take off my morion so they could see my face clearly. At that, I asked my arms bearer for my hat, and, with it, I took off my morion. I went closer so that they might see and clearly recognize me, even taking the kerchief from my head. They said that when the Spaniards were in the kingdom, they had made peace with the Apaches and later gone out and killed them. They said I would do the same with them, to which I replied that the Apaches were not Christians but traitors who, while at peace, came in to better assure their thefts and killings, as they had done when the Spaniards lived in the land. They themselves came out of their homes to defend and guard their lives and those of their wives and children in them. What they had of clothing and horses, the Apaches took away with them. Even with the care the Spaniards had taken, in the pueblos where no soldiers lived or served, the Apaches succeeded in killing and robbing them, carrying off their property and their wives and children for slaves.

So that they might believe that peace was sure and I would pardon them in the name of his majesty, the king, our lord, I would offer as a witness the image of the Blessed Virgin on the royal standard, which I again showed them, taking it anew in my hand. Bracing myself in the stirrups, I effectively made the gestures necessary because of their disbelief. Taking the rosary from my pocket, I showed them a holy cross of Jerusalem I had placed on it, telling them that I took as my witnesses the holy cross and the Virgin, our most holy Lady, whose image I carried on the royal standard they were looking at. I would pardon them in his majesty's name, and they should believe me and come down and shake hands with me. I also brought the three fathers so that they might absolve them of the great sin they had committed of having left our holy faith.

They replied to this that although they believed what the governor and the fathers told them was true, they had had to work very hard, having been ordered to build the churches and homes of the Spaniards, and they were whipped if they did not do what they were told. The Spaniards and citizens had done this, and they indicated and named Javier, Quintana, and Diego López,[41] asking whether they had come with us. I said they had not, and I did not know whether they were already dead. They could be assured that they would no longer come here.

One of the Indians, who I later found out was named Antonio and had been given the surname Bolsas, was very fluent in Spanish and was on top of the big rampart above the gate. He spoke for everyone, who, with their lances, heavy spears, bows, arrows, and large lances,[42] also occupied some other ramparts. Whenever the men-at-arms made any movement, the Indians quickly became excited, thinking war was about to break out.

The rest of the camp and provisions arrive
Nota bene

At this time, the rest of the men of the camp and the provisions arrived. I ordered them to halt on the llano beyond the milpas and within sight of the fortress, about a musket shot away, and that the bronze stone mortar and the cannon should also be placed with the camp. It should be garrisoned with the squad of cavalry, muleteers, and some allies, all together, and no one was to move without my order.

The governor orders his camp quartered away from the milpas

Antonio Bolsas spoke for the traitorous, rebel Indians, using as an excuse for their uprising that the devil was at work in their thoughts. Finally, he stated that the guilty had already died and the living were not at all guilty and most of them had been young men then. I replied that they could all be assured that I had already told them I was pardoning them in his majesty's name. I repeated this, with the Blessed Virgin and the holy cross I was showing them as my witnesses, and that I was telling them the truth.

At this, one of the Indians came out through the gate with his lance, leather shield, bow, and arrows, as if to say they were unafraid and were there. I replied to him that he should calm himself, approach me, and shake my hand. He responded in a different way, until as a result of what those above said to him in his language, he went back in, having first said that two of the three fathers who came should follow. Father fray Cristóbal Barroso and Father fray Francisco Corvera dismounted and wanted to enter, at which I, the governor and captain general, seeing that they were already below the rampart and Father fray Cristóbal was hurrying to enter, said to them, "Your reverences, stop!" shouting and calling them to return. I so ordered and requested, and the fathers, with much courtesy and care, obeyed me. I told them it was not the time for them to do such a thing, since the Indians were seen to be so rebellious and possessed by the devil. Once inside, they could kill them, and there would be no way to save their lives, with which we would all risk losing ours.

Warriors from neighboring pueblos came toward the flanks and corners

At that time, the squads on both flanks and corners spotted many men on horses and foot coming from the neighboring pueblos. Without a doubt, they would have rushed us from behind. When I arrived, an Indian, or someone in the milpas or torreones, had gone to warn the pueblos. Their men came, as I say, as fast as possible on foot and horseback with their weapons, most of them with lances on long shafts. According to what I later asked them, they have an Indian blacksmith who makes the lances for them. I ordered the captain of the presidio to leave the siege operations with a squad and, without going far, intercept those men and prevent them from passing. The other squad was to do the same on the other side, while I remained holding the position and siege of the fortress with the men from the third squad and the allies distributed among several positions.

The captain carried out my order, as did the leader of the second squad. The rebels, who were paying close attention to everything going on, sensed that we might keep them from being aided and so raised a great uproar from their ramparts, saying over and over that their men were on the way and that we would see. I replied to them that I did not fear them though they were all together, but pitied them because they did not believe in my good intentions. I had already told them that the devil was deceiving them. If I had wanted to kill them, I would not have said the alabado, but, as soon as I arrived, without making a sound or awakening them with the alabado, I would have made sure they were dead. I would not have allowed time for the men coming to their aid to find them alive. To favor them, as they may judge for themselves, I have not ordered them killed, because I only wish for them to become Christians again. I come to pardon them, as I have told them. They were rebellious and did not heed my kind words, but stubbornly persisted in securing themselves in their fortifications, bringing many round stones, painting themselves red, and making gestures and demonstrations so as to bring on war.

Seeing that they had many small reservoirs in front of the fortress near the gate, but noticing that since they had no water in them they had conduits going inside, I, the governor and captain general, ordered four men from my squad to go immediately to higher ground to divert and cut off the water from the ditch that was used in the fortress.

He cut off their water by diverting it

They did so, taking Indian allies and tools at my order to carry it out, as was done. The besieged rebels were saddened and greatly regretted it, asking why, if we had come in peace and as friends, we were depriving them of water. I answered them that, as far as I was concerned, peace was certain. So that they might see it was so, they should come down from the ramparts and come out to give me the peace. They were defiant and repeated that the fathers should come inside, and that afterward they would begin to come out. The fathers also said they all wanted to go in.

He restrains the fathers, who do not enter because they may be killed

Father fray Miguel Muñiz asked me for permission to do that, but I thanked him and said, "Father, it is not time for your reverence and the other fathers to enter, because the rebels are treacherous and can commit an atrocity against your reverences and even kill you. It is wrong for me to place you at such risk or consent to your going in."

Seeing that it was about eleven o'clock in the morning, and that they were persevering in new demonstrations, some coming out and others entering, I decided neither to risk anything else nor waste time, since I had for my part justly carried out the actions of a loyal Catholic vassal of his majesty by requesting his vassals to render proper obedience and vassalage to him, our holy faith, and Divine Majesty. In addition, I had forty men in the plaza and surrounding positions, with others guarding the entrances. The Indian allies able to take up arms were involved in the siege and numbered some fifty to sixty, since the rest were at the camp guarding the horses and supplies. Thus, I said through the interpreters that I was going to advise them once more of the peace I had required of them in his majesty's name. I was going again to wait for the peace without harming them, pardoning them all. I was reassuring them of it with our Lady, the Blessed Virgin, and the holy cross as my witnesses.

> The governor and captain general requires and gives the period of one
> hour to give the peace and render obedience
> Period of one hour to give the peace

I was giving them a period of one hour in which to decide and determine to render their obedience and give the peace. If they did not, I would consume and destroy them by fire and sword, holding nothing back. Thus, I make known, require, and give them the period of one hour, so that afterward they may not complain about their misery.

They replied in the desperate terms that are of record that I should do whatever I wanted. I ordered all the camp and the reverend fathers to come with me to the camp for breakfast and to arrange for the men-at-arms to do so at the same time. I carried that out, sending chocolate and biscuit to everyone. I ordered them to set out and take supplies of bullets and powder and the artillery captain to take the large, bronze stone mortar and the cannon down to the plaza, loaded to my satisfaction.

> The governor's preparations for the decision to start fighting, because
> the period of one hour had passed

When we were about to go to the plaza to begin the war, since about two hours had been spent sending refreshments and breakfast to the squads at their posts, and changing the horses for me and my escort, the sergeant and other soldiers arrived, bringing two Indians on horseback and one on foot, with their weapons, arrows, lances, and leather shields.

Two Indians arrived from the pueblos of Tesuque, Santa Clara, and San Lázaro

I received them with kindness, and they told me they were from the pueblos of Tesuque, Santa Clara, and San Lázaro.[43] Having word of my arrival, they were coming in response to the call from the rebellious, besieged traitors in the villa. They were all coming because they had learned of my arrival. They had been advised about it by some Indians from the villa who had gone to a dance at Santa Clara Pueblo.

I replied to them that I had not come for the reason they thought, to kill them, rob them, and carry off their women and children, but to pardon them so they might again become Christians. That was why the king, our lord, had sent me and why I had brought the fathers along with me. They should tell all the people of their pueblos to be calm and not leave them, because they were safe. So that they might believe me, I showed them the image of our Lady, the Blessed Virgin, which was on the royal standard, using it and the holy cross as witnesses to my truthfulness and good intentions.

The Indian chief Domingo, a Tewa, also arrives

After this, another soldier arrived, accompanied by a prominent Indian, their chief, who said his name was Domingo of the Tewa nation. I treated him with kindness and said the same things to him that I had said to the other three, adding in their presence that I had come to change neither their governors nor their captains, but to keep the ones they had since they were pleased with them. I had to leave them, because I had only come, and the king had only sent me, so that they might render him obedience as his vassals, which they were. I had come to pardon them so they might again be Christians. Thus, I ordered him to tell everyone, assuming that the people of the villa were subject to him and he should enter it to tell and counsel them. I would wait in the plaza for him to come out, since the period of one hour I had given them to come out of the fortress and render their obedience had already passed. If not, I was going to destroy the villa and fortress once and for all. For that reason, I was ordering that the large harquebuses, whose small wagons were being drawn by mules, be brought up, as he could see.

I told him many other things very gently and with all kindness, and the Indian responded warmly. I saw he had a heart that could be reduced. From this, I was certain that I could successfully convey my good intentions to the rebels through him. To better assure them, he was going, having already spoken with me. I had given him the explanation that would at last convince them to believe. It then occurred to me to take him at my side and enter the besieged plaza.

Having arrived there, I told him, with the rebels who remained on their ramparts hearing me, "Tell them, your children, who clearly understand what I have told them and what I have also told and ordered you to tell them. I must carry out my decision, based on their reply, because it is already late. The day will not end before what remains to be done is settled. This is why you have already seen that I have ordered the large harquebuses to be brought up." Then, their captain, Domingo, went in to speak to them.

Nota bene

He found them as rebellious as I had, and they paid little attention to him, remaining on the ramparts, not abandoning them. They spoke to him from there and defied him, neither accepting nor being assured about my proposal. During this time, the artillery captain entered with the cannon, the large stone mortar, and the wagoners. I ordered the pieces set in position and adjusted so that their operation and charges would be effective. The men aimed at the ramparts, so that at the same time, they could be free to mine the facade of the fort and pack the blastholes with the two small cases of gunpowder I had prepared to blast open breaches. We could then advance from all sides, and the few men who make up my camp could make the assault in greater safety. Their number was insufficient to assault an open pueblo, much less a walled and fortified place like the present one. Nevertheless, bravery and eagerness moved them. I received from each equally the enthusiasm and joy with which they heeded not the risk and danger to their lives, but their love as vassals of his majesty and Catholics. Thus, they made no complaint about the risk resulting from our lack of security because we had already been seen.

The ramparts are abandoned, with only a few rebels remaining

Squads of them continued to come from everywhere on foot and horseback, with weapons at the ready. We had already seen that a large squad of from forty to fifty Indians had taken the mesa at the right-hand corner of the fort.[44] It was necessary to send two squads to stop them. I remained at the siege operations in the plaza with the rest of the men, in order to quell the rebels' pride. As soon as they saw the cannon and stone mortar, they immediately abandoned the ramparts. I saw only a few loopholes occupied by the rebel Indians.

At this time, the Indian Domingo came to me, the governor and captain general. He told me very sadly that he had already told his people how good peace would be for them, reminding them of what had happened at Zia Pueblo. They should not be fools, but believe me. If they did not, he was tired of talking to them and responding to everything. They might want to die, but neither he nor the people of his pueblo did. He saw they were not obeying him, so he came out, taking his leave of them and told me he could not do anything with them. This is what he said to me and for his part, there was nothing more he could do.

They return to the ramparts

The Indians returned to their ramparts, occupying them in safety when they saw me at the siege operations in their plaza, speaking with their captain. I, the governor and captain general, went to the interpreters again, also ordering my royal alferez and secretary of government and war to come. Nearby and in front of the gate of the ramparts, speaking loudly, I again exhorted, persuaded, and warned them, saying it was now necessary for them to reply to me with their decision about whether they wanted to become Christians again, rendering the obedience and submission owed to our holy faith and to the king, our lord. I ordered them to come down and render obedience to the Divine and human majesties, reassuring them of a pardon, with our Lady, the Blessed Virgin, as my witness. I showed them her image on the royal standard, as I had so many times before. I showed it to them again and said they should give me their reply immediately. One person should speak for them all and they should not all speak at once, so that I might decide on peace or war. They replied that they would give me the peace if I returned to my camp with all the men, removed the large harquebuses, and came back with all the men unarmed. In that way, when we returned without our weapons to the plaza, they would come out to give me peace.

I replied that I was neither afraid of them nor humbled as they

were, confined, besieged, without water, and subject to my burning
them out and killing them all, which I could have done in the time
that had passed since I arrived. Domingo repeated what he had said
to them, and the fathers spoke to them through interpreters from the
plaza below their ramparts.

Nota bene

Two unarmed Indians came out to give me the peace. I received
them, shaking their hands, and, dismounting, embraced them. At
that time, the reverend father, fray Francisco Corvera, entered the
patio of the fortress, followed by the captain of the presidio, and then
by the reverend father, Miguel Muñiz, who emerged on the ramparts. The Indians, although frightened, began to come out to give
me the peace, which I gave them all, with all my love. I dismounted
and embraced them, shook their hands, and spoke words of tenderness and love, so that they might be reassured about my good intentions and greeting. In that way, they might make the others who had
not come down understand, although some women, young and old,
did come down.

When the plaza was empty, since they had immediately returned
to the fortress, the captain of the presidio came to inform me and
ask whether the squads should allow the people who had been detained
to enter, as well as those who, as is of record, were again seen on the
mesa. I replied to the captain that he and the squad that had been
with me should come with me. I also ordered my secretary of government and war to accompany me.

When I arrived at the mesa, I found a large squad of Indians from
the villa on foot and horseback who had gone to the dance at Santa
Clara Pueblo. I also found the captain of that pueblo with most of
his people. Drawing near to them, I said, "Praise be the blessed sacrament." Through the interpreters, I welcomed them and gave them
the peace in the manner referred to. I embraced them and shook
their hands after they had dismounted and laid their weapons aside.
I told them to order the people of their pueblo not to leave their
houses, because they were safe there, and that they could continue
living there as they always had with the same governor and captains,
if they were pleased with them. I also told them that the only thing
his majesty, the king, our lord, who was their lord and lord of all the
land, wanted was for them to be Christians again and not idolaters.

With that they were satisfied, and I took my leave of them. I returned to the plaza, ordering the captain of the fortress and all the rebels to wear crosses around their necks and set up a large cross in the middle of the patio of their house. Since it was after four or five o'clock in the afternoon, I withdrew with the fathers to eat, leaving the men distributed around the plaza and sides of the fortress. I also left the order that, unless they had a new one from me, they should not let any Indians enter the fortress. Re-forming with them, they could strengthen themselves and lay an ambush, which they could secure from outside, and attack the camp or horses. We could fear that some calamity might occur from this. In spite of peace, we should not leave our fear aside, but be diligent and vigilant, by dint of the sense of duty as good soldiers and his majesty's loyal vassals.

At the camp, seeing some Indians coming and going, I thought to put some trust in fortune, because God Our Lord had seen fit to provide a successful beginning. To better assure them that I did not fear them, and of the peace I had given and they had received, and the pardon I had granted them in his majesty's name, I decided to command and order as I did. I ordered the captain of the presidio to go to the plaza and gather the men-at-arms he had left at the siege operations and have them come by virtue of my order. I also ordered the artillery captain to move the cannon and large, bronze stone mortar, taking the mules to transport them. This was all carried out in the manner referred to. So that the entrada and what occurred during it; how the siege that was laid against the fortress in the plaza of the villa was raised; the questions, answers, and reports; and everything that has been referred to may be of record, as it is of record to the letter, so that its truth may be of record for all time, I signed it with the military leaders, war officials, citizens who knew how, and my secretary of government and war, on the said day ut supra.

Don Diego de Vargas Zapata Luján Ponce de León
Cristóbal de Tapia
Roque Madrid
Francisco Lucero de Godoy
José Gallegos[45]
Don Fernando de Chaves
Antonio Jorge
Alonso García
Pedro Hidalgo
Diego Arias de Quirós

Juan López Holguín
Diego Zervín[46]
Before me, Alfonso Rael de Aguilar, secretary of government and war

> Order the governor and captain general gives to his men-at-arms after
> having raised the siege laid in the plaza of the villa of Santa Fe against
> the fortress and walled pueblo

On 13 September 1692, the captain of the presidio, by virtue of
my order, gathered the men-at-arms with whom I had laid siege and
cordoned off the plaza and in it the fortress of the villa of Santa Fe.
The artillery captain brought the bronze cannon and large stone mortar and set them on their carriages at a place that faces the villa about
a musket shot away. I, the governor and captain general, designated
it as the plaza de armas for as long as I am present in this area, as it is
convenient for holding audience to listen to and receive the rebel
nations of the surrounding pueblos and provinces of this district and
kingdom in peace.

They have heard of my arrival from the Indians gathered today at
this outpost, who have spoken to me, and been received in peace.
Through these eyewitnesses, I have assured the others that they should
come to see me, in safety and without fear. I shall listen to and pardon them in his majesty's name, reassuring them in every way.

Because they are treacherous Indians and so accustomed to their
apostasy and freedom, they can join with others, so that, rebel and
allied, they may commit some outrage. We are so few, with the sierras so near and the montes surrounding us, that for our defense and
safety, I ordered that tonight the horses and mules should have two
squads on guard and not be allowed to wander, but be kept together,
though there may be little pasture. The other two squads are to change
horses immediately, leaving them saddled and bridled, and keep their
weapons at the ready, so that if there is a surprise attack, everything
will be battle ready to make war on the enemy. All the men of this
camp are to keep, fulfill, and carry out this order. So that they may
be informed about it, I order the captain and the alferez to notify
them. So that it may be of record, they signed it with me, the governor and captain general, and my secretary of government and war.
Don Diego de Vargas Zapata Luján Ponce de León
Roque Madrid
Juan de Dios Lucero de Godoy
Before me, Alfonso Rael de Aguilar, secretary of government and war

The governor and captain general goes to examine the fortress and see whether the holy cross is in place

Today, Sunday, 14 of the present month of the current year, the Day of the Exaltation of the Holy Cross,[47] I, the governor and captain general, spent the night with the vigilance required and the men-at-arms on guard duty. They told me that many people had come and gone from the fortress all night long and it would be risky to enter in my finery, as I had dressed, without weapons. Nevertheless, I told them I was going to be present at the absolution the reverend missionary fathers were going to grant the rebel, apostate Indians and that no one should fire without my order. They should remain on horseback in the plaza of the villa with only the leaders, their captain, and the citizens entering with me and the missionary fathers.

In this manner, I left, marching from the plaza de armas toward the fortress. When the alferez arrived with the royal standard, I ordered him to enter with me, the fathers, and the men-at-arms indicated. Once inside, I found a cross slightly shorter than a man's height set up on the patio. Within view of the Indians, I knelt on one knee and kissed the cross.

There were only eight or ten Indians on the patio because they were so afraid and suspicious. They said the men who had come with me should not come in, because the women were afraid and crying, and the boys and girls were frightened. I did this to please them and so that they might not think I was afraid of them. They were standing on the drawbar they used to close the gate. Once assured in this manner, they began to come down from their houses, which are high and have pole ladders. They put the ladders in place to come down, and when they go up, they raise them and put them in their houses, remaining safe there as though walled in, since no one can come in.

Revalidation of his majesty's possession of this kingdom and its vassals, ordering that the royal standard be raised in sign of this

Once all the people had come down and assembled, I told them through the interpreters that they could be calm, now that they knew my good intentions, and content that they would be pardoned and reduced to our holy faith and the king, our lord (may God keep him). They were his vassals, and in his royal name, I was returning to revalidate and reclaim his possession not only of this kingdom, provinces, and all the land, but also of them. This was because he was their lord and rightful king, and no other, and they should consider themselves fortunate to be his vassals and have such a king, lord, and sovereign monarch.

I also ordered the alferez to raise the royal standard three times, while I, the governor and captain general, told and ordered them to repeat three times, "Long live the king, our lord (may God keep him), Carlos II, king of all the Spains, all this New World, and the kingdom and provinces of New Mexico," which they said three times. "These are his kingdom and provinces and his vassals, newly reduced and conquered." They responded three times, "May he live for many years and reign happily." Having done so, with great rejoicing and showing their happiness, they threw their hats in the air, and the religious, the reverend missionary fathers, knelt and offered a prayer of thanksgiving.

All the populace was in front of the holy cross to hear the Te Deum.[48] The holy water having already been prepared, they then absolved them of their apostasy. This was preceded by a sermon the reverend father, fray Francisco Corvera, gave through an interpreter. After he granted absolution, which the Indians received kneeling with their hands together, some of them sang and repeated the alabado. When the ceremony was over, I embraced each of them again, shook their hands, and was greatly pleased by hearing them repeat the alabado to the women and children.

I took my leave of them and ordered the leaders to advise the men-at-arms not to shoot. This was so that the people expected from the other pueblos, would not think the peace had been broken because they heard shots, not knowing they would be made in celebration, and turn back and leave because of this novelty. I therefore gave the order so as not to risk the disturbance their flight might cause. So that what has been referred to—the possession, the absolution, and the rest—may be of record, I signed it with those who knew how and my secretary of government and war.

Don Diego de Vargas Zapata Luján Ponce de León
Roque Madrid
Don Fernando de Chaves
Antonio Jorge
Francisco Lucero de Godoy
Juan de Dios Lucero de Godoy
José Gallegos

Pedro Hidalgo
Before me, Alfonso Rael de Aguilar, secretary of government and war

He continues the actions of that day, 14 September

Today, Sunday, 14 September, at about noon, the Indian Domingo, principal leader of this pueblo, came and gave me the information that don Luis of the Picuris nation,[49] governor of all the pueblos of the Tewas and Tanos and to whom they give obedience, has sent word that he will come to see me tomorrow. He had gone to see the Navajo Apaches, who had sent for him. I kindly welcomed him, assuring him that don Luis could come to see me without fear.

He sends him a rosary as a safe-conduct

I sent him a rosary with Domingo, telling him, among other things, that as a Christian, I was sending him that rosary with the holy cross as my witness that I was coming to give him and all his people a sure peace. So that it may be of record, I signed it with the captain of the presidio, the alferez, and my secretary of government and war.
Don Diego de Vargas Zapata Luján Ponce de León
Roque Madrid
Juan de Dios Lucero de Godoy
Before me, Alfonso Rael de Aguilar, secretary of government and war

He continues on the same day, Sunday, 14 September 1692, when Indians from the three pueblos, San Lázaro, San Cristóbal, and Tesuque come to give the peace

On that day, Sunday, 14 of the present month of the current year, at this plaza de armas at about four o'clock in the afternoon, the captain and some Indians from the pueblos of San Lázaro, San Cristóbal, and Tesuque came before me, the governor and captain general, to see me and give me the peace. I spoke warmly to them, and they were happy, according to what the interpreters told me. So that it may be of record, I signed it with the captain of the presidio, the alferez, and my secretary of government and war.
Don Diego de Vargas Zapata Luján Ponce de León
Roque Madrid
Juan de Dios Lucero de Godoy
Before me, Alfonso Rael de Aguilar, secretary of government and war

On Monday morning, the governor and captain general sends another message to don Luis with the Indian, Antonio Bolsas, because he heard he is afraid he has been called in order to be captured

Today, Monday, 15 September of the current year, at sunrise, the Indian, Antonio Bolsas, arrived at my tent and told me that don Luis el Picurí, to whom they have given obedience while the Spaniards were not living here, was in San Juan Pueblo and already knew I was in this villa and what had happened. He was happy about the peace I, the governor and captain general, had given them and the pardon they had received in his majesty's name. He was also happy that the Indians could again be Christians, but, as he had been their head and leader, he feared they would seize him because they told him that the king, our lord, had ordered me to capture and take him to him.

Because Antonio Bolsas speaks Spanish, I questioned and answered him endlessly, replying to don Luis's doubts, occasioned by the mistrust and fear his great transgression caused. The last thing I said was, "Leave right away for Tesuque Pueblo. If you hurry, you may find don Luis there. Your leader and captain, Domingo, told me yesterday, Sunday, that he had said to tell me that although he might return late from seeing the Apaches at his pueblo of San Juan, he would travel all night to arrive at Tesuque today and then come on to see me. You will find him there, because Domingo speaks the truth and will have told him and given him the rosary I sent with him as a sign and as witness that he can come safely without fearing I may harm him. You will tell him the same."[50] With this, he left. So that it may be of record, I signed it with the captain, the alferez, and my secretary of government and war.

Don Diego de Vargas Zapata Luján Ponce de León
Roque Madrid
Juan de Dios Lucero de Godoy
Before me, Alfonso Rael de Aguilar, secretary of government and war

The governor goes with the fathers to the fortress to hear the mass that the absolved apostates were advised would be said in its patio, where they are advised and ordered that they should select compadres by tomorrow, when the fathers will baptize the children and many others

On the same day, Monday, 15 September of the current year, I, the governor and captain general, found that the enramada I had ordered the absolved apostate rebels to set up yesterday, Sunday, was already prepared and in it, the altar to celebrate thanksgiving for being newly reduced to and conquered for our holy faith. The mass was celebrated with the people who accompany me.

The reverend missionary father, fray Francisco Corvera, gave another sermon through an interpreter to those recently reduced. He told and exhorted them with very effective words and fervent, holy zeal that the parents and others should bring the infants and boys and girls born since they rebelled against the holy faith and were separated and apostate, so that they might have the privilege of becoming Christians through baptism. His reverence and the other fathers did so. They would be godfathers to those who selected and indicated them to be. They would do likewise with me, the governor and captain general, and the rest of the soldiers and Spaniards who come with the camp.

When the sermon was over, the mass continued. Afterward, the Santo presignum crucis,[51] the Our Father, the Hail Mary, and the Alabado were prayed through the principal interpreter for the actions recorded in these proceedings, Pedro Hidalgo.

I, the governor and captain general, again exhorted them with friendly words that every morning, just as they eat, they should pray in front of the holy cross, making the sign of the cross first, saying their prayers, the Our Father, the Hail Mary, the Salve, and the Alabado. They should do the same in the afternoon at the hour when the Spaniards pray vespers. They should do this with everyone present; the ones who know the prayers should pray with them. For this, I ordered those who know the prayers to be in charge and report to me, should God and the king, our lord, see fit to order me to return to see them when the fathers and Spaniards come. I looked to see whether they were wearing the crosses at their necks, as I had ordered them, and almost all were. I ordered all those who did not have crosses to put them on, so that the devil might leave and flee them. I also ordered them to call on Jesus, Mary, and Joseph when they were at war, out working, or sick, because in that way, they would have every relief. They should not forget to do so. They agreed, answering yes and nodding their heads.

With all said and done, I took leave of them, as did the fathers. We were all very happy about having managed to return the Indians to the veneration and exaltation of the name of Our Lord, Jesus Christ, and His adoration in the holy sacrifice of the Mass. This was a very moving experience for all, for not so long ago, it was thought that those Indians would not have this opportunity again. Because the day was stormy, it was not possible for the missionary fathers to carry out holy baptism. So that everything referred to may be of record, I signed it with the interpreter, the captain of the presidio, the alferez, and my secretary of government and war.

Don Diego de Vargas Zapata Luján Ponce de León

Roque Madrid

Juan de Dios Lucero de Godoy

Pedro Hidalgo

Before me, Alfonso Rael de Aguilar, secretary of government and war

Monday afternoon, 15 September, the Indian, don Luis Picurí, arrives to render obedience

On the same day, Monday, 15 September of the current year, at about five o'clock in the afternoon in this plaza de armas, the men-at-arms and I saw a squadron of Indians approaching along the camino real from Tesuque Pueblo, advancing out of the monte and mountain ranges that surround this villa. The ones in front were on foot and fully armed. Others followed them on horseback, also fully armed and advancing. Most of them had leather jackets. They halted within sight of the fortress and villa until various Indians went out to receive the squadron, and together directed their march to this plaza de armas.

Style of clothing don Luis wears and manner in which he arrives to render obedience

Shortly thereafter, a captain came with two other Indians, sent by don Luis Picurí, the leader of the pueblos and nations cited in these proceedings, asking permission to see me. Replying to his request, I said I wished this and would receive him with love. The captain returned to give him the message. On the other side of the arroyo, about sixty paces away, don Luis dismounted from the horse he had come on and walked with his escort, all dressed in animal hides, as is their custom. On his forehead, near the crown of his head, he was wearing a palm-straw band that looked like a diadem. It was woven like a cordon, and in the middle, above his forehead, was a heart-shaped shell. [52]

At about twenty paces from my tent, he stopped. I ordered a squad of soldiers to flank me and the alferez to be present with the royal standard. He bowed three times, kneeling each time. When he arrived at the entrance of my tent to do so, I came out, received, and embraced him. He showed me a small, silver image of Christ he had in his hands with a small piece of taffeta, which I saw had the printed image of Our Lady of Guadalupe. He was also wearing around his neck the rosary I had sent him. In a pouch of relics, he had an Agnus Dei,[53] which I was told he wore. I welcomed him through the interpreters and gave the peace, telling him he would be safe. So that he might better understand my good intentions and that I was not going to harm him at all, I showed him the image of the Blessed Virgin, which was on the royal standard; the holy cross of the rosary; and the one that I had sent him, all of which I took as my witnesses that the peace I was offering him in the name of the two majesties was sure. He replied that he believed it was so. I ordered him to enter my tent, greeting him kindly with warm words and chocolate, which he drank with the fathers, the others who were present, and me.

The last thing I told him was that I was going to leave him as governor and he would have to report to me and see that the Indians were good Christians. That was why I had been sent and what his majesty asked of and ordered me. I said I needed nothing and was asking him for nothing, because I had brought what was necessary and the wherewithal to buy whatever I needed. I said I had not come to make a profit, but for their good and so that they might again become Christians, vassals obedient to his majesty, as they were and had an obligation to be. He was very powerful, and they should recognize this.

The captain of the Picurí nations

When he appeared to be satisfied, and because night was falling, I ordered that he be given one of my saddle horses. He received it quite happily and asked me through the interpreters to receive the trifle he was giving me, not because I needed it, but as a symbol of peace. I replied that I was receiving it, so that he would be content and assured of my good intentions. With this, he left, saying he would return in the morning to talk with me at length. The gift was various animal skins. So that don Luis's having rendered obedience and the rest that is referred to may be of record, I signed it with Pedro Hidalgo and the artillery captain, Francisco Lucero de Godoy, who were the interpreters, and the witnesses, the captain of the presidio, its alferez, and my secretary of government and war.

Don Diego de Vargas Zapata Luján Ponce de León

Roque Madrid

Juan de Dios Lucero de Godoy

Francisco Lucero de Godoy

Pedro Hidalgo

Before me, Alfonso Rael de Aguilar, secretary of government and war

> Tuesday, 16 September, in the morning, don Luis again visits the governor and captain general and discusses the conditions of the peace with the pueblos that obey him and the war against the enemy

Today, Tuesday, 16 of the present month of the current year, at about eight o'clock in the morning, don Luis Picurí came to see me, the governor and captain general. I gave him a public audience in my tent and some breakfast, which he had with the reverend missionary fathers. He brought with him the captains and principal Indians from the pueblos and nations who obey him, the Tewas, Tanos, and Picuris.

I, the governor and captain general, ordered the interpreters to assist me. They were present to satisfy and reply to him and satisfy me about all the points and proposals he might make to me so that this matter of the reduction and conquest, of such great importance, might finally be concluded with the submission and obedience I sought to secure from those nations, so that they might be subject to the Divine and human majesties. Seeing a great crowd of people around my tent, I, the governor and captain general, began to speak again of my sure and loyal good intentions and word, in which they could trust. I had told them I would do them no harm. The Indians of their pueblos and nations should also be assured. To listen to and speak with him, it was first necessary for the fathers to absolve him and the men who were present as his guards and followers.

Thus, he and the rest obediently knelt, and one of the reverend fathers, Father fray Francisco Corvera, took up his manual[54] and then absolved them, with Fathers fray Cristóbal Alonso Barroso and fray Miguel Muñiz assisting. When absolution was finished, and they had received it, I embraced him and shook his hand, saying that now he was a child of God, since he and the rest who were present were absolved and pardoned.

I again sat down with the others and told him I needed to visit the pueblos, because I had to give an account to the king, our lord, who ordered me to do so. I would take the fathers with me, so that I would pardon and the fathers would absolve those who received me of their free will, gave me the peace, and believed me. Also, those who had separated from their wives, whom, as Christians, they had received and been given according to the holy sacrament of marriage, would necessarily be ordered and made to return to live with their wives, putting aside and turning away from them any other women they might be with.

I also told him that all the children and boys and girls born and raised since the uprising would have to be baptized as Christians, which they had to become. The reverend fathers would do this with all their love, because that was what I had brought them for. The pueblos and people who did not believe me, obey, and comply with all I told them and what his majesty the king, our lord, ordered, I would destroy once and for all. The others who had obeyed me and rendered their obedience should neither speak against nor oppose me, for those who were good would be dear to my heart and I would esteem them greatly.

I told him all this through the interpreters, and he replied that it would be difficult to go to the pueblos inasmuch as most of their people had left, seeking shelter on the mesas and in the mountain ranges. What I could do, since this villa had now surrendered, was go to El Paso and within a year, return once and for all with the fathers. Then he would have everyone back together at their pueblos, and they would render the obedience he said they would.

I answered this, saying to him that I could not do such a thing because that would be too long for me. Going to them, I would wait for them to come down from their pueblos. I was not afraid of them and had to give an account to the king, our lord, of having visited them and subjugated the rebels. I would send for more men, whom I had left behind to wait for me so as not to frighten the Indians.

He makes a proposal about the enemy nations and asks to be helped in winning their friendship and if not, make war against them

He discussed my proposal with the captains and the Indians in his retinue. He decided that, since the Pecos nation is numerous and friendly with his enemy, the Apaches they call Faraones, as is the

Taos nation, the most distant in this kingdom, I would go to these two pueblos and districts to see whether I could unite them as his allies. If not, he would assist me with some men, so that with mine, we could make war against them until we were victorious, so that his people might be free and safe from the enemy.

> The governor and captain general agrees with what he proposes about helping him until the day of the departure and campaign against the enemy

Having returned, with the time spent on the two journeys, the people in his charge from the nations and pueblos of the Tewas, Tanos, and Picurís will have come down and will be together. I shall see and visit them then, so that he may leave and be completely satisfied about me.

> Note bene
> Our Lady of Remedies has been their patroness and advocate in the undertaking

He should not be judged by fear of his proven treachery, notwithstanding my trust in Blessed Mary, the Queen, Our Lady of Remedies[55] and advocate, who has also been the pilgrim and the patroness of this undertaking. I trust, as I repeat, in her Divine Majesty, although our numbers are few and at this time I have had no information about the men from Parral.

I told him in regard to this matter that Saturday, the twentieth of the present month, after having attended mass, which the fathers will say to our Lady for success, I shall go out with my camp to the district of the Pecos and once and for all leave it in friendship or free of the enmity they have for don Luis.

> He decided on Saturday for the other entrada to the Pecos and the Taos

Immediately after, Our Lord seeing fit to give me success, I shall go to the district and nation of the Taos and do the same. Upon my return, I shall make a tour of inspection. Leaving on the trip, I shall also go on to the nation of the Jemez and the Keres of San Felipe, who they also say make war upon him.

With that and my promise to defend them in the manner referred to, I am very pleased, as are the rest of the captains and Indian leaders of his retinue. He asked my permission, which I gave with my approval, for his people to enter with their trade goods, such that he was in the plaza de armas all day into the afternoon, speaking and being friendly with everyone. He left before the sun set, asking my permission to do so, and said he was going to gather his chosen warriors to be with them on Friday. I should let him go in the company of the sergeant and his brother-in-law, a soldier of this presidio's company, so that they might see their relatives in San Juan Pueblo. I gave it to him, asking them first if they wanted to go for a period of two days, without counting today. So that what has been referred to may be of record, I signed with the interpreter, the witnesses, the captain of the presidio, the alferez, and my secretary of government and war.

Don Diego de Vargas Zapata Luján Ponce de León

Roque Madrid

Juan de Dios Lucero de Godoy

Pedro Hidalgo

Before me, Alfonso Rael de Aguilar, secretary of government and war

Account of the second mass celebrated the Day of the Stigmata, 17 September, when 122 infants and children of various ages and both sexes were baptized after mass

Today, the seventeenth of the present month, the day on which the Feast of the Stigmata[56] of our father St. Francis, is celebrated, the newly reduced people were advised, that after celebrating mass on the patio of the fortress in the enramada erected for the first mass, the reverend fathers would be ready to administer the holy sacrament of baptism to all the unbaptized infants and boys and girls born since their uprising and apostasy from our holy faith.

Having thus admonished them on Monday of this week, the day of the first mass, as is of record, I, the governor and captain general, went on to the fortress and villa in the company of the reverend missionary fathers, military leaders, war officials, interpreters, and some soldiers, entered the patio of the fortress, and was present to hear the mass the reverend missionary father, fray Miguel Muñiz, celebrated. Through an interpreter, Pedro Hidalgo, he preached a sermon to the Indians of the fortress, repeating how necessary holy baptism was for them to enjoy heavenly bliss, since without it they could not see

God and become Christians. Thus, he ordered all those who might have unbaptized children—and the rest of the people who might have unbaptized infants and boys and girls—to select compadres so that they might have them and not hesitate choosing whomever they wanted.

When the sermon and mass were over, the three reverend fathers began to administer the holy sacrament. José, the captain and leader of the fortress, and his wife Juana asked me, the governor and captain general, to be godfather to their three daughters of various ages. I named the eldest of the three children Isabel; the second, Francisca; and the youngest, María. Their names will be of record in the entry of the registry and book the reverend father, fray Francisco Corvera, president of the religious, kept. I was godfather to another three infants. Their mothers brought them to me so that I might carry them in my arms, as I did, to receive the water of holy baptism, which they did. I was godfather to them and later to three more infants.

Nota bene: 122 baptized

The fathers, military leaders, war officials, soldiers, and interpreters were godfathers to many infants, since 122 are baptized this morning, as is of record in the registry that as president, the reverend father, fray Francisco Corvera, has in his possession. The aforesaid were godfathers with me, the governor and captain general, to almost all of them. The ceremony ended in general rejoicing and solace. So that it may be of record, I signed it with the interpreter and witnesses, the captain of the presidio, its alferez, and my secretary of government and war.

Don Diego de Vargas Zapata Luján Ponce de León
Roque Madrid
Juan de Dios Lucero de Godoy
Pedro Hidalgo
Before me, Alfonso Rael de Aguilar, secretary of government and war

Wednesday, 17 September, in the afternoon, don Lorenzo, brother of don Luis Picurí, governor of the pueblo of the Picuris, comes to render obedience

On Wednesday, 17 September, at about four o'clock in the afternoon, don Lorenzo arrived at this plaza de armas. He is current governor and captain of the nation and pueblo of the Picuris. He is said to be, and said he was, the brother of don Luis, leader and head of these nations.

> The current governor and captain, don Lorenzo, brother of don Luis Picurí

I received don Lorenzo and the people he brought with him with the same kindness as I had his brother. I made the same gestures and said the kind words I had to his brother. I assured him of the peace he and his men had humbly given. I told him through the interpreter, Sgto. mayor Alonso García, that I would aid him in everything and leave him as governor, as he was, of his nation and would aid and favor him against his enemies.

He said the Pecos and the Faraón Apaches and their supporters, the Taos, Jemez, and Keres of San Felipe, Santo Domingo, and Cochiti, all made war on him and did harm, as his brother had said. Informed of the war I was about to begin, he said that should I not achieve the pacification of the enemy nations, he would also provide men to aid in the war. He told me he delayed to await his brother, and that with my permission, tomorrow, Thursday, his men would enter this plaza de armas with their trade goods. I agreed to this and gave him a horse. He reciprocated with some skins. I was happy to receive them and gave him many thanks. So that it may be of record, I signed it with the interpreter and witnesses, the captain of the presidio, the alferez, and my secretary of government and war.

Don Diego de Vargas Zapata Luján Ponce de León

Roque Madrid

Juan de Dios Lucero de Godoy

Alonso García

Before me, Alfonso Rael de Aguilar, secretary of government and war

> Thursday, the eighteenth, arrival of the sergeant and soldier who went in his company to the pueblo of San Juan and the rest who are on the road

Today, Thursday, 18 September, at sunset, the sergeant, Juan Ruiz de Cáceres, and his brother, Miguel Luján,[57] arrived at this plaza de armas, before me, the governor and captain general. They went with my permission in the company of don Luis Picurí, with his consent and at his request. They informed me that by the time they had arrived at the pueblos through which they passed and at San Juan, they found the people had withdrawn to the mesas. As soon as don Luis ordered them to come down, they did. He then told them what I had said and arranged with him, and they were very content. Don Luis said he kissed my hand and sent to tell me that tomorrow, Friday, in the afternoon, he would be with the men who had to go to war and campaign against their enemies. So that the arrival and the information referred to may be of record, I signed it with the captain, the alferez of the presidio, and my secretary of government and war.

Don Diego de Vargas Zapata Luján Ponce de León

Roque Madrid

Juan de Dios Lucero de Godoy

Before me, Alfonso Rael de Aguilar, secretary of government and war

A soldier finds the bronze cannon buried when they left the land

Today, Saturday, 20 September, I, the governor and captain general, awoke ill, which prevented me from leaving. I was awaiting don Luis as well, who was to come with his men as he had pledged to me, when a soldier named Francisco Márquez[58] of the company from the El Paso presidio arrived. He reported to me that he had found the bronze cannon that for all this time he had made every effort to locate. Even the captain of the presidio himself had gone to try to find it where it was when they had left the kingdom because of the Indians' uprising. He searched, but was unable to find it. From this, it was concluded that the rebels had moved it to where it was now, as the captain saw.

They found a bronze cannon 7 spans long

I ordered the artillery captain to go get it with the small wagon for the large stone mortar, which he did, and leave it in this plaza de armas. When he came with the cannon, I examined it. It is more or less 7 spans long.[59] From what I saw, the priming hole in the chamber must have burst, because it is plugged for more than a short span,[60] and another priming hole of the same size has been drilled. Having given the soldier my thanks and a reward for his find, I am taking this cannon on campaign. So that it may be of record, I signed it with the captain of the presidio, its alferez, and my secretary of government and war, and the artillery captain, Francisco Lucero de Godoy.

Don Diego de Vargas Zapata Luján Ponce de León
Francisco Lucero de Godoy
Roque Madrid
Juan de Dios Lucero de Godoy
Before me, Alfonso Rael de Aguilar, secretary of government and war

Arrival of don Luis, his brother don Lorenzo, and his captains with the men of his retinue

Immediately after on this day, don Luis Picurí, his brother don Lorenzo, his captains, and the men of his retinue arrived at this plaza de armas before me, the governor and captain general, where I was after attending mass. I greeted them kindly with chocolate, which they drank with me and the reverend missionary fathers. Since it was already late and because of my indisposition, I told them that tomorrow, Sunday, after mass, we would leave on the campaign decided upon for the district of the Pecos and they and their men might go rest. With that, we would leave the following day at the appropriate time for a day's journey so as to make the entrada at a propitious moment. So that it may be of record, I signed it with the captain of the presidio, its alferez, the interpreter, and my secretary of government and war.

Don Diego de Vargas Zapata Luján Ponce de León
Roque Madrid
Pedro Hidalgo
Juan de Dios Lucero de Godoy
Before me, Alfonso Rael de Aguilar, secretary of government and war

He informs me that the Tewa Indians who left to reconnoiter the land have discovered a trail of their enemies, the Keres Indians

On the same day, month, and year, a little before midday, before me, the governor and captain general, the captain of the presidio, Roque Madrid, informs me that the Tewa Indians, who had left this villa to reconnoiter the land and the entradas of the enemies, saw some twenty tracks of the Keres Indians, who are from Santo Domingo Pueblo and with whom they are at war. Because of this information, don Luis Picurí warned the captain of the presidio that they should take care with their horses. In order to have his herd secure, he asked the captain to order the leaders of his guard to meet it. So that it may be of record, I signed it with the captain and the alferez of the presidio. I ordered that they inform everyone in the camp about this information. The squad leaders of the horse guard should be notified, so that tonight, each might take the necessary care so that the enemy might not surround us, lying in ambush, the more so since we are surrounded by mountain ranges. I sign it with my secretary of government and war.

Don Diego de Vargas Zapata Luján Ponce de León
Roque Madrid
Juan de Dios Lucero de Godoy
Before me, Alfonso Rael de Aguilar, secretary of government and war

> Letter the governor and captain general leaves for the captain he left appointed in the pueblo of El Paso, so that he might lead the fifty soldiers his excellency ordered to come to the pueblo from the presidios of Parral for this conquest

It is certain that, had we not been so fortunate in the conquest and reduction to our holy faith of these Indians and nations of this villa and principal town of Santa Fe, I would have endangered myself, the camp, and men-at-arms who follow me, had I trusted in the aid of the fifty soldiers from Parral, of whom I appointed you captain.

Divine mercy, however, permitted my entrada to this villa on 13 September and the siege I laid at daybreak to the fortress in its plaza. Its rebels gave me reason enough to begin war. I thought their reduction hopeless, though I tolerated their excesses in everything. Looking to the greater service of both majesties, it was possible by means of the Divine to successfully overcome their rebelliousness. They were stubborn unbelievers, but my repeated, effective arguments, which were pure and full of the fervent spirit of a Catholic's zeal, could not persuade them.

My intent was achieved. I attribute the parting of the shadows of their blindness to the aurora and guiding light of my thoughts and, finally, the protectress of our holy faith, the one who might see to everything, the most holy Mary of Remedies. She protected this enterprise and guided my steps to conquer such a devil, removing us at once from danger and recovering for us the pleasure of happiness achieved at seeing those Indians who, having surrendered, left their fortress to render obedience to me in its plaza and to the Divine Majesty as well. I was there on his majesty's behalf to receive it for him.

I have waited for you until today. Having despaired of your coming, with the protection and guidance of the most holy Mary, I am going to make my entrada to the pueblos of Galisteo and the Pecos district, which among these nations is rebellious. If they are still in rebellion and in league with the Apaches, I order that as soon as you arrive, you should follow in the direction of my tracks to help me with whatever God may see fit to give me.

I leave this for you with a trustworthy person from the camp, so that with every precaution, you may receive and read it, carrying out the order. May God keep you many years. Villa of Santa Fe, principal town of the kingdom of New Mexico, newly reduced and conquered for the royal crown, 21 September 1692.
Don Diego de Vargas Zapata Luján Ponce de León
Capt. Juan Páez Hurtado

> Departure from this villa of Santa Fe with all the camp and don Luis Picurí and his brother don Lorenzo, with the captains and men of his retinue, to make a dawn attack on their enemies, the rebel Pecos

Today, Sunday, day of the glorious St. Matthew, 21 September, at sunrise, don Luis Picurí, his brother don Lorenzo, the Indian Domingo, and the captains and leaders of their retinue came to this plaza de armas with many Indians from the pueblos of their nations who were not absolved. They were going to join the Pecos nation, their enemies, apostates and rebels against the royal crown.

The reverend missionary father, fray Miguel Muñiz, absolved them, don Lorenzo, and Domingo. Once they had been absolved, the reverend father, fray Cristóbal Alonso Barroso, celebrated mass for the whole camp. I attended with those present. Once the mass was over, I repeated to them through the interpreter that they should be very happy at having heard it again. I gave the captains and the reverend fathers breakfast and chocolate.

When the camp had prepared itself and mounted, I, the governor and captain general, did so and left, marching from the villa and plaza de armas between eight and nine in the morning and halting in the pueblo of Galisteo, where I ordered the leaders and war officials to make this information known to the camp.

> The scouts will be sent ahead to the pueblo of Galisteo to see whether there are any enemy and water holes

I sent two Indian war scouts ahead on foot to the pueblo of Galisteo to see whether any of the enemy was there and examine its water holes, which were used for supply when it was inhabited by the Tano nation, today living in the villa of Santa Fe. They supplied themselves ingeniously with water from some pools and reservoirs they made. Somewhat more than 2 leagues before arriving at the pueblo, the scouts came, explaining that there were neither enemies nor water for the camp.

> He halts within view of Galisteo, spending the night in an unprotected arroyo

It was necessary to halt with the camp in an arroyo within view of and on the direct road to the pueblo of Galisteo. I gave the order that with the rising of the morning star, the camp should begin to prepare to continue and carry out the entrada to Pecos Pueblo. So that it may be of record and that the march was 8 leagues, I signed it with the captain of the presidio, the alferez, and my secretary of government and war.
Don Diego de Vargas Zapata Luján Ponce de León
Roque Madrid
Juan de Dios Lucero de Godoy
Before me, Alfonso Rael de Aguilar, secretary of government and war

> The captain of the reinforcements from Parral arrives when the governor and captain general was about to leave for the pueblo of Pecos to subdue or reduce it by force of arms

Today, Monday, 22 September 1692, I, the governor and captain general, was about to mount my horse before sunrise when, with the camp, I heard two shots. Since I had given the order that none of the men-at-arms was to shoot when the password, which was "Praise the Lord," expired, I realized that it could be the customary salvo that any squad or men-at-arms coming to carry out an order make to a guard post and camp.

On 22 September, those from Parral arrived at the villa of Santa Fe

A short time later, Juan Páez Hurtado, appointed in these war proceedings as captain of the fifty soldiers for reinforcements from the presidios of Parral, arrived. He had come ahead by virtue of my letter-order, which he received in the villa of Santa Fe, a copy of which is of record in these proceedings, dated yesterday, Sunday, 21 September. It was sunset when the captain arrived at the villa, as he says, with six soldiers from his company. He had come ahead to report that he had arrived, had left the horses in that villa to spend the night so that they might recover somewhat, and the men of his company would be here by this afternoon, Monday.

Order the governor and captain general gives

For that reason, I ordered the postponement of the march and entrada to Pecos Pueblo, in order to do it the next day, Tuesday, with the whole camp together, to accomplish its reduction or submission by force of arms. I ordered the military leaders and war officials to communicate this decision and the reason for it. Through an interpreter, I also ordered the Indians, don Luis and don Lorenzo, to send their swiftest Indians out as scouts. All day long they might be in the lomas and mesas that surround us to reconnoiter the enemy, the Apaches and the Pecos, who, though hostile and enemies of the newly reduced rebel nations that follow me, try to win their friendship. So that the arrival of the captain, the reason for the postponement of the march, and the order contained herein may be of record, I signed it with the captain of the reinforcements and those present with me in these proceedings, the captain of the presidio, the alferez, and my secretary of government and war.
Don Diego de Vargas Zapata Luján Ponce de León
Roque Madrid
Juan de Dios Lucero de Godoy
Juan Páez Hurtado
Before me, Alfonso Rael de Aguilar, secretary of government and war

I received the certification that the fifty soldiers arrived at El Paso on Friday, 5 September, at nine o'clock in the morning

On Monday, 22 September, the captain of the reinforcements gave me, the governor and captain general, the certification he requested from the cabildo, justicia y regimiento of this kingdom of New Mexico, which resides in the jurisdiction of El Paso, for which I had left Mre. de campo Luis Granillo, as my lieutenant governor and captain general. In accord with my order, he appeared before the cabildo, asking the time and date of the arrival of the fifty soldiers from the presidios of Parral with their leader at the plaza de armas of the pueblo of El Paso.

Proceedings

So that the time of their arrival at the pueblo of El Paso and their having passed muster in its plaza de armas may be of record, I, the governor and captain general, order the original certification, signed and sealed by those who are of record in it as members of the cabildo, justicia and regimiento, placed in these proceedings. So that it may thus be of record that I provided it, I so ordered and signed it with the witnesses, the captain of the presidio, the alferez, and my secretary of government and war.
Don Diego de Vargas Zapata Luján Ponce de León
Roque Madrid
Juan de Dios Lucero de Godoy
Before me, Alfonso Rael de Aguilar, secretary of government and war

I received the certification

The cabildo, justicia y regimiento of the villa of Santa Fe, New Mexico, that today is located and meets in the jurisdiction of El Paso for his majesty.

On 5 September, the fifty soldiers from Parral arrived at El Paso

I certify and attest that today, Friday, 5 September 1692, at about nine o'clock in the morning, the camp of fifty soldiers from the presidios of Pasaje, El Gallo, Cerro Gordo, and San Francisco de Conchos passed muster, as is customary, before Mre. de campo Luis Granillo, lieutenant governor and captain general of this kingdom and provinces of New Mexico for the current lord governor and captain general for his majesty, don Diego de Vargas Zapata Luján Ponce de León. The fifty soldiers came well supplied with weapons and horses, as is of record in the list they presented before the lieutenant, which is of record in the declaration and muster, and that we attest to having seen and I requested from the lieutenant. So that it may be of record, we ordered him to send the present document, signed with our names, sealed with the seal of the villa, and signed by the secretary of the cabildo. Given in El Paso on this day, month, and year. It is on ordinary blank paper, as the stamped kind is unavailable here.

Francisco de Anaya Almazán

Antonio Montoya

Antonio Lucero de Godoy[61]

Diego de Montoya[62]

Before me, to which I attest, Tiburcio de Ortega,[63] secretary of the cabildo

> One of the Indian scouts arrives and brings information about having seen two tracks of the enemy Apaches and a horse that, since it was tired, was set loose last night

On Monday, 22 September, I, the governor and captain general, was informed through an interpreter by a Tano Indian who said his name was Nicolás, one of the scouts who had been newly reduced and sent, that he had seen and examined two tracks left by two Apaches who came to scout us last night. Also, he and two other companions had found a horse the enemy had left behind because it was tired. I said I would give it to him and he should share in it equally with his two companions. So that the rest may be encouraged and take heart, I favored him by shaking his hand and embracing him. I gave him this gift and spoke to him very warmly. So that it may be of record, I signed it with the witnesses, the captain of the presidio, the alferez, and my secretary of government and war.

Don Diego de Vargas Zapata Luján Ponce de León

Roque Madrid

Juan de Dios Lucero de Godoy

Before me, Alfonso Rael de Aguilar, secretary of government and war

> Departure from this place to make a dawn attack at Pecos Pueblo tomorrow

Today, Monday, 22 September, having been informed about the rough road and the distance from this campsite and arroyo of the abovementioned pueblo, and within sight of Galisteo, I, the governor and captain general, ordered the captain of the presidio and reinforcements that the military leaders should bring up the horses, war officials, and squad leaders of the guard at five o'clock in the afternoon to ready the men. In fulfillment of that order, and since they were ready, I left marching with the camp and arrived at about nine or ten o'clock at night, after a march of about 3 leagues, at a stretch of vega and llano surrounding a mountain. The Indian scouts said there was nowhere else we could stop with the horses and camp and be undetected by the rebels and apostates of Pecos, since they were not far away. For this reason, I called a halt there, ordering the military leaders to have the camp ready at dawn to go besiege the rebels and their pueblo. So that it may be of record, I signed it with the captain of the presidio, the alferez, and my secretary of government and war.

Don Diego de Vargas Zapata Luján Ponce de León
Roque Madrid
Juan de Dios Lucero de Godoy
Before me, Alfonso Rael de Aguilar, secretary of government and war

Entrada to the pueblo of the Pecos

Today, Tuesday, the twenty-third of the present month, 1692, the military leaders were mounted on their horses, and the camp, men-at-arms, and reverend apostolic missionary fathers carrying out the above order were about to mount up. I, the governor and captain general, asked Father fray Miguel Muñiz to absolve me and grant absolution to the men-at-arms who were present. I received it kneeling, as did the rest.

I left there marching. I had previously given the order to all the people mentioned above that, upon entering the pueblo through its plaza and corners, they should all say "Praise be the most holy sacrament" five times. The signal I would give them to shout "Santiago"[64] and begin the battle would be to unsheathe my sword.

Having marched a little more than a league, we saw the tracks of two Indians on horseback. We realized they had gone into the mountains either last night or early this morning, because the tracks led back to the pueblo.

Having gone down a loma and barranca, we saw the pueblo. As we advanced, I ordered the captain of the presidio to take the men-at-arms from his presidio with him for the siege. The sargento mayor was to go with the captain and reinforcements who had come from Parral. The other military leaders were to come with me, the governor and captain general, with the six citizens from El Paso to complete the siege and assist in detaining rebel fugitives and reserves.[65]

In a short time, we saw two columns of smoke rising, apparently from the pueblo, from which it could be seen that it was inhabited. We had only gone a short distance when the friendly Indian warriors who had advanced cried out to the camp that the rebels were leaving on horseback and already coming. As this information spread, I commanded and ordered the general adjutant of the kingdom, Domingo Varela, to pass the word on and tell the squadron that when the fighting broke out, the rebels, who we had determined were coming on horseback, should be unhorsed, captured, and killed. The men must be careful, because the rebels could be coming with Apaches.

Going at a full gallop to the pueblo, which is wide open with very large three-story houses, it was found to be abandoned, though well supplied with all sorts of vegetables and maize. Realizing that the two on horseback whose tracks are referred to in this entrada doubtlessly would have come to give information about having discovered us, I immediately ordered the men-at-arms and military leaders to follow the tracks, without anyone stopping.

They followed the route solely by the cloud of dust they thought they had seen. I, the governor and captain general, closed up the squadron and flanks of those men on guard. Increasing the pace, their squads spread over the mountain and range bordering the milpas across the river from the pueblo. Its ravines, slopes, and barrancas had caused the men-at-arms as well as their leaders to spread out.

I remained with the alferez, my secretary of government and war, and the six citizens. Since a soldier I found in a barranca told me that the track the men-at-arms were following was old, so that they might carefully examine it, I told and ordered him to go as fast as possible and tell them that I was ordering all who were not following new tracks of the rebel nation that had abandoned the pueblo to rejoin me. If they were following a new one, they should do so until they could bring me as captives the people they might find.

After the soldier left with that order, I, the governor and captain general, was going down a deep barranca with my escort, when one of my servants saw tracks left by children. A short while later, he heard an harquebus shot, and I had to conclude from the echo and sound that the shot had been fired in the mountain range. At that moment, we encountered the soldier with whom I had sent the order coming down the mountain with a prisoner, an old Indian woman. I told Pedro Hidalgo, the interpreter in these proceedings, to ask the Indian woman where and when the people of her pueblo had fled, to inform and call them. She said that the younger people had fled six days ago with the word of my arrival at the villa of Santa Fe. They wanted neither to go see me, nor allow the older people of the pueblo, who said they would go and come down to see me and give me the peace, to do so. The few of them who were outside beyond the milpas this morning had word from those Indians that we were coming. They fled as soon as they heard.

After going on somewhat farther, another soldier arrived. He brought a prisoner, an old Indian who was naked and looked about sixty years old. I ordered the an Indian woman, who was carrying some hides, to give him one to cover himself. Speaking through the interpreter who spoke to and questioned him, the Indian said the same thing the Indian woman had said, declared, and replied. Seeing that there was little to lose and much to gain by the experience, I wanted to have a good talk with the Indian through the interpreter, which I did. I said to him that he should go and, assuming he could find his people, tell them I had come to pardon them in his majesty's name so they might again be Christians. They should come down, and I would receive them peacefully, leaving their pueblo and milpas alone without doing them any harm. As assurance and a sign, I gave him a rosary, which I placed around his neck. So that the men-at-arms would not kill him, I had him make a cross a little more than a span long. I put the superscription of one of my letters on it and told him to carry it in his hand, so that with it and with the rosary I had put on him, he could show it to them. He could go assured that they would not take his life. At this, he was very content. I embraced him and shook his hand, reassuring him and repeating that he should believe me. I would wait in the pueblo either for him and his people or the reply they might give him.

In the meantime, the captain of the company of reinforcements arrived with many of his soldiers. They brought another two prisoners along with them, one of them a very old man. It was necessary to carry him on the croup of a horse so that he might make it to the pueblo. The men-at-arms arrived without the captain of the presidio with the information that he had gone in another direction with the military leaders and the men-at-arms. On the mountain, they had found many animal hides and pelts the rapidly withdrawing rebels had left among the woods and thickets of the rocky terrain.

There are twenty-seven prisoners

When the men of the camp re-formed, the captain of the presidio arrived. Counting the captives, women, infants, children of all ages, and the old man, with the nine brought in by the military leaders, twenty-seven were captured.[66] My secretary of government and war counted them in my presence and that of the leaders and war officials. So that the entrada, the pursuit of the enemy, and what happened may be of record, I signed it with those who were present at my side, the captains and military leaders, along with my secretary of government and war.

Don Diego de Vargas Zapata Luján Ponce de León
Roque Madrid
Juan de Dios Lucero de Godoy
Pedro Hidalgo
Cristóbal de Tapia
José de Gallegos
Don Fernando de Chaves
Antonio Jorge
Juan Páez Hurtado
Martín de Alday
Before me, Alfonso Rael de Aguilar, secretary of government and war

Arrival of an old Indian from the fugitive rebels of this pueblo, sent by the old Indian prisoner mentioned herein, to whom the cross and rosary were given to bring the rebels down to this pueblo of the Pecos

On 23 September 1692, at about three or four in the afternoon, an old Indian arrived at this pueblo of the Pecos. Before me, the governor and captain general, he said through interpreters that he was from this pueblo and nation. He came with that cross in his hand, sent by the old Indian mentioned in the entrada on the previous page. I, the governor and captain general, had given him the rosary and put it around his neck when he was taken prisoner on the mountain. First, the cross was to safeguard his person, so that the men-at-arms in my charge would not kill him. Second, this was so

that he might also assure the fugitive Pecos rebels who have abandoned their pueblo that I was not coming to do them any harm because
of their great crimes, as they thought, but only to pardon them in
his majesty's name. He had sent me for that and also so that they
might render the obedience they should to his royal person and again
become Christians and be reduced to our holy faith, for that was
what I ordered them. I had told him that through the interpreter
and repeated it to this Indian who came into my presence.

He said that the women and old people said they should not leave
the pueblo. The young men, who defend them against the enemy
who harm them and take part in war, made them go out and leave
their homes. They left with their women and children six days ago.
Only eleven people stayed. They were in their milpas with their wives
and children when, very early this morning, two Indians warned them
that the Spaniards were coming. The fear the boys and girls felt made
them run away. The old Indian I had set free and to whom I had
given the holy cross had sent him with it to advise me that he was
the governor of this pueblo. Since his people were very scattered,
and those who had left first far away, it would take time to advise
them and make them return, telling them he had seen me and what
had happened.

I told the old man through the interpreter that he should return to
look for the governor. To better assure him that he had seen me and
told his people about what I had told him, I gave him the rosary. I
also put it around his neck, treated him kindly, and spoke to him
warmly. I told him I would be waiting for him all day tomorrow,
Wednesday, and he should go and tell them that as soon as they
arrived, they could come back to live in their houses. Although he
saw me living in this house and my men in others, as soon as his
people arrived, we would leave them all unoccupied. My men and I
also had slept outside. While I had been in the villa I had slept out
in the open. He could ask the leaders who were present from the
villa whether everything I had told him was true, and they would
tell him so. They all assured him of it, each one on his own, which
completely satisfied the old man.

I also told him to tell them that I had come to reconcile them
with the Tanos and Tewas who were coming with me, so they might
be as brothers and not harm one another. I made all that understood
through the interpreter. I spoke to him, and he, having understood,
was very pleased and satisfied. So that it may be of record, I signed it

with the interpreter, Sgto. mayor Alonso García, the witnesses, the captain of the presidio, the alferez, and my secretary of government and war.

Don Diego de Vargas Zapata Luján Ponce de León

Roque Madrid

Juan de Dios Lucero de Godoy

Pedro Hidalgo

Alonso García

Before me, Alfonso Rael de Aguilar, secretary of government and war

> The Indian allies who went to patrol the countryside bring back prisoners during the course of the day: three prisoners, Indian women from this pueblo

Today, Wednesday, 24 September, some swift Indian warriors who had gone out to reconnoiter the countryside, the mountain ranges, and montes that surround this pueblo in the course of the day brought into my presence three Indian women. One, with a infant at her breast, said they had left this pueblo because the men had. They had gone out of fear of finding themselves alone. All three, when they came to see me, greeted me saying, "Praise be the blessed sacrament," speaking clearly and distinctly. I ordered the interpreter to tell them that no one was going to do them any harm. They would be left in this their pueblo and houses, so that they would have what they needed to feed themselves. They should be very content about the Indians having brought them. I ordered the squad leader of the guard to return their houses to them. So that it may be of record, I signed it with the captain of the presidio, the alferez, and my secretary of government and war.

Don Diego de Vargas Zapata Luján Ponce de León

Roque Madrid

Juan de Dios Lucero de Godoy

Before me, Alfonso Rael de Aguilar, secretary of government and war

> Arrival of an old Indian, sent by the first prisoner on the day of the entrada and campaign to this land and pueblo of the Pecos

On that day, the twenty-fourth of the present month, at about six o'clock in the afternoon, an old Indian, who appeared to be more than sixty, arrived at this pueblo before me, the governor and captain general. At my order, the interpreters and some principal Indians of those newly reduced asked first where he had been. He said he was hidden in the milpas and was coming to see me. I told him that the people of this pueblo had done wrong by abandoning it and fleeing, leaving their houses. He said the older people did not want to leave. Their governor, the old Indian to whom I had given the cross, was sending me word with him of having assembled some of his people and that tomorrow he was expecting others he had sent for. As soon as they were together, he would come and bring them down to this pueblo, so that they might see me. Since the old man said he was very tired, I ordered him to spend the night here. I told him he could go early in the morning and tell the old governor I was waiting for him, and because of that, I was not leaving.

So that he could verify that it was true that he had seen me, I put a rosary around his neck. He was spoken to in such a way as to allay his fear, so that they would not fear for their safety. So that it may be of record, I signed it with the captain of the presidio, the alferez, and my secretary of government and war.

Don Diego de Vargas Zapata Luján Ponce de León

Roque Madrid

Juan de Dios Lucero de Godoy

Before me, Alfonso Rael de Aguilar, secretary of government and war

> A very swift Indian woman from among the prisoners offers to go and tell the old man, who will only come a short way, that she will go and tell the people they can come right now

Today, Thursday, the twenty-fifth of the present month, before me, the governor and captain general, an offer was made to go see and talk to the old governor. We were waiting for him to come down to the pueblo today with the people he has gathered, according to the information brought at his command and the message given to me by the aforementioned old man. An Indian woman, one of the prisoners, offered to go of her own free will. She said she was leaving her daughter and mother prisoners as security that she would return and that her father was governor of this pueblo and very reasonable. She would go, because the old man would take a long time to arrive.

So that they might believe what she told them, I gave her permission to go and placed a rosary around her neck. I ordered four Indians to go with her, accompanying her as far as she might say. So that it may be of record, I signed it with the captain, the alferez of the presidio, and my secretary of government and war.

Don Diego de Vargas Zapata Luján Ponce de León
Roque Madrid
Juan de Dios Lucero de Godoy
Before me, Alfonso Rael de Aguilar, secretary of government and war

> The Indian woman returns, and the governor and captain general orders her to go again with the captain of the presidio and twelve soldiers as an escort, to leave her at the tracks of the rebels

On the same day, at eleven, the aforementioned Indian woman arrived, saying that she was afraid to go further. She had gone through the monte, calling out to the people of this pueblo, and had neither discovered nor seen a single one. So that she might manage to see and speak with them, assuring them they could return without fear to this their pueblo, I ordered the captain of the presidio of El Paso and the sergeant to escort the Indian woman immediately with a squad of twelve soldiers as far as she would tell them. They carried this out, returning at about five o'clock in the afternoon.

The captain and sergeant stated before me, the governor and captain general, that they had gone some 3 leagues along the riverbed with the Indian woman. Seeing some of the rebels' tracks there, the Indian woman told them they should return and she would go on alone, so that the Indians would not see them and run away. They should not wait, because she would return to give them a report without fail. So that it may be of record and that a short time later, after the arrival of the captain and sergeant, the Indian woman arrived, saying she had gone looking for the Indians, but had not found them, although she had looked carefully, I signed it with the captain, the alferez, and my secretary of government and war.

Don Diego de Vargas Zapata Luján Ponce de León
Roque Madrid
Juan de Dios Lucero de Godoy
Before me, Alfonso Rael de Aguilar, secretary of government and war

> A young Indian from this pueblo arrives to present himself before me, the governor and captain general, and I ordered him to go see his people, so that they may come down tomorrow, for I am waiting for them to see me

Immediately after, a young rebel Indian from this pueblo presented himself before me, the governor and captain general. I treated him kindly and gave him a rosary, which I hung around his neck. Through the interpreters, I ordered him, since he was swift, to go tell the people of this pueblo that they could safely come down and come to see me. I would be waiting for them tomorrow. I had already sent word with the three old men who had seen me, giving each a rosary as a sign, and done likewise with the Indian woman. He should see the ones who were prisoners. He would find them content. After he saw them and was welcomed, he left with my message. So that it may be of record, I signed it with the captain of the presidio, the alferez, and my secretary of government and war.

Don Diego de Vargas Zapata Luján Ponce de León

Roque Madrid

Juan de Dios Lucero de Godoy

Before me, Alfonso Rael de Aguilar, secretary of government and war

> The Indians and soldiers bring three other old Indian women and a youth who said he had been a captive since the uprising

During the course of the same day, the Indian allies and soldiers brought before me, the governor and captain general, three Indian women, two of whom were apparently more than one hundred years old, and a young man who said he had been a captive since the uprising. He is the son of Cristóbal de Anaya,[67] whom the Indians killed at that time. So that it may be of record, I signed it with the captain, the alferez, and my secretary of government and war.

Don Diego de Vargas Zapata Luján Ponce de León

Roque Madrid

Juan de Dios Lucero de Godoy

Before me, Alfonso Rael de Aguilar, secretary of government and war

The governor and captain general sends an Indian of the Keres nation on that day to those from San Felipe mentioned in these proceedings and to go on to those from Santa Ana and Zia, sending a letter with a cross on it to its captain, El Malacate, and a rosary as a sign of peace

On the same day, month, and year, an Indian of the Keres nation I had brought with the camp from the pueblo of El Paso asked for permission to go on to the mesas of the abandoned pueblo of Santa Ana. They say the Keres Indians who fled and escaped from Santa Ana Pueblo are living on the lomas they call the Cerrito Colorado. It was said that the Indians who escaped and were away from their pueblo of Zia joined them with the governor they call Antonio Malacate.[68]

To not waste time in sending someone ahead and ensure that the Indians do not rise up when they learn I am here, I, the governor and captain general, gave permission to the Indian, because he was trustworthy and had his wife in the pueblo of El Paso. I placed a rosary around his neck as a sign I was sending him and gave him a letter with a cross on it for the governor, Antonio Malacate. I also sent him a rosary and word that I would go in peace to his pueblo, his people should not leave, and they should come down with their captains to see me at Santo Domingo Pueblo. I repeated that he could come down without fear. The Indian carried that message with many other arguments to better satisfy them. So that this action may be of record, I signed it with the captain of the presidio, the alferez, and my secretary of government and war.

Don Diego de Vargas Zapata Luján Ponce de León
Roque Madrid
Juan de Dios Lucero de Godoy
Before me, Alfonso Rael de Aguilar, secretary of government and war

The swift young Indian arrives accompanied by another from this pueblo with the report that he does not know where its people have gone

Today, Friday, 26 September, at about four o'clock in the afternoon, the swift young Indian arrived. He had appeared before me yesterday, Thursday afternoon. After giving him a rosary, I had ordered him to go see whether he could find the fugitive, rebel people of this pueblo. He said he had only found the young man he brought with him. I asked him his name, and he said it was Juan Pedro.[69] He did not know about the rest of the people, who had gone off in different directions, because the young men disagreed with the opinion of the old men of this pueblo. The latter said they should come to see me and they would. For that reason, the former were about to kill them. The other Indian, having been asked his name, said it was Agustín Sebastián and told me the same thing. I ordered them taken to the captives and detained until I decide tomorrow, if nothing changes, what will be of greatest service to both majesties. So that it may be of record, I signed it with the captain, the alferez, and my secretary of government and war.

Don Diego de Vargas Zapata Luján Ponce de León

Roque Madrid

Juan de Dios Lucero de Godoy

Before me, Alfonso Rael de Aguilar, secretary of government and war

> Information the Tewa Indian Domingo gives of having spoken with three Pecos Indians from this pueblo from which is inferred their rebelliousness and continued apostasy

On that day, the twenty-sixth of the present month, the Indian Domingo, captain of the Tewas, mentioned in these proceedings, came before me, the governor and captain general. He said he was giving me an account of how he, accompanied by others he chose from his nation, had left very early to see whether they could find the Indians of this pueblo to advise them that they could return to it safely. They found only three high up in the mountains and ranges. He told them they could come down. Thinking they were not safe, they told him they did not want to return to their pueblo and that those who had made friends with the Spaniards, who were a pack of liars, were a bunch of old women. They wanted neither peace nor friendship with them. Some would go to the Taos and some to the Apaches. Although he said more to them, they paid no attention and fled shouting through the mountains. So that this information may be of record, I signed it with the captain of the presidio, the alferez, and my secretary of government and war.

Don Diego de Vargas Zapata Luján Ponce de León

Roque Madrid

Juan de Dios Lucero de Godoy

Before me, Alfonso Rael de Aguilar, secretary of government and war

The governor and captain general orders the secretary of government and war to count the prisoners and captives of this pueblo in his presence and that of the interpreter and tell them what is of record about these proceedings

Today, Saturday, 27 September, I saw that the Indians of this pueblo are firm in their rebellion against coming here. To leave and go on to the others without wasting time, I, the governor and captain general, ordered the secretary of government and war, accompanied by the captain of the presidio, the alferez, and the interpreter, to count and examine the Indian prisoners who, from the day of the entrada to this pueblo, have been taken captive while we have been here and patrolled their land.

Having carried out the order, my secretary of government and war and those mentioned above said they had seen and counted the captives. They consisted of the following: two young Indians, an old man, thirteen women, and twelve boys and girls and infants, twenty-eight in all.

Twenty-eight captives from this pueblo are given their freedom

They were given their freedom, and their houses were restored to them, so they may remain in possession of them, their pueblo, and their milpas. They were ordered to tell this to the Indians of this pueblo when they return. A cross was left for them, placed as a sign of peace, and some were left painted on the walls of their houses. They were also ordered to tell them to come see me, the governor and captain general, in the villa, their pueblos, or wherever I might be in this kingdom. I shall listen to them and receive them in peace. To assure the safety of the peace and their persons, I would leave them a cross about a half-vara long and another drawn on blank paper folded like a letter. Everything that was referred to occurred in the presence of the witnesses. So that it may be of record, I signed it with my secretary of government and war, and with those witnesses, done ut supra.

Don Diego de Vargas Zapata Luján Ponce de León

Roque Madrid

Juan de Dios Lucero de Godoy

Pedro Hidalgo

Before me, Alfonso Rael de Aguilar, secretary of government and war

Departure from the pueblo of the Pecos for the villa of Santa Fe

Immediately after, having carried out the above action, I, the governor and captain general, was unable to execute the reduction and bringing together of the Indians of Pecos in their pueblo, which they had abandoned. This was with the exception of leaving the women, children, and the three old Indian men referred to free and leaving their pueblo without having destroyed or laid waste to it by ordering it burned. I have proceeded with such mature and prudent understanding that even the kivas they have, of which there are many in that pueblo, have been neither burned nor buried, just as their grains and milpas have not.

Eight people were found captive and are leaving with their relatives

Since the rest of the pueblos are distant and need to be reconnoitered, I, the governor and captain general, ordered the captain of the presidio and the other leaders to prepare the men-at-arms and the camp to leave with the people who were found captive, taking their relatives. These are the three Tewa women with three infants, whose brothers and relatives from the pueblo of Ysleta del Sur are taking them; a captive Spanish-speaking Jumano woman; and a captive, Cristóbal de Anaya's son, whose uncle, the artillery captain, Francisco Lucero de Godoy, is taking with the charge of teaching him to be an armorer.

So that the departure from this pueblo and the actions taken may be of record, postponing those their persistent rebelliousness and contumacy may require, I signed it with the captain, the alferez of the presidio, the captain of the artillery, and the interpreter, together with my secretary of government and war.

Don Diego de Vargas Zapata Luján Ponce de León
Francisco Lucero de Godoy
Roque Madrid
Pedro Hidalgo
Juan de Dios Lucero de Godoy
Before me, Alfonso Rael de Aguilar, secretary of government and war

The governor and captain general arrives at the villa of Santa Fe from the pueblo of the Pecos with the camp, except for the artillery captain, who had to spend the night in the mountains because of the rough road

Today, Saturday, 27 September, at about three o'clock in the afternoon, I, the governor and captain general, arrived at this villa of Santa Fe. I established my quarters on the plaza de armas, which I had designated at the time of the siege and entrada. So that it may be of record, I signed it, the march having been 8 leagues, all mountains and ranges. There are some difficult passes that forced the artillery captain to delay in the middle of the journey with a squad of ten soldiers remaining as his escort. So that it may be of record, I signed it with the witnesses, the captain of the presidio, its alferez, and my secretary of government and war.

Don Diego de Vargas Zapata Luján Ponce de León

Roque Madrid

Juan de Dios Lucero de Godoy

Before me, Alfonso Rael de Aguilar, secretary of government and war

Departure for the pueblo of Tesuque

Today, Monday, 29 September, after having attended the mass of the Feast of the Archangel, St. Michael,[70] I, the governor and captain general, left this villa of Santa Fe with the camp for the pueblo of Tesuque, which was a doctrina, according to what they say, of this villa.

When I arrived at that pueblo, a distance of about 3 leagues, the Indian Domingo, mentioned in these proceedings, the principal leader of this pueblo, came out to receive me. Upon entering the plaza, I found the people of this pueblo arranged in two lines, with a young man in the first holding a cross. In this manner, I entered the plaza, which has three cuarteles, with two-story dwellings. Through the interpreter, I treated them kindly and embraced them all, shaking their hands and saying the alabado first, to which they responded without any rebelliousness.

After a short time, as I was in the plaza, I called the Indian Domingo and ordered him to assemble all his people, telling them I was ordering them to come down. When that was done, I had the alferez real go out with the squadron of soldiers and military leaders, ordering them to form a rank with just their swords, facing the Indians. I took the position in the middle, ordering the interpreter and my secretary of government and war to be present. I told the interpreter that he should state in the language the Indians speak that I had come from very far away to see them by order of the king, our lord, who was also theirs and no other. I told them through the interpreter what was referred to, which is of record in the proceedings of 14 September in the villa of Santa Fe, revalidating and reclaiming the possession that his majesty, the king, our lord (may God keep him), has of this pueblo, land, and its inhabitants, who are his vassals. As a sign, I ordered the alferez to raise the royal standard three times, with everyone repeating and saying three times, "Long live the king, our lord, Carlos II, king of all the Spains, this New World, and the kingdom of New Mexico that has newly been reduced and conquered for his royal crown and our holy faith, whose vassals these are." Everyone answered with much rejoicing and happiness, "Viva," many times and "May the good fortune of his monarchy increase."

After that was said, I told them through the interpreter that I was bringing the reverend missionary fathers with me, so that they might absolve them all of the great sin they had committed in having separated themselves from our holy faith and the other crimes they had committed during the uprising. By virtue of the pardon, I had brought the image of the Blessed Virgin on that royal standard, which I showed them. Because they were Christians, as they had been and all their children should be, the reverend fathers would baptize them, for which they should select compadres according to their wishes. I would also be one. The reverend missionary father, fray Francisco Corvera, aided by the others, absolved them. They also baptized all the Indians' boys and girls, children, and infants. I, the governor and captain general, was godfather to a daughter of Captain Domingo, as well as to other people who gave me their children so that I might take and hold them, so that they might be baptized. The leaders, soldiers, and other people of this camp did likewise.

Seventy-four infants and boys and girls of all ages were baptized

The reverend fathers having attended to and finished this with great joy, counted the baptized of all ages and both sexes, seventy-four people. So that this may be of record, I ordered them all to wear crosses and pray the four prayers in the afternoon and morning, to which they replied they would. I told and ordered them that those who had separated from their wives should receive the holy sacrament of marriage, returning to them, and if they were with others, they should leave them.

So that everything referred to may be of record, I signed it with the interpreter and witnesses, the captain of the presidio, the alferez, and my secretary of government and war.

Don Diego de Vargas Zapata Luján Ponce de León

Roque Madrid

Juan de Dios Lucero de Godoy

Pedro Hidalgo

Before me, Alfonso Rael de Aguilar, secretary of government and war

Entrada to the pueblo of Cuyamungue

Today, Tuesday, 30 September, I, the governor and captain general, entered this pueblo of Cuyamungue[71] with the camp. The distance was about 2 leagues. Its captain, whose name is Juan, came out to receive me with the Indians, men as well as women and children of that pueblo. They had put up arches for me and had their crosses at the entrance of the pueblo.

Having dismounted in the plaza, as did the men-at-arms who were following me, I spoke to him, and the interpreter made the captain and the other Indians understand everything referred to and contained herein about my coming and inspection. They were happy about my coming and about returning to our holy faith. They were also overjoyed that the new possession should be revalidated and pronounced in favor of his majesty, the king, our lord, Carlos II (may God keep him).

Thirty baptized today, 30 September

The reverend father, fray Francisco Corvera, absolved them, with the reverend missionary fathers attending and helping. All three fathers then went on immediately to baptize the boys and girls, children, and infants. I, the governor and captain general, was godfather to Captain Juan's daughter and many others, as were the other soldiers. Once it was over, the reverend father saw that the number of people baptized, of all ages, male and female, was thirty.

I went on with the camp to the pueblo of Nambe. So that it may

be of record, I signed it with the interpreter, the captain, the alferez
of the presidio, and my secretary of government and war.
Don Diego de Vargas Zapata Luján Ponce de León
Roque Madrid
Pedro Hidalgo
Juan de Dios Lucero de Godoy
Before me, Alfonso Rael de Aguilar, secretary of government and war

Entrada to the pueblo of Nambe

Today, Tuesday, 30 September, I, the governor and captain general, arrived with this camp at the pueblo of Nambe. In the same
manner and form referred to, its people and captain, whose name is
Alonso, came out to receive me. I dismounted in the plaza, which
has three cuarteles. They rendered their obedience, which I received,
as did the camp, with great rejoicing. I revalidated and reclaimed
possession for his majesty, the king, our lord (may God keep him),
of this land and his vassals who have been newly reduced and conquered for the Divine and human majesties.

Fifty-one children of all ages, male and female, were baptized

Through the interpreter, I made them understand what had
occurred in the earlier pueblos, to which reference has been
made. They were absolved of their apostasy by the reverend father,
fray Francisco Corvera, who, together with the other reverend missionaries, baptized the boys and girls, children, and infants born
since their uprising. I, the governor and captain general, was
chosen as godfather to Captain Alonso's daughter and several other
Indian children, as were those of the camp. Once it was over, the
reverend father found that there were fifty-one people of all ages
baptized, male and female.

So that it may be of record, I signed it with the interpreter, the
captain, the alferez of the presidio, and my secretary of government
and war. It was 2 leagues away.
Don Diego de Vargas Zapata Luján Ponce de León
Roque Madrid
Juan de Dios Lucero de Godoy
Pedro Hidalgo
Before me, Alfonso Rael de Aguilar, secretary of government and war

Entrada to the pueblo of Pojoaque

Today, Tuesday, 30 September, I, the governor and captain general, went to spend the night at this pueblo of Pojoaque and entered it with the camp at about five o'clock in the afternoon. Its captain, whose name is Gregorio, came out to receive me with the people of his pueblo, which has two cuarteles. I dismounted in the plaza, and they rendered their obedience.

After I found the crosses set up, I told them about my coming and the rest of record in these proceedings. I also made them understand through the interpreter that his majesty (may God keep him) and no other was lord of that land and that, although they had risen up, he was their king and natural lord. In that respect, they were his vassals. As a sign of this, I was returning to pronounce and reclaim possession. In the manner referred to, I took possession of it, and it was solemnized jointly by me, the governor and captain general, and the camp.

There are forty-eight children and infants baptized

The reverend missionary, fray Francisco Corvera, absolved them as he had the others with the assistance of the reverend missionary fathers who then baptized them all: boys and girls, children, and infants. I was godfather to the infants and children of some Indians and the children of other women, as were the people the Indians selected from the camp.

After the father counted them, it was seen that forty-eight people of all ages, male and female, had been baptized. So that it may be of record and that its distance was about 1 league, I signed it with the captain, the alferez of the presidio, my secretary of government and war, and the interpreter.

Don Diego de Vargas Zapata Luján Ponce de León
Roque Madrid
Pedro Hidalgo
Juan de Dios Lucero de Godoy
Before me, Alfonso Rael de Aguilar, secretary of government and war

Entrada to the pueblo of Jacona

Today, Wednesday, 1 October of this year, 1692, I, the governor and captain general, entered this pueblo of Jacona[72] with the camp.

Its captain and people received me in the same manner as the rest. Having dismounted in their plaza, I saw one cuartel where the Indians live. Through the interpreter, I made them understand what is of record that I had told the other pueblos, confirming in their presence the possession referred to in favor of his majesty.

Eighteen children, male and female, of all ages were baptized

Father fray Francisco Corvera absolved them of their apostasy and baptized the children and other people who were unbaptized. I, the governor and captain general, was godfather to a boy, son of the captain, whose name is Diego, and to others, as were the soldiers. The reverend father found that he had baptized eighteen children of all ages, male and female.

The distance was about 1 league, more or less. So that this may be of record and that I went on to the pueblo of San Ildefonso to spend the night, I signed it with the interpreter, the captain, the alferez of the presidio, and my secretary of government and war.

Don Diego de Vargas Zapata Luján Ponce de León
Roque Madrid
Pedro Hidalgo
Juan de Dios Lucero de Godoy
Before me, Alfonso Rael de Aguilar, secretary of government and war

Entrada to the pueblo of San Ildefonso

On Wednesday, 1 October, I, the governor and captain general, entered this pueblo of San Ildefonso with the camp. Its captain and the Indians came out to see me in the same manner as the others.

Having dismounted in the plaza, I saw a large cross in it. It has four very good cuarteles. They all rendered their obedience with great warmth. I decided to spend the night there to wait for some people who were probably off at their milpas and out gathering firewood. During the afternoon, I could go on to carry out everything here that has been referred to at the other, earlier pueblos.

101 boys and girls of all ages are baptized

At about three o'clock in the afternoon, with the information that the people were assembled in the plaza, I left for it with the alferez

San Ildefonso Pueblo, John K. Hillers, c. 1880
    Museum of New Mexico

real and the royal standard, the military leaders, officials, and soldiers. Having arrived there, through the interpreter I told them and their captain, Francisco, whom they obey, what has been referred to about the other, earlier pueblos. In that manner, I also revalidated and proclaimed the king's possession of this land, kingdom, and its inhabitants. I told those present that he and no other was their king and natural lord. Thus, they understood that they were newly reduced and conquered. As is of record, Father fray Francisco Corvera granted them absolution from their apostasy in the same way as to the others, accompanied by the other reverend missionary fathers. Then, they all assisted in baptizing the boys and girls and children. Having completed the baptism, they saw the number was 101 children of all ages, male and female.

I, the governor and captain general, was godfather to Captain Francisco's daughter and many others, as were the men-at-arms and soldiers. So that it may be of record, I signed it with the captain, the interpreter, the alferez of the presidio, and my secretary of government and war. It is some 2 leagues away.

Don Diego de Vargas Zapata Luján Ponce de León
Roque Madrid
Juan de Dios Lucero de Godoy
Pedro Hidalgo
Before me, Alfonso Rael de Aguilar, secretary of government and war

Entrada to the pueblo of Santa Clara

Today, Thursday, 2 October, I, the governor and captain general, entered this pueblo of Santa Clara with the camp. The Indians received me in the manner referred to in the earlier ones. Having entered the plaza, I dismounted and saw it had four cuarteles. With the people assembled, I spoke to them through the interpreter, who made them and the captain they obey and whom they call Diego understand about my coming and the rest repeated at the earlier pueblos. In that same manner, I revalidated and proclaimed his majesty's possession of this land, kingdom, and its inhabitants who have been newly reduced and conquered for his royal crown and our holy faith.

Eighty-nine children of all ages and both sexes are baptized

The reverend father, fray Francisco Corvera, accompanied by the reverend missionary fathers, granted them absolution from their apostasy. Having done so, he baptized the infants, children, and boys and girls. I, the governor and captain general, was godfather to the captain's son and many others their parents gave me, as were the other people of the camp. Eighty-nine people of all ages and both sexes were seen to have been baptized.

So that it may be of record and that the distance was 2 leagues, I signed it with the captain, the interpreter, the alferez, and my secretary of government and war.

Don Diego de Vargas Zapata Luján Ponce de León

Roque Madrid

Pedro Hidalgo

Juan de Dios Lucero de Godoy

Before me, Alfonso Rael de Aguilar, secretary of government and war

Entrada to the pueblo of San Juan

On Thursday, 2 October, I, the governor and captain general, entered this pueblo of San Juan with the camp. Don Luis Picurí, the governor and leader of its inhabitants and the other Tewa and Tano nations, and his brother, don Antonio, had come out to receive me more than a league before arriving there. I received them in a friendly manner. They advanced with the other Indians to do the same. They had their cross, a flag like a banner, and many crosses placed at the entrance to their pueblo, as well as one in their plaza, where they had provided a new room with an enramada in the form of a corridor for me and the three reverend fathers.

The men-at-arms and I dismounted. I ordered don Luis to order his captains to bring all the people who were absent. Once they were all together, they might all be absolved. All the children and those not there yet could be baptized.

Everyone assembled, and I ordered the men-at-arms to form a rank and the alferez to hold the royal standard. The interpreter was present, and I told them of my coming and the rest of record about the earlier pueblos. They happily received the words said to them and celebrated the possession I revalidated and proclaimed in favor of his majesty, both of this kingdom, its land, and of them, his vassals, who had been newly reduced and conquered for the royal crown and our holy faith.

Seventy-six people of all ages are baptized

The reverend father, fray Francisco Corvera, assisted by the other reverend missionaries, also absolved them and went on to baptize the people and children. I, the governor and captain general, was godfather to don Luis's son and others, as were the men-at-arms. Their number was seen to be seventy-six people of all ages, male and female.

Also, a woman married to Cristóbal Nieto,[73] who lives in Sonora, was found in this village. His relatives recognized her with three sons and daughters, all of whom she had had during this time. There was also another captive found, an unmarried woman named Juana de Arzate, to whose son I was godfather. There was also another captive, an unmarried Spanish woman, a daughter of Nevares, a soldier now at the presidio of Janos, and one from the Tiwa nation of Isleta Pueblo. He is the brother of Juan Moro, who has come with the camp. So that this may be of record and that its march and distance was about 2 leagues, I signed it with the captain, the interpreter, the alferez, and my secretary of government and war.

Don Diego de Vargas Zapata Luján Ponce de León
Pedro Hidalgo
Juan de Dios Lucero de Godoy
Before me, Alfonso Rael de Aguilar, secretary of government and war

Entrada to San Cristóbal Pueblo

Today, Friday, 3 October, I, the governor and captain general, ordered the camp and men-at-arms to remain in this pueblo of San Juan, so that I might rapidly visit and make an entrada to the pueblos of San Cristóbal and San Lázaro.[74] If God sees fit, I shall return here to spend the night.

Thus, I left with two squads, the military leaders, the interpreter, and my secretary of government and war, together with the reverend missionary fathers, fray Francisco Corvera and fray Cristóbal Alonso Barroso, with whom I entered San Cristóbal Pueblo, about 3 leagues away. Captain Francisco and his people received me in the same manner as in the others.

Having entered the plaza, which had four cuarteles, we dismounted. I told them what is contained herein through the interpreter. On behalf of his majesty, I revalidated the possession of this pueblo and its inhabitants, his vassals, who have newly been reduced and conquered for the royal crown and our holy faith.

> There are sixty-six baptized, children and boys and girls of all ages and both sexes

The reverend father, fray Francisco Corvera, absolved them and baptized the children and other people who were unbaptized. I, the governor and captain general, was godfather to Captain Francisco's son. Many who came in my company were godfathers to the rest as well. It was seen that the number of those baptized was sixty-six boys and girls and children of all ages and both sexes.

A Tiwa Indian from Isleta who was with my camp found his wife with two small children in the pueblo. Through Sgto. mayor Alonso García, procurator general for the Indians and nations from El Paso, he asked me to order them to turn her over to him. He wanted her to be handed over because she was his wife. Having assured her that no harm would be done her, I gave her to him. The Indian was very content to have found his wife.

Also, another Indian woman of the Piro nation was found with a small child. She is married to an Indian from the pueblo of El Paso who came with the camp. His relatives asked that she be handed over to return her to her husband. So that it may be of record, I signed it with the interpreter, the procurator general, the captain of the presidio, the alferez, and my secretary of government and war.

Don Diego de Vargas Zapata Luján Ponce de León
Roque Madrid
Alonso García
Juan de Dios Lucero de Godoy
Pedro Hidalgo
Before me, Alfonso Rael de Aguilar, secretary of government and war

> Entrada to the pueblo of San Lázaro

Today, Friday, 3 October, I, the governor and captain general, entered the pueblo of San Lázaro with the men-at-arms and reverend fathers. They and their captain, don Cristóbal Yope, received me with a large cross. There were others at the entrance to their pueblo. In the center of the plaza, which has four cuarteles, they had placed another cross in front of which they had prepared an enramada for the reverend fathers and me.

After everyone had dismounted and the people of the pueblo had assembled at my order, I told them what is of record that I ordered the interpreter to tell, as he had done in the other pueblos, which I repeated to him. I was revalidating and reclaiming, in his majesty's name, his possession of this kingdom, its lands, and Indians. The people of this pueblo are his vassals, newly reduced and conquered for his royal crown and our holy faith.

Eighty-nine are baptized, children and boys and girls of all ages and both sexes

After Father fray Francisco Corvera had granted and they had received absolution, they presented their children and other people so that they might be baptized, which he did. I, the governor and captain general, was godfather to a daughter and a son of Captain don Cristóbal and others. So were the men-at-arms. Having finished, it was seen that there were eighty-nine people and children of all ages.

Though I wanted to go, they asked me to wait, saying they would give me something to eat. I accepted this courtesy, as did my men. So that this may be of record and that I returned to San Juan Pueblo, 4 leagues away, I signed it with the interpreter, the captain, the alferez of the presidio, and my secretary of government and war.

Don Diego de Vargas Zapata Luján Ponce de León

Roque Madrid

Pedro Hidalgo

Juan de Dios Lucero de Godoy

Before me, Alfonso Rael de Aguilar, secretary of government and war

Order the governor and captain general leaves for the artillery captain in San Juan Pueblo regarding departing from it for Picuris and Taos

Today, Saturday, 4 of the present month of October, I concluded the inspection of the preceding pueblos of the Tewa and Tano nations. It is necessary to go on to the districts and pueblos of the nations of the Picuris and Taos, which are from 20 to 22 leagues from this pueblo of San Juan. The road is very rough and through mountain ranges. It is impossible to transport the two cannon and the large bronze stone mortar.

So that they and some victuals may remain in San Juan Pueblo with some degree of safety, I, the governor and captain general, order the artillery captain to attend to everything, his guard remaining under his charge. So that he may have an escort, I am leaving him ten soldiers from the two groups of the men-at-arms of this camp, with their weapons, munitions, and horses, including those that are exhausted. He may not leave this pueblo without my order, and these men will be here for whatever order I may give. So that it may be of record, I signed it with the artillery captain and the witnesses, the captain, the alferez of the presidio, and my secretary of government and war in attendance.

Don Diego de Vargas Zapata Luján Ponce de León
Roque Madrid
Juan de Dios Lucero de Godoy
Francisco Lucero de Godoy
Before me, Alfonso Rael de Aguilar, secretary of government and war

Departure from this pueblo of San Juan for that of Picuris
He calls a halt to spend the night with the camp next to the river

Today, Saturday, 4 October, at about two o'clock in the afternoon, I, the governor and captain general, left with the camp for Picuris Pueblo. Having gone about 3 leagues, I called a halt in a cove that borders the Río del Norte to spend the night, since it was a good spot for the camp.

So that it may be of record, I signed it with the captain of the presidio, the alferez, and my secretary of government and war.

Don Diego de Vargas Zapata Luján Ponce de León
Roque Madrid
Juan de Dios Lucero de Godoy
Before me, Alfonso Rael de Aguilar, secretary of government and war

Arrival at the pueblo of Picuris

Today, Sunday, 5 October, I, the governor and captain general, arrived with the camp at this pueblo of Picuris. About a quarter of a league before entering it, the Indians had placed several arches and crosses along the road. At its entrance, their captain and leader, don Lorenzo; his brothers, don Luis Picurí and don Antonio; their children; other principal Indians of his retinue; and the people of the pueblo were waiting for me. I greeted them all, saying the alabado, to which they answered, "Forever."

I entered the pueblo, which is composed of four very large, tall separate cuarteles, three or four stories high, with adobe walls, covered passageways, and palisaded windows. I saw that they had provided me an enramada next to one of them, where I dismounted. I rested there, as did the reverend fathers.

Through the interpreters, I ordered don Lorenzo to have all the people assembled in front of the enramada, where I had my quarters. I came out and ordered the alferez to be at my side with the royal standard, having arranged the soldiers from the squads of the vanguard in a rank with the military leaders. Through the interpreter, I told the captain and other Indians and people about my coming and the rest that is of record about the earlier pueblos, returning to revalidate and reclaim the possession his majesty, the king, our lord (may God keep him), has of this pueblo and its inhabitants, his vassals. Through the interpreter, I ordered and told them all that they should wear crosses, should pray, and I was bringing the three reverend fathers to absolve them and baptize their children and other people who might be unbaptized. They would first be absolved from the great sin they had committed of having separated themselves from our holy faith.

Eighty-six of all ages are baptized

Immediately after, I asked the reverend father, fray Francisco Corvera, to absolve them, which he did in the manner referred to in the other pueblos, with the two others assisting. Then, all three baptized the people and children on that day. There were eighty-six in all.

I, the governor and captain general, was godfather to Captain don Lorenzo's daughter and many others whose parents gave them to me. The men-at-arms were as well. So that it may be of record that they are newly reduced and conquered for our holy faith and the royal crown, the march and distance were 8 leagues, and the road very rough, I signed it with the interpreters, the captain, the alferez of the presidio, and my secretary of government and war.
Don Diego de Vargas Zapata Luján Ponce de León
Roque Madrid
Juan de Dios Lucero de Godoy
Pedro Hidalgo
Before me, Alfonso Rael de Aguilar, secretary of government and war

Departure from this pueblo for that of Taos

Today, Monday, 6 of the present month of October, notwithstanding the fact that at dawn everything was covered with snow and the day stormy, I ordered the captain of the presidio to give an order for the men-at-arms and camp to be ready to leave before midday. Because they were ready, I left at about that time.

Having gone about 4 leagues on a very rough road with persistently bad weather, at that distance I called a halt at an appropriate campsite for the camp. So that it may be of record, I signed it with the captain, the alferez of the presidio, and my secretary of government and war.

Don Diego de Vargas Zapata Luján Ponce de León

Roque Madrid

Juan de Dios Lucero de Godoy

Before me, Alfonso Rael de Aguilar, secretary of government and war

Departure from this outpost of Miranda, in order to make a dawn attack on the pueblo of the Taos

Today, Tuesday, 7 October, 1692, I, the governor and captain general, and the men-at-arms of this camp were ready to leave this outpost of Miranda. Because of the denseness of the mountains and ranges, they had quartered and spent the night there yesterday at my order, so as not to be noticed by the Taos.

The Tewa, Tano, and Picuris nations of this kingdom of New Mexico have asked me to destroy these rebels, their enemy, once and for all and burn their pueblo, since they have been repeatedly raided by them, their inhabitants killed, and they cannot live safely in their pueblos or land. When their children and wives go out of their houses, they are clubbed. They all said the same thing at San Juan Pueblo.

Through the interpreter, Pedro Hidalgo, I promised them my complete assistance in this regard, coming in person for that purpose, either making friends of them or overcoming them if they did not render obedience. With regard to this, I ordered and directed the men in the camp to be very careful in battle.

I left with them and the missionary fathers at four o'clock in the morning. Having gone about 4 leagues at full gallop and passed an arroyo in a llano, in sight of the pueblo I asked for absolution from the reverend father, Cristóbal Alonso Barroso, which the entire squadron and I received. I ordered the captain of the presidio to cordon off and lay siege to a cuartel with his company. The captain of the reinforcements was to do the same with the people of his company to the other cuartel of this pueblo. The military leaders and my secretary of government and war would assist me in whatever might develop.

Entering in that manner with the men divided into three squads, siege was laid to the two large cuarteles with their ramparts and adobe wall. They saw that no one was there. We looked toward the mountain ranges to the east of this pueblo, where smoke appeared to be rising. As a result of seeing those smoke signals, I felt obliged to send don Luis the Picurí and his brother, don Lorenzo, with his men to reconnoiter that mountain range. As soon as the horses arrived so I could change mounts, I would follow him.

After about an hour had passed, an Indian sent by don Luis came to advise me, giving me word of having found the people of this pueblo of the Taos. They were in a funnel-shaped canyon in the center and way into the range, on top of which some of the Taos rebels were standing watch. With that information, I left with the men on the same mounts at full speed for that place without waiting for the horses.

A Spanish-speaking rebel Indian arrived at the foot of the mountains. When asked his name, he said it was Josefillo and that they call him the Spaniard. I embraced him and shook his hand, telling him that the people of his pueblo had acted badly in having gone to the sierra, leaving their homes when the extreme cold and snow appeared. They should be told I was coming to pardon them. The king was sending me for that reason, and I was bringing the image of the Blessed Virgin on the royal standard. He should tell them I was coming for that reason only and so that they might again become Christians. I was bringing the fathers along with me for that, so that they might absolve them and baptize the children and other people who might be unbaptized.

He understood, since I repeated it to him. I told him many other things and that he should go and tell them. So that they might believe him, I was giving him the rosary I hung around his neck. He left.

A short while later, six other Indians came, arriving before me at the foot of the sierra and surrendering their weapons. I dismounted and received them. I embraced them, and we shook hands. They joyously heard what I told them through the interpreter. I told the two who spoke the best Spanish that they should go make the people come down. For that, I was giving them rosaries and placing them around their necks as a sign of peace and pardoning them all, so that they could come down safely. They left.

Having taken that action, after a short while I saw that many of those people were coming down in groups. Among them were their captains, and the one they obey. He is their head, whose name is Francisco Pacheco. I told them they should come to their pueblo and sent word with some of them to advise the others to come down, as their captains and men were already doing.

After they had arrived in the plaza, I made them understand through the interpreters in clear words they could understand about my coming. The only thing that prevented the men, women, children, and other people who were now satisfied from coming down by tomorrow was that they did not want to leave behind the clothes they had taken to the sierra. Nevertheless, I told them that most of them could come down today, so that they could be in their homes in the pueblo and the men-at-arms would not occupy them.

After they repeated many difficulties, all born of the suspicion and fear they had about my intentions, I persuaded them to come down by treating the captains and governors kindly. I made them friends publicly in the plaza, with don Luis, don Lorenzo, and the rest of the Picuris, Tewas, and Tanos. I had them embrace and shake hands as friends, which they did, settling their differences while they embraced one other.

At about four o'clock in the afternoon, other Indians came down with the women, children, and boys and girls of this pueblo. Arriving before me, they greeted me, saying, "Praise be." I received them with great kindness and embraced them, shaking everyone's hands, telling them why I had come, which is repeated in these proceedings and entrada. Finally, after they understood through the interpreters, I ordered them to go rest because it was late, and tomorrow the remaining people would come. When they were together, I would speak to them and do what might be of service to both majesties. So that what is referred to may be of record, I signed it with the captains, the alferez of the presidio, the interpreter, and my secretary of government and war.

Don Diego de Vargas Zapata Luján Ponce de León
Juan Páez Hurtado
Roque Madrid

Juan de Dios Lucero de Godoy
Pedro Hidalgo
Before me, Alfonso Rael de Aguilar, secretary of government and war

> The people, having finished coming down from the sierra, render their obedience to me, the governor and captain general, who, in his majesty's name, revalidates the possession of this pueblo, and the children and people are absolved and baptized by the fathers

Today, Wednesday, 8 October, the Indians Josefillo the Spaniard and Francisco Pacheco, the governor of the pueblo of the Taos, gave me word that the people who had not come down from the sierra before were all together now. Therefore I, the governor and captain general, ordered that they make them come to the plaza, descending from their cuarteles.

When they had done so, I went out. Having first ordered the men-at-arms, the alferez with the royal standard, and my secretary of government and war to be present, I repeated through the interpreters to the Indians in the middle of the plaza what is of record that I said to them yesterday. I finally said that his majesty the king (may God keep him) was their lord, as is no Indian among them. Although he was lord and master of this land and them, his vassals, he asked for nothing. As a sign of taking possession again, I was ordering the royal standard in my hand raised. Also, the people were to say along with me, three times, "Long live the king, our lord, Carlos II, king of the Spains and of this New World, this kingdom of New Mexico, this land, and the pueblo of the Taos, whose inhabitants are his vassals." In the manner referred to, I revalidated the possession, telling them that I was bringing the fathers so that they might grant them absolution.

> Ninety-six children and boys and girls of all ages and both sexes were baptized

Father fray Francisco Corvera went on to do so at my request, assisted by the other two reverend fathers. Together they baptized the children and the other people who were unbaptized. When they had finished, ninety-six of all ages and both sexes were seen to have been baptized.

I ordered them all to wear crosses and pray the four prayers. Those not living with their wives should return to them and separate from

Taos Pueblo, B. H. Guernsey, 1878

others they might be with, and those who were unmarried should marry, if they wished. So that everything referred to may be of record, I signed it with the interpreter, the captain, the alferez of the presidio, and my secretary of government and war.

Don Diego de Vargas Zapata Luján Ponce de León

Roque Madrid

Juan de Dios Lucero de Godoy

Pedro Hidalgo

Before me, Alfonso Rael de Aguilar, secretary of government and war

> Word Josefillo and Governor Pacheco give of having heard two Indians from this pueblo who appear before me say they came from Zuni and there was a gathering to ambush me, waiting along the road when I leave with the men-at-arms

Today, Wednesday, 8 October, at about four o'clock in the afternoon, Pedro Hidalgo, principal interpreter on this campaign, came before me, the governor and captain general, to say that Josefillo the Spaniard and the governor and captain of this pueblo of the Taos, Francisco Pacheco, had told him they wanted to see me and give me a report about what they knew. I ordered them to enter my tent and be seated. I told them I would hear with pleasure and love whatever they might want to tell me.

They said to the interpreter that we were now like brothers and friends, since they were once again Christians. They told me that two young men, natives of the pueblo of the Taos, had come from the province of Zuni. On the return trip to Acoma they had encountered a large gathering that all the captains from the nations of Zuni, together with those from Moqui, the Jemez, Keres, Pecos, Faraones, Coninas from the Cerro Colorado, and many others from other places had held for three days and nights. They had heard them say it would be some time before the Spaniards left this kingdom, and in the interim, they should prepare their supplies. Thus, they would lie in ambush along the road to fall upon the horses, the camp, and me, the governor and captain general.

Having seen and understood this, I thanked them and treated them kindly. I told don Luis, don Lorenzo, and the other Indians that since those nations were their enemies, to be safe and live quietly in their pueblos with no one doing them harm, they should assemble the young men from their pueblos, those who were fastest, bravest, best armed, and had the best horses. They would go with me and the camp to the pueblos of the nations that border theirs, the Pecos and the Keres of Cochiti, Santo Domingo, San Felipe, Santa Ana, and Zia and Jemez, so that they might render their obedience as they had done before. Upon doing so, I would pardon, and the fathers would absolve them and baptize the children and other people who might be unbaptized. If not, we would destroy them all. I ordered them to be at the villa of Santa Fe a week from tomorrow, Thursday, for the departure. From there they would go with me to the pueblo and district of the Pecos, since the people of Taos from this pueblo were their friends.

I told their governor, Francisco Pacheco, that two swift young men could go. I would give them a cross drawn on a piece of paper and a rosary for each one to wear around his neck as a safe conduct that I was going in peace to see and pardon them. The fathers were going to do the same as they have in this pueblo and the others. They should give them this message.

With respect to this decision, they agreed with my opinion and accepted the departure, which would be a great relief for them and leave them secure and content. I repeated my kind treatment, guaranteeing my good intentions, greatly esteeming and loving them. I told them I wanted them to go with me not because I feared them, but so as to leave them as friends and secure, for this is what I had done in this pueblo. They said this is how they understood it to be. So that what was decided because of the information may be of record, I signed with the interpreters, the captain, the alferez of the presidio, and my secretary of government and war.

Don Diego de Vargas Zapata Luján Ponce de León
Roque Madrid
Pedro Hidalgo
Juan de Dios Lucero de Godoy
Before me, Alfonso Rael de Aguilar, secretary of government and war

Departure from the pueblo of the Taos

Today, Thursday, 9 October, I left the Indians of this pueblo reassured in their tranquility, pleased at having seen me and returned to our holy faith. On my order, they turned over their captives, two women with seven children of all ages, male and female, and a Tiwa Indian who is leaving for El Paso. Upon arriving there (if our Lord sees fit), he will marry one of the two Piro women, by whom he has three children. She is being taken by her brothers.

I, the governor and captain general, spent the night at the Miranda campsite with the men and the next day at the pueblo of the Picuris, where I was received very kindly and humbly. So that this arrival may be of record and that I went 10 leagues in two days, I signed it with the captain, the alferez of the presidio, and my secretary of government and war.

Don Diego de Vargas Zapata Luján Ponce de León
Roque Madrid
Juan de Dios Lucero de Godoy
Before me, Alfonso Rael de Aguilar, secretary of government and war

Arrival of the three young Indian men from Taos Pueblo who are going to Pecos to bring them down to the villa to see me, the governor and captain general

Today, Friday, after I, the governor and captain general, arrived with the camp at the pueblo of the Picuris, the principal interpreter, Pedro Hidalgo, came before me with three Indians from the pueblo of the Taos. They are the ones I had arranged for their governor, Francisco Pacheco, to send me before going on to the pueblo of the Pecos. The interpreter gave them the message they are to carry.

So they may recognize that I am sending them the message and will not be suspicious, I gave each of them rosaries that I put around their necks and also a cross more than a vara long with another drawn on a piece of blank paper as a sign of peace and that I would await each and every one in the villa of Santa Fe. So that it may be of record, I signed it with the interpreter, the captain of the presidio, its alferez, with my secretary of government and war.

Don Diego de Vargas Zapata Luján Ponce de León
Roque Madrid
Juan de Dios Lucero de Godoy
Before me, Alfonso Rael de Aguilar, secretary of government and war

Arrival at San Juan Pueblo

Today, Saturday, 11 October, I, the governor and captain general, arrived with the camp at about three o'clock on the return from Taos. I found that nothing worth mentioning in these proceedings had happened to the artillery captain and the soldiers I had left. The distance traveled was 9 leagues by the shortcut of the funnel-shaped canyon, over a very difficult road through that mountain range. I signed it with the witnesses, the captain, the alferez of the presidio, and my secretary of government and war.

Don Diego de Vargas Zapata Luján Ponce de León

Roque Madrid

Juan de Dios Lucero de Godoy

Before me, Alfonso Rael de Aguilar, secretary of government and war

Arrival at San Ildefonso Pueblo

Today, Tuesday, 14 October, I, the governor and captain general, arrived with the camp at San Ildefonso Pueblo. Its inhabitants received me again with the same kindness as when I had entered the first time. So that it may be of record, I signed it with the captain, the alferez of the presidio, and my secretary of government and war.

Don Diego de Vargas Zapata Luján Ponce de León

Roque Madrid

Juan de Dios Lucero de Godoy

Before me, Alfonso Rael de Aguilar, secretary of government and war

Arrival at the villa of Santa Fe

Today, Wednesday, 15 October, I, the governor and captain general, arrived at this villa of Santa Fe with the camp. The inhabitants received me with great kindness. So that it may be of record, I signed it with the captain, the alferez of the presidio, and my secretary of government and war.

Don Diego de Vargas Zapata Luján Ponce de León

Roque Madrid

Juan de Dios Lucero de Godoy

Before me, Alfonso Rael de Aguilar, secretary of government and war

Proceedings of transmittal to the most excellent lord viceroy, Conde de Galve

In the villa of Santa Fe, newly reduced and conquered for our holy faith and the royal crown, principal city of the kingdom of New Mexico, on 16 October 1692, don Diego de Vargas Zapata Luján

Ponce de León, governor and captain general of this kingdom, its lands and provinces, and castellan of its fortress and presidio for his majesty, has achieved by means of divine favor and at his own expense the reduction and conquest for our holy faith and the royal crown of this villa since 13 September of the present year, when he made an entrada to it with his majesty's arms.

> Thirteen pueblos conquered with that of the villa, Tewas, Tanos, Picuris, and Taos

The difficulties and rebellion of its inhabitants are referred to in what is of record in these proceedings, as are those of the other pueblos of the Tewas, Tanos, Picuris, and Taos. There are thirteen pueblos, including that of the villa.

It is also of record that during that time, an entrada was made on Tuesday, 23 September, to the pueblo of the Pecos. Rebellious in their apostasy, they abandoned the pueblo, whose population, judging from its cuarteles and plazas, would be fifteen hundred Indians.

The day the men-at-arms of the camp patrolled the mountains and ranges, which resulted in only a few prisoners, is of record. The number of prisoners increased with the repeated patrols made by the men-at-arms in the course of the five days of the siege against the pueblo. Having seen that it was useless, and so as not to waste time, they gave the prisoners their freedom. They numbered thirty people and six other captives who left with their relatives. Also, a soldier from among the horse guard found a bronze artillery piece.

So that the circumstances, actions, patrols, entradas, arrangements, and orders I, the governor and captain general, gave, made, and decided upon for the entrada, reduction, and conquest, and the letters written to the most excellent lord viceroy (may God keep him), may be of record for your excellency, the most excellent lord, the Conde de Galve, representative of the king, our lord; lord viceroy, governor and captain general of all this kingdom and that of New Spain; president of the Royal Audiencia and court of Mexico, I ordered my secretary of government and war to copy them to the letter for your excellency and his majesty, the king, our lord (may God keep him). As his loyal vassal, I reverently place the victory at his royal feet. I would hope, if it is possible, that it would be all that remains to be reduced and conquered for his royal crown in this New World.

At present, those who have again been reduced to our holy faith and the royal vassalage of his majesty are the Tewa, Tano, Picuris, and Taos nations, who live in the thirteen pueblos and villa mentioned. There and in all of them, I, the governor and captain general, revalidated, reclaimed, and proclaimed the new possession for his majesty of this kingdom, its lands, provinces, and inhabitants, who are his vassals.

So that what was done, reduced, and conquered, and the success of this enterprise to date may be of record for the most excellent lord viceroy, I send these military proceedings to your greatness with the letter. My secretary of government and war will copy the proceedings and the letter exactly, so as not to risk the originals, which will remain with me, as the road is so long and the land so dangerous. So that the proceedings of transmittal may be of record, I signed it with the witnesses, the captain, the alferez of the presidio of El Paso, and my secretary of government and war.

Don Diego de Vargas Zapata Luján Ponce de León
Roque Madrid
Before me, Alfonso Rael de Aguilar, secretary of government and war

Letter to the most excellent lord viceroy, the Conde de Galve, written with the military proceedings of the conquest of the villa of Santa Fe and its twelve pueblos, sent with the proceedings from the villa on 16 October 1692

Most excellent sir,

Sir, at the time I departed El Paso on 21 August, I left a letter written to your excellency, informing you of this. In the letter, I told your excellency that we must not risk the conquest promised to you and the other lords of the royal junta, already affirmed and made known throughout New Spain, New Biscay, Sonora, and other places and reported in the opinion I prepared in response to your excellency's directive, in which I pointed out how advantageous and necessary it is. Having experienced and seen this kingdom, it may be of the greatest savings to the royal treasury. Putting aside considerations of the enemy, the peril to my life, and the difficulties of such superior forces that some hasten to say once and for all are invincible, I decided to risk everything. It would be better for me to be accused of being bold than cowardly, so as not to put my honor into question. I departed and fulfilled my promise.

I left the letter of record in these proceedings for your excellency and the order to my lieutenant governor and captain general. This was so that in case the fifty soldiers your excellency ordered to come arrived, he could send them on to me immediately with the captain I had provided. They could come within two weeks to reinforce me at the villa, to which I made an entrada on the day referred to, 13 September. The happy outcome of this resulted in my being able to overcome the remaining difficulties. I resolutely refused to recognize the manifest danger of continuing with so few men in a land inhabited by such treacherous people who that day so rebelliously and obstinately demonstrated their hate, anger, and rancor. They shouted that they would continue the battle for five days and fight until they killed us all, and we would not be able to escape as we had the first time. Although the camp on that day numbered forty soldiers and fifty Indians, at times I remained within sight of the fortress with but twelve men. Because the surrounding districts and pueblos had been warned, there were many groups coming down to the villa to their aid from the various mesas and mountain ranges. So that they might not go on to encourage the rebels to begin the war, I thought it advantageous to have the men who could have guarded me scatter the Indians through the mountains. I would remain exposed to the risk that, seeing me so alone in the plaza, they might have the audacity to come out to attack the squad.

The siege lasted from four o'clock in the morning to three o'clock in the afternoon. It was necessary to take that much time to break down their contumacy, so they might abandon the unbelievers who replied to me. Finally, I managed to get them to submit to the Divine and human majesties. They were absolved from their apostasy and returned to his majesty, the king, our lord (may God keep him), in new possession of the villa. I inspected, entered, made surrender, and conquered its pueblos for the Divine and human majesties.

In this way, I revalidated and proclaimed possession for his majesty along a distance of 36 leagues. In them, 969 people and children born since the time of their uprising were baptized. I found, most excellent sir, that to achieve the purpose of his majesty's royal, Catholic zeal, assure the permanence of our holy Catholic faith, and prevent their rebelling again, the land and its inhabitants must have settlers and presidios. To do otherwise would be to risk losing everything that will be expended. I know that, unless five hundred families and one hundred presidial soldiers come here, it will be like casting a grain of salt into the sea.

Of the families who can be counted are one hundred at El Paso and fifty soldiers from the presidio. As to the citizens your excellency and the Royal Treasury Junta seek, you should not harbor any great hopes. It would be easier for the Inquisition to forgive the Jews than force the citizens to leave the places where they live and are well established. Thus, you could sift through the jails of Mexico City, Querétaro, Zacatecas, Guadalajara, and Rosario and send craftsmen here: gunsmiths, carpenters, and barbers. Miners, vagrants, and vagabonds in the reales can come to this land to explore the mines. There are many whose ores I have seen. The families from El Paso should be considered with regard to security and of better quality, but not in terms of economy. Without corresponding support and assistance from the royal treasury, they will be unable to move. Thus, they would be incredible burdens, blind and crippled.

I am leaving on this date with some allied Indian warriors who go willingly to make war against the nations of their enemies, contiguous for some 30 to 40 leagues. They have abandoned the pueblos where they were living so as to be safe from their enemies, being better off in the rough country of the mountain ranges, mesas, and cañadas. I have two aims and intentions. The first is the idea I have followed in this conquest of seeing whether I can reduce them to our holy faith and manage to make friends with them, as I did with the nation of the Taos. If my good intention is not achieved, and theirs is such that they remain rebellious and contumacious, I shall leave them destroyed and annihilated once and for all. Then these nations and the citizens his majesty (may God keep him) may see fit to send here as settlers may live safely wherever they are. They will be hard pressed just to defend themselves from the Apaches, who are many and have widespread rancherias.

If, after ending the war with the Jemez and Keres, I have enough horses able to travel the more than 300 leagues on the round trip to the provinces of Zuni and Moqui, I shall go on to the Cerros Colorados and mercury mine to investigate what is said about it. Once and for all, I shall finish with the matter of vassalage to his majesty being given in the kingdom of New Mexico, so that with a complete report, you may decide and determine to settle it.

As far as I am concerned, I shall be satisfied and glory in the fact that no one has had the boldness to do what I have done up to now through divine will. I shall live safe in the knowledge that no one will censure my actions when I report triumphs through divine mercy.

Once achieved, the word will spread like wild fire, so that from now on ability will enslave envy. Confronting the greatest difficulty, I shall be able to say that no one should lose hope when valor accompanies unadorned disinterest.

I place myself at the feet of your excellency's nobility, not to demand remuneration, but to tell you that with humble affection the least of your servants places and offers his works at your feet. Without them and without risk, one neither achieves nor acquires victories. I endlessly render my victory in this kingdom to your nobility, telling you that I hope to seal it with good fortune at Zuni and Moqui, though I have some doubts. I say that there is nothing left for me but to serve in order to be worthy of the honor princes owe their servants. So, I trust your excellency will do what is necessary to make his majesty, the king our lord, aware of my son, who was a menino of the queen our lady who died and the reigning one.[75] May God keep your most excellent person in increasing nobility many happy years. From this villa of Santa Fe, principal city, kingdom of New Mexico, newly reduced and conquered for our holy faith and the royal crown, on 16 October 1692.

Most excellent lord, your humblest servant kisses your hand,

Don Diego de Vargas Zapata Luján Ponce de León

Most excellent lord viceroy, the Conde de Galve

Alfonso Rael de Aguilar, Certification, Santa Fe, 16 October 1692, DS.

This agrees with the original, which remains in the possession of lord don Diego de Vargas Zapata Luján Ponce de León, governor and captain general of this kingdom and provinces of New Mexico, castellan of its fortress and presidio for his majesty, by whom I was ordered to make an exact transcription of the copy of the military proceedings recorded in this conquest of New Mexico, to send to the most excellent lord, the Conde de Galve, viceroy, governor, and captain general of all this New Spain. It is exact, true, corrected, and in order. Capt. Roque Madrid and Afz. Juan de Dios Lucero de Godoy, were present. It is on ordinary blank paper, as the stamped kind is not available here. This copy is on 138 folios, in whole and in part. Done in this villa of Santa Fe, principal city of the kingdom of New Mexico, newly reduced and conquered for the royal crown, on 16 October 1692.

In testimony of the truth, I make my customary signature and rubrica.

Alfonso Rael de Aguilar [rubrica]

Secretary of government and war

Diego de Vargas to the Conde de Galve, Santa Fe, 16 October 1692, LS.

Most excellent sir,

Sir, I have held this point in reserve, so that I alone would be the first your excellency seeks out in the selection of a head ecclesiastic. This is so that this kingdom may convalesce quickly from the illness caused by the Indians recently reduced and converted to our holy faith from their apostasy, and so that they may be dissuaded from the license in which they have lived, blind slaves of the devil, with the abuses of their heathenism that as idolaters they have followed. So that such deep roots may be cut away and torn from their hearts, he who will govern in spiritual matters must have the appropriate manner and method to reintroduce the rudiments of our holy faith in place of their superstitious abuses. I thus express to your excellency's nobility that the custos of this kingdom should have the necessary prudence and talents.

With similar wisdom in choosing a person who has these qualities and experience, I find the reverend father, fray Francisco de Vargas, appropriate, because of his great service to both majesties, and worthy, because of his talents and merits. He has lived in this region nearly thirteen years, having served as custos for a three-year term in El Paso. He has given justified and competent satisfaction in his term of office, also having the manner and civility, such that the citizens, settlers, and Indian nations esteem and love him. He was very mindful of the governors, my predecessors, and likewise of me, when I arrived at the end of his term as custos. He remains in the convento he rebuilt in the pueblo of the Manso nation, which he reduced to the faith and whose church he built. In obedience to his prelates, he is ministering to doctrinas. Likewise, in attention to what I express to your excellency on this point, it would serve your greatness to intercede so that the very reverend father commissary, on his authority, would choose him and confer the office on him, ordering him to send the letter patent of such custos.

I assure your excellency that this father is not involved and does not agree with this suggestion. He only wishes that the happy success in what I have achieved at such great risk should be enjoyed, considering that people of such character need the prudence of their pastor and ecclesiastical minister to govern their souls. I have done no more than my duty in expressing to your excellency my opinion on both matters. I feel no reservation in having made this representation to your excellency, so that you may consider what you think most appropriate in everything. May God keep your most excellent person many happy years. Done in this villa of Santa Fe, 16 October 1692.

Most excellent sir, your truest and humblest servant kisses your hand,

Don Diego de Vargas
Zapata Luján Ponce de León [rubrica]

Lord viceroy, the Conde de Galve
Villa of Santa Fe, 16 October 1692
Received on 21 November
Don Diego de Vargas Zapata Luján

Diego de Vargas to the Conde de Galve, Santa Fe, 16 October 1692, LS.

Most excellent sir,

Sir, I want to work in everything with the certainty of pleasing your excellency. As soon as I return to El Paso (Our Lord seeing fit), if it pleases your excellency, I shall order the fifty soldiers your ordered sent from the presidios of Parral where their families are and their captains will need them, to return and in everything carry out the orders you may give me, which will be the most effective. May God keep your most excellent person in your increasing nobility. I entreat you to reply by courier as soon as possible, so that I shall not be isolated here. With the Río del Norte freezing, the excessive snows, and the winter's ice, my horses may be destroyed, most of them dying, leaving me at any rate, on foot. From this villa of Santa Fe, 16 October 1692.

Most excellent sir, your humble servant who venerates you kisses your hand,

Don Diego de Vargas
Zapata Luján Ponce de León [rubrica]

Most excellent lord viceroy, the Conde de Galve
Villa of Santa Fe, 16 October 1692
Received 21 November
Don Diego de Vargas Zapata y Luján

*Luis Pérez Granillo to the Conde de Galve, El Paso,
23 October 1692, LS.*

New Mexico
Most excellent sir,
   Sir, my passions do not excuse me, as lieutenant general of this kingdom, from reporting to your excellency that today, on this date, two couriers arrived, sent by my governor and captain general from the villa of Santa Fe in New Mexico. One went on with dispatches for your excellency with the information about his having conquered most of the kingdom of New Mexico, for which I give thanks to God. To your excellency, I give many congratulations for its conquest during your term of government. With regard to this outpost, I inform your excellency that all is quiet, glory be to God, whom I ask to keep your most excellent person for many centuries. El Paso and 23 October 1692.

The least of your servants kisses your excellency's feet,

Luis Pérez Granillo [rubrica]

———

El Paso, 23 October 1692
Received 21 November
Luis Pérez Granillo

> *Cabildo of Santa Fe to the Conde de Galve,*
> *El Paso, 24 October 1692, LS.*

Most excellent sir,

Sir, Wednesday, 24 October, this cabildo received the letter and report our governor and captain general of this kingdom, don Diego de Vargas, made. In it, he informed us of the state of the new conquest of the kingdom of New Mexico and the villa of Santa Fe, as he will relate at greater length to your excellency in the dispatch he sends. It is certain, most excellent sir, that having examined its contents, we cannot refrain from offering your excellency the thanks and congratulations owed for the successful return to the faith and pacification of that unfortunate kingdom. This has required much diligence and care from your most excellent person as a prince so devoted to the honor of God and increase of his majesty's royal crown. Under his royal protection, we are ready and very obedient, as loyal vassals of the king, our lord (may God keep him), to comply with and obey your excellency's orders as his representative.

Thus it is, most excellent sir, that we only ask your excellency to safeguard us and give us the aid and forces to defend and guard the royal crown in the new conquest of New Mexico and for the preservation of Christianity. We, all the settlers of this kingdom, will have our spirits uplifted and find ourselves enriched by the best means your excellency, as so sovereign a prince with the junta of your royal acuerdo, may adopt for the preservation and increase of the new conquest. Thus, we cannot but inform your excellency how happy these poor settlers will be with word of relief resulting from your excellency's royal largess. We lay at your excellency's feet so many and such very great efforts and misfortunes we have suffered for twelve years in the defense of Christianity. This has been bought with our blood, both in this region and in the new conquest of the province of Sonora, Casas Grandes, and its districts. This was with the aim of achieving the good fortune of returning the kingdom of New Mexico to the yoke of evangelical law.

Today you can already see that in most of that kingdom, obedience is rendered to his majesty (may God keep him). Trusting in your excellency's royal protection, we ask and beg with all humility that you see fit to send us the cedula of honors his majesty (may God keep him) granted to this cabildo, to comply and obey according to what is contained therein. Likewise, prostrate at the feet of your most excellent person, we ask you to please help this kingdom with the cedula of exemptions and liberties granted to children, grandchildren, and descendants of conquerors and first settlers of this kingdom. What your excellency sent us is the contract for conquest the adelantado, don Juan de Oñate,[76] made. The cedulas, together with the capitulations, which are the ones we need, did not come. In everything, this cabildo awaits the favor of the royal largess of your most excellent person. May God keep you for many happy years, as is wished, in your greatest nobility.

El Paso, 24 October 1692

Most excellent sir, this cabildo, justicia y regimiento kisses your excellency's feet, with all humility,

Francisco de Anaya Almazán [rubrica]
Don Juan García de Noriega [rubrica]
Antonio Montoya [rubrica]
Diego Montoya [rubrica]
Don Pedro Ladrón de Guevara [rubrica]
Tiburcio de Ortega, [rubrica]
Secretary of the cabildo

The justicia, cabildo and regimiento of El Paso, 24 October 1692
Received on 21 November
They ask to be sent his majesty's cedula, in which various privileges were conceded to that cabildo, so that they may be kept and likewise the other one of prerogatives and exemptions that ought to be retained for the descendants of conquerors and first settlers of those provinces.

*Fray Joaquín de Hinojosa to the Conde Galve, El
Paso, 24 October 1692, ALS.*

Most excellent sir,
    This is matter for loving rejoicing, because of the conversion of so many apostates reduced to the faith and the many baptized children.

The heavenly spirits and the blessed are giving thanks to the Most High for His mercies with celestial joy. Because of the conversion of a single soul, the joys of the church triumphant are many. For this reason, my humility ought not to diminish now, but be much encouraged to give many thanks to Our Lord God, as I and your excellency's chaplains all do with repeated pealing of bells and solemn masses of thanksgiving. Public prayers and supplications have been continuous. Due thanks are owed to your excellency's nobility. Your actions and inspiration have achieved the success, so wished for, of now possessing most of the kingdom of New Mexico in peace. The governor and captain general, don Diego de Vargas Zapata Luján Ponce de León, continues this, having followed the wise decision of demanding peace from the pueblos before bloodying weapons. Thus, without expending a single shot, today he is in possession of it. Moreover, this will be more esteemed for having been achieved during your excellency's term. Time and again, its preservation is successful because of your excellency's most outstanding wisdom. I and every religious of this holy custody know this to be so secure that in the name of all my seraphic Order, and with all humility, I give the thanks I owe to your excellency, whose greatness is most essential for the future.

Nota bene

The fifteen priests here today are insufficient; many more are necessary for such vast lands. I shall not trouble your excellency with further writing, because the governor and captain general will give you the necessary, specific information. I only ask that our Divine Majesty keep for us the human majesty of our Catholic monarch, in the possession of the entire terrestrial sphere, which, with your excellency's life, is assured. May God so will, with the happiness that I, a humble chaplain, request. El Paso, 24 October 1692.

Your humble chaplain kisses your excellency's feet,
as always,

Fray Joaquín de Hinojosa [rubrica]

————

El Paso, 24 October 1692
Received 21 November
Fray Joaquín de Hinojosa

———

Mexico City, 21 November 1692
To the lord fiscal, with the copy of the proceedings of the matter and those preceding it, the letters written by both the governor and other individuals from El Paso and its cabildo, and the record of the letter last written to the governor about the return of the soldiers of New Biscay to their presidios, so that, for now, with an examination of everything, he requests what may correspond to the surest and quickest sending of this courier, setting aside the rest, which requires lengthier consideration, arrangements, and preparations for the preservation of what is restored, for after the dispatch has been sent. [Galve's rubrica]

Dr. Juan de Escalante y Mendoza, Fiscal's reply, Mexico City, 21 November 1692, DS.

Most excellent sir,

His majesty's fiscal has examined this letter from the governor of New Mexico, don Diego de Vargas, of 16 October of this current year, along with two others of the same date; those from the lieutenant general and from the cabildo, justicia y regimiento of El Paso; and from the father, fray Joaquín de Hinojosa, along with the copy of the one your excellency wrote to the governor on the fifth of the current month and the copy of the proceedings you send with it, and those that were previously done, about the entrada to the villa of Santa Fe. In accord with your excellency's decree and the rapid dispatch of this courier, he says that what will be decided for now is to thank the governor for what he has done on the entrada, as is always understood from his great sense of duty and noble lineage. Its prosecution is expected with greater advances, which will be in your excellency's care. This is to favor him in everything that may be your concern and inform his majesty so that he may honor him and reward so singular a military exploit, which is and will be perfectly achieved, very much in the service of and pleasing to both majesties. Regarding this end and the wished for aim of this recovery, your excellency will likewise see fit to issue dispatches so that the governor of Parral, don Juan Isidro de Pardiñas, may find a way to provide support with people of the presidios or in some other way from the provinces, putting all his effort into aiding him. He will take part in these actions, writing to the presidial captains with whom he will confer as those who have the matter at hand, the experience in and knowledge of both kingdoms, and all supplies that may be accessible and available for this aid. He will again proclaim the orders sent to him so that the settlers who left and may remain in those districts will resettle New Mexico. He will send a list of all the settlers so that a decision can be made about what must be done with them. It is time for them to return.

He will also have proclaimed in Parral, Sonora, Sinaloa, and wherever it seems necessary that all the individuals and families who may want to go to the settlement referred to will, as first settlers, be given the privileges of nobles, and lots and lands will be distributed among them,[77] if, by this method, it would be easier for some to go. This is all that occurs to the fiscal for now.

In the meantime, with more judicious reflection and according to what may result from these affairs and the new information from the governor, don Diego de Vargas, your excellency will provide the measures you may judge most effective. With the benefit of your counsel he may be advised and encouraged to continue with discretion to carry out everything he may see as conducive to the permanence, preservation, and continuation of this enterprise, because he is currently engaged in it. According to don Diego de Vargas, one hundred presidial soldiers are necessary in the villa of Santa Fe. Your excellency has the royal cedula of 21 July of the past year of 1691 (which is in these proceedings on page 188) in which his majesty, considering that the state of things may require other measures, orders you apply your great fervor to what is most certain after reflecting on everything. You will be able to decide the point about men for the presidio according to necessity.

For now, twenty-five or thirty men may be assembled with salaries on the royal treasury's account. They may attend to the necessary military operations and orders of the governor, until your excellency decides, with more judicious reflection in the general junta as his majesty provides for in the royal cedula, what ought to be done for the permanent and sure preservation of what has been conquered. Without these measures, this will be difficult.

He proposes the father, fray Francisco de Vargas, for custos, informing you that he is the most appropriate, and this suggestion ought to be heeded. It is understood that this governor, having performed so signal a service as the restoration of New Mexico with all zeal, knowledge, and experience, and wishing for the best for the successful completion of his plan, will have looked to the father for the office of custos. In consideration of this, your excellency will see fit to request and charge the most reverend commissary general of the Order of St. Francis to appoint him and send him his letter patent, which the current courier may carry.

With respect to the prerogatives of the cabildo, your excellency will order that the cedulas it cites, which refer to it, be searched for and a copy of them sent when convenient. With regard to the representation of Father fray Joaquín de Hinojosa about fifteen ministers being too few, the governor will inform you what he may find out and may occur to him about this matter. Your excellency above all will decide what is most fitting and, as always, the best. Mexico City, 21 November 1692.

Dr. don Juan de Escalante y Mendoza [rubrica], fiscal

———

Villa of Santa Fe, 24 October 1692
Received on 21 November
Don Diego de Vargas Zapata y Luján
He says that on 13 September of this year, he carried out the promised entrada to the villa of Santa Fe, principal town of the kingdom of New Mexico, which remains reduced to his majesty's obedience.

Copy of the letter written on 5 November of this year, 1692, by the most excellent lord, Conde de Galve, my lord viceroy, governor, and captain general of this New Spain, to don Diego de Vargas Zapata y Luján, governor of the kingdom of New Mexico

I am concerned about both the result of your entrada to the villa of Santa Fe in New Mexico and the reports the captains of the presidios of New Biscay have made to me about their lack of soldiers to respond to the Indian hostilities visited upon their cordilleras because they went to garrison that presidio during the entrada. It has occurred to me to order you to restore them to the presidios they belong to as soon as possible and advise me of the state of the referred to enterprise and its events. By the enclosed dispatch, you will come to know what his majesty has ordered about the Indians' superior numbers you referred to and the fiscal's reply with his opinion. You should conform to all its points with the punctuality you are accustomed to give in the royal service. May God keep you many years. Mexico City, 5 November 1692.

The Conde de Galve

This agrees with the letter referred to

Mexico City, 21 November 1694

Don Juan Francisco de Vargas

Manuel de Lodeña [rubrica]

General junta, Mexico City, 24 November 1692, DS.

In the general junta held on 24 November 1692 by the most excellent lord, Conde de Galve, viceroy, governor, and captain general of this New Spain, with the lords don Francisco Fernández Marmolejo, don Jacinto de Vargas Campuzano, don Agustín Félix Maldonado,[78] and don Pedro de la Bastida,[79] judges of this royal audiencia; as well don Gerónimo Chacón[80] and don Manuel Suárez Muñiz,[81] judges of the royal criminal chamber of this court; don Andrés Pardo de Lago, don Mateo Fernández de Santa Cruz, and don Manuel de Tovar, comptrollers of the Royal Tribunal of Accounts; don Sebastián de Guzmán and don José de Urrutia, treasury officials of the royal treasury of this court; and don Fernando de Deza y Ulloa, comptroller general of tributes of this kingdom; his majesty's fiscal present: We have examined in this junta the letter from the governor and captain general of New Mexico, don Diego de Vargas, of 16 October of the current year, with two others of the same date; those from the lieutenant general of El Paso; from the cabildo, justicia y regimiento; from Father fray Joaquín de Hinojosa; with the copy of the one your excellency wrote to the governor on the fifth of the current month; the copy of the proceedings that he sent with it and what was done previously about the entrada to the villa of Santa Fe; and the royal cedula, dated 21 July of the past year 1691, placed with them and lately sent by his majesty. We examined the emended report of the proceedings and the letters referred to from the governor and captain general, don Diego de Vargas Luján y Zapata. He had pledged his noble lineage and great sense of duty to the entrada to the villa of Santa Fe of the provinces of New Mexico and its restoration. He undertook, achieved, and conquered it by such unusual means, discretion, and plans that not only have his outstanding triumph and advances been worthy of admiration, but also the circumstances praiseworthy and notable. With sound judgment, he took note of every measure and prudently foresaw every unexpected event to achieve it completely. With this, he made himself worthier of the happiness and successes of so much glory. Since it results in the glory of God Our Lord and his majesty's greater gratitude, he is thanked repeatedly for this with the very singular appreciation and esteem of your excellency and the lords minister of this junta, although without being able to state in detail to him the pleasure and thanksgiving he has caused in the entire kingdom. He will be kept in mind in order to care for and esteem him, as a person who by his deeds proclaims and repeats those of his predecessors. With word of his honorable methods, his excellency assures him how much it was his responsibility to communicate so singular a heroic feat to his majesty (may God keep him) with his report and proceedings. This is so that he may reward him in accord with such great merit, recommending him and his son, so that he may obtain in equal measure what his royal will justly decides to give in return for his acts. In the interim, his excellency will attend to assisting him in everything however way he can.

He should be immediately informed that his judgments are agreed with, as so appropriate to everything that has occurred. In such a brief time, orders and aid wherever needed can be neither deliberated nor decided upon. Only the one who is at present engaged in this will be able to decide. Having entrusted to him all the outcome referred to, arrangements will be left completely to his consideration and discretion. With his zeal, he will advise and arrange how the villa of Santa Fe and the rest of the reduced pueblos should remain for their preservation, with the protection and defense he may deem appropriate. In the areas around the outposts he may leave military leaders and soldiers he trusts and chooses, selecting them from the fifty he has from Parral without worrying about returning them to their presidios, the people under his command, or those he took with him from El Paso. Thus, they or the others can remain at his disposal wherever he may assign them. At his discretion, he will also arrange to take the families he proposes from El Paso to protect and defend the places he may need to secure. He will pay for their transport and aid as he deems adequate, so that they will willingly accept his assistance, either as presidial troops with soldiers' salaries or in another form he may devise instead. Because of the enormous distance from this city to those provinces, what is equitable and suitable cannot be decided here. It is up to the governor to plan and advise their composition and preservation and what will be necessary to support El Paso, what is acquired anew, and the area from one place to the other, so that everything may be expedited and what is gained, maintained.

On the first occasion that presents itself, he will send a report of what he may have done, how it is being supported and will be preserved for the future, the means and people necessary for everything, and where the presidio he proposes will be needed, reflecting on it with his great zeal and application. Because his majesty's cited royal cedula treats this case and has the same intent, send a copy of it to him. Informed of its contents, he may report to us about its particulars and see whether, in the present state of the matter, it can be carried out. He has the means to preserve those provinces, and they must be applied under his direction.

For now, this junta will provide the aid that can be sent, although he has said that none would be necessary. Send a draft up to the amount of 12,000 pesos on the treasuries of Zacatecas, Sombrerete, or Durango, whichever seems to him the most expedient and closest. With it, he may either aid the people who had to remain to defend those outposts or transport and sustain the families he may have taken from El Paso. If more people beyond those of his presidio and the fifty men from Parral are needed, he will send agents to seek out the rest from Sombrerete, Zacatecas, Durango, and Parral, or the closest places. He will be able to achieve this by paying them as he does the rest of the presidial soldiers. With this incentive and attraction, it may be that they will be easily found, proceeding in all with his generous spirit. His excellency and this junta are prepared to aid him fully for a complete success, so that the provinces will remain perfectly secured once and for all, without any contingency, happenstance, or fears of the barbarians being able to disturb them. The governor has noted that it is also this junta's decision that the people and families be sought out from the areas he proposes, as well as others to be decided upon, with all diligence for this end, as necessity demands, and because this is a matter very much in his majesty's service. Everything referred to is now ready for the sending of the courier, which urgency presses.

He has also made the petition and request to the most reverend father commissary general to send the letter patent of custos to the reverend father, fray Francisco de Vargas. On the governor's recommendation—over and above the fact that the reverend father is worthy—this has been attended to with great esteem in this junta.

We are also of the opinion that the governor and captain general should give many thanks in his excellency's name to all the religious who have aided him, and for the manner in which they have attended and accompanied him, expecting no less from their holy Rule.[82] They will continue with the same zeal in the future, persevering in it, for the greater security of the reduced. He will also thank all the military leaders, soldiers, other people, and citizens of the group who participated in the battle. He will encourage and promise them that they will be attended to in accord with each one's merits and effort made in the action referred to. They will willingly continue to support it with the aid and assistance made to them from the royal treasury. They and their families will be rewarded with the honors corresponding to first settlers, both those his majesty may grant in the royal cedula they ask to have searched out, as will be done, and the others thought advantageous for their use and comfort.

Because of what was done with the settlers who left the provinces of New Mexico and the villa of Santa Fe at the time of their loss, they replied that, once restored, they would return. Since that time has arrived, dispatches should be sent notifying them that they should do so immediately. They will be treated as the rest who are in those provinces and declared first settlers and noble. Lots and lands will be distributed to them. These orders will be sent to the governor of Parral, so that for his part, all effort and speed will be applied to comply with them, having them proclaimed throughout his jurisdiction where the settlers currently reside. The governor of Parral should also be advised that if the governor of New Mexico comes to him with an urgent request, he should send help with all speed. The captains of the presidios of Parral, which are near New Mexico, should do the same, having been so ordered. So that the agents or military leaders the governor, don Diego de Vargas, may send to seek out and enlist the necessary people may do so freely and effectively wherever they go, judges and magistrates should aid and favor them in all that is conducive to this end. With a warning about the responsibility not to delay a matter so much in his majesty's service, the treasury officials of the treasuries referred to, or the one he may choose from the three, should aid the governor with the draft in the amount of 12,000 pesos from whatever funds available in the royal treasury without delay, obstruction, or impediment. As for the rest of the points about arrangements and preparations for the preservation of what is restored and the other religious requested, let all the proceedings be taken to the fiscal. In the interim, the governor will also report about Father fray Joaquín de Hinojosa's proposal about the ministers required, in addition to those in the provinces today. Thus, it was decided and rubricated with his excellency.

Rubricated [five rubricas]

His excellency, Lords Marmolejo, Vargas, Maldonado, Bastida, Chacón, Muñiz, Pardo, Santa Cruz, Tovar, Guzmán, Urrutia, and don Fernando Deza

---

*AGN, Historia 37:6. 138 folios, 275 written pages. Transcripts of journal and correspondence from 16 August to 28 November 1692 published in Maas, *Misiones*, 188–260, with omissions. Translation of journal from 21 August to 16 October 1692 published in Espinosa, *First Expedition*, 48–165.

1. At Robledo, also known as La Cruz de Robledo, the expedition entered the southern end of the Jornada del Muerto, the 145-km dry stretch of the camino real. The name commemorates the death of Pedro Robledo who, with his family, accompanied Juan de Oñate on his 1598 expedition. This site is east of the present-day village of Rincon. Michael P. Marshall and Henry J. Walt, *Rio Abajo: Prehistory and History of a Rio Grande Province* (Santa Fe, 1984) (hereinafter RAP):235, 237.

2. Drum and bugle accompanied military announcements. The caja, or drum, used in the seventeenth century was typically a brass cylinder whose ends were fitted with rings to hold and tense cowhide drumskins by means of a cord that zigzagged from top to bottom. The clarín, or trumpet, resembled a bugle, a brass horn with one or two loops and no valves.

3. This was the twelfth anniversary of the outbreak of the 1680 Revolt.

4. Diego de Luna was born about 1633 in New Mexico, the son of María Jaramillo. An alferez in 1680, he was mustered at La

Salineta in September where he was accompanied by his extended family (with the exception of his wife, Elvira García) and servants, some thirty people in all. Luna enlisted as a settler the following year. Holding the rank of captain, he was still with the family at Corpus Christi de Ysleta in 1687, when they were described as extremely poor. Captain Luna was ordered to assemble his men for the return to New Mexico in 1692. In August of that year, he was living in Ysleta with his wife, Elvira García, and three children: Antonio, fifteen; Nicolás, five; and Gregoria, twenty-four. Espinosa, "Population of El Paso," 61–84. NMFA, 63:317–19. Hackett and Shelby, *Revolt*, 1:150; 2:76, 98. NMF, 65, 214.

5. Diego Arias de Quirós was a native of Asturias and the son of Juan de Quirós Prieto and Inés Arias. After the reconquest, he received a grant of land just east of the Governor's Palace in Santa Fe. A member of the Confraternity of Our Lady of the Conquest, he married María Ana Montoya, widow of Nicolás Márquez, on 20 July 1694. At that time, he was serving as royal alferez of Santa Fe. Arias de Quirós's wife died in 1712, and he married María Gómez Robledo two years later at San Ildefonso. He served as alcalde mayor and alcalde ordinario in Santa Fe into the late 1720s. NMF, 134. NMR, 118.

6. A captain and squad leader during the 1692 Vargas campaign, Juan López Holguín was the son of Salvador Holguín and Magdalena Fresqui and the only survivor of the prominent López Holguín family to return to New Mexico after the Revolt. His first wife, María Luján, died in 1693 at El Paso. In 1695, he married Juana Martín de Salazar, widow of Francisco de Apodaca, in Santa Fe. López Holguín was a member of the Confraternity of Our Lady of the Conquest. Alcalde mayor of San Diego de los Jémez, he died there in the 1696 uprising. NMF, 244. CRG, 68, 251.

7. Juan Ruiz de Cáceres, a native of New Mexico born about 1657, enlisted in the presidio of El Paso on 23 September 1681. He served as an interpreter of the Tewa language during the 1681 Otermín campaign. He was still living in 1698. NMF, 99. Hackett and Shelby, *Revolt*, 1:clviii, clxxiv; 2:137, 195, 232, 237, 383.

8. A pedrero, or large, bronze stone mortar, was a breech-loading artillery piece designed to shoot stone balls or bags of rocks. The design of the pedrero changed little if any from the fifteenth to the eighteenth century. Three reloadable, removable chambers were usually supplied for each gun. Each chamber held the powder and had a vent for lighting. Although the pedrero had limited range, the reloadable chambers permitted relatively rapid firing. Leonid Tarassuk and Claude Blair, eds., *The Complete Encyclopedia*

of Arms and Weapons (New York, 1982):363.

9. About 17 km north of El Paso.

10. Estero Largo lay approximately 170 km north of El Paso. Judging from its name, it was a marshy area along the Rio Grande, where high water spread out along the relatively flat river bottom. Hackett and Shelby, *Revolt,* 1:cxxv.

11. Born in Motrico (Guipúzcoa) in 1652 or 1653, Lázaro de Mizquía came to New Mexico in 1677 as an officer in charge of convicts. Mizquía remained and married María Lucero de Godoy. He passed muster before Mre. de campo Tomé Domínguez de Mendoza at San Lorenzo de la Toma in September 1681. During the 1696 revolt, while alcalde mayor of Taos, Mizquía managed to escape with his life. CRG, 71, 254, 268, 270, 295. NMF, 74. Hackett and Shelby, *Revolt,* 2:37, 109–10, 200.

12. At Ancón de Fray García, some 25 km north of El Paso, the Rio Grande could be forded. An ancón is a bay or beach in the middle of a wide stream or river, the bend of a river, or a sheltered cove. Rubén Cobos, *A Dictionary of New Mexico and Southern Colorado Spanish* (Santa Fe, 1983):86. Hackett and Shelby, *Revolt,* 1:cxxi; 2:190.

13. Sgto. mayor Cristóbal de Tapia owned land about 8.5 km south of Isleta Pueblo before 1680. At the time of the 1692 El Paso census, Tapia was married to Juana Valencia. They had no children of their own, but two orphans were members of their household. He was mayordomo of the Confraternity of Our Lady of the Conquest in 1692. NMF, 106. Espinosa, "Population of El Paso," 61–84.

14. San Diego, some 22 km north of Robledo, was the first campsite after beginning the Jornada del Muerto, one of the few where water could be obtained, because of access to the river. RAP, 243.

15. Ojo del Perrillo, Los Charcos del Perrillo, or El Perrillo was named at the time of the Oñate expedition, when, on 23 May 1598, a dog with muddy paws signaled the existence of water nearby. RAP, 237.

16. Las Peñuelas has been tentatively identified as a site on the east bank of the Rio Grande south of the water hole of El Muerto, opposite the gap in the Caballo and Cristóbal ranges. RAP, 237.

17. The water hole of El Muerto was about 30 km north of Las Peñuelas. RAP, 242.

18. The outpost of Fray Cristóbal, near present-day San Marcial, was at the northern end of the Jornada del Muerto and provided access to the river. The name is said to have originated because a nearby mountain resembled the face of fray Cristóbal Salazar, the commissary of the Franciscans on the 1598 Oñate

expedition. The name refers to a general area, not a specific site. RAP, 237, 240–41.

19. La Cruz de Anaya was about 30 km from the Rio Grande, two days' travel south of Fray Cristóbal. Otermín and Vargas used it as a campsite. At the southern edge of the malpais, the site is probably what is known today as Tucson Springs. RAP, 241.

20. Senecú, the southernmost Piro pueblo, was destroyed on 23 January 1675 by Apaches. The priest, fray Alonso Gil de Avila, was killed and the church, ruined. The survivors fled to the mission of Nuestra Señora del Socorro. The general area around Senecú evidently supplied salt to the mines of Parral during the seventeenth century. Capt. Alonso García de Alvarez, Gov. Bernardo de Mendizábal et al., Lawsuit, San Martín, 20 Jan. 1662, AHP, 1662B. RAP, 237.

21. The outpost of Juan García may have been named for the Juan García, who appeared on the list of reinforcements being sent to Oñate in New Mexico that was recorded on 29 August 1600 at San Bartolomé in the Santa Bárbara district. Hammond and Rey, *Oñate*, 1:556.

22. Socorro, originally the Piro pueblo of Pilabó, was by 1626 the site of Nuestra Señora del Socorro mission. By the 1640s, with a population of some six hundred people, it was the principal settlement of the middle Rio Grande area, serving the two visitas of Alamillo and Sevilleta as well as two nearby estancias. Spaniards fleeing in 1680 were briefly sheltered there. When they departed, they took most of the Indians to the El Paso area. RAP, 248.

23. Alamillo, a Piro pueblo, lay more than 85 km south of Isleta Pueblo. On their march from El Paso to Isleta Pueblo, on 30 November 1681, Governor Otermín and his men found that the church, convento, and crosses at Alamillo had been burned. The Spaniards put to the torch what remained and continued their march. Hackett and Shelby, *Revolt*, 1:c; 2:206. RAP, 237.

24. Sevilleta, another Piro pueblo situated north of Socorro on a bluff overlooking the Rio Grande, dated from the fourteenth century. During Otermín's 1681 return, it was still uninhabited, probably because of the threat of Apache raids. Evidence that a kiva had been constructed, however, indicated that some of the Piro who had remained behind may have tried to live there. A final unsuccessful attempt by the Piro to reoccupy the pueblo was made in 1698. RAP, 247.

25. Capt. Felipe Romero, a native of New Mexico born about 1639, married Jacinta de Guadalajara y Quirós. Romero and Bartolomé Gómez Robledo were accused of killing cattle belonging to Alamillo Pueblo in 1661. Having fled the Pueblo Revolt with his wife, six sons, and four

daughters, Romero enlisted as a soldier before Governor Otermín in El Paso on 24 September 1681. The following month, he and his son, Sebastián, were mustered before Otermín at Ancón de Fray García. Romero's estancia was near the pueblo of Alamillo at San Antonio de Sevilleta. Romero and his wife were deceased by 1695. NMR, 8:1559. NMF, 97. Hackett and Shelby, *Revolt*, 2:104, 198.

26. The outpost of Las Barrancas and hacienda of Francisco Gómez Robledo stood north of Sevilleta and about 45 km south of Isleta Pueblo. RAP, 257.

27. Established around 1662, the hacienda of Tomé Domínguez de Mendoza II was south of Isleta Pueblo on the west side of the Rio Grande, which flowed farther to the east than it does today, somewhat northwest of the present-day village of Tomé. Domínguez lost many of his family members and much of his property in 1680 and incurred some hostility from other refugees who charged him with profiteering. Tomé and his family were living in San Bartolomé in New Biscay by 1684, where they remained. List of former New Mexicans Living in Sonora and New Biscay in 1684, n.p., n.d., AHP, 1684D. Surveyor General's New Mexico Land Grant Records, San Clemente and Nicolás Durán de Chaves Grants. NMF, 25.

28. The feast of the birth of the Virgin Mary, 8 September.

29. The hacienda of Juan Domínguez de Mendoza was located approximately 13 km south of Alameda. Domínguez de Mendoza was born in Mexico City between 1629 and 1634. He was the son of Tomé Domínguez I and Elena Ramírez de Mendoza and brother of Tomé Domínguez de Mendoza II. His father had been a resident of New Mexico at least as early as 1641. Juan served in numerous military and civil capacities throughout his forty-four years of service. In 1669, he was granted an encomienda in the pueblo of Las Humanas. Fourteen years later, he led an expedition to the Jumano Indians, who ranged along the Rio Grande from El Paso almost as far south as the Big Bend. In 1685, Domínguez led a desertion plot with other members of his family and apparently fled to New Spain. The viceroy gave Domínguez permission to travel to Spain that same year. He and his son, Baltasar, were shipwrecked, and the elder Domínguez died in Madrid. Servicios personales del maestre de campo Juan Domínguez de Mendoza, n.p., c1643–95, Biblioteca Nacional de Madrid, Ms. 19258. Albert H. Schroeder, "Pueblos Abandoned in Historic Times," in *Handbook*, 9:240. NMF, 25–26. Hackett and Shelby, *Revolt*, 2:cxli.

30. Sgto. mayor Alonso García de Noriega II, the son of Alonso García, the lieutenant general of the Río Abajo region, fled Isleta Pueblo with his father and the rest of the family in 1680 before

Governor Otermín and the other survivors from Santa Fe could reach it. Born in New Mexico around 1650, García de Noriega II accompanied Otermín during his attempted reconquest. Before participating in Vargas's expeditions of 1692 and 1693, García served in operations against the Mansos, Sumas, and Apaches in the El Paso and Casas Grandes regions. He was married twice, first to Ana Jorge de Vera, with whom he had four sons, and then to María Luisa Godines, who was widowed in 1696 when Alonso died in Sevilleta of an Apache arrow wound. NMF, 34, 181. Naylor and Polzer, *Presidio and Militia*, 1:508 n9.

31. The hacienda of Mejía, within the present-day city of Albuquerque, was contiguous to the hacienda of Doña Luisa. The area, south of Central Avenue and north of the Barelas Bridge, was primarily marshland, sometimes used for grazing. No individual named Mejía has been associated with the hacienda. Vélez de Escalante, Extracto de Noticias. Marc Simmons, *Albuquerque: A Narrative History* (Albuquerque, 1982):10, 41.

32. North of Mejía, the outpost of Doña Luisa lay in the area called the Bosque Grande, the Bosque Grande de Doña Luisa, or the estancia de doña Luisa de Trujillo, which extended from the southern boundary of Alameda Pueblo to the marsh of Mejía or Pedro López. Doña Luisa may

have been Lucía de Montoya, who may have married Francisco de Trujillo around 1663. NMF, 108. CRG, 54. Adams and Chávez, *Missions*, 145 n1.

33. St. Nicholas of Tolentino, an Italian Augustinian known for his powers of healing and devoted care of the ill, died on 10 September 1305 and was canonized in 1446. Herbert Thurston and Donald Attwater, eds., *Butler's Lives of the Saints* (1798–1800; rpt., New York, 1956), 3:524–27.

34. Diego Varela de Losada, born about 1650 in New Mexico, passed muster in 1680 with his brothers and sisters, two children, and various others. In 1684, he accompanied the Domínguez de Mendoza expedition to Texas. Varela married María Ana Fresqui, but apparently did not return to New Mexico with the reconquest. In 1709–10, he was living at Guadalupe del Paso. Hackett and Shelby, *Revolt*, 1:144. NMR, 11:2055. NMF, 111.

35. Puaray, a Southern Tiwa pueblo, stood about 4 km north of Sandia Pueblo. Hackett and Shelby, *Revolt*, 1:xlix.

36. At Las Bocas, west of Santa Fe in the Santa Fe River canyon below San Ildefonso Springs, streams unite to form the Río de las Bocas, which joins the Rio Grande north of Santo Domingo at the settlement of Cieneguilla. As the Río de las Bocas nears the Rio Grande, the bed widens into a wash large enough for a road.

Adams and Chávez, *Missions*, 41.
Myra Ellen Jenkins, personal
communication, 12 Jan. 1989.

37. Bandelier said of Cieneguilla:
"We met with a considerable [ruin]
at the Cienega, near where the
Santa Fe stream enters a narrow
defile called the 'Bocas.' This is the
pueblo of Tzi-gu-ma, or
Tzi-gu-may. Until 1680, this
village, under the name of 'La
Cienega,' belonged to the
ecclesiastical jurisdiction of the
mission of San Marcos." Bandelier
believed it to have been a
Tano-Tewa village. Harrington,
"Ethnogeography," 468–69.

38. Santa Fe had been
established as a villa in 1610 in
accordance with the Royal
Ordinances of 1573 and
instructions of the viceroy, Luis de
Velasco II, to Governor Peralta.
The ordinances stipulated that the
casas reales should be built around
a square or rectangular plaza;
streets oriented to the four cardinal
directions; lots assigned to settlers
for house, garden, and fields, and
to religious authorities for churches
and hospitals; water regulated; and
commons provided.

Santa Fe's plaza was rectangular
and about twice the size of the
present-day one, perhaps as large
as 175 by 265 m. The north and
west boundaries of the plaza were
about where they are today; the
south at about Water Street,
former course of the Río
Chiquito, later an acequia; and the
east paralleled the facade of the
present cathedral. At the time of

the Pueblo Revolt, one thousand
settlers and 5,700 livestock were
sheltered in the plaza and casas
reales surrounding it.

The interior of the plaza was
modified by the Indians after 1680
by constructing a cuartel, which
divided the plaza into two smaller
ones. There were four towers and
one entrance, on the south, at the
original entrance of the camino
real. The cuartel was destroyed by
Gov. Pedro Rodríguez Cubero in
1697. Cordelia Thomas Snow,
"The Plazas of Santa Fe, New
Mexico," *El Palacio* 94 (Win.
1988):40–51. Hammond and Rey,
Oñate, 2:1087–91. Zelia Nuttall,
"Royal Ordinances Concerning the
Laying Out of New Towns," HAHR
4 (Feb. 1921):743–53.

39. Pedro Hidalgo, a New
Mexico native, was born around
1646. On 10 August 1680, he
accompanied Father Sánchez de
Pro to Tesuque Pueblo, where they
encountered Tesuque warriors who
killed the Franciscan, the first
recorded victim of the Pueblo
Revolt. Hidalgo escaped to warn
Santa Fe residents and retreated to
El Paso. He passed muster with a
family of eight. In El Paso, he was
a scribe to the friars and an officer
of the Confraternity of Our Lady of
the Conquest. Hidalgo did not
resettle in New Mexico. He died
sometime before 1705. NMF,
47–48. CRG, 60.

40. Sebastián de Monroy
Mondragón, born in New Mexico
about 1655, fled to El Paso in
1680. He was poor and married

with a family of three. He returned to New Mexico in 1693. NMF, 75. CRG, 60.

41. Francisco Javier, Luis de Quintana, and Diego López are repeatedly named in the declarations of Indians questioned in 1681 by Antonio de Otermín concerning the 1680 Revolt. They are identified as the ones who whipped and otherwise mistreated their servants and burned kivas. Their actions may have been a primary catalyst for the revolt. All three had been directly involved in the hangings of four medicine men and the beating of forty-three others in 1675 during the governorship of Juan Francisco Treviño. Hackett and Shelby, *Revolt*, 2:238, 239, 250, 309. CRG, 61.

42. Jaras grandes, translated here as large lances, were long, wooden lances with fire-hardened tips thrown or held as weapons. The term is from the Arabic ŝa'ra, meaning brush or bramble.

43. San Lázaro, originally a Tano pueblo in the Galisteo Basin, was abandoned after 1680, when the residents settled north of Santa Fe in the Santa Cruz drainage. When the Spaniards founded the villa of Santa Cruz in 1695, they pressured the Tanos to move. This resettlement was short-lived, however, and many from that region moved to First Mesa in Hopi country, probably sometime in 1701. Michael B. Stanislawski, "Hopi-Tewa," in *Handbook*, 9:600. Schroeder, "Pueblos Abandoned," in *Handbook*, 9:247–48.

44. This mesa was the west end of the ridge where Ft. Marcy was later sited by Gen. Stephen Watts Kearny in 1846, soon after the occupation of Santa Fe by the United States. Lt. Jeremy F. Gilmer, *Plan of Santa Fé, New Mexico* (Santa Fe, 1847).

45. José Gallegos was a native of Parral, probably baptized there on 22 March 1657. His parents were Afz. Diego Gallegos and Catalina de Rivera. Diego was born around 1600 in Durango, the son of Luis Gallegos de Terrazas, a freighter, and Pascuala de Rueda. Diego arrived in Parral early in 1649, where he worked as a struggling cattleman and silver miner. His two brothers, Antonio Gallegos and Juan Burruel de Luna, worked in silver extracting and re- fining in Parral during the 1650s.

José came to New Mexico about 1675. His wife, Catalina Hurtado, was the daughter of Capt. Andrés Hurtado and Bernardina de Salas. At the time of the Pueblo Revolt, José was absent from the colony with the Leyba party, but his wife and children were in the Bernalillo area. They managed to escape unharmed.

He fled the El Paso colony for a time, but eventually returned. The 1692 census showed him living there with his wife and five children: Antonio, five; Juan, seven; Nicolás, five; Diego, three; and Juan, three. José and his family had returned to New

Mexico by October 1694. In 1696, he was among the New Mexico settlers listed as dead or missing; his wife was listed as a widow in the 1697 Santa Fe census. Diego de Vargas, Census of Santa Fe, Santa Fe, 1 May 1697, AGI, Guad. 141:20. AASF, Diligencias matrimoniales, 1694:20. NMF, 31, 53, 179. Census of Spaniards living in the Jurisdiction of Santa Bárbara, Parral, 10 July 1649, AHP, 1649A. Diego Gallegos, Will, Parral, 27 June 1657, AHP, 1656B. Gerald J. Mandell, A History of the Gallegos Family. LDS, Parral, Baptisms, 152529.

46. Little is known about the soldier Diego Zervín, but by early 1696, he was listed as missing from the New Mexico colony and had reportedly made his way to the Philippines. CRG, 239 n25.

47. The Feast of the Exaltation of the Holy Cross was celebrated between 13 and 14 September. Originally called Encaenia, it was given its later name in the sixth century. This liturgical feast, always connected with the finding of the True Cross and the dedication of churches at the sites of the Holy Sepulcher and Calvary in Jerusalem, was dropped from the reformed calendar by Pope John XXIII in 1966. NCE, 3:479.

48. The Te Deum is a hymn of praise sung since the sixth century during mass and extraliturgical ceremonies such as consecration,

ordination, and military victories. While in the patio of the walled pueblo of Santa Fe, Vargas granted possession of an unspecified site for a church and convento to Corvera. On taking possession, the Franciscan celebrated the rendering of salt water for the exorcism and absolution of apostasy. BNM 4:1 (22/454.1) translated in Espinosa, *Pueblo Indian Revolt of 1696*, 63–65. NCE, 13:954–55.

49. Don Luis el Picurí, also known as Luis Tupatú, was one of the original leaders of the 1680 Revolt, along with Popé. By the following year, Tupatú, who seemed to have been highly respected by many of the Pueblos, had become their superior chief. KCC, 241. Hackett and Shelby, *Revolt*, 2:274, 296.

50. Here, Vargas uses the second-person, familiar form of address. In his personal correspondence, he reserved this form to express affection as parent to child and as close friend.

51. These prayers figure prominently in the Vargas journals. The Way of the Cross, or Stations of the Cross, is a private devotional centered on fourteen representations of Christ's sufferings on the way to Calvary. From the fourteenth century, when the Franciscans were given custody of the holy places, the Order saw as part of its mission the enhancement of devotion to those places and to the Passion of Christ. Originally, only Friars Minor Observants could erect the Stations

of the Cross. It later became common for them to appear in all Franciscan conventos, chapels, and the churches they served. The devotion consists of moving from station to station, meditating on Christ's Passion and death. It can be performed individually or in common with a leader. At each station one Our Father, one Hail Mary, and one Glory be to the Father are said. The Our Father (Pater Noster) is commonly known as the Lord's Prayer. The Hail Mary is: "Hail Mary full of Grace, the Lord is with thee, blessed art thou amongst women. Blessed is the fruit of thy womb Jesus. Holy Mary, Mother of God, pray for us sinners now and at the hour of our death. Amen." The Glory be to the Father (Gloria Patri, Lesser Doxology) is: "Glory be to the Father, and to the Son, and to the Holy Spirit. As it was in the beginning, is now, and ever shall be, world without end. Amen." The Salve regina is one of the oldest Marian antiphons, a response that may be sung or chanted as a part of the liturgy. Every recitation entitles the worshiper to a partial indulgence. John A. Hardon, *Pocket Catholic Dictionary* (Garden City, N.Y., 1988):162, 392. NCE, 6:898; 10:29–30.

52. Palm-straw, or yucca-fiber, headbands have been found in various Southwestern archaeological sites. Some were burden bands worn across the forehead and attached to a basket carried on the back. Others were used for adornment or as a base for feathers and other ornamental objects. Saltwater shells, such as abalone and olivella, were traded into the Southwest from coastal groups in California as well the Cocopas, Seris, and Papagos along the Gulf of California. Fray Marcos de Niza reported in 1538 that some of the latter groups wore shells on their foreheads. Shells were worked into varied shapes. A headband and other ritual objects were sometimes buried with medicine men or men of high ceremonial status in the Puebloan Southwest. Ann M. Palkovich, *Pueblo Population and Society: The Arroyo Hondo Skeletal and Mortuary Remains* (Santa Fe, 1980):61. George P. Hammond and Agapito Rey, eds. and trans., *Narratives of the Coronado Expedition 1540–1542* (Albuquerque, 1940):67. William H. Holmes, "Art in Shell of the Ancient Americans," *Second Annual Report of the Bureau of Ethnology* (Washington, D.C., 1883):255–64. Richard I. Ford, "Inter-Indian Exchange in the Southwest," in *Handbook*, 10:713. Virginia M. Roediger, *Ceremonial Costumes of the Pueblo Indians: Their Evolution, Fabrication, and Significance in the Prayer Drama* (Berkeley, 1961):156. Winifred S. Reiter, "Personal Adornment of the Ancient Pueblo Indians," (M.A. thesis, Univ. of New Mexico, 1933).

53. An Agnus Dei, or Lamb of God, was a medal or token made

from the wax of Paschal candles or from those used in the Purification season during Lent. Dust from the relics of saints was added to the wax. On one side the image of the Lamb of God and the words Agnus Dei were stamped, and, on the other, the image of Christ, the Virgin Mary, or a saint, with appropriate inscription and name of the reigning pope. The pope blessed the medal, which was used as protection against Satan, temptation, sudden death, and illness. Jovian P. Lang, *Dictionary of the Liturgy* (New York, 1989):19.

54. The manual referred to was most likely either the *Missale Romanum* (1570) or the *Breviarium romanum* (1568). The missal and breviary contained the order of the mass; the propers, ceremonies, and texts related to fixed feasts; the commons, ceremonies, and texts that dealt with other feasts; and the lessons that were used in the celebration of the Eucharist. The missal also contained a long description of how to celebrate the Mass. The missal and breviary remained essentially unchanged from shortly after the Council of Trent (1545–63) until the Second Vatican Council (1963–65). Davies, *Dictionary*, 98–101. NCE, 8:880.

55. Our Lady of Remedies was Vargas's special protector. Throughout the 1692 expedition, the alferez of the company carried a banner that bore on one side an image of Our Lady of Remedies. Vargas requested her mediation to bring about the return of the Pueblo Indians to the faith. According to Vargas, as embellished by Carlos de Sigüenza y Góngora, Our Lady of Remedies made a miraculous intercession, though not an apparition, at Awatovi on 19 November 1692. After successfully carrying out the largely ceremonial reconquest, Vargas referred to her as Our Lady of the Conquest. This modification of nomenclature follows that of Hernán Cortés, who carried an image of Our Lady of Remedies and referred to her as Our Lady of the Conquest as well. Some confusion in this matter results from the fact that the Our Lady of the Conquest venerated in Santa Fe to the present day is actually an image of Our Lady of the Rosary. The cult of Our Lady of Remedies is confined to Spain and Latin America. Notable images can be found in Bolivia, Colombia, Guatemala, Mexico, and Peru. Rubén Vargas Ugarte, *Historia del culto de María en Iberoamérica y de sus imágenes y santuarios más celebrados* (Madrid, 1956), 1:300, 370–71, 393, 397; 2:158, 285. J. Manuel Espinosa, "The Virgin of the Reconquest of New Mexico," *Mid-America* 18 (Apr. 1936):79–87. Espinosa, *First Expedition*, 213 n11.

56. According to St. Bonaventure, St. Francis received the stigmata on his hands, feet, and side in 1224 after contemplation of

the Passion of Christ. Upon his death in 1226, his followers could see the stigmata on his body. The stigmata are considered a visible sign of participation in Christ's Passion and associated with a state of emotional ecstasy. They are not considered a miracle by the Catholic church. NCE, 13:711–12. Paul Sabatier, *The Life of St. Francis of Assisi* (New York, 1930):286–96.

57. Miguel Luján was actually the brother-in-law of Juan Ruiz de Cáceres and was married to Elena Ruiz de Cáceres. By 1695, both Luján and his wife were dead. NMFA, 63:247.

58. Francisco Márquez, twenty-two years old and married, passed muster in 1681. His wife was Estela Luján, with whom he had a daughter, Rosa Isabel. NMFA, 63:368. NMF, 70, 220.

59. The term cuarta, or span, was the distance between thumb and tip of the little finger with hand spread, equal to one-fourth of a vara, about 22 cm.

60. A jeme, or short span, was the distance between thumb and tip of the index finger with hand spread, about 18 cm.

61. Afz. Antonio Lucero de Godoy's grandfather, Mre. de campo Pedro Lucero de Godoy, probably established the family in Santa Fe in the 1620s. Antonio's father, Juan Lucero de Godoy, held a variety of posts in the military and civil government of New Mexico and resided at Pueblo Quemado near Santa Fe.

The alferez was born between 1640 and 1645. At the outbreak of the Pueblo Revolt, he, his parents, three brothers, and four sisters fled south. One of his brothers was Juan de Dios Lucero de Godoy II, whose name also frequently appears in these documents. In 1681, Antonio enlisted as a colonist and in 1693, returned upriver. He was dead by 1712. NMF, 61, 209.

62. Born around 1658, Capt. Diego de Montoya passed muster in 1680 with his wife and two children. Montoya returned to Santa Fe with his wife in 1693. He apparently moved to the Bernalillo area around 1695–96. NMF, 78, 236. Hackett and Shelby, *Revolt*, 1:145; 2:60, 111. Autos de Guerra de la Reconquista de Nuevo México, 17 Dec. 1693–5 Jan. 1694, Ritch Collection.

63. Tiburcio de Ortega, born about 1655 in New Mexico, was listed with the other refugees in 1680 as a scribe along with his wife, Margarita Otón; two children; his mother; siblings; nephews; nieces; and servants. Between 1692 and 1712, he held the post of protector of the Indians at El Paso. He was in Santa Fe in 1694, but, the following year, was serving as scribe for the religious in El Paso. A councilman and alguacil mayor in August 1696, Ortega was imprisoned in 1711 for opposing exploitation of the Indians. By 1715, he occupied the office of alcalde mayor of Jemez, Zia, and Santa Ana pueblos. NMF,

82, 246. NMFA, 64:126. Cutter, *Protector*, 51, 52. CRG, 271.

64. Spaniards invoked St. James, or Santiago, the patron saint of Spain, when they began a battle.

65. The term sobresalientes, translated here as reserves, refers in a military context to those leaders or soldiers designated to respond to troop requirements dictated by the flow of battle.

66. Vargas uses the word pieza here simply as captive, not in the sense of piezas de Indias, a measure by which African slaves were counted. James F. King, "Evolution of the Free Slave Trade Principle in Spanish Colonial Administration," HAHR 22 (Feb. 1942):36.

67. The young man referred to here is probably the Francisco de Anaya Almazán, who was the son of Cristóbal de Anaya Almazán and would have been about twenty-nine years old in 1692.

68. Malacate, from the Nahuatl malacatl, was an epithet meaning spindle or winch, figuratively, a person in constant motion.

69. Though Indians received Spanish given names at baptism, often those of their godparents or the saint whose feast day it happened to be, few Pueblos received surnames.

70. The feast of the Archangels Michael, Gabriel, and Raphael.

71. The Tewa pueblo of Cuyamungue, 20 km north of Santa Fe, was abandoned sometime in the early 1700s.

Schroeder, "Pueblos Abandoned," in *Handbook*, 9:250.

72. A small Tewa-speaking pueblo about 30 km northwest of Santa Fe, Jacona was abandoned in 1696.

73. Petrona Pacheco, possibly the daughter of Juan Pacheco and Antonia de Arratia, was the wife of Cristóbal Nieto and had been captured with their five daughters and a son at the time of the Pueblo Revolt. Nieto was present in El Paso on 25 August 1680 at the junta de guerra that installed Pedro de Leyva as the commander of the relief party. He appears in two musters, one the same year opposite La Salineta and the other at Ancón de Fray García, the following year. He enlisted as a settler in 1681 and was apparently unaware his wife had survived the revolt, for he was described as a widower. In 1697, Nieto was given a grant of land in the Santa Fe area by Gov. Pedro Rodríguez Cubero. The title was revalidated by Nieto's request on 5 August 1700. Cristóbal Nieto, Petition for revalidation of lands, Santa Fe, 5 Aug. 1700, SANM I. Hackett and Shelby, *Revolt*, 1:37, 147, 176; 2:120, 192. NMF, 81, 242, 252.

74. The Tano inhabitants of the pueblos of San Cristóbal and San Lázaro in the Galisteo basin had relocated north of Santa Fe sometime after the 1680 Revolt.

75. Vargas's son, Juan Manuel, was page to María Luisa de Borbón (1662–89) and Mariana de

Neoburgo (1667–1740). RBC, 47, 49, 113 n100, 147, 149, 273.

76. The contract of don Juan de Oñate for the discovery and conquest of New Mexico was made in Mexico City on 21 Sept. 1595 by Viceroy don Luis de Velasco II. There are copies in AGI, Patronato 22; and AGI, México 20, 23, 25, and 26. A transcript and translation are in Hackett, *Historical Documents*, 1:224–55, and another translation, in Hammond and Rey, *Oñate*, 1:42–57. For a complete biography of Oñate, see Marc Simmons, *The Last Conquistador: Juan de Oñate and the Settling of the Far Southwest* (Norman, 1991).

77. A number of laws concerning first settlers dealt with solares, or lots. In dividing available land for a new town, sufficient land for lots, commons, and enclosures was set aside, as was land for people already living at the site. In theory, the remaining land was divided, with a fourth going to the founder and the rest to be shared among the other settlers. Lots were divided among settlers, continuing out from those set aside for the principal plaza. RECOP, Lib. 4, tít. 6, ley 6 and Lib. 4, tít. 7, leyes 7, 11, 16, 17.

78. Agustín Félix Maldonado de Salazar began his career as a judge on the Audiencia of Santo Domingo, where he served from 14 May 1667 to 4 December 1672. He was then appointed fiscal of the Audiencia of Guadalajara, but, because of poor health, was allowed to stay in Santo Domingo. In 1676, he went to Guadalajara not as fiscal, but as judge (20 March 1676–21 July 1678). He was promoted to criminal judge of the Audiencia of Mexico and arrived in Mexico City in May 1680, serving as criminal judge from 13 November 1680 to 23 December 1686. His last appointment came on 17 April 1686, when he became judge. While in Mexico City, Maldonado, who never married, lived on the Calle del Reloj. He died on 3 August 1696 and was buried in the Church of San Francisco. Robles, *Diario*, 3:48. Rubio Mañé, "Gente de España," 111. Schäfer, *Consejo Real*, 2:447–48, 458, 462, 496.

79. Lic. Pedro de la Bastida was a member of the Council of the Indies from 16 December 1697 to 24 August 1699; he died in office. He had served as judge on the Chancellery of Granada, civil fiscal for the Audiencia of Mexico (24 July 1681–21 December 1686), and judge on the Audiencia of Guadalajara (6 April 1680–24 July 1681). He was married to María Agustina de Vergara. Robles, *Diario*, 2:289. Schäfer, *Consejo Real*, 1:366; 2:458, 464, 496. RBC, 68, 194, 198.

80. Gerónimo Chacón Abarca was born in Salamanca in the parish of San Julián on 2 October 1640. He held a chair at the University of Salamanca before being appointed judge of the Audiencia of Santo Domingo (23

December 1672) and later, interim
judge of Guatemala (17 April
1678). His last post was as senior
criminal judge (20 February 1686)
of the Audiencia of Mexico, from
which he retired on 30 December
1697.

On 21 May 1672, he married
doña Luisa Mojica, a native of
Madrid, in the Madrid parish of
San Sebastían. They had at least
one son, Gerónimo Chacón y
Mojica, born in Santo Domingo
on 9 February 1675. Schäfer,
Consejo Real, 2:448, 462.
Lohmann Villena, *Americanos*,
1:125.

81. Manuel Suárez Muñiz was
appointed supernumerary criminal
judge to the Audiencia of Mexico
on 5 November 1687 and was
serving in the post as late as 1696.
In 1695, he was granted a robe in
the Order of Calatrava. His wife
was María Teresa Saravia y
Medina. Rubio Mañé, "Gente de
España," 158. Robles, *Diario*,
3:267. Schäfer, *Consejo Real*,
2:127, 462.

82. The Rule of St. Francis, the
regula bullata, was approved by
Pope Honorius III (1216–27) in
1223 in the bull *Solet annuere*. It
regulates Franciscan life and
provides for the observance of the
vows of obedience, chastity, and
poverty. Its purpose is to encourage
following the Gospel, which is the
essence of Franciscan life. The
Rule consists of twelve chapters
with twenty-four precepts and a
number of admonitions. The
precepts, which are the letter of the
Rule, give guidance; the
admonitions, which are the spirit,
caution them. David Flood and
Thaddée Matura, *The Birth of a
Movement: A Study of the First
Rule of St. Francis* (Chicago,
1975):63–107. NCE, 6:39–40.

The Viceroy Congratulates Vargas,
24 November 1692.*

The Conde de Galve leaves no doubt. He is elated by the news of what Governor Vargas has achieved. Concluding his directive, which repeats the wording recorded in the junta of 24 November, the viceroy adds a personal note of appreciation and support. Then, in a letter of transmittal the same day, he confides in don Diego that he considers the restoration of New Mexico the most praiseworthy event of his viceregal administration.

The Conde de Galve to Diego de Vargas, Directive (conclusion), Mexico City, 24 November 1692, C.

I agreed with all the items this decision of the general junta contains and includes. It seemed appropriate to me to add in this dispatch, as is done (so that the governor and captain general, don Diego de Vargas Luján y Zapata, may understand the contents, how he is to fulfill what refers to him, and be aware of all that is proposed to him) that I appreciate and esteem him greatly, offering him whatever may be pleasing and advantageous to him in the interim. His majesty (may God keep him), having seen my report and the proceedings I shall send him, will reward him out of his Catholic zeal as he deserves, and I hope. With this dispatch, another is being sent separately for the draft and disbursement of the 12,000 pesos, as well as a copy of the royal cedula and three other dispatches, so that with them, he may decide the proper procedure, as I trust he will. Mexico City, 24 November 1692.

The Conde de Galve

Mexico City, 24 November 1692
By command of his excellency
Don Diego Velásquez de la Cadena

Report on the order at the end of it

Recorded. His excellency is pleased to give thanks to the governor and captain general of New Mexico, don Diego de Vargas, for his victory and the conquest and restoration of the villa of Santa Fe and the pueblos of its district. For their preservation, it has been decided to leave all the means up to his arrangement in the manner that general junta's decision included in this dispatch refers to.

> Directive and order from his excellency, with the agreement of the royal junta, decided upon and in response to having seen the notice and copy of the military proceedings from the conquest of the villa of Santa Fe and the twelve pueblos in its district

There are some papers about this in the possession of the lord fiscal and letters from the viceroy to which this should be added, as the lord secretary ordered.

The Conde de Galve to Diego de Vargas, Mexico City, 24 November 1692, C.

By means of the dispatches enclosed, you will see what was resolved. I have seen the letters and copy that accompanies them about the restoration of that villa and the districts of its cordillera, for which I repeat my thanks and congratulations. I assure you that for me this information has been, of all I have managed to achieve during my government, the most admirable and praiseworthy in the service of both majesties; it is of the highest order. To make it more commendable in my estimation, I have had the good fortune that you achieved and brought about that restoration through your diligent effort and at so little expense. I hope from your prudence and obligations that you will continue in the arrangement of the matter, so that what has been gained may not be lost. I shall continue to attend to this for you, making provisions for the preservation of obedience and the Catholic religion in that country. I shall try to do everything possible with all due haste. It seems to me that to put them in order, it would be advantageous, in the case of any sudden occurrence requiring a change in the decision, for you to advise me about everything that may occur to you. The soldiers under contract and citizens of the El Paso presidio should be encouraged with a reward for their services. The granting of the privileges they lack will be clarified for them as soon as they have established themselves. May God keep you many years. Mexico City, 24 [November] 1692.

Sir, I repeat with affection and delight the proper thanks for the prudence, valor, and wisdom with which you have achieved such a fortunate outcome. I most sincerely assure you that I shall reciprocate, so that a service of such magnitude may be rewarded. I shall present this to his majesty at the time of the next packet boat.

The Conde de Galve
Don Diego de Vargas Zapata Luján Ponce de León

*AGI Guadalajara 139:6. 3 folios, 5 written pages. Translated in Espinosa, *First Expedition*, 290–95.

With receipt in Mexico City of the news from Santa Fe, don Diego de Vargas at last gains the upper hand over the governor and captains of New Biscay. The viceroy orders them to support Vargas in every way. They will cooperate in recruiting and enlisting people for the reoccupation of New Mexico or face the consequences.

*The Conde de Galve to Diego de Vargas,
Directive, Mexico City, 24 November 1692, DS.*

Don Gaspar de Sandoval Cerda Silva y Mendoza, Conde de Galve; gentleman of the bedchamber; comendador of Zalamea and Ceclavín in the Order and Knighthood of Alcántara; of his majesty's council; his viceroy, lieutenant, governor and captain general of this New Spain; and president of its royal audiencia; and so forth: I have seen in the general junta I held today the information that the governor and captain general of the provinces of New Mexico, don Diego de Vargas Zapata y Luján, communicated to me with an authorized copy of the proceedings in which he reports the victory of the conquest and reduction of the apostate rebel Indians of the villa of Santa Fe and another twelve pueblos of its environs. I have greatly appreciated and esteemed the way and circumstances in which he achieved it, for which I have given him many thanks, promising to assist him in whatever might be his pleasure, leaving at his disposition and orders everything that might be conducive to maintaining and preserving what has been acquired.

Likewise, he should request for himself, if need be, all the people who seem necessary to him, acquiring and seeking them out in all the areas, places, and jurisdictions closest to the provinces of New Mexico or in those that occur to him, enlisting those he might find at the salary of presidial soldiers, or other aid he might consider more appropriate.

At present, I order all his majesty's judges and justices of any jurisdictions, areas, or places where people sent by Gov. don Diego de Vargas, or the holders of his power of attorney, with his orders to this effect to obey them, since they are given by virtue of this my order. Not only should they aid and help them in whatever way may be conducive to this, but they should also help them find the people they are seeking and transport them wherever the governor decides, since this would result in the greatest service to his majesty and the preservation of what has been acquired. This is with the understanding that acting to the contrary will result in serious charges against them, as well as the corresponding penalties. So that obedience to this order may be of record, they will give a receipt of it to the holder of the power of attorney so that it may be shown. The original will be returned so that it may be of record. Mexico City, 24 November 1692.

The Conde de Galve [rubrica]

———

By order of his excellency
Don Pedro Velázquez de la Cadena [rubrica]
[rubrica]

———

To the holders of power of attorney or people to whom the governor of New Mexico turns over this order (should it be necessary to avail himself of it) and his own order, the justices should give every aid they may request for the end expressed herein.
Signed [rubrica]

*AGN, Historia 38:1. 1 folio, 2 written pages.

ADDITIONAL FRANCISCAN PRIESTS FOR NEW MEXICO AND A NEW FATHER CUSTOS, November 1692.*

For the time being, Governor Vargas is a hero. Franciscan superiors in Mexico City are at pains to show the viceroy why don Diego's request to have fray Francisco de Vargas named father custos is unfair to the newly appointed man. The friars bid, at the same time, for the customary government subsidy to outfit, transport, and provision for three years twenty more missionary priests for New Mexico. Unwilling for the moment to take the permanence of the reconquest for granted, viceregal authorities counter with a year and a half's support for twelve additional Franciscans.

Fray Diego de Trujillo to the Conde de Galve, Mexico City, [November] 1692, ALS.

Fray Diego Trujillo, minister provincial of this Holy Province of the Holy Gospel and Custody of New Mexico, says that, through God's mercy and the success of the governor of the kingdom of New Mexico, the happy reduction to our holy Catholic faith of the Indians who had abandoned the faith at the time of the general uprising has been achieved. In accord with this, he needs ministers for the preservation of the converted pueblos and those expected to be converted and reduced in the future.

Therefore, since it is his duty as prelate of the religious present to see to ministering to the Indians, he expresses to your excellency this just request. He asks that you decide, should you see fit and agree it is in the service of both majesties, for as many as around

twenty priests to go now, while the rest of the pueblos are being reduced. Thus, I express, ask, and request, trusting that because of your excellency's singular zeal, you will provide what is most fitting.
Fray Diego Trujillo [rubrica]
Minister provincial

———

Mexico City, 24 November 1692
To the fiscal [Galve 's rubrica]

Juan de Escalante y Mendoza, Fiscal's reply, Mexico City, 25 November 1692, DS.

Most excellent sir,
   His majesty's fiscal states that the decision about this matter and the sending of twenty religious to New Mexico the reverend father provincial of the Order of St. Francis proposes depends upon favorable word from the governor of that kingdom and the permanence of its conversion. Until he confirms this with the report he has been ordered to make, sending them will be delayed, postponing it until the occasion arrives when they are judged necessary. Your excellency will then take the appropriate measures and in all things order what you may see fit, which will be, as always, the best. Mexico City, 25 November 1692.
Dr. don Juan de Escalante y Mendoza [rubrica]
Mexico City, 25 November 1692
As the lord fiscal proposes [Galve's rubrica]

Fray Diego Trujillo to the Conde de Galve, Mexico City, [November] 1692, ALS.

Most excellent sir,
   Fray Diego Trujillo, minister provincial of this Province of the Holy Gospel and Custody of New Mexico, as prelate of this custody and provinces says that he has expressed to your excellency their need for religious ministers to assist in the administration of the holy sacraments to the thirteen pueblos, which, as is of record today in the

report from the governor and the custos of those provinces, have rendered obedience to his majesty, as well as to those other pueblos that as of today he will have already reduced. There are three priests in the villa of Santa Fe, and they will have gone with the governor to the provinces he has told your excellency about. Because it is so large a ministry, even if those who remained in El Paso had gone, they would not have been able to give the spiritual nourishment that today those souls need after twelve years of separation. Necessarily, as it should be understood, they were as men who have lived as they wished. Most excellent sir, supposing that some of the clergy referred to might have gone to the villa of Santa Fe, it is of no less harm to leave the pueblos of El Paso without someone to minister to them.

In this regard, I must ask you, notwithstanding what the fiscal proposed, to see fit for now to order that, if not the twenty religious I have indicated to your excellency, then ten or twelve priests be sent in the interim until the second courier comes. He will be delayed at least more than four months, because of the distance to the provinces of Zuni and Moqui, more than 250 leagues beyond El Paso, and from here 650, and the time the governor will be delayed in the reconnoitering he must do of the land and mines, according to his report. This can be done today with some convenience to you since the wagons transporting his majesty's alms to the religious there are about to leave and cannot delay any longer because of the great expense they are causing. I believe this is in the service of both majesties and a comfort to those poor religious, which is the reason for this petition. Your excellency will decide whatever you may see fit, which will be, as always, the best.

Fray Diego Trujillo [rubrica]

———

Mexico City, 26 November 1692
To the lord fiscal [Galve's rubrica]

Juan de Escalante y Mendoza, Fiscal's reply,
Mexico City, 27 November 1692, DS.

Most excellent sir,
Sir, in view of the new request and petition the reverend father provincial of our father St. Francis makes, his majesty's fiscal says

that, should your excellency see fit, you should send your decision to the junta where the decision to postpone the religious' going to New Mexico until another time originated, so that the junta, with the reasons expressed at hand and after having considered them, may decide what is appropriate, about which your excellency will order, as always, the best. Mexico City, 27 November 1692.
Dr. don Juan de Escalante y Mendoza [rubrica]

––––––

Mexico City, 27 November 1692
As the lord fiscal asks
[Galve's rubrica]

The Conde de Galve to the Franciscan Commissary General, Mexico City, 24 November 1692, DS.

Don Gaspar de Sandoval Cerda Silva y Mendoza, the Conde de Galve; gentleman of his majesty's bedchamber; comendador of Zalamea and Ceclavín in the Order of Alcántara; viceroy; governor and captain general of this New Spain; and president of its royal audiencia: I have examined in the general junta the information that, with a copy of the proceedings, the governor and captain general of the provinces of New Mexico, don Diego de Vargas Luján y Zapata, sent me. He reports the victorious conquest and reduction of the apostate rebel Indians of the villa of Santa Fe, with another twelve nearby pueblos. I greatly regarded and esteemed the way and circumstances in which he achieved this. I have repeatedly thanked him for this, promising him to attend to whatever may please him, because he is so worthy.

As he states in his letter, he asks that a letter patent of custos for those provinces obtained from the very reverend father commissary general of the Order of St. Francis be sent to Father fray Francisco de Vargas. He suggests to me that all the necessary qualities of care and virtue recognized as appropriate for that ministry come together in this religious. In accord with what was decided in the general junta, for the present I entreat and charge the most reverend father commissary general of the Order of St. Francis to grant the appointment to the religious, fray Francisco de Vargas, sending him the letter patent so that he may immediately begin that ministry and so that the governor may achieve his end, which is considered as just as his sense of duty is great. This must be done in such a way that the courier, who is to be sent with all haste because time is of the essence, may carry the letter patent to him. Mexico City, 24 November 1692. The Conde de Galve [rubrica]

———

By his excellency's order
Don Pedro Velázquez de la Cadena [rubrica]

———

Rubricated [rubrica]
About the request and charge to the most reverend father commissary general of the Order of St. Francis, so that he may send the letter patent of custos for the provinces of New Mexico to Father fray Francisco de Vargas

Fray Juan de Capistrano to the Conde de Galve,
Mexico City, 26 November 1692, LS.

Most excellent sir,

In obedience to your excellency's order, in which you see fit to direct me to give the letter patent of custos for New Mexico to Father fray Francisco de Vargas, who just completed his term in that post a year ago, I inform your excellency that, because of the death of his successor, who died more or less five months ago, I gave the letter patent of custos to Father fray Salvador de San Antonio.[1] He is a man of talent and virtue who has been in that custody more than ten years and knows the languages of some of those nations. The letter patent to this individual was confirmed by the provincial chapter of this province at the canonical election held in this convento on the twenty-second of this month.

The father custos is already in possession of his office and has begun his ministry, according to his letter, which I received with this courier from that custody. I have now informed the governor of that kingdom, don Diego de Vargas Luján y Zapata, about this election in a letter, which I also sent to your excellency. In it, I told and notified him of the talents of the father custos and that he was going instructed by me so that he and his subjects might be under his direction in what concerns service to both majesties. I believe that if the governor, don Diego de Vargas, knew the man was coming and were acquainted with him, he would not make such a request of your excellency, because everything promised and expected from Father fray Francisco de Vargas is necessarily found in the other man too. He would not have made the request had he known of the canonical election of the present officeholder.

Given this, great wrong would be done to him by removing him without cause, because he already offered himself in the service of both majesties. Thus, while venerating your excellency's order, it seems to me that, should your excellency see fit, we should wait until the governor has experienced the current father custos's manner of working. If, knowing of this decision, he asks for another, I shall be the first to concur in giving him satisfaction in everything possible, because I have long known of the faithful work of the governor, don Diego de Vargas, both in his duties as soldier and as a judge who looks so dutifully to the service of both majesties and my Order. Moreover, Father Vargas writes that he has built a new mission, which he is developing. It seems fitting to me that he should attend to this calling, for which I shall reward him at the proper time in accord with his merits. This is my opinion, unless your excellency gives me a new order, which I shall always obey. Convento Grande of San Francisco. Mexico City, 26 November 1692.
Fray Juan de Capistrano [rubrica]

———

Mexico City, 26 November 1692
Put this with the proceedings the lord fiscal has. [Galve's rubrica]

Junta of the Treasury, Mexico City, 28 November 1692, DS.

In the Junta of the Treasury held by the most excellent lord viceroy, the Conde de Galve, on 28 November 1692 with lords don Jacinto de Vargas Campuzano and don Agustín Félix Maldonado, judges of this royal audiencia; don Andrés Pardo and don Mateo de Santa Cruz, comptrollers of the Royal Tribunal of Accounts; and don Sebastián de Guzmán and don Antonio de Deza, knight of the Order of Santiago, treasury officials of this court; with his majesty's fiscal present: We have examined the preceding petition from the father procurator of the provinces of New Mexico, along with the proposal from the reverend father provincial of the Order of St. Francis, about the suitability of and need for sending at least twelve religious priests to those provinces to care for the reduced apostate Indians. It was unanimously decided that, although it had already been determined to await favorable word from that kingdom's governor, the opportunity and reasons the reverend father relates nevertheless convincingly argue for sending the priests. Since to put off the inconveniences and increased expenses in transporting the religious with the hope that God Our Lord will permit the permanence of the reductions with greater increases for the future, it is thus unanimously decided to agree to the reverend father provincial's suggestion.

This is done bearing in mind his majesty's royal orders and his Catholic zeal not to worry about incurring slightly greater or lesser expense. The twelve religious priests should be appointed and paid the customary amount for their journey from the funds of the royal treasury. If the end to which they direct themselves is not accomplished, payments will be suspended, just as they will be continued as necessary, if those reductions are established and continue. It was so decided and rubricated with his excellency. Make this information known to the governor and captain general of New Mexico and have him send further word, which is awaited with the same happiness as the first. Also, give him an account of the most reverend father commissary general's response to the dispatch, in which he was charged with sending the letter patent of custos to Father fray Francisco de Vargas, so that the governor may understand the reverend father commissary general's just expression and reasons and know that his request has been dealt with. There is no doubt that because of his zeal he will conform to the reverend father's reply, which is so just and correct. Put this with the proceedings about the matter. Rubricated [three rubricas]

His excellency; Lords Vargas, Maldonado, Pardo, Santa Cruz, Guzmán, Deza

Fray Francisco Farfán to the Conde de Galve,
Mexico City, [28 November] 1692, LS.

Most excellent sir,

By your excellency's order of 28 November, with the agreement of the general junta, you ordered the treasury officials of this court to make a draft and pay in advance what is due as stipend to each and every one of the twelve religious I² am to lead in the wagons of the custody of New Mexico, as has been done and has been the practice until now with the others in those provinces. For this, the general junta prepared the proceedings so that they might be taken to the accounting office of the royal treasury and the draft, which I place in your excellency's hands with due compliance, could be sent. The draft was signed, sent on by the comptroller, recorded in the factor's office, and signed by him, as is customary. When the draft arrived for the treasurer's signature, he said that what was decided in the junta was one year's advance payment and not the three the draft refers to. The orders in the accounting office follow the manner and form your excellency's directive provides, by which every three years, which is when the wagons come for these contributions, it is arranged for these stipends to be paid in advance.

Because of this, as procurator general of this custody, I have carried out the business of the preparations. I have charged to my own account the most necessary things for their transportation and provided provisions, animals for their conveyance, and everything else. This is so that the wagons may leave from one day to the next, because of the great expense they cause and so as not to lose a minute by taking advantage of the opportune time before the rains begin.

For this, I request and ask your excellency to see fit to order the draft, after the treasurer signs it, put into effect as it should be, as is of record in the order, without any argument. If it is not sent to me, I shall not be able to convey the religious, and many inconveniences and delays to the custody will follow. I thus justly await the favor of your excellency's nobility and zeal.

Fray Francisco Farfán [rubrica]

Junta of the Treasury, Mexico City, 28 November 1692, DS.

In the Junta of the Treasury that on 28 November 1692 the most excellent lord viceroy, the Conde de Galve, held with the lord ministers don Jacinto de Vargas Campuzano and don Agustín Félix Maldonado, judges of this royal audiencia; don Andrés Pardo and don Mateo de Santa Cruz, comptrollers of the Royal Tribunal of Accounts; and don Sebastián de Guzmán and don Antonio de Deza, knight of the Order of Santiago, treasury officials of this court; with his majesty's fiscal present: Having examined in this junta the preceding petition from the father procurator of the provinces of New Mexico, it was unanimously decided that with regard to the dispatch of 28 November, referred to therein, the decision and draft should be taken to mean that payment should be made to each one of the twelve religious in advance, according to what their stipend amounts to for a year and a half, the amount that seemed most appropriate for now, until they can be assured, as they hope, of more certain word of the permanence and security of what has been reduced.

It was so decided and rubricated with his excellency.
Rubricated [three rubricas]
His excellency; Lords Vargas, Maldonado, Pardo, Santa Cruz, Guzmán, Deza

Up to this point, a copy of all these proceedings was made for the packet boat of January 1693. [Velázquez de la Cadena's rubrica]

*AGN, Historia 37:6 (cont.)

1. Born in Puebla around 1639, fray Salvador Rodríguez de San Antonio was in New Mexico as early as 1664, evidently returning to the Convento Grande before 1680. He was appointed custos in 1684 and arrived in El Paso in 1685. During his second term as custos, he accompanied Vargas on the 1693 entrada. He resigned as custos in 1694 and returned to El Paso. Adams and Chávez, *Missions*, 338. EBARN.

2. Born in Cadiz around 1643 to Juan Farfán of Jérez de la Frontera (Cadiz) and Isabel García of Cadiz, fray Francisco Farfán took the habit in Mexico City at the Convento Grande on 7 July 1661. He later professed there on 7 July 1662.

At the time of the Pueblo Revolt

in 1680, fray Francisco Farfán was assistant to the guardian of the Santa Fe convento, fray Francisco Gómez de la Cadena. He fled to El Paso with the other refugees and during the next three years, served in the El Paso missions.

Farfán was procurator in Mexico City in 1693 and led a group of settlers to El Paso. He arrived in Santa Fe in June 1694 and served for short periods from 1697 to 1703 at Santa Ana, Acoma, Pecos, San Ildefonso, and San Felipe. In 1701, Farfán was serving as vice-custos and, in this capacity, had the priests announce the excommunication of individuals interfering with ecclesiastical immunity. Adams and Chávez, *Missions,* 333. KCC, 232. Rosa Figueroa, Becerro.

Ritual Repossession of the Pecos, Keres, Jemez, Acoma, Zuni, and Moqui Indians; Summary; and Letter of Transmittal to the Viceroy, 16 October 1692–10 January 1693.*

As Diego Varela, the courier, rides toward Mexico City with news of Vargas's triumph to date, Governor Vargas resumes his campaign. The weather and the Indians' disposition grow harsher. He is at pains to conserve and use wisely his small, tired force and, at the same time, to persuade residents of defensive, mesa-top pueblos that they should submit, even if ritually.

Three times he relates the story—first in his campaign journal, then in summary form, and finally in a letter to the Conde de Galve—each time warming to the heroism of his theme. Others may have wished to restore New Mexico, but only Diego de Vargas, by divine providence and zealous attention to the king's service, has achieved it. He repeats his claim to have carried out the reconquest at his own expense, which is only partly true, since both companies of presidial soldiers are salaried.

Yet, even allowing for exaggeration, Vargas's feats among the ill-disposed western Pueblos are astonishing. He trusts in the protection of Our Lady of Remedies and refuses to be provoked. Repeatedly, he places himself in harm's way, and the Indians seem to respect him for it.

507

Diego de Vargas, Campaign journal, 16 October–
27 December 1692, DS.

Departure of the courier with the copy of the previous proceedings,
up to today's date

On 16 October 1692, the courier, Diego Varela, general adjutant
of the men-at-arms of this kingdom, carried the copy of the military
proceedings, including what was done, reduced, and conquered in
this kingdom of New Mexico. So that it may be of record, I, the
governor and captain general, signed it with the captain, alferez, and
my secretary of government and war.
Don Diego de Vargas
Zapata Luján Ponce de León [rubrica]

Roque Madrid [rubrica]
Juan de Dios Lucero de Godoy [rubrica]
Before me,

Alfonso Rael de Aguilar [rubrica]
Secretary of government and war

Departure of the artillery captain with the men-at-arms from this villa
of Santa Fe, as is of record

On 16 October, I, the governor and captain general, having to go
on to the pueblo of the Pecos and the Keres and Jemez nations, ordered
the artillery captain, because of the rough road and circuitous route
of more than 10 leagues, to go to Santo Domingo Pueblo with the
two cannon and the large bronze stone mortar. Under his command,
he should take the Indian allies from El Paso, the captives who are
leaving this kingdom with their relatives for those regions, and the
packtrain. I also ordered the captain of the reinforcements of men-
at-arms from Parral to give him two squads from the company. With
its horses, he might go as an escort with the artillery captain. Likewise, a squad from the El Paso presidio's company should go, taking
the horses and mules of these men. Its captain will carry everything
out in this manner. So that the departure with the people referred to
may be of record, the artillery captain to whom I give the order will
go to Santo Domingo Pueblo and when he arrives there, halt with

the men, until I, the governor and captain general, arrive at the pueblo with the rest of the camp. So that it may be of record, I signed it with the artillery captain, the captain, and the alferez of the El Paso presidio, together with my secretary of government and war.

Don Diego de Vargas Zapata
Luján Ponce de León [rubrica]

Roque Madrid [rubrica]
Juan de Dios Lucero de Godoy [rubrica]
Francisco Lucero de
Godoy [rubrica]
Before me,

Alfonso Rael de Aguilar [rubrica]
Secretary of government and war

> I, the governor and captain general, appoint, choose, and name don
> Luis Picurí as governor of the nations of this kingdom

Immediately after, I, the governor and captain general, to depart this villa for the rest of the nations to reduce and conquer them for the royal crown and our holy faith, must leave named and chosen a governor whom the reduced and conquered nations, as are the thirteen pueblos of Taos, Picuris, Tewas, Tanos, with this villa, will obey. From them, I choose, appoint, and name as governor don Luis Picurí. In the presence of the captains of these nations, I gave him the title, ordering my secretary of government and war to expedite it. Likewise, I gave him the cane signifying that he was their governor.[1] Before he was received into office, he swore the oath by God Our Lord and the sign of the cross to use his office faithfully and legally. Through the principal interpreter, I made him understand what he had to do in the service of both majesties. So that it may be of record, I signed it with the interpreter, the captain, the alferez of the presidio, and my secretary of government and war.

Don Diego de Vargas
Zapata Luján Ponce de León [rubrica]

Roque Madrid [rubrica]
Juan de Dios Lucero de Godoy [rubrica]

Before me,

Alfonso Rael de Aguilar [rubrica]
Secretary of government and war

I, the governor and captain general, finally depart from this villa of
Santa Fe for the pueblo of the Pecos, where I made my entrada today

Today, Friday, 17 October 1692, I, the governor and captain
general, with the rest of the men-at-arms of the two companies; the
military leaders and officials; the principal interpreter; the two
reverend missionary fathers, fray Francisco Corvera and fray Cristóbal
Alonso Barroso; and my secretary of government and war left this
villa of Santa Fe, principal town of the kingdom of New Mexico.
All its inhabitants remained there and in their pueblos, because
they had not gathered their harvests. The bad weather has prevented them from leaving to go with me, the governor and captain
general, to the nations of the Pecos, the Keres, and the Jemez,
as had been decided.

The baptized are 248 people and children of all ages and both sexes

With the men, I entered the pueblo of the Pecos at about two in
the afternoon. All the people were waiting for me at its entrance,
having received me with arches and having a large, very well made
cross there. All received me, saying the Praised be, at which I responded
to them with much pleasure. The men of my company all came
together, accompanying me to the plaza of the cuartel where I was
during the first entrada, which is of record in these proceedings. Having dismounted, I made them understand through the interpreter,
Pedro Hidalgo, about my coming, which had been repeated in the
rest of the pueblos. In the same way, I reclaimed, revalidated, and
proclaimed on behalf of his majesty the possession of this pueblo, its
land, and its inhabitants, his vassals. I, the governor and captain
general, asked Father fray Francisco Corvera to absolve them of apostasy, which he did with the reverend Father fray Cristóbal Alonso
Barroso. Both also baptized the individuals and children who were
unbaptized. I, the governor and captain general, was godfather to a
child of their captain, whom they obey, as I was to many others, as
were the men-at-arms. When the reverend fathers were finished, they
counted as baptized 248 individuals and children of all ages and
both sexes.

The natives were very joyful, as was I, the governor and captain
general, for having again reduced and conquered them through the
efforts I made and sought to make, which are of record in these proceedings. So that everything and this entrada may be of record, I

signed it with the interpreter, the captain, the alferez of the presidio, and my secretary of government and war.

Don Diego de Vargas
Zapata Luján Ponce de León [rubrica]

Roque Madrid [rubrica]

Juan de Dios Lucero de Godoy [rubrica]
Pedro Hidalgo [rubrica]

Before me,

Alfonso Rael de Aguilar [rubrica]
Secretary of government and war

The Pecos ask the interpreter to ask me to leave them appointed a governor and other officials, as they had them when the Spaniards were living here

Today, Saturday, 18 October, the interpreter, Pedro Hidalgo, told me that the elders and prominent people of this pueblo of the Pecos all together have said to him that they ask me to leave them people appointed to hold offices, as when the Spaniards were living here. In this way, they asked me to leave them appointed. In consideration of this, I, the governor and captain general, ordered him to call them all together with the rest of the inhabitants. When they were together, I said to them through the interpreter that they should freely elect the Indians to serve in the offices of governor, his lieutenant, an alcalde, his alguacil, two fiscales,[2] and two war captains. They did so, presenting them before me. I received their oath to faithfully fulfill the duty of their offices, which, through the interpreter, I ordered and told them was for the greater service of both majesties. The reverend father received the oath from the two fiscales for the holy church who were named and elected. Those elected and named in this way were happy with the possession of their offices, as they gave us to understand. So that it may be of record, I signed it with the interpreter, the captain, the alferez of the presidio, and my secretary of government and war.

Don Diego de Vargas
Zapata Luján Ponce de León [rubrica]

Roque Madrid [rubrica]
Juan de Dios Lucero de Godoy [rubrica]
Pedro Hidalgo [rubrica]
Before me,

Alfonso Rael de Aguilar [rubrica]
Secretary of government and war

Departure from the pueblo of the Pecos and entrada into Galisteo Pueblo

Today, Saturday, 18 October, though it had been snowing and raining until two in the afternoon, I, the governor and captain general, departed from this pueblo of the Pecos at about three in the afternoon, despite the bad weather, with the men-at-arms who follow me and the reverend missionary fathers. I took my leave of the Indians and repeated to them that they should pray and live as Christians, which they promised to do. I departed, as joyful as the people were, for leaving them reduced and quiet in their pueblo. At about nine at night, I arrived at Galisteo Pueblo and saw that it was abandoned and its houses in ruins, although most of the walls are still standing. The march covered 6 leagues of rough road. I spent the night there with the men. So that it may be of record, I signed it with the captain, the alferez of the presidio, and my secretary of government and war.

Don Diego de Vargas
Zapata Luján Ponce de León [rubrica]

Roque Madrid [rubrica]

Juan de Dios Lucero de Godoy [rubrica]

Before me,

Alfonso Rael de Aguilar [rubrica]
Secretary of government and war

Entrada into San Marcos Pueblo and departure for Santo Domingo

Today, Sunday, the nineteenth, I, the governor and captain general, after having attended mass with camp, left Galisteo Pueblo and, at a distance of about 3 leagues, entered the pueblo of San Marcos.[3] I found it abandoned and some rooms and walls of its cuarteles and dwellings still standing. Likewise, the walls of the convento and the church, as well as the nave, are sound. Immediately after, I went with the camp to Santo Domingo Pueblo, a distance of 7 or 8 leagues. In it, I found the artillery captain and the men-at-arms who were in his escort, with the provisions and the captives, who are leaving with their relatives. I ordered them to leave from the villa Thursday, the sixteenth of the present month, as is of record in these proceedings. So that my arrival and that I rejoined the camp may be of record, I signed it with the captain, the alferez, and my secretary of government and war.

Don Diego de Vargas
Zapata Luján Ponce de León [rubrica]

                                                    Roque Madrid [rubrica]

Juan de Dios Lucero de Godoy [rubrica]

                                                              Before me,

Alfonso Rael de Aguilar [rubrica]
Secretary of government and war

> The governor and captain general finds the Keres Indian, whom, on
> Friday, 26 September, of this present year, as is of record in the pro-
> ceedings, he sent from the pueblo of the Pecos with the letter, cross,
> and rosary, to Antonio Malacate, captain of those people of the Keres
> nation who left Zia, who are in the pueblo of Santa Ana; and Fran-
> cisco the cantor comes in the company of the Indian

Today, Sunday, I, the governor and captain general, having arrived
at Santo Domingo Pueblo, found there the Keres Indian, whom, as
is of record in these proceedings, I sent from the pueblo of the Pecos
on 26 September of this present year, with the letter, cross, and a
rosary, so that it might be taken and given to Antonio Malacate,
captain and leader of the Keres Indians who left Zia Pueblo and live
in Santa Ana Pueblo, to whom it was given. He was ill and sent in
his place to see me the Spanish-speaking Indian cantor, named Francisco, who was from the pueblo and knows how to read and write.
He told me that the captain was ill, he was waiting for me and the
men to come, and they are joyful about my coming and the letter
and the pardon I told them about in it. So that he may be better
assured, I gave him a rosary, put it around his neck, and ordered
him to go, taking a cross I ordered him to make, to see the Indians
of his Keres nation. They had left their pueblos of Cochiti and San
Felipe and are in Cieneguilla[4] on the other side of the sierra. This
was so as to tell their captains to come down with him to see me and
go on with them to the sierra and site where they have their pueblo.
I ordered the Indian to go in their company and with another from
the camp named Bartolo, who is of the same nation. So that this action
and the success of the previous one may be of record, I signed it with
the captain, the alferez, and my secretary of government and war.
Don Diego de Vargas
Zapata Luján Ponce de León [rubrica]

                                                    Roque Madrid [rubrica]

Juan de Dios Lucero de Godoy [rubrica]

Before me,

Alfonso Rael de Aguilar [rubrica]
Secretary of government and war

> Arrival of the Indian Francisco the cantor, who took the message to
> the Keres of Cieneguilla

Today, Monday, 20 October, at about five in the afternoon, the
Indian Francisco the cantor arrived. It is of record that yesterday,
Sunday, I, the governor and captain general, sent him with the message to the Indians of his Keres nation who are in Cieneguilla and
on the mesa of the sierra of their pueblo, Cochiti. He told me their
captains were coming with him to see me, and through the Indian
Bartolillo, I spoke to four captains and the man who is their principal leader whom they obey. He told me his name was Juan, and I
treated them all kindly, embracing them and shaking their hands. I
ordered them to return to their pueblo and tell everyone to be assured
of my good intentions. I only came to see and know them in order
to pardon them and so that they would again become Christians. I
gave them many other suitable explanations so that they may be convinced and all await me in their pueblo. I gave him a rosary that I
placed around his neck, and he left with the Indians, with great pleasure at having seen me. So that it may be of record, I signed it with
the captain, the alferez of the presidio, and my secretary of government and war.
Don Diego de Vargas
Zapata Luján Ponce de León [rubrica]

Roque Madrid [rubrica]

Juan de Dios Lucero de Godoy [rubrica]

Before me,

Alfonso Rael de Aguilar [rubrica]
Secretary of government and war

> Arrival at Cieneguilla and the pueblo of the Keres
> The governor and captain general sees that conveying the pack ani-
> mals, cannon, horses and other equipment, and the captives will be
> an obstacle because of the rough road and passage, so he orders the
> artillery captain and the sargento mayor to go to the outpost referred to

Today, Tuesday, 21 October, because of the distance and rough road on the direct route to the site of Cieneguilla, and so that some soldiers accompanying the citizens, captives, and some Indians to El Paso may leave directly, I, the governor and captain general, ordered the artillery captain and the sargento mayor to go with the men and the cannon in his charge. They should all await me at the abandoned hacienda that was Cristóbal de Anaya's. Having carried out the departure from Santo Domingo Pueblo in this way, I, the governor and captain general, left with five squads of the two companies. Having gone a distance of 3 leagues, I passed Cochiti Pueblo. I went by its sierra and mesa without stopping, a distance of about another 3 leagues, and found most of the people of the pueblo there. I climbed the mesa and saw that the Keres Indians had set up a large cross and arches. All the people of the pueblo were a musket shot away. I received them with all kindness, and they greeted me, saying the Praised be. I walked to the pueblo's plaza, which has three cuarteles and another large, separate one, where they had prepared a house for me. I did not enter it until after having told all the people on the plaza of my coming and likewise having revalidated and proclaimed possession for his majesty and telling them his royal will, as is of record for the previous pueblos.

103 people of all ages and both sexes are baptized

Likewise, in the company of the other reverend fathers, Father fray Francisco Corvera granted absolution and went on to baptize the individuals and children who were unbaptized. I, the governor and captain general, was godfather to the captain's child, to whom the name Carlos was given in honor of the king, our lord (may God keep him). I was godfather to many others, as were the men-at-arms. One hundred and three people and children of all ages were baptized and the Indians rejoiced.

Asking them how many pueblos they were from and why they had withdrawn to that rugged, steep, mountainous range, they said they were from the three pueblos of Cochiti, San Marcos, and San Felipe. They had left their pueblos and moved to settle there out of fear of the ambushes their enemies, the Tewas, Tanos, and Picuris, laid for them. With the coming of the Spaniards, which I assured them would be in a short time, they would again go down to their pueblos. I took my leave of them, and they all remained very happy. They gave me and the men tortillas and other kinds of food. So that this entrada may be of record, I signed with the captain, the alferez, and my secretary of government and war.

Don Diego de Vargas
Zapata Luján Ponce de León [rubrica]

Roque Madrid [rubrica]

Juan de Dios Lucero de Godoy [rubrica]

Before me,

Alfonso Rael de Aguilar [rubrica]
Secretary of government and war

Entrada into Cochiti Pueblo, on returning from the Keres of Cieneguilla

Today, Tuesday, 21 October, I, the governor and captain general, went with the camp from Cieneguilla to Cochiti Pueblo, a distance of about 3 leagues, to spend the night. So that it may be of record, I signed it with the captain, the alferez of the presidio, and my secretary of government and war.

Don Diego de Vargas
Zapata Luján Ponce de León [rubrica]

Roque Madrid [rubrica]

Juan de Dios Lucero de Godoy [rubrica]

Before me,

Alfonso Rael de Aguilar [rubrica]
Secretary of government and war

Arrival at the abandoned hacienda of Cristóbal de Anaya, where he joins the camp

Today, Wednesday, 22 October, I, the governor and captain general, arrived with the camp at this tumbledown, abandoned hacienda of Cristóbal de Anaya. I found the sargento mayor and artillery captain there with the men-at-arms and the rest of the camp, by virtue of my order of the day before yesterday, Monday, in the pueblo of Santo Domingo, as is of record. So that it may likewise be of record, I signed it with the captain, the alferez of the presidio, and my secretary of government and war. The distance is 7 leagues.

Don Diego de Vargas
Zapata Luján Ponce de León [rubrica]
Juan de Dios
Lucero de Godoy [rubrica]

Roque Madrid [rubrica]
Before me,

Alfonso Rael de Aguilar [rubrica]
Secretary of government and war

Order the governor and captain general gives to the sargento mayor
and the artillery captain

Today, Thursday, 23 October, since the direct route to the Keres
nations of the abandoned pueblos of Santo Domingo and Zia is different from that to the Jemez, I, the governor and captain general,
order the sargento mayor and the artillery captain to go with two
squads of the men from Parral and from the presidio of El Paso as
escort, taking the Indian allies and captives and the tired horses with
the provisions. Together as a body, they should go in two days' march
to the outpost and hacienda of Mejía to join the campaign captain,
whom I left in that outpost on 10 September of this year. They will
halt there until I, the governor and captain general, Our Lord seeing
fit, return from reducing and conquering those nations. So that it
may be of record, I signed it with the captain, the alferez, and my
secretary of government and war.
Don Diego de Vargas
Zapata Luján Ponce de León [rubrica]

Roque Madrid [rubrica]

Juan de Dios Lucero de Godoy [rubrica]

Before me,

Alfonso Rael de Aguilar [rubrica]
Secretary of government and war

Entrada to the abandoned Keres Pueblo of Zia

Today, Thursday, 23 October, I, the governor and captain general, arrived at Zia Pueblo with the men-at-arms numbering five squads,
the leaders of the two companies, and fifty Indians. We found the
pueblo, which my predecessor, Gen. don Domingo Jironza Petrís
de Cruzate, had razed, in ruins.

A soldier finds a buried bell, which the governor and captain general orders Capt. Roque Madrid to leave buried

In the pueblo, a soldier found a large bell buried. By my order, Capt. Roque Madrid of the El Paso presidio reburied it, so that it can be found when his majesty (may God keep him) may see fit for it to be found. I spent the night in the pueblo. The distance was 7 to 8 leagues. So that it may be of record, I signed it with the captain, the alferez of the presidio, and my secretary of government and war. Don Diego de Vargas
Zapata Luján Ponce de León [rubrica]

Roque Madrid [rubrica]

Juan de Dios Lucero
de Godoy [rubrica]

Before me,

Alfonso Rael de Aguilar [rubrica]
Secretary of government and war

Entrada to the nation of the Keres of Zia, who have their pueblo on the mesa of the Cerro Colorado

Today, Friday, 24 October, after traveling 4 leagues, I, the governor and captain general, entered this Keres pueblo of Zia, which is on the mesa of the Cerro Colorado, whose ascent is very steep and rocky. After the Indians saw me and the camp, most of them came down to the first mesa to receive me. Having gone up, I found that they had set up arches and crosses, in accord with the message and letter I had sent them and Antonio Malacate, the captain and leader whom they obey.

123 men, women, and children of all ages are baptized

With the other captains and elders, he received me with all reverence. They all had crosses in their hands and on most of the houses of the cuarteles of the plaza, where they had prepared a ground-level room for me. With the people of the pueblo on the plaza, I told them through the Indian Bartolo, who acted as interpreter, about my coming and took possession for his majesty, as in the other pueblos. The reverend fathers absolved and baptized them, as is stated. I, the governor and captain general, was godfather to Antonio Malacate's child, whom I named Carlos, in honor of the king, our lord (may God keep him), and to many others. I instructed his parents to call him this. It was seen that 123 of all ages, male and female, were baptized.

Then I ordered them to return to settle the pueblo, because the walls were sturdy and good, and the church, likewise, had all its nave and the capilla mayor was sound. They lack nothing but the timbers, which I advised them to cut next month. They told me that they did not have what was needed to cut them. I told them to go to the outpost of Mejía where I had the rest of the men and that I would give them a new saw so that they would have what they needed to cut the timbers for the church and convento. I did not ask them to build a house for me, but only to erect the church and the convento for the fathers, which they agreed to do. They seemed very joyful and happy with their dances and war cries. So that the reduction and conquest of the pueblo for both majesties may be of record, I signed it with the captain, the alferez of the presidio, and my secretary of government and war.

Don Diego de Vargas
Zapata Luján Ponce de León [rubrica]

Roque Madrid [rubrica]

Juan de Dios Lucero
de Godoy [rubrica]

Before me,

Alfonso Rael de Aguilar [rubrica]
Secretary of government and war

> The captain, Antonio Malacate, asks that, considering he is old and ill, a new captain and governor for the Indians be left appointed

Immediately after, I, the governor and captain general, saw that his request was just, since he was prevented from exercising and attending to his office. In my presence and that of the witnesses, and with the attendance of my secretary of government and war, the elders and Indians of the Keres nation in this place and mesa of the Cerro Colorado presented to me as chosen and named a tall, robust Indian. I asked him what his name was, and he said, Cristóbal. Through the interpreter Bartolo, I had him swear the oath to use his office well, making him understand the care I was ordering him to take of the Indians and what is necessary for the greater service of both majesties. With the greatest respect, he pledged to obey and serve in what he will be ordered in everything. So that it may be of record, I signed it with the captain, the alferez of the presidio, and my secretary of government and war.

Don Diego de Vargas
Zapata Luján Ponce de León [rubrica]

Roque Madrid [rubrica]

Juan de Dios Lucero
de Godoy [rubrica]

Before me,

Alfonso Rael de Aguilar [rubrica]
Secretary of government and war

> The governor and captain general goes on to spend the night within sight of the old pueblo of the Jemez

Immediately after the governor's election, I took my leave of the Indians, whom I again ordered to come down from the mesa and settle their pueblo of Zia, and they said they would. I went on to stay the night within sight of the old pueblo of the Jemez, which is abandoned. The march seemed to be about 2 leagues. So that it may be of record, I signed it with the captain, the alferez of the presidio, and my secretary of government and war.

Don Diego de Vargas
Zapata Luján Ponce de León [rubrica]

Roque Madrid [rubrica]

Juan de Dios Lucero
de Godoy [rubrica]

Before me,

Alfonso Rael de Aguilar [rubrica]
Secretary of government and war

> Entrada to the mesa of the pueblo of the Jemez

Today, Saturday, 25 October, I, the governor and captain general, went to the pueblo of the Jemez, which is on the high mesas, 3 leagues from the one they abandoned, and whose ascent is very difficult. On going up the cuesta, more than three hundred Indians, with bows and arrows, came out to receive me. Likewise, on the mesa and loma of its ascent, more than two hundred remained, all with their weapons. They all joined together in a great cry, as is their custom in war, ambush, and battle. In the same way, they put themselves in the midst of the five squads of soldiers and the thirty or forty Indians of the men-at-arms I took from El Paso, throwing dirt in their eyes and making all the gestures they use in their fighting. When Capt. Roque Madrid told them to be still, they replied that it was in token of celebration of my coming,[5] and in the same way, the people continued among my men. With them, I ascended the cuesta on horseback.

When I was on top of the mesa, I saw many people. The only precaution I took was for the men to have their weapons ready, although I could not help but remember the information of record in these proceedings that the Taos Indians gave me the day of their arrival about the junta they had been at and that these natives of Jemez were the instigators. Dissembling, I went about the length of an harquebus shot to where I found their captain and governor, who is called Sebastián, who had a cross in his hand. He was waiting for me at the entrance of the arch, as were another five Indians, leaders and elders of the pueblo.

When they saw me, they knelt to receive me. I dismounted out of respect for the holy cross they had and greeted them all, saying the Praised be. I shook their hands, and they embraced me. I went to the plaza of their pueblo where I entered, followed by my men and the people of the pueblo. I saw that it has two plazas, one with an entrance that leads to the other, garrisoned and closed, and each with four cuarteles. In this way, I found myself afoot and hemmed in by the crowd. Because they were suspicious, some had not laid down their weapons. Others were bewildered, while others prepared a great war dance.

Presently, I said to Captain Sebastián, who had the holy cross in his hand, as well as to the other elders who accompanied him, that I saw in their faces a troubled look. Despite the fact that I was the one who should have been and was troubled because I had entered with so few men, I neither spoke a word nor made a gesture that might cause them to think I was afraid of them and knew their evil intention. I thus ordered, as I had in the other pueblos, the women, children, and all the people who might be in the pueblo to come down. Although in the others they were all there to receive me, in this pueblo, only the armed Indians were present. Nevertheless, much later, some others came out from their cuarteles and came down, although few in number for so many warriors.

Seeing that there were no more, as their captains told me, and having ordered them to leave their weapons on the ground, most of them put them at their feet. Through a Spanish-speaking Indian from the pueblo, a war captain named Francisco, I told them in their Jemez language of my coming and did likewise for the Keres Indians of the pueblo of Santo Domingo through the Indian Bartolo, already referred to. I reclaimed and revalidated the royal possession that his majesty (may God keep him) has, both of the land and of his vassals, which they are. To even greater effect, I told them they were his vassals alone and were they not loyal and good, they would not be safe anywhere, for his power was great, and other reasons to persuade them that what I told them was true. I said this while I was walking among them.

117 of both sexes are baptized

When I was finished, the reverend fathers granted them absolution in the manner referred to in the other pueblos. They went on to baptize the children and the rest of the people who were unbaptized. I was godfather only to some unmarried Indian women and widows, in case they gave me cause to begin fighting. Having counted the number baptized, there were 117 of all ages and both sexes.

Once that was finished, they asked me to come up to a second-story room to eat. So that they would not suspect the bad opinion I had formed and was forming of them, I went up, and they fed me, the officials and war leaders, and fathers with more courtesy than anywhere else. I left afterward, and several Apaches who came out of the house formally rendered me their obedience. In its passage-way, I spoke to them, telling them that in the coming year I would return (God Our Lord giving me life) and that they should tell those of their nation and rancheria that if they were not Christians, I did not want their friendship. They accepted what I told them and replied that they were satisfied. I inferred from the fact that the Apaches were lodged in the house and that many others were in the houses of the second plaza that the report from the Taos about the aforementioned junta was true.

Taking my leave of them, I told them they should go down to live in the pueblo they had abandoned; that I was going to pass by it that night; and that they should bring me some supplies, for which I had paid them in pinole and mutton. They agreed to do so the following morning. I left, giving thanks to God for success in the reduction and conquest of the Indians, going on to spend the night at a camp-site opposite their abandoned pueblo, having traveled about 6 leagues round-trip. So that what is referred to may be of record, I signed it with the captain, the alferez of the presidio, and my secretary of government and war.

Don Diego de Vargas
Zapata Luján Ponce de León [rubrica]

Roque Madrid [rubrica]

Juan de Dios Lucero
de Godoy [rubrica]

Before me,

Alfonso Rael de Aguilar [rubrica]
Secretary of government and war

Entrada to the pueblo of Santa Ana

Today, Sunday, 26 October, after mass they brought me the supplies referred to above, although because of the short notice, there were very few. Nevertheless, I valued this as a sign of their vassalage and obedience. I treated those who brought them kindly and sent gifts to all. I went on to spend the night at this abandoned pueblo of Santa Ana, a march of about 7 leagues. So that it may be of record, I signed it with the captain, the alferez, and my secretary of government and war.

Don Diego de Vargas
Zapata Luján Ponce de León [rubrica]

Roque Madrid [rubrica]

Juan de Dios Lucero
de Godoy [rubrica]

Before me,

Alfonso Rael de Aguilar [rubrica]
Secretary of government and war

The governor and captain general arrives at the outpost of Mejía, where he joins the camp and sargento mayor

Today, Monday, 27 October, I, the governor and captain general, arrived at this abandoned hacienda of Mejía, which I had chosen on 10 September for the reserve of the provisions and for the horses to regain strength. I found everything, with the men and the leaders in charge of them having arrived safely and the leader appointed to guard this outpost having successfully done so. So that my having joined the camp there and the march of about 8 leagues may be of record, I signed it with the captain, the alferez of the presidio, and my secretary of government and war.

Don Diego de Vargas
Zapata Luján Ponce de León [rubrica]

Roque Madrid [rubrica]

Juan de Dios Lucero
de Godoy [rubrica]

Before me,

Alfonso Rael de Aguilar [rubrica]
Secretary of government and war

> The governor and captain general thinks it advantageous to send the captives, wagons, and carts with the bronze cannon to El Paso and orders that what is contained here be prepared and a muster and list of the captives be made

Today, Tuesday, 28 October, wishing for my part to carry out in every way the most difficult tasks to the greater service of his majesty and review and close the books on the conquest and reduction of all the inhabitants and nations of this kingdom, I, the governor and captain general, have just reduced and conquered New Mexico at my expense for our holy faith and the royal crown. The pueblos of the nations reduced and conquered number seventeen, and in them 1,560 children, boys and girls, men, and women of all ages and both sexes have been baptized. Only the provinces of Zuni and Moqui, which they say are more than 100 leagues from this outpost, remain. Inasmuch as the Indian allies I took from El Paso are injured and their horses are tired; the winter weather here is severe and there has already been some snow and heavy frost this month, which wear out the horses and make them stiff; and so that the men and ten citizens who have followed me from the pueblo of El Paso may not lose the horses, I order the artillery captain and the sargento mayor to ready the wagons, oxen, and mules for the transport of the carts and bronze cannon. At the same time, I name eight soldiers from the company of the El Paso presidio, whom I order to go as escort, and as their leader, Diego Zervín, leader of one of the squads of that company, since he is an excellent and careful soldier.

At the same time, a muster and list of the captives is to be made, so that they may go to the pueblo of El Paso with the men, their relatives, with whom they have departed from the reduced and conquered kingdom. I order the muster held in the presence of the sargento mayor, Cristóbal de Tapia, so that in his charge he may take it and hand it over to my lieutenant governor and captain general in the pueblo of El Paso, with the attendance of the illustrious cabildo of this kingdom residing there, giving him a copy of the muster, so that he may take it, signed in my hand and countersigned by my secretary of government and war. Thus, for all time, the number, condition, and ages of the captives may be of record in these proceedings. So that what is referred to and the order may be of record, I signed it with the captain, the alferez of the presidio, and my secretary of government and war.

Don Diego de Vargas
Zapata Luján Ponce de León [rubrica]

Roque Madrid [rubrica]

Juan de Dios Lucero
de Godoy [rubrica]

Before me,

Alfonso Rael de Aguilar [rubrica]
Secretary of government and war

List of the people found in the pueblos of New Mexico at the time of its conquest and reduction in this present year 1692, who are going to El Paso in the charge of Sgto. mayor Cristóbal de Tapia, so that in its plaza de armas, he may make the presentation by this list before my lieutenant governor and captain general, with the attendance of the most illustrious cabildo of the kingdom, and so that at all times, it may be seen that the people referred to in it are in the pueblo of El Paso and its district, until his majesty, the king, our lord (may God keep him), may decide and order.

Capt. Roque Madrid from this presidio takes Petrona, married to Cristóbal Nieto, citizen and resident in Sonora, with five daughters and two sons

José Domínguez[6] takes his sister, Juana Domínguez, with four daughters and one son

List of former captives being escorted to El Paso, 29 October 1692, Vargas Journal (SANM II:53)
State Records Center and Archives, Santa Fe

No 4   Una drana hiparytas Con Una niña   No 3

No 1   In muchacho hijos hijos ——————— No 2

El Sargto Inos Cruz de Cazary Uba, aun
Indio llamado Hoome Con su beama
Antonia y dize ser sus suinos ——————— No 1

No 1   & Iuan Indio tiguas de Magdalena Uena
Una India llamada Mana & tiene de
Madre y de Mando enotro Pueblo ——— No 1
asimismo Uena otra India llamada Ca
thalina soltera Con Una hija q dize ser
su beama ——————— No 2

asimismo Uena Una India India Presidias
mada Isauel Conus hijos q tiene ens
otro Pueblo ——————— No 1
Fran Indio del Pho de Magdalena Uena
No 1   aun Madre llamada elena Con Una hijas No 1
mas lacha Una hija grande llam Mas ——— No 1

No 1   & Un hijo grande llamado Fran Co
mas otro hijo de lacha llam de Iuane — No
Mas Uena Una India Pary llamada tos

No 1   & Isauel Con Un hijo ——————— No 1
mas Uena dos hijas de lacha Isauel No 2
Un India & mas Entiguas Uena a suuire
en llamaou Isauel Con Una hija Iths
No 1   hijo ——————— No 2

asimesmo Uena En lucomp a Inynos.
tiguas llamdo Isuan qieba acauar Cons
No 1   sepa India ——

_____   Anttonio Indio delas tiguas Uena asus _____
4 1 1   4 3 3

Varony / Muger Caballo En San Xptobal llam.^{do} del Rem.^{to}
U11 / U.1 Juzia En d.^{ha} lisa y d.^{ho} hijo ————— U.2
gran Indio del Paso llena a su b.^{nia}
U.1 llamada Maria con dos hijas y d.^{os} U.3
muchacho asimismo Una a yun.^{ta}
Indio tigua llamado Juan queba acasan
U.1 En otra India al Paso ———————— U.
asimismo Una Yn Indio llamado Pedro
U.1 q. tiene asu muger Pedrasu.^{la} En los sierras de
Paso aqui pues del Paso d.^{ha} Indio
llamado fran.^{co} del nazon q.^e g.^r
tiene asi Maese en eve q.^{ue} y an my
q.^e ba en fuerson q.sa Una India lla
nasa Una d.mas q.sa En d.ho
jo d.na hija d.na q.^{ue} La llena pa.^{es} ——— U.2
U.2 Casarse en otros q.^{ue}s
asimism ba Una India humanes
llamada Juanona q. de ballo q.^{ue}
continua en los q.^{ue}s d.tiguas llam.^{da} U.1
Paso Un Indio d.nes
Sebastian Gobero ——————— U.
U.1 asimesmo dos yndios tiguas que se
U.1 > primeron en busca de los españoles
a esta haz.^{da} de Mexia llamada la
Una y la otra tigua q. pasan
a la yg.^{ca} cresta con su Qaxy choys ——— U.2
U.Fin
d.ha lista se hizo segun se refiere en esta Juris.^{on}
el bueno d.ho Sargento may.^{or} d.Catasia Rond.

Testigos el Capp.n del Pressidio de el gar.te Juan

Luz de Chavez y lo firm.ó con.migo secretar.io

de gou.no y guerra. Enel va ba...

D.n Fran.co de Coron.do...

que el Alferez... y ...los an...enm...

enmienda = Vale =

El Sargento Vargas

Capta de San Ponze de Leon / Xptoual de tapia

Roque madrid

Antonio...

Thomas...

... dg q que...

Juan Holguín, soldier, takes two daughters of José Nevares, soldier of Janos, who are his kinswomen or relatives

Francisco Márquez, soldier, takes his aunt Lucía, wife of Pedro Márquez,[7] resident in Casas Grandes, with a grown daughter

Francisco de Almazán Saez takes a mulatta named María, with three daughters and one son

Diego García,[8] soldier of this presidio, takes Juana, his relative, with a daughter and a young boy, her children

Sgto. Juan Ruiz de Cáceres takes an Indian named Tomé with his sister Antonia, and he says they are his cousins

Esteban, a Tiwa Indian from Ysleta, takes an Indian named María, who has her mother and husband in that pueblo. He also takes another Indian named Catalina, unmarried, with a child, who says she is her sister. He also takes an old Indian named Isabel, with the children she has in that pueblo

Francisco, an Indian from Ysleta Pueblo, takes his mother, named Elena, with a son, a grown daughter named María, a grown son named Francisco, and another of her sons named Juan. He takes an Indian relative named Isabel with one son and two of her daughters

Juan, an Indian of the Tewa nation, takes his sister-in-law, named Isabel, with a daughter and a son and also takes in his company a Tewa Indian named Esteban, who is going to marry that Indian woman

Antonio, an Indian from Ysleta, takes his wife, named Lucía, whom he found in San Cristóbal, with a daughter and a son

Francisco, an Indian from El Paso, takes his sister, named María, with two daughters and one son and also takes to El Paso a Tewa Indian named Juan, who is going to marry that Indian woman. He also takes an Indian named Pedro, who has his father and mother in Ysleta

An Indian named Francisco from the Piro nation goes to the outpost of El Paso. He has his mother in that pueblo. Also, an Indian named Ana from the Piro nation accompanies him with a son and a daughter. He says he takes her to marry her in that pueblo

A Jumano Indian named Antonia also goes. She was a captive among the Pecos

An Indian of the Tiwa nation named Sebastián, unmarried, goes

Likewise, two Tiwa Indians go, one named Juana and the other Lucía, who came in search of the Spaniards at this hacienda of Mejía. They are going to Ysleta with their relatives

The list was made, as is related, with the attendance of the afore-mentioned sargento mayor, Cristóbal de Tapia. The captain of the presidio and the sargento, Juan Ruiz de Cáceres, were witnesses. They signed it with my secretary of government and war at this hacienda of Mejía, today, Thursday, 29 October 1692.
Don Diego de Vargas
Zapata Luján Ponce de León [rubrica]

Cristóbal de Tapia [rubrica]
Roque Madrid [rubrica]

Before me,
Alfonso Rael de Aguilar [rubrica]
Secretary of government and war

Departure of the sargento mayor and artillery captain with the people in their charge for El Paso

Today, Wednesday, 29 October, the people going to El Paso left this outpost, provisioned with meat, pinole, and biscuit; and the soldiers and citizens with chocolate, sugar, tobacco, and soap, so that they can make it to the pueblo of El Paso. So that this may be of record and that the escort of the oxen and the carters were also provisioned in this way, I signed it with the captain, the alferez of the presidio, and my secretary of government and war.
Don Diego de Vargas
Zapata Luján Ponce de León [rubrica]

Roque Madrid [rubrica]

Juan de Dios Lucero
de Godoy [rubrica]

Before me,

Alfonso Rael de Aguilar [rubrica]
Secretary of government and war

Departure of the governor with the two companies for the provinces of Zuni and Moqui and entrada to the pueblo of Isleta

Today, Thursday, ~~29~~-30 October, I, the governor and captain general, leave from this outpost of Mejía with eighty-nine soldiers; the leaders and war officials of the two companies; and thirty swift Indians, the only ones able to leave for the entrada, conquest, and reduction of the provinces of Zuni and Moqui. I arrived at this pueblo of Isleta, which is on the other bank of the Río del Norte. It is abandoned and in ruins, except for the nave of the church, the walls of which are still standing. So that this march may be of record and that it seemed to be 5 leagues, I signed it with the captain, the alferez of the presidio, and my secretary of government and war.

Don Diego de Vargas
Zapata Luján Ponce de León [rubrica]

Roque Madrid [rubrica]

Juan de Dios Lucero
de Godoy [rubrica]

Before me,

Alfonso Rael de Aguilar [rubrica]
Secretary of government and war

Arrival at the Río Puerco

Today, Friday, 31 October, I, the governor and captain general, arrived with the camp at this place they call the Río Puerco.[9] Because the water at the crossing was so deep, it was necessary to carry the load of provisions across on our shoulders. The march was 7 to 8 leagues. So that it may be of record, I signed it with the captain, the alferez of the presidio, and my secretary of government and war.

Don Diego de Vargas
Zapata Luján Ponce de León [rubrica]

Roque Madrid [rubrica]

Juan de Dios Lucero
de Godoy [rubrica]

Before me,

Alfonso Rael de Aguilar [rubrica]
Secretary of government and war

Arrival at the laguna next to the mesas that descend from the arroyo of San Felipe

Today, Saturday, 1 November 1692, after mass, I, the governor and captain general, having gone about 1 league, arrived with the camp at a laguna in which they say they have never seen water. It seems it was formed by the springs from the lomas and mountain range that surround it and the flooding of Los Quelites arroyo. Since the horses and mules have come without having drunk because the water from the other river was filthy, I stopped. The day's storm with

its heavy shower kept me from going on from this flatland and campsite. So that it may be of record, I signed it with the captain, the
alferez of the presidio, and my secretary of government and war.
Don Diego de Vargas
Zapata Luján Ponce de León [rubrica]

                                            Roque Madrid [rubrica]

Juan de Dios Lucero
de Godoy [rubrica]

                                                       Before me,

Alfonso Rael de Aguilar [rubrica]
Secretary of government and war

    Arrival at El Pozo

    Today, Sunday, 2 November, I, the governor and captain gen-
eral, arrived with the camp at this water hole of El Pozo. It was just
luck that it had any water, and the horses drank, although with difficulty. The march was about 10 leagues. So that it may be of record,
I signed it with the captain, the alferez of the presidio, and my secretary of government and war.
Don Diego de Vargas
Zapata Luján Ponce de León [rubrica]

                                            Roque Madrid [rubrica]

Juan de Dios Lucero
de Godoy [rubrica]

                                                       Before me,

Alfonso Rael de Aguilar [rubrica]
Secretary of government and war

    Arrival at the peñol of Acoma, occupied by the rebel Keres nation,
    who killed four religious in their uprising

    Today, Monday, 3 November, because of the shallow water hole,
I, the governor and captain general, departed with this camp from
this campsite at eleven in the morning. Having gone up some rough
road and cuesta and marched about 1 league, I discovered and they
pointed out to me the hill they call the peñol of Acoma. In a little
while, we descried at a distance the smoke that the enemies, the
treacherous, uprisen, and apostate traitors of the Keres nation,
made on it.

In order to go examine it and face the enemy, I changed horses and ordered the leaders and officials of the two companies to come with me with five squads. I stopped within sight of another peñol, on the right side of the road and bajada and apparently higher. Ordering the men of the squads to come, I marched with the leaders. Before arriving at the peñol, about a musket-shot away, I ordered them to follow me in rank, and as I would go saying the Praised be, they should say it too.

I reached the peñol, which the enemy was occupying, and said the Praised be in a loud and clear voice, and at the same time, those who were accompanying me said and repeated it. We heard the enemy say, "Forever," at which I spoke to them through an interpreter, saying to them that I came to pardon them. I repeated everything I said to them and what is of record in the other pueblos. Suspicious and afraid, they replied to me they did not believe I would pardon them. At that, I had to show and tell them that, with the most holy Virgin whose image I showed them on the royal standard and the holy cross of the rosary as my witnesses, they could safely come down to see me and I would pardon them.

Nevertheless, they repeated various questions, and their bringing up an Indian from among those of my camp was not enough for them to be sure of my truthfulness. He shook their hands, embraced them, and told them everything that had happened in the other pueblos. They had another Indian, one from Zuni, come up and another from Moqui, who had both come with me from Jemez Pueblo. The Moqui Indian, who came from that place with his sister, who had been a captive of the Apaches, even had her come up.

When everyone was up there, after many repeated questions, with even the reverend fathers having said to them they could safely come down, as I had told them, after a little while they told me to go to the other side of the peñol where they have their way up. Having gone around it, we went up by the sand bank, which is the path they have to the entrance. I stopped there, leaving the men-at-arms in reserve below. Understanding they would come down, the enemy was occupying the ramparts, without wanting to reply or say a word. It was found that they had their gate and entrance to the peñol all blocked off with stone they brought up to fortify it and close it off as soon as they glimpsed me and my men, in order to prevent entry, since it will and would be impossible to ascend except through it. I told them that, seeing that they did not believe me, they should send me the Indians who had gone up. At this, one of them replied that he would call them, since they were talking with the people.

Nevertheless, much time passed, such that I repeated my order three times. After a long while, my Indians came down. One, a coyote[10] from Zuni named Ventura, brought me a gift of a melon, a cooked squash, and some tortillas. He said they were sending them to me, saying they would all talk that night and in the morning, I should return and they would send me their answer. Although the newly appointed sargento mayor dismounted and, together with the first Indian, ascended as far as the blocked gate, telling them in their language to come down, he could not persuade them. I repeated to them with effective words that they should be convinced of my truthfulness, and they again said to me that they would talk together that night and reply to me through the one to whom they had given the message.

In the midst of this, one of the soldiers who had arrived at the water hole where the camp had to stop came, bringing as a prisoner an enemy Indian, who was carrying a load of firewood. Within their view, I treated him kindly, shook his hand, embraced him, and gave him his freedom, telling him to tell them not to be afraid. Despite acting in this way, it was not reason enough to remove their fear, since they repeated to me that that night they would decide what they had to reply to me. They warned me to be careful, because all the Apaches were waiting for me to kill me and all the men. Thus they advised me, at which I told them that only those who were Christians were my friends. I was not afraid of the Apaches and tomorrow would wait for them at the water hole. Since the sun had already set, I was going and would send the Indian Ventura to them. So that everything referred to and the more than five hours spent on the demands and replies may be of record, I signed it with the captain, the alferez of the presidio, and my secretary of government and war.

Don Diego de Vargas
Zapata Luján Ponce de León [rubrica]

Roque Madrid [rubrica]

Juan de Diego Lucero
de Godoy [rubrica]

Before me,

Alfonso Rael de Aguilar [rubrica]
Secretary of government and war

The governor and captain general sends the Indian Ventura with the cross as a sign of peace, so that the enemy Keres of the peñol of Acoma can give him their reply

Today, Tuesday, 4 November, at sunrise I, the governor and captain general, called the aforesaid Ventura, a coyote from Zuni. I ordered him to go and carry the holy cross, which I gave him, and a letter in which I told the Keres Indians of the peñol of Acoma I had come to pardon them so that they might again become Christians, as they had been. I had brought the fathers in my company to absolve them and baptize the children. As a sign of peace and as witness to my truthfulness, I was sending the holy cross. Thus, without fear of my doing them any harm, all could see me, and they could open the gate they had to ascend the peñol. I awaited their reply, and the aforesaid coyote went, accompanied by the Moqui Indian, both informed of everything. So that the action may be of record, I signed it with the captain, the alferez of the presidio, and my secretary of government and war.
Don Diego de Vargas
Zapata Luján Ponce de León [rubrica]

Roque Madrid [rubrica]

Juan de Dios Lucero
de Godoy [rubrica]

Before me,

Alfonso Rael de Aguilar [rubrica]
Secretary of government and war

Reply the coyote Ventura brings, and the decision that by virtue of it the governor and captain general makes

Today, Tuesday, 4 November, Ventura, the coyote Indian, returned at about ten in the morning with the verbal reply to the letter and message I, the governor and captain general, had given him and said and repeated to him that he had to give and say to the enemy Keres Indians, uprisen rebels and treacherous apostates on the peñol of Acoma. He told me he had told them everything I had ordered him to say and likewise delivered the letter, which they had listened to attentively when a Spanish-speaking Indian, native of the peñol, read it. He had also given them the holy cross he had received, and in this manner, he, as all the rest, kissed it. They replied to me that at present, they were very afraid, because they were alone and had as their only friends the Navajo Apache, whom they would advise when I had left on my journey to Zuni. I should advise them when I return, and then they would see me and talk. As a result of that reply, I, the governor and captain general, because of the shallowness of the water hole in the campsite where I was, and because there was not another one, and since even this one did not have enough water for the large number of this camp's horses, mules, and cattle, set the men-at-arms to the task of cleaning it with shovels and hoes for tools. While they were engaged in this, which scarcely had the effect of relieving the horses, and, thus unable to maintain myself in that campsite without leaving it because of the lack of water for both the horses and the men, I heard the reserve adjutant, José de Madrid,[11] say he had discovered a small water hole.

The governor and captain general goes to reconnoiter a small water hole with the leaders and war officials of the two companies

To find out whether it was sufficient, I mounted my horse and ordered the leaders and the war officials of the two companies to come with me to see whether there was enough water to stay on that frontier and go conquer the enemy, whose fortifications on that peñol are impregnable. Having done so and gone about 1 league, I saw that the water hole had scarcely an arroba of water. I saw that the enemy all remained on the summit of the peñol on the lookout from their ramparts.

Because it seemed to me that for them to recognize my good will and that I was not afraid to go talk to them and repeat what I had written them and sent Ventura, the coyote Indian, to say, I went up to and nearly below the ramparts and greeted them, saying to them the Praised be, and so forth. I began to speak to them, at which they replied to me to go where they had their way up, where I had been yesterday afternoon. Having arrived there, all the people of the peñol came, assuming positions in front of and on the ramparts. I told them again with effective and gentle words of my coming and was sorry they did not believe me. I was a Christian and they were as well. Because of that, I was moved to compassion for them. I repeated my reasons, saying to them that I came to pardon them, and that the king, our lord (may God keep him), sent me for that from so great a distance and so that they might be Christians, which was what he wanted of them and nothing else.

I also did not come to ask them to give me anything at all. They should be assured that what I said to them was true and not false, to which the Spanish-speaking Indian, whom they obey and have for their leader, replied for all. I asked him what his name was, and he said it was Mateo. I replied to and calmed all his doubts and suspicions. Fearful and obstinate, however, he remained doubtful, saying that two Manso Indians and other Apaches had told him and his people that when I, the governor and captain general, came, they should not believe me, because although I would tell them that I came in peace to listen and see, under that pretext I would order them all shot with harquebuses and hanged.

I told them this account was false and that the Mansos and Apaches were liars. The reason for their trying to prevent them from being our friends was that they were enemies of the Christians. Since they did not trust me enough to come down from the peñol, so that they might see I trusted them and how few men came with me, they should open for me the entrance that they had blocked, and I would go up. Then, I dismounted and approached, as did the leaders and my secretary of war and government with me. To listen and reply in answer to the complete disbelief in their assertions, I sat down, as the rest did, on the flat stones and large rocks that are at the entrance. Persisting, I stood up to tell them to come down, since they did not want to open the entrance. Mateo, with the consent of the Indians, wanted to hurry down by one side of it. Since it was very steep, he said we should come by the footpath they have and that they would come down that way. I went there with the men and people mentioned and saw him coming down. When he was at the end of the path, the leaders went up to receive him.

They embraced him, and most of those Indians, all without their weapons, came down. As a result, so not to lose the opportunity, I decided to go up by the very difficult part of the ascent, calling to the reverend missionary fathers, who did so as well. I reached the mesa of the peñol with the leaders and men mentioned. It is so broad and spacious that it has two plazas. One divides the third cuartel in the middle. All three cuarteles are so extensive that they have a long horse track along the length of the plaza.

Having approached the first cuartel on the first plaza, I ordered the captain of the El Paso presidio to set up a cross. With the many people of the pueblo before it, through the Spanish-speaking Indian, I repeated the reason for my coming and the pardon, of which I assured them in his majesty's name. He and no other was their king and natural lord. They were his vassals and he lord of that peñol and all that land. His power was great, and were they not good they would not be safe. As a sign of his possession of them and their pueblo, I took the royal standard in my hands, reclaiming, reaffirming, and proclaiming the royal possession on behalf of his majesty in the manner referred to in the rest of the pueblos.

The baptized are 87 people of all ages and both sexes

Afterward, the reverend father, fray Francisco Corvera, with the father, fray Cristóbal Alonso Barroso, granted them absolution, which they all received kneeling. They went on to baptize the children and the rest of the individuals who were unbaptized. I was compadre to one of Captain Mateo's sons, whom I named Carlos in honor of the king, our lord, and to many others, as were the men and leaders referred to. Once this was finished, the number of the baptized was seen to be eighty-seven individuals and children of all ages, male and female.

Afterward, I ordered them all to put crosses around their necks and pray morning and evening before the holy cross I ordered them to set up in their plaza. It must have been about vespers when everything mentioned was finished. I went to see their holy church, whose appellation was that of San Esteban, patron saint of their pueblo. I found it to be very large, and it seemed to be even larger than the Convento de San Francisco in that court, both in the length of the church and in the height of its walls. In thickness, these are about a vara and a half. They are still standing and intact, except for the holes made for the windows and clerestories of the church.

After seeing it, since it was already night, I took leave of the Indians and my compadre Mateo. I embraced and caressed him, saying and repeating to him to see that they all prayed and that those who knew how taught those who did not.

Thanking God, I went down the peñol as best I could. Everyone was very pleased at having achieved the reduction and conquest in the manner referred to. Only fifteen men went up—military leaders, officials, and my secretary of government and war among their number—without Indian allies, because they had deserted me and scarcely fifteen remained. So that the undertaking may be of record, I signed it with the leaders and my secretary of government and war.

Don Diego de Vargas
Zapata Luján Ponce de León [rubrica]

          Roque Madrid [rubrica]

Martín de Alday [rubrica]

          Juan de Dios Lucero

de Godoy [rubrica]
Juan Páez Hurtado [rubrica]

          Before me,

Alfonso Rael de Aguilar [rubrica]
Secretary of government and war

> The governor and captain general goes to the water hole to spend the night, the sargento and the men-at-arms having cleaned it as well as they could

Immediately after having come down from the peñol and pueblo of Acoma, where the Indians have two cisterns from which they maintain themselves, I, the governor and captain general, went with some caution with the leaders to the shallow water hole referred to, where the camp was quartered. The sargento of the El Paso company reported to me that in the course of the day, he, with the men-at-arms, had continued cleaning, so that the spring, which was low, would produce some water tonight.

> Order the governor and captain general gives to the leaders of this camp

With this information, I ordered and commanded the captains and the sargento mayor to be at that water hole tomorrow, Wednesday, when the password expired. This was only to water the animals of the pack trains and the horses the men-at-arms had to saddle up for the departure from this place and march to the first water hole that might be found on the road to the pueblo of the province of Zuni. So that this order may be of record, I signed it with the captains, the sargento mayor, the alferez of the presidio, and my secretary of government and war.

Don Diego de Vargas
Zapata Luján Ponce de León [rubrica]

          Roque Madrid [rubrica]

Juan Páez Hurtado [rubrica]

Juan de Dios Lucero

de Godoy [rubrica]

Before me,

Alfonso Rael de Aguilar [rubrica]
Secretary of government and war

Arrival at the water hole of the Nacimiento River

Today, Wednesday, 5 November, I, the governor and captain general, arrived with the camp at this water hole and campsite of the river that descends from Nacimiento spring, which is to the south along the road to the pueblo of Zuni. So that it may be of record, and its march having been 5 leagues, I signed it with the captain, the alferez of the presidio, and my secretary of government and war.

Don Diego de Vargas
Zapata Luján Ponce de León [rubrica]

Roque Madrid [rubrica]

Juan de Dios Lucero
de Godoy [rubrica]

Before me,

Alfonso Rael de Aguilar [rubrica]
Secretary of government and war

Arrival at Nacimiento spring

Today, Thursday, 6 November, I, the governor and captain general, went with the camp to this water hole at Nacimiento spring. Its march is from 2 to 3 leagues. So that it may be of record, I signed it with the captain, the alferez, and my secretary of government and war.

Don Diego de Vargas
Zapata Luján Ponce de León [rubrica]

Roque Madrid [rubrica]

Juan de Dios Lucero
de Godoy [rubrica]

Before me,

Alfonso Rael de Aguilar [rubrica]
Secretary of government and war

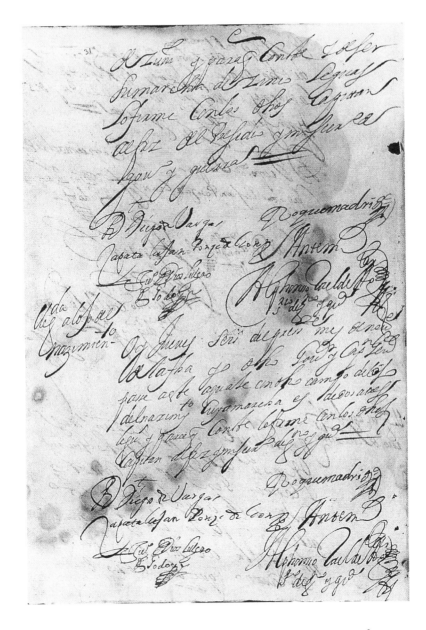

Arrival at Nacimiento spring, 6 November 1692, Vargas Journal
(SANM II:53)
    State Record Center and Archives, Santa Fe

The governor and captain general sends Ventura, the coyote Indian, and gives him provisions, so that he may take the letter about the governor's arrival to the Zuni Indians

Today, Friday, 7 November, since the province of Zuni is 25 leagues away from this campsite, so that its Indians may know of my arrival and my going immediately to see them, I, the governor and captain general, ordered Ventura, the coyote Indian of that nation, to go immediately with my letter for its captains and Indians, so that it may be given as a sign of peace, bearing as a sign the holy cross marked on it. I also put a rosary around his neck. Giving him the necessary provisions of a good mule and supplies, I also gave him the appropriate message and many other explanations, which I told him. This was so that they might be informed of my good will and not leave their homes and go away from their pueblo, but await me there all together. Fully informed about everything, he took leave of me, carrying out his journey. So that it may be of record, I noted it as a completed action and signed with the captain, the alferez, and my secretary of government and war.

Don Diego de Vargas Zapata
Luján Ponce de León [rubrica]

Roque Madrid [rubrica]

Juan de Dios Lucero de Godoy [rubrica]

Before me,

Alfonso Rael de Aguilar [rubrica]
Secretary of government and war

Arrival at Las Peñuelas

Today, Friday, 7 November, I, the governor and captain general, arrived with the camp at this place they call Las Peñuelas. Since it was already late and there was no water hole until El Morro, which is 14 to 15 leagues away, I stopped in this campsite, breaking the journey halfway. So that it may be of record, I signed it with the captain, the alferez of the presidio, and my secretary of government and war.

The campsite at El Morro
(above) and Vargas inscription
by Richard H. Kern, 1849
　From James H. Simpson,
　*Journal of a Military
　Reconnaissance* (1852)

Don Diego de Vargas Zapata
Luján Ponce de León [rubrica]

Roque Madrid [rubrica]

Juan de Dios Lucero
de Godoy [rubrica]

Before me,

Alfonso Rael de Aguilar [rubrica]
Secretary of government and war

Arrival at the water hole of El Morro

Today, Saturday, eighth of the present month, I, the governor
and captain general, arrived with the camp at this place of El Morro,[12]
a very large, extended peñol, at the foot of which is a hollow like an
inverted cupola in which rainwater collects. Depending on whether
it has rained, there is a chance of finding water there. God saw fit
that at present it had abundant water. Thus, this camp was aided,
and the horses, mules, and other livestock, in such a fashion that
there was enough for the return (God seeing fit). So that it may be of
record, I signed it with the captain, the alferez of the presidio, and
my secretary of government and war.
Don Diego de Vargas
Zapata Luján Ponce de León [rubrica]

Roque Madrid [rubrica]

Juan de Dios Lucero
de Godoy [rubrica]

Before me,

Alfonso Rael de Aguilar [rubrica]
Secretary of government and war

Arrival at this water hole of Ojito de Zuni

Today, Sunday, 9 November, after having attended mass, notwithstanding the continued bad weather, I, the governor and captain general, left with the camp from the water hole at El Morro and
arrived at this one, which they call Ojito de Zuni. The march was
more or less 6 leagues. So that it may be of record, I signed it with
the captain, the alferez of the presidio, and my secretary of government and war.

Don Diego de Vargas
Zapata Luján Ponce de León [rubrica]

Roque Madrid [rubrica]

Juan de Dios Lucero de Godoy [rubrica]

Before me,

Alfonso Rael de Aguilar [rubrica]
Secretary of government and war

Arrival of the captains and some Zuni Indian leaders, sent by the Indians to see me

Today, Sunday, at about four o'clock in the afternoon, ten or twelve Indians on horseback and two on foot from the Zuni nation arrived here, Ojito de Zuni. They presented themselves before me, the governor and captain general. I received them with kindness and through a Spanish-speaking Indian from the camp, a native of that nation, asked them various and repeated questions. They replied to me that by virtue of my letter, which I had sent to them with the coyote Indian, Ventura, and they had received, they came to see and welcome me on behalf of the leaders, elders, and Indians of the province of Zuni. They all were very pleased and satisfied. One Spanish-speaking Indian from among them named Alonso repeated what the interpreter said and translated. I treated them kindly, and they me, bringing me as a gift mutton, some melons, and tortillas. They spent that night with the people of the camp, very content. So that it may be of record, I signed it with the captain, the alferez of the presidio, and my secretary of government and war.

Don Diego de Vargas
Zapata Luján Ponce de León [rubrica]

Roque Madrid [rubrica]

Juan de Dios Lucero
de Godoy [rubrica]

Before me,

Alfonso Rael de Aguilar [rubrica]
Secretary of government and war

Arrival within sight of the peñol, on whose mesa the Indians of the pueblos of Zuni are found to have settled, having abandoned those they had

Today, Monday, 10 November, I, the governor and captain general, arrived with the camp within view of the large peñol[13] on which at present the Indians of the Zuni nation and the pueblo of Halona[14] are found to have settled and be living. The aforementioned Indians who came to welcome me approached me. I wanted to go on to stop at the old pueblo, but they told me that they had not yet completely harvested their milpas and there was not enough firewood there. On this llano, the horses had pasture and water all around, and the people also had firewood. To please them, I stopped, quartering the camp there. They also told me they were going to see their people and order the way up to the peñol prepared. I told them that in order for them to have time, God seeing fit, I would tell them tomorrow, Tuesday, when I would go up to their pueblo. So that it may be of record, and that the march was from 4 to 5 leagues, I signed it with the captain, the alferez of the presidio, and my secretary of government and war.

Don Diego de Vargas
Zapata Luján Ponce de León [rubrica]

Roque Madrid [rubrica]

Juan de Dios Lucero
de Godoy [rubrica]

Before me,

Alfonso Rael de Aguilar [rubrica]
Secretary of government and war

Word that last night, Monday, the Apaches fell upon the cattle and carried off 16 head

Today, Tuesday, 11 November, at the dawn watch, the alferez of the El Paso presidio, and, a little later, the captain of this company told me, the governor and captain general, that last night, with the unexpected bad weather and storm, the cunning enemy Apache had raided a group of cattle that must have wandered off from the rest. Neither the cavalry squad, which was coming the same way, nor those who were guarding the herd sensed the enemy. Thus, the Apache seized the opportunity and carried off a group of sixteen head. Because of the harshness of the weather, the great fatigue of the horses, and so as not to risk failure by going in pursuit of the enemy to punish their daring, I did not make the effort. For these reasons and with legitimate cause, I am leaving it, should God see fit for me to return here, to be carried out against the rancherias of those Apaches of the Faraón nation. So that it may be of record, I signed it with the captain, the alferez of the presidio, and my secretary of government and war.

Don Diego de Vargas Zapata
Luján Ponce de León [rubrica]

Roque Madrid [rubrica]

Juan de Dios Lucero
de Godoy [rubrica]

Before me,

Alfonso Rael de Aguilar [rubrica]
Secretary of government and war

Entrada to the pueblo of the Zuni nation, which is on the peñol

Today, Tuesday, 11 November, I, the governor and captain general, ordered the captains of the two companies to prepare five squads and their leaders and war officials with their weapons and horses to ascend the peñol and enter the pueblo that the Indians of the pueblos of the Zuni nation have on its mesa. Once prepared, I, the governor and captain general, mounted, as did my secretary of government and war. I ordered the cavalry lieutenant and leaders to march with the men in four files. In this order, I arrived at the peñol, at the edge of which the people of the pueblo were standing. Since the way up was so steep and long, and because of the danger of its rough stretches, it was necessary to go up on foot, which although very difficult, was accomplished.

Once I, the governor and captain general, and the men were on top, I saw the mesa was very spacious and about 2 leagues long. I remounted my horse to go enter the pueblo, where the Indians received me with all the people, whom I saw were numerous. Once I had dismounted, I greeted them all, saying the Praised be. All the people came up to embrace me and shake hands with me. I received them with complete love and spoke to them. I was in their plaza, which has at present three cuarteles, and first ordered a large cross set up there. Next, through an interpreter, who was the Indian I had brought, a native of that nation, I ordered the captains and elders to have all the people gather and bring their children and boys and girls for baptism. When they had gathered, I told them of my coming and the rest, which is of record, that I had sent the coyote Indian, Ventura, to tell them. The king, our lord, was lord of that peñol, their pueblo, and all this land and kingdom, and they and everyone else were his vassals. I reclaimed the possession in the manner referred to in the rest of the pueblos, proclaiming it on his majesty's behalf.

The baptized are 294 children, boys and girls, and women of all ages

Afterward, I asked the reverend father, fray Francisco Corvera, aided by the reverend father, fray Cristóbal Alonso Barroso, to grant them absolution, which they did. They received absolution and were baptized. I was compadre to a child of their captain and governor, whom they obey, and many others, as were the men-at-arms. The baptized were of all ages, male and female, and numbered 294.

Furnishings of divine worship from the holy church that are revealed

Then, my compadre the governor and the captains asked me to come up. In a room of the second floor and terrace, I entered and found an altar set with two large, lighted tallow candles. I removed some pieces of vestments with which they had covered the following ornaments of divine worship:[15]

First, two images of Christ Jesus[16] crucified of cast bronze, a little larger than a half-span, each one on a wooden cross

Another image of Christ Jesus crucified on a wooden cross, with a Capuchin St. Francis at his feet, also painted, the cross a little less than 2 spans

A painting in oil on canvas of St. John the Baptist, the size of 3 spans

A monstrance of gilded silver and the small case at the center of the monstrance with a crystal broken

Three chalices of wrought silver, two with patens, and the cups gilded on the inside

Another large chalice, completely gilded, with enamel on the cup and foot, with paten

A missal in very good condition, not one of the very modern ones

A bound book of Holy Week

Handing over of different books

A book entitled *Favores del Rey del Cielo hechos a su Esposa Santa Juana de la Cruz*[17]

Another book entitled *Segunda parte del itinerario historial*, in which the life of Christ is treated

Another book entitled *Los libros de la madre Santa Teresa de Jesús*

Another book entitled *Historia eclesiástica política natural y moral*

Another book entitled *Manual de administrar los sacramentos a los españoles y naturales de esta Nueva España*

Another book entitled *Instrucción espiritual para animar al que a la religión viene y profesa en ella*

Another without parchment binding and missing some pages entitled *Meditaciones del amor de Dios*

Another book, with the title on the first page because the rest are missing, *Primera parte de la venida de Cristo y de su vida y milagros*

Another book entitled *Manual de administrar los santos sacramentos a los naturales y españoles de esta Nueva España*

Another book entitled *Declaración copiosa de la doctrina cristiana compuesta por orden del beatísimo padre Clemente Octavo*

Another book entitled *Directorium curatorum instrucción de curas útil y provechoso para los que tienen cargo de ánimas*

Another book entitled *Confesionario en lengua mexicana y castellana*

Another book missing pages at the beginning and the end entitled *Declaración de la doctrina cristiana*

Another book entitled *Mementos de la misa*

Another book entitled *Obras de Quevedo*

Candlesticks and bells

Two brass candlesticks

Two bells without clappers

A tiny little bell

Another book[18] was found, for Sunday and Advent, without a cover.

These furnishings, as stated, and books, which the captains, Juan, Esteban, and Ventura handed over willingly, were found in the room. I embraced them closely, gave many thanks, and promised to favor and aid them with all my heart, so great was the tenderness aroused in me and those present in my company for having recovered the images of Christ Jesus and the sacred vessels, considering the risks and travails suffered on that journey worthwhile. So that the Indians might be satisfied that removing the furnishings and carrying them away with me was not because I mistrusted them, I told them I was taking them so that the father custos in El Paso might reconsecrate them. I was leaving the two large bells for them. When God saw fit,

I would return in the company of the priest indicated by his majesty, the king our lord, and I would return to them the furnishings for the church and convento I would order them to build for the father.

They were very pleased and content with these explanations. They asked me to come eat what they had prepared for me, which I did, in the company of the reverend missionary fathers. They were all astonished at the Indians' action, which was taken in no other pueblo of the kingdom or villa, where the Indians said that everything had been lost and destroyed and carried off by the Apaches. At sunset, I arrived from the peñol at the place designated the plaza de armas and camp for my men, having gone about 3 leagues round-trip. So that the entrada and what was referred to in it, and the Indians humbled and conquered for our holy faith and the royal crown, may be of record, I signed it with the military leaders and officials and my secretary of government and war.

Don Diego de Vargas Zapata
Luján Ponce de León [rubrica]

Roque Madrid [rubrica]

Martín de Alday [rubrica]

Juan de Dios Lucero de Godoy [rubrica]

Juan Páez Hurtado [rubrica]

Before me,

Alfonso Rael de Aguilar [rubrica]
Secretary of government and war

> The governor and captain general sends the Moqui Indian he brought with him from the pueblo of the Jemez and another Moqui Indian who had come to say that the Apaches have stirred up the people

Today, Wednesday, 12 November, as soon as I arrived at this campsite, I, the governor and captain general, was informed by the Moqui Indian that he had found someone from the province of Moqui. He had told him that, despite the arrival there of his companion, whom I, the governor and captain general, had sent from the pueblo of the Jemez and to whom I had given a rosary and holy cross to carry as a sign of peace to the Indians of his pueblo and the rest of the province of Moqui, the Navajo Apaches had warned them that they should not believe me. With the guarantee of peace I was going to kill them all and take away their women and children. They had believed that rabble-rouser to the extent that they had sent their livestock away to the mountains to protect them.

I thought it would be advantageous to persuade them the report was false, since only the devil could work in such a way as to convince them to disbelieve me, preventing them from benefiting from the pardon and absolution offered and freely granted to them and their children, whom they have had and raised since the uprising. In virtue of all this, I gave him a letter for those Indians and for an Indian, Miguel, from Awatovi Pueblo who knows how to read and write. In it I assured them, by virtue of the holy cross that was drawn on it, that they would be pardoned. They should not believe what was reported by that rabble-rouser, and my intention was only to assure them in every way. He should repeat this and many other explanations to the other Indians, since they had witnessed what I had done in the rest of the pueblos and, at present, in this pueblo of Zuni province. They should all be peaceful in their homes and pueblos. I gave each of them a rosary, mule, and supplies for the road, and they left, happy to comply with what they were ordered to do. So that it may be of record, I signed it with the captain, the alferez of the presidio, and my secretary of government and war.

Don Diego de Vargas
Zapata Luján Ponce de León [rubrica]

Roque Madrid [rubrica]
Juan de Dios Lucero de Godoy [rubrica]
Before me,

Alfonso Rael de Aguilar [rubrica]
Secretary of government and war

A captain from the Salinero Apache Indians arrives with some people from his rancheria

Today, Thursday, 13 November, while I, the governor and captain general, was walking in this outpost and plaza de armas, at about two o'clock in the afternoon, a captain of the Salinero Apaches arrived here with eight or ten Indians. Through an interpreter, they said they had come to see me and tell me they had always come in peace, and continued to come peacefully, into the Zuni territory and province. They were friends of the Zuni people and very happy for the Spaniards to be their friends. The captain came up to embrace me and shake my hand, and the others came to surrender their weapons. I told them I would be their friend if they were good. I also said that if they were good, as they say they are, they should go to kill the Faraón Apaches who had carried off some of my cattle. If they were caught, they would say that it was not they, but the Salinero Apaches, who had stolen them. I could never be certain whether they or the others had stolen them. I could only say what the people of this province had told me.

He replied differently, telling me that he had come to see me so that I might go safely to Moqui and that the Apaches, who were many, would not appear on the road and harm me. I replied to this that I was not afraid of them, and if they did come out, I had the soldiers he saw with me. I suggested various things to him so that he and his men would become Christians, since they were our friends, as they said, and friends of the Indians of Zuni province. He was confused by this and did not reply, except to say that because he was not afraid, he went everywhere. I took my leave of him, having seen that the time I spent was wasted. I treated him with kindness and ordered that he be given biscuit and a hand of tobacco. So that it may be of record, I noted it as a completed action, which I signed with the captain, the alferez of the presidio, and my secretary of government and war.

Don Diego de Vargas
Zapata Luján Ponce de León [rubrica]

Roque Madrid [rubrica]
Juan de Dios Lucero de Godoy [rubrica]
Before me,

Alfonso Rael de Aguilar [rubrica]
Secretary of government and war

> Order the governor and captain general gives to the captains of the two companies in which he indicates the men-at-arms from each company who must remain to guard the horses, mules, livestock, and provisions that are staying as support and reserves here in Halona Pueblo, Zuni province, for the reasons expressed in it

Today, Friday, 14 November, with regard to having to go humble, reduce, and conquer the provinces and pueblos of Moqui and obtain accurate information there about the almagre, the location of the cerro that contains the vein whose ore is thought to be mercury, and the distance to it, according to the information given in the court of Mexico to the most excellent lord viceroy, the Conde de Galve, I, the governor and captain general, must complete these actions by virtue of his greatness's letter sent last October 1691.

With the extended march, I, the governor and captain general, have made as of the date of this letter for the reduction and conquest of the entire kingdom of New Mexico, I have also humbled, conquered, and reduced to our holy faith and the royal crown the Keres nation, which is on the peñol of Acoma, and the Zuni nation, which is on the peñol of this province. The march for this conquest was very lengthy and continuous and it was necessary to do extensive scouting in this kingdom because the Keres and Jemez nations have abandoned their pueblos, moving them to different mesas and mountainous ranges, whose entradas and ascents are of record. There I, the governor and captain general, humbled, reduced, and conquered with great travail and continuous march. Only my fervent zeal in the service of both majesties could have taken from me consideration of the difficulties in such harsh weather, paying no attention to the risks, fears, and inconveniences. I had only eighty-nine soldiers in two companies, with their leaders and war officials, since the Indian allies have all deserted me and the few I ordered separated so that they would not be wounded have fled.

With respect to the fact that most of the horses and mules are unable to go on to Moqui province, and so as not to lose any and that some may arrive at El Paso, I thought and continue to think it was appropriate that each of the military leaders of the two companies should separate out the animals that the men-at-arms of their company think are unable to go on. I also order the capitán, cabo y caudillo of the presidial company of El Paso to set aside ten soldiers with the leader of their squad; and the capitán, cabo y caudillo of the company from the body of men-at-arms from New Biscay to likewise set aside whichever of the men's horses may be disabled with fifteen soldiers with the leader of their squad. These captains and leaders will deliver everything, as is stated. They are to be sent to the campaign captain, Rafael Téllez Girón,[19] so that the twenty-five men from the two war squads; their freight, horses, mules, and little other stock still alive; as well as the provisions, pack animals, and muleteers may be his responsibility. He will go to the abandoned old pueblo of Halona, since it has better pastures, and there the men-at-arms, supplied with ammunition and food, will remain during my absence in the province of Moqui. Its road has so few water holes, which are far apart, that it is impossible to take more than the most indispensable horses and mules. So that this report and order may be of record, I place it as a proceeding I provided, with the attendance of the captains who immediately carried out its contents and signed it with me, the governor and captain general, and my secretary of government and war.

Don Diego de Vargas
Zapata Luján Ponce de León [rubrica]

Juan Páez Hurtado [rubrica]

Juan de Dios Lucero
de Godoy [rubrica]

Roque Madrid [rubrica]
Before me,

Alfonso Rael de Aguilar [rubrica]
Secretary of government and war

Departure of the governor and captain general for the province of Moqui

Today, Saturday, 15 November, after the leaders of the companies had carried out the previous order and the campaign captain in the proceedings having delivered the horses, mules, other livestock, provisions, and ammunition and understood his duty to properly guard everything, I, the governor and captain general, ordered the leaders to ready the remaining men-at-arms of both companies with their officials.

The camp spends the night without water 6 leagues away

Once ready, I left with them, sixty-three in number, and arrived with the camp and the two reverend missionary fathers at a place in the middle of the woods 6 leagues away, where I stopped and spent the night without water, since the water hole was very far away. So that this march may be of record, I signed it with the war officials, the captain of the presidio, the alferez, and my secretary of government and war.

Don Diego de Vargas
Zapata Luján Ponce de León [rubrica]

Roque Madrid [rubrica]

Juan de Dios Lucero de Godoy [rubrica]

Before me,

Alfonso Rael de Aguilar [rubrica]
Secretary of government and war

Arrival at the water hole of El Entretenimiento

Today, Sunday, 16 November, I, the governor and captain general, arrived with the camp at the water hole of El Entretenimiento, having come about 6 leagues. So that it and the great difficulty in providing the horses and mules with the little available water, may be of record, I signed it with the captain, the alferez of the presidio, and my secretary of government and war.
Don Diego de Vargas
Zapata Luján Ponce de León [rubrica]

Roque Madrid [rubrica]

Juan de Dios Lucero
de Godoy [rubrica]

Before me,

Alfonso Rael de Aguilar [rubrica]
Secretary of government and war

Arrival at the water hole of Los Chupaderos

Today, Monday, 17 November, I, the governor and captain general, arrived with the present camp at the nearly dry water hole of Los Chupaderos. Its march was from 8 to 9 leagues. So that it may be of record, I signed it with the captain, the alferez of the presidio, and my secretary of government and war.
Don Diego de Vargas
Zapata Luján Ponce de León [rubrica]

Roque Madrid [rubrica]

Juan de Dios Lucero
de Godoy [rubrica]

Before me,

Alfonso Rael de Aguilar [rubrica]
Secretary of government and war

Arrival at the water hole of Magdalena

Today, Tuesday, 18 November, I, the governor and captain general, arrived with the camp at this water hole of Magdalena, which is so low that almost all the horses and mules went without water, since it is a very small spring among some rocks. Its march was about 9 leagues. So that it may be of record, I signed it with the captain, the alferez of the presidio, and my secretary of government and war.

Don Diego de Vargas
Zapata Luján Ponce de León [rubrica]

Roque Madrid [rubrica]

Juan de Dios Lucero
de Godoy [rubrica]

Before me,

Alfonso Rael de Aguilar [rubrica]
Secretary of government and war

Entrada into the first pueblo of Moqui province, which is called San Bernardo de Aguatuvi

Today, Wednesday, 19 November, I, the governor and captain general, left the campsite and water hole of Magdalena, where I had found two Indians from Awatovi Pueblo,[20] which is in Moqui province. One of them said his name was Salvador, and the other, a youth, said his was Sebastián and that he was the son of Miguel, to whom I had written. He said that his father had waited for me yesterday, Tuesday, at that campsite. Because his father saw that I was not coming and it was already late, after sunset, he went home. He had left them to wait for me and give me a message on his behalf. I ordered them also to advise him immediately about my arrival. The son was going to tell his father about this. Then, I treated him kindly and placed a rosary around his neck and Salvador's.

Today, Wednesday, between about one and two o'clock in the afternoon, I, the governor and captain general, arrived at this pueblo. Four Indians, with leather jackets and weapons and riding very good horses, came out about 2 leagues to receive me. They welcomed me and I treated them kindly. After traveling a little more than a league, they advanced and went to their pueblo. As a result, I, the governor and captain general, was going without the suspicion I might have had, were it not for the circumstances and the following causes of record in these proceedings. This was that when I made the entrada to the pueblo of the Keres nation of Zia, Santa Ana, and Santo Domingo (which I located, humbled, reduced, and conquered on the mesas of the Cerro Colorado and whose captain is Antonio Malacate) and the entrada to and ascent of the mesa, three Indians advanced and came out to receive me. Two were from Moqui province. The elder was named Pedro; the second, Sebastián; and the third was a coyote named Ventura, a Spanish-speaking Indian and native of Zuni province and Halona Pueblo. These Indians were very happy and content to have found me. I also was very pleased that they could go and be eyewitnesses to the manner in which I behaved toward the Indians, inhabitants of the pueblos I entered. They saw my entrada to the Keres nation, and, on the following day, the entrada I made to the mesas of the Cerro de la Cañada of the Jemez nation.

On that afternoon, all three Indians came with me, the governor and captain general, to where I had established my camp. The coyote Indian Ventura said that one of the two Moqui Indians who accompanied him was offering and wanted to go advise his pueblo and Zuni province and that he would go there from Moqui province. He would give them word about everything I had done in the two entradas to those nations and that they could be assured and receive me without fear in their pueblos and provinces. I told him that seemed very good to me and they should return to see me in the morning. I would outfit them and tell them the message to give to the people in those provinces.

With this, on the following day, Sunday, they came to the camp very early, and I told them the message. I gave Pedro a rosary and cross and outfitted him with supplies and an elk hide that he asked me for to cover himself. He left very content, saying that in five days he would be in his land. The other Indian, Sebastián, remained with the coyote Indian, Ventura, and accompanied me to Zuni Pueblo. Ventura recognized his sister among the three captives who had fled from the Apaches and been found in the road by soldiers from my camp. The Apaches had captured her from their pueblo when she was very young. I brought her, and she came very contentedly, to this pueblo of Awatovi.

On the entrada I made to Zuni Pueblo, I also found two more Indians, natives of Moqui Pueblo, who readily talked to me. They had also been witnesses to the entrada and the warmth and the kindness with which I had treated the Indians. In the afternoon, they came to see me at the camp. They told me that the Faraón Apaches had told them that I entered the pueblos of New Mexico under the guise of peace and then killed everyone and they should not believe me, because I bore them ill will. For that reason, the Indians of Moqui province had fled to the mountains, taking their livestock and horses. They had come to see what I was doing. After seeing, they wanted to leave immediately, so they could go down to their pueblos. The Indian Sebastián asked me to outfit him with a mule and supplies, and I gave them to him. To his friend, one of the two Indians, he said he should bring his sister to me. He came with the other, and I gave both of them mules and supplies. I put rosaries around their necks and gave them the letter for the Indians of this entire province and for Miguel, head and leader of the people of this pueblo of Awatovi.

For these reasons, and because of having found those Indians at the campsite of Magdalena and the report they gave me, I, the governor and captain general, left for this campsite, so lacking in misgivings that, although the horses were very fatigued and had had very little to drink since they left Zuni Pueblo, there was reason enough to bring scarcely thirty soldiers with my secretary of government and war, the military leaders, and many of the men-at-arms on mules. We had scarcely noticed the pueblo they call San Bernardo de Aguatuvi when, before arriving at it, on the slope of a mesa a little less than a league from it, a large and very numerous squad of Indians on foot and horseback came out from it, with a loud cry, to receive me. They were all well prepared, with all their weapons; they even had harquebuses and a horse pistol.[21] In a short time, their numbers increased, so that their men on foot and horseback came to seven or eight hundred Indians. They all gave signs of wanting to make war, provoking us with their gestures for that purpose. I tolerated this so that I might, with persuasive arguments aided by divine assistance, turn their diabolical questions against them, which I tried three times from that distance.

All these people were talking and told the Indian Miguel, the Spanish-speaking head of this pueblo, and another Indian named Pancho, who had been raised by Father Espeleta, to ask me whether the Spaniards were going to harm them when they came and offer various other explanations of their uprising. I replied that they should calm themselves and be assured that the king our lord, had sent me from afar just to pardon them, since they were going to become Christians once again, and for that reason I had brought the priests with me. I also repeated to them that I had brought the image of the holy Virgin on the royal standard. Thus, in order to be able to receive her in their pueblo, everyone should lay down his weapons and dismount.

Although it is true that, rebellious and stubborn, they discussed it among themselves for more than an hour, at last I told the Indian Miguel, seeing that he had respect and goodwill for the Spaniards, "Dismount and lay down your weapons, and with that those children will do the same." He did so and talked to them and told them what I ordered him. Finally, I told him that he should make them be quiet. Did they not remember from when they were Christians that, in order to receive a saint and the Virgin, they should all be very reverent, silent, and on their knees, and that they should therefore kneel? By means of divine will, I was able to get them to do so.

Seeing that a man on foot could scarcely enter the door to the plaza of their walled pueblo, I was forced to dismount. I also ordered the alferez with the royal standard, the military leaders, and my secretary of government and war to do so. I reclaimed possession for his majesty, that mob of people present already reduced and humbled. I did the same in the plaza of the pueblo, where I ordered them to kneel again and receive the holy Virgin, and revalidated and proclaimed royal possession on his majesty's behalf of this land, kingdom, pueblo, and its Indians. Then I repeated to them through the interpreters, the Indians Miguel and Francisco, that the fathers were tired and that tomorrow morning they would grant them absolution and baptize the children. The men and their captains who were here at this junta from other pueblos should go to them and tell their inhabitants that I, along with the fathers, would go see them. They should not fear that I would harm them.

Wanting me to come, Miguel asked me to go up to his house to eat. I told him to bring the food out, because I could not leave my men alone. He did so, bringing food out for me, the fathers, and the men. I told him I was going to sleep at the water hole. Although he insisted I remain at his pueblo, I repeated to him that I could not leave my men alone, inasmuch as they had advised me at Zuni that the Salinero Apaches would come, and I should be careful. With this, he told me that he would show me a good place near the water hole. He mounted his horse and came to show me, about an eighth of a league from the pueblo, where he told me I could stay because there was no better place, since it was very uncomfortable on account of the heaviness of the frost, and there was no firewood for heat. So that what is referred to may be of record, I signed it with the captain, the alferez of the presidio, and my secretary of government and war.

Don Diego de Vargas
Zapata Luján Ponce de León [rubrica]

                              Martín de Alday [rubrica]

Juan de Dios Lucero
de Godoy [rubrica]

                              Juan Páez Hurtado [rubrica]
                              Roque Madrid [rubrica]
                              Before me,

Alfonso Rael de Aguilar [rubrica]
Secretary of government and war

Second entrada into the pueblo of Awatovi, on the following day

Today, Wednesday, twentieth of the present month,[22] I, the governor and captain general, ordered the military leaders and war officials of both companies to prepare fifty men with their weapons and horses to go up and enter the pueblo of Awatovi. The rest of the men are to remain guarding the horses pastured around the camp that I have indicated as my plaza de armas. Once the men had mounted up, I did so as well and ordered both companies to form four files and be alert in the plaza of the pueblo during the time the reverend missionary fathers spent there, dismounted, granting absolution to the Indians and baptizing the children and people who were unbaptized.

Having given that order, I entered the plaza with the men-at-arms following me. The cuartel of that plaza is divided so that one can enter through it. Once inside, the reverend fathers and I dismounted. I ordered my alferez to do so as well and told the Indians about my coming, ordering them to set up a cross in the plaza, which they did immediately. In front of it, I asked the reverend father, fray Francisco Corvera, to absolve them, which he did, assisted by the other father, fray Cristóbal Alonso Barroso. Then, the reverend fathers baptized the children and other unbaptized people.

122 people of all ages and both sexes are baptized

I, the governor and captain general, was godfather to a son and daughter of the leader and captain, Miguel. Calculating their number, it was seen there were 122 baptized. Afterward, I appointed Miguel as their governor in their presence, telling them to obey him in every way. I had him swear the oath to properly exercise his office, which he did and I received, before God Our Lord, and the sign of the cross. Then, he asked me to go up to his house and eat, which I did to please him and the Indians and so that they might not think I was afraid of them. So that it may be of record, I signed it with the captain, the alferez of the presidio, and my secretary of government and war.

Don Diego de Vargas
Zapata Luján Ponce de León [rubrica]

Martín de Alday [rubrica]

Juan de Dios Lucero
de Godoy [rubrica]

Juan Páez Hurtado [rubrica]
Roque Madrid [rubrica]
Before me,

Alfonso Rael de Aguilar [rubrica]
Secretary of government and war

> Word the Indian Miguel gives that the Indians of all the pueblos are armed and prepared to kill me and the men-at-arms and only waiting for me to go to their pueblos so they may carry it out

Today, Thursday, 21 November, the Indian Miguel, my compadre, came to my tent. Accompanied there by the reverend father, fray Francisco Corvera, he said that he had to speak to me alone, but was afraid to because there were many Indians in the camp and they should not see him. I replied to this that he should return in the afternoon, when, with no one around, he could tell me what he had to say. He knelt at the father's feet and, lowering his head, kissed the father's hands. Holding them tightly and crying a river of tears, he told him it was a miracle they had allowed him to live. He was well aware they would kill him after I left with the men-at-arms. I consoled and encouraged him and told him to return in the afternoon.

He was in my tent a little after four, and I had Sgto. mayor Antonio Jorge, the captain of the presidio of El Paso, and my secretary of government and war come. The reverend father, fray Francisco Corvera, was also present. I told him he could tell me what he said he had to that morning, because the entrance of the tent was closed and I had ordered the soldiers of my guard to remove anyone around it. With the assurance that no one had seen him enter, he began the following explanation.

Part of the statement of Miguel regarding the Hopi pueblos, 21 November
1692, Vargas Journal (SANM II:53)
   State Records Center and Archives, Santa Fe

He said that, although he did not know how to speak as well as he should to give me a report about what had happened since he received the letter I had sent him and all the Indians of Moqui province, he would give me a report and explain it as well as he could. He said he immediately gave the word in the letter to the Indians in Awatovi Pueblo, who obey him, and also notified the people in the other pueblos, four in number, which are named Walpi, Shongopavi, Mishongnovi, and Oraibi. They all came on Sunday and had a large junta: the captain, head of Walpi Pueblo, whose name is Antonio; those from Oraibi; and Pedro, Antonio's son, who is captain of the pueblo of Shongopavi and the one they obey. Antonio persuaded them, after he had come from the pueblo of the Jemez, that the men from all the pueblos could surely kill all the Spaniards. This was reinforced by the true account from his brother Sebastián who brought his sister back, accompanying me as far as Zuni, whence he advanced. He said we were few in number, because I had left some of the men I had with me in the province of Zuni and sent most to El Paso, also taking the tired horses.

Regarding all that has been referred to about that information and that Antonio and his two sons were the cause of the uprising in that province, with little resistance to the obstacles suggested, all the Indians accepted Antonio's and his two sons' proposal. When they received us, they should all be prepared and make war on us, so that, when we defended ourselves, they would kill us all. Miguel, the witness, gave his opinion about this, saying they should see it was not right, because they had come from so far away, so that they might become Christians. For that reason, the blessed fathers were coming to baptize their unbaptized children and absolve them from their great sin because of the evil they did during the uprising. Neither he nor those of his pueblo had to do such a thing. If they did not wish to obey him, he would join the Spaniards. He knew they were going kill him, but might do with him whatever they wanted.

This was how the junta was held. Many people came on the following day, such that twice as many people as they had seen had gone away because the pueblo could not feed them. On the following day, Monday, he came to the water hole of Magdalena with his son, Sebastián, to receive me and give me this report so that, based on it, I might decide about the entrada. Missing him, they had found out he had come to see me. All the people of the pueblos had become angry with him. The people from his pueblo sent the Indian Salvador to see him. He had left the message for me with him. He gave it to me and an order to his son to advise me as soon as he arrived at the water hole. As soon as he returned to the pueblo, many of the people from the other pueblos quarreled with him, threatening him that the Spaniards would leave and letting him know they would kill him because he had been so pleased about their coming. So that this information and that I assured him I would take him and his children with me may be of record, I signed it with the witnesses and my secretary of government and war.

Don Diego de Vargas
Zapata Luján Ponce de León [rubrica]

Roque Madrid [rubrica]
Before me,

Alfonso Rael de Aguilar [rubrica]
Secretary of government and war

Entrada into Walpi Pueblo, called San Bernardino

Today, Thursday, 22 November, during the entire entrada I made here to the pueblo of Awatovi in Moqui province I experienced the following: great clamor and crowds of Indians, war preparations they had made with all their weapons, gestures with which they tried to provoke us to make war on them, and demonstrations of their perverse intention, which they were unable to hide. On the entrada, I had recourse to wisdom and the persuasive arguments with which I tried to convince them about my coming and my goodwill, which was not treacherous like theirs. Because of their great crime, they deserved the corresponding punishment. Having seen how few men-at-arms we were, they thought the occasion opportune to repeat their crime. So that they might fully understand that I neither feared them nor failed to tell them the truth about the reason for my coming, I, the governor and captain general, finally decided to go on and make the entrada to the rest of the pueblos, notwithstanding the above information.

According to the reports from their Indians and the people from the camp who came and went here, however, there is no water hole in the pueblos where the horses can drink, because the only water the Indians have to supply themselves with is in pools that are so shallow there is scarcely enough for them. In accord with what has been referred to, I ordered the military leaders of both companies to have fifteen soldiers with their leader guard the horses at this camp-site and water hole of Awatovi. They should remain with the horses around the camp and supplies I was leaving with the muleteers. The forty-five remaining soldiers and military leaders should be ready with their weapons and mounted on their best horses, with the warning that they will have to ride them today from 12 to 13 leagues without water to drink, until they return to this water hole tonight, should God see fit, since I had to make the entradas to the three pueblos of Walpi, Mishongnovi, and Shongopavi.

As soon as the men had mounted and were ready in that fashion, as well as the military leaders and my secretary of government and war, I, the governor and captain general, mounted, as did the rever-end missionary fathers, for this entrada. Then, I ordered the leaders to take the companies arranged in four files. The soldiers and their leaders, alert to any evil intention of the Indians, should have their weapons ready. No one should either act rashly or begin the fight without my order.

In this manner and order, I marched about 3 leagues until we arrived at a very high mesa where the first pueblo is, which they call Walpi. As soon as its Indians descried me, they came down, accom-panied by many others from the other pueblos, on foot and horse-back, with all kinds of weapons, to the middle of the cuesta and ascent, which is long and very rough. I went to all of them, saying they should go back up and leave their weapons, if I had not already ordered them to leave them in the previous pueblo, Awatovi.

Having gone up on top to Antonio, their captain and leader whom they obey, I ordered him to tell and order all his Indians to enter the pueblo, leaving their weapons in their houses, and come out with-out them to receive me, because otherwise I could go no further. I repeated this to him and so ordered. He did so, although he looked somewhat ill at ease. In spite of the fact that some of his people in the crowd had laid down their weapons, since most of them still had them, I repeated my request, asking Antonio why some of them had not laid down their weapons. He replied to this that the people from his pueblo were the ones who had laid down their weapons, and that I could see they did not have them. The rest who had them were from all the other pueblos.

I pretended not to notice and ordered half the men to enter the plaza with me and the fathers. The lieutenant general of the cavalry remained outside with the other half. Having entered the plaza of the pueblo, as stated, I dismounted, as did the reverend fathers. I ordered the alferez and my secretary of government and war to do so. Through the Indian Miguel, my compadre, who served as interpreter, I told them about my coming and proclaimed possession on his majesty's behalf, both of the pueblo and them, his vassals. I ordered a cross set up in the plaza and that everyone was to wear crosses around their necks. They should pray the four prayers in the morning and afternoon. If anyone had any furnishings from the church, they should hand them over to the captain so that he could give them to me. I would not become angry; rather I would greatly appreciate it. I was ordering them to build their church gradually and a convento for the father. I neither wanted nor was I ordering them to build me a house, because, as they had seen, I slept out with my men.

81 baptized of all ages and both sexes

Having told them everything referred to, I told and asked the reverend father, fray Francisco Corvera, to absolve them, which he did immediately, assisted by the reverend father, fray Cristóbal Alonso Barroso. Then, they went on to baptize the children who had been born and raised since their uprising. They numbered eighty-one of all ages, male and female.

I also asked who the pueblo's saint was, and they said his name was San Bernardino. I repeated to them with all my love that they should pray, be Christians, and build their church, telling them to stay with God. I was leaving, content for having seen them. With this, the Indian Antonio asked me to go up to his house and eat. Although there were many Indians from outside with their weapons on the terraces of the houses of the pueblo, so that it might seem to him that I was neither afraid of them nor suspicious of their ill will, I went up, and they fed me.

After taking my leave of them, having repeated everything to them and charged them to be Christians, I said goodbye. Mounting my horse, I gave the order to the military leaders for the men-at-arms to leave, descending the cuesta to go to the pueblo of Mishongnovi, 3 leagues away. So that what is referred to, and of having left the pueblo of Walpi humbled, reduced, and conquered in the manner referred to for our holy faith and the royal crown, may be of record, I signed with the leaders, the alferez of the presidio, and my secretary of government and war.

Don Diego de Vargas
Zapata Luján Ponce de León [rubrica]

                                    Martín de Alday [rubrica]

Juan de Dios Lucero
de Godoy [rubrica]

                                    Juan Páez Hurtado [rubrica]
                                    Roque Madrid [rubrica]
                                    Before me,

Alfonso Rael de Aguilar [rubrica]
Secretary of government and war

Entrada to the pueblo of Mishongnovi, called San Buenaventura

Immediately after on the same day, Thursday, 22 November, having gone down the cuesta of the pueblo of Walpi, I went with the camp, the reverend missionary fathers, and my secretary of government and war to the pueblo of San Buenaventura de Mishongnovi. Having traveled somewhat more than 3 leagues, once dismounted I saw it was also on a mesa, whose ascent and entrance were even worse than the previous one. Similarly, there was a crowd of Indians who had gone on in advance to this pueblo.

I entered the plaza and found Pedro in the middle of it, and in his hand he had the cross I had given him as a sign of peace to come from Jemez Pueblo. Through my compadre, Miguel, who served as interpreter, I ordered him to speak to their two captains and heads whom they obey in that pueblo. The two other captains, one named José and the other Sebastián, were beside him. I had made the Indians surrender their weapons and stand without them next to their wives and children in the plaza. I had them come down from their houses where they were all on their terraces and roofs and set up a cross in the plaza. I ordered the same thing I had said and repeated to the Indians of the previous pueblos of Awatovi and Mishongnovi[23] and, in that form, repeated and proclaimed royal possession on his majesty's behalf.

37 are baptized, of all ages and both sexes

The reverend fathers absolved and baptized the children and other unbaptized people. I was godfather, as I had been in the other pueblos, to the children the Indians brought me, as were the men-at-arms. I repeated, ordered, and charged them with everything referred to and took leave of them, after having calculated that the number baptized, of all ages, male and female, was thirty-seven.

So that the entrada, reduction, and conquest may be of record, I signed it with the captain, the alferez of the presidio, and my secretary of government and war.

Don Diego de Vargas
Zapata Luján Ponce de León [rubrica]

Martín de Alday [rubrica]

Juan de Dios Lucero
de Godoy [rubrica]

Juan Páez Hurtado [rubrica]
Roque Madrid [rubrica]
Before me,

Alfonso Rael de Aguilar [rubrica]
Secretary of government and war

Entrada to the pueblo of San Bernabé de Jongopavi

Immediately after, I, the governor and captain general, went on with the camp, the reverend missionary fathers, and my secretary of government and war to this pueblo, whose Indians said it was called San Bernabé de Jongopavi. I saw it immediately, after having traveled about a league. It is on a mesa steeper and higher than those where the previous pueblos are. A crowd of Indians had preceded us to its ascent, although those of this pueblo were all together, without weapons, with many women and children.

Having entered their plaza, I, the governor and captain general, first ordered them to set up a cross there. After the reverend missionary fathers and I had dismounted, I ordered my secretary of government and war to do so with the alferez. Through the Indian Miguel, my compadre, appointed as my trusted interpreter, I told them about my coming and all the circumstances and the wish of his majesty the king, our lord (may God keep him), on whose behalf and in whose royal name I reclaimed and proclaimed the new possession referred to, as in the previous pueblos, ordering them everything of record I had told and ordered their Indians.

The baptized number 33, male and female of all ages

At my request, the reverend fathers absolved them and baptized the children and other unbaptized people. Having completed this, the number of those baptized was seen to be thirty-three males and females of all ages.

I took leave of them with all my love since it was already vespers, returning to the campsite and plaza de armas I had indicated at the water hole of Awatovi. The entrada to the three pueblos was a round trip of 13 to 14 leagues. On their return, many of the horses had become very tired, since they had not had any water, were already quite fatigued, and because of the harshness of the season and frosts. So that having humbled, reduced, and conquered that pueblo for our holy faith and the royal crown may be of record, I signed it with the captain, the alferez of the presidio, my secretary of government and war, and the other military leaders.

Don Diego de Vargas
Zapata Luján Ponce de León [rubrica]

Martín de Alday [rubrica]

Juan de Dios Lucero
de Godoy [rubrica]

Juan Páez Hurtado [rubrica]
Roque Madrid [rubrica]
Before me,

Alfonso Rael de Aguilar [rubrica]
Secretary of government and war

Actions taken regarding the route of the journey toward Cerro Colorado, where there is almagre, or cinnabar

On 23 November 1692, I, the governor and captain general, don Diego de Vargas Zapata Luján Ponce de León, wishing in every way the greatest service for his majesty the king, our lord (may God keep him), don Carlos II, king of all the Spains, of this New World and land, the provinces of Moqui, and kingdom of New Mexico, made an entrada to them and their pueblos on the date of this letter, as is of record in the military proceedings. I achieved their reduction and conquest for the holy faith and royal crown. In his nobility, the most excellent lord viceroy of this kingdom and all New Spain, the Conde de Galve, ordered and advised me to inquire, verify, and seek out in detail and with precision where the Cerro Colorado is. This is where the Indians of this province take the ore they call almagre or cinnabar, with which they paint themselves. It leaves a purplish, greasy luster when rubbed in the palm of the hand and is good for the eyes when it is cold, or to preserve a good complexion and hide smallpox scars. I have bartered for the little ore the Indians have brought me in order to send it to him. To begin the trip and examine and investigate with certainty, I am at present prevented by the difficulty of the water holes, the time it would take to go to the cerro, and the uncertainty of places that might have water. In the presence of the witnesses who signed, the captain, the alferez of the presidio of El Paso, and Sgto. mayor Antonio Jorge, I made the following investigation and verification, inquiring and seeking extrajudicially to obtain information from various Indians, in order to see from their accounts whether it is all the same.

Declaration of Francisco, a Spanish-speaking Indian from the pueblo of Oraibi, raised by Father fray José de Espeleta

There appeared in my presence, of the witnesses below, and of my secretary of government and war an Indian who understands and speaks Castilian. He was raised by the reverend father, fray José de Espeleta, whom he served until he died here. The Indian said his name was Francisco and he has been as far as the salinas, which can be reached on foot in fourteen days when the days are long, that is to say, in the late summer months.[24] In front of the salt bed is the cañada and then the river. The river can be forded, but it runs high when the snows in the mountains melt and in the rainy season, when the water comes down from the Sierra Prieta there. When the high water subsides, the river can be forded.

The cerro that has almagre is on the other side and can be seen from there. He has not gone up it and knows the way as far as the river. Through Francisco, I also asked an Indian from the Zuni nation who was present whether he had been there. He said he had been there twice. I asked him what his name was, and he said Pedro. Since the sargento mayor understands the Zuni language, I had him accompany me as interpreter with Francisco and asked the Indian the following questions.

Declaration from the Zuni named Pedro

I asked him how many days it takes to get to the mine and how many water holes there will be in those ten days. He stated the first water hole is about 10 leagues away, where Father fray José de Espeleta had his conversion. Wheat was also sown there. Nearby, before it, was the water hole where the many Coninas live.[25] Before that one, is another small pool that has water when it rains. From this little pool, it will take a day to get to the bajada, which has water. It is so deep, however, that it is boxed in to the extent that horses cannot drink there. It is very deep, but one can cross it on foot and leave the animals on this side.

The cerro is very high and steep. It takes longer than from morning to afternoon to get there. They extract the ore, which is about an estado[26] down, and sleep on the cerro, which has no water. The following day, they take a long time in coming down. Asked for information about the vein, he declared, "It is this wide," taking a melon for comparison. "The good part of it is the mature part." Similarly, "It is this wide," he stated, making a circle with his thumbs and forefingers, meaning it is round like an eye. Sometimes, it loses or changes color, and he showed me the dust he had on his boot.

This information was the declaration he made through the interpreters, who had ably made him understand the questions, to which he answered what is of record for them. So that the actions taken may be of record for his excellency, the most excellent lord viceroy (may God keep him), I am sending this with the letter of transmittal enclosed with it. So that it may be of record, I signed it with the captain, the alferez of the presidio, the sargento mayor, and my secretary of government and war.

Don Diego de Vargas
Zapata Luján Ponce de León [rubrica]

                                    Antonio Jorge [rubrica]

Juan de Dios Lucero
de Godoy [rubrica]

                                    Roque Madrid [rubrica]
                                    Before me,

Alfonso Rael de Aguilar [rubrica]
Secretary of government and war

When I, the governor and captain general, was about to leave with the camp for the pueblo of Oraibi, the only one that remains, the military leaders came to speak to me about the total exhaustion of the horses and what is of record, and for this reason, I ordered them all to leave for the province of Zuni

Today, Sunday, 24 November, I, the governor and captain general, gave the order to the military leaders to prepare all the men-at-arms, horses, and pack animals carrying the provisions to leave and go on to the last pueblo of Moqui province, called Oraibi, which still has not surrendered. It is 8 or 9 leagues from Awatovi Pueblo. The military leaders of both companies came to me to indicate it was impossible to go on because of the condition of the horses and mules. Just from yesterday's march, Thursday, returning at night from having humbled and conquered the pueblo of San Bernabé de Jongopavi, which, as is of record, was done that day, most of the horses were tired, and some of the soldiers had to return on the haunches of their comrades' horses.

I had also reconnoitered and seen that along the entire patrol of the three pueblos I had humbled and conquered on that day, a round trip of 13 to 14 leagues, no water hole had been found for the horses because there was none, and the land was very dry. Similarly, there was no water in the pueblo of Oraibi, because its Indians supplied themselves from a pool scarcely sufficient for their needs.

The leaders were making these proposals and explanations because it would be risky since, in fact, all the horses and mules could be lost. They explained and said that so I might be aware of the risk.

The governor and captain general decides, as a result of their explanation, to return and withdraw, having obtained information and a sample from the cerro of the almagre and its ore or metal to send to his excellency with the proceedings

In this regard, my compadre, Miguel, told me the same thing. I had, by the grace of God, achieved the reduction and conquest and delivered the four pueblos of this province of Moqui to his majesty's vassalage. I had, at great risk and expense, entered them and persisted at the pueblo of Awatovi, establishing the camp at its water hole. I had inquired and sought information about the cerro where there is almagre or cinnabar, as well as having bartered for the ore. This was so that the most excellent lord viceroy, the Conde de Galve, may order an assay of the sample, which he so greatly wishes for, to see whether it has the quality thought to be mercury. So as not to risk losing the horses and mules and being left on foot without mounts, in a land with so many enemies, and lacking only the pueblo of Oraibi in this province of Moqui, I, the governor and captain general, postponed the entrada for now, since the weather and the current condition of all the horses and mules have made it impossible.

I shall make the entrada whenever the time his excellency, the most excellent lord viceroy, or his majesty (may God keep him) orders me to go on and reconnoiter the cerro. In this regard, I ordered the military leaders to leave when they and the camp were mounted with the provisions and everything prepared for the march, taking the route and march to the first water hole, which is on the road to the province of Zuni. I was returning there to join the camp and men-at-arms I had left with the campaign captain in charge. I, the governor and captain general, with the alferez, some soldiers and leaders, and my secretary of government and war, went on to the pueblo of Awatovi with my secretary of government and war. I called my compadre, Miguel, its governor, and the Indians and told them the reason, referred to above, for my return, departure, and inability to go on to the pueblo of Oraibi and they should tell its Indians so. I took leave of them, and the women and children came out to say goodbye to me and all the men with much emotion. So that the departure and the reason, referred to above, may be of record, the military leaders, the captains, the alferez of the presidio of El Paso, and my secretary of government and war signed with me.

Don Diego de Vargas
Zapata Luján Ponce de León [rubrica]

Martín de Alday [rubrica]
Juan Páez Hurtado [rubrica]

Juan de Dios Lucero
de Godoy [rubrica]

Roque Madrid [rubrica]
Before me,

Alfonso Rael de Aguilar [rubrica]
Secretary of government and war

Arrival within sight of the water hole of Magdalena where the governor and captain general spends the night with the camp

Today, Sunday, 24 November, at about ten o'clock at night, I, the governor and captain general, arrived with the camp at the foot of the mesa and mountain where the water hole of Magdalena is. As it is a campsite with firewood and pasture, I spent the night there with the camp. So that it may be of record, I signed it with the captain, the alferez of the presidio, and my secretary of government and war.
Don Diego de Vargas
Zapata Luján Ponce de León [rubrica]

                                            Roque Madrid [rubrica]

Juan de Dios Lucero de Godoy [rubrica]

                                                    Before me,

Alfonso Rael de Aguilar [rubrica]
Secretary of government and war

Arrival at the water hole of Los Chupaderos

Today, Monday, 25 November, I, the governor and captain general, arrived with the camp at the water hole of Los Chupaderos, which is shallow. Many of the horses were tired, because most of them did not drink at the previous water hole, and the heavy frost has exhausted them. So that it may be of record, I signed it with the captain, the alferez of the presidio, and my secretary of government and war.
Don Diego de Vargas
Zapata Luján Ponce de León [rubrica]

                                            Roque Madrid [rubrica]

Juan de Dios Lucero de Godoy [rubrica]

                                                    Before me,

Alfonso Rael de Aguilar [rubrica]
Secretary of government and war

At the water hole of Los Chupaderos on that day, 25 November, at about vespers, two Indians from Zuni arrived with this letter from the campaign captain I had left in the pueblo of Halona in that province. Having read it, I replied to him that, God willing, I was going to aid him on Wednesday, because it was impossible to leave at present, since the horses were exhausted and had had almost nothing to

drink for two days. So that it may be of record, I signed it with my secretary of government and war.
Don Diego de Vargas
Zapata Luján Ponce de León [rubrica]
Before me,
Alfonso Rael de Aguilar [rubrica]
Secretary of government and war

Sir,

That your lordship's health is very good will please me greatly. Mine is good, thank God, for whatever your lordship may wish to order me in whatever may please you. Sir, I advise your lordship that El Bermejo gave me information about a junta that had been formed to attack us. El Bermejo himself had a report from the Apaches about how there was an argument by which they say the junta was undone. Seven of El Bermejo's animals were carried off. Four were returned, and I sent the Salinero captain's son and his brother to go for the three that were carried off. I told them that the peace was feigned, and they went and brought them.

They say they caught up with them one day beyond the salinas. They also say that they argued with them and told them the Spaniards and their Indians were already going. If they did not want to lose their children, women, and fine captives for three animals, they should hand them over since the captain was going to kill those who stole the animals.

El Bermejo, Ventura, and the governor, your compadre, will be pleased if you enjoy good health. The governor and El Bermejo have come more than three times to insist that we come to the foot of the peñol to help if an ambush is launched. Because the pastures are far away, I have not moved there, since it will appear as weakness. Nothing more, but may God keep your lordship the many years I wish. 22 November 1692.

Your most affectionate servant kisses your hand,

Rafael Téllez Girón [rubrica]

Lord governor and captain general, don Diego de Vargas

Arrival at the water hole of El Entretenimiento and departure from it
by the governor and captain general with thirty soldiers and their military leaders to aid the campaign captain, Rafael Téllez Girón

Today, Tuesday, 26 November, I, the governor and captain general, arrived with the camp at this water hole they call El Entretenimiento. It is only a deep hole about 3 varas wide, and much time is
needed to water the horses. Scarcely four can drink at one time, and
their owners must carefully lead them by their halters. With this
delay, it must have been about vespers when I, the governor and
captain general, became concerned because of the information I
received in the letter from Capt. Rafael Téllez Girón. I left him, as
is of record in these proceedings, in Halona Pueblo, Zuni province,
with men-at-arms to guard the tired horses and mules, the pack animals, provisions, and other army stores, to swiftly make the entrada,
reduction, and conquest of the province of Moqui I accomplished
through divine favor. I thank God Our Lord for having moved me
to leave there in time, because only two days later, while traveling,
the information I refer to in that letter about the plans of the enemy
Apache reached me.

Order that the governor and captain general leaves for the captain of
the El Paso presidio

Should the enemy unite their forces in order to attack, our force
would not be adequate to resist their fierceness, and we would run
the risk of losing the men and horses. In attention to this and so as
not to waste time, I, the governor and captain general, ordered the
captain of the El Paso presidio, Roque Madrid, to give me thirteen
soldiers with their leader from the squads of men-at-arms in his charge.
They should be the best equipped and bring along two saddle horses,
so that, with the one they were riding, they would bring three. I also
ordered Capt. Juan Páez Hurtado to separate in the same way another
thirteen soldiers with their leader from the men of New Biscay. Sgto.
mayor Antonio Jorge; the lieutenant general of the cavalry, Martín
de Alday; the general adjutant, Francisco de Anaya Almazán; and
Sgto. Juan Ruiz de Cáceres from the El Paso company should all
prepare themselves in this way with their weapons and horses. I ordered
Capt. Roque Madrid to stay with the rest of the men-at-arms, horses,
mules, pack animals, and provisions to bring them in his charge to

Halona Pueblo, Zuni province, in two days, as is required and necessary.

I, the governor and captain general, advised him of the new state of things he might find there, and the captain will do so as well in order to decide what is advantageous for the royal service. With the men-at-arms mentioned, the military leaders, and their war officials present, it must have been about nine o'clock at night when I, the governor and captain general, mounted my horse and marched with the men the greater part of the night as far as the monte, 5 leagues before arriving at Zuni province. It was necessary to stop, having marched 8 or 9 leagues. So as not to risk the horses with the extended march from the water hole of Los Chupaderos, which they left without having been watered, I stopped until dawn today, Wednesday, 26 November. With the camp, I remounted my horse and arrived at about nine o'clock in the morning at Halona Pueblo, Zuni province, where the campaign captain came out to receive me. He repeated to me his concern as a result of the certain word of the junta the Apache nation was trying to form. So that the reinforcements and I having joined the others may be of record, I signed it with the military leaders, the alferez of the presidio of El Paso, and my secretary of government and war.

Don Diego de Vargas
Zapata Luján Ponce de León [rubrica]

Roque Madrid [rubrica]

Juan de Dios Lucero de Godoy [rubrica]

Before me,

Alfonso Rael de Aguilar [rubrica]
Secretary of government and war

Arrival of the captain of the presidio of El Paso with the rest of the men-at-arms

Today, Thursday, 27 November, the capitán, cabo y caudillo of the presidio of El Paso, Roque Madrid, arrived with the rest of the men-at-arms. I left him, the horses, mules, pack animals, and provisions on the Tuesday night I left from the water hole of El Entretenimiento, which is of record in these proceedings. Many of the camp's animals and the men-at-arms had become tired from the lack of water and harshness of the heavy frost. The distance was about 13 leagues. So that the arrival and the camp's already being together

and united may be of record, I signed it with the captain, the alferez of the presidio, and my secretary of government and war.
Don Diego de Vargas
Zapata Luján Ponce de León [rubrica]

Roque Madrid [rubrica]

Juan de Dios Lucero de Godoy [rubrica]

Before me,

Alfonso Rael de Aguilar [rubrica]
Secretary of government and war

Departure from this abandoned pueblo of Halona

Today, Saturday, 29 November, having given the horses a rest yesterday and the stormy weather of these days having made me stay in this campsite, I, the governor and captain general, decided to leave with the camp to find a better place next to the peñol to spend the night. I shall leave this province of Zuni at once, tomorrow, Sunday, by the grace of God, withdrawing to the presidio of El Paso because of the great harshness of the weather. I leave finished, through divine favor, the entrada, reduction, and conquest of all the kingdom of New Mexico and its provinces of Zuni and Moqui, of record in these proceedings.

So that the camp may know of this departure and withdrawal, I order the military leaders thus to communicate it, immediately making the men-at-arms ready with their weapons, horses, pack animals, provisions, ammunition, and livestock. This is so that they may move everything today and depart from this pueblo to the other bank of the arroyo next to the peñol I am indicating as the plaza de armas from which to make the march and withdrawal, as stated, tomorrow, Sunday, God seeing fit. My secretary of government and war will make this order known, reading it to the leaders and war officials of this camp. So that it may be of record, I signed it with the captain, the alferez, and my secretary of government and war.
Don Diego de Vargas
Zapata Luján Ponce de León [rubrica]

Roque Madrid [rubrica]

Juan de Dios Lucero de Godoy [rubrica]

Before me,

Alfonso Rael de Aguilar [rubrica]
Secretary of government and war

The governor and captain general's arrival within sight of the peñol of Zuni in fulfillment of the preceding order

Today, Saturday, 29 November, in fulfillment of the preceding order, the military leaders readied the men-at-arms of their companies, the pack animals, provisions, livestock, horses, mules, and other army supplies. I, the governor and captain general, left, marching to the place mentioned in the order. I quartered the camp for the night within sight of the peñol. So that it may be of record, I signed it with the captain, the alferez of the presidio, and my secretary of government and war.

Don Diego de Vargas
Zapata Luján Ponce de León [rubrica]

Roque Madrid [rubrica]

Juan de Dios Lucero
de Godoy [rubrica]

Before me,

Alfonso Rael de Aguilar [rubrica]
Secretary of government and war

Word the sargento mayor gives to the governor and captain general of having heard from a Zuni Indian about the route he knows to get to the pueblo of Senecú in a week

Today, Saturday, 29 November, Sgto. mayor Antonio Jorge presented himself before me, the governor and captain general, in this place I have indicated as the plaza de armas. He said to me that an Indian from Halona Pueblo on the peñol had experience in having traveled the direct route and road from the water hole of El Morro, two days' journey from this place. Paying him well, he will point out the way to go and take me and the camp to the pueblo of Senecú. I, the governor and captain general, saw of what great profit it would be to all this kingdom, as well as his majesty (may God keep him), if, through God's will, almagre or cinnabar containing enough high quality mercury to pay for itself is found. This road would be of great advantage for its transport, if it is, as the Indian told the sargento mayor, so level that wagons can travel on it. There are enough water holes that from El Morro, only a day and a night would be spent without water. There is water for the men, although not for the horses, but by noon the following day, one reaches an arroyo that crosses the road and has plenty of water. From there, for the following four days' journey, there is water at the stopping places. On the last day, one reaches the pueblo of Senecú.

With word of this and the great saving of more than 50 to 60 leagues, with some stretches of very rough road, and of poor, widely spaced, shallow water holes, some with the risk of having no water (since they only have it if there have been many and repeated rains in that season of the year), I acted according to what has been referred to and ordered the sargento mayor to bring me the Indian. I wanted to question and examine him about the route. A short time later, he brought him. In the presence of my secretary of government and war, the governor, two Spanish-speaking Indians, and captains from the pueblo, I had him tell me what is of record he told the sargento mayor regarding his knowledge of the road referred to from the water hole of El Morro two days' journey from this place and Zuni province. He spoke in accord with what is of record about this information. He only added that because during this season the days were short, one could travel but a short distance. He said and repeated that a week was needed to arrive at the pueblo of Senecú. I asked him what he wanted to be given, and he replied that because it is a land at such risk from the Apaches, he asked that two Indians from the pueblo accompany him on the return to his pueblo from the pueblo of Senecú. He must be given a horse and another for each Indian and a buffalo hide and they must be given supplies for the round trip.

I said to him, good, that I did not object. He should come tomorrow with those two Indians, should God see fit, and I would order him given three of my own horses and the hides when he arrived at the pueblo, and the agreement was made. He said his name was Agustín, El Cabezón. The two captains, Agustín, El Bermejo, and Alonso agreed to accompany him. Since they were Spanish-speakers and honorable Indians, I immediately treated them kindly and encouraged them to come. They offered to go in my company with Agustín, El Cabezón. So that what has been referred to may be of record, I noted it as a completed action, which I signed with the sargento mayor and my secretary of government and war.

Don Diego de Vargas
Zapata Luján Ponce de León [rubrica]

Roque Madrid [rubrica]
Juan de Dios Lucero de Godoy [rubrica]

Before me,

Alfonso Rael de Aguilar [rubrica]
Secretary of government and war

> Immediate departure from this province of Zuni and withdrawal to
> the pueblo of El Paso

Today, Sunday, 30 November, by my order the three horses charged
to my account were given to the Indians mentioned in the completed action on the reverse for them to go by way of the shortcut I,
the governor and captain general, intend to leave newly discovered
for the greater aid of this kingdom and service of his majesty, the
king, our lord (may God keep him). The camp was fully prepared
and ready to march. I, the governor and captain general, immediately left this place and Zuni province, taking my leave of its Indians
who, with great love, shook my hand and embraced me.

> The governor and captain general stops with the camp to spend the
> night in this place at the water hole Ojito de Zuni

Having arrived at their water hole of Ojito de Zuni, 5 leagues away,
I stopped with the camp to spend the night there. So that it may
thus be of record, I signed it with the captain, the alferez of the pre-
sidio, and my secretary of government and war.
Don Diego de Vargas
Zapata Luján Ponce de León [rubrica]

Roque Madrid [rubrica]

Juan de Dios Lucero de Godoy [rubrica]

Before me,

Alfonso Rael de Aguilar [rubrica]
Secretary of government and war

> An Indian sent by the governor of Halona Pueblo on the peñol in
> Zuni province arrives who says that we should be careful that night,
> because they have seen the tracks of the Apaches who are coming to
> attack us

Today, Sunday, 30 November, a swift runner arrived after vespers at Ojito de Zuni water hole. He said through the Spanish-speaking
Indian Alonso, who is from Zuni province and Halona Pueblo on

its peñol, that his governor sent him to tell me and all the men of this camp to be careful that night. The people who left to reconnoiter his pueblo's land saw and discovered the tracks of the Apache enemy who at night surrounded my camp. They have also seen the tracks of the enemy coming, following our camp.

Order the governor and captain general gives to the military leaders

With this information, I, the governor and captain general, immediately made this known to the military leaders and war officials of this camp, summoning them to my presence and telling them to order everyone to be careful and prepared with their weapons and a saddled horse, and that they should be, too. In the same way, I would be prepared. The camp should be gathered together, and the night watch should be rotated and repeat their watches in order to be aware of the enemy and resist them in such a way that they do not triumph through the carelessness of our being unprepared. In attention to this, everyone went to carry out the order. So that it may be of record, I signed it with the leaders, the alferez of the presidio, and my secretary of government and war.

Don Diego de Vargas
Zapata Luján Ponce de León [rubrica]

Roque Madrid [rubrica]

Juan de Dios Lucero
de Godoy [rubrica]

Before me,

Alfonso Rael de Aguilar [rubrica]
Secretary of government and war

Explanation of the two captives who arrived with their brothers and children at this water hole, so that it may be of record for all time they are accompanying them to El Paso

At this water hole on the said day, month, year, and at that hour, the two soldiers who had remained in Halona Pueblo on the peñol in Zuni province arrived. With permission from me, the governor and captain general, they had gone there, because they said they had found their sisters living in that pueblo. Since the uprising of the kingdom of New Mexico, their bad fortune brought them wandering to it. Their brothers had the good fortune of finding them alive, and the sisters asked them to get them out of there and take them along. So that it may be of record in these military proceedings, I made a list for the muster they passed with the help of my secretary of government and war and the witnesses below, carrying this out in this way.

The reserve adjutant, José Madrid, presented his sister, who said she is unmarried and her name is Lucía, with two sons, one about twelve years old and the second, six (3)

Martín Hurtado,[27] presidial soldier of the company from El Paso, brings his sister, who says she is a widow and her name is Juana Hurtado, with two daughters and a son, the oldest named María Naranjo, about fourteen; the second, eight or nine years old; and the little boy must be three years old (4)

The two soldiers bring the seven (7) male and female captives referred to on this list and muster. So that it may be of record, I noted it as a completed action, which I signed with the captain, the alferez of the presidio, and my secretary of government and war.

Don Diego de Vargas
Zapata Luján Ponce de León [rubrica]

Roque Madrid [rubrica]

Juan de Dios Lucero de Godoy [rubrica]

Before me,

Alfonso Rael de Aguilar [rubrica]
Secretary of government and war

Arrival at the water hole of El Morro

Today, Monday, 1 December 1692, I, the governor and captain general, arrived with the camp at the water hole of El Morro, although the day has been very stormy. Its march has been about 6 leagues. So that it may be of record, I signed it with the captain, the alferez of the presidio, and my secretary of government and war.

Don Diego de Vargas
Zapata Luján Ponce de León [rubrica]

Roque Madrid [rubrica]

Juan de Dios Lucero de Godoy [rubrica]

Before me,

Alfonso Rael de Aguilar [rubrica]
Secretary of government and war

Departure from the above place to take the shortcut with the aid of the Zuni Indian who accompanies me, the governor and captain general

Today, Tuesday, 2 December, I, the governor and captain general, spent last night with the camp with great care, because of the previous information about the enemy Apache and the harshness of the weather, the rain- and snowstorm that has been with us from last night until eight o'clock this morning. Since I saw it was already clearing up, I ordered the camp to get ready to continue the march. Once they and the Indian, Agustín, El Cabezón, were prepared, I mounted my horse, and the camp and I followed him. I noticed that he took the road to the south, and after a league, we descried various mountain ranges from a loma. He said one was called the Sierra Prieta, and another, branching off from it, the Peña Larga. He said the rancheria of the Colorado Apaches[28] was located in this one and that they planted maize. A river or arroyo went by its slope.

Taking the southeast route from the low part of this loma, going up and down several lomas of malpais, having gone about 4 leagues, I entered by a mountain between some hills. Having gone from it and down several lomas, because it was already late and a snowstorm threatened, I had to stop on the mountain close to the hills. I spent the night without water, although what snow there was helped both the camp and the horses some. The march was about 6 leagues. So that it may be of record, I signed it with the captain, the alferez of the presidio, and my secretary of government and war.

Don Diego de Vargas
Zapata Luján Ponce de León [rubrica]

Roque Madrid [rubrica]

Juan de Dios Lucero
de Godoy [rubrica]

Before me,

Alfonso Rael de Aguilar [rubrica]
Secretary of government and war

The new route and second day's journey continue

Today, Wednesday, 3 December, I, the governor and captain general, with the camp in the campsite above, went on, despite the harshness of the weather. The wind- and snowstorm was extreme. All night long on this mountain the storm beat at us and punished the men-at-arms of the horse guard and night patrol. Despite the care their leaders took, they could not fail to suffer the misfortune that the enemy might endure such a severe storm, enjoying the good luck they had because of the mountain and the mountain ranges.

The enemy Apache stole fourteen horses and left one wounded

Surrounding us, they successfully separated a small group of horses in the midst of some woods. With the darkness of the night, the horses were carried off. Had they not been detected, the theft would have been even greater. They took fourteen horses and left one wounded with a sword such that it died in the morning.

From the tracks seen by the leaders, officials, and war leaders, we could tell that they had surrounded us. Having seen the heavy guard and sentries of the men-at-arms, they had not dared attack the camp. I ordered it to be readied and leave at nine in the morning. When we had gone about 2 leagues, the Indian always following the south-east road and route, the mountain came to an end. Crossing a llano, going down various lomas of malpais on it that were very long (they must have been 4 leagues long without counting the 2 of the moun-tain), the route curved toward the left at the place where the malpais erupts in the form of a mountain range. Having gone about 1 league, we ascended a high loma to where there is a large cañada filled with royal pine.[29]

After having gone through it for more than a league, we came down from the mountain to a very large cañada. Because Agustín said the water hole was 3 leagues away and it was already late, I stopped at this campsite. The march was from 8 to 9 leagues. So that it may be of record, and that the camp went without water, I signed it with the captain, the alferez, and my secretary of government and war.
Don Diego de Vargas
Zapata Luján Ponce de León [rubrica]

Roque Madrid [rubrica]

Juan de Dios Lucero de Godoy [rubrica]

Before me,

Alfonso Rael de Aguilar [rubrica]
Secretary of government and war

Arrival at the ciénaga of La Cebolleta cañada

Today, Thursday, 4 December, by virtue of the Indian taking the southeast route in the same cañada, and having gone 3 leagues through it, I, the governor and captain general, found a ciénaga in the cañada they call La Cebolleta. Since the storm was violent with snow and wind, the horses had gone three days without water because of the harshness of the storm, and there having been no water hole in the two previous days' journey, I had to stop. So that it may be of record, I signed it with the captain, the alferez of the presidio, and my secretary of government and war.

Don Diego de Vargas
Zapata Luján Ponce de León [rubrica]

Roque Madrid [rubrica]

Juan de Dios Lucero de Godoy [rubrica]

Before me,

Alfonso Rael de Aguilar [rubrica]
Secretary of government and war

Fourth day's journey, the camp, horses, and mules spending the night without water

Today, Friday, 5 December, the night, which was the same as the previous day with a snowstorm and very strong, freezing winds, was spent with great discomfort. The snow alone having stopped and the storm with its harsh wind continuing, nevertheless I, the governor and captain general, ordered the camp to prepare itself to continue the march.

When it was ready, I, the governor and captain general, left with the Indian, following the cañada, which is very spacious, hilly, and with fine pastures and many royal pines and savins. Following the same route toward the right and the southeast, although not so far within, having come down various mesas and gone through the cañada for 2 or 3 leagues, the Indian came out to a hilly llano that seemed more than 3 leagues wide. Coming down some mesas and lomas and having reached a mesa, we descried the Sandia and Salinas mountains.[30] This way down is very steep and deep, with many sharp, rugged rocks.

From this way down, a llano following the woods is entered. Having gone on about 2 leagues, since it was already late and the water hole far away and uncertain, I stopped on the mountain with the camp. The men-at-arms and I had to remain without water. Because the Indian guide had also assured us there was enough in the water holes for both, no water was brought along. So that the fourth day's journey, which was 7 or 8 leagues, may be of record, I signed it with the captain, the alferez of the presidio, and my secretary of government and war.

Don Diego de Vargas
Zapata Luján Ponce de León [rubrica]

Roque Madrid [rubrica]

Juan de Dios Lucero
de Godoy [rubrica]

Before me,

Alfonso Rael de Aguilar [rubrica]
Secretary of government and war

The fifth day's journey of this shortcut

Today, Saturday, 6 December, having spent the night with the camp without water, at dawn I, the governor and captain general, ordered it to prepare to leave in search of a water hole. The Indian guide went on ahead to reconnoiter the route. Shortly after dawn, I left this place with the camp, following the same southeastern direction. The road was the same, with hilly plains and mesas, always going down. After having gone about 3 leagues, a very well traveled path was found, which was the one the Indian said yesterday had to be on the way to the water hole. In attention to this, following the path, I went down a large barranca with very rocky terrain, and, dropping down to a llano, having gone about 4 leagues, a very small freshwater spring was found from which the people of the camp could quench their thirst, the horses and mules going on without drinking. From this mesa, the Ladron and Magdalena mountains[31] could be seen. Having reached an arroyo with many alamos, it was found to be dry. Because it was already late, and the camp had gone 9 to 10 leagues, I stopped. So that it may be of record, I signed it with the captain, the alferez of the presidio, and my secretary of government and war.

Don Diego de Vargas
Zapata Luján Ponce de León [rubrica]

Roque Madrid [rubrica]

Juan de Dios Lucero
de Godoy [rubrica]

Before me,

Alfonso Rael de Aguilar [rubrica]
Secretary of government and war

The sixth day's journey of this shortcut continues

Today, Sunday, 7 December, I, the governor and captain general, had stayed awake all night because the horses and mules had had no water in two days and because of the harshness of the storm, with its intense cold and strong winds. Capt. Roque Madrid told me that a Piro Indian from among those of the camp had told him that, going in the direction of El Alamillo for more than 20 leagues along the river, in addition to the 5 from this dry arroyo, a water hole would be found. Although the water was very salty, the horses could satisfy their thirst. The proposed end of following the current shortcut had not been achieved, because the horses were becoming very tired, although I had intended to secure their relief by having them walk as little as possible. Having attended mass at about five o'clock in the morning, I, the governor and captain general, called the military leaders to the entrance to my tent. With the attendance of my secretary of government and war, I informed them of the information and the inconvenience mentioned of ordering the march to go in that direction in search of the water hole. Given that the Magdalena Mountains had come into view, the march should be made where the Indian guide said to reconnoiter the location of the route and a fixed place where it begins. He was of the opinion that it should be followed, since he could not be so unlucky that, out of a 12-league distance they might march, a water hole would not be found. Should it be shallow, we would stop there for the camp to spend the night, sending the horses and mules to the river, even if they had to travel all night. I gave this order, since they, with the Indian, had promised me to follow the shortcut.

At dawn, the camp prepared itself and was already on the march when the sun was rising. At a distance of about a league, a small spring was found, which had a curbstone like that of a well. The Indian guide pointed it out and went on ahead, following that path and direction. At the small spring, some of the saddle horses were watered. The camp went on following the Indian along a large mountain surrounded by lomas. Having gone up and down lomas for a distance of about 5 leagues, another small spring was found on the road and path. Some saddle horses were also watered, and the herd of horses had the good luck to find snow in those lomas and shady places in parts of the mountain. Though hardened by the frosts, it was about to melt. They immediately broke some off to eat as best they could, and it served to keep them from weakening altogether.

Following the march and direction, the camp came out on to a llano with fewer mountains. The Gila and Magdalena mountains came into view. The Indian guide followed the path. Having gone about 5 leagues on the route and way out, following the direction of the crest of the sierra, which seemed to go out to the Río del Norte, it was seen to be correct. On the rise in front of the sierra, I found a very old pueblo. The faces of some walls and parts of two kivas made of stone placed by hand were standing. This pueblo was large. Looking to the right toward the Gila Mountains, about an eighth of a league away, the water hole from which the people of the pueblo supplied themselves was seen next to some tall reeds. This was seen to be so, when I, the governor and captain general, went with the men-at-arms and found and saw it was a spring. Half the camp could spend that night and water some animals. In effect, almost all the saddle horses drank.

I pressed the Indian to find out where the large water hole was. He said and indicated from the road that it was in the ravine of those sierras. He said that it must be 2 leagues away and he was tired from having gone so far that day. At that, I became angry with him, ordering the leaders and war officials to go and take him, whether he wanted to go or not. They were not to come back until he had shown them the water hole. Since it was already about four o'clock in the afternoon, they went to carry this out.

A short time later, the camp arrived with its two herds of horses. So as not to waste time, I ordered four squads from the two companies to prepare themselves. I ordered the adjutant to go and take the horses, ordering each of the rest of the men to set aside his favorite horse, as well as the mules from the pack trains. All the rest should go with the other horses. After ordering the men to provision themselves, the adjutant left with the four squads of eleven men each. He took a Piro Indian from the camp so that he could show him the path that night, and he could be at the Río del Norte on the following day, should no water hole with enough water be found. If he found one, he should stop there, since the next day, through the grace of God, I would leave with the rest of the camp along the same trail.

After I gave him this order, he left immediately. The military leaders went to the sierra with the Indian to reconnoiter the water hole. They arrived with the sargento, explaining that the water hole the Indian spoke of was about 2 leagues away and the horses and mules that remained could drink there. I immediately ordered the sargento to go with a squad from the two companies to the water hole, taking the horses and mules I had ordered set aside for the men-at-arms of the camp. I ordered him to return from the water hole at midnight, since we would be without horses in this dangerous land. He carried it out in that way. So that what has been referred to concerning to-day, Sunday, the sixth day's march, may be of record, I signed it with the military leaders, the alferez of the presidio, and my secretary of government and war. The march was about 12 leagues.

Don Diego de Vargas
Zapata Luján Ponce de León [rubrica]

Roque Madrid [rubrica]

Juan de Dios Lucero
de Godoy [rubrica]

Before me,

Alfonso Rael de Aguilar [rubrica]
Secretary of government and war

The governor and captain general takes his leave of the Indian and continues his march, following the adjutant's trail

Today, Monday, 8 December, I, the governor and captain general, after having attended mass with the camp, called the Indian guide and the three Zuni Indians who had come in his company. I treated them kindly, giving them their buffalo hides, and ordered them provisioned for their return. They said to me that, because they were afraid of the Apaches, they wanted to return by way of the peñol of Acoma. I should give them a letter so that the Keres of that peñol might give them safe passage. I did so, writing to my compadre Mateo and telling him the reason for not having returned, charging him to make his people pray and make everyone wear crosses. They were very satisfied with this letter I gave them.

I left this campsite and water hole, which I called La Purísima

Concepción[32] for having discovered it on the eve of this most holy day. Having left within sight of the Magdalena Mountains, we came out after a little less than half a league. The crest was on the right, and it dropped to a llano that seemed more than 12 leagues wide. We discovered what they call the Sierra del Socorro. Following the trails of the horses and mules that had gone the previous night with the adjutant, and having gone 5 or 6 leagues, I went up the sierra, passing its mesas, lomas, and way down, crossing it along the trails. At a distance of 2 or 3 leagues, I found the adjutant in the ravine at the foot of the sierra with the men-at-arms, horses, and mules, because they had found a very wide arroyo where he had halted so that I, the governor and captain general, might decide what I saw fit.

Because it was late, the camp had come a long way, and the horses and mules were very tired from the repeated, extended marches, I stopped at that pass, having joined up with all the camp, which arrived safely, though with the loss of some horses and mules. So that this march, which must have been 8 or 9 leagues, and what is referred to about this day may be of record, I signed it with the captain, the alferez of the presidio, and my secretary of government and war.

Don Diego de Vargas
Zapata Luján Ponce de León [rubrica]

Roque Madrid [rubrica]

Juan de Dios Lucero
de Godoy [rubrica]

Before me,

Alfonso Rael de Aguilar [rubrica]
Secretary of government and war

Arrival at the pueblo of Socorro

Today, Tuesday, 9 December, notwithstanding the appearance of the great windstorm and snows, the day being overcast everywhere; because this campsite is unprotected; the lomas have no pasturage for the horses; and there is no firewood with which the wretched men-at-arms might protect themselves against the harshness of the weather, as it was snowing, I left this campsite to look for the pueblo of Socorro, which is the closest one. After a distance of about 2 leagues' march, I entered it. The church's walls, which are still standing, are very strong, more than two varas and a span wide. I spent the night in a cell of its convento. Its door and a piece of the upper front wall were fallen down. So that it may be of record, I signed it with the captain, the alferez of the presidio, and my secretary of government and war.

Don Diego de Vargas
Zapata Luján Ponce de León [rubrica]

Roque Madrid [rubrica]

Juan de Dios Lucero
de Godoy [rubrica]

Before me,

Alfonso Rael de Aguilar [rubrica]
Secretary of government and war

Arrival within view of the pueblo of Senecú

Today, Wednesday, 10 December, I, the governor and captain general, arrived on this side of the Río del Norte. In addition to the heavy frosts, today at dawn it was snowing. Within view of and a distance away from the pueblo of Senecú, I stopped, having marched 9 to 10 leagues. So that it may be of record, I signed it with the captain, the alferez of the presidio, and my secretary of government and war.

Don Diego de Vargas
Zapata Luján Ponce de León [rubrica]

Roque Madrid [rubrica]

Juan de Dios Lucero
de Godoy [rubrica]

Before me,

Alfonso Rael de Aguilar [rubrica]
Secretary of government and war

The governor and captain general sends the campaign captain with two soldiers to the pueblo of El Paso with word of his arrival nearby

Today, Thursday, 11 December, so that the citizens of El Paso might be consoled at having the weapons of their presidio nearby for their defense, I, the governor and captain general, thought it appropriate to send the campaign captain, Rafael Téllez Girón, with two soldiers so that they might be at that outpost quickly, within three days. Once they were ready with their weapons and leaders, I ordered them supplied. I gave letters to the leader for the illustrious cabildo of that republic; the very reverend prelate, vice-custos of that holy custody; and my lieutenant governor and captain general. I gave them the word of my success and that I would be ready for the defense of that district with the weapons of its presidio within nine days, God Our Lord seeing fit. I ordered them to advise me of the state that country was in. So that this dispatch may be of record, I noted it as a completed action, which I signed with the captain, the alferez of the presidio, and my secretary of government and war.

Don Diego de Vargas
Zapata Luján Ponce de León [rubrica]

Roque Madrid [rubrica]

Juan de Dios Lucero
de Godoy [rubrica]

Before me,

Alfonso Rael de Aguilar [rubrica]
Secretary of government and war

> Arrival before Fray Cristóbal, coming by this side of the river from Socorro and Senecú so as not to risk that there might not be water in the 30-league distance to San Diego

Today, Thursday, 11 December, having issued today's dispatch, which is of record, I, the governor and captain general, and the camp departed along this side of the river from the pueblos of Socorro and Senecú, so as not to risk the lack of water, going by the road from Fray Cristóbal to San Diego. There is no certain water hole, but the chance of its having rained might make one in the low-lying ground and ciénaga, where it collects, even if it were insufficient to supply a camp such as this one. Following this route for this reason and having gone about 7 leagues, I stopped on the lowlands on this side of the river, within view of a hill that is before Fray Cristóbal. So that this march may be of record, I signed it with the captain, the alferez, and my secretary of government and war.

Don Diego de Vargas
Zapata Luján Ponce de León [rubrica]

Roque Madrid [rubrica]

Juan de Dios Lucero de Godoy [rubrica]

Before me,

Alfonso Rael de Aguilar [rubrica]
Secretary of government and war

Arrival on this bank of the river within view of the hills of El Muerto and Las Peñuelas

Today, Friday, 12 December, having gone with the camp along this bank of the Río del Norte 6 to 7 leagues, along a very rough road with mesas, lomas, and sandbanks, I, the governor and captain general, stopped at the riverbank. From this campsite, one can see the sierras of El Muerto and Las Peñuelas and the camino real for wagons that is on the other bank. So that this march may be of record, I signed it with the captain, the alferez of the presidio, and my secretary of government and war.
Don Diego de Vargas
Zapata Luján Ponce de León [rubrica]

Roque Madrid [rubrica]

Juan de Dios Lucero
de Godoy [rubrica]

Before me,

Alfonso Rael de Aguilar [rubrica]
Secretary of government and war

The governor and captain general leaves quickly with twenty soldiers and military leaders, leaving Capt. Roque Madrid to come with the rest of the camp and the tired horses that are coming

Today, Saturday, 13 December, since the horses and mules are tired from the extended and continuous march, as well as from the harshness of the stormy weather, and having lost some on this campaign, to ensure that most do not run the risk of being lost, I, the governor and captain general, ordered the two captains of the two companies to select from each one of the companies ten soldiers from among the best equipped, so that they, with the military leaders, the adjutant, and the sargento of the El Paso company, together with my secretary of government and war, may accompany me.

Order he leaves for Capt. Roque Madrid so that, within a period of ten days, he may go to El Paso with the rest of the camp

I order Capt. Roque Madrid to come with the rest of the camp, horses, mules, and pack animals. I leave him supplies for the men-at-arms and order him, within a period of ten days, since it is 50 leagues from this place to El Paso, to arrange their march within

that time. So that it may be of record, I sign it with the captain, the alferez of the presidio, and my secretary of government and war.
Don Diego de Vargas
Zapata Luján Ponce de León [rubrica]

Roque Madrid [rubrica]

Juan de Dios Lucero de Godoy [rubrica]

Before me,

Alfonso Rael de Aguilar [rubrica]
Secretary of government and war

> The governor and captain general crosses the river with the men-at-arms for the outpost they call San Diego; after 2 leagues, he encounters the enemy Apache, and the captain of the reinforcements is wounded; and what is referred to

Today, 16 December, I, the governor and captain general, with the men-at-arms who come in my company, quickly crossed the Río del Norte for the outpost they call San Diego. I had advanced with eight of the men, among them my secretary of government and war; the lieutenant general of the cavalry; the sargento mayor; and the reserve alferez and newly appointed campaign captain, Juan Lucero de Godoy. Having gone somewhat more than 2 leagues, we saw some people, the first. They were headed for the place of San Diego, in the same direction as our march. We understood them to be the men from El Paso, who, when they had word I was near, would come to receive me with the fresh supplies I had ordered sent from my house.

Continuing on our march, a short time later, we saw, quickening our pace, that those we had seen were turning their horses around. At that, everyone urged on their horses, and the swiftest, who overtook them, were Capt. Juan Páez Hurtado of the men-at-arms of the reinforcements from Parral; the lieutenant general of the cavalry, Martín de Alday; and the campaign captain, Juan Lucero de Godoy. The men from El Paso, having fled from the mounted Apaches, saw that my men and I were approaching. The three leaders overtook and were able to prevent two Apaches on foot from fleeing by surrounding them. The Apaches began immediately to shoot their arrows so violently that by the time I, the governor and captain general, arrived with the rest, the aforementioned captain had already been shot through the left leg with an arrow. Both Apaches attacked the lieutenant's horse, which was shot with four arrows and died that night. They shot another arrow through the neck of the horse belonging to the campaign captain.

The governor and captain general gives an order to the cavalry lieutenant for four soldiers to shoot the Indian, the captured enemy Apache

One of the Indians died, and I did not allow them to finish killing the other until his statement had been received. He gave it after he arrived with the wounded captain. Because he had lost so much blood, I had to stop 2 leagues away in the place they call Robledo. There, asked whether he knew the Apaches had come into the pueblo of El Paso to steal and do damage, the Apache Indian said that this month, he and a companion had entered and stolen two horses, and he knew nothing else. I said to the reverend father president, fray Francisco Corvera, that he should urge the Indian on, if he wanted to become a Christian. I then had to order him shot. The reverend father baptized him and gave him the name Agustín. Once this was over, I gave an order to the cavalry lieutenant for four soldiers to go and take the Indian to one side at the outpost and for them to shoot him immediately, giving him a clean death.

So that the event referred to may be of record, I signed it with the cavalry lieutenant and the campaign captain, with the attendance of my secretary of government and war.

Don Diego de Vargas
Zapata Luján Ponce de León [rubrica]

Martín de Alday [rubrica]
Before me,

Alfonso Rael de Aguilar [rubrica]
Secretary of government and war

Arrival of the governor and captain general at the pueblo of El Paso

Today, Saturday, 20 December 1692, I, the governor and captain general, entered this pueblo of El Paso with the men-at-arms at about eleven o'clock in the morning. The illustrious cabildo, justicia and regimiento of this kingdom; most of the citizens who live here; the reverend father vice-custos, fray Joaquín de Hinojosa; the father guardian of this pueblo; and my lieutenant governor came out to receive me. Accompanied by them, I entered this holy temple, the church of Our Lady of Guadalupe, to give proper thanks to His Divine Majesty for my successful arrival, a victory achieved through our Lady's most holy intercession.

I dismounted in this plaza de armas, and when my lieutenant general arrived, I asked him whether the enemy Apache had raided and entered many times. He said to me that in the two times they had entered, they had carried off twenty horses and head of cattle. Nothing else had happened, and even with that loss, he had been fortunate during my four months' absence on campaign. So that it may be of record, the military leaders, the lieutenant general of the cavalry, the sargento mayor, the campaign captain, the alferez of the presidio, and my secretary of government and war signed it with me.
Don Diego de Vargas
Zapata Luján Ponce de León [rubrica]

                              Juan Páez Hurtado [rubrica]

Arrival of Capt. Roque Madrid with the rest of the camp

Today, Monday, 22 December, at about noon, Capt. Roque Madrid, whom I left with the rest of the camp on the thirteenth in the place of record in these proceedings (as is the order to him), arrived at the plaza de armas of this pueblo of El Paso. Although he fulfilled and carried out the contents of the order despite the fatigue of the horses, he could not help but lose some. So that it may be of record, I signed it with the captain of the presidio, the campaign captain, and my secretary of government and war.
Don Diego de Vargas
Zapata Luján Ponce de León [rubrica]

Representation of the reverend father president, asking that he be given the sacred vessels and books the Indians of Zuni handed over, as is of record

In the pueblo of El Paso of New Mexico on 27 December 1692, the reverend father, fray Francisco Corvera,[33] missionary and apostolic minister of this holy custody of our father St. Francis of this kingdom, of the chaplains of the army who went on the conquest that I, don Diego de Vargas Zapata Luján Ponce de León, governor and captain general of this kingdom of New Mexico, castellan of its fortress and presidio for his majesty, through the grace of God, have just accomplished and from which I have just returned: The reverend father president appeared before me, the governor and captain general, asking me to give him the images of Christ Jesus, the sacred vessels, the books, and everything else of record they gave me on 11 November in the entrada I made to the peñol, to whose extensive mesa the Indians of the province of Zuni had withdrawn and upon which they had built their pueblo.

Proceedings

I, the governor and captain general, have seen his request, and it is justified. It is being put into effect in the presence of the witnesses who sign and in the presence of my secretary of government and war. The very reverend father minister, fray Salvador de San Antonio, custos of this holy custody, was also present, and I delivered to him what the Indians gave me, the governor and captain general, the day of the entrada, as is of record. My secretary of government and war referred to it and read it entry by entry at my order.

Delivery and receipt by the reverend father president

The reverend father president accepted the sacred vessels, images of Christ Jesus, and books as delivered, his will satisfied. I, the governor and captain general, asked him to tell the very reverend father president minister custos how I promised those Indians (as is of record when they were handed over) they would return the sacred vessels to their pueblo for divine worship in the holy church that would be built in it. So that what is referred to and the receipt contained herein may be of record, I, the governor and captain general, signed it with the witnesses of the entrada and of the handing over, with my secretary of government and war.
Don Diego de Vargas
Zapata Luján Ponce de León [rubrica]

Fray Francisco Corvera [rubrica]

Martín de Alday [rubrica]

Roque Madrid [rubrica]

Juan García de Noriega [rubrica]
Antonio Lucero de Godoy [rubrica]

Lázaro de Mizquía [rubrica]
Before me,

Alfonso Rael de Aguilar [rubrica]
Secretary of government and war

*Diego de Vargas to the Conde de Galve, Transmittal
summary, El Paso, 8 January 1692, DS.*

Proceedings of transmittal

In the pueblo of El Paso, kingdom of New Mexico, on 8 January
1693, don Diego de Vargas Zapata Luján Ponce de León, governor
and captain general of this kingdom, castellan of its fortress and presidio for his majesty: He has come from leaving completely and fully
reduced, humbled, and conquered for our holy faith and the royal
crown the Indians of the kingdom. He sent to his excellency, the
most excellent lord viceroy of the entire kingdom of New Spain, the
Conde de Galve, a copy of the military proceedings of what was conquered until last 16 October 1692. At present, with a review of the
military proceedings, in pursuance of the conquest, it is of record that
the following day, 17 October, leaving a governor chosen for the nations of the Tewas, Tanos, Picuris, and Taos, and having made this
choice in the villa of Santa Fe, he left there, despite his lack of allies
from these nations.

On 8 October, he had arranged and come to an agreement with
the governors of those pueblos, by virtue of the information of record for the afternoon of that day in the military proceedings, that
the two young men who arrived returning from Zuni province gave
him. Because of the rain- and snowstorms that had suddenly occurred, the Indians were hindered in gathering their maize. This
was the reason they were unable to comply with what was decided
and agreed to that afternoon, which was to leave in the company of
the governor and captain general for the nations whose captains had
assembled at the junta held for three days and nights for the rebellious, uprisen, apostate, treacherous nations of the Pecos, Keres, Jemez,
Apache, Zuni, and Moqui to ambush me.

Without the Indian allies, I might have hesitated about the entrada
to these nations, and even more so, lacking the Indian allies I took
from this pueblo of El Paso and its district and the ten citizens and
thirty soldiers. Also, because the horses were exhausted, carrying freight
difficult, and the Indian allies tired, I sent the captives, whose list is
of record, in the charge of the sargento mayor, Cristóbal Tapia. The
cannon, wagons, and provisions went in the charge of the artillery
captain so that, unburdened, I would be able to complete the recon-

noitering of those nations that, plotting, wished to destroy me and the camp.

Putting aside these considerations, however, and trusting and placing the matter in God's hands, as His cause only, blindly and without fear of facing such considerable risks and force, I left that villa of Santa Fe on 17 October, having with kindness taken my leave of its Indians, telling them to obey their governor and pray morning and night. After the Indians had promised to comply fully with what I said to them, I left that villa for those nations, experiencing with the Jemez nation the truth about their evil intention, which I pretended not to notice and overcame, as is of record from the entrada on 25 October. On the twenty-seventh, having joined the camp in the outpost of Mejía, I considered and decided to send to El Paso the ten citizens, captives, and cannon with an escort of eight soldiers, and also the Indian allies, in order to go on to the vast provinces of Zuni and Moqui and the peñol of Acoma with eighty-nine soldiers, including among them the military leaders and war officials. Having seen on the twenty-eighth that it was advantageous to decide in this way, I immediately carried it out, giving the orders and provisions of record from that day, as well as the list of captives who left this kingdom. Their departure was carried out on the twenty-ninth. Once the men and I, the governor and captain general, were supplied, on the following day, the thirtieth, I continued my route toward the peñol of Acoma.

On 3 November, it is of record that I came face to face with the enemy, the Keres nation of that peñol, who were rebellious and unbelieving from that day until the following one, the fourth of that month. I succeeded in reducing, humbling, and conquering them, going up the steep ascent of the peñol until I reached the entrance of its mesa, accompanied by the men referred to on that entrada. This was of even greater consequence because of the impregnability of that peñol. It is of record, as is public and well known, what that triumph cost its first conqueror after having won that land and kingdom.

Having won the laurels of that surrender, I left for the province of the Zunis, whose Indians, having abandoned all their pueblos, went to live on their peñol, since it was impregnable, even more so than the previous one. The mesa of that peñol of Zuni must be 2 leagues long. The Indians have their pueblo on it, as is of record from the entrada and ascent I made to it on 11 November. What the Indians did to distinguish themselves on that day, also of record, is in the proof of their handing over the images of Christ Jesus, the monstrance and sacred vessels, the missal, and the books. This evoked from me, the governor, and those who were present the tenderness and pleasure of discovering and receiving what was handed over. This should be considered by a Catholic heart: not having suffered the risks and travails of the journey, but having had much good fortune.

Going to examine the horses of the men-at-arms on the fourteenth, they were found to be so tired that they gave almost no hope of departure from that province. To see the Moqui nation, 40 leagues away, I ordered the leaders to take twenty-five soldiers aside to remain as an escort for the horses that might be unable to make the march. Carrying this out, and also leaving one of the packtrains and the muleteers under the orders of the leader and the appointed campaign captain with supplies to maintain themselves in that outpost, ammunition, and cattle, I left on the fifteenth of that month. I spent the night 6 leagues away without water with the men-at-arms I took, who numbered sixty-three soldiers, including the military leaders, the war officials, and my secretary of government and war.

In the 40 leagues referred to, there were three water holes. The first sustained a very few horses and the camp, though with great difficulty. Only with care can a few saddle horses drink in the next two. We were able, despite the loss of horses and mules on the march, in addition to the harshness of the weather and ice storms, to enter on 19 November the first pueblo of Moqui province. A little less than a league away, at the ascent to a mesa, a squadron of Indians, apparently more than seven or eight hundred, came out on foot and horseback to receive me, provoking us to make war so they could make use of their treachery.

The circumstances and conditions deserved much consideration and were worthy of being attended to by a miracle from the most holy Virgin, Our Lady of Remedies.[34] She helped me to convince them and stop their furor, as is of record from all the events of the entrada, its circumstances and the manner in which I overcame, reduced, and conquered them, neither fearing nor paying attention to their great number. I found the information from the Taos Indians to be true. I not only overcame them, as I relate, but also made them surrender their weapons and kneel twice at the entrance to their pueblo. I also had two to three hundred dismount for this reason, but not the ones on horseback who were prepared and equipped with all their weapons and leather jackets.

I, the governor and captain general, entered the pueblo on foot, because its door was so small and narrow that one could scarcely fit in sideways. There, accompanied by the leaders, my secretary of government and war, and the alferez, I proclaimed, revalidated, and reclaimed for his majesty the new possession of that pueblo, the province, and its Indians, having them surrender their weapons and kneel. I did this accompanied by only eight of the leaders and officials, so that the Indians might see I was not afraid of them. Since it was late, I delayed the entrada with the fathers, the president, and the chaplain until the following day, so that the reverend fathers might absolve them of their apostasy and baptize the children and those they had raised. Telling everyone in the pueblo to be prepared to carry out what has been referred to, I took my leave. I received the same kindness the governor and head of the pueblo, an Indian loyal to the Divine and human majesties and very reverent to our holy faith, requested from me.

Having taken my leave, I established my camp a quarter-league away at the water hole of that pueblo. On the following day, 20 November, having prepared five squads, I made the entrada with them to the plaza of the pueblo where its people were, with many from the rest of the pueblos who had come to be with those Indians. The reverend fathers, the president fray Francisco Corvera and fray Cristóbal Alonso Barroso, absolved them and baptized their children and the other unbaptized people. After I told them again about my coming and had taken my leave, the governor asked me to come up to his house and eat. I did so, so that they might think me neither fearful nor suspicious of their evil intentions. Thus, I went up, as did the fathers, the leaders, and my secretary of government and war. He fed us very politely. I took my leave of them all, embracing them and shaking their hands with great kindness, having become a compadre to the Indian Miguel and others.

The following day, Thursday, the twenty-first, the Indian governor Miguel gave me information about the junta the Indians from all the pueblos of the province had held to kill me and the men-at-arms, as is of record in the proceedings. Their treacherous intent is given in detail in his report. Having warned me about it, he was telling and giving me an account so that, with that information, I might see whether it was appropriate for me to return. If I were to go on, it would be with the necessary caution, since my life was at risk because of the treachery they had decided upon. Although that information could have afflicted me, and though I had such a small number of men (seventy-three, as has been referred to), I decided to go on at any price to humble, reduce, and conquer the pueblos of that province. It was because of that decision the entrada had been made there. Thus, I told him that God Our Lord and the most holy Virgin would help me and that on the following day, Friday the twenty-second, he should be here early to go with me and serve as interpreter.

On the appointed day, 22 November, in the plaza de armas I had indicated and the campsite at that water hole, I left with fifty soldiers, taking only powder and bullets, and they, their best and most satisfactory horses. I warned them that on that day, they had to make the entrada to the three pueblos of Walpi, Mishongnovi, and Shongopavi, a round-trip distance of 13 or 14 leagues, without watering the horses. The Indians supplied themselves from water holes, like wells, with little replenishment, which is all they have at their pueblos. They take the water out with gourds to supply themselves and water their animals in gourd bowls, according to the flow.

We went first to the pueblo of Walpi, which is on a very high mesa whose ascent is very dangerous. I found it crowded with many people on foot and horseback, fully armed and making war cries. Proceeding on to climb the mesa, breaking through the squadron of Indians, and stopping them with effective arguments until I arrived within sight of the entrance, I found their governor there, somewhat disturbed. He could scarcely reply to what I said to him through the interpreter, Miguel, who warned him to order his men to lay down their weapons. At last, as a sign of obedience and humility, he did so. The interpreter said, using my effective arguments and with persuasive insistence, that the Indians belonging to that pueblo should lay down their weapons, which they did. The governor said to me that those from his pueblo were the ones without weapons. The others I saw with their weapons had come from the other pueblos. For that reason, I entered the plaza of the pueblo of Walpi, where I made the revalidation and possession on behalf of his majesty. The reverend fathers absolved them and baptized the children and unbaptized people.

I went on to the second pueblo, where I found the Indians had left, and it was in the same condition. It had a very rugged ascent and was on another mesa. I went on to the third, whose ascent is longer and whose mesa is larger and more extensive. In this one, I found the Indians were humbler, since both the men and women came out to receive me, without weapons. I noticed, however, that they disdained having the men-at-arms as compadres, in spite of the fact that I, the governor and captain general, was compadre to some. Once the ceremony was over, I took my leave of them at vespers, finding I had to return about 7 leagues to my encampment. I did in fact return that night to Awatovi Pueblo, with so many of the horses so tired that some soldiers had to ride double with their comrades.

The following day, Saturday, I had to give them a day of rest, in order to make the entrada to the last pueblo, Oraibi, on Sunday, 24 November. On the day mentioned, Saturday, 23 November, as is of record in the proceedings, one may find the account of the action I completed regarding the route to Cerro Colorado, where the almagre or cinnabar is. On the same day, I also bartered for some from the Indians of Moqui province.

On the day mentioned, Sunday, I found out from the Indians about the distances and water holes on the way to Oraibi Pueblo. Since there were no water holes along the entire route nor in the pueblo, which was 9 or 10 leagues away, I had to delay the departure in order to take the horses that had been watered, waiting until eleven o'clock. At that time, I ordered the camp and provisions prepared in order to go, spending the night without water, making the entrada on the following day. When we were about to march, the military leaders came to explain to me, as is of record from the departure of that day, that I should see that I could not make that entrada, because it would risk losing the camp, since there was no water for the horses. They explained and brought this to my attention after having seen the miserable condition of the horses.

In attention to that well-founded argument, it would be necessary to spend three days without water (the day of the departure, the stay, and the return) to make the entrada. The harshness of the frosts had exhausted the horses. With regard to what had been said and of having achieved the entrada, reduction, and conquest of that province, and having bartered for the ore, I ordered the camp to leave for Zuni province. I, the governor and captain general, went with the military leaders, some soldiers, and my secretary of government and war to Awatovi Pueblo and ordered their head and governor, Miguel, to call his people. I told them I was returning for the reason referred to and they should so tell the people of Oraibi. So as not to use up the water they had in their pool for their sustenance, I would return, God seeing fit, when there was water. I took leave of them and my compadre, Miguel.

Having arrived on Monday, 25 November, at the water hole of Los Chupaderos, I received the letter, of record in the proceedings, from the campaign captain. He gave me information about the intention of the Apaches, who had a junta to attack him, and he was so advising me. For that reason, and because we had just arrived without having watered most of the horses for two days, on the following day, Tuesday, I left with the necessary caution. Arriving at the water hole of El Entretenimiento at sunset, I ordered thirty soldiers to be ready to leave at nine o'clock that night. The military leaders and I, the governor and captain general, left with them, traveling that night until Wednesday, the twenty-sixth.

Very early in the morning, I arrived at the pueblo and campsite of Halona to join the campaign captain. I found him concerned about the enemy. He told me about the many tracks they left, which they found in the mornings, and that were there when I arrived. The Indians of its peñol also repeated their concern. On Saturday, the twenty-ninth, having decided to leave for the arroyo of the peñol, I went with the men-at-arms to improve my position and be near the road for the final departure. Sgto. mayor Antonio Jorge obtained information from a genízaro[35] Zuni, nicknamed Agustín, El Cabezón, that in a week he could take us by a road that would come out above the pueblo of Senecú—a shortcut that would be of great value.

Carrying this out, I had this Indian brought to me to question him and arrange for the payment he requested, the agreement for which is of record in the proceedings for that day. It would be very useful to try the shortcut and new route, since more than 50 to 70 leagues could be saved, if it is true the ore has mercury, as is thought. It would also provide some relief to the pack animals and for the current miserable condition of the camp's horses and mules. Thus, since the Indian had affirmed that he would take me and bring me out at Senecú in a week, I gave an order that night that on the following day, Sunday, the camp, pack animals, and provisions should be ready. Once they were, I left with the Indian.

The information is of record for that night that the enemy Apache was about to act upon their junta's design. On Tuesday, 2 December, they fell upon a group of horses from one of the herds, because it was a stormy night with wind and snow, as is of record in the proceedings. Continuing along the shortcut, I, the governor and captain general, and the camp were forced to melt snow for drinking water, since we had not had any for two days and nights. We found none—though the Indian had assured us that we would. The horses had been without water for three days. The snow was divine providence to prevent us from perishing, because the shortcut went through very dry country. The Indian had doubtlessly gone through there in the rainy season, when there was sure to be water.

To save 30 leagues, though, which was what was saved, one cannot run the great risk of dying. The shortcut can only serve for sending a courier with ten men, traveling lightly. I also do not think it advantageous, because it is a land of great danger, numerous rancherias, and terrain broken by malpais and many dunes, all reasons that prevent travel in that land. This is what I think about that experience.

Finally, I, the governor and captain general, arrived at this pueblo of El Paso, on Saturday, 20 December, and the captain of its presidio with the rest of the camp, on Monday, 21 December.[36] The only bad luck they had, as was referred to, was that the captain of the reinforcements from Parral was returning badly wounded by the enemy Apache on the sixteenth, as is of record in the proceedings. Everyone was returning happy about the victory and conquest, as is of record in the proceedings, having completely reduced, humbled, and conquered the kingdom of New Mexico, its pueblos, the provinces of Zuni and Moqui, and the peñol of Acoma. With the villa of Santa Fe, this makes twenty-three in which, as is of record, I, the governor and captain general, as their new restorer and conqueror, revalidated and again proclaimed on his majesty's behalf his possession of them. I was awarded the trophy of having made the Indians surrender to his royal crown, vassalage, and our holy faith.

In all the kingdom of New Mexico and the provinces of Zuni and Moqui, 2,214 people of all ages, male and female, of both sexes are baptized

In addition, 2,214 people and children of all ages, male and female, were baptized. Likewise, 74 captives who were slaves in that kingdom have been freed and are enjoying the liberty to return to their brothers, relatives, and spouses. About all that has been referred to, my humility places victory at his excellency's feet, the most excellent lord viceroy, the Conde de Galve. Would that I were able to give greater trophies to his majesty, increasing his monarchy, without requesting compensation for expenses, because those I have had are offered as a gift, as I have written before and repeat with these proceedings of transmittal.

As for the military proceedings of the war from 16 October to the present and the letter of transmittal for the most excellent lord viceroy, the Conde de Galve, I am ordering my secretary of government and war to copy, take, and put them in order word for word, so that the transmittal may be of record for his greatness. Thus, I provided and signed with my secretary of government and war on the said day, month, and year ut supra.

Don Diego de Vargas Zapata
Luján Ponce de León [rubrica]

Before me,

Alfonso Rael de Aguilar [rubrica]
Secretary of government and war

Diego de Vargas to the Conde de Galve, El Paso, 10 January 1693, C.

Most excellent sir,

Sir, in prosecution of this conquest, I left the villa of Santa Fe on 17 October and on the same day achieved the surrender of the nation and pueblo of the Pecos. With gestures, they made it understood they were satisfied I told them the truth and were happy to return to the Catholic religion and the obedience they should render. I went on to the other nations of the Keres and Jemez. In the latter, I found that the information referred to in the proceedings for 8 October about the Taos Indians was accurate, since the Jemez Indians sought an army. Their allies, the Apaches, were hidden in the houses and cuarteles of their pueblo. They also tried to bring together the Keres under Captain Malacate the day before. On their mesa in the Cerro Colorado, I humbled and conquered them, and they refused to join and cooperate in treachery. This was related to me by Bartolo, a Keres Indian, who served as interpreter.

Although the Jemez nation, because of their actions, angered me and the men-at-arms with whom I entered their pueblo, I repressed it as well as I could. At times, I pretended not to notice their excesses, which included repeatedly throwing dirt in our eyes. They also came out completely armed. Splitting up, some remained on the lower part of the ascent, and others spread out along the loma of the mesa, which was also occupied by many fully armed Indians. Finally, the reduction was achieved, and they said they had entertained me in that fashion because of my entrada, hiding their treacherous spirit. I went on to the other nations of the Keres, with the good results of reducing and conquering for our holy faith and the royal crown four pueblos: the Pecos; the Keres of Cochiti and San Felipe on the mesa of La Cieneguilla; the Keres of Santo Domingo, Santa Ana, and Zia on the mesa of the Cerro Colorado; and the Jemez on the mesa of La Cañada. The four pueblos mentioned are living at those places and are from the district and kingdom of New Mexico and the villa of Santa Fe. The pueblos, including the villa, in which they have eked out a living, number seventeen.

Having achieved the conquest, I went on to join the camp at the outpost of Mejía on 27 October. When I arrived, I found the leaders who had carried out the order about their arrival. Seeing the number of captives, the Indian allies I took from the pueblo of El Paso, the ten citizens, and the difficulty of wagons and artillery carriages without animals to draw them (those that had them before did not have enough), it would be no little chore to reach El Paso. Adding to this was the consideration of the sixty-six people coming out of captivity in that kingdom enjoying freedom with their relatives, brothers and sisters, and spouses. Thus, I decided by myself, without consulting a war junta, because I could see it was impossible to go on to the peñol of Acoma and the provinces of Zuni and Moqui, since the horses and mules were unable.

Apart from these considerations and mindful of the importance of that battle, I removed the obstacle referred to. I ordered the leaders appointed on the twenty-eighth to prepare the Indian allies, the captives of record from the list of the general muster, and the ten settlers, everyone well supplied, with eight soldiers and the leader I gave them as an escort, for the twenty-ninth. I gave them the order of record for that date about their departure. They were to return to the pueblo of El Paso, taking the information about the enterprise and conquest achieved and of my remaining with only eighty-nine soldiers, including in that number the military leaders, officials, and my secretary of government and war.

I was staying with those men to overcome and conclude once and for all the difficulties of that campaign. The risks were continuous, with the additional difficulty caused by the scarcity of water holes over the whole distance. They existed only as a result of occasional rain and were usually quite shallow. Added to this was the harshness of the frosts and snow. Never had a similar corps or troop of men-at-arms passed through that country before. The people from that land thought it impossible and the entrada risky. Undertaking it at any cost and trusting to luck, I rushed forth to make the entrada, resigning myself completely to divine will and that of the sovereign queen, Mary, our most holy Lady of Remedies, guide and protector of the present enterprise.

Thus, I left the outpost of Mejía on 30 October, catching sight of the impregnable peñol of Acoma on 3 November. The Keres nation lives and has its pueblo on the mesa. Because of their strong position, they replied incredulously, doubting what I told them. Finally, as is of record in the proceedings, on the following day, the fourth, I went up the peñol with only nine soldiers, including my secretary of government and war. Its conquest was an even greater triumph, because when this land was won by its first conqueror, it took fourteen years and the best soldiers of the kingdom to reduce it to our holy faith and royal vassalage.

At last, on the eleventh, I entered and went up the peñol of Kiákima in Zuni province. On that mesa, which is more than 2 leagues long, the Indians from the five pueblos of the Zuni nation are living, having abandoned their pueblos because of the Apaches, their enemies. To live safely, they are resigned to servitude to many Apache rancherias that come to eat their food, and, when they leave, carry off the horses they want. Having gone up the peñol, an even stronger position than the previous one, I entered the pueblo, where, humbly and with kindness, the Zunis showed themselves to be more polite than the others. Informing me that they had the holy vessels and images of Christ Jesus, a painting of St. John the Baptist, a missal, and books in a room on the terrace of an Indian woman's house, I went up there.

I entered the room, through a door that gave no more light than a shuttered window. The leaders, my secretary of government and war, and the Indian captains of that nation entered as well. I found an altar set up, with the images of Christ Jesus, the monstrance, and the holy vessels covered with some scraps of vestment, with two large, tallow candles burning. I knelt to uncover and receive the images of Christ Jesus that evoked in me and those present great pleasure and tenderness for having restored to our power the furnishings and having had the good fortune of such a discovery. My heart said to me that, having had such a victory, the risks and travails suffered had been nothing.

As a sign of esteem, I stood up, embracing the captains, shaking their hands. With persuasive words, I assured them sincerely that I would serve them in whatever way I could for their respect and veneration of the monstrance and those furnishings of record from their inventory in the proceedings. I told them I would take them so that the reverend father custos, whoever he might be, could reconsecrate them. They would be saved for the church he would order them to build.

I returned to the plaza de armas and campsite indicated. The enemy Apache had attacked one very dark and stormy night where the cattle were and carried off sixteen head without their absence being noticed until dawn. Although I could have ordered two squads of soldiers to leave and overtake them, I did not want to delay the departure for Moqui province. Thus, out of necessity, since the horses were completely tired and worn out, on 14 November, I ordered the leaders to separate all those belonging to the men-at-arms and unable to go on the march and to make a list of twenty-five soldiers with the leader and campaign captain of record from the order. They were to be given ammunition, provisions, and pack animals.

Once it was done, as is stated, I left on 15 November with sixty-three soldiers, with the military leaders, officials, and my secretary of government and war among their number. Over a distance of 40 leagues, there are three water holes before one arrives at the first pueblo of Moqui province, which is called San Bernardo de Aguatuvi. As is of record from our arrival on 19 November, the denunciation by the Taos was seen to be true, because of the squadron of fully armed Moqui Indians mounted and on foot at the ascent to their mesa. They numbered more than seven or eight hundred Indians and through their rebellious gestures gave many signs they wanted and planned to kill me and the men-at-arms. Because the horses had scarcely drunk over that distance, since the water holes were shallow and difficult to reach and there were heavy frosts, they were at the point of collapse. This made it necessary for most of the men-at-arms, though there were few, to ride mules. They were very spread out and separated, so that there scarcely seemed to be more than twenty or thirty soldiers and leaders accompanying me, with my secretary of government and war.

Returning to the traitorous Moqui Indians, their large army immediately joined and surrounded us, hurling countless insults, throwing dirt in our eyes and giving furious war cries. Shooting to scatter them and drawing swords, at a distance of 1 league, we stopped three times to wait for the men-at-arms, who were coming all spread out. This was so they might arrive and help, at least in part, in the last stage of the fight, since they could not assist in the first attack. I saw this as unavoidable, although, availing myself of all my knowledge and tolerating this audacity, I said, ordered, and commanded the men-at-arms not to begin fighting until they saw me begin.

I had the Indian Miguel, head of the pueblo, tell them, since he could speak Spanish, that I came in peace, showing them as authority and proof the most holy Virgin of Remedies. On that day, I received even greater favors from her most holy patronage. Only with the aid of her divine presence could I lessen the ferocity of the treacherous barbarians. I replied to their diabolical propositions, whose subtleties were as acute as they were carefully thought out, influenced as they were by hell and ministers of the devil, who, I have no doubt, were present, held within the hearts of those barbarians.

I convinced them in such a way that I humbled, reduced, and conquered them. I approached the entrance to the pueblo, about a musket shot away, finding myself on ground suitable for whatever skirmish might have been offered. I ordered them with imperious words to lay down their weapons if they were Christians and receive the divine Lady, our mother, on their knees and commanded those who were mounted to dismount. I achieved this, although only with repeated urging and resolute words, saying to them they should do so and agree they were Christians and not to let the devil deceive them. Having made everyone kneel, I took the royal standard from the alferez's hand and, from my horse, told them about my coming. Showing them the most holy Lady, Mary, and having said various words concerning the possession that his majesty, the king, our lord (may God keep him), had of them and that province, I dismounted and entered the plaza of their pueblo, accompanied by the military leaders, the alferez, and my secretary of government and war, through a gate so narrow that it was necessary to enter sideways.

Entering the plaza, I revalidated the possession proclaimed for his majesty in the same way. Since it was late, I told them I was going to the water hole of their pueblo and on the following day would return with the priests. Having established the camp at the water hole and designated it as a plaza de armas, several bands of Indians came together there. I had them bring me firewood, since the area had no trees at all. They had their weapons, and I told them I would burn their bows and arrows to get warm. With that, some went to bring firewood, and others remained to spend that night with the camp, which, besieged and surrounded by so many enemies, took precautions.

The following day, the twentieth, as is of record, I made the entrada to the pueblo again, accompanied by the reverend fathers, the president and the chaplain of this army, who absolved the Indians and baptized their children and the other unbaptized people. I was godfather to two children of the Spanish-speaking Indian, Miguel, and to many others given to me by their parents, as were the men-at-arms. The Indians came to their senses and changed their intention, since they told me and my compadre Miguel to go up and eat in their governor's house, which I did with the reverend fathers, some of the leaders, and my secretary of government and war. The rest did so with the men-at-arms, treating them as friends. I took my leave of them, repeating to them that they should pray and build their church. I returned to the plaza de armas, pleased with this reduction and conquest, having considered reduction to our holy faith lost without risking the loss of many souls.

On the following day, the twenty-first, my compadre Miguel came to see me. In the presence of the reverend father president, fray Francisco Corvera, as is of record, he knelt and, crying a river of tears and kissing his hands and holy habit, told him that he well knew that since he came to me, they would kill him for the good he had done for the Spaniards and because he had not wanted to cooperate in killing me and the men-at-arms. He was warning me that all the men of the pueblos had been waiting to do so, so that I would refuse to make the entrada to them. The governor of Walpi Pueblo, Antonio, was prepared for this with those men and his sons. Then, I told him that I was not afraid and had to make the entrada because I had come for this purpose and the Virgin, our Lady, would help me. Because he speaks Spanish, I ordered him to be mounted early the next day, the twenty-second, to go with me as interpreter to the pueblos of Walpi, Mishongnovi, and Shongopavi. I was already informed that there was no water hole in them or on the round trip of 30 to 40 leagues.

He thus came promptly on the stated day, the twenty-second. Once the military leaders with the five squads were mounted on their most satisfactory horses, with powder, ball, and their weapons, I left for the pueblos without further difficulty. The high mesa where the pueblo of the Indians of Walpi is located is about 3 leagues away. Having gone up by a very dangerous road, I found it totally covered from one side to the other with a large squadron of Indians, mounted and on foot, all intermingled, fully armed, giving furious war cries and throwing much dirt in our eyes. With all my skill I tried to overcome them, without rushing to attack them, rather distracting them and ordering them to lay down their weapons. With effective arguments, I made the Indians, who were from this pueblo, carry this out, their governor and the Indian Antonio satisfying me that those without weapons were their responsibility and from this pueblo. The rest had come to be present for my entrada.

So that they would judge me neither afraid nor suspicious of their depraved and treacherous intention, I entered the plaza of their pueblo with half the men-at-arms, leaving the rest outside. I dismounted in the plaza with the alferez and my secretary of government and war. The people of the pueblo were there, and I made them first set up a holy cross. After I had repeated and revalidated the new possession in his majesty's favor, the reverend fathers absolved and baptized their children and the other people. I was also godfather to the children of the governor, Antonio, and to his son's child.

Once this was finished, he asked me to come up to eat at his home. I did so with the fathers, although from the disturbed state in which I found him at first, I could infer it was a trick to more safely achieve what had been agreed to: killing me and the men-at-arms. To put aside their impression that my compadre Miguel had revealed the treason and their junta's conspiracy to me, with a happy countenance I went up with the reverend fathers, some leaders, and my secretary of government and war. I very readily ate some eggs cooked in their style and some melon. I took my leave of him and embraced him, seeing that, as a result of the words I spoke to him, he was regaining the color he lost because of his disturbed state, assuring him that I knew nothing of what he had intended.

I went on to the second pueblo, Mishongnovi, which is on another very high mesa and whose ascent is of the worst sort. The people of the pueblos already occupied it, making the same gestures and movements to provoke me, although we paid no attention other than to attend to carrying out what was referred to. Entering the plaza, I found in it the three captains with three small crosses in their hands and saw that one of them was the one I had sent them as a sign of peace with the word of my entrada. So they might recognize the reverent worship due the holy cross, I dismounted, knelt, and kissed it. I ordered them to set up a large cross in the plaza. Once this was done and the people of that pueblo, men without weapons, women, boys and girls, and children were there, I spoke and repeated the possession in his majesty's favor to them in the same way. The reverend fathers absolved and baptized them, as in the rest of the pueblos.

When this was finished, I went to the third pueblo of Shongopavi, which is on another mesa, wider, as is its ascent. In it, I saw the Indian men were humbler and more polite, since they came out to receive me without their weapons, as did the people of the pueblo, the women, boys and girls, and children. I dismounted in their plaza and ordered another holy cross set up, carrying out in the same way the new possession and saying to them what is of record for the previous ones. The fathers absolved and baptized them. Since it was already vespers, I took my leave of them.

In the 7 leagues I traveled to return to the plaza de armas and water hole of Awatovi, many of the horses became tired, so some soldiers rode double with their companions. Arriving when it was quite late, I had to remain the following day, the twenty-third, in that campsite. There I made the report of record in these proceedings of the route from the sierra of the Cerro Colorado, where the mine with almagre or cinnabar is. It is thought to have signs of mercury, as they have informed your excellency. This is a matter of such value, as is everything else in your excellency's care, in accord with your great zeal. The weather and the condition of the horses, however, made it impossible to go discover that cerro and its mine. I therefore bartered for the ore to see whether the decision about its discovery should be made based on its assay.

I have no doubt, from its appearance, that it must have not just some mercury content, but a considerable amount. This cannot be known because the mark of mercury ore has the distinction of being invisible, while that of silver or any other ore is not. Nevertheless, it is seen that it contains mercury from the signs of that ore: weight; wetness; greasiness; and rubbing it on the hand, which leaves a purplish luster. This will be part of a more complete examination. Not only experience in the profession of silver refiner and miner, according to what has been referred to, but also empirical consideration and speculation held it to be so. There will be no shortage in that court of those expert in this knowledge who can determine the quality of the ore, since they will also foresee that whatever ore may be found will be of value.

I bartered for and acquired the sample I send to your excellency from many Indians, though it is in short supply. It is impossible to know whether it is definitely taken from the purest part of the vein or mixed together afterward, a judgment that will be made during the assay of the content that may result. Our Lord has seen fit to provide this ore, since it may be by this means that he seeks to relieve our great monarch and lord (may God keep him), Carlos II, and preserve those Indians who will obey him and the Catholic religion. Thus, I shall esteem with my proper and fervent zeal the successful achievement of the completed action regarding the ore.

I spent that day, the twenty-third, in this activity. On the following day, the twenty-fourth, I was informed of the distances and the water holes on the way to the last pueblo of that province, the one called Oraibi. The Indians told me it was 9 or 10 leagues and there was no water. The pueblo did not have any either, other than a well from which, as in the others mentioned, they draw water with gourds to maintain themselves and their horses, which they water from gourd bowls. Because of its slow flow, they are only able to keep them alive by putting them far away in summer pastures.

Having watered the horses at eleven o'clock, I decided that day, the twenty-fourth, to go on and spend the night on the road, make the entrada on the following day, and then return on the third, although it might be late at night. The leaders presented me with the reasons of record for that day and departure. I also understood their justification and having recognized it, refused to place the camp at risk, after having enjoyed such successes. During the rainy season, his majesty seeing fit, an entrada will be made, and the province entered and settled once and for all, leaving the missionary to attend them. I told the Indians of Awatovi Pueblo that they should tell that to those of Oraibi. So as not to use up the water in the well, which was necessary to keep them from perishing, and so that the men-at-arms would not cause them any difficulty, I returned without making an entrada into that pueblo. I trusted Our Lord would let me do so someday.

Having told them these and many other reasons, I took my leave and left with the men-at-arms on that day to return to the province of Zuni. On the second day of the march, the twenty-fifth, the courier arrived at vespers. He had been sent by the campaign captain I left on the fifteenth in Halona Pueblo, Zuni province. Of record in the letter is the information referred to of having expected the enemy Apache. With this information, I left the following day to make the direct journey to that pueblo.

The following day and night I traveled about 26 leagues, arriving at sunrise within view of Halona Pueblo to aid him with thirty soldiers, the military leaders, and my secretary of government of war. I found that campaign captain was vigilant so that the enemy would not ambush him and carry off the horses, since he was in a place where he feared it could be done. He thanked me again for coming and spoke of the enemy tracks they had discovered and the great junta they had prepared to attack me. Upon my arrival, and that of the rest of the camp on the following day, the twenty-eighth, I left to find a better campsite on the twenty-ninth, within view of the peñol of Zuni.

That night I made an agreement with a genízaro Indian and arranged for the crossing by the new route that I had discussed with the sargento mayor. Having paid him on the thirtieth, I left Zuni province at once, taking my leave of the Indians, who were eager for my quick return. That night, 5 or 6 leagues away, they sent me word that the large junta of the enemy Apache was following me. For that reason, the whole camp and I were on watch the entire night. [37]

Having followed the new route, it is of record that the enemy managed to carry off a small herd of fourteen horses on 2 December because the night was dark and stormy. They left one so badly wounded it soon died. Finally, after ten days, the route ended at Socorro Pueblo. It was divine providence that the snows continued, for these served as repeated, I mean, melted water at some places for the camp and me. The horses were able to go without water for three days and a night.

The reason I took that route was to see whether it was shorter, so that his majesty might exploit and work the mine should the ore show signs of mercury, as was thought. We had saved 30 leagues. Should the matter be pursued, a route farther north where water holes can be found should be sought, because there are none along the way the Indian brought me.

Having arrived within sight of Senecú, 70 leagues from this pueblo of El Paso, I sent three soldiers with word I was at that place. On the eleventh of the present month, the camp and I saw that the river was already frozen in that area. On the following day, since the cold was excessive, I decided to go on to the pueblo of El Paso so that the men-at-arms could winter there or nearby, should your excellency wish to order them to withdraw to the presidios of New Biscay, or remain until the kingdom is settled, after having conquered all its rebels, its villa of Santa Fe, the peñol of Acoma, and its provinces of Zuni and Moqui.

There are twenty-three pueblos, including the villa, where the Indians of those nations live in want. Two thousand two hundred and fourteen adults and children, male and female of all ages, were baptized. Seventy-four captives, slaves of those barbarians, are now free to come to live with their relatives, brothers and sisters, and spouses.

The conquest has been accomplished without firing a shot.[38] I remain proud of having achieved it without deaths on either side, arriving and victoriously entering this outpost of El Paso four months later, less one day, on 20 December, having traveled, as will be of record in the proceedings, more than 600 leagues on the campaign. I render many times over everything that has been referred to that is of record, with the proper zeal of my courtesy as a servant of your excellency and as a loyal vassal of the king, our lord (may God keep him).

My greatest glory has been to conclude the conquest referred to so completely, as I offered it, and to clear up the matter of the ore by sending some of it. At the same time, I can proudly say that what has been achieved is what any other governor who had been in this post would have considered and hoped for. To your excellency or your successors the decisions of the lords minister of the royal junta would seem be as tenuous as the results of the delay, further advancing my argument that this enterprise would have been completely disregarded and left in the ashes of oblivion. I have made this brief digression about all this to your excellency, not to make it seem more important than it is, but to assess the triumph that merits a just defense. To its opponents who may seek to diminish this glory, its victory will be what the nobility of your excellency most values.

At his majesty's royal feet, I courteously speak to you again of the enterprise, hoping its preservation may be achieved for the increase of Christianity and the royal crown. May God keep your excellency's person many happy years in increasing greatness, as I wish.

El Paso, 10 January 1693.

Most excellent sir, your humblest and most obligated servant kisses your excellency's hand,

Don Diego de Vargas Zapata Luján Ponce de León

Most excellent sir, the Conde de Galve

———

This copy agrees with the military proceedings don Diego de Vargas Zapata Luján Ponce de León, governor and captain general of the kingdom and provinces of New Mexico, its new restorer, conqueror, and castellan of its fortress and presidio for his majesty, made and carried out on the campaign, conquest, reduction, and pacification achieved at his cost and expense. He ordered me to copy them to the letter to send them to the most excellent lord viceroy, the Conde de Galve, viceroy of all this New Spain, so that what was done in the conquest may be of record for his greatness. The copy is accurate and true, corrected and in the proper order, with the lieutenant general of the cavalry, Martín de Alday, and José Contreras[39] present for this. Done in this pueblo of El Paso on 12 January 1693. The copy is on 130 folios and ordinary blank paper, because the stamped variety is not available here. In testimony of the truth, I make my usual signature and rubrica.

Alfonso Rael de Aguilar, secretary of government and war

———

*SANM II:53. 125 folios, 249 written pages. Text from BNM 4:5 (22/455.1) has been used to supplement the translation. Translated in Espinosa, *First Expedition*, 166–277. Portions are translated in Twitchell, *Spanish Archives*, II:85–86; *The Leading Facts of New Mexican History* (1911), 1:360–80; *Old Santa Fe: The Story of New Mexico's Ancient Capital* (Santa Fe, 1925):87–150; and *Old Santa Fe: A Magazine of History, Archaeology, Genealogy and Biography* 1 (Jan., Apr. 1914):288–307, 420–35. Some texts and summaries of others are published in *Documentos para la historia de México*, 3d series (1856), 1:129–30.

1. In the 1620s, the bastón, or cane of office, topped with a silver head and adorned by a cross, was first given by the Spanish crown to the governors and other Spanish officers of each pueblo as symbols of their authority. The Pueblos received new canes from Vargas,

the Mexican government when it won independence from Spain, President Lincoln in 1863, and New Mexico Gov. Bruce King in 1981. Juan Carlos I, king of Spain, also presented a new set of canes to nineteen pueblo governors on 30 September 1987 during his visit to Santa Fe.

The cane is kept in the governor's house and used on ceremonial occasions in the kiva and elsewhere. Traditionally, it is blessed every 6 January, the feast day of the Three Kings, before being passed on to the new governor. The authority of the office is believed to reside in the cane. Without it, the official has no power. Fred Eggan and T.N. Pandey, "Zuni History, 1850–1970," in *Handbook*, 9:478. Sando, "Jemez Pueblo," in *Handbook*, 9:424. Nancy S. Arnon and W.W. Hill, "Santa Clara Pueblo," in *Handbook*, 9:301. Cheryl Wittenauer, "Pueblo leaders receive canes," *The New Mexican*, 30 Sept. 1987.

2. Fiscales were appointed by Indian elders to ensure fulfillment of community tasks, make general announcements, and report those absent from church services. Ignaz Pfefferkorn, *Sonora: A Description of the Province* (Albuquerque, 1949):266–67.

3. San Marcos Pueblo was located in the Galisteo basin about 4 km from the turquoise mines in the Cerrillos area. Gaspar Castaño de Sosa on his 1590 expedition identified the inhabitants as Keres.

San Marcos was also referred to as Yates or Yatez. The pueblo was abandoned in 1680, when its inhabitants joined the Tanos in the attack on Santa Fe. Schroeder, "Pueblos Abandoned," in *Handbook*, 9:244–47.

4. Cieneguilla, also known as the "old pueblo of Cochiti," was built on the Potrero Viejo sometime after 1683 by Keres from Cochiti, San Felipe, and San Marcos. In the 1880s, Bandelier described the ruin as two stories high in some places and well preserved. The pueblo was burned during Vargas's recolonizing expedition in 1693, and Bandelier noted that charred wood and maize were evident at the site. Adolph F.A. Bandelier, *Final Report of Investigations Among the Indians of the Southwestern United States, Carried on Mainly in the Years from 1880 to 1885* (Cambridge, Mass., 1890–92), 2:171, 177.

5. This display may represent a form of military salute or welcome similar to greeting customs witnessed by American military officers among the Pueblos during the midnineteenth century. In 1846–47, Gen. Stephen Watts Kearny and his staff were invited to visit Santo Domingo where they were met by village leaders outside the pueblo. They were told that young men, dressed for war, were coming to receive them and cautioned not to fire. In a cloud of dust and with war whoops, warriors swept by the soldiers on each side at full speed, firing volleys under

the horses' bellies. This mock battle continued as they accompanied the troops to the village. Three years later, Lt. J.H. Simpson reported a similar scene at Zuni. Norman B. Humphrey, "The Mock Battle Greeting," *Journal of American Folklore* 54 (July–Dec. 1941):186–90.

6. José Domínguez de Mendoza, born around 1657 in New Mexico, was the natural son of Ana Velázquez and one of the Domínguez de Mendoza brothers, possibly Tomé II or Antonio. When the Pueblo Revolt began, he was with the Leyva party that had gone south to meet the supply train. In April 1682, he married Juana López, a native of New Mexico and daughter of Sgto. mayor Diego López and María de Juárez. José Domínguez left El Paso sometime in 1682, but returned to take part in the reconquest. He was an alferez and a widower in 1692 when he recovered his sister, Juana Domínguez, and her children from captivity. By 1705, he was a captain and remarried. Nine years later, he resided in Santa Cruz. He was dead by 1727. NMF, 27, 169–70. NMR, 3:435.

7. Pedro Márquez was a native of New Mexico, from Nambe, born about 1640. He survived the revolt of 1680 with one son, but his wife and daughter were abducted. Assuming they had perished, Márquez reported in a 1681 muster that he was a widower. NMF, 69–70.

8. Also a native of New Mexico, Diego García Holgado was married and twenty-six or twenty-eight years old in 1681. The Juana mentioned here was Juana de Apodaca. NMF, 33.

9. The Rio Puerco is a major north-south tributary of the Rio Grande that has cut a broad valley west of the Llano de Albuquerque, joining the Rio Grande approximately 28 km south of Belen. RAP, 3.

10. The word coyote had several meanings. In New Mexico it usually referred to a person of Indian and mestizo parents. The term also was used for a go-between, or native of a particular place.

11. José de Madrid, son of Lorenzo de Madrid and a native of New Mexico, passed muster in 1681 at the age of about twenty-two years. He was married to María Trujillo. Madrid died sometime in the first decade of the 1700s. NMF, 68.

12. Either on this occasion or on the return trip in December 1692, Vargas's name was inscribed on El Morro.

13. This was Dowa Yalanne, or Corn Mountain. At its base was Kiákima. Woodbury, "Zuni Prehistory," in *Handbook*, 9:469, 471–72.

14. Halona (halona·wa, or red-ant place) was the prehistoric and historic village on the site of present-day Zuni Pueblo. Woodbury, "Zuni Prehistory," in *Handbook*,

9:467. Eggan and Pandey, "Zuni History," in *Handbook*, 9:481.

15. Here, unexpectedly, Vargas came across church furnishings that had been respectfully preserved by the Pueblos after the 1680 Revolt. According to Zuni oral tradition, the Zunis had become very fond of one particular missionary serving at Hawikuh in 1680. They spared his life under the condition he adopt their customs and dress. According to one account recorded by Frank Hamilton Cushing in the 1880s, the friar was still living with the Zunis atop Corn Mountain when Vargas arrived in 1692. This friar, whom the Zunis called Kwan Tátchui Lók`yana ("Juan Gray-robed-father of us"), was summoned by the elders as the Spaniards approached. Giving him some charcoal and a deerskin whitened with prayer meal, the elders asked him to write the Spaniards a message to the effect that the Zunis were good to those who were good to them and did not meddle in their affairs. They would not injure the Spaniards if their women, children, and old people were not harmed. The friar was given permission to rejoin his countrymen, but chose to stay and did not disclose to the Spaniards that he was there. He wrote on the deerskin only that the fathers of the Ashiwi [Zuni] were good now and would meet the Spaniards in peace. The deerskin "letter" was hurled over the mesa's edge toward the Spaniards. Soon after receiving it, according to the account, Vargas and his men were cordially welcomed on the top of the mesa, where they then found the preserved altar and books.

Fray Juan de Val, serving at Halona, was killed in 1680, but Vetancurt mentions that an unnamed friar serving at Hawikuh escaped, although the church was burned. A fray Juan Galdo of Seville, who professed in Mexico City on 6 July 1659, was serving at Hawikuh and Halona in the early 1670s. There is no mention of this fray Juan in the documents relating to the Revolt. Adams and Chávez, *Missions*, 197 n2. Vetancurt, *Teatro mexicano*, 3:275. Frank Hamilton Cushing, "Outline of Zuni Creation Myths," in *Thirteenth Annual Report of the Bureau of Ethnology, 1891–92* (Washington, D.C., 1896):330–31. Frederick Webb Hodge, *History of Hawikuh, New Mexico: One of the So-called Cities of Cíbola* (Los Angeles, 1937):102–105.

16. Christ Jesus is used in this text as the translation of Cristo Nuestro Bien. The origin of the word Christ is the Latin Christus, corresponding to the Greek Χριστός meaning anointed, which was used in turn to translate the Hebrew *māšîah* from which Messiah came. Greek-speaking pagans being converted to Christianity, however, did not fully understand the concept of the Messiah and further confused the Greek word for anointed with a similar sounding

personal name, Χρηστός, meaning good or kind, and assumed that Christ was part of Jesus's proper name. Jesus, the Christ, was thus transformed, incorrectly, into Jesus Our Good. NCE, 3:627.

17. These books have been tentatively identified by Eleanor B. Adams and France V. Scholes, "Books in New Mexico, 1598–1680," NMHR 17 (July 1942):226–70, in the following fashion:

Fray Pedro Navarro, *Favores de el Rey de el cielo, hechas a su esposa la Santa Juana de la Cruz*, Madrid, 1662

P. Alonso Andrade, S.J., *Itinerario historial que debe guardar el hombre para caminar al cielo*, 2 vols., Madrid, 1642, and later editions

Los libros de la M. Teresa de Jesús, Salamanca, 1558, and later editions

Fray Pedro de Contreras Gallardo, *Manual de administrar los Santos Sacramentos a los españoles y naturales desta nueva España conforme a la reforma de Paulo V*, Mexico City, 1638

Fray Diego de Estrella [Fray Diego de San Cristóbal], *Meditaciones devotísimas del amor de Dios*, Salamanca, 1576, 1578

Primera parte de la venida de Cristo y su vida y milagros, see Andrade, *Itinerario historial*, above

Manual de administrar los santos sacramentos a los naturales y españoles de esta Nueva España, see Contreras Gallardo, *Manual de administrar*, above

One of the Spanish versions of St. Roberto Francesco Romolo Bellarmino (1542–1621), *Dichiarazione più copiosa della dottrina cristiana*, [Rome?], 1598

Either Dr. Luis Juan Villeta, *Libro intitulado Directorium Curatorum compuesto por el ilustre y reverendíssimo Sr. D. Fr. Pedro Martyr Como Obispo de Elna, nuevamente traduzido de la lengua Cathalana en vulgar castellano*, Barcelona, 1566 and possible later editions; or St. Roberto Francesco Romolo Bellarmino, *Directorium Curatorum*

Confesionario en lengua mexicana y castellana, by fray Alonso de Molina (*Confesionario breve en lengua castellana y mexicana*, Mexico City, 1565, and *Confesionario mayor en la lengua mexicana y castellana*, Mexico City, 1578) or fray Juan Bautista

Declaración de la doctrina cristiana, probably the same as Bellarmino, *Dichiarazione*, above

Pedro de la Fuente, *Instrucción de religiosos y declaración de los mementos de la misa*, Seville, 1616

Francisco de Quevedo y Villegas (1580–1645), possibly *Partes primera y segunda de las obras de D. Francisco de Quevedo*, Madrid, 1659

18. Probably a book of sermons or devotions for the Sundays of

Advent. Adams and Scholes, "Books," 261.

19. A native of New Mexico, Rafael Téllez Girón was born about 1660 to José Téllez Girón and Catalina López Romero. Rafael's father, from Cuyoacán, held encomiendas at San Felipe and Cochiti in 1661. In 1680, José took his wife, his son Rafael, and their other six children to El Paso. Rafael enlisted as a soldier on 9 September 1681. In December of that year, he was appointed Piro interpreter. In 1682, Rafael married Mariana Montoya de Esparza, with whom he had two children, José and Catalina. In 1684, he again mustered before Jironza. Rafael was back in El Paso in 1694 and did not return upriver. He was living at San Lorenzo del Paso in 1711. Hackett and Shelby, *Revolt*, 2:141, 188, 242. Naylor and Polzer, *Presidio and Militia*, 1:517. NMR, 10:1882. NMFA, 64:188. NMF, 106.

20. Although unavoidably confusing, Indian pueblos are referred to in Spanish when they appear with the Spanish name of their patron; all other usage is in English, for example, San Bernardo de Aguatuvi and Awatovi Pueblo.

21. In the late seventeenth century, a pistolete, or horse pistol, was described as a short firearm designed to be held in one hand. The caliber was not fixed, but could be as large as 22.5 mm. The gun, usually from 30 to 45 cm long, had a range of about 40 paces. Charles J. Ffoulkes, ed., *Gaya's Traité des Armes*, 1678 (London, 1911):27.

22. This was actually Thursday. Although Vargas on occasion recorded the incorrect date, he was for the following week unusually confused.

23. He meant Walpi.

24. Meses mayores, or late summer months, refer to the period before harvest.

25. A mission to the Coninas (Havasupai) was attempted in the early 1660s about 60 km west of Oraibi. By 1665, there were thirty or forty baptized Indians. Forbes, *Apache*, 157–58.

26. An estado equaled 7 pies, the height of a man, or approximately 2 m.

27. Martín Hurtado was a native of New Mexico, born about 1659 to Andrés Hurtado and Bernardina de Salas (Trujillo). He was evidently their only son who returned with the reconquest. He was married to Catalina Varela Jaramillo. Hurtado was a captain in 1709 and alcalde mayor of Albuquerque in 1714. He was buried in Albuquerque on 17 Oct. 1734. NMF, 49, 50, 197.

28. Apparently some of the Gila Apaches who ranged southwest of Acoma were referred to as Colorado Apaches. These should not be confused with the Plains Apaches, or Vaqueros, also called Colorado Apaches, who lived on the Río Colorado, or Canadian River. Opler, "Apachean Culture," in *Handbook*, 10:390.

29. The royal pine is the common name of the pino piñonero, or Mexican Piñon (*Pinus cembroides*).

30. Today's Sandia and Manzano mountains.

31. The Ladron Mountains, so named because they served as a refuge for alleged Navajo and Apache horse thieves, are 40 km northwest of Socorro, while the Magdalena Mountains are west of Socorro and south of present-day Magdalena.

32. The solemnity of the Immaculate Conception is celebrated on 8 December.

33. At Doña Ana, Vargas granted Father Corvera possession of the religious authority to administer the sacraments over the missions of Acoma, Zuni, and Moqui. BNM 4:2 (22/456.2) translated in Espinosa, *Pueblo Indian Revolt of* 1696, 66–68.

34. Throughout Vargas's reconquest, Mary was invoked in her role as intercessor. In Catholic theology, she is considered the mediatrix of all graces. Mary occupies a middle ground in the hierarchy of beings between God and humankind. Mary's mediation serves to bring about reconciliation and has two forms. Ontological mediation results from divine motherhood—dignified and intensified by her virginity—and plentitude of grace. Moral mediation comes from the fact that Mary contributed to the reconciliation of God and humankind through her son and because through her intercession in heaven she obtains and is the dispensatrix of the grace that God chooses to bestow on humankind, of whom she is the spiritual mother. By her association with the redemptive work of Christ, Mary is also known as coredemptrix. Juniper B. Carol, ed., *Mariology* (Milwaukee, 1961), 1:32–44. José M. Bover, *María mediadora universal o soteriología mariana estudiada a la luz de principios mariológicos* (Madrid, 1946):34–49. NCE, 9:359. *Liturgy of the Hours*, 1368.

35. In New Spain, the term genízaro was sometimes used in the sense of mestizo, or a person of mixed Indian and non-Indian blood. In eighteenth- and nineteenth-century New Mexico, it became a specialized ethnic term for a group derived from detribalized Plains Indians, mostly women and children, who had been captured during intertribal raids and ransomed to Spanish households to be used as servants and herders. The children of these servants, the actual genízaros, followed local Hispanic customs, losing their tribal identity. During the latter part of the eighteenth century, the term genízaro assumed military connotations when genízaro settlements were established as buffers between Spanish villages and Plains Indian raiding parties, and genízaro men became active in the militia. Robert Archibald, "Acculturation and Assimilation in Colonial New

Mexico," NMHR 53 (July 1978):210–14. Fray Angélico Chávez, "Genízaros," in *Handbook*, 9:198–99.

36. This should read Monday, 22 December.

37. Because the conclusion of this document is missing from SANM II:53, the remainder of the translation is based on the copy in BNM 4:5 (22/455.1), 2 folios, 3 written pages. Translated in Espinosa, *First Expedition*, 275–77.

38. Vargas chose here to ignore shots that killed one or both of the Apaches on 16 December.

39. Born around 1646 to Andrés de Contreras and María de Salinas y Valdés of San Luis Potosí, José Contreras passed muster at El Paso in 1684. His first wife was Magdalena de Carvajal (or García); his second was María de Valencia, whom he married in 1693. Naylor and Polzer, *Presidio and Militia*, 1:517.

Glossary

alcalde de primer voto   One of two magistrates chosen yearly by the cabildo

alcalde mayor   In New Spain, a district administrator with extensive political and judicial authority; also known as a corregidor in both New Spain and South America

alcalde ordinario   Civil magistrate elected yearly by the cabildo

alcaldía mayor   District administered by an alcalde mayor

almagre   Usually translated as red ocher; here used in the sense of a mercury-bearing ore, or cinnabar

arroba   Measure of weight equivalent to .25 quintal or 25 libras; as a liquid measure, equivalent to 16.13 liters

Cámara of the Council of the Indies   Subcouncil of the Council of the Indies, responsible for making appointments to offices in the Indies

capitán, cabo y caudillo   Military leader of unspecified rank

casas reales   Principal government building and residence of president of the audiencia

conde   Title of nobility equivalent to a marqués in Spanish- and Portuguese-speaking countries; not equivalent to the title of count in the English nobility

Council of the Indies   Supreme administrative body that handled the affairs of the New World

definitorio   The four-man council of a Franciscan custody or province whose members were selected by the custos

doctrina   A parochial jurisdiction; specifically, an Indian parish

doctrinero   A parish priest

duquesa   Duchess in Spanish- and Portuguese-speaking countries; not equivalent to the title of duchess in the English nobility

encomienda   Royal grant giving an individual the right to Indian tribute in exchange for his provision of protection and Christian instruction to the Indians

fanega   Dry-weight measure equivalent to approximately 35 liters; also a measure of land equaling about .6 hectare

fiscal   Royal prosecutor

flota   One of the two fleets that were customarily sent each year from Cadiz or Sanlúcar de Barrameda, Spain, to Veracruz, New Spain, carrying Spanish products and passengers, and transporting New World products and passengers back to Spain; corresponding fleet for Tierra Firme (Peru) was known as the Galeones

future   Individual's right of succession in employment at some time in the future

hacienda   Landed estate, larger than a rancho, that combined stock raising and agriculture

in verbo sacerdotis   With the word of a priest

junta   Meeting of the viceroy and ministers of an audiencia; meeting of civil or military officials

Junta of the Treasury   Body for dealing with serious financial matters and composed of the viceroy, senior audiencia judge, fiscal, comptroller of the Tribunal of Accounts, and senior treasury official

justicia mayor   Lieutenant appointed to serve in the absence of a governor or alcalde mayor

league   Approximately 4.2 kilometers

licenciado   Licentiate

litis   Lawsuit

maestre de campo   Field-grade officer

marqués   Marquess in Spanish- and Portuguese-speaking countries

menino   Page

milpa   Planted field

peñol   A mesa or stone outcrop

peso   Spanish unit of money equal to 8 reals

plaza de armas   Site where an army camps and musters in formation when it is on campaign or where garrisoned troops muster and drill

quintal   Hundredweight

rancho   Small, rural landholding that produced much the same sort of products as the hacienda, but on a smaller scale

real   Mining camp

tercio   Half a pack animal's load, or carga, divided into two tercios, when the load goes as bundles (fardos). A carga weighs about 135 kilograms

Tribunal of Accounts   Audit court responsible for monitoring all public accounts except those for the alcabala, tribute, and mercury

verbo ad verbum   Literally

villa   Chartered municipality superior in size, status, and privileges to a pueblo, but inferior to a ciudad

your reverence   In Spanish, vuestra paternidad

Works Cited

ARCHIVAL MATERIALS

Archive of the Archdiocese of Santa Fe, New Mexico (AASF)
    Diligencias Matrimoniales
    Loose Documents, Mission, 1680–1850
Archivo de Hidalgo del Parral (Chihuahua), Mexico (AHP)
Archivo General de Indias, Seville, Spain (AGI)
    Audiencia de Guadalajara (Guad.)
    Audiencia de México
    Contaduría
Archivo General de la Nación, Mexico City, Mexico (AGN)
    Civil
    Historia
    Inquisición
    Provincias Internas
    Reales Cédulas
Archivo General de Notarías del Distrito Federal, Mexico City, Mexico
    (AGNot.)
Archivo Histórico de Protocolos de Madrid, Spain (AHPM)
Archivo Histórico Nacional, Madrid (AHN)
    Clero
    Osuna
The Bancroft Library, University of California, Berkeley
    Mexican Manuscripts
Biblioteca Nacional de México, Mexico City, Mexico (BNM)
    Archivo Franciscano, New Mexico Documents
Biblioteca Nacional, Madrid, Spain
    Manuscritos
Church of Jesus Christ of Latter-day Saints, Genealogical Library, Salt
    Lake City, Utah (LDS)
    Collection of ecclesiastical records: Durango, Mexico City, Parral,
    and Puebla

Harold B. Lee Library, Brigham Young University, Provo, Utah (BYU)
    Spanish New Mexico Collection
The Henry E. Huntington Library, San Marino, California (HL)
    Rare Books
    Ritch Collection
The John Carter Brown Library, Providence, Rhode Island
New Mexico State Records Center and Archives, Santa Fe, New Mexico
    Spanish Archives of New Mexico (SANM): Series I and II
The Newberry Library, Chicago, Illinois
    Ayer Collection
Parish of Santa María la Blanca, Villas de los Palacios y Villafranca
    (Seville), Spain

OTHER WORKS

Acosta, José de. *Historia natural y moral de las Indias.* 1590. Mexico
    City: Fondo de Cultura Económica, 1940.
Adams, Eleanor B. "Fray Silvestre and the Obstinate Hopi." NMHR 38
    (Apr. 1963):115–16.
Adams, Eleanor B., and Fray Angélico Chávez, eds. and trans. *The Mis-
    sions of New Mexico, 1776: A Description by Fray Francisco Atanasio
    Domínguez, with Other Contemporary Documents.* Albuquerque: Univ.
    of New Mexico Press, 1975.
Adams, Eleanor B., and France V. Scholes. "Books in New Mexico,
    1598–1680." NMHR 17 (July 1942):226–70.
Agricola, Georg. *De Natura Fossilium (Textbook of Mineralogy).* 1546. Rpt.
    Trans. Mark Chance Bandy and Jean A. Bandy. The Geological Soci-
    ety of America, Special Paper, 63. New York: Geological Society of
    America, 1955.
Alegre, Francisco Javier. *Historia de la Provincia de la Compañía de Jesús
    de Nueva España.* Ed. Ernest J. Burrus and Félix Zubillaga. Rome:
    Institutum Historicum Societatis Jesu, 1960.
Alessio Robles, Vito. *Coahuila y Texas en la época colonial.* Biblioteca
    Porrúa, 70. 2d ed. Mexico City: Porrúa, 1978.
Alfonso X, El Sabio. *Primera Partida según el manuscrito Add. 20.787 del
    British Museum.* Ed. Juan Antonio Arias Bonet. Valladolid: Univ. de
    Valladolid, 1975.
Almada, Francisco R. *Diccionario de historia, geografía y biografía sonorense.*
    Chihuahua: Ruiz Sandoval, 1952.
Almirante, José. *Bibliografía militar de España.* Madrid: Manuel Tello,
    1876.
———. *Diccionario militar: Etimológico, histórico, tecnológico.* Vol. 1.
    Madrid: Depósito de la Guerra, 1869.

Alonso Barba, Alvaro. *Arte de los metales. En que enseña el verdadero beneficio de los de oro y plata por azogue, el modo de fundirlos todos y como se han de refinar y apartar unos de otros.* Biblioteca Boliviana, 8. La Paz: Publicaciones del Ministerio de Educación, Bellas Artes y Asuntos Indígenas, 1939.

Alonso-Cadenas López, Ampelio, Julio de Atienza et al. *Elenco de grandezas y títulos nobiliarios, 1981.* Madrid: Ediciones de la revista *Hidalguía,* 1981.

Andreski, Stanislav. *Syphilis, Puritanism and Witch Hunts: Historical Explanations in the Light of Medicine and Psychoanalysis with a Forecast about AIDS.* London: Macmillan, 1989.

Anthony, John W., Sidney A. Williams, and Richard A. Bideaux. *Mineralogy of Arizona.* Tucson: Univ. of Arizona Press, 1977.

Arteaga y Falguera, Cristina. *La Casa del Infantado: Cabeza de los Mendoza.* 2 vols. Madrid: Duque del Infantado, 1944.

Bakewell, P.J. *Silver Mining and Society in Colonial Mexico: Zacatecas, 1546–1700.* Cambridge Latin American Studies, 15. Cambridge: Cambridge Univ. Press, 1971.

Bancroft, Hubert Howe. *History of Arizona and New Mexico, 1530–1888.* 1889. Rpt. Albuquerque: Horn and Wallace, 1962.

Bandelier, Adolph F.A. *Final Report of Investigations Among the Indians of the Southwestern United States, Carried on Mainly in the Years from 1880 to 1885.* 2 vols. Papers of the Archeological Institute of America, American Series, 3–4. Cambridge, Mass.: John Wilson and Son, 1890–92.

Bargalló, Modesto. *La minería y la metalurgia en la América española durante la época colonial.* Mexico City: Fondo de Cultura Económica, 1955.

Barrett, Elinore M. *The Mexican Colonial Copper Industry.* Albuquerque: Univ. of New Mexico Press, 1987.

Beaglehole, Ernest. *Notes on Hopi Economic Life.* Yale University Publications in Anthropology, 15. New Haven: Yale Univ. Press, 1937.

Beardsley, Charles. *Guam Past and Present.* Tokyo: Rutland, 1964.

Beneyto Pérez, Juan. *Historia de la administración española e hispanoamericana.* Madrid: Aguilar, 1958.

Beninato, Stephanie. "Popé, Pose-yemu, and Naranjo: A New Look at Leadership in the Pueblo Revolt of 1680." NMHR 65 (Oct. 1990):417–35.

Béthencourt, Francisco Fernández de. *Historia genealógica y heráldica de la monarquía española: Casa Real y grandes de España.* 10 vols. Madrid: Establecimiento Tipográfico de Enrique Teodoro, 1902.

Biringuccio, Vannoccio. *The Pirotechnia of Vannoccio Biringuccio.* 1540. Rpt. Trans. Cyril S. Smith and Martha T. Gnudi. New York: The American Institute of Mining and Metallurgical Engineers, 1942.

Bloom, Lansing B. "New Mexico under Mexican Administration, 1821–1846." *Old Santa Fe* 1 (July 1913):3–49; 1 (Oct. 1913):131–75; 1 (Jan. 1914):235–87; 1 (Apr. 1914):347–68; 2 (July 1914):3–56; 2 (Oct. 1914): 119–69; 2 (Jan. 1915):223–77; 2 (Apr. 1915):351–80.

———. "The Vargas Encomienda." NMHR 14 (Oct. 1939):366–417.

Bolton, Herbert Eugene. *Rim of Christendom: A Biography of Eusebio Francisco Kino, Pacific Coast Pioneer.* 1936. Rpt. Tucson: Univ. of Arizona Press, 1984.

———, ed. and trans. *Kino's Historical Memoir of Pimería Alta: A Contemporary Account of the Beginnings of California, Sonora, and Arizona, by Father Eusebio Francisco Kino, S.J.* 2 vols. in one. 1919. Rpt. Berkeley: Univ. of California Press, 1948.

Bover, José M., S.J. *María mediadora universal o soteriología mariana estudiada a la luz de principios mariológicos.* Madrid: Consejo Superior de Investigaciones Científicas, 1946.

Boyd, E. "The Use of Tobacco in Spanish New Mexico." *El Palacio* 65 (June 1958):103–106.

Brading, D. A. *Miners and Merchants in Bourbon Mexico: 1763–1810.* Cambridge: Cambridge Univ. Press, 1971.

Bromley Seminario, Juan. "La ciudad de Lima durante el gobierno del Virrey Conde de la Monclova." *Revista Histórica* (Lima) 22 (1955–56):142–62.

Burkholder, Mark A., and D.S. Chandler. *Biographical Dictionary of Audiencia Ministers in the Americas, 1687–1821.* Westport, Conn.: Greenwood, 1982.

Burrus, Ernest J., S.J. *Juan María de Salvatierra: Selected Letters about Lower California.* Los Angeles: Dawson's Book Shop, 1971.

———. *Kino and Manje: Explorers of Sonora and Arizona, Their Vision of the Future.* St. Louis: Jesuit Historical Institute, 1971.

———, ed. and trans. *Kino Reports to Headquarters: Correspondence from New Spain with Rome.* Rome: Institutum Historicum Societatis Jesu, 1954.

———. "Francesco Maria Piccolo (1654–1729), Pioneer of Lower California, in the Light of Roman Archives." HAHR 35 (Feb. 1955):61–76

———, ed. "A Tragic Interlude in the Reconquest of New Mexico." *Manuscripta* 29 (Nov. 1985):154–65.

Campos Rebollo, Mario Ramón. *La casa de los Franciscanos en la ciudad de México: Reseña de los cambios que sufrió el Convento de San Francisco de los siglos xvi al xix.* Mexico City: Colección, 1986.

Cárdenas y Cano, Gabriel de [Andrés González de Barcia Carballido y Zúñiga]. *Ensayo cronológico para la historia general de la Florida.* Madrid: En la Oficina Real y a costa de N. Rodríguez Franco, 1723.

Carol, Juniper B. O.F.M., ed., *Mariology.* 3 vols. Milwaukee: Bruce Publishing, 1961.

Carrera Stampa, Manuel. "The Evolution of Weights and Measures in New Spain." HAHR 29 (Feb. 1949):2–24.

Casado Fuente, Ovidio. *Don Francisco Cuerbo y Valdés, governador de Nuevo México, fundador de la ciudad de Alburquerque.* Oviedo: Instituto de Estudios Asturianos, 1983.

Charney, Paul. "The Implications of Godparental Ties Between Indians and Spaniards in Colonial Lima." *The Americas* 47 (Jan. 1991): 295–314.

Chauvet, fray Fidel de Jesús, O.F.M. *Franciscanos memorables en México: Ensayo histórico, 1523–1982.* Vol. 1. Mexico City: Centro de Estudios Bernardino de Sahagún, 1983.

———. *San Francisco de México.* Mexico City: Tradición, 1985.

Chaves, Ireneo L., trans. "Instructions to Governor Peralta by the Viceroy." NMHR 4 (Apr. 1929):178–87.

Chávez, Fray Angélico, O.F.M. *Archives of the Archdiocese of Santa Fe, 1678–1900.* Publications of the Academy of American Franciscan History, Bibliographical Series, 3. Washington, D.C.: Academy of American Franciscan History, 1957.

———. *Chávez: A Distinctive American Clan of New Mexico.* Santa Fe: William Gannon, 1989.

———. *New Mexico Roots Ltd.: A Demographic Perspective from genealogical, historical and geographic data found in the Diligencias Matrimoniales or Pre-Nuptial Investigations (1678–1869) of the Archives of the Archdiocese of Santa Fe; Multiple data extracted, and here edited in a uniform presentation by years and family surnames.* 11 vols. Santa Fe: n.p., 1982.

———. *The Origins of New Mexico Families in the Spanish Colonial Period in Two Parts: The Seventeenth (1598–1693), and the Eighteenth (1693–1821) Centuries.* 1954. Rpt. Santa Fe: William Gannon, 1975.

———. "Addenda to New Mexico Families." *El Palacio* 62 (Nov. 1955): 324–39; 63 (May–June 1956):166–74; 63 (July–Aug. 1956):236–48; 63 (Sept.–Oct. 1956):317–19; 63 (Nov.–Dec. 1956):367–76; 64 (Mar.–Apr. 1957):123–26; 64 (May–June 1957):178–90; 64 (July–Aug. 1957):246–48.

———. "Pohé-yemo's Representative and the Pueblo Revolt of 1680." NMHR 42 (Apr. 1967):85–126.

Cobos, Rubén. *A Dictionary of New Mexico and Southern Colorado Spanish.* Santa Fe: Museum of New Mexico Press, 1983.

Corominas, Joan, in collaboration with José A. Pascual. *Diccionario crítico y etimológico castellano e hispánico.* 5 vols. Biblioteca Románica Hispánica, V. Diccionarios, 7. Madrid: Gredos, 1980.

Cortés Alonso, Vicenta. *La escritura y lo escrito: Paleografía y diplomática de España y América en los siglos xvi y xvii.* Madrid: Ediciones Cultura Hispánica, Instituto de Cooperación Ibero-Americana, 1986.

Cox, L.M. *The Island of Guam*. Washington, D.C.: Gov. Printing Office, 1926.

Crouch, Dora P., Daniel J. Garr, and Axel I. Mundigo, eds. and trans. *Spanish City Planning in North America*. Cambridge, Mass.: The MIT Press, 1982.

Cushing, Frank Hamilton. "Outline of Zuni Creation Myths." In *Thirteenth Annual Report of the Bureau of Ethnology, 1891–1892*. Washington, D.C.: Gov. Printing Office, 1896.

——. *Zuni: Selected Writings of Frank Hamilton Cushing*. Ed. Jesse Green. Lincoln: Univ. of Nebraska Press, 1979.

Cutter, Charles R. *The Protector de Indios in Colonial New Mexico, 1659–1821*. Albuquerque: Univ. of New Mexico Press, 1986.

Davies, J.G., ed. *A New Dictionary of Liturgy and Worship*. London: SCM Press, 1986.

Diccionario de autoridades. Biblioteca Románica Hispánica, V. Diccionarios. 3 vols. 1726–37. Facs. ed. Madrid: Gredos, 1979.

Diccionario enciclopédico Espasa-Calpe. 8th ed. rev. 12 vols. Madrid: Espasa-Calpe, 1978.

Diccionario de la lengua española. 18th ed. Madrid: Espasa-Calpe, 1956.

Diccionario Porrúa de historia, biografía y geografía de México. 4th ed. 2 vols. Mexico City: Porrúa, 1976.

Dirección General de Ordenación del Turismo. *Urbanismo español en América*. Madrid: Editora Nacional, 1973.

Documentary Relations of the Southwest I, II, Biofile, and Geofile.

Documentos para la historia de México. 3d ser. 1. Mexico City: Vicente García Torres, 1856.

Domínguez Ortiz, Antonio. "Regalismo y relaciones iglesia-estado en el siglo xvii." In *Historia de la Iglesia en España*. Ed. Ricardo García-Villoslada. 5 vols. Biblioteca de Autores Cristianos, 16–22. Madrid: EDICA, 1979–80.

Dozier, Edward P. "Spanish-Catholic Influences on Rio Grande Pueblo Religion." *American Anthropologist* 60 (June 1958):441–48.

——. "Rio Grande Pueblos." In *Perspectives in American Indian Culture Change*. Ed. Edward H. Spicer. Chicago: Univ. of Chicago Press, 1961.

Dussel, Enrique. *A History of the Church in Latin America: Colonialism and Liberation, 1492–1979*. Trans. and rev. Alan Neely. Grand Rapids, Mich.: William B. Eerdsman, 1981.

Edwards, Paul, ed. *The Encyclopedia of Philosophy*. New York: Macmillan, 1967.

Ellis, Florence H. "Comments on Four Papers Pertaining to the Protohistoric Pueblos, AD 1450–1700." In *The Protohistoric Period in the North American Southwest, AD 1450–1700*. Eds. David R. Wilcox and W.

Bruce Masse. Anthropological Research Papers, 24. Tempe: Arizona State Univ. Press, 1981.

Enciclopedia de la cultura española. 5 vols. Madrid: Editora Nacional, 1962–68.

Enciclopedia universal ilustrada europeo-americana. 70 vols. Barcelona: Hijos de J. Espasa, 1907–30.

Escalona Agüero, Gaspar de. *Gazofilacio Real del Perú: Tratado financiero del Coloniaje.* 1647. Rpt. Biblioteca Boliviana, 2d ser., 1. La Paz: Editorial del Estado, 1941.

Escriche, Joaquín. *Diccionario razonado de legislación y jurisprudencia.* 4 vols. Ed. Juan B. Guim. Bogotá: Temis, 1977.

Escudero, José Antonio. *Los secretarios de estado y del despacho, 1474–1724.* 2d ed. 4 vols. Estudios de la historia de la administración. Madrid: Instituto de Estudios Administrativos, 1976.

Espinosa, fray Isidro Félix de. *Crónica de los Colegios de Propaganda Fide de la Nueva España.* 1746–47. Rpt. New ed. with notes and introduction by Lino G. Canedo. Washington, D.C.: Academy of American Franciscan History, 1964.

Espinosa, J. Manuel. *Crusaders of the Río Grande: The Story of Don Diego de Vargas and the Reconquest and Refounding of New Mexico.* 1942. Rpt. Salisbury, N.C.: Documentary Publications, 1977.

———. *First Expedition of Vargas into New Mexico, 1692.* Coronado Cuarto Centennial Publications, 1540–1940, 10. Albuquerque: Univ. of New Mexico Press, 1940.

———, ed. and trans. *The Pueblo Indian Revolt of 1696 and the Franciscan Missions of New Mexico: Letters of the Missionaries and Related Documents.* Norman: Univ. of Oklahoma Press, 1988.

———. "The Legend of Sierra Azul, with Special Emphasis upon the Part It Played in the Reconquest of New Mexico." NMHR 9 (Apr. 1934): 113–58.

———. "Population of the El Paso District in 1692." *Mid-America: An Historical Review* 23 (Jan. 1941):61–84.

———. "Report of the Finance Committee of the Government of New Spain, March 28, 1692, Officially Authorizing Governor Vargas to Reconquer New Mexico." NMHR 14 (Jan. 1939):76–81.

———. "The Virgin of the Reconquest of New Mexico." *Mid-America: An Historical Review* 18 (Apr. 1936):79–87.

Farfán, fray Agustín. *Tractado breve de medicina.* 1592. Facs. ed. Madrid: Ediciones Cultura Hispánica, 1944.

Ferguson, T.J., and E. Richard Hart. *A Zuni Atlas.* Norman: Univ. of Oklahoma Press, 1985.

Fernández Duro, Cesáreo. *Don Diego de Peñalosa y su descubrimiento del reino de Quivira. Informe presentado a la Real Academia de Historia por el capitán de navío Cesáreo Fernández Duro.* Madrid: Manuel Tello, 1882.

Ffoulkes, Charles J., ed. *Gaya's Traité des Armes, 1678.* 1678. Rpt. Tudor and Stuart Library. London: Clarendon Press, 1911.

Fisher, Lillian Estelle. *Viceregal Administration in the Spanish-American Colonies.* Berkeley: Univ. of California Press, 1926.

Flood, David, O.F.M., and Thaddée Matura, O.F.M. *The Birth of a Movement: A Study of the First Rule of St. Francis.* Trans. Paul Schwartz, O.F.M., and Paul Lachance, O.F.M. Chicago: Franciscan Herald Press, 1975.

Florescano, Enrique, and Alejandra Mereno Toscano. *Bibliografía general del maíz en México.* 3d ed. Mexico City: Instituto Nacional de Antropología e Historia, 1987.

Flynn, Maureen. *Sacred Charity: Confraternities and Social Welfare in Spain, 1400–1700.* Ithaca: Cornell Univ. Press, 1989.

Forbes, Jack D. *Apache, Navaho, and Spaniard.* Norman: Univ. of Oklahoma Press, 1960.

———. "Unknown Athapaskans: The Identification of the Jano, Jocome, Jumano, Manso, Suma and Other Indian Tribes of the Southwest." *Ethnohistory* 6 (Spr. 1959):97–159.

Fuller, J.F.C. *From the Defeat of the Spanish Armada, 1588 to the Battle of Waterloo, 1815.* Vol. 2 of *A Military History of the Western World.* 3 vols. Ed. J.F.C. Fuller. New York: Funk and Wagnalls, 1955.

Galloway, Patricia K., ed. *La Salle and his Legacy: Frenchmen and Indians in the Lower Mississippi Valley.* Jackson, Miss.: Univ. Press of Mississippi, 1982.

Galván Rivera, Mariano. *Ordenanzas de tierras y aguas, o sea formulario geométrico judicial.* 4th ed. Mexico City: Librería del Portal de Mercaderes, 1851.

García Carraffa, Alberto, and Arturo García Carraffa. *Diccionario heráldico y genealógico de apellidos españoles y americanos.* 88 vols. Madrid: Nueva Imprenta Radio, 1943.

García Oro, José, O.F.M. *Cisneros y la reforma del clero español en tiempo de los Reyes Católicos.* Biblioteca "Reyes Católicos." Estudios, 13. Madrid: Consejo Superior de Investigaciones Científicas, Instituto Jerónimo Zurita, 1971.

Garcilaso de la Vega, El Inca. *Comentarios reales de los Incas.* 1609. Rpt. Buenos Aires: Emecé, 1943.

Gerhard, Peter. *A Guide to the Historical Geography of New Spain.* Cambridge: Cambridge Univ. Press, 1972.

———. *The North Frontier of New Spain.* Princeton: Princeton Univ. Press, 1982.

Gibson, Charles. *The Aztecs under Spanish Rule: A History of the Indians of the Valley of Mexico, 1519–1810.* Stanford: Stanford Univ. Press, 1964.

Gilmer, Lt. Jeremy F. *Plan of Santa Fé, New Mexico.* Santa Fe: U.S. Corps of Engineers, 1847.

Golmayo, Pedro Benito. *Instituciones del derecho canónico.* 2 vols. Madrid: Gabriel Sánchez, 1896.

González Holguín, Diego. *Vocabulario de la lengua general de todo el Perú llamada lengua qquichua o del inca.* 1608. Rpt. Lima: Santa María, 1952.

Griffen, William B. *Indian Assimilation in the Franciscan Area of Nueva Vizcaya.* Anthropological Papers of the University of Arizona, 33. Tucson: Univ. of Arizona Press, 1979.

Guadalajara, Tomás de. *Historia de la tercera rebelión tarahumara.* Ed. Roberto Ramos. Chihuahua: Sociedad Chihuahuense de Estudios Históricos, 1950.

Guthrie, Chester Lyle. "Riots in Seventeenth-Century Mexico City: A Study of Social and Economic Conditions." In *Greater America: Essays in Honor of Herbert Eugene Bolton.* Ed. Adele Ogden and Engel Sluiter. Berkeley: Univ. of California Press, 1945.

Gutiérrez, Ramón A. *When Jesus Came, the Corn Mothers Went Away: Marriage, Sexuality, and Power in New Mexico, 1500–1846.* Stanford: Stanford Univ. Press, 1991.

Gutiérrez Coronel, Diego. *Historia genealógica de la Casa de Mendoza.* 2 vols. Ed. Angel Gómez Palencia. Biblioteca Conquense, 3. Cuenca: Instituto Jerónimo Zurita del Consejo de Investigaciones Superiores y Ayuntamiento de la Ciudad de Cuenca, 1946.

Hackett, Charles Wilson, ed. *Historical Documents relating to New Mexico, Nueva Vizcaya, and Approaches thereto, to 1773.* 3 vols. Washington, D. C.: Carnegie Institution of Washington, 1923–37.

———, ed., and Charmion Clair Shelby, trans. *Revolt of the Pueblo Indians of New Mexico and Otermín's Attempted Reconquest, 1680–1682.* 2 vols. Coronado Cuarto Centennial Publications, 1540–1940, 8–9. Albuquerque: Univ. of New Mexico Press, 1942.

Hammond, George P., and Agapito Rey, eds. *Don Juan de Oñate: Colonizer of New Mexico, 1595–1628.* 2 vols. Coronado Cuarto Centennial Publications, 1540–1940, 5–6. Albuquerque: Univ. of New Mexico Press, 1953.

———, eds. and trans. *Narratives of the Coronado Expedition 1540–1542.* Coronado Cuarto Centennial Publications, 1540–1940, 2. Albuquerque: Univ. of New Mexico Press, 1940.

Hanke, Lewis, ed., in collaboration with Celso Rodríguez. *Los virreyes españoles en América durante el gobierno de la Casa de Austria: México.* Biblioteca de Autores Españoles, desde la formación del lenguaje hasta nuestros días (continuación), 277. Madrid: Atlas, 1978.

Hardon, John A., S.J. *Pocket Catholic Dictionary.* Garden City, N.Y.: Doubleday, Image Books, 1988.

Haring, C. H. *The Spanish Empire in America.* 1947. Rpt. New York: Harcourt, Brace and World, 1963.

Harrington, John P. "The Ethnogeography of the Tewa Indians." In *Twenty-Ninth Annual Report of the Bureau of American Ethnology, 1907–1908.* Washington, D.C.: Gov. Printing Office, 1916.

———. "Notes on the Names Moqui and Hopi." *American Anthropologist* 47 (Jan.–Mar. 1945):177–78.

Hendricks, Rick. "Levels of Discourse in Early Modern Spanish: The Papers of Diego de Vargas, 1643–1704." *North Dakota Quarterly* 58 (Fall 1990):124–39.

———. "Road to Rebellion, Road to Reconquest: The Camino Real and the Pueblo-Spanish War, 1680–1696." In *Essays on the History of the Camino Real de Tierra Adentro.* Ed. Gabrielle Palmer. Santa Fe: The Camino Real Project, 1989.

———. "Forgotten Lessons and Missing Links: Bandelier as a Pioneering Scientific Historian." Paper delivered at the Bandelier Sesquicentennial Conference, Albuquerque, New Mexico, 7 Aug. 1990.

———. "Franciscan Ritual in Seventeenth-Century New Mexico: Possession of Churches." Paper delivered at the World History Association, Rocky Mountain Regional Conference on Religion in World History, Snowbird, Utah, 8 June 1990.

———. "Observations on Pueblo-Spanish Relations in the Vargas Era." Paper delivered at the New Mexico Historical Society Annual Convention, Socorro, New Mexico, 15 Apr. 1989.

Hill, W.W. *An Ethnography of Santa Clara Pueblo, New Mexico.* Albuquerque: Univ. of New Mexico Press, 1982.

Hodge, Frederick Webb. *History of Hawikuh, New Mexico: One of the So-called Cities of Cíbola.* Publications of the Frederick Webb Hodge Anniversary Publication Fund, 1. Los Angeles: Southwest Museum, 1937.

———, George P. Hammond, and Agapito Rey. *Fray Alonso de Benavides' Revised Memorial of 1634.* Coronado Cuarto Centennial Publications, 1540–1940, 4. Albuquerque: Univ. of New Mexico Press, 1945.

Holmes, William H. "Art in Shell of the Ancient Americans." In *Second Annual Report of the Bureau of Ethnology.* Washington, D.C.: Gov. Printing Office, 1883.

Hough, Walter. "A Collection of Hopi Ceremonial Pigments." *Annual Report of the Smithsonian Institution, 1900.* Washington, D.C.: Gov. Printing Office, 1902.

Hughes, Anne E. *The Beginning of Spanish Settlement in the El Paso Dis-*

trict. 1914. Rpt. University of California Publications in History, 1. Berkeley: Univ. of California Press, 1935.

Humphrey, Norman B. "The Mock Battle Greeting." *Journal of American Folklore* 54 (July–Dec. 1941):186–90.

Iriarte de Aspurz, Lázaro, O.F.M. Cap. *Franciscan History: The Three Orders of St. Francis of Assisi.* Trans. Patricia Ross. Chicago: Franciscan Herald Press, 1982.

Jenkins, Myra Ellen. "Taos Pueblo and its Neighbors, 1540–1847." NMHR 41 (Apr. 1966):85–114.

John, Elizabeth A. H. *Storms Brewed in Other Men's Worlds: The Confrontation of Indians, Spanish, and French in the Southwest, 1540–1795.* College Station: Texas A & M Univ. Press, 1975.

John, Eric, ed. *The Popes: A Concise Biographical History.* New York: Hawthorn, 1964.

Jones, Oakah L. *Nueva Vizcaya: Heartland of the Spanish Frontier.* Albuquerque: Univ. of New Mexico Press, 1988.

Kelley, J. Charles. "The Historic Indian Pueblos of La Junta de los Ríos." NMHR 27 (Oct. 1952):257–95.

Kessell, John L. *Kiva, Cross, and Crown: The Pecos Indians and New Mexico, 1540–1840.* Washington, D.C.: National Park Service, U.S. Dept. of the Interior, 1979.

————, Rick Hendricks, Meredith D. Dodge, Larry D. Miller, and Eleanor B. Adams, eds. *Remote Beyond Compare: Letters of don Diego de Vargas to His Family from New Spain and New Mexico, 1675–1706.* Albuquerque: Univ. of New Mexico Press, 1989.

————. "Spaniards and Pueblos: From Crusading Intolerance to Pragmatic Accommodation." In *Columbian Consequences: Archaeological and Historical Perspectives on the Spanish Borderlands West:* 1. Ed. David Hurst Thomas. Washington, D.C.: Smithsonian Institution Press, 1989.

King, James Ferguson. "Evolution of the Free Slave Trade Principle in Spanish Colonial Administration." HAHR 22 (Feb. 1942):34–56.

Kinnaird, Lawrence. "The Spanish Tobacco Monopoly in New Mexico, 1766–67." NMHR 21 (Oct. 1946):328–39.

Lang, Jovian P. *Dictionary of the Liturgy.* New York: Catholic Book Publishing, 1989.

Lange, Charles H. *Cochití: A New Mexico Pueblo, Past and Present.* Austin: Univ. of Texas Press, 1959.

Lanning, John Tate. *Academic Culture in the Spanish Colonies.* London: Oxford Univ. Press, 1940.

Lapedes, Daniel N., ed. "Soil." In *McGraw-Hill Encyclopedia of Food, Agriculture and Nutrition.* New York: McGraw-Hill, 1977.

Lausen, Carl, and E.D. Gardner. *Quicksilver (Mercury) Resources of Ari-*

zona. Arizona Bureau of Mines Bulletin, 122. Mineral Technology Series, 29. Tucson: Univ. of Arizona Press, 1927.

Leonard, Irving A. *Don Carlos de Sigüenza y Góngora: A Mexican Savant of the Seventeenth Century.* University of California Publications in History, 18. Berkeley: Univ. of California Press, 1929.

The Liturgy of the Hours According to the Roman Rite. New York: Catholic Book Publishing, 1975.

Lohmann Villena, Guillermo. *Las minas de Huancavelica en los siglos xvi y xvii.* Publicaciones de la Escuela de Estudios Hispano-Americanos de Sevilla, 50. Seville: Escuela de Estudios Hispano-Americanos de Sevilla, 1949.

―――. *Los americanos en las órdenes nobiliarias, 1529–1900.* 2 vols. Madrid: Consejo Superior de Investigaciones Científicas, Instituto "Gonzalo Fernández de Oviedo," 1947.

Lynch, John. *Spain under the Habsburgs.* 2 vols. 2d ed. New York: New York Univ. Press, 1984.

Maas, P. Otto, O.F.M. *Misiones de Nuevo Méjico: Documentos del Archivo General de Indias (Sevilla) publicados por primera vez y anotados.* Madrid: Hijos de T. Minuesa de los Ríos, 1929.

Madoz, Pascual. *Diccionario geográfico-estadístico-histórico de España y sus posesiones de ultramar.* 16 vols. Madrid: P. Madoz y L. Sagasti, 1845–50.

Mandell, Gerald J. "A History of the Gallegos Family." Albuquerque, New Mexico, 1991.

Manje, Juan Mateo. *Luz de tierra incógnita en la América septentrional y diario de las exploraciones en Sonora.* Publicaciones del Archivo General de la Nación, 10. Mexico City: Talleres Gráficos de la Nación, 1929.

Manrique Chávez, Antonio. *El maíz en el Perú.* Lima: Fondo del Banco Agrario del Perú, 1987.

Margadant S., Guillermo F. "Mexican Colonial Land Law." In *Spanish and Mexican Land Grants and the Law.* Ed. Malcolm Ebright. Manhattan, Kans.: Sunflower Univ. Press, 1989.

Marshall, Michael P., and Henry J. Walt. *Rio Abajo: Prehistory and History of a Rio Grande Province.* Santa Fe: Historic Preservation Division, 1984.

McGregor, John C. "Burial of an Early American Magician." In *Proceedings of the American Philosophical Society* 86 (Feb. 1943):270–98.

Menéndez Pidal, Ramón. *El P. Las Casas y Vitoria con otros temas de los siglos xvi y xvii.* 2d ed. Madrid: Espasa-Calpe, 1966.

Molina, fray Alonso de. *Vocabulario en lengua castellana y mexicana y mexicana y castellana.* 1555–57. Rpt. 2d ed. Mexico City: Porrúa, 1977.

Montgomery, Ross Gordon, Watson Smith, and John Otis Brew. *Franciscan Awatovi: The Excavation and Conjectural Reconstruction of a 17th*

Century Spanish Mission Establishment at a Hopi Indian Town in Northeastern Arizona. Cambridge, Mass.: Peabody Museum, 1949.

Moore, John Preston. *The Cabildo in Peru under the Hapsburgs: A Study in the Origins and Powers of the Town Council in the Viceroyalty of Peru, 1530–1700.* Durham: Duke Univ. Press, 1954.

Moorhead, Max L. *New Mexico's Royal Road: Trade and Travel on the Chihuahua Trail.* Norman: Univ. of Oklahoma Press, 1958.

———. *The Presidio: Bastion of the Spanish Borderlands.* Norman: Univ. of Oklahoma Press, 1975.

Muro Orejón, Antonio, ed. *Cédulas de Carlos II, 1679–1700.* Vol. 1 of *Cedulario americano del siglo xviii: Colección de 248 disposiciones legales indianas desde 1680 a 1800, contenidas en los Cedularios del Archivo de Indias.* Seville: Escuela de Estudios Hispano-Americanos de Sevilla, 1956.

Navarro García, Luis. *Don José de Gálvez y la Comandancia General de las Provincias Internas del norte de Nueva España.* Publicaciones de la Escuela de Estudios Hispano-Americanos de Sevilla, 148. 2d ser. Seville: Escuela de Estudios Hispano-Americanos de Sevilla, 1964.

———. *Sonora y Sinaloa en el siglo xvii.* Publicaciones de la Escuela de Estudios Hispano-Americanos de Sevilla, 176. Seville: Escuela de Estudios Hispano-Americanos de Sevilla, 1967.

———. "El Real Tribunal de Cuentas de México a principios del siglo xviii." *Anuario de Estudios Americanos* 34 (1977):517–35.

Naylor, Thomas H., and Charles W. Polzer, S.J., comps. and eds. *Pedro de Rivera and the Military Regulations for Northern New Spain, 1724–1729: A Documentary History of His Frontier Inspection and the Reglamento de 1729.* Tucson: Univ. of Arizona Press, 1988.

———. *The Presidio and Militia on the Northern Frontier of New Spain: A Documentary History, 1570–1700.* Vol. 1. Tucson: Univ. of Arizona Press, 1986.

The New Catholic Encyclopedia. 18 vols. New York: McGraw-Hill, 1967–79.

The New Mexican. 30 Sept. 1987.

The New Oxford Annotated Bible with the Apocrypha. New York: Oxford Univ. Press, 1973.

Nuttall, Zelia. "Royal Ordinances Concerning the Laying Out of New Towns." HAHR 4 (Feb. 1921):743–53.

Ocaranza, Fernando. *Establecimientos franciscanos en el reino misterioso de la Nueva México.* Mexico City: n.p., 1934.

Ortiz, Alfonso. *The Tewa World: Space, Time, Being, and Becoming in a Pueblo Society.* Chicago: Univ. of Chicago Press, 1969.

———, ed. *Southwest.* Vol. 9 of *The Handbook of North American Indians.* Washington, D.C.: Smithsonian Institution, 1979.

———, ed. *Southwest*. Vol 10 of *The Handbook of North American Indians*. Washington, D.C.: Smithsonian Institution, 1983.

———. "Popay's Leadership: A Pueblo Perspective." *El Palacio* 86 (Win. 1980–81):18–22.

Palkovich, Ann M. *Pueblo Population and Society: The Arroyo Hondo Skeletal and Mortuary Remains*. Santa Fe: School of American Research, 1980.

Palomino de Castro y Velasco, Antonio. *El museo pictórico y escala óptica*. 1715. Rpt. Madrid: Aguilar, 1947.

Pandey, Triloki Nath. "Images of Power in a Southwestern Pueblo." In *Anthropology of Power: Ethnographic Studies from Asia, Oceania, and the New World*. Eds. Raymond D. Fogelson and Richard N. Adams. New York: Academic Press, 1977.

Pearce, T.M. *New Mexico Place Names: A Geographical Dictionary*. Albuquerque: Univ. of New Mexico Press, 1965.

Pérez de Villagrá, Gaspar. *Historia de la Nueva México*. Alcalá de Henares: Luis Martínez Grande, 1610.

Peterson, Harold L. *Arms and Armor in Colonial America, 1526–1783*. New York: Bramhall House, 1956.

Pfefferkorn, Ignaz. *Sonora: A Description of the Province*. Trans. Theodore E. Treutlein. Albuquerque: Univ. of New Mexico Press, 1949.

Piccolo, Francesco Maria. *Informe del estado de la nueva cristiandad de California 1702 y otros documentos*. Ed. Ernest J. Burrus. Colección Chimalistac de libros y documentos acerca de la Nueva España, 14. Madrid: José Porrúa Turanzas, 1962.

Plá Cárceles, José. "La evolución del tratamiento 'vuestra-merced.' " *Revista de Filología Española* 10 (Jul.–Sept. 1923):245–80.

Pontificale Romanum: Ritus Solemnis pro Dedicatione Ecclesiae et Consecratione sive unius sive plurium altarium tam fixorum quam portatilium. Cincinnati: Sumptibus, Chartis et Typis Friderici Pustet, 1890.

Porras Muñoz, Guillermo. *La frontera con los indios de Nueva Vizcaya en el siglo xvii*. Mexico City: Fomento Cultural Banamex, 1980.

Puckett, Fidelia Miller. "Ramón Ortiz: Priest and Patriot." NMHR 25 (Oct. 1950):265–95.

Recopilación de leyes de los reynos de las Indias. 4 vols. 1681. Facs. ed. Foreword by Ramón Menéndez y Pidal, a preliminary study by Juan Manzano Manzano. Madrid: Cultura Hispánica, 1973.

Reeve, Frank D. *History of New Mexico*. 3 vols. New York: Lewis Historical Publishing, 1961.

Reiter, Winifred Stamm. "Personal Adornment of the Ancient Pueblo Indian." M.A. thesis. Univ. of New Mexico, 1933.

Ribadeneira y Barrientos, Antonio Joaquín de. *Manual compendio de el regio patronato indiano, para su más fácil uso en las materias conducentes a la práctica: Dedicado al rey nuestro señor d. Fernando VI, El Amado.* Madrid: Antonio Marín, 1755.

Riley, Carroll L., and Joni L. Manson. "The Cíbola-Tiguex Route: Continuity and Change in the Southwest." NMHR 58 (Oct. 1983):347–67.

Rituale Romanum. Madrid: Typografía Regia, 1776.

Rivera Cambas, Manuel. *Los gobernantes de México: Galería de biografías y retratos de los virreyes, emperadores, presidentes y otros gobernantes que ha tenido México, desde Hernando Cortés hasta el C. Benito Juárez.* 2 vols. Mexico City: J. M. Aguilar Ortiz, 1872–73.

Robles, Antonio de. *Diario de sucesos notables, 1665–1703.* Ed. Antonio Castro Leal. 3 vols. Colección de Escritores Mexicanos, 30–32. Mexico City: Porrúa, 1946.

Roca, Paul M. *Paths of the Padres Through Sonora: An Illustrated History and Guide to Its Spanish Churches.* Tucson: Arizona Pioneers' Historical Society, 1967.

Roediger, Virginia More. *Ceremonial Costumes of the Pueblo Indians: Their Evolution, Fabrication, and Significance in the Prayer Drama.* Berkeley: Univ. of California Press, 1961.

Roscoe, William. *The Life and Pontificate of Leo the Tenth.* 2 vols. 5th ed. London: Henry G. Bohn, 1846.

Ruano, Eloy Benito. "Nuevos datos biográficos sobre don Francisco Cuervo y Valdés, fundador de Alburquerque (Nuevo México)." *Boletín del Instituto de Estudios Asturianos* Oviedo: Instituto de Estudios Asturianos, 1984.

Rubio Mañé, J. Ignacio. *El Virreinato.* 4 vols. 2d ed. Mexico City: Fondo de Cultura Económica, 1983.

———. "Gente de España en la ciudad de México: Año de 1689." Sobretiro del *Boletín del Archivo General de la Nación,* 2d ser., 7. Mexico City: Archivo General de la Nación, 1966.

Sabatier, Paul. *The Life of St. Francis of Assisi.* Trans. Louise Seymour Houghton. New York: Charles Scribner's Sons, 1930.

Salmón, Roberto Mario. "Frontier Warfare in the Hispanic Southwest: Tarahumara Resistance, 1649–1780." *Mid-America: An Historical Review* 58 (Oct. 1976):174–85.

Sanchez, Jane C. "Spanish-Indian Relations during the Otermín Administration, 1677–1683." NMHR 58 (Apr. 1983):133–51.

Sánchez Bella, Ismael. "El Tribunal de Cuentas de México, siglo xvii." In *Memoria del Cuarto Congreso Venezolano de Historia del 27 de octubre al 10 de noviembre de 1980.* 3 vols. Caracas: Academia Nacional de la Historia, 1983.

Santamaría, Francisco J. *Diccionario de mejicanismos.* 3d ed. Mexico City: Porrúa, 1978.

Santo Tomás, fray Domingo de. *Lexicón, o vocabulario de la lengua general del Perú*. 1560. Facs. ed. Lima: Instituto de Historia, 1951.

Sariñana y Cuenca, Isidro. *Oración fúnebre*. Mexico City: Viuda de Bernardo Calderón, 1681.

Schäfer, Ernesto. *El Consejo Real y Supremo de las Indias: Su historia, organización y labor administrativa hasta la terminación de la Casa de Austria*. 2 vols. Seville: Centro de Estudio de Historia de América, Univ. de Sevilla, 1935; Escuela de Estudios Hispano-Americanos, 1947.

Scholes, France V. *Church and State in New Mexico, 1610–1650*. Historical Society of New Mexico. Publications in History, 7. Albuquerque: Univ. of New Mexico Press, 1937.

———. *Troublous Times in New Mexico, 1659–1670*. Historical Society of New Mexico, Publications in History, 11. Albuquerque: Univ. of New Mexico Press, 1942.

———. "Civil Government and Society in New Mexico in the Seventeenth Century." NMHR 10 (Apr. 1935):71–111.

———. "Problems in the Early Ecclesiastical History of New Mexico." NMHR 7 (Jan. 1932):32–74.

——— "The Supply Service of the New Mexican Missions in the Seventeenth Century." NMHR 5 (Jan. 1930):93–115; 5 (Apr. 1930):186–210; 5 (Oct. 1930):386–404.

Schwaller, John Frederick. *The Church and Clergy in Sixteenth-Century Mexico*. Albuquerque: Univ. of New Mexico Press, 1987.

Sheridan, Thomas E., and Thomas H. Naylor, eds. *Rarámuri: A Tarahumara Colonial Chronicle, 1607–1791*. Flagstaff: Northland Press, 1979.

Sigüenza y Góngora, Carlos de. *Alboroto y motín de México del 8 de junio de 1692: Relación de don Carlos de Sigüenza y Góngora en una carta dirigida al almirante don Andrés de Pez*. Ed. Irving A. Leonard. Mexico City: Talleres Gráficos del Museo Nacional de Arqueología, Historia y Etnografía, 1932.

———. *Libra astronómica y filosófica*. 1690. Rpt. Ed. Bernabé Navarro. Nueva Biblioteca Mexicana, 2. Mexico City: Centro de Estudios Filosóficos, Univ. Autónoma de México, 1959.

Siméon, Rémi. *Diccionario de la lengua nahuatl o mexicana redactado según los documentos impresos y manuscritos más auténticos y precedido de una introducción*. 1885. Rpt. 2d ed. Trans. Josefina Oliva de Coll. Colección América Nuestra, América Antigua, 1. Mexico City: Siglo Veintiuno, 1981.

Simmons, Marc. *Albuquerque: A Narrative History*. Albuquerque: Univ. of New Mexico Press, 1982.

———. *The Last Conquistador: Juan de Oñate and the Settling of the Far Southwest*. Norman: Univ. of Oklahoma Press, 1991.

————. "Governor Cuervo and the Beginnings of Albuquerque: Another Look." NMHR 55 (July 1980):189–207.

————, and Frank Turley. *Southwestern Colonial Ironwork: The Spanish Blacksmithing Tradition from Texas to California.* Santa Fe: Museum of New Mexico Press, 1980.

Snow, Cordelia Thomas. "The Plazas of Santa Fe, New Mexico." *El Palacio* 94 (Win. 1988):40–51.

Solórzano Pereira, Juan de. *Política indiana.* Biblioteca de Autores Españoles, desde la formación del lenguaje hasta nuestros días (continuación), 252–56. Madrid: Atlas, 1972.

Sonnichsen, C.L. *Pass of the North: Four Centuries on the Rio Grande.* El Paso: Texas Western Press, 1968.

Spicer, Edward H. *Cycles of Conquest: The Impact of Spain, Mexico, and the United States on the Indians of the Southwest, 1533–1960.* Tucson: Univ. of Arizona Press, 1962.

————. "Spanish-Indian Acculturation in the Southwest." *American Anthropologist* 56 (Aug. 1954):663–84.

Stephen, A.M. "Pigments in Ceremonials of the Hopi." In *The International Folk-Lore Congress of the World's Columbian Exposition.* 1898. Rpt. Ed. Helen Wheeler Bassett and Frederick Starr. International Folk-Lore Association, Archives, 1. New York: Arno Press, 1980.

Tarassuk, Leonid, and Claude Blair, eds. *The Complete Encyclopedia of Arms and Weapons.* New York: Simon and Schuster, 1982.

Thomas, Barnaby. *After Coronado: Spanish Exploration Northeast of New Mexico, 1696–1727.* Norman: Univ. of Oklahoma Press, 1935.

Thurston, Herbert, S.J., and Donald Attwater, eds. *Butler's Lives of the Saints.* 1798–1800. Rpt. New York: P.J. Kennedy and Sons, 1956.

Twitchell, Ralph Emerson. *The Leading Facts of New Mexican History.* Cedar Rapids, Iowa: Torch Press, 1911.

————. *Old Santa Fe: The Story of New Mexico's Ancient Capitol.* Santa Fe: Santa Fe New Mexican Publishing Corp., 1925.

————, comp. *The Spanish Archives of New Mexico: Compiled and Chronologically Arranged with Historical, Genealogical, Geographical, and Other Annotations, by Authority of the State of New Mexico.* 2 vols. Cedar Rapids, Iowa: Torch Press, 1914.

————, ed. "The Reconquest of New Mexico, 1692: Extracts from the Journal of General d. Diego de Vargas Zapata Luján Ponce de León." In *Old Santa Fe: A Magazine of History, Archaeology, Genealogy, and Biography* 1 (Jan., Apr. 1914):288–307, 420–35.

Upham, Steadman. "Population and Spanish Contact in the American Southwest." Paper delivered at Disease and Demographics: New World Peoples Before and After 1492, Smithsonian Institution, Washington, D.C., 2–3 Nov. 1989.

Uyá, Jaime, ed. *Fuero juzgo o libro de los jueces.* 1815. Rpt. Barcelona: Zeus, 1968.

Vargas Machuca, Bernardo de. *Milicia y descripción de las Indias.* 1599. Rpt. 2 vols. Madrid: Librería de Victoriano Suárez, 1892.

Vargas Ugarte, Rubén., S.J. *Historia del culto de María en Iberoamérica y de sus imágenes y santuarios más celebrados.* 3d ed. Madrid: Talleres Gráficos Jura, 1956.

Venegas, Miguel. *Juan María de Salvatierra of the Company of Jesus: Missionary in the Province of New Spain, and Apostolic Conqueror of the Californias.* Ed. and trans. Marguerite Eyer Wilbur. Cleveland: Arthur H. Clark, 1929.

Vetancurt, fray Agustín de. *Teatro mexicano: Descripción breve de los sucesos exemplares de la Nueva-España en el nuevo mundo occidental de las Indias.* 4 vols. Colección Chimalistac de libros y documentos acerca de la Nueva España, 8–11. Madrid: José Porrúa Turanzas, 1961.

Vitoria, Francisco de. *Relecciones sobre los indios y el derecho de guerra.* Comp. Guillermo Malavassi Vargas. San José, Costa Rica: Alma Mater, 1988.

Walz, Vina. "History of the El Paso Area, 1680–1692." Ph.D. diss. Univ. of New Mexico, 1951.

Warner, Ted. J. "Don Félix Martínez and the Santa Fe Presidio, 1693–1730." NMHR 45 (Oct. 1970):269–310.

Weddle, Robert S. *Wilderness Manhunt: The Spanish Search for La Salle.* Austin: Univ. of Texas Press, 1972.

West, Elizabeth Howard. "The Right of Asylum in New Mexico in the Seventeenth and Eighteenth Centuries." Ed. with additional notes by Eleanor B. Adams. NMHR 41 (Apr. 1966):115–53.

West, George A. *Tobacco, Pipes and Smoking Customs of the American Indians.* 1934. Rpt. Westport, Conn.: Greenwood, 1970.

West, Robert C. *The Mining Community in Northern New Spain: The Parral Mining District.* Ibero-Americana, 30. Berkeley: Univ. of California Press, 1949.

Whitaker, Arthur Preston. *The Huancavelica Mercury Mine: A Contribution to the History of the Bourbon Renaissance in the Spanish Empire.* Harvard Historical Monographs, 16. Cambridge, Mass.: Harvard Univ. Press, 1941.

Wilcox, David R. "Changing Perspectives on the Protohistoric Pueblos, AD 1450–1700." In *The Protohistoric Period in the North American Southwest, AD 1450–1700.* Eds. David R. Wilcox and W. Bruce Masse. Anthropological Research Papers, 24. Tempe: Arizona State Univ. Press, 1981.

Williams, Jerry L., and Paul E. McAllister, eds. *New Mexico in Maps.* Albuquerque: Univ. of New Mexico Press, 1979.

Wilson, Christopher M. "The Santa Fe, New Mexico Plaza: An Architec-
tural and Cultural History, 1610–1921." M.A. thesis. Univ. of New
Mexico, 1981.

Wilson, John P. "Awatovi—More Light on a Legend." *Plateau* 44 (Win.
1972):125–30.

Woywod, Stanislaus. *A Practical Commentary on the Code of Canon Law.*
New York: Joseph F. Wagner, 1957.

Index

NOTE ON THE INDEX

Entries and subentries are alphabetical with the following exceptions. Spanish geographical names incorporating the articles "el," "la," or "del" are alphabetized by the name rather than the article, though the articles appear in the index. Surnames with "de la" and "del" are alphabetized by "de la" and "del." General references precede those modified by subentries.

References to note numbers follow the number of the page on which the note begins, or on which the item indexed appears, and are preceded by a "n." Definitions of terms are indexed by the page reference followed by a "d." Numbers in in bold type are references to illustrations.

Cities, towns, and other inhabited places in Spain are identified by their modern provinces in parentheses, those in New Spain, the focus of the book, by colonial designations. Hence, El Paso and the Hopi pueblos, for example, are listed as parts of New Mexico, as they were in the seventeenth century. Other Latin American and European cities and towns are given with their modern locations.

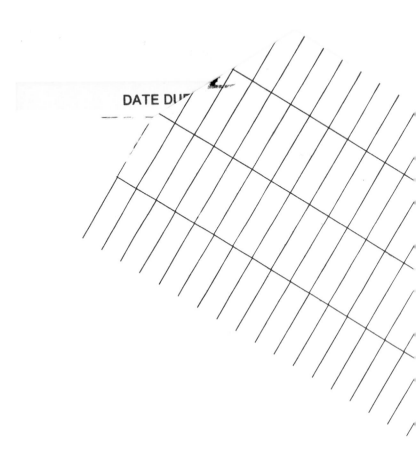

DATE DUE